TAKING IT ALL IN

Pauline Kael is that rarity, a marvellous writer who is also a marvellous critic. Among her other books are *Kiss Kiss Bang Bang*, *Going Steady*, *Reeling*, *Deeper into Movies* (which won the National Book Award in the USA) and *When the Lights Go Down*. A native of northern California, she began writing for *The New Yorker* in 1967.

'The most interesting and invigorating film critic around' *The New York Times*

'One of the most honest, articulate, waspish, sometimes infuriating but certainly informed film critics in the business' *San Francisco Chronicle*

D1494025

Pauline Kael

TAKING IT ALL IN

An Arena Book

Published by Arrow Books Limited
62-65 Chandos Place, London WC2N 4NW

An imprint of Century Hutchinson Ltd

London Melbourne Sydney Auckland
Johannesburg and agencies throughout
the world

First published in Great Britain
by Marion Boyars Publishers Ltd 1986

Arena edition 1987

All material in this book originally appeared in
The New Yorker

Printed and bound in Great Britain by
The Guernsey Press Co Ltd
Guernsey, C.I.

ISBN 0 09 948170 7

Contents

Author's Note

The hit movies make the most noise in the culture, and the hits of the early eighties have often been just TV in a souped-up form. But when I looked over the titles of the hundred and fifty films I reviewed for *The New Yorker* between June 9, 1980, and June 13, 1983, it was a shock to discover how many good ones there were. Only a very few of the movies I liked were box-office successes—*E.T.*, of course, and *Tootsie*, and *Star Trek II: The Wrath of Khan*, and to a lesser extent *Dressed to Kill*, *Atlantic City*, *My Dinner with André*, *Excalibur*, and *Diva*. In the eighties, films that aren't immediate box-office successes are instantly branded as losers, flops, bombs. It's almost as if they'd never been born. And some of the new movies that meant the most to me were in this doomed group: *The Stunt Man*, *Blow Out*, *The Devil's Play-ground*, *Pennies from Heaven*, *Melvin and Howard*, *Shoot the Moon*, and *Come Back to the 5 & Dime Jimmy Dean, Jimmy Dean*. There were many others that didn't attract anything like the audiences they deserved—movies such as *Barbarosa*, *Local Hero*, *Used Cars*, *All Night Long*, *Dragonslayer*, *Honeysuckle Rose*, *Tales of Ordinary Madness*, *Personal Best*, *Pixote*, *Diner*, *Three Brothers*, *The Flight of the Eagle*, *Smash Palace*, *The Year of Living Dangerously*, *Leap Into the Void*, and the superb *The Night of the Shooting Stars*. That's an impressive array, and I would like to think that maybe the reviews in this book would induce a few readers to catch some of the films they've missed.

This collection starts up after a gap of a year, part of which I spent in Los Angeles. What I learned during those months is summed up in the piece *Why Are Movies So Bad?* (An additional, brief note on further developments in the industry precedes the review of *Raiders of the Lost Ark*.) What I also learned during my time away was how much I missed the quickening of the senses involved in reviewing.

It has become a ritual for me to express my gratitude to William Shawn, Editor of *The New Yorker*, and William Abrahams of Holt, Rinehart and Winston. I have come to take these two for granted—I want them to know that I love being able to. And I thank my daughter Gina and her son William for astonishing me (all the time).

TAKING IT ALL IN

Devolution

*I*f Stanley Kubrick's *The Shining* is about anything that you can be sure of, it's tracking: Kubrick loves the ultra-smooth travelling shots made possible by the Steadicam. This marvellous invention—an apparatus that stabilizes the camera so that the camera operator's body substitutes for a dolly—was used to dramatic effect in *Rocky* (the sequence of the triumphal leaping run up the steps) and in *Bound for Glory* (the tour of the migrant workers' camp), but it has probably never been used so much or so insistently as it has been in *The Shining*. In at least one sequence Kubrick uses it spectacularly: we glide behind Danny (Danny Lloyd), the boy in peril (he looks about five), who is at the center of the film, as he pedals his low-rider tricycle up and down the corridors of the huge Overlook Hotel, where most of the action takes place. Some of us in the audience may want to laugh with pleasure at the visual feat, and it is joined to an aural one: the sounds of the wheels moving from rug to wood are uncannily exact. We almost want to applaud. Yet though we may admire the effects, we're never drawn in by them, mesmerized. When we see a flash of bloody cadavers or observe a torrent of blood pouring from an elevator, we're not frightened, because Kubrick's absorption in film technology distances us. Each shot seems rigorously calculated, meticulous, and he keeps the scenes going for so long that any suspense dissipates. Kubrick's involvement in film technology led to the awesomely impressive effects of *2001*, and to the tableau style of *Barry Lyndon*, which some people found hypnotic, but it works against him here. Over and over, the camera tracks the characters, and by the climax, when we're running around in the hedge maze on the hotel grounds, the rhythmic sameness has worn us down. It's like watching a skater do figure eights all night, or at least for two hours and twenty-six minutes. (Less two minutes of highly expendable footage that the director cut after the film's opening.)

The story, loosely adapted from a pulp gothic by Stephen King, is about a former teacher, Jack Torrance (played by Jack Nicholson), who wants to write; he takes the job of winter caretaker at an isolated hotel in Colorado that was built on Indian burial ground, and moves in with his wife, Wendy

(Shelley Duvall), and Danny, their son. The child is already somewhat traumatized, because of an episode in the past when his father—drunk at the time and in a violent temper—grabbed him and dislocated his shoulder. Since that injury, Danny has had a psychic sensitivity—"the shining"—and he has visions that make him afraid of the hotel, especially of Room 237. The hotel's departing black cook, Halloran (Scatman Crothers), who also "shines," explains to him that events in the past leave traces that can be dangerous to those with "the gift," and cautions him to avoid that room. However, Torrance, though he has been warned that a previous caretaker got "cabin fever" and slaughtered his two small daughters and his wife before taking his own life, is elated about the place; it gives him a happy sense of déjà vu. So the Torrances are left alone for the winter, to be snowbound in what is quite obviously a haunted hotel.

It took nerve, or maybe something more like hubris, for Kubrick to go against all convention and shoot most of this gothic in broad daylight. Probably he liked the idea of our waking into a nightmare instead of falling asleep into one. And, having used so many night shots in *A Clockwork Orange* and so much romantic lighting in *Barry Lyndon*, he may have wanted the technical challenge of the most glaring kind of brightness. The hotel sets, which were built on the sound stages at the EMI-Elstree Studios, outside London, have enormous windows; the elegant, simple interiors are decorated in something like a blend of Navajo and Art Deco, and flooded with simulated sunshine. There isn't a dark corner anywhere; even the kitchen storerooms have a fluorescent boldness. But the conventions of gothics are fun. Who wants to see evil in daylight, through a wide-angle lens? We go to *The Shining* hoping for nasty scare effects and for an appeal to our giddiest nighttime fears—vaporous figures, shadowy places. What we get doesn't tease the imagination. Visually, the movie often feels like a cheat, because most of the horror images are not integrated into the travelling shots; the horrors involved in the hotel's bloody past usually appear in inserts that flash on like the pictures in a slide show. In addition, there are long, static dialogues between Torrance and two demonic characters—a bartender and a waiter—who are clearly *his* demons: they are personified temptations, as in a medieval mystery play, and they encourage him in his worst impulses. (They also look as substantial as he does.) The taciturn bartender (played by Joe Turkel, who was Private Arnaud in *Paths of Glory*) is lighted to look satanic; he offers Torrance free drinks. The loathsome, snobbish English waiter (Philip Stone) goads Torrance to maintain his authority over his wife and child by force. During these lengthy conversations, we seem to be in a hotel in Hell. It's a very talky movie (a Hell for some movie-lovers). Clearly, Stanley Kubrick isn't primarily interested in the horror film as scary fun or for the mysterious beauty that directors such as Dreyer and Murnau have brought to it. Kubrick is a virtuoso technician, and that is part of the excitement that is generated by a new Kubrick film. But he isn't just a virtuoso technician; he's also, God help us, a deadly-serious metaphysician.

It is said that an audience will always give a movie the benefit of the doubt for the first half hour; at *The Shining*, I think we give it longer than that—from forty-five minutes to an hour. For one thing, it has a wonderful opening sequence that promises the kind of movie we are hoping it will be— ominous horn music with synthesized sounds of snake rattles and bird trills which suggest cosmic terror, and helicopter views of a car seen from high above, like a caterpillar being observed by God, as Torrance drives up the mountain roads for his job interview at the Overlook. And then there's Nicholson himself. He has a way of making us feel that we're in on a joke—that we're reading the dirty, resentful thoughts behind his affable shark grins— and he gives the first hour of the film its buzz. But Kubrick uses Nicholson in the most obvious way. The character of Jack Torrance—a man in a rage about his own inadequacy, the sort of man who plays genius to his wife, tells her that she has wrecked his life, jeers at her, and makes her unsure of him, unsure of herself—fits Nicholson all too snugly, and his performance begins to seem cramped, slightly robotized. There's no surprise in anything he does, no feeling of invention. This is true of everyone in the film—the actors appear to be merely Kubrick's tools, and you get the feeling that they have been denied any free will. Nicholson's acting, though, suffers the most, because there are so many shots of him looking diabolic—his eyebrows like twin Mt. Fujis hovering in his forehead—and so many echoes of his other freaks, in *Carnal Knowledge* and *The Fortune* and *Goin' South*. There's nothing he can do with the role except express the gleaming-eyed hostile undercurrents of incipient madness while waiting to go whole-hog crazy. It's a long wait, in an underpopulated movie. (Once the Torrances are isolated for the winter, we have nothing but quickly glimpsed horrors and those moral-temptation demons for diversion.) And when Torrance does turn violent and attempts to reënact the crimes of the earlier caretaker, the tone of Nicholson's performance seems too grinningly rabid for the movie he's in: axe in hand and slavering, with his tongue darting about in his mouth, he seems to have stumbled in from an old A.I.P. picture. He's borderline funny—which he isn't meant to be—and finally, in spite of his great talent, tiresome, a mixture of Richard III and the Big Bad Wolf huffing and puffing.

The family theme—that is, a boy child's primal fears that his father will hurt his mother and him—doesn't jell: we don't feel the give-and-take of familial stresses, we don't feel that Jack and Wendy Torrance are married or that Danny is their child. When the three are together in the car driving to the hotel and we could get some sense of how they interact, Kubrick and his coscenarist, the novelist and critic Diane Johnson, use the scene instead to have Jack answer the boy's question about what the Donner Party was. (In case we didn't know that the mystery in this movie is the higher mystery. The Donner Party has become the literary person's equivalent of such *National Enquirer* stories as "My Mother Ate My Child.") The little boy who plays Danny has a clear face and a grave, unchildish voice; he has a lovely calm, trancelike quality. But each scene in the movie is so carefully structured to serve a purpose and he performs so precisely that he begins to seem like a puppet, and we don't feel anxious about his fate, as we would with a child whose terror wasn't so muted. Wendy, the drudge who does the work at the hotel while Jack sits at his typewriter, is a woebegone, victim role until this woman, who has been driven into hysteria, must pull herself out in order to protect her child. Though at the start Shelley Duvall seems not quite there, as if her lines were being spoken by someone else in another room, she becomes much stronger. We can feel that she's held down; she usually brings a more radiant eccentricity to her parts. But she looks more like a Modigliani than ever, and even in this role, which requires her to have tears welling in her Raggedy Ann eyes almost constantly, she has her amazing directness and her odd, flip gallantry. There's a remarkable moment when Wendy picks up her child and screams at her husband. And in what is probably the most daringly sustained series of shots Wendy, who is carrying a baseball bat in case she needs it with Jack, backs away as he moves toward her; he keeps advancing, she brandishes the bat as she backs away across a room and up a staircase, finally swinging the bat in front of her to keep him at a distance. It's a ghoulish parody of a courtship dance, staged with hairbreadth timing (though overextended), and Duvall is superbly simple even when Wendy is palsied with terror. Yet Duvall isn't entirely convincing as a mother; she's more like a very conscientious nurse.

The Torrances don't really seem to interest Kubrick anyway—not as individuals. At first, we get the impression that the horrors and demons are simply hallucinatory embodiments of Jack's impulses to kill his wife and son, and that Danny, with his shining, is picking up warnings. When Danny shines, he often waggles his forefinger and talks in the guttural voice of an imaginary playmate, Tony, who, Danny says, "lives in my mouth"; Tony is given to croaking "Redrum," in the manner of "Beware the ides of March." Jack took a vow not to drink after the violent incident with his son, but when Wendy accuses him of mistreating the boy again, he begins to frequent the Gold Room of the hotel, where he gets high on (imaginary?) booze, has conversations with the (imaginary?) bartender, and mingles with the (imaginary?) guests at revels that suggest the twenties. He is almost seduced by a tall, slim nude who comes out of her bath in Room 237, but when they're in each other's arms kissing, he sees in the mirror that she's a fat, rotting crone—and at the same instant she's back in her tub yet still standing there laughing at him. Danny's behavior and Jack's activities all seem explainable by Jack's madness. But Danny has been bruised on the neck, and he says that it was the crone, trying to strangle him, and after Jack has become crazily violent and is chasing Danny, even Wendy catches sight of a couple of depraved creatures in a bedroom. (Kubrick has an odd sense of morality: it's meant to be a hideous debauch when she sees the two figures in the bedroom—one of them, wearing a pig costume, looks up at her while he or she is still bent over the genitals of a man in evening clothes on the bed.) Soon Wendy, like

Danny, sees the blood pouring from the elevator, and other apparitions, and hears people chanting. Do the tensions between father, mother, and son create the ghosts, or do the ghosts serve as catalysts to make those tensions erupt? It appears to be an intertwined process. Kubrick seems to be saying that rage, uncontrollable violence, and ghosts spawn each other—that they are really the same thing. He's using Stephen King's hokum to make a metaphysical statement about immortality. The Torrances are his archetypes; they are the sources and victims of monsters that live on.

Kubrick mystifies us deliberately, much as Antonioni did in *The Passenger*, though for different purposes. The conversations between Jack and his demons are paced like the exposition in drawing-room melodramas of fifty years ago; you could drop stones into a river and watch the ripples between words. (In one of these scenes, with Jack and the waiter conversing in a men's room, the movie comes to a dead halt, from which it never fully recovers.) Kubrick wants to disorient us. At a critical moment in the action, there's an abrupt cut to the images on the TV news that Halloran, the cook, is watching in Florida, and the audience is bewildered—it's as if the projectionist had made a mistake. In one scene, Jack, in bed, wears a sweatshirt; the lettering across it is reversed, so we assume we're seeing a mirror image. But then Wendy enters the room and goes over to him, and we never move away to see the mirror. *The Shining* is also full of deliberate time dislocations. Two little sisters (who seem the deliberate re-creation of a Diane Arbus photograph) appear before Danny; we naturally assume that they are the butchered daughters of the earlier caretaker. But they are wearing twin party dresses of the twenties, and we have been told that the daughters were killed in the winter of 1970. Jack says that he injured Danny three years ago, and Wendy says that it happened five months ago. The waiter, whom Jack first meets at a twenties party, has the same name as the murderous caretaker of 1970. (There is no mention of who has taken care of the hotel the winters since then.) The film is punctuated with titles: suddenly there will be a black frame with "Tuesday" on it, or "3 o'clock," or "Saturday"; after the first ones, the titles all refer to time, but in an almost arbitrary way. Jack says that he loves the hotel and wishes "we could stay here forever, ever, ever." And at the very end there's a heavy hint of reincarnation and the suggestion that Jack *has* been there forever, ever, ever. I hate to say it, but I think the central character of this movie is time itself, or, rather, timelessness.

Even the methodical use of tracking patterns is thematic—a visual representation of the repetitive, cyclical nature of experience. Probably Kubrick meant to draw us into the swirling movement from the start and make the evil palpable—and then, as we gradually became disoriented in time, we were supposed to accept the mystic inevitability of the ugly theme (the timelessness of murder). But since we are not drawn in, we're not effectively disoriented—just fed up. We wait for revelations—the events that will connect the different types of parapsychological phenomena we've been observing—

and since we don't get those revelations, the picture seems not to make any sense. So when, at the very end, we're hit over the head with reincarnation, it has no emotional resonance. It just seems like a dumb finish.

Much of the film appears to be structured in terms drawn from Freud's essay *The "Uncanny."* (Danny's creation of a double in order to protect himself, Jack's immediate feeling of being at home in the hotel, the maze, etc.), but we don't actually feel this psychological patterning; it doesn't connect up subconsciously as we watch the movie. And what of the redrum blood pouring from that elevator? There isn't any gothic, dream logic that we respond to when we see the bleeding elevator, and no one ever takes an elevator in this movie. Is it possible that Kubrick intends something as banal as rivers of blood running throughout time, rising and subsiding? Probably most of us go to a gothic eager to be manipulated by someone with finesse. But we don't know how to read Kubrick's signals; it may be that he simply doesn't know us well enough anymore to manipulate us successfully. Again and again, the movie leads us to expect something—almost promises it—and then disappoints us. Why give us a tour of the vast hotel kitchen, with an inventory of the contents of the meat locker, when nothing much takes place there? (Couldn't we at least have a touch of comic relief—Shelley Duvall, like a female Buster Keaton, covering miles in an area designed for the preparation of banquets in order to cook a meal for three?) At one point, the child escapes from the hedge maze and runs into his mother's arms, and we're afraid that his father is going to loom up just behind him—and then we see Jack in the middle of the maze. The clumsiest part of the movie involves a promise that is clearly broken. When Jack is becoming dangerous, Danny tries to get help in the only way he can, by sending psychic messages to Halloran. The film then crosscuts between the mother and child in their ordeal and Halloran in his apartment in Florida, Halloran trying to make contact with the hotel by phone, Halloran trying to have the Forest Service make contact with the hotel by radio, Halloran flying to Denver, Halloran in the air, landing at the Denver airport, renting a car and driving to Boulder, tricking a friend in order to borrow a Sno-Cat, in the Sno-Cat driving through a storm, driving, driving (always seen in profile, looking like a sculptured Indian), approaching, finally arriving. He walks toward the entrance (with his dear, bowlegged gait), comes in the door, walks inside (still bowlegged), and calls out and calls out—the scene is prolonged. And nothing decisive to the movie comes of all this. Halloran travelled all that way and we were subjected to all that laborious crosscutting (which destroyed any chance for a buildup of suspense back at the hotel) just to provide a sacrificial victim and a Sno-Cat? The awful suspicion pops into the mind that since we don't want to see Wendy or Danny hurt and there's nobody else alive around for Jack to get at, he's given the black man. (Remember the scene in *Huckleberry Finn* when Huck tells Tom's Aunt Sally that he arrived on a steamboat and that a cylinder head had "blowed out." "Good gracious!" she says. "Anybody hurt?" "No'm. Killed a nigger." "Well, it's lucky; because sometimes people do get hurt.") But, at the same time, Halloran is the only noble character in the movie. Too noble. Something doesn't sit right about the way the movie ascribes the gift of shining to the good black man and the innocent child (the insulted and the injured?), and having Halloran's Florida apartment decorated with big pictures of proud sexy black women gives the film an odor of sanctity. The waiter referred to Halloran as a "nigger cook"; the demons in this movie are so vicious they're even racists.

The Shining seems to be about the quest for immortality—the immortality of evil. Men are psychic murderers: they want to be free and creative, and can only take out their frustrations on their terrified wives and children. The movie appears to be a substitution story: The waiter denies that he was the caretaker, but there has always been a caretaker. And if the waiter is telling the truth, it's Jack who has always been the caretaker. Or maybe Jack is so mad that he has hatched this waiter, in which case Jack probably *has* always been the caretaker. Apparently, he lives forever, only to attack his family endlessly. It's what Kubrick said in *2001*: Mankind began with the weapon and just went on from there. Redrum ("murder" backward). Kubrick is the man who thought it necessary to introduce a godlike force (the black slab) to account for evolution. It was the slab that told the apelike man to pick up the bone and use it as a weapon. This was a new version of original sin: man the killer acts on God's command. Somehow, Kubrick ducked out on the implications of his own foolishness when he gave *2001* its utopian, technological ending—man, reborn out of science, as angelic, interplanetary fetus. Now he seems to have gone back to his view at the beginning of *2001*: man is a murderer, throughout eternity. The bone that was high in the air has turned into Jack's axe, held aloft, and Jack, crouched over, making wild, inarticulate sounds as he staggers in the maze, has become the ape.

What's increasingly missing from Kubrick's work is the spontaneity, the instinct, the lightness that would make us respond intuitively. We're starved for pleasure at this movie; when we finally get a couple of exterior nighttime shots with theatrical lighting, we're pathetically grateful. As Wendy, trying to escape from Jack, opens a window and looks at the snowstorm outside, and then as she pushes Danny out and he slides down the snowbank, we experience, for a second or two, the spectral beauty we have been longing for. Earlier (in the film's most imaginative, chilling scene), when Wendy looked at the pile of manuscript that her husband had been working on, she found only one sentence, "All work and no play makes Jack a dull boy," typed over and over. Well, all work and no play makes Stanley a dull boy, too. He was locked up with this project for more than three years, and if ever there was a movie that expressed cabin fever, this is it.

June 9, 1980

Why Are Movies So Bad?

or, The Numbers

*T*he movies have been so rank the last couple of years that when I see people lining up to buy tickets I sometimes think that the movies aren't drawing an audience—they're inheriting an audience. People just want to go to a movie. They're stung repeatedly, yet their desire for a good movie—for *any* movie—is so strong that all over the country they keep lining up. "There's one God for all creation, but there must be a separate God for the movies," a producer said. "How else can you explain their survival?" An atmosphere of hope develops before a big picture's release, and even after your friends tell you how bad it is, you can't quite believe it until you see for yourself. The lines (and the grosses) tell us only that people are going to the movies—not that they're having a good time. Financially, the industry is healthy, so among the people at the top there seems to be little recognition of what miserable shape movies are in. They think the grosses are proof that people are happy with what they're getting, just as TV executives think that the programs with the highest ratings are what TV viewers want, rather than what they settle for. (A number of the new movie executives come from TV.) These new executives don't necessarily see many movies themselves, and they rarely go to a theatre. If for the last couple of years Hollywood couldn't seem to do anything right, it isn't that it was just a stretch of bad luck—it's the result of recent developments within the industry. And in all probability it will get worse, not better. There have been few recent American movies worth lining up for—last year there was chiefly *The Black Stallion*, and this year there is *The Empire Strikes Back*. The first was made under the aegis of Francis Ford Coppola; the second was financed by George Lucas, using his profits from *Star Wars* as a guarantee to obtain bank loans. One can say with fair confidence that neither *The Black Stallion* nor *The Empire Strikes Back* could have been made with such care for visual richness and imagination if it had been done under studio control. Even small films on traditional subjects are difficult to get financed at a studio if there are no parts for stars in them; Peter Yates, the director of *Breaking Away*—a graceful, unpredictable comedy that pleases and satisfies audiences—took the project to one studio after another for almost six years before he could get the backing for it.

There are direct results when conglomerates take over movie companies. At first, the heads of the conglomerates may be drawn into the movie business for the status implications—the opportunity to associate with world-famous celebrities. Some other conglomerate heads may be drawn in for the girls, but for them, too, a new social life beckons, and as they become socially involved, people with great names approach them as equals, and it gets them crazy. Famous stars and producers and writers and directors tell them about offers they've had from other studios and about ideas they have for pictures, and the conglomerate heads become indignant that the studios they control aren't in on these wonderful projects. The next day, they're on the phone raising hell with their studio bosses. Very soon, they're likely to be summoning directors and suggesting material to them, talking to actors, and telling the company executives what projects should be developed. How bad are the taste and judgment of the conglomerate heads? Very bad. They haven't grown up in a show-business milieu—they don't have the background, the instincts, the information of those who have lived and sweated movies for many years. (Neither do most of the current studio bosses.) The conglomerate heads may be business geniuses, but as far as movies are concerned they have virgin instincts; ideas that are new to them and take them by storm may have failed grotesquely dozens of times. But they feel that they are creative people—how else could they have made so much money and be in a position to advise artists what to do? Who is to tell them no? Within a very short time, they are in fact, though not in title, running the studio. They turn up compliant executives who will settle for the title and not fight for the authority or for their own tastes—if, in fact, they have any. The conglomerate heads find these compliant executives among lawyers and agents, among lawyer-agents, among television executives, and in the lower echelons of the companies they've taken over. Generally, these executives reserve all their enthusiasm for movies that have made money; those are the only movies they like. When a director or a writer talks to them and tries to suggest the kind of picture he has in mind by using a comparison, they may stare at him blankly. They are usually law-school or business-school graduates; they have no frame of reference. Worse, they have no shame about not knowing anything about movies. From their point of view, such knowledge is not essential to their work. Their talent is being able to anticipate their superiors' opinions; in meetings, they show a sixth sense for guessing what the most powerful person in the room wants to hear. And if they ever guess wrong, they know how to shift gears without a tremor. So the movie companies wind up with top production executives whose interest in movies rarely extends beyond the immediate selling possibilities; they could be selling neckties just as well as movies, except that they are drawn to glamour and power.

This does not prevent these executives from being universally treated as creative giants. If a studio considers eighty projects, and eventually twenty of them (the least risky) go into production, and two of them become runaway hits (or even one of them), the studio's top executive will be a hero to his company and the media, and will soon be quoted in the *Los Angeles Times* and *The New York Times* talking about his secret for picking winners—his intuitive understanding, developed from his childhood experiences, that people want a strong, upbeat narrative, that they want to cheer the hero and hiss the villain. When *Alien* opened "big," Alan Ladd, Jr., president of the pictures division of Twentieth Century-Fox, was regarded as a demigod; it's the same way that Fred Silverman was a demigod. It has nothing to do with quality, only with the numbers. (Ladd and his team weren't admired for the small pictures they took chances on and the artists they stuck by.) The media now echo the kind of thinking that goes on in Hollywood, and spread it wide. Movie critics on TV discuss the relative grosses of the new releases; the grosses at this point relative to previous hits; which pictures will pass the others in a few weeks. It's like the Olympics—which will be the winners?

*T*here are a lot of reasons that movies have been so bad during the last couple of years and probably won't be any better for the next couple of years. One big reason is that rotten pictures are making money—not necessarily wild amounts (though a few are), but sizable amounts. So if studio heads want nothing more than to make money and grab power, there is no reason for them to make better ones. Turning out better pictures might actually jeopardize their position. Originally, the studios were controlled by theatre chains—the chains opened the studios in order to have a source of supply. But the studios and the theatre chains were separated by a Supreme Court order in 1948 and subsequent lower-court rulings; after that, the studios, operating without the protection of theatres committed in advance to play their product, resorted to "blind bidding" and other maneuvers in order to reduce the risk on their films. It's only in the last few years that the studios have found a new kind of protection. They have discovered that they can get much more from the sale of movies to television than they had been getting, and that they can negotiate presale agreements with the networks for guaranteed amounts before they commit themselves to a production. Licensing fees to the networks now run between $3,000,000 and $4,000,000 for an average picture, and the studios negotiate in advance not only for network showings and later TV syndication (about $1,500,000 for an average picture), and for pay television (between $1,000,000 and $1,500,000), but for cable TV, the airlines, cassettes, and overseas television. And, of course, they still sell to foreign distributors and to exhibitors here, and much of that money is also committed in advance—sometimes even paid in advance. So if a film is budgeted at $8,500,000, the studio may have $14,000,000 guaranteed and—theoretically, at least—show a profit before shooting starts, even if $4,000,000 is allowed for marketing and advertising. And the studio still has the possibility of a big box-office hit and *really* big money. If a picture is a large-scale adventure story or has superstars, the licensing fee to the networks alone may be between $15,000,000 and $25,000,000, and the total advance guarantees may come to almost double the budget. Financially, the only danger in an arrangement like this is that if the film goes seriously over budget the studio can still lose money. That's why directors who have the reputation of always coming in on schedule are in steady demand even if they've had a long line of box-office failures and their work is consistently mediocre, and why directors who are perfectionists are shunned as if they were lepers—unless, like Hal Ashby, they've had some recent hits.

The studios no longer make movies primarily to attract and please moviegoers; they make movies in such a way as to get as much as possible from the prearranged and anticipated deals. Every picture (allowing for a few exceptions) is cast and planned in terms of those deals. Though the studio is very happy when it has a box-office hit, it isn't terribly concerned about the people who buy tickets and come out grumbling. They don't grumble very loudly anyway, because even the lumpiest pictures are generally an improvement over television; at least, they're always bigger. TV accustoms people to not expecting much, and because of the new prearranged deals they're not getting very much. There is a quid pro quo for a big advance sale to television and theatres: the project must be from a fat, dumb best-seller about an international jewel heist or a skyjacking that involves a planeload of the rich and famous, or be a thinly disguised show-business biography of someone who came to an appallingly wretched end, or have an easily paraphrasable theme—preferably something that can be done justice to in a sentence and brings to mind the hits of the past. How else could you entice buyers? Certainly not with something unfamiliar, original. They feel safe with big-star packages, with chase thrillers, with known ingredients. For a big overseas sale, you must have "international" stars—performers who are known all over, such as Sophia Loren, Richard Burton, Candice Bergen, Roger Moore, Clint Eastwood, Burt Reynolds, Alain Delon, Charles Bronson, Steve McQueen. And you should probably avoid complexities: much of the new overseas audience is subliterate. For a big advance sale to worldwide television, a movie should also be innocuous: it shouldn't raise any hackles, either by strong language or by a controversial theme. And there must be stars, though not necessarily movie stars. It has recently been discovered that even many Americans are actually more interested in TV personalities than in movie ones, and may be roused from their TV-viewing to go see a film with John Denver or John Ritter. In countries where American TV series have become popular, our TV stars may be better known than our movie stars (especially the ones who appear infrequently). A 1979 Canadian film, *Running*, starring Michael Douglas, who has appeared in a TV series and was featured in *The China Syndrome*, cost $4,200,000; by the time it was completed, the various rights to it had been sold for over $6,000,000. The lawyer-financier who set up the production of *Foolin' Around*, which stars Gary Busey, said he would not have made the picture without the television insurance of a supporting cast that included Tony Randall, Cloris Leachman, and Eddie Albert. Nobody needs to have heard of these independently packaged pictures for them to be profitable, and, in some cases, if it were not contractually necessary to open the film in theatres in order to give it legitimacy as a movie, it would be cheaper not to, because the marketing and advertising costs may outstrip the box-office revenue (unless that, too, was guaranteed). On productions like these, the backers don't suffer the gamblers' anxieties that were part of film business in the fifties and sixties, and even in the early seventies. Of course, these backers don't experience the gamblers' highs, either. Movie executives now study the television Q ratings, which measure the public's familiarity with performers, and a performer with a high rating (which he attains if he's been in a long-running series or on a daytime quiz show) is offered plum movie roles—even if this means that the script will have to be completely rewritten for his narrow range or bland personality.

*T*here is an even grimmer side to all this: because the studios have discovered how to take the risk out of moviemaking, they don't want to make any movies that they can't protect themselves on. Production and advertising costs have gone so high that there is genuine nervous panic about risky projects. If an executive finances what looks like a perfectly safe, stale piece of material and packs it with stars, and the production costs skyrocket way beyond the guarantees, and the picture loses many millions, *he* won't be blamed for it—he was playing the game by the same rules as everybody else. If, however, he takes a gamble on a small project that can't be sold in advance—something that a gifted director really wants to do, with a subtle, not easily summarized theme and no big names in the cast—and it loses just a little money, his neck is on the block. So to the executives a good script is a script that attracts a star, and they will make their deals and set the full machinery of a big production in motion and schedule the picture's release dates, even though the script problems have never been worked out and everyone (even the director) secretly knows that the film will be a confused mess, an embarrassment.

Another new factor makes a risky project still riskier; if a movie doesn't have an easily paraphrasable theme or big stars, it's hard to sell via a thirty-second TV commercial. (The networks pay a lot for movies, but they get much of it back directly from the movie industry, which increasingly relies on TV commercials to sell a film.) It's even hard for the studio advertising departments to figure out a campaign for newspapers and magazines. And so, faced with something unusual or original, the studio head generally says, "I don't know how to market it, and if I don't know how to market it, it will lose money." The new breed of studio head is not likely to say, "It's something I feel we should take a chance on. Let's see if there's somebody who might be able to figure out how to market it." Just about the only picture the studios made last year that the executives took a financial risk on was *Breaking Away*. And despite the fact that it cost what is now a pittance ($2,400,000) and received an Academy Award Best Picture nomination, Twentieth Century-Fox didn't give it a big theatrical re-release (the standard procedure for a nominated film) but sold it to NBC for immediate showing, for $5,000,000. So a couple of weeks after the Awards ceremony, just when many people had finally heard of *Breaking Away* and might have gone to a theatre to see it, it appeared, trashed in the usual manner, on television. The studio couldn't be sure how much more money might come in from box offices, and grabbed a sure thing. In order to accept the NBC offer, the studio even bypassed pay TV, where the picture could have been seen uncut. It was almost as if *Breaking Away* were being punished for not having stars and not having got a big advance TV sale. And the price was almost insulting: last year, Fox licensed *The Sound of Music* to NBC for $21,500,000, and licensed *Alien* to ABC for $12,000,000, with escalator clauses that could take the figure up to $15,000,000; Columbia licensed *Kramer vs. Kramer* to ABC for nearly $20,000,000, and United Artists got $20,000,000 for *Rocky II* from CBS. But then how do you summarize in a sentence the appeal of a calm, evenhanded film about fathers and sons, town boys and college boys, and growing up—a modest classic that never states its themes, that stirs the emotions by indirection, by the smallest of actions and the smallest exchanges of dialogue?

*I*f a writer-director conceives a script for a fiery young actor—K., a young man with star potential who has not yet had a role that brought him to the consciousness of the public—and shapes the central character to bring out K.'s volatility and ardor, he is likely to be told by the studio head, "K. doesn't do anything to me." That rules out K., even if the studio head has never seen K. act (and chances are he wouldn't remember him if he had). The studio head doesn't care if K. could become a star in this part; he wants R., because he can get a $4,000,000 network sale with the impassive, logy R., a Robert Wagner type who was featured in a mini-series. And if the point is pressed, the studio head may cut off discussion with some variation of "I must know what I'm doing, or I wouldn't be in this job." If he is feeling expansive, he may go on with "I won't say that you can't make a good film with K., and some people—some critics and your friends—will like it. But a good picture to me is a successful picture—one that will make money." If the writer-director still persists, it's taken as a sign of stupidity. A finer-grained executive—one of the rare ones who loves movies—may put it to him this way: "I like K., I like you, I like the script. But I can't recommend it. It's an expensive picture, and the subject matter makes it a long shot. And if I back too many long shots that don't come in, I'm out on my ass." That's the distillation of executive timidity, and maybe it's better to get it from the coarser man: you can have the pleasure of hating him—you aren't made to sympathize with his plight. Since all the major studios basically play by the same rules, the writer-director will wind up with a picture that is crucially miscast and has a vacuum at its center. By the time it is released and falls by the wayside, and he is publicly humiliated, K., disgusted at not having got the part, may have accepted a dumb role in a TV series and become a hot new TV personality, whom all the movie studios are propositioning.

Chances are that even if the writer-director had been allowed to use K., he would have been completely enraged and demoralized by the time he started shooting, because the negotiating process can stretch on for years, and anyone who wants to make a movie is treated as a hustler and an adversary. "Studios!" said Billy Wilder, paraphrasing an old complaint about women. "You can't make pictures with 'em, and you can't make pictures without 'em." Everybody in the movie business has the power to say no, and the least secure executives protect themselves by saying no to just about anything that comes their way. Only those at the very top can say yes, and they protect themselves, too. They postpone decisions because they're fearful, and also because they don't mind keeping someone dangling while his creative excitement dries up and all the motor drive goes out of his proposal. They don't mind keeping people waiting, because it makes them feel more powerful. I'm describing trends; of course, there are exceptions—those who are known (and sometimes revered) for quick decisions, like David Picker in his United Artists days, and Daniel Melnick in his brief stints at M-G-M and Columbia, and David Begelman at Columbia and now at M-G-M. But most of the ones who could say yes don't; they consider it and string you along. (Hollywood is the only place where you can die of encouragement.) For the supplicant, it's a matter of weeks, months, years, waiting for meetings at which he can beg permission to do what he was, at the start, eager to do. And even when he's got a meeting, he has to catch the executive's attention and try to keep it; in general the higher the executive, the more cruelly short his attention span. (They're television babies. Thirty seconds is a long time to them.) In this atmosphere of bureaucratic indifference or contempt, things aren't really decided—they just happen, along bureaucratic lines. (Generally, it's only if a picture is a hit that executives talk about having given it the go-ahead. They all angle for credit in the media.) During the long wait, the director has lost the cinematographer he wanted and half the performers; in order to get the necessary approvals, he has agreed to actors he knows are wrong, and he has pared down the script to cut costs, chopping out the scenes that once meant the most to him but that he knows he can't get in the tight, ten-week shooting schedule he has been forced to accept. And then, at the last minute, a few days before shooting is to start, the studio is likely to slice the budget further—and he's down to a nine-week schedule, which means trimming the camera moves that were half the reason he'd been eager to work on the idea in the first place. Is it any wonder if the picture that comes out has a sour spirit?

It may just barely come out anyway. If there's an executive shakeup during production or after the film is completed (and shakeups take place every few months), the new studio head has nothing to gain if the film succeeds (he can't take credit for initiating it); he may find it to his strategic advantage for the film to fail. The executives—bed-hoppers, who go from one berth to another—have no particular loyalty to the studio, and there isn't the lower-echelon executive stability to launch a film initiated during the old regime with the same care as one initiated during the new regime. It all depends on the signals that come from the top.

*I*f a big star and a big director show interest in a project, the executives will go along for a $14,000,000 or $15,000,000 budget even if, by the nature of the material, the picture should be small. And so what might have been a charming light entertainment that millions of people all over the world would enjoy is inflated, rewritten to enlarge the star's part, and overscaled. It makes money in advance and sends people out of theatres complaining and depressed. Often, when people leave theatres now they're bewildered by the anxious nervous construction of the film—by the feeling it gives them of having been pieced together out of parts that don't fit. Movies have gone to hell and amateurism. A third of the pictures being made by Hollywood this year are in the hands of first-time directors, who will receive almost no guidance or help. They're thrown right into a pressure-cooker situation, where any delay is costly. They may have come out of sitcoms, and their dialogue will sound forced, as if it were all recorded in a large, empty cave; they may have come out of nowhere and have never worked with actors before. Even if a director is highly experienced, he probably has certain characteristic weaknesses, such as a tendency to lose track of the story, or an ineptness with women characters; he's going to need watching. But who knows that, or cares enough to try to protect the picture? The executives may have hired the director after "looking at his work"—that is, running off every other reel of one of his films. They are busy people. Network executives who are offered a completed movie commonly save time by looking at a fifteen-minute selection from it—a précis of its highlights—which has been specially prepared for them. God forbid that they should have to sit through the whole thing.

What isn't generally understood is how much talent and hard work are wasted—enough, maybe, to supply the world with true entertainment. A writer who is commissioned to adapt a book and turns in a crackerjack script, acclaimed by the studio executives, who call him a genius, then stands helplessly by as the studio submits it to the ritual lists of the stars and the directors whom they can get the biggest guarantees on. And as, one by one, the stars and directors who aren't right for the project anyway take months to read it and turn it down, the executives' confidence in the script drains away. If a star expresses tentative interest, contingent on a complete rewrite, they will throw out the snappy script and authorize a new script by a sodden writer who has just had a fluke hit, and when the star decides to do something else anyway, they will have a new script written for a different star, and another and another, until no one can remember why there was ever any interest in the project. It may be shelved then, but so much money has already gone into it that in a couple of years some canny producer will think it should be brought back to life and reworked to fit a hot new teen-ager from television—who eventually will decide not to do it, and so on. To put it simply: A good script is a script to which Robert Redford will commit himself. A bad script is a script which Redford has turned down. A script that "needs work" is a script about which Redford has yet to make up his mind. It is possible to run a studio with this formula; it is even possible to run a studio *profitably* with this formula. But this world of realpolitik that has replaced moviemaking has nothing to do with moviemaking. It's not just that the decisions made by the executives might have been made by anyone off the street—it's that the pictures themselves seem to have been made by anyone off the street.

The executives are a managerial class with no real stake in the studio; they didn't build it, it's not part of them, and they're moving on—into a bigger job at another studio, or into independent production (where there's more money), or to form their own companies. The executives just try to hold things together for the short period that they're going to be around; there isn't even an elementary regard for the conservation of talent. And, as in any chaotic bureaucracy, the personalities and goals of those at the top set the tone for all the day-to-day decisions; the top executives' apathy about the quality of movies infects the studio right down the line. The younger executives who are pushing their way up don't want to waste their time considering scripts that may not attract a star. For them, too, a good picture is a picture that makes money, and so after *The China Syndrome* clicked at box offices, they could be heard talking about what a wonderful craftsman its director, James Bridges, was, and after *The Amityville Horror*, with its unbelievably clunky script, by Sandor Stern, showed big grosses, they wanted to sign up Stern as a writer-director. At the bottom as at the top, the executives want to score; they want a hit, not just for the money but for the personal pleasure of the kill.

*P*art of what has deranged American life in this past decade is the change in book publishing and in magazines and newspapers and in the movies as they have passed out of the control of those whose lives were bound up in them and into the control of conglomerates, financiers, and managers who treat them as ordinary commodities. This isn't a reversible process; even if there were Supreme Court rulings that split some of these holdings from the conglomerates, the traditions that developed inside many of those businesses have been ruptured. And the continuity is gone. In earlier eras, when a writer made a book agreement with a publisher, he expected to be working with the people he signed up with; now those people may be replaced the next day, or the whole firm may be bought up and turned into a subdivision of a textbook-publishing house or a leisure-activities company. The new people in the job aren't going to worry about guiding a writer slowly; they're not going to think about the book after this one. They want best-sellers. Their job is to find them or manufacture them. And just as the studios have been hiring writers to work on screenplays, they are now beginning to hire writers to work on novels, which the publishers, with the help of studio money, will then attempt to promote to best-sellerdom at the same time that they are being made into movies. The writer Avery Corman has suggested "the horrifying prospect of a novelist being fired from his own book." It won't horrify the people who are commissioning these new books—pre-novelizations.

There are certain kinds of business in which the public interest is more of a factor than it is in the manufacture of neckties. Book publishing, magazines and newspapers, movies and television and live theatre—these are businesses, of course, but traditionally the people who work in them have felt privileged (by birth or ability or talent or luck, or by a combination of those factors). That has been true not only of the actors and journalists but of the entrepreneurs and the managers. There have always been a few businessmen in these fields who had the sensibility of artists (without the talent or the drive); if they had a good critical sense and a generous nature, they were appreciators of artists and didn't resent them. And so they became great producers in the theatre and movies, or great book and magazine editors. Contemporary variants of these people insist on being celebrity-artists themselves, and right now they all seem to be writing and directing movies.

In movies, the balance between art and business has always been precarious, with business outweighing art, but the business was, at least, in the hands of businessmen who loved movies. As popular entertainment, movies need something of what the vulgarian moguls had—zest, a belief in their own instincts, a sentimental dedication to producing pictures that would make their country proud of their contribution, a respect for quality, and the biggest thing: a willingness to take chances. The cool managerial sharks don't have that; neither do the academics. But the vulgarians also did more than their share of damage, and they're gone forever anyway. They were part of a different America. They were, more often than not, men who paid only lip service to high ideals, while gouging everyone for profits. The big change in the country is reflected in the fact that people in the movie business no longer feel it necessary to talk about principles at all. They operate on the same assumptions as the newspapers that make heroes of the executives who have a hit and don't raise questions about its quality.

When the numbers game takes over a country, artists who work in a popular medium, such as the movies, lose their bearings fast. There's a pecking order in filmmaking, and the director is at the top—he's the authority figure.

A man who was never particularly attractive to women now finds that he's the padrone: everyone is waiting on his word, and women are his for the nod. The constant, unlimited opportunities for sex can be insidious; so is the limitless flattery of college students who turn directors into gurus. Directors are easily seduced. They mainline admiration. Recently, a screenwriter now directing his first picture was talking about his inability to find a producer who would take some of the burden off him; he said he needed a clone— someone who would know what was in his mind and be able to handle a million details for him. But anyone observing this writer-director would know that he needs a real producer, and for a much more important reason: to provide the sense of judgment he has already lost. Nobody really controls a production now; the director is on his own, even if he's insecure, careless, or nuts. There has always been a megalomaniac potential in moviemaking, and in this period of stupor, when values have been so thoroughly under-mined that even the finest directors and the ones with the most freedom aren't sure what they want to do, they often become obsessive and grandilo-quent—like mad royalty. Perpetually dissatisfied with the footage they're compulsively piling up, they keep shooting—adding rooms to the palace. Megalomania and art become the same thing to them. But the disorder isn't just in their heads, and a lot of people around them are deeply impressed by megalomania. What our directors need most of all, probably, is a sense of purpose and a subject that they can think their way through. Filmmakers want big themes, and where are the kinds of themes that they would fight the studios to express? It's no accident that the two best recent American movies are both fantasy fairy tales—childish in the fullest, deepest sense. Working inside a magical structure, Carroll Ballard in *The Black Stallion* and Irvin Kershner in *The Empire Strikes Back* didn't have to deal with the modern world; they were free to use the medium luxuriantly, without guilt. You can feel the love of moviemaking—almost a revelry in moviemaking—in their films, as you can also in Walter Hill's *The Long Riders*, despite its narrative weaknesses and a slight remoteness. But we don't go to the movies just for great fairy tales and myths of the old West; we also hope for something that connects directly with where we are. Part of the widespread anticipation of *Apocalypse Now* was, I think, our readiness for a visionary, climactic, sum-ming-up movie. We felt that the terrible rehash of pop culture couldn't go on, mustn't go on—that something new was needed. Coppola must have felt that, too, but he couldn't supply it. His film was posited on great thoughts arriving at the end—a confrontation and a revelation. And when they weren't there, people slunk out of the theatres, or tried to comfort themselves with chatter about the psychedelic imagery. Trying to say something big, Coppola got tied up in a big knot of American self-hatred and guilt, and what the pic-ture boiled down to was: White man—he devil. Since then, I think, people have expected less of movies and have been willing to settle for less. Some have even been willing to settle for *Kramer vs. Kramer* and other pictures that seem to be made for an audience of over-age flower children. These pictures express the belief that if a man cares about anything besides being at home with the kids, he's corrupt. Parenting ennobles Dustin Hoffman and makes him a better person in every way, while in *The Seduction of Joe Tynan* we can see that Alan Alda is a weak, corruptible fellow because he wants to be President of the United States more than he wants to stay at home communing with his daughter about her adolescent miseries. Pictures like these should all end with the fathers and the children sitting at home watching TV together.

The major studios have found the temporary final solution for movies: in technique and in destiny, their films *are* television. And there's no possibility of a big breakthrough in movies—a new release of energy, like the French New Wave, which moved from country to country and resulted in an international cross-fertilization—when movies are financed only if they fall into stale categories of past successes. But once the groups that are now subsidizing studio-made films begin to weary of getting TV shows when they thought they were buying movies, there should be a chance for some real moviemaking. And when the writers and directors have confidence in what they want to express, if they can't find backing from the studios they ought to be able to find backers outside the industry who will gamble on the money to be made from a good picture, once it is completed. It's easier to make money on movies now: there are more markets, and we know now that the films themselves have a much longer commercial life than early moviemakers could have guessed. The studios may find that they need great moviemakers more than the moviemakers need them. Billy Wilder may be right that you can't make pictures with 'em, but of course he's wrong that you can't make pictures without 'em. There are problems both ways, but there may be fewer problems without them, and less rage.

It would be very convincing to say that there's no hope for movies—that audiences have been so corrupted by television and have become so jaded that all they want are noisy thrills and dumb jokes and images that move along in an undemanding way, so they can sit and react at the simplest motor level. And there's plenty of evidence, such as the success of *Alien*. This was a haunted-house-with-gorilla picture set in outer space. It reached out, grabbed you, and squeezed your stomach; it was more griping than entertaining, but a lot of people didn't mind. They thought it was terrific, because at least they'd felt something: they'd been brutalized. It was like an entertainment contrived in Aldous Huxley's *Brave New World* by the Professor of Feelies in the College of Emotional Engineering. Yet there was also a backlash against *Alien*— many people were angry at how mechanically they'd been worked over. And when I saw *The Black Stallion* on a Saturday afternoon, there was proof that even children who have grown up with television and may never have been exposed to a good movie can respond to the real thing when they see it. It was a hushed, attentive audience, with no running up and down the aisles and no traffic to the popcorn counter, and even when the closing credits came on, the children sat quietly looking at the images behind the names. There may be a separate God for the movies, at that.

June 23, 1980

Muckrakers and Saints

*A*t the beginning of *Brubaker,* a group of convicts are being transported to Wakefield State Penitentiary. Among them is Robert Redford, who is clearly not just another convict, because during the drive to the prison and for the first days there he is a silent presence, registering the signs of low corruption, and responding to the acts of cruelty—the rapes, the lashings, the beatings—with tense, anguished compassion. It's close to half an hour before Redford identifies himself as the new warden, Henry Brubaker. This incognito prologue—a speeded-up season in hell—shows us the prison from the underside, from the point of view of the bludgeoned, terrified prisoners. They are controlled by gun-carrying convict guards, who, with the connivance of the prison administrators and the prison board, supply slave labor to nearby farms and businesses, and sell most of the food intended for the men. This section is one violent spasm after another: *Midnight Express* without Turks. It vividly establishes the need for a warden who will clean up the place, and it demonstrates that Brubaker is courageous enough to risk entering this medieval torture chamber as a powerless prisoner. The device is dependent on Redford's saying almost nothing. But he's the film's center of consciousness; whenever something happens, there's a cut to his silent reaction, and there are many lingering shots of him suffering for those who suffer. He's like Vincent de Paul sharing the agony of the galley slaves.

Wakefield prison is set in an unidentified Southern state; the actors speak with a pan-Southern accent—the more corrupt the character, the thicker the accent. Brubaker, of course, isn't a Southerner; he's an outsider. We're not told where he comes from, but when he gets cleaned up and into his plaids and corduroys and broad-brimmed hats, we can see what he is. He's the fearless, selfless white knight of the Westerns—Gary Cooper, flexing his jaw righteously, or Alan Ladd, the mysterious stranger in *Shane.* Brubaker is the mythic redeemer, who has come to clean out the evil infestation and then ride off alone into the sunset. But he hasn't ridden into a small Western town, where the good settlers are struggling against the rustlers and the land-grab-bers—he has been plunked down in a situation out of the old Warners muck-raking prison pictures.

Stuart Rosenberg, who replaced the first director (Bob Rafelson), made his reputation with an earlier prison picture, *Cool Hand Luke*, in 1967; *Brubaker* is considerably better. From the dramatic excitement Rosenberg brings to almost all the scenes, there is every indication that this project roused him from the apathy of the films he directed in the intervening years (*The April Fools, Move, WUSA, Pocket Money, The Laughing Policeman, The Drowning Pool, Voyage of the Damned, Love and Bullets, The Amityville Horror*). The movie was suggested by the experiences of Thomas O. Murton as superinten-dent of Tucker Prison Farm, in Arkansas, in 1967–68, which were reported in the 1969 book *Accomplices to the Crime*, by Murton and Joe Hyams; the fic-tionalized script, by W. D. Richter, has offhand dialogue with a warm, funny tone which is lost, however, when the characters make speeches for us. And Rosenberg worked with one of the greatest modern cinematographers—Bru-no Nuytten (who did Marguerite Duras's *The Truck* and André Téchiné's *French Provincial*). This film doesn't have the forced, hothouse atmosphere of *Cool Hand Luke*. Visually, it has a marvellous ease; it moves with such freedom that you give all your attention to the story being told—except when Rosenberg violates this freedom by fixating the camera on someone. Despite some perplexing scenes, which are probably the result of Rosen-berg's taking over a project that had been shaped for a different director and trying to mold the material his way, there are individual sequences in this movie that are probably the best work he has ever done on the screen. Yet there isn't a believable minute in it.

Installed in the warden's office, Brubaker asks his clerk, Purcell (Matt Clark), some questions, and as the sour, resentful clerk answers, the camera subjects him to prolonged close scrutiny, so that we won't fail to perceive every nuance of his double-dealing cowardliness. The gang of trusties who have been running the prison—the armed convicts who buy special privi-leges for themselves by beating the other prisoners to make them work hard-er—are never anything but sadistic, ruthless, totally conscienceless. One of them is well played by Tim McIntire, who, with his Southern-looking plump cheeks and his compressed little eyes, is like a redneck Harry Lime. Another (Everett McGill) is a tall, baby-faced menace with a cold stare that seems to have been handed down through generations of overzealous actors trying to make an impression. He is the chief sadist when this gang tortures and kills an old black man and strings him upside down at the top of the prison flag-pole. The old man, Abraham (played lovingly by Richard Ward, who died right after giving this demonstration of the glory of an actor's craft), was the prison's coffinmaker; he is killed because he has promised to show Brubaker where on the prison's farmland (fifteen thousand acres) two hundred bodies have been hidden in unmarked graves.

There's a sequence in which Woodward (M. Emmet Walsh), a jes'-folks local businessman, comes to pay his respects to the new warden, bringing a chocolate prune cake made by his wife. Woodward has been enriching himself by using convict labor at his logging mill, and, having contracted to build a new roof on a prison barracks, he put up one that collapsed. As he talks to Brubaker, trying to charm him but also using veiled threats, the camera moves in close, so that we won't miss any detail of his oily, folksy hypocrisy. And that's the only side there is to Woodward. The bad guys are totally bad. Nothing casual happens in this movie, and what we first see in a character is all we'll ever see. When Brubaker is called before the prison board to explain the reforms he has set in motion, each member of the board reveals his special interest in maintaining the prison as a nest of corruption, and the chairman is that veteran mealymouthed politician Murray Hamilton. (By now, all you have to do is point a camera at him and his pores ooze duplicity.)

The high point of the movie, dramatically and emotionally, comes toward the end of the prologue: a black prisoner (Morgan Freeman) who is in the hole—the death-row cell block, where the men are allowed out into the light for only a few minutes one day each year—breaks out of his dungeon, grabs a young prisoner (David Keith) and starts to strangle him. Brubaker (still in convict guise) intervenes. The tension in this scene comes largely from Morgan Freeman's superb control: he makes you feel the psychotic urgency of the situation. It's typical of the way the film is constructed that we are caught up in Morgan Freeman's intensity and then he's dropped from the movie. There's no follow-through on most of the issues that are raised, either. Brubaker announces that a new barracks roof will be put up by the prisoners themselves, and we expect to see what happens. Does he succeed? We don't find out. It's almost as if the moviemakers thought that once the expectation had been set up, it would be banal to fulfill it. (Or is it merely that the later scenes these plot threads were meant to connect with weren't shot, or were shot and then cut?) After that wham-bam prologue, with its mysterious blond stranger, the audience expects the hero to take some sort of vengeance on the guards who committed those grisly brutalities, and when he doesn't the film loses momentum. Once Brubaker starts to clean up the place, we don't know how much time is passing, or what he's actually getting done, or if the alliance of the armed convict guards and the businessmen is balking him at every turn. We never quite get the feeling that Brubaker is in charge.

On the day of Brubaker's arrival at Wakefield, he saw a young convict, bleeding from a horrible big wound in his chest, who had been dumped on the floor of a bus as if he were a sack of garbage. After Brubaker takes over the warden's office, he asks his sneaky clerk what has become of the man. The clerk replies evasively that he will look into the matter, and some time later Brubaker reminds him about it. Yet after Abraham the coffinmaker is killed, Brubaker doesn't attempt to put pressure on anyone else to tell him where the bodies are buried. His response, instead, is to take the electrical gadget with which Abraham was tortured and give himself a shock of pain. (Peter O'Toole burned himself in *Lawrence of Arabia*—blonds have all the fun.) Then he goes out digging with a team of men and finds four buried coffins, which the prison board is able to explain away as bodies from long ago, when there might have been a paupers' cemetery on the grounds. Brubaker announces that he's calling in the media, but there's no follow-through on that, either—there are no newspapermen like Redford himself in *All the President's Men*, eager to uncover a scandal. (Is he the only hero anywhere?) And all the time we keep expecting the body of that young man who disappeared to turn up; if it did, Brubaker would have the proof of recent crimes which he needs, and the prison board, and the governor, whose special assistant put Brubaker in as warden, would be forced to back him. But Brubaker seems to forget all about that wounded man. The audience sits there wondering when the other shoe is going to drop, not knowing that the moviemakers have thrown it out the window.

The film is at its most puzzling when Brubaker, having stormed out of a meeting with the prison board at the local Hilton Inn, makes a speech about "pseudo reformers," and how they're the worst—worse, even, than the mercenary business people and politicians who sit on the board. We don't know what he's talking about—there haven't been any reformers around, pseudo or otherwise, except for him. Then, as Lillian Grey (Jane Alexander), the governor's special assistant, urges him to learn how to obtain what he wants from the board, we get the idea. Now we understand why Jane Alexander is always lighted so glaringly and shot in closeup, with dry, prissy lips and a tight face. She's this movie's fall guy: the liberal, the one who thinks you can accomplish changes by compromise. (Brubaker, though, has charged that murders have been committed at the prison, and what liberal would condone murder?) Later, a senator (played by John McMartin, a specialist in characters so gelatinous that even Murray Hamilton recoils from them) gives Brubaker a last chance to keep his job. The senator is empowered to offer Brubaker everything he needs to improve the lives of the men at Wakefield if he will just knock off searching for bodies. Brubaker, of course, refuses and is fired; he is replaced by a hard-line warden, who will undo everything he has tried to do. And Brubaker, the moral symbol, walks off alone. He came to redeem us, but we were beyond redemption, and so he failed. The picture flirts with the adolescent revolutionary view that the prison can't be improved, because the whole society is rotten. And it says that the evil is so all-encompassing that even the mythic American hero is futile now. It's like the John Wayne films where the wishy-washy liberals compromise and sell out their friends but the Wayne heroes prove their purity by being steadfast and winning. Only, Brubaker proves his purity by losing.

It's the mythic quality that gets this film in trouble: Brubaker's defeat is supposed to be a moral victory, but there's not much lift in that for an audience that has been witnessing the brutalities that will once again be inflicted on the prisoners. So some people in the audience are bound to ask, Why doesn't Brubaker accept the senator's deal and protect the men of Wakefield instead of saving his own intransigent, saintly soul? But this whole moral dilemma is a phony. The movie sets up a situation in which only two paths are open to Brubaker: he can fight evil single-handedly and fail, or he can compromise and align himself with the forces of evil. So, of course, it's morally necessary for him to fail. If we feel dissatisfied with this, it's because we know that it's only in mythic stories—or in simplistic, cartoon ones—that people are all evil or all good and the liberal who thinks there's a middle ground is the snake trying to corrupt the hero so he'll stop fighting evil. And we also know that the kinds of sociological data about graft and crime that we've been getting in this movie don't belong to the fairy-tale world of the Westerns: they're part of a world where situations are never that clear-cut. (If you turn to *Accomplices to the Crime*, you find that in the experiences that "suggested" the movie the warden brought in aides whom he'd worked with before, so that he wouldn't be completely surrounded by hostile convict guards, and he called in the press almost immediately, and also sought and received help from legal groups. It wasn't one man against "the system.") At the very end of the movie, there's a big scene: As Brubaker walks away from Wakefield, the men are in the yard listening to the new, hard-line warden speak to them over the loudspeaker system. That solid, great actor Yaphet Kotto, who plays Dickie Coombes, the leader of the black prisoners, begins to clap, honoring the departing figure, and then all the men in the yard move toward the wire fence, applauding rhythmically. Too late, they have come to appreciate an honest man; they're honoring the saint who tried and failed. Brubaker's eyes fill with tears as he goes off. Then there's a postscript, a title informing us that two years later twenty-four of the inmates, led by Coombes, filed suit for cruel and inhuman punishment, that their treatment was declared unconstitutional, and that the governor was not reelected. After making us feel that nothing could be done, the movie turns around and says, O.K., Brubaker failed, but the prisoners got the message and changed things. We've been watching a fictional movie about a fearless legendary hero and then this postscript is thrown at us, as if the fiction film were factual. It may be meant as a sop, so the movie won't seem a downer, but all it does is undercut Brubaker's moral victory—making him seem like a quitter when he goes off into the metaphoric sunset.

The central problem with this movie is that as it has been directed it supports Brubaker's view of himself a hundred per cent and turns him into a man for all seasons. But suppose that Redford's eyes were a little too shiny as he spurned the senator's offer, and maybe—dread thought—*his* lips were dry when he appeared before the members of the board, and they looked recognizably human and he sounded pious. Maybe then we could see how a man who was basically sound could undercut his own cause by an excess of indignation, and by the feeling that he was right and everyone else was wrong—and weak and crooked besides. With just a slight difference in emphasis, or even a different way of lighting Redford, the movie could have been about a strong yet self-righteous man who didn't know how to gain allies, or when to fight and when to bargain, and so lost when he held the cards to win. Then the prisoners would learn not so much from Brubaker's noble example as from his goofing up.

In a number of earlier movies, Redford interiorized emotion so much that he became inexpressive; now that he's trying to show emotion, there's no energy in it. In the many cuts to him clenching his strong jaw to hold in his angry tension, as his eyes flinch from the suffering he sees, you feel that he isn't tense at all. He's an intelligent, hip actor, but saintliness without passion makes him seem vacant. When Brubaker arrives at Wakefield and discovers that a bribe to the barber will keep him from having his head shaved, prison style, he slips the barber five dollars and receives an immaculate windswept coiffure; is this Brubaker's vanity, or Redford's, or the moviemakers' anxiety to preserve his Goldilocks image? We know it isn't Brubaker, because there is no Brubaker. There is only a movie star who doesn't show the toughness to reorganize a prison like Wakefield. Robert Redford isn't a man of action; he's essentially a romantic actor who needs a co-star to play off. (When he's the only star, he seems to be in love with himself.) He's the wrong kind of actor for a prison movie, and so, possibly somewhat unconsciously, as the Arkansas scandals were being simplified for the sake of drama, the central figure was mythologized, softened, honeyed. Our interest shifts to the other actors—such as David Keith as the prisoner threatened by the death-row psychotic, because Keith (who looks a lot like Charlie Starkweather) has a few likable moments explaining how he got into trouble as a kid, and there's a gleam of humor in him.

Though *Brubaker* often seems to be at cross-purposes with itself, in its glamour-ridden way it's still grappling with something, and it's far more stirring than any of the dozen or so other movies that have opened in the last few weeks. It's a movie that probably couldn't have been made without a star of Redford's magnitude, yet his presence distorts the material, and *Brubaker* may also be the rare case of a movie that actually suffers commercially because of the popularity of its star. Redford has become so strongly identified with solar energy and ecological and moral causes that when people learn he's in a picture about prison reform they may assume that it's a dull, earnest film, and stay away. Charles Bronson in a prison movie, or Clint Eastwood, wouldn't scare them off like this—but then, of course, Bronson or Eastwood wouldn't be playing the warden, or at least not this warden. You're held by this movie, even when you're arguing with it, because there's power in the subject and in many of the performances, but that final clapping for Brubaker is troubling; there's something about it that suggests canned applause. You come out a little angry about Brubaker's purity, about Redford's purity. It seems to be a two-hour commercial for a man running for governor, for senator, or for God.

*I*t has taken all these years for Aretha Franklin to reach the screen—and then she's on for only one number! Getting her into *The Blues Brothers* was the smartest thing that the director, John Landis, did; letting her get away after that number was the dumbest. When she sings "Think," while wearing a waitress's uniform in the soul-food café she runs, she smashes the movie to smithereens. Her presence is so strong she seems to be looking at us while we're looking at her. She's so completely there, and so funny, as she waggles a threatening finger at her lover, the cook (Matt "Guitar" Murphy), who's considering leaving her to rejoin his old band, led by the Blues Brothers (Dan Aykroyd and John Belushi), that you can't come down enough to respond to what follows. And the deadpan singing by Aykroyd and Belushi that seemed so funky on "Saturday Night Live" is very drab. Back in the late sixties, the popular-culture critic Albert Goldman wrote, "It takes only one record like Aretha Franklin's virtuoso treatment of 'I Can't Get No Satisfaction,' written by Mick Jagger of the Rolling Stones, to remind us of the great gap that exists between those who have soul and those who merely pay it the compliment of imitation." And Goldman explained this, too: "She releases every tightly creased irony of the blues and dispels the old stale atmosphere of patiently endured female sorrow. Lacking even a trace of self-consciousness, she cries out in ecstasy or anger, in bewilderment or terror, achieving the beauty of a perfectly realized emotion. Indeed, her naturalness is as much a matter of the spontaneity with which she lets fly every phrase as it is of the depth and solidity of her feelings. At another time, in another society, this complete freedom from emotional restraints might appear a dubious value. A Victorian would have called it hysteria. Today, it seems like a state of grace." When the Blues Brothers take Matt Murphy with them and leave Aretha behind, you know that the moviemakers don't know what they're doing.

This musical slapstick farce, set in Chicago, is good-natured, in a sentimental, folk-bop way, but its big joke is how overscaled everything in it is, and that one sequence that's really alive is relatively small-scale. John Landis has a lot of comic invention and isn't afraid of silliness, but in terms of slapstick craft he's still an amateur. This showed in *Animal House*, but it didn't seem to matter as much there: the sloppiness was part of the film's infantile gross-out charm. Here he's working with such a lavish hand that the miscalculations in timing are experienced by the audience as a form of waste. There are funny moments: Aykroyd's parody version of the theme song from "Rawhide"; Henry Gibson's expression of dreamy surprise when the Pinto that he and a sidekick are in is wafted high in the air over the city and slowly drops. There are also sequences that just miss: the jiveass jumping at the church presided over by James Brown, with Belushi feeling the power of the Lord and doing handsprings down the center aisle; Aykroyd and Belushi prancing in a circle around Ray Charles as he sings "Shake Your Tailfeathers," like stage Indians around a totem pole—Aykroyd with his tiny, jerky speed freak's steps

26

(the essence of white gracelessness), and Belushi with his lumbering hot shuffle; Cab Calloway shedding his janitor's garb and appearing in white tails to sing "Minnie the Moocher," in a silvery Deco set (but there are too many cuts interrupting the actual song). The script, by Aykroyd and Landis, keeps the jokes coming, and maybe it wouldn't matter much when they miss if almost all the musical numbers weren't staged so disappointingly. And maybe the jokes missing *and* the musical numbers fizzling wouldn't matter *too* much if only Aykroyd and Belushi really clicked together, in the slightly hallucinated way you expect them to. But the fun has gone out of their hipster-musicians act. Possibly it was only good for a few skits. There's nothing going on between them and the taciturn style doesn't allow them to show enough personality for a full-length movie. When Aykroyd loses his mask for a few seconds in a posh-restaurant scene, he becomes more appealing; they're more like the Marx Brothers here than the Blues Brothers, and their looseness is a relief.

Does the film traduce the great black rhythm-and-blues musicians in the cast? Only inadvertently, by not knowing how to use them. Since Aretha Franklin transcends the film's incompetence, one can perhaps forgive Landis (who is still in his twenties) for the somewhat patronizing casting of the black performers. No doubt he would do something comparable with Benny Goodman and Hoagy Carmichael and Gene Krupa. (Amateurism crosses color lines.) A chief ingredient of the film is noisy car crashes, pile-ups, and demolition scenes: the Blues Brothers antagonize so many individuals and organizations in the course of rounding up their old band that thousands of vehicles chase them and converge on unlucky streets and plazas. The movie is probably more fun for people who drive than for people like me. Even when I laugh at car stunts, I'm not having a good time—I'm just giving in. I blot them out instantaneously, the way one forgets pain.

July 7, 1980

Boys and Girls

The Blue Lagoon tries to reinstate the benighted idea that "nature intended" sexual intercourse to be beautiful—to be the tender and innocent culmination of romantic love. Set at the turn of the century, this film imputes to "nature" man's most hypocritical forms of sentimentality. The central and virtually the only characters are two little cousins; shipwrecked, they grow up alone together on a South Sea island. The passage of the years is indicated by having the children go swimming; as they cavort among the shimmering fish, we catch a glimpse of pubic hair and hear islandy music—rhapsodic strings, golden-toned horns—and two tall, bronzed adolescents (Brooke Shields and Christopher Atkins) emerge from the water. In order for us to understand that the children's development is natural (rather than the result of familial and social nurture), there are frequent inserts of birds and reptiles and crustaceans in magnified closeup, like the shots of insects that were peppered throughout *Days of Heaven*, which was shot by the same cinematographer, Nestor Almendros. Bizarrely, these creatures start making their cameo appearances even before the children reach the island. Along with the magic-of-nature mystique and the phosphorescent underwater sequences of the children swimming as if they were another sensuous form of marine life, the film has an inevitable, built-in prurience: all we have to look forward to is, When are these two going to discover fornication? And so each teasing sign of maturation—the sprouting hair on the boy's body, the girl's first menstrual period—becomes the occasion for audience cheers, applause, derision. The director, Randal Kleiser, and his scenarist, Douglas Day Stewart, have made the young boy and girl clean and innocent by emptying them of any dramatic interest. Watching them is about as exciting as looking into a fishbowl waiting for guppies to mate.

This picture seems to have been directed by a young teen whose vision of Eden is blissful lazy days at a summer camp with the boy or girl of one's dreams and no camp counsellors to say no to anything. It's conceivable that Kleiser's love scenes may, like the ones in Zeffirelli's *Romeo and Juliet*, be taken as romantic poetry by the swooniest thirteen-year-olds in the movie audience: when the boy kisses the girl and they begin—finally—to caress each other, their exertions are intercut with two birds, and after they gracefully commingle (i.e., much lyrical panning over the intertwined healthy young bodies), there's a sudden insert of sea anemones undulating passionately. Then the boy and the girl go into the water, and when they see a turtle with another turtle on its back they smile knowingly, as if to say, "The whole world is in love." It's Disney nature porn. First we wait for these two to discover sex; then we may wish they hadn't—their innocent idyll seems to go on forever. (And we've got so used to inserts that when we see two dolphins who are actually in the same shot as the boy we may become rattled—is something going to come of this?) Except for some of the underwater footage, this picture looks and sounds like a Hollywood nineteen-fifties South Sea adventure, or a pop-camp Elvis Presley film, such as *Blue Hawaii* (and in profile Brooke Shields, with her slight self-conscious sneer, resembles Presley, whose approach to acting was about the same as hers—casually wooden). The cinematography is so inexpressive that we seem to be looking at the scenic wonders of a vacation spot in a travelogue. No doubt this was what Almendros thought was wanted—but why? From the camera artist who in his

European films seemed to know so much about sunlight that he could make it tap-dance for him, there's an implicit condescension in this Kodachrome, *National Geographic* look. Or is it merely that Almendros was trying to oblige Kleiser with a "natural"—impersonal—style?

Kleiser has directed his two featured players in the same impersonal manner: they're like suburbanite teens lounging around the shopping mall looking at amphibious gear. In still photographs, Brooke Shields' young beauty has suggestiveness, mystery. In moving pictures, she seems too complacent, too earthbound to be an actress. (This isn't a matter of youth: Jodie Foster had tension and control when she was even younger, and Diane Lane has such an adult grasp of acting that she's already an accomplished performer.) In this movie, the blossoming Brooke Shields is generally photographed against floral backgrounds, and the director doesn't pass up the Nabokov shot: nymphet picking up butterfly. The boy, who might be a kid left over from the Brady bunch, is sometimes posed so that he looks like a dreamy-eyed junior muscleman. As a child, the boy is meant to enchant us by his coy mispronunciation: "San Forisco," twice. As an adolescent, he's more contemplative: "I wonder what fish think about"—that's what he thinks about. He has inklings of what human society might mean; when he realizes that the savages on the other side of the island practice human sacrifice, he says, "I don't understand why people have to be so bad to each other." The movie is taken from a popular novel of 1908 (which was adapted to the screen once before, in 1949, with Jean Simmons), with most of the original attitudes intact. The boy shows signs of intellectual curiosity, examining a skeleton, and asking himself such questions as Where does the moon go? The boy hopes they can leave the island. But the girl has her lover and, in due course, her infant—she glows with womanly fulfillment. There is no doubt that in the moviemakers' minds, she's closer to nature. Woman is content to romp and pick flowers (this film is heavy on vegetation); it's man who strives to understand. (When the boy is puzzled about why the girl had the baby, he's got good reason to be: there's nothing resembling penetration in their lovemaking—the way they rub limbs, all they'd produce is friction.)

Helplessly, Kleiser compounds this felony of a movie by introducing a whole series of concluding devices. Suddenly, after all these years, the boy's father (who is the girl's uncle) turns up in a ship, searching the seas for them, the little holy family somehow find themselves drifting in a tiny rowboat, with a shark circling; there are also poisonous berries that the toddler has brought into the boat. Rescue, drifting, the shark, poison—any one of these would be enough to end the picture; Kleiser put them all together, in the hope, probably, of an *Elvira Madigan* finish. But when the lovers in *Elvira Madigan* took their own lives, it was because they knew that they couldn't sustain their love once they were subjected to worldly pressures. Here it's as if the lovers were too pure for our world—and they knew it. But how could they know it? They're taking their lives to satisfy Kleiser's and Stewart's fantasy that they are untouched by the corruptions of civilization. At the beginning of the picture, the little girl referred to her mother's dying with the Victorian euphemism—her mother had "gone to Heaven." At the end, Kleiser proves himself a Victorian child at heart: his three innocents are shown in perfect serenity. They have drifted in the ocean in an open boat, they have taken poison, but when they are found by the rescue party they have suffered no burns and no retching or gastrointestinal pain. They simply fell asleep and went to Heaven. If your thirteen-year-old falls for this, watch out: you may have the kind of rotten kid who will grow up to like *Fame*.

· · · · ·

*A*aron Latham's article "The Urban Cowboy," featured on the September 12, 1978, cover of *Esquire*, was subtitled "Saturday Night Fever, Country & Western Style," and it was quite clearly a set of variations on the *Saturday Night Fever* theme—how working-class kids, frustrated by their boring jobs and their whole daytime existence, found another, more glamorous way to live at night. For the Bay Ridge kids who worked at low-paying jobs, the disco palace was a Saturday-night world only. Latham's young hardhats who worked in the petro-chemical plants around Houston made high wages and could go out every night, but they didn't find the release of the Bay Ridge kids. According to Latham, their nighttime fantasy life was pathetically empty. Their headquarters was a vast honky-tonk, Gilley's, which featured a mechanical bucking bull that the men paid to ride. The article laid on the symbolism and the ironies: these anomic young Southwesterners had no way to prove their manhood except by dressing up in boots and jeans and cowboy hats and trying to live out the myths of the West by riding this mechanical bull. And the twist was that although the bull broke the men's bones and gave them excruciating pain in the testicles, women got sexual pleasure from riding it. The article featured a young couple who met at Gilley's and celebrated their wedding there; he was a champ on the bull, and the marriage broke up because she began to outperform him and wouldn't give it up. The article had an ominous view of what was going on between the sexes: "The honky-tonk cowgirls keep putting more and more pressure on the honky-tonk cowboys. . . . Once the bullring was the simplest of the simple entertainments at Gilley's. Either you rode the bull or you got bucked off. You beat the bull or it beat you. It was perfect for an urban cowboy who never beat anything beyond the walls of the saloon. But then Eve entered the bullring. The cowboys were no longer simply measured against the bull, they were measured against the cowgirls." And the young ex-wife is quoted: "My favorite thing is to watch all the guys fall off. Then I get up and ride it." Latham, watching her ride, comments, "She clung to the bull, which pounded her harder than any man had ever been able to." I hated the article: it was smartass-glib about manual laborers' lives in a way that one could never be about one's own life. If these hardhats' dreams are so pathetic, what about the dreams of someone who pushes a mechanical bull to the center of his literary ripoff—as if it were central to the lives of young Southwesterners—and then rides the symbolic overtones in all directions?

That article is a bad seed for a movie: James Bridges, who directed *Urban Cowboy*, from a screenplay he wrote with Latham, can't extricate himself from the symbolism. The film views the young hero, Bud (John Travolta), as a victim of social dislocation: he's rootless and ignorant, his conception of manhood is based on a mythology that no longer applies. But on the assumption (false, I think) that the audience believes in those antiquated macho values and wants to see them on the screen, the movie also tries to reactivate the cowboy mythology. Bud spends the whole movie trying to learn how to ride that stupid mechanical contraption. And when he succeeds, the film views it as his triumph. In order to set up the conditions for this, the writers have dredged up an ex-convict villain out of an ancient Western—a lean, mean hombre whose lips curl with pleasure when he inflicts pain. Bud wins his manhood: he defeats the villain on the bucking machine, and he beats him up in a fistfight as well.

At the beginning, Bud, a bearded farm boy, leaves home and goes to Houston to stay with his Uncle Bob (Barry Corbin) and Aunt Corene (Brooke Alderson), because his uncle, who works in one of the plants, can help him get a job. On Bud's first night in town, his uncle and aunt take him out to Gilley's—a barnlike roadhouse that is essentially just a bigger version of any beer drinkers' country-and-Western hangout. On the second night, he returns on his own, but now he's dressed in a complete fancy dude's outfit, with a dark, feathered Stetson, and the camera slowly moves up his boots and jeans and deep-green Western shirt and then catches his newly clean-shaven face in profile, for a Valentino smolder. Suddenly, he's a knowledgeable gaucho stud; a few seconds later, he's a callow kid again. Bridges seems willing to do almost anything for an immediate effect, and this happens all through the scrappily edited picture. When Bud and Sissy (Debra Winger), the girl he meets at Gilley's, get married, it seems to happen just a couple of days after they've met—and probably Bridges intends it to seem that fast, so we'll understand how hot and impulsive they are, and how unprepared for responsibilities. Yet when they pose for their wedding pictures, it's in a large, elaborately costumed group—Bud in an extraordinary white tuxedo, with a ruffled shirt, white patent-leather cowboy boots, and a big white hat. He looks like a dude prince. The shot instantly evokes Travolta's white suit at the disco dance contest in *Saturday Night Fever*, but his regalia here looks much more movie-star expensive. (Travolta's first wedding on the screen is an historic occasion, like Deanna Durbin's first screen kiss, so of course he has to be all in white.) A minute later, Bud is carrying his bride over the threshold, or whatever it's called, of their mobile home, and we're back to blue-collar rootlessness, and take-out dinners from McDonald's.

A week after the wedding, Bud and Sissy quarrel and split, and each has an affair—Bud with Pam, a rich sophisticate, played by Madolyn Smith, and Sissy with the villain, played by Scott Glenn. But these kids who met and married practically in the same breath have a deep and lasting love, and get back together. Fundamentally, they're the characters in romantic thirties movies who had to suffer before resolving their misunderstandings, except that, with Latham's metaphorical setting giving the story its slant, they're retarded versions of thirties characters. Much of the time, Bud is slackjawed and uncouth; then he has a speech explaining that he isn't dumb—and I think we're meant to take him at his word—because he has "feelings." We're embarrassed, the way we are in life when someone says, "You think I'm dumb, don't you?" and we're forced to deny it.

Of course we think he's dumb: Bridges and Latham have written him dumb. (A standard Texan's boast would be beyond his conversational powers.) Worse, they've written him weak. Vulnerability has been a catchword in the movie industry ever since various people decided that it was the secret of Marilyn Monroe's appeal, and it has often been invoked to explain Travolta's success. But vulnerability has to be played off against a swaggering ego or some sass or a self-protective shell, or it's merely infantile. You get the feeling that if anybody slapped Bud he'd start crying. Travolta seems to get younger in every picture; this time, he comes across as a hurt little kid of about fourteen. He has demonstrated great flair in comedy and in dance sequences, a gift for cockiness, and a rare ability to let something emotionally naked show through. What he hasn't yet demonstrated is a core of strength, and because he doesn't come across as strong, he especially needs effrontery or a streak of opportunism in his roles, so he won't seem just blubberingly sensitive—as he did in *Moment by Moment*—or lamebrained. Actually, though *Moment by Moment* was a much worse movie than *Urban Cowboy*, Travolta was more confident in it than he is here. As Bud (even the name infantilizes him), he seems whipped, anxious, scared; he shows the sick bewilderment of an actor who can't get a fix on his character. Who could? Bud is written inconsistently.

The subject suggests satire, or even farce, and this keeps peeping through the film's attempts at raw heat. In the most effective moments, satire and sultriness work together. When Bud first does a two-step with Sissy, his hold on her is formal and his face is earnest, yet his leg movements are so snaky that the effect is comic. Later, he has a very funny self-pitying glower as he watches her dancing with the sinewy villain—a man so tough he looks as if he'd ejaculate bullets. This masochistic comedy number, set to "Stand by Me," with Bud glowering longingly at Sissy while he's dancing with Pam (whom he's hardly aware of), and Sissy staring at him in misery while dancing with the soulless baddie, is probably the best-directed sequence in the movie. But the story is posited on hot blood, and the country music, which is mostly safe and tired, doesn't supply enough impetus or excitement. And Bud doesn't seem to have sexual energy bottled up, the way Tony Manero did in *Saturday Night Fever*. Bud's quick marriage would be very puzzling if Debra Winger's Sissy didn't have such warm huskiness in her voice and if she weren't so steamy. With soft, still unformed cheeks and the clear eyes of a child, she has a quality of flushed transparency. When she necks on the dance floor—and she's a great smoocher, with puffy lips like a fever blister—her clothes seem to be under her damp skin. (She's naked all through the movie, though she never takes her clothes off.) It's Debra Winger, rather than Travolta, who has the movie's big turn-on number: she does an exhibitionistic routine on the mechanical bull that's reminiscent of Rita Hayworth's strip song in *Gilda*. She writhes and does all sorts of stunts, like a circus bareback rider, but in slow, sensual motion. This routine has no more to do with the story than Travolta's Valentino pose does, but it's the one time that the bucking machine serves any visual purpose. Sissy is given some fake torrid bits—such as a flamboyant moment when she pulls open the villain's shirt, as if to devour his leathery chest—but she's the only fluid, sustained character. When she thinks Bud doesn't care about her, and the sadistic villain smashes her in the face, we understand why she doesn't leave him: she feels so alone she doesn't think she has anyplace to go. Madolyn Smith's role as the slumming rich bitch Pam is a series of camp howlers, and, like Richard Gere in *American Gigolo*, Pam is redeemed by love—in her case, when she realizes that Bud truly loves Sissy. (She learns about love vicariously.) Somehow, the actress brings a fillip of sexy humor to her moth-eaten lechery. Scott Glenn has maybe the most unsayable lines in the movie (example: "You can't expect a man like me to be faithful to any woman"), and when he appears wearing a black fish-net T-shirt over that taut, hairless chest, the camera seems to be making goo-goo eyes at his pectorals. Glenn was the soldier trying to protect the Ronee Blakley character in *Nashville*, and as the musician who hooked up with Candy Clark he gave the ill-fated *More American Graffiti* some relaxed charm. Here he's so wickedly proficient at stone-faced hokum that he's like a parodist, taking off Clint Eastwood, Gary Cooper, Humphrey Bogart, and even David Carradine. Twitching his stern cheek muscles, he's a cartoon of a he-man. (He even has a cartoon name, Wes Hightower.)

The way Bridges directs these four performers, they don't seem to be in the same film. But then the scenes don't even seem to have been written for the same picture. There are vague hints that Bud is uneasy about Sissy's wanting to do things that aren't traditional for women, but is he eager to win the bucking contest at Gilley's so he can outride Wes or so he can outride Sissy? It's all blurred. The marriage broke up when he yelled at her that they lived "like pigs" in their shiny new mobile home and that a man expected his wife to clean and cook (the debris is from takeout junk food). Sissy said *she* worked, too; they whacked each other, and that was it. Later, as a gesture of love, she came back and scrubbed the place, but he didn't know, because the slyly possessive Pam took the credit for it. Sissy may be a feisty little thing who likes to drive trucks and show off on the bucking machine, but when it comes down to it she's womanly—she cleans up the dirty dishes. (Bud, who was living there after she left, never made a move toward the mess which would demonstrate that *he* was growing up.) *Urban Cowboy* has no center, but there's always one damn thing or another happening, so the picture moves along, and that may be what saves Bridges here, as it did also in his last film, *The China Syndrome*, which was paced—like an old Saturday-afternoon serial—to prevent restlessness. In *The China Syndrome*, why did Jack Lemmon break down when the TV cameras were finally on him? There wasn't any more preparation for that sudden collapse than there is for Bud's sudden jealous rage about his wife, which seems to erupt two seconds after the marriage ceremony. The characters in these movies do whatever is necessary to advance the plot; if they didn't crack up or yell on cue, the plot might chug along without them. And when Bridges wants hysterics, he doesn't protect the performers by keeping the camera at a discreet distance. Lemmon's overacting was useful in the first part of *The China Syndrome*—it perked things up. But by the end, when he pulled out all the stops and became haggard and dazed, his performance might have been impressive if only he hadn't been in closeup so much of the time. In *Urban Cowboy*, the more hollow the scene, the closer the camera gets; the director tries to bludgeon his way past the unmotivated actions—emphasizing them, the way French women (it's said) emphasize their worst features, to make them seem striking, distinguished.

Stuck with the problem of how to make their common-man Bud a hero, Bridges and Latham devised that stock villain for him to pummel. But they still must have felt that they needed to give the picture "heart." And so they became even more shameless. In a sequence that takes place at the petrochemical plant during the time when Bud and Sissy are separated, jolly, loving Uncle Bob, his chubby gut stuffed with homely wisdom, tells Bud, "Sometimes even a cowboy's got to swaller his pride." The equipment that Uncle Bob is standing on is struck by lightning an instant later, and though it's really Bridges and Latham who should have been hit, let's be grateful for any mercies we receive. Bud, who has been training for the upcoming contest, with Uncle Bob, a onetime rodeo rider, coaching him, is too disheartened by Bob's death to want to compete. But after the funeral Aunt Corene, who has been quirkily funny up to this point, turns gallant (in maudlin closeup) and tells Bud that he's got to do it for Uncle Bob, and, for luck, she gives him her most cherished possession, the buckle that Bob had won in a rodeo. Ride a mechanical bull for dear, dead Uncle Bob? James Bridges, Aaron Latham, have you been riding a head-pounding machine?

July 21, 1980

Master Spy, Master Seducer

In *Dressed to Kill*, a suspense comedy about sex and fear, set in Manhattan, everybody is spying on everybody else, or trying to. And the director, Brian De Palma, who also wrote the script, is the master spy. In two early De Palma pictures, Robert De Niro played an underground filmmaker who made Peep Art movies, and in the second one he also tried to get into the action. At the start of *Sisters* (1973), a blind girl is taking off her clothes; a well-dressed black man catches sight of her—will he go on watching? It turns out that they are both part of a TV game show called "Peeping Toms." The beginning of *Carrie* (1976) is like an adolescent boy's dream of sneaking into the girls' locker room at high school and hiding there, unseen, as the girls strip and soap themselves and brush their hair in the misty, steamed atmosphere. Now, at the opening of *Dressed to Kill*, Kate Miller (Angie Dickinson), a beautiful, aging golden blonde, married yet frustrated, and longing to be made love to, is in her shower, at her most defenseless, smiling ever so slightly in pleasure, and as the camera moves around her she seems to have an aureole—an auto-erotic glow. We in the audience are put in the position of voyeurs inside Kate's languorous masturbation fantasy, sharing her secrets. (In some shots, she has been given the dream body an aging woman might have in her fantasies.)

Over the years, De Palma has developed as an artist by moving further into his material, getting to deeper levels of erotic comedy and funnier levels of violation. If he has learned a great deal from Hitchcock (and Welles and Godard and Polanski and Scorsese and many others), he has altered its nature with a funky sensuousness that is all his own. The gliding, glazed-fruit cinematography is intoxicating but there's an underlay of dread, and there's something excessive in the music that's swooshing up your emotions. You know you're being toyed with. The apprehensive moods are stretched out voluptuously, satirically—De Palma primes you for what's going to happen and for a lot that doesn't happen. He sustains moods for so long that you feel emotionally encircled. He pulls you in and draws the wires taut or relaxes them; he practically controls your breathing.

Has any other moviemaker mastered new skills with each picture the way Brian De Palma has? Born in 1940, he has been making movies since his sophomore year at Columbia, in 1959, and gaining visual strength; now, in his thirteenth feature film, he has become a true visual storyteller. He knows where to put the camera and how to make every move count, and his timing is so great that when he wants you to feel something he gets you every time. His thriller technique, constantly refined, has become insidious, jewelled. It's hardly possible to find a point at which you could tear yourself away from this picture.

A few minutes in, De Palma stages an almost perfect love comedy, in miniature: Kate Miller, whose day began with a bout of miserable thumping intercourse with her husband, Mike (Fred Weber), to the accompaniment of the weather report on the radio, followed by a session with her analyst, Dr. Elliott (Michael Caine), who rejected her sexual invitation, sits on a bench in a room at the Metropolitan Museum. This woman, who looks—as they used to say—"made for love," is visibly aching for it. Distracted, dreaming away the time, she watches a little Oriental girl skip off from her mother and her mother's male companion, who a moment later run after her. She glances up at a portrait of a woman (by Alex Katz) that seems to look back at her, contemplatively, as if to say, "So what are you going to do now?" A handsome stud of perhaps thirty-eight, in dark glasses, a casual gray pullover, and a well-tailored dark jacket, sits down next to her. Unable to meet his eyes, Kate looks down at her hand, in two-toned gloves with strips of leather running up the fingers, and then she looks farther down, to his expensive two-toned leather shoes. It's commodity fetishism. Kate takes off a glove, exposing the diamond on her third finger, left hand, and the man disappears. Perceiving with dismay that she has driven him off, she gets up, dropping her glove, and looks for him. The camera (the Panavision version of the Steadicam) darts from gallery to gallery as she searches anxiously. But when the man, having backtracked, picked up her glove, and put it on, touches her shoulder with his gloved hand, she is so startled she bolts away. Then, realizing that he meant to return the glove and that her frayed nerves had made her look a panicky fool, Kate follows him. The man teases her, leading her in a chase through the rooms, with contemporary paintings as witnesses to the cat-and-mouse courtship game. The music here is subdued (the friend next to me whispered, "It sounds like Bernard Herrmann on Quaaludes"), and though it becomes more frantic the chase still has an eerie sheen of culture. With almost no words, this loveplay edged by the man's contemptuous assurance goes through so many permutations that it suggests a speeded-up seduction out of *Les Liaisons Dangereuses*—a hundred pages turned into a visual scherzo. The quick sequence is extraordinarily revealing: when Kate, hopelessly outmaneuvered, stands indecisively in galleries that have two or three entrances, you can see that she's vulnerable to attack from any direction. The desperation in Kate's sexual loneliness makes it possible for Angie Dickinson to show a much warmer expressive range than might be expected—you can read every nuance of desire, embarrassment, and trepidation on her face.

There's very little dialogue altogether in *Dressed to Kill*; what talk there is is casual, funny, and often good-naturedly off-color. Most of the film's humor, though, is visual, and it's not innocent at all. Visual humor is generally slapstick; this isn't. You could try to single out the gags that make *Dressed to Kill* visually funny, but describing the gags wouldn't convey its humor. What makes it funny is that it's permeated with the distilled essence of impure thoughts. De Palma has perfected a near-surreal poetic voyeurism—the stylized expression of a blissfully dirty mind. He doesn't use art for voyeuristic purposes; he uses voyeurism as a strategy and a theme—to fuel his satiric art. He underlines the fact that voyeurism is integral to the nature of movies. In the Metropolitan sequence (the interiors are actually the Philadelphia Museum of Art), we catch glimpses of figures slipping in and out at the edges of the frame, and there are other almost subliminal images; we're playing hide-and-seek along with Kate, and her pickup. Later, there's a visually layered police-station sequence: the principal characters—Mike; Dr. Elliott; Kate's whiz-kid son, Peter (Keith Gordon); a loud, brash investigator, Detective Marino (Dennis Franz); and a pretty, investment-minded hooker, Liz Blake (Nancy Allen)—are in different rooms or in the hallway, but they can see each other through the glass partitions, and the interplay among these people, most of whom have never met before, seems to be happening on about eighteen different levels of deception, eavesdropping, and all-around peeping. And there's a subway chase, in which the reddish-blond Liz, who has witnessed a murder and is being pursued by the killer, stands, for protection, near a couple of young black men playing a tape recorder, but then they're joined by their pals, and the gang of hoods turns on her; everybody has designs on poor Liz. In this paranoid urban nightmare of a sequence, it's once again now-you-see-it-now-you-don't, as hidden figures scurry by. Throughout the film, De Palma plays with the visual theme of outside and inside voyeurism (the person peeking through windows is always much safer than the person who sneaks inside), and he also keeps dividing things in two—often the screen itself. This film has some of the most graceful use of the split screen (and screen-within-the-screen devices) in recent years, especially when the image is divided between Dr. Elliott at his place and Liz at hers; she gets a tip from her stockbroker on one phone and raises the necessary money by arranging a "date" with her escort service on another—for her, Phil Donahue on the TV is just a background noise, while the doctor, watching the same show, is giving it close attention.

De Palma's sense of humor makes him the least respectable of the front-rank American directors. He presents extreme fantasies and pulls the audience into them with such apparent ease that the pleasure of the suspense becomes aphrodisiacal. And he does what Hitchcock always said he wanted to do—such as have Cary Grant really be a murderer at the end of *Suspicion*. (Hitchcock came closest to actually doing it when he bumped off Janet Leigh in *Psycho*.) De Palma goes ahead and takes the risks all the time. Yet though he draws the audience in by the ironic use of sentimental conventions, when he explodes the tension (the shocks are delivered with surgical precision), those people in the audience who are most susceptible to romantic trickery sometimes feel hurt—betrayed—and can't understand why the rest of us are gasping and laughing. Life plays obscene jokes on soft, creamy-pink Kate Miller, who wants nothing more than to give and receive pleasure; just when she's happy and sated and feels grateful, she discovers something so humiliating that she gets the cold shakes. Life also played obscene jokes on the teenage Carrie (Sissy Spacek), who wanted only to be accepted by the other kids at school. Life played a brutally dirty trick on the father (Kirk Douglas) in *The Fury* (1978), who wanted only to be reunited with his son. Like Hitchcock, like Polanski, like Buñuel, De Palma has a prankish sense of horror. Most parodists of gothic tricks flatten them out (as in *High Anxiety*); De Palma's humor heightens them—he's probably the only American director who knows how to use jokiness to make horror more intense. Through visual storytelling, he can get at the currents of sexiness and fear and guilt that were the hidden strength of the great silent horror films, but he taps those currents for a different purpose. De Palma replays film history as farce. He has kept the dirty fun of a bad boy at the center of his art. It gives his work a lurid, explosive vitality.

Dressed to Kill isn't as imaginatively dark as *The Fury*: the evil was luxuriant in that one—nightshade in bloom. There's nothing here to match the floating, poetic horror of the slowed-down sequence in which Amy Irving and Carrie Snodgress are running to freedom: it's as if each of them and each of the other people on the street were in a different time frame, and Carrie Snodgress's face is full of happiness just as she's flung over the hood of a car. And the story told in *Dressed to Kill* doesn't have the richness of the pop fairy-tale theme of *Carrie*. It's a thinner-textured movie, but—perhaps because De Palma did the writing by himself—it's all of a piece in a way that those films weren't. His dialogue is much more sly than that of the scenarists he has generally worked with—there are no flat, laughable lines like the ones that marred *The Fury*.

There are no weak performances, either. In the pivotal role of Dr. Elliott, Michael Caine demonstrates once again what an unself-centered actor he is: he's willing to be reserved and a little creepy—he does no reaching for sympathy, and he never turns on the charm. Clearly, he's considering the total effect rather than just his own part, and he's willing to strengthen the picture by providing authority and letting the women shine. The element that gives the movie its balance may be the director's liking for the characters played by Nancy Allen (she was the blond viper, Chris, in *Carrie*) and Keith Gordon. He first paired the two in *Home Movies*, the primal-family slapstick comedy that he filmed at Sarah Lawrence, using students and professionals, during the break he took after making the excitingly hellish *The Fury* (which must have been like working in a danger zone). In this anomalous, often very funny comedy, Keith Gordon played an adolescent filmmaker, who was given

Star Therapy by the Maestro (Kirk Douglas) who told him that he behaved like an extra, and that he had to learn to put his name above the title, because "Everyone is the star in the movie of his own life." (Keith Gordon had a plaintive moment when he said, "I didn't get a script.") Working on a family theme in light, knockabout terms seems to have loosened De Palma and brought him a simpler, streamlined touch. In *Home Movies*, Keith Gordon won the sexy girl played by Nancy Allen—a night-club ventriloquist with a lewd rabbit—but he seemed almost presexual. In carrying these two performers over as the hero and heroine of *Dressed to Kill*, De Palma has made this innocence work for him. As Nancy Allen plays her, Liz Blake must be the most practical, out-in-the-open girl since the young, gum-chewing Ginger Rogers. In the Paris setting of *Roberta*, Ginger was said to have the best figure in Europe, and no one in a theatre was ever heard to deny it; if Nancy Allen were to play that role, there wouldn't be any rebuttals this time, either. Liz Blake is everybody's target, and four-eyed Peter, who's obsessed with computers, is the teen-age prodigy who rescues her. (As a boy, De Palma, who started out at Columbia in physics and then switched to fine arts, used to design computers for science fairs; he was married to Nancy Allen last year.) Peter has the preoccupied seriousness of an adolescent eccentric, but he becomes a person to reckon with right before our eyes, and it's easy to see why Liz grows fond of him. Even when she says things like "I'll miss having you on my tail," they're spoken in an oddly straightforward way; if she knows more about sex, he knows more about everything else. Nancy Allen is a breezy comedienne, and Keith Gordon is a great young straight man. *Dressed to Kill* seems to have merged De Palma's two sides: he has created a vehicle in which he can unify his ominous neo-Hitchcock lyricism with the shaggy comedy of his late-sixties *Greetings* days, when he used to let background jokes dominate the foreground. Without the misfit romance and the many casual bits, such as the rapid changes of expression on a young cabdriver's face and the changes of clothing on Detective Marino (winner, hands down, of the worst-dressed-cop award), *Dressed to Kill* would be too chic, too stylish. It needs every bit of its shag. This picture is such a unified, confident piece of work that De Palma can even make the image hazy and provide a stylized chorus of observers out of Bedlam—giving it away that something isn't really happening—and still you're terrified.

De Palma has been able to retain control of most of his films by working in the suspense genre, on a small budget. His development has been mostly outside the industry, or on its margins, and, with only a few exceptions, such as *The Fury*, which cost six million dollars, he has worked on minuscule budgets or small ones; *Dressed to Kill*, which is being released by Filmways (the new name for A.I.P.), came in at six and a half million. (The average cost of a major studio movie this year is nine million.) De Palma knows how to get style on the cheap. Though he didn't have his usual editor, Paul Hirsch (who was busy on *The Empire Strikes Back*) and worked with Jerry Greenberg, the timing of the cuts in the Metropolitan sequence and in the subway sequence is daringly precise. And the way that cinematographer Ralf Bode's images connect with the slightly debauched music—it's like a rhapsody on forties movies—by Pino Donaggio seems exactly right. (Donaggio also did the scores for *Carrie* and *Home Movies*.) The whole film gives you the feeling of evenly controlled energy. De Palma shows the kind of restless intelligence which suggests that he will want to work in many different forms, and certainly he needs more chances to work on a larger scale, as he did in *The Fury*. But he doesn't have to move away from thrillers to prove he's an artist. In his hands, the thriller form is capable of expressing almost everything—comedy, satire, sex fantasies, primal emotions.

There is a peculiarity about *Dressed to Kill*: when the explanation comes, it's weightless. You've probably already figured out most of it anyway, and since everything else plays on several levels, this scene, which has only one, seems prosy and obligatory. You recognize how carefully the murder motive was prepared and how everything fits together, but the explanation has no tingle: you don't feel its connections with what makes the picture frightening. The explanation scene in *Psycho* was even prosier, and there is a slight suggestion of parody here, but more likely the resemblance is an homage; the kicker is that it's an homage to—arguably—Hitchcock's worst scene. The parody comes right after it, in the restaurant scene, when Liz plays teacher to Peter, and a woman at a nearby table (a pantomime role, by Mary Davenport, who was Keith Gordon's mother in *Home Movies*) overhears such bewildering clinical information being delivered in a matter-of-fact tone that her face crumples. Here De Palma sabotages the rational explanation, which goes rattling on. Then, at the end, he uses a ploy—a pause and then a starting up again—that resembles the endings of *Carrie* and *The Fury*, but to get a different psychological effect. In those pictures, he jolted the audience out of the gothic atmosphere, and most of us left the theatre laughing. This time, the spell isn't broken and he doesn't fully resolve our fear. He's saying that even after horror has been explained, it stays with you—the nightmare never ends.

August 4, 1980

Craft

*I*n *Honeysuckle Rose*, Dyan Cannon is a curvy cartoon—a sex kitten becomes a full-blown tigress. Her hair is a great tawny mop, so teased and tangled that a comb would have to declare war to get through it; her blouse is filled to capacity, and her jeans are about to split. She has never looked better. Dyan Cannon has always brought a blaze to her roles—a charge of comic lust. Her face was quick to register lecherous eagerness and petulant disappointment; playing sexpot bitches, she used her physical equipment so completely that you couldn't really be sure whether you were laughing with her or at her. (I remember how the audience's spirits sank after she was killed early in *Doctors' Wives*.) Now, past forty, she has finally had a chance to drop the bitchery and show some acting range, and she's sexier than ever. As Viv, who has been married for fifteen years to Buck Bonham (Willie Nelson), a country-and-Western singer, she is so full of energy and humor and knowingness that she gives the audience hope: if this is maturity, then life looks pretty good. Having stumbled onto this affirmation, the director, Jerry Schatzberg, knows what he's got, and doesn't overplay his hand and wreck it.

Schatzberg lacks a theatrical instinct for involving the audience, and the script of *Honeysuckle Rose*, which is credited to three writers (but which, reportedly, many others also worked on), seems almost nonexistent, with story points undeveloped or left dangling, and crucial scenes so underwritten that the actors look starved for a line of dialogue. For the first ten minutes, you can't tell where the picture is heading: it's all movement and atmosphere, with too much jumpy crosscutting between Buck and his backup band in their tour bus on the Southwestern highways and Buck with the band performing at concerts. But then Buck, alone in the bus except for a mare he's bringing home as a week-late tenth-birthday present for his son Jamie (Joey Floyd), arrives at his ranch in central Texas—the Honeysuckle Rose—and is greeted by the boy and the pulchritudinous Viv. And soon they're all off to the Bonham Family Annual Reunion, where several generations—hundreds of people—gather for a picnic and a party. It's a long, hot day, with men throwing horseshoes, little kids skinny-dipping, practical jokes, a chase after an armadillo, flirtations and seductions, games of dominoes, eating and drinking and dancing, and small boys in hiding watching a couple make love. The members of the band and their families are there, and you enter into the world of back-roads country people and feel the folk roots of their music. In the evening, Viv sings, in a good torchy blues voice; Buck joins in and, face to face, they harmonize on Kris Kristofferson's song "Loving Her Was Easier." There's real voltage between them—they look as if they belong together. When the party's over, Viv and Buck, relaxed and at peace, collect Jamie from among the sleeping children at the back of the big dance hall, and Buck carries him to their pickup truck. The frames have been packed with activity, but now, as the lights that have been strung up go out, we see just the truck moving along through the deserted picnic ground, and, tied to it, trotting by its side, Jamie's mare.

After you've been to a batch of movies that look as impersonal and as indifferently made as most TV shows, Schatzberg's care for the visual frame and for movement seems an affirmation, too. The music and the imagery move together. That's where the work of Schatzberg and his team, which includes Richard Baskin as music supervisor, shines. Right from the start, with the Willie Nelson song "On the Road Again," the score seems to have much more energy than the country music in *Coal Miner's Daughter* or *Urban Cowboy*. Nelson has a fine reedy voice, and subtle phrasing like that of a great blues singer. The songs (they're by several composers) don't have the rhythmic monotony of much of the country music in recent films; they're livelier, jazzier, and the images hop to the roustabout melodies or drift with the more poignant ones. Collaborating with the gifted cinematographer Robby Müller (who shot Wim Wenders' *The American Friend* and Bogdanovich's *Saint Jack*), Schatzberg, who used to be a photographer, makes the people—all of them—look beautiful, in a special, transparent way. This isn't a picture with extras dressed up in somebody's idea of what Texas peasants wear. You feel that you're seeing regional Americans as they are, without awkwardness on their part. The color is realistic, yet so joyful it's almost hallucinatory.

Like last year's *The Rose*, *Honeysuckle Rose* seems conceived and designed in color, but in a contrasting—almost opposite—way. *The Rose*, which is about an orgiastic rock-and-roll singer (Bette Midler) in the last stages of burning herself out, is set in the smoky, psychedelic night world of a young star who has leapt into the big money. Her story is told in hot Day-Glo pinks and reds and lavenders, with orange for her frizzy halo. She sings frenziedly, trying to reach her emotional limits; she lives in planes, and when she lands she totters on high heels and blinks, bleary-eyed, at the sunshine. *Honeysuckle Rose* is about a survivor—a regional idol who has never quite attained national stardom. With a short reddish beard, like a tramp's two-week stubble, and long hair with a headband, and a small diamond stud in one ear, Willie Nelson's Buck Bonham suggests a benign Sam Peckinpah; he's more like an amiable, slightly out-of-it eccentric than a performer. (That seems to be the key to the personal style of a lot of enduring stars.) Buck and his band travel companionably in their tour bus; dust (not smoke) is their element, and the movie seems color-coördinated to Willie Nelson's hippie-Indian earth-tone clothing—blues and browns and dark reds and greens, with an occasional dash of yellow. (The faded blue of the concertgoers' jeans is so pervasive it complements the skies.) *The Rose* was shaped to tear you up, and as one of the Dionysiac stars who ascended to fame in the sixties, and O.D.'d, all within a few years, Bette Midler gave a paroxysm of a performance—it was scabrous yet delicate, and altogether amazing. What *Honeysuckle Rose* wants to do isn't clear; nobody appears to have been sure what kind of picture it should be, and that may be why so few people have seen it—even the ads don't provide a clue.

Willie Nelson, who made a likable film début last year as Redford's crony in *The Electric Horseman*, isn't a bad actor; his open, casual manner protects him against false moves, and he has a calm, rascally sexual magnetism. He acts "natural"—there's nothing complacent about Buck Bonham, but he isn't fighting with himself or with anybody else. If there were fights, that was in the past; approaching fifty, Buck has a grizzled dignity. The film is very sensual in its color, in the looks that the two central women characters exchange with Buck, and in the music itself. Yet there are no big dramatic conflicts, and Buck isn't written to project much emotion, with the result that the movie seems to lack a center, and Willie Nelson comes across as rather limp. His singing has a much stronger emotional current than his acting. (It's the reverse with Bette Midler.) Partly, that's because he doesn't bring an actor's tension to his scenes (he tends to express deep feelings by an owlish, sweet-Jesus stare); mostly, it's because the lyrics in this movie are so much more eloquent than the dialogue that he can't help losing some of his magnetism whenever he's just talking.

We can see that life on the road is the answer to Buck's restlessness. He enjoys the rowdiness of travelling with his band. (Most of the musicians are members of Nelson's actual backup band, and the byplay among them is unforced and funny throughout the movie.) And Buck revels in the highs that he shares with the crowds at his concerts. He basks in their affection, he's intoxicated by it—at times, when he's kissing girls in the audience, he's like a politician who has sold himself on his own spiel. Buck is on the road playing one-night stands about three hundred days a year; he doesn't get to his ranch to see Viv very often. (She complains that he treats Jamie and her like an audience, that he pops in and sings a song.) He wishes that she would travel with him again, the way she did before they had the boy, but basically he doesn't want any change in his life. Buck will keep going as long as he can. The film makes us understand that he's afraid not to get back on the road—he likes to take over the wheel of the tour bus and feel that he's on his way.

The change comes when Buck's guitarist, Garland (Slim Pickens), decides to retire and stay on his farm, and Viv suggests that Garland's daughter Lily (Amy Irving), who is on her summer vacation from college and has been giving Jamie guitar lessons, can fill in for a few weeks until the new guitarist arrives. The audience can call the shots: we are a few too many jumps ahead of Viv and Buck—maybe they don't go to the movies. The story is *Intermezzo* out West—one more revamping of the 1936 Swedish film, featuring Ingrid Bergman, that was remade in 1939 to introduce Bergman to Americans and other English-speaking audiences. She played a young pianist who had been giving lessons to the child of a famous violin virtuoso and then, as accompanist, went on a concert tour with the violinist himself—the melancholy Gösta Ekman in the Swedish version, and Leslie Howard, who in profile was a ringer for Ekman, in the American version. The serious-minded, fresh-faced girl was, of course, irresistibly swept up into an adulterous affair with the guilt-ridden married man. (In 1968, there was an unmemorable version, an English production in color, called *Interlude*, with Oskar Werner and Barbara Ferris.) In the Bergman-Howard version, it was clear that the whole weight of social conventions was on the illicit lovers' consciences; when the violinist went back to his wife, it was because he had to—though he still loved the young girl. The amusing switch this time is that in modern America the musician—Willie Nelson now—is not bound by conventions: when he gives up Lily, it's because he knows he has more going with Viv. And the audience doesn't need any convincing: though Amy Irving, a soft, witchy actress, has never looked more radiant, Dyan Cannon's lustiness blows her off the screen.

As the *Intermezzo* material is used here, it has lost its droopy moral dilemma. Lily, who takes to wearing Indian headbands like Buck's, isn't the guileless girl that Ingrid Bergman played. Buck may not be a big-time star, but he's the big star of Lily's fantasy life, and she practically rapes him. (She tells him, "I've gone to bed with a song of yours since I was nine years old," and, looking at him—her dewy almond eyes clouded by desire—she muses, "It must be strange bein' everybody's hero.") Soon he's trotting around with her like a college boy carrying her books, and onstage, while they're performing, they can't keep from eying each other. They draw sexual excitement from the crowds, and there's an element of exhibitionism in the way they share their intimacy with those crowds. Ingrid Bergman's victim role made audiences love her and weep for her; Amy Irving's role probably makes audiences hate her and want her to lose out. Schatzberg himself doesn't appear to like Lily; her bland plaintiveness seems icky. This movie doesn't create a big fuss about adultery. The affair is treated the way affairs are treated in country ballads—in terms of cheating and anger, and as the most common of tragicomedies.

Maybe Schatzberg thought he could get by without much of a script (he may even have had more and subverted it) because Willie Nelson's music itself is, as the rock critic Ken Tucker has put it, "one long meditation on both the salvation and the dangers of marriage and parenthood." The story points are, in fact, made in the songs, and for Schatzberg, who had just come off *The Seduction of Joe Tynan*, where there was nothing *but* script (and Rip Torn's juicy performance), the temptation must have been strong to do something visual and to improvise. The danger is that people who demand action and a strong story may think there's nothing going on in the film. A friend of mine who became passionate about Dyan Cannon but hated the picture said, "Dyan Cannon proves that life *can* exist in a vacuum." There is an awful lot going on in this movie, though, if you are willing to adjust to its picaresque approach and its lackadaisical rhythm. A character like Sid (Charles Levin), the smart, sensible young road manager, who's hip to everything that's happening, wouldn't be nearly as funny in a more tightly structured narrative. And Slim Pickens, who has come to sound even more endearingly hoarse and scratchy than Andy Devine, thrives in this atmosphere. As the outraged father whose tender Lily has been ravished, this huge man, with his great gut slopping over his belt, goes looking for Buck equipped with a gun and a bottle of tequila; first he shoots at Buck and then they get soused together. It's a slapstick lampoon of everything that was prissy and pure in the middle-class setting of *Intermezzo*.

Possibly there's no way to star Willie Nelson in a movie without falsifying his essence unless you're willing for the movie to be relaxed at its center. In its loose, non-linear way, *Honeysuckle Rose* has *more* going on than most movies—it's just that what's going on is understated, and sometimes a little screwed up. The early scene of Buck and Viv smearing ice cream on each other and on Jamie seems completely miscalculated; there's too much cross-cutting during the guest appearance by Emmylou Harris; and Lily's big moment—her tearful apology for her thoughtlessness—just dribbles away, because she has no words to speak and nothing to do. There are also incidents that don't quite make sense. At one point during the big family reunion, Buck brings Jamie onstage to play guitar for him while he sings, and Jamie suddenly breaks off and runs out; when his father goes after him to find out what is wrong, Jamie says he doesn't have any music in him. Jamie's playing was a little uncertain for a moment, but he didn't make any glaring mistake that would explain why he got so impatient with himself; later, this crisis is just as suddenly resolved, without explanation. From what we can see, it's not Jamie who lacks a musical sense—it's Amy Irving's Lily who has no music in her. When Lily is part of the band, she looks as if she really loves being onstage in front of people, but her singing is breathy and almost inaudible, and in her guitar playing you don't feel any connection between her and the instrument—she looks tentative and listless. Probably all Amy Irving could hope for in this poorly written role is to be touching—and she isn't; she can't seem to get enough of a handle on her character to give it inflections. Despite her beauty and sultriness, she becomes tiresome, and when she and Willie Nelson sing together, her passivity makes him look passive. They seem to be one person, in a peculiarly wrong way: there's no sexual tension between them—it's puppy love. Worst of all, Amy Irving doesn't suggest the strength of a country musician.

Luckily, Dyan Cannon does. After Viv hears about what's going on between Buck and Lily, she goes to Amarillo and pays them a surprise visit: she strides into the arena with her mass of tangled curls bouncing. Buck and Lily are on the stage singing, and she watches from backstage. They're face to face, in the same position she and Buck were in when they harmonized at the family reunion. Buck and Lily are so aroused from heating up the crowd that they sing with their faces touching, mouth to mouth, and climax in a kiss. Viv has caught them flagrante delicto; the true adultery is not what Buck does with Lily in bed (he has admitted sleeping with other women)—it's how he sings with Lily. Viv marches onto the stage and makes a speech that is maybe one of the high points of movie kitsch. This is the kind of scene you rarely get anymore—like Norman Maine, in the 1954 *A Star is Born*, drunkenly whacking his wife in the face while she's making her Academy Award acceptance speech—and it doesn't belong in this low-key, rambling film. But it's ridiculously enjoyable, and it makes the whole movie come together.

August 18, 1980

Who and Who

A lot of people who saw *Jules and Jim*—especially those who picked up on it several years after its release, when it had become a revival-house favorite—went to see it repeatedly. It was their link between European bohemianism and the American counterculture, and they returned to it with new friends and lovers, in the hope that the people they saw it with would be stirred as they had been. Some of them must have come out thinking "I wish it was us"—wanting to be Jules and Jim and Catherine living in that "whirl-pool of days," from before the First World War to the burning of the books, that is celebrated in Catherine's song, "Le Tourbillon." Paul Mazursky's new *Willie & Phil* is an homage to the movie that provoked those longings, and also an overview of the psychosocial fashions of the seventies.

The picture starts inside the Bleecker Street Cinema just as *Jules and Jim* is ending; we hear Delerue's orchestration of "Le Tourbillon" and a bit of narration before Mazursky takes over as narrator to tell us, "The year was 1970." Two young men meet coming out of the theatre. Willie, a high-school English teacher who plays jazz piano, is performed by Michael Ontkean, a tall, gentle actor with almost invisible eyes, who gives the impression that he's politely sleepwalking through the entire decade. Phil, a go-getting fashion photographer, is played by Ray Sharkey, a spry, skinny-faced actor who suggests a grown-up Dead End Kid. Sharkey perks up some of the scenes with frisky gestures and vocal tricks—he has his own streetwise bravura—but there's no hint of anything going on upstairs. He's the damnedest thing to watch: a hollow dervish, a windup-toy actor. Sharkey may be doing too much to compensate for Ontkean's not doing anything; at times it comes out as impatience—he seems to be saying, "Come on, Ontkean, you're in this picture, too." Actually, neither one of them seems to be in the picture; they don't connect with each other or with anything around them. We have no idea why Willie and Phil become inseparable friends, beyond their having met at *Jules and Jim*, and the descriptions of their affinity provided by the narrator come in the form of second-generation epigrams: "They were having a good time, but they were miserable. They were looking for answers, but they didn't know what the questions were." (Is that why they seem so blank?)

When Willie and Phil both fall in love with Jeannette (Margot Kidder), a girl from Kentucky who is broke and needs a place to stay, we have no idea why *her*, rather than any other stray pretty girl in Washington Square. We don't get a clue to what they think they see in her. Mazursky has directed Margot Kidder to be flip and matter-of-fact. At the start, wearing a miniskirt and Phil's cap, she has a chic, gamine look, and she has her usual physical equipment: the angular face with wide eyes, high cheekbones, and that strange come-on of hers—a curlicue upper lip that pulls back over her gums. She has the face of a starved milkmaid, and long, long legs. Her Jeannette is practical, confident, and open-minded, with no fears or hangups about sex. She moves in with Willie, but she's fair in her dealings with men: as soon as she finds a job—selling nail polish at Bloomingdale's—she pays half the rent on Willie's apartment. (She must be a wizard of finance.) Mazursky apparently wants to demystify modern women. On the surface, he appears to be saying that women now see things more clearly than men, that they're not confused by intellectual doubts or by guilts and fears, as men like Willie and Phil are—that they trust their feelings, as Jeannette does. But though Willie and Phil marvel at Jeannette's energy, she never suggests the vitality that persuades them to live on her terms. Margot Kidder overworks her mouth, and her harsh, twangy voice is unpleasing; she sounds like the coal miner's other daughter. What's wrong is more basic, though: she goes through the motions, yet she doesn't seem to be in the movie, either. Jeannette doesn't live up to what Willie and Phil say about her, and they don't live up to what the narrator says about them.

Directors who are deeply in love with a particular film or a film genre or a film master may make an homage to what they love which strikes many viewers as completely soulless. Jacques Demy's *The Young Girls of Rochefort* and Peter Bogdanovich's *At Long Last Love* are predecessors of *Willie & Phil*; I doubt if the men who made these movies have any grasp of why some of us may find them embarassingly flimsy. There's no texture to the lives of the characters in them; it's as if the films were made in a time warp. Mazursky's strength has always been in the way he brought you close to his characters, whose obsessions came through in even their most casual conversations. But Willie and Phil don't seem part of the counterculture chic of the seventies— they go through their fads and changes on about the same level as the couple in *Same Time, Next Year*. The picture is free of the ideological jargon that weighed down Mazursky's last film, the popular *An Unmarried Woman*, but its lightness is creepy. These lives seem to have no shape, and no stress. Mazursky's theme song, Cole Porter's "What Is This Thing Called Love?," is a particularly awkward device, since the characters look as if they were together for want of anything better to do.

An homage to a master film artist is a hapless project for a man who isn't a visual director. (Probably only in comedy can someone be a major director, like Mazursky, with an original, distinctive style, and not be strongly visual.) Mazursky's films generally look like mud, though *Alex in Wonderland*, in

1970, with cinematography by Laszlo Kovacs, and *Blume in Love*, in 1973, with cinematography by Bruce Surtees, did have sunlight and some spaciousness. This time, Sven Nykvist is the cinematographer, and, yes, there's more light and clarity than Mazursky got in his last couple of pictures, but the imagery is stiff and pictorial. Without a director who knows exactly what he wants, Nykvist tends to create still-lifes, and his austerity and super-realism don't go with the material. In the interiors—especially when Willie and Phil and Jeannette take LSD—the underpopulated, near-abstract images, with figures against bare walls, almost fight the material. (Sometimes the images suggest Godard, though without his bold, primary colors.) When Jeannette takes Willie to meet her family in Kentucky, we get the standard landscape with horse; when the shots are meant to be lyrical, they're overrich—at sunset, Jeannette and Willie stand at the barn, their heads outlined with an orange glow. It's burnished innocuousness. Visually, the film has no spirit; it's in color without being in color.

In Mazursky's best work, everyone is satirized, and the characters' foolishness makes them more likable. Mazursky brings people to life only when he makes fun of them. But he presents everything that Jeannette does at face value, and having held back his feelings about her (or not having sorted them out), he muffles his satiric feelings about the men and the triangular situation. The whole movie becomes neutral. Actually, Mazursky did a variant of *Jules and Jim* in *Blume in Love*; we could feel the drunken rapport and affection between George Segal and Kris Kristofferson, who were involved with the same obstinate woman (Susan Anspach). In that film, it was clear that Segal (Blume) was so berserkly in love with this woman that what she actually was was irrelevant. He was an obsessed romantic fool, and we laughed at him with great affection. This time, Mazursky has given up his own comic perspective; instead, we get highfalutin lines delivered straight. When Jeannette, before going to bed with Willie for the first time, says, "Never tell me that you love me. Just love me," she's a pain beyond endurance. When she tells Willie that she probably won't mess around with Phil anymore and Willie says, "Promise you won't make any promises," he's as phony as she is. But we're not cued to laugh. It's Mazursky's imitation of what he must think the French are like in these situations: in their sentimental lives, far from the eyes of foreign viewers, they still have subtitles. This is another case of a clown playing Hamlet: Mazursky is trying to make a romantic classic. Suppose the picture were told from the point of view of a hip girl: There are two guys who are enamored of a movie called *Jules and Jim*. When they meet the girl, who moves in first with one and then with the other, the guys conclude that they're now living *Jules and Jim*. The girl could spend the entire movie pointing out that they're not. But in *Willie & Phil* Mazursky himself thinks they are. (At the close, when the two men return to the Bleecker Street Cinema and you see the marquee, you almost expect a double bill of *Jules and Jim* and *Willie & Phil*.)

My guess is that *Willie & Phil* is so weak for the same reason that parts of *An Unmarried Woman* sagged with sincerity: Mazursky draws away from poking fun at women's efforts toward freedom and independence. As a comedy writer-director, Mazursky may be a casualty of the women's-liberation movement. When Jeannette has a baby girl and names the child Zelda, and when, still at the hospital, she announces, "As soon as we get home, I want to take violin lessons," we expect some payoff to these references. (*Jules and Jim* was, after all, a tribute to a magical madwoman.) But no, we see Jeannette a little later living on a subsistence farm with Willie and she *has* learned to play the violin, and Zelda is treated like an adored, happy pet throughout. Actually, Zelda shows less will of her own than the cat in *Harry & Tonto*—she never inconveniences her mother or the two men in the slightest. (This appears to be an indication of the benefits of growing up in an environment where everyone loves everyone else.) The men show no anxiety about letting Jeannette make the major decisions about their lives; they don't question her sudden announcements or try to argue with her. This creature without guilt or doubt is stronger than both of them; she suggests the male view of the feminine principle—simple, direct, a natural little beastie. And at the same time she represents women's striving for self-realization. These three characters are so burdened by what Mazursky thinks they should be that they have none of the spontaneity of the people in *Jules and Jim*. The liveliest, funniest performance—it's just a small one—is by Kaki Hunter, as Jeannette's cutie younger sister, Patti (the same name as the adolescent daughter in *An Unmarried Woman*, but I don't know why). In bed with Phil, Patti is avid for sex in a way that Jeannette never is. She doesn't represent anything; she's pure fluff—Mazursky's invention—and her freedom shines. (You wonder why Phil doesn't run off with her and forget Jeannette.)

Mazursky must have felt the need to renew himself by trying something different, but he doesn't appear to know why he's making this Frenchy *Design for Living*. He seems to be looking for an escape from his principal characters: he drags in ethnic humor, and never lets up on it. In a sequence in Brooklyn, Willie's Jewish parents pressure him to get married; they're noisy, nagging stereotypes (Jan Miner is the mother) that even TV has tired of. In the Kentucky sequence, Jeannette's Protestant family reacts coyly to Willie's being Jewish; Mazursky writes these scenes as if he thought no Jew had ever got below the Mason-Dixon Line before. Then Phil's Italian Catholic parents weigh in, and Julie Bovasso is a screeching nightmare of a mother who lusts to see her son respectably settled down, having kids. She's such a violent cartoon that she *is* funny. Besides, her raging refusal to understand the loving threesome strikes a note of sanity: we in the audience don't understand it any better. When Phil has become a successful director of TV commercials, with a house in Malibu, shared with Jeannette and Zelda (who is Willie's daughter), Willie returns from communal farming in Maui and mystic explorations in India and moves in, too. Mazursky sets up scenes in which Jeannette, who has become a film editor, goes up to bed early, leaving Willie and Phil to their nightly discussions in the hot tub. This isn't a ménage-à-trois movie in the sexual sense, and you hardly expect the two men to make love, but you do expect them to bitch about her high-handedness, or to compare notes, or to ask, "What does she want?" (as in Bertrand Blier's *Get Out Your Handkerchiefs*). Or maybe you expect Willie to show a little resentment and ask, "Did she bring her violin to Malibu?" There's nothing—only acceptance of whatever Jeannette does. This movie is One Plays, the Others Listen.

It could be that the theme of *Jules and Jim*, which preoccupies Mazursky—woman as the source of life and art, and woman as destroyer—is just what he can't handle. Near the beginning, Jeannette says, "Our destinies are interlocked forever." But they're not. Ultimately, Jeannette doesn't need either of the men. In Malibu, she announces that it's time for them all to go their separate ways, and she heads East to pursue her career in film, taking the docile, cooing Zelda (who barely talks—she knows the answers, so she doesn't have to ask questions). In our last view of Jeannette, she's having a fling with Igor, a six-foot-tall Russian émigré who loves to dance and has a bright, flashing gold tooth. Is Mazursky saying that she was always a fool, or is this his idea of romantic whimsy? The narrator informs us that Willie and Phil got married and led "ordinary lives." That's a real wet blanket thrown over the seventies and the picture. And did Jeannette have an extraordinary life or was she also ordinary? Are we to admire her freedom? If we're left with nothing but questions, it may be because buried inside this tepid movie there's the complaint of a man who feels whipped, a man who's saying, "You go along with everything a woman wants and then she leaves you for a Russian dancer with gold in his teeth." If this is Mazursky's complaint, it might have been a great subject for him if he had brought it to the surface, where he could treat it with irony, as Blier did in *Get Out Your Handkerchiefs* (which possibly influenced *Willie & Phil* more than *Jules and Jim* did). There's certainly more ease between the two men than there is between either of them and Jeannette. The ad for *Willie & Phil* does bring out the film's latent subject: we see the open mouth of a giant goddess who is holding two men in the palm of her hand. They reach up to her with their offerings—one with a bottle of wine, the other with a bunch of flowers. She may be breathing life into these dwarf suitors or preparing to devour them along with their gifts. Either way, she's a source of awe and terror. All through the picture, Mazursky has been trying to demystify what he experiences as mystifying. This movie is a little monument to screwed-up notions of what women are.

·   ·   ·   ·   ·

Airplane! is cheerfully clunky and there are laughs in it, but it's so forgettable that the morning after I'd been to it, when I read a rave review, my first thought was "Oh, I've got to see that." If you were a teen-ager in the late fifties and read the movie lampoons in *Mad* and watched a lot of TV series shows and a lot of cheapie old movies on television and remembered parts of them all jumbled into one dumb movie—that's *Airplane!* It's compiled like a joke book. The three writer-directors (Jim Abrahams and David and Jerry Zucker) keep the gags coming pop pop pop, and the picture is over blessedly fast, and it's unpretentious—God is it unpretentious. It's manic from the effort to keep going whatever the quality. Most of the picture is staged and shot and mistimed with the same lack of skill as the air-disaster movies that it's patterned on. In addition to a pair of young lovers (Julie Hagerty, a misty-eyed sugarpuss, and Robert Hays), it features deadpan manly authority heroes such as Leslie Nielsen and Peter Graves and Robert Stack and Lloyd Bridges, who have aged to look like Republican ranchers. Each of these stoics has one gag that is repeated, with variations, throughout the picture; it takes a trouper not to slide downhill—Nielsen, surprisingly, keeps his footing best.

. . . . .

*R*obert Duvall plays the Bruce Dern role in the slice-of-family-life melodrama *The Great Santini* (called *The Ace* on Home Box Office). Duvall is Bull Meechum, a lieutenant colonel in the Marine Corps and a military psychopath. It is 1962, and the United States isn't involved in any major war; Bull, a flying ace primed for battle, gets drunk at the Officers' Club and lets off steam in crude practical jokes and in hostile "jesting." He treats his four children like little commandos to be trained and is particularly rough on the oldest—Ben (Michael O'Keefe, in the Richard Thomas role), a high-school basketball star who is just turning eighteen. Bull blames his wife (Blythe Danner) for being too gentle with the boy and making him soft. But when he and Ben have a basketball contest—one-on-one—in their back yard, and the lithe, quick Ben beats him, he turns mean. Refusing to accept defeat, he follows the boy inside the house, and demands another game; walking up the stairs right behind the boy, he tries to goad him by bouncing the ball, hard, off the boy's head and calling him "my sweetest little girl." That night, Ben looks down from his window and sees his father, alone in the rain, obsessively practicing basketball shots; turning from the window, Ben says to his mother, "I was praying we'd all go to war again, so King Kong out there could fight somebody besides me."

When Bull is whacking Ben's head with that ball, the movie has found (in Pat Conroy's autobiographical novel, *The Great Santini*, on which it is based) a strong metaphor for the ugly competitiveness inside a father's determination to toughen up his son. This sequence probably reaches just about everybody in the audience; it's the only one that hits home, though. *The Great Santini* (Bull's nickname for himself) is warmed over and plodding. Ostensibly, the Meechum family lives in Beaufort, South Carolina (the site of a Marine air station), where Pat Conroy grew up, and where, in fact, most of the movie was shot, but as it was written for the screen and directed by Lewis John Carlino *The Great Santini* takes place in the TV land of predictability: that plain of dowdy realism where a boy finds his manhood by developing the courage to stick to his principles and stand up to his father. Almost inevitably, since this is the South, the principles involve friendship with a saintly black—Toomer (Stan Shaw), who is crippled and has a stammer, or at least a hesitation, and is martyred by redneck stupidity and cruelty. The chief redneck villain—for simplicity's sake, he's called Red (David Keith)—is so mean he even shoots Toomer's dawg. Like the TV dramas that are honored for their seriousness, this film divides people into "them" and "us": "them" includes infantile macho militarists and sniggering rednecks; "us" is the good characters and the viewers, who perceive the insensitivity. One of the differences between drama and TV drama is that in the former we feel ourselves capable of being "them"—we feel dangerously close to "them"—while in the latter we look on and feel how remote we are from those brutes. The thoughtful kid Ben and the boozer Bull seem to belong to different species, as do Toomer and his tormentors.

Clearly, this is Ben's account of his youth, and we see his father through his eyes. But the movie protects Ben himself. His friendship with the disadvantaged Toomer (the son of the Meechum family's housekeeper) is presented in a series of rustic idylls; if Ben liked Toomer but were also using him for his own sanctimonious purposes—to antagonize his father—we might see more going on in him: some mixed motives, some crossed circuits. And maybe the actor could suggest something more than the irreproachable sensitive juvenile who's growing straight and strong. Michael O'Keefe stays in character throughout, yet he's a little pinched, and his face seems colorless and inexpressive. Blythe Danner comes close to creating a believable woman out of an idealized mother figure, and she brings in shadings that help to suggest a real family, but as the genteel Southerner who mediates between her uncouth Northerner husband and their children, the finest young actress in the American theatre is confined to an essentially undramatic role. (She doesn't have a single scene that is really hers.) The only member of the family who has been conceived with any originality is the young teen-ager Mary Anne Meechum (Lisa Jane Persky), a budding insult comic who is on to her father and taunts him the same way he taunts the children.

Robert Duvall has usually suggested a Midwestern Christian Scientist—somebody with a smooth forehead and gritted teeth—and he was a fine Eisenhower on television (*Ike*). In *Apocalypse Now*, his cartoon of stiff-necked lunacy was a flamboyant vaudeville turn—an actor's delight. But it could be that he is one of those actors who are stars when they play character parts (as in *Apocalypse Now*) but character actors when they play star parts; some element of excitement seems to be missing—we don't have star empathy with him. Perhaps because of the overexplicit writing and directing, Duvall's Bull isn't driven in a way that would really frighten us for him when he walks onto the court during a high-school game and bawls out his son, or when he pretends to throw up in front of high-ranking officers and their wives, or when he smirks as he tells his squadron, "I want you to look on me like I was, well—God." Duvall tries to suggest a powerhouse showoff, but the booming voice and the leers seem too controlled; he's skillful, but he doesn't draw us inside. (He's always "them.") Bull Meechum is so monotonously "on" that when he's up in his plane it seems as if it would be a blessing to everybody—especially the audience—if he crashed. And a movie in which we feel that way about the central character has something terribly wrong with it. *The Great Santini* has one mood throughout, like *Long Day's Journey Into Night* scored for ocarina.

· · · · · ·

I wish that Steven Spielberg had trusted his first instincts and left *Close Encounters of the Third Kind* as it was. In his new, reëdited version, *The Special Edition*, he has made some trims, put in some outtakes, and shot a few new bits. But if you saw it before and loved it, you may be bothered all the way through—not just because you miss some of the scenes that he has taken out (you miss even what you didn't think was great) but because the slightly different outtakes that Spielberg has substituted for the shots you remember keep jarring you. You can see why most of these outtakes weren't used originally, and some of them have the wrong lighting for where they've been inserted. A new image—a ship in the desert—isn't a bad idea, but it's not a good shot, and it duplicates other material. Also, when pieces are taken out, other pieces don't fit together as well as they did. For example, Roy Neary (Richard Dreyfuss) no longer makes a commotion outside his house which gets the neighborhood buzzing, but when his wife drives off with the children, the neighbors are still gathered around watching. Now when little Barry is taken off by the spaceship, his mother doesn't go to the authorities; she never mentions her missing child to anyone. And now, since the footage of the government hearing about UFOs is gone, the ruthlessness of the Air Force and Army men who keep the cranks and dreamers away from their objective is puzzling. And the most perplexing omission: in the recutting of the end, the shot of the red-clothed astronauts ascending the stairway to heaven has been lost, and it looks as if Roy were the only one who goes up to enter the mother spaceship.

It's true that the action is swifter and more streamlined, but I didn't mind the diversionary scenes of the original; they had their own scruffy charm, and part of what we love in fairy tales is their eccentricity. It's also more clear now from the beginning that Roy has become alienated from his family; his character is easier to understand, and there's more preparation for his leaving. Despite these changes, the structure, which was clumsy, is still clumsy—but does that really matter much in this huge toy of a movie?

The only really serious flaw in *Close Encounters* is one that can't be changed by cosmetic editing: in a picture with such a childlike vision, it seems wrong—unjust—that the cranks, the misfit dreamers, and the crazies who received the signals and fought their way to the mountain are not allowed to board the craft. In an ideal fairy tale, these unhappy people, whose lives have been empty on this earth, would find themselves and each other in sci-fi heaven. They were invited and they should have gone—not just the astronauts and/or the one token dreamer, Roy. That would have been a perfect fairy-tale wrapup; now the only human gesture we experience at the end is Truffaut as the blissed-out French scientist making a hand sign to the cosmic visitors. The recut ending is so prolonged it loses some of its magic; it's less awesome now and more desolate. Roy appears to board alone, and in the added footage he enters the huge craft and it's empty. There's no one to welcome him; he's standing in what might as well be a deserted Loew's Palace, and with a heavenly choir on the track which ought to be sent straight to hell.

Close Encounters of the Third Kind is one of the most euphoric comedy fantasies ever made. It will probably be a wonderful movie in any version, but I hope that this *Special Edition* will not replace the original—that the original will also be available to audiences. I want to be able to hear the true believer Roberts Blossom tell people that he has seen Bigfoot as well as flying saucers. It may not seem like a big loss, but when you remember something in a movie with pleasure and it's gone, you feel as if your memories had been mugged.

September 1, 1980

Australians

*T*he great Australian film *The Chant of Jimmie Blacksmith*, which was made in 1978 and has finally opened here, has almost nothing in common with the other Australian films of recent years. All of them partake of some of the fascination of movies set in unfamiliar terrain, but this one is large-scale and serenely shocking, with the principal characters shot against vast, rolling landscapes that are like wide, wide versions of the flat, layered backgrounds in Chinese wash drawings. *The Chant of Jimmie Blacksmith* was adapted from Thomas Keneally's novel, which is based on the case of Jimmy Governor, a half aborigine who went on a rampage and killed seven whites in 1900, the very year of Federation. (His hanging was delayed until after the ceremonies, so as not to embarrass the proud young nation by reminding it of what had been done to the natives.) The movie is about the cultural chasm that divides the natives and the European-spawned whites, and it's horribly funny, because the whites are inadequate to their own cruelties. The emotional effects of what these displaced Irish and Scottish and English do are much larger than the people themselves. The director, Fred Schepisi (pronounced Skepsee), has a gift for individualizing every one of the people on the screen; it takes him only a few licks to let us perceive how they justify themselves to themselves. Men who were at the bottom in Europe now command thousands of acres. Scrabbling tightwads, these white landowners got where they are by self-denial. Penny-pinching is a moral tenet to them, and they don't regard cheating the helpless aborigines as cheating, because the aborigines don't know how to save their money anyway. The aborigines live in the remnants of a tribal society with an elaborate structure of claims: men are obliged to give a share of their earnings to their kin, even if their kin are drunken and diseased and want the money only to go on a binge. And men offer their wives to visiting kin as a form of hospitality. To the whites, giving money away is unfathomable laxity, and since the black women are so easily available the white men treat the aboriginal settlements as brothels. The black women don't even have to be paid for their services, except with a bottle of cheap sherry for their husbands. The settlements are conveniently situated on the outskirts of the towns, far from the eyes of white women and children.

Jimmie Blacksmith (Tommy Lewis) is a product of one of these visits to a tin shanty, and because he learns quickly and is half white, the Reverend Mr. Neville (Jack Thompson), who runs the Methodist mission school, and Mrs. Neville (Julie Dawson) take him into their home when he's of an age to be useful. They train him to be polite and docile and teach him how important it is to gain a good reputation for work. Jimmie goes through his tribal initiation rites, but he grows up determined to escape the debased existence of aborigines in their hovels by working hard, buying land, and, as Mrs. Neville has advised him, marrying a nice white girl off a farm, so his children will be only a quarter black and the next generation scarcely black at all.

Sent out into the world, with the blessing of the Nevilles, he's a half-caste Horatio Alger figure, determined to show that his word is his bond and that he will stick to a job until it's done. Proper and well-mannered, he looks for work among clerks and prospective employers who call him Jacko and refer to him as a boong, a darkie, and a nigger. He doesn't take offense: these whites don't understand yet that he's different from the uneducated blacks. He smiles, so that they will see how willing he is, and eventually he gets his first job—making a post-and-rail fence to mark the boundaries of a huge farm. As he digs holes in the hard, dry earth, the vistas are lonely and bare; far in the distance, delicately etched trees look pale blue. After months of backbreaking work, Jimmie finishes the job, is underpaid, and is ordered off the property; denied a letter of recommendation as well, he flares up and tells the man that he knows why—it's because the man can't write. Jimmie is knocked flat. He goes from one fence-building job to the next, and we see how his employers react to his eagerness to prove himself a good worker. No matter how long and hard he works or how servile his behavior is, he never wins the civility or praise he longs for. These isolated farmers are terse, close-mouthed, as if even a little companionable chat would be profligacy, a waste. They can't resist finding fault with Jimmie's work and shorting him on his pay; thrift and mistrust have become second nature to them. Besides, they need to see him fail: it confirms the necessity of keeping the savages in their place. Since the aborigines have no legal rights, the farmers can feel gener-ous-hearted for paying any part of what was agreed to. When Jimmie com-plains, he looks slightly wall-eyed from terror. The farmers show their fears in their tight faces whenever there's more than one black on their land. Jimmie has a half brother, laughing Mort (Freddy Reynolds), a teen-age aborigine who giggles with contentment. He walks enormous distances to come be with Jimmie and give him a hand on his jobs, but this additional presence upsets the bosses, who accuse Jimmie of turning their land into "a blacks' camp."

When Jimmie visits his tribal shantytown with Mort, a claim is made on them for money; Mort gives his little bit happily, but Jimmie flings a roll of bills down on the ground in disgust, because his inability to save money eats away at his hopes. He gets a job as a tracker and general underling with the New South Wales Mounted Police; barefoot in a thick, outsize uniform, he's a caricature of a policeman. He thinks of the uniform very righteously, though, and when the police raid a settlement, trying to find out which of the aborigi-nes stabbed a debauching white man, Jimmie does just what his boss, Con-stable Farrell (Roy Barrett), tells him to do: he rides in smashing his club down on the head and shoulders of anyone within range. Then he proves his diligence by turning in the culprit—an old friend. It isn't until the brutish Constable Farrell gets boozed up and tortures and kills the prisoner that Jim-mie wakes from his illusion that he is part of the master race. Barrett is so strong an actor that when the constable's full sadism comes into play you want to cower in your seat; Jimmie is forced to understand that he is as pow-erless as the mutilated corpse.

He runs off and finds work as a sweeper and cook's helper at a shearing contractor's, where a dim-witted, rutting servant girl (Angela Punch), a blond waif who has been coupling with the goatish cook (played by Thomas Ken-eally), presents herself to him, half naked. She becomes pregnant, and so he gets himself a white wife. His next employer, Newby (Don Crosby), allows him to put up a one-room shack, where he and his bride can live while he builds a fence around the Newby domain. Beyond him, there are always the pastel hills—so remote they're almost part of the sky—and the faint blue trees. The immensity of the plains mocks Jimmie's hope of gaining a good reputation; trying to improve himself, he's like a hair-raisingly foolish cross between Jude the Obscure and Gunga Din. Jimmie's pathetic wife brings him his only chance of realizing his ambition to have a home, like a white man. Yet when he hears the first cries of his wife's baby, his bare feet grip the earth in dance steps that suggest an atavistic rite. Unconsciously, he seems to be expressing his continuity with nature and his tribe. Mort arrives in a spirit of celebration, accompanied by a cousin and by Jimmie's uncle Tabidgi (Steve Dodds), a tribal elder, who is worried about Jimmie's marriage to a white woman and has brought him a talisman to keep him safe. They stay on and on, with the uncle sousing while Mort helps with the work, until Newby raises the familiar cry that the place is being turned into "a blacks' camp." Mrs. Newby (Ruth Cracknell) and Miss Graf (Elizabeth Alexander), a young schoolteacher who lives with the Newbys, want to save Jimmie's wife from the fate of living among blacks anyway, and so Newby tries to get rid of Jimmie and his black kin by starving the whole group out. Jimmie is baffled by the whites' hatred, baffled that these people—the only ones on his travels who have ever shown him any kindness—are humiliating him by denying him money for groceries and are trying to persuade his wife to leave him and become a servant to Miss Graf, who is getting married. They represent what he wanted a white wife for—he wants to be them. And so, of course, they enrage him the most.

When Jimmie explodes, you may feel a sudden chill that is quite unlike what you have felt at other films, because his actions don't come out of conscious militancy or a demand for political justice. They come out of helplessness and frustration. The speed of Jimmie's first, irrevocable action makes the image seem like something happening in a delirium; his motion is so fast you replay it in your head and it stays with you—an insane ritual. It's as if he had let his unconscious take over. Jimmie acts on the level on which he has been experiencing the insults and the condescension. After the first explosion, he says he has declared war. But even then he doesn't wage war directly against the men: he attacks the men's most prized possessions—their robust, well-fed women, their pink-and-white children. His prime target—though only semiconsciously—is the supercilious schoolie, Miss Graf. She is everything plump and prissy that Jimmie has aspired to. Her immaculate, high-toned respectability represents sexuality to him, just as the "gins"—the unpaid black prostitutes lying on the dirt floors of their hovels—represent it to the ranchers. His war is race war, sex war—a freakish parody of textbook war which is probably an accurate reflection of the forces let loose in colonial uprisings. It's a conflict between two debased, threatened cultures—one individualistic, one tribal—and it's Jimmie, rather than a full-blooded aborigine, who explodes because he has tried the individualistic white way and has been rejected. He and Mort go back over the hundreds of miles he has covered; he retraces his steps to take revenge for each humiliation he has suffered.

If the film has a hero, it's Mort, who loses his happy laugh when he is drawn into Jimmie's war, and never fully regains it. We feel for Jimmie, but we don't love him as we love Mort, who is instinctively kind and selfless. Mort is something like the noble Indians and Negroes of American literature, but he's not a warrior or a mighty hunter. There's nothing overtly heroic about him; he's essentially passive and relaxed—a loyal, easy-going bum in ragged tweeds. This bum makes us see what the Europeans have destroyed; he's the simplest yet the most civilized person in the movie. The tribalism he accepts means that he doesn't have to prove himself, like the tormented Jimmie: he is part of everything. Jimmie suffers from the perils of Christian individualism; he wants respect, property, whiteness, and his failure rots him and twists him. Mort has nothing yet feels rich. We understand Jimmie and his divided soul only too well, but we don't *understand* Mort—he's both transparent to us and totally mysterious. People in ethnographic documentaries sometimes combine these qualities, but this is just about the only time I have ever seen primitive mystery made flesh in an acted movie. It couldn't have simply happened this way through a lucky accident of casting, because, of course, the past eighty years have taken their toll of tribalism. (Now it is having a *conscious* resurgence, and it's no more simple or instinctive than re-awakened tribal consciousness among American Indians or the neo-African movements among American blacks.) Mort became a Methodist, but it rolled right off him. Jimmie was so flagrantly naïve that he believed what the white missionaries taught the blacks; he's their patsy. The Reverend Mr. Neville comes to understand this, in horror and confusion: he has been giving his life to destroying the blacks. Yet how could Jimmie have improved his lot except by being the good native grateful to work for the whites? The alternative was drunkenness, and death at an early age from consumption or pneumonia.

The Chant of Jimmie Blacksmith is a triumph of casting and of coaching. With a shooting schedule of only fifteen weeks, and locations requiring that the crew travel five thousand miles, Schepisi had the job of blending a large company of the finest (white) stage and screen performers with aborigines— most of them nonprofessionals who were trained while the film was being made. (The star, Tommy Lewis, was a nineteen-year-old half-caste college student.) The professionals had to be really skillful, so as not to dominate their scenes with the amateurs; there are fine shadings in the work of actors such as Brian Anderson, who plays the objective-minded butcher and hangman, and Peter Carroll, who plays the wheezing red-haired McCreadie, an intelligent, neurasthenic schoolteacher who is taken hostage by Jimmie and is then carried piggyback to safety by Mort. The aboriginal performers—the men, particularly—come through vividly. They have the advantage of their unusual (to us) physiognomies. At times, Freddy Reynolds (Mort) and some of the others—whose features are not African, yet whose skins are dark—look like the actors in blackface who played Negroes in *The Birth of a Nation* and other early American films; they seem so different from American blacks that it sometimes throws you off when they're referred to by the same epithets. Two professionals among them are wonderful as sots: Jack Charles as the murdered prisoner, and Steve Dodds as the dazed Tabidgi, who is tried for murder and simply says, "You'd think it would take a good while to make up your mind to kill someone and then to kill them, but take my word for it, it only takes a second." (Of all the turn-of-the-century locations, only one arouses suspicion: the graffiti in a deserted sacred place are disconcertingly bright and much too legible—the four-letter desecrations spell irony.)

Schepisi, who was born in Melbourne on December 26, 1939 (his grandfather was an immigrant from a small island north of Sicily), began working in advertising at fifteen and went on to TV commercials and government documentaries. In 1970, he made a half-hour short called *The Priest*, which was part of the omnibus film *Libido*, and five years later he completed an autobiographical feature, *The Devil's Playground*, about his early-teen years in a Catholic seminary. (Keneally, a friend of his, played a priest.) An epic is not easily made, especially one that deals with the queasy emotions that attend the creation of a society built on racial oppression, yet *Jimmie Blacksmith* is only Schepisi's second feature; it's a highly sophisticated production, made in Panavision (the cinematographer was Ian Baker), and one of the rare movies in which a wide screen is integral to the conception. Schepisi has trimmed fourteen minutes since the film was shown at Cannes in 1978, and though wide-screen imagery is difficult to edit for speed, he has achieved a glancing, leaping emotional progression that's very calm, very even. The score, by Bruce Smeaton, never crowds the viewer's emotions but is right there when it's needed. Schepisi picked great material, and in mapping out the screenplay he took much of the dialogue right from the book. This is generally a mistake, but not with Keneally, who is a dramatist as well as a novelist. He writes dialogue that jumps up from the page, bites you on the nose, and makes you laugh.

Published here in 1972, Thomas Keneally's novel is no longer in print; the library copy that I read hadn't been checked out since January, 1973. How did this book slip into neglect? Was it because the literary-publicity machine was in its modernist phase, when the most highly honored novels were intricate literary puzzles? Or did the thought "arid," so closely associated with Patrick White, smudge the wrong Australian? I began the novel around one in the morning, intending to read only a few chapters before going to bed. Although it's a short book (just a hundred and seventy-eight pages), I stayed up until five, reading it slowly, because I didn't want to diminish the pleasure by going too fast. The book is like Nat Turner's story as a great lusty ironist—an Irish Nabokov, perhaps—might have written it. I didn't want to lose the full shape of the story by interrupting it until the next day; anyway, I had to read it in one sitting, because the rhythms propel you forward. They're oral rhythms—not just in the dialogue but in the prose cadences. The book itself is the chant, and it's inexorable. The novel and the movie add to each other. Keneally's passion comes out in barbaric, pixillated humor; Schepisi's vision is less comic, but his work is visually impassioned, and it, too, seems inexorable. The smooth, high-strung tone is set right at the start, and I don't think there's an inexpressive frame of film in the entire movie. Schepisi's chant has a different rhythm: Keneally writes spiccato, Schepisi's moviemaking is legato. Keneally writes with the comic virulence of an Irish-Australian observing the stingy Scots, who can't open their fists even when they're the lords of a great land; Schepisi sees the meanness set against the expanses, sees the patterns of dark to light, with the people at the dark bottom of the image and the birds flying from the pastels to the whiteness at the top. Each, in his way, makes you feel that he has captured a nation's rhythm.

In recent years, the movies with the clearest social vision appear to be those rooted in a particular time and place: in the Sardinia of the Taviani brothers' *Padre Padrone*, with its patriarchal system; in Francesco Rosi's *Christ Stopped at Eboli* (which gave you the feeling that the camera arrived in the remote, mountainous peasant village with Carlo Levi in the thirties and left with him, and that the land and the people returned to darkness). Maybe it's because movies spouted so much humanitarian ideology in the past, and Hollywood showed us so many faceless throngs, that these exact, personal visions bringing us up close to their subjects have special, ecstatic force. *The Chant of Jimmie Blacksmith* is a dreamlike Requiem Mass for a nation's lost honor; that Schepisi should have financed it partly by his work in TV commercials is a joke that all moviemakers can appreciate. Keneally's book is full of jokes. A sample: "Press cartoonists sketched the nascent motherland. . . . In one hand she held perhaps a tome with a title such as 'British Civilization,' in the other a blank parchment entitled 'The Fresh New Page of Democracy.' She rather resembled Miss Graf."

.   .   .   .   .

*I*t makes very good sense that the Australians, who are involved in a concerted effort to bring new life to their film industry, are asking the question "Where did we come from?" But you don't get very far in investigating your roots by taking minor late-Victorian and post-Victorian novels such as *My Brilliant Career* and *The Getting of Wisdom* and re-creating them on the screen in their own terms, or in what the re-creators think are their own terms. That's the "Masterpiece Theatre" approach: it can be done skillfully, so that the novel unfolds in a leisurely, soothing way, and this can be very charming if the performers are likable—*My Brilliant Career* has considerable charm—but it's essentially taxidermy. If the book is still alive, they kill it and stuff it.

I found last year's *My Brilliant Career* somewhat bewildering. The impoverished, sixteen-year-old heroine, Sybylla, spends most of the movie pursuing a wealthy, aristocratic bachelor—a tall, thin "man of the world." He seems to be the only thing on her mind; she publicly displays her jealousy, and she is a thoroughgoing sexual tease. But when she has him half crazy and he proposes, she hits him with a whip. It seems she just wants to be friends with him—she apparently has no sexual appetite, because she intends to have her own career as an artist. Were we suffering from the same delusion of a hot flirtation that he was, or is Sybylla a very confused girl? It's obvious that the appeal of this material to the modern women filmmakers (the director Gillian Armstrong, the writer Eleanor Witcombe, the producer Margaret Fink) must be in Sybylla's desire for independence, but shouldn't they clarify what is going on with their heroine? From the evidence of the film, the book, which was written by a sixteen-year-old girl, is a gothic feminist fantasy: feisty Cinderella wins Prince Charming but turns him down and goes off to fulfill herself. Judy Davis, who plays Sybylla, suggests a blooming, broad-faced version of Katharine Hepburn's tomboy Jo in *Little Women* (an autobiographical portrait of Louisa May Alcott), and the lines are often beauts. Sybylla's aunt to Sybylla: "You have a wildness of spirit which will trouble you all your life." Prince Charming's mother to her son, of Sybylla: "She makes other women look insipid." Though the movie—tasteful, slow, pictorial—doesn't go any deeper into the material than this sort of feminine self-infatuation, Sybylla is treated as if she were a precursor of the new woman: a model of the woman who resists conventional blandishments. What she's a precursor of is the feminist novelists who write princess fantasies.

The Getting of Wisdom, which was made in 1977 but has just recently opened here, was also adapted by Eleanor Witcombe, from another Australian woman's autobiographical novel set in the eighteen-nineties. It's far less enjoyable; it's cultured—a foreign film in English. The impoverished heroine this time is Laura Rambotham (Susannah Fowle), a girl from the back country, who's highly precocious and a gifted musician. At thirteen, she comes to Melbourne, and she spends five years there at the Presbyterian Ladies College, a "select" school for the daughters of the wealthy, where the teachers sneer at her because her mother runs a post office in the bush, and the girls are harpies. Laura almost succumbs to snobbery, but she has her brains and her talent and her intrepid nature to see her through. (She's so confident of her intellectual and artistic superiority that she doesn't need any social snobbery.) Small, dark, with large, observant eyes and a slight, forbidding overbite, Laura is gauntly intense. There's something a little poisonous about her, and we spend the whole movie looking at her big eyes as she perceives the low follies around her. Clearly, we're meant to care for her more than I did. It's easy to read the signals: she impulsively says what's on her mind, she's imaginative, and so on. But this self-infatuated fantasy is presented in the guise of harsh realism, and the faithful, meticulous period re-creation makes it hard for us to connect with Laura or with anything else. *My Brilliant Career* and this film had the same accomplished cinematographer—Don McAlpine—but he doesn't get any chances for pastoral romanticism here. The director this time is a man—Bruce Beresford—whose attitude toward the material is cold and literal, as if we were in need of a muckraking exposé of the Victorian education of ladies.

The movie shows no particular interest in what the other girls go through. It's strictly a careful rendering of Laura's adolescent horrors: her wanting to belong; her defensiveness about her poverty; how she becomes ashamed of her family; her sensitivity to the repressiveness and hypocrisy and pettiness of the staff; how she learns to get along and conceal her feelings; how the schoolgirl crush she develops on a rich, lushly beautiful older student causes her to neglect her studies; her cheating in a history exam; her triumph (winning a scholarship for two years of study in Leipzig with a famous music teacher); her sense of liberation when she graduates. You feel, This is just what people must have got from the book when they read it—that school is a horrible rite of passage, and what counts isn't what you learn in your classes (which is all memorizing) but what you learn about how to get close to the powerful, so their power will rub off on you, and how to stay clear of the helpless and weak, so their failure won't infect you. It is learning this principle of contagion that is supposed to prepare you for the outside world. And so Laura is equipped to make her way—Little Miss Machiavelli, concealing her finer impulses. (The title of the movie is, I assume, ironic.) But why go to a movie to see the kind of proud-headstrong-heroine novel that we all read long ago? And were fed up with long ago. This movie is intelligent, and it has been visually designed so that the limited setting won't seem too claustrophobic, but in a way it's worse than a bad movie—it has the mustiness of the books that drive you out of the house in search of something trashy with a little life to it. Having been through so many men's coming-of-age literary autobiographies on film, do we have to plow through the same tediousness with women? We always know the end: they go off to write the book.

September 15, 1980

As Swift as Buzzard Flies

The Stunt Man catches you up with its rowdy, satirical opening sequence: between the snaps of clapper boards with the credits, we see a series of paranoid reactions to chance happenings, with one reaction sparking the next. All nature is a powder keg of grievances. On a sunny, bright day, a po-

lice car honks at a dog sleeping in the middle of the road, the dog snarls viciously, and the movie is off and spinning. A telephone lineman throws a
rock at a big buzzard; darting away, the buzzard hits a helicopter carrying a
cameraman and a movie director, and somebody in the plane (the pilot or
the cameraman) rasps out, "That God damn crazy bird . . . he was trying to
kill us!" The voice of the not yet visible director, Eli Cross (Peter O'Toole), is
heard: "That's your point of view. Should we stop and ask the bird what his
was?" Then Cross takes a bite from an apple and tosses it away; the apple
lands on the roof of a café and rolls down onto the top of the police car,
which is just being parked, giving the two policemen a start. Inside the café, a
trucker reaches out to make a pass at a waitress, and the pet Chihuahua that
she carries close to her breast snaps at him ferociously. A scroungy-looking
young man with stubble on his chin, Cameron (Steve Railsback), sees the policemen coming in, and, terrified, he goes to the pinball machine, where he
finds a free ball; the policemen come over and put handcuffs on him, but he
bolts out the door and keeps going, while they shoot at him. A short distance
away, he knocks down the telephone lineman, grabs the man's tool belt, and
heads for the woods, where he uses the tools to split the handcuffs apart.
Running past the sawhorse barricades closing a road, he starts across a river
bridge and tries to hitch a ride in the only car in sight—a shiny, glamorous
old Duesenberg. The young, yellow-haired driver, who is alone, stops, and
Cameron thinks he's being picked up, but when he gets in, the driver shoves
him out with his foot and speeds away, leaving him sprawling and bruised;
then the Duesenberg turns around and heads right toward him. Thinking that
the driver means to kill him, Cameron grabs a construction bolt and throws it
at the car, hitting the windshield. But the car doesn't come near him. By the
time he picks himself up—a few seconds only—it has disappeared and the
bridge is deserted. Looking down, he sees bubbles where the water has
closed over the Duesenberg, and, hearing an engine above, he looks up and
sees the helicopter, which comes down close. Cameron runs across the
bridge and through fields until he comes to an oceanside resort area. He cuts
off the legs of his jeans, so that he'll look like a vacationer in shorts, and joins
the crowd that is watching a movie crew prepare to shoot a war scene on the
beach. There's a non-stop quality about this chain-reaction prologue. The music—cheery, jangling, circusy music, by Dominic Frontiere—might almost be
driving Cameron on. It seems to pick him up and keep him whirling; he gets
only a short breather before he's in movement again. The music doesn't
reach any kind of completion: it's a repeated vamp that starts up—loud and
boisterous—each time the mood of the film is frazzled and everything is in
motion.

Eli Cross's first, disembodied words state the theme of *The Stunt Man*:
it's about the paranoia of snap judgments. All through the movie, people
grasp only a fragment of a situation, and misinterpret what is going on because they perceive that fragment in terms of their fears that everything—a

buzzard, an apple, a yellow-haired man in a Duesenberg—is against them. The film itself is designed to demonstrate how difficult it is for Cameron—or you—to know what's really happening. You joyride through this picture, sorting out what you're seeing as it races ahead. At first, the thought may cross your mind that the cameraman in the helicopter is photographing Cameron, and that he's part of a movie being made; this thought gets discarded fast, as you realize that Cameron intruded on the making of a movie, and that Burt, the man in the Duesenberg who shoved him out and spun the car around, was a stunt man, doubling for the blond hero. Burt didn't have time for more civil behavior because his drive had to be coördinated with the helicopter—and he had intended to go over the side of the bridge. (He had also intended to survive, of course, but Cameron's cracking his windshield was a factor he hadn't taken into account.) When Cameron shows up at the beach, Eli Cross, who recognizes him from the bridge, pretends to the police that he was the driver of the Duesenberg, and that nobody got killed. Cross, who has a permit to shoot for three more days at the resort, doesn't want the police to close him down, so he protects Cameron. The actors and crew know perfectly well that Cameron is a stranger, but Cross decrees that because of Burt's return from the bottom of the river he is henceforth to be known as Lucky Burt, and everyone complies, shortening it to Lucky. When Cameron is afraid that he won't be able to fool the police, Cross reassures him: "You will be disguised as a stunt man who doubles for an actor who plays an American flier who poses as a German soldier who, like yourself, is a fugitive." Clean-shaven, wearing makeup, and with yellow hair, Cameron becomes the stunt man.

Working with material that could, with a few false steps, have turned into a tony reality-and-illusion puzzle, the director, Richard Rush, has kept it all light-headed and funny—it's slapstick metaphysics. *The Stunt Man* is a virtuoso piece of moviemaking: a sustained feat of giddiness that is at the same time intense. Rush isn't afraid to hook you and to keep hooking you. Despite the elaborateness of what he and his scenarist, Lawrence B. Marcus (best known for *Petulia*), were aiming at, he didn't forget what he'd learned in exploitation pictures, when his subjects were hippies, drugs, and motorcycles. Rush uses the pacing and exhilarating, so-bright-it's-luminous visual style he developed on A.I.P. releases in the late sixties, when he was working with the cinematographer Laszlo Kovacs on such pictures as *Psych-Out* and *Hell's Angels on Wheels* and *The Savage Seven*. Those movies were crude with a special, hopped-up American trashiness; that was true, too, of such later Rush films as the more ambitious (and more disreputable) *Getting Straight* and *Freebie and the Bean*. Rush is a kinetic-action director to the bone; visually, he has the boldness of a comic-strip artist, and maybe because *The Stunt Man* is about subjects close to him—paranoia and moviemaking, which may be the subjects closest to almost all dedicated moviemakers—there's a furious aliveness in this picture. The cinematographer, Mario Tosi, has brought back the airiness and energy of that early Kovacs lighting (which even Kovacs has lost). There's nothing delicate or subtle in this movie, but there's nothing fussy or dim in it, either. The music is the film's motor; it starts up with the varoom of Rush's motorcycle gangs.

The Stunt Man suggests what Truffaut's *Day for Night* might have been if its director-hero had been a flamboyant fire-eater instead of a modest, self-effacing clerk, or what Fellini's *8½* might have been if its director-hero had been John Huston or David Lean rather than "Guido," and if he had been seen from the slapstick, satirical outside rather than from the soft, warm inside. There is, of course, a reason for Eli Cross's being heard before he is seen: in the beginning was the word. And when Peter O'Toole lets out his strong, raucous voice, you know that there's only one cock-a-doodle-doo man on this movie set, and he's it. He doesn't need a megaphone. O'Toole's Eli Cross may be as definitive a caricature of a visionary movie director as John Barrymore's Oscar Jaffe in *Twentieth Century* (1934) was of theatrical genius. Cross is a shameless manipulator, who tricks people to get what he wants, but probably he long ago lost track of the difference between what he wants and what his legend requires of him. He plays to his own legend, and he does it with the crazed strength of the totally self-centered. The only thing that matters to him is the movie he's at work on, and, like Oscar Jaffe, this God is on his uppers: He needs a hit. But there's something that means much more to Cross than box-office success: his most basic need is to do something mad—and to be acclaimed and vilified for it, of course.

Remarkable as O'Toole has often been in gentle roles (as in the 1969 *Goodbye, Mr. Chips*), it's great to see him playing a hellion. Using his words like a cat's playthings, pouncing on them, teasing, and then showing his claws, he gives a peerless comic performance. It's apparent that Eli Cross has been conceived by Rush and Marcus and O'Toole as a protean figure—a man who has in him all the basic human attributes. He's fierce-tempered and tough; like Sam Peckinpah, he carries teeth-gnashing orneriness to an art form. Yet he's also an Audrey Hepburn gamine—ethereal and fey. The chief of police (Alex Rocco), who is enraged by his high-handedness, yells at him that he's a "fruit with a camera." Yes, of course he is. Eli Cross could be called almost anything and it wouldn't be wrong and it wouldn't insult him. He's a capering showoff with a tricky glint in his eyes. He opens them wide, like someone sincere and insincere; he mesmerizes whomever he's talking to. Eli Cross acts all the time, and he's completely aware of his craggy magnificence—he holds his gaunt, high-boned face to the light the way the other Hepburn does. (O'Toole has acted with both.) Wearing a black turtleneck and black pants, and with his arms hanging at his sides holding his chest together, he's a spiffy Hamlet. He never wears an ordinary shirt; in his knits and the high-necked blouses that emphasize his thinness and height, he's a slinky dowager. Perhaps it's not that no human possibilities are closed to him but that no glamorous poses are closed to him. (Directors and stars often fight because they're competing for the same pose.) Yet Cross *does* live in another world. O'Toole revels in the histrionics of this thick-skinned, thin-skinned, dreamlit optimist, who chews a hunk of bubble gum as if it were a plug of tobacco. Seated in the basket chair of his crane, Cross drops down into the film frame to say something to Lucky, or he swings in from the side and floats off again. He's always hovering overhead, dangling from his helicopter or his crane; he uses his basket chair like a divinity's kiddie car, popping into the frame to make a grand entrance. Cross is on top of everything, dominating everyone's life; he knows what everyone is doing, whom they're sleeping with, and what they're thinking—and which ones are out spreading vicious gossip, and why. To the cast and the crew he is God the Father as a son of a bitch.

Cross turns his visage into a heroic, world-weary mask, but Cameron has only a stricken, naked face. Cross has a use for Cameron beyond hiding the fact of Burt's death from the police: with his director's hyper-intuitiveness— the one attribute that all fanatic movie directors seem to share or, at least, to pride themselves on—Cross detects in Cameron's animal desperation something of the madness he needs for his film. As Steve Railsback plays Cameron-Lucky, the role suggests James Dean's crushed loners, with a trace of Tommy Lee Jones in this fugitive's inability to trust anyone. Rush and Marcus tease the audience and build suspense by withholding information: for most of the movie, all we know about Cameron is that he spent two years in 'Nam. (Vietnam today is used as a catchphrase—a plot convenience—the way the Foreign Legion used to be.) And his quick physical responses—which convinced Cross that he could replace the stunt man—tell us of his will to live. But, just as Cameron doesn't know how to interpret the situations in which he finds himself, we don't know if he's a perverse, brutal murderer or merely a kid who got into trouble. Railsback (he played Manson on TV in *Helter Skelter*) manages to suggest a pure, lacerated sensibility that would fit either of these explanations, and many others as well. It's far from easy to make a scared, self-pitying man with terrible judgment appealing, but Railsback does it. He's helped by the physicality of his role (though much of it is, no doubt, an illusion provided by stunt men doubling for him). Rush takes a sizable liberty with the way movies are actually made—shot by shot, with considerable time spent in moving the camera and arranging the lights and setting up all the elements. Instead, he presents the scenes of Lucky's stunts as if they were shot together in continuous long takes, so we see a chase (reminiscent of a chase in *Gravity's Rainbow*) in which he is pursued by German soldiers and shot at by planes while he runs across rooftops, slides down turrets, leaps from tower to balcony, crashes through a skylight to fall on a brothel bed between two naked bodies, and is caught by carousing Huns in the beer hall downstairs, who sadistically toss him around over their heads—and all the time that insistent, vamping music is driving the action forward. The shifting camera angles in what is presented as if it were accomplished as fast as we're seeing it give the moviemaking sections of the film a hurtling, exhilarating speed; Rush is well-named. (Actually, superlative editing was needed to achieve the effect of these long takes, which parallel the chain reactions of the opening; it was done by Jack Hofstra and Caroline Ferriol.)

Lucky gets tipsy on his own prowess and on the thought of the big money that the stunt master (Chuck Bail) tells him he has coming for it. He falls in love with stardom, in the person of Nina (Barbara Hershey), the actress who is the heroine of the movie being made, and when they're together he gets up from her bed, puts on her wig, and holds her costume in front of him—he entertains the fantasy of doubling for her as well as for the hero. Maybe it's the location that has got to him: most of the picture was shot around the Hotel Del Coronado, near San Diego—the same gabled and turreted romantic folly that figured in *Some Like It Hot*. If there were such a thing as a masterpiece of a location, the Hotel Del Coronado as it is used in *The Stunt Man* would be it. The cameras are positioned so skillfully that this location satisfies the needs of the film we see being shot as well as the more complex needs of the film we're seeing. When the crew is photographing soldiers being blown up on the beach, with ancient little planes flying over the water and strafing them, we also see the hotel that will not be visible in the shots, and during Lucky's stunts we take in how the illusion of the First World War period can be created from a few bits of roof, with the parking lots and the palm trees kept out of the compositions.

Starting with the misunderstood bird, and the apple falling on the top of the café, this movie is in love with sky and roofs, planes and cranes; it touches earth as little as possible, except in the character of Sam, the dumpling screenwriter, who is designed to be the Sancho Panza to Cross's Don Quixote. Sam—the practical worrywart whose dialogue Cross throws out as he improvises his way toward madness—may be the best role Allen Goorwitz has had, and the best performance he has given since he (when he used the name Allen Garfield) and Robert De Niro did a comedy routine together in De Palma's *Hi, Mom!* back in 1970. The conversations between squat Sam and lean, tall Cross are a comedy routine, too, with Sam claiming that his "magical madhouse" scene is better than *Marat/Sade*, and Cross throwing it out anyway. Goorwitz's byplay and timing are impeccably deceptive: at first you think Sam is a quintessential jerk; a little later he doesn't seem quite so dumb; and by the time he's offering Lucky advice he has actually become lovable and wise.

There are also scenes that might touch earth if the music didn't drive the picture forward. (We move on so fast we don't hear the thud.) I have men friends who like Barbara Hershey's flower-child persona; one of them said, "I always wanted to get to know her—I felt if I met her she'd be mine." "What about her acting?" I asked. "What acting?" he said. If Barbara Hershey isn't perceived as an actress (and very likely she isn't by most people), it's probably a mistake to cast her as one. Nina, I assume, is meant to keep us guessing about when she's playacting and when she isn't, but Hershey, whose technique consists primarily of an affected naturalness, playacts all the time. She certainly doesn't have the style to deliver a line such as "I *am* the movies." Her performance gets off to a bad start: Nina is first seen made up as an elderly woman, but the camera is too close for us to be fooled, she moves all wrong, and whoever did her rubbery, wrinkled makeup might as well have signed his name across her forehead. And when the ruthless Cross plays a rotten trick on Nina in order to get her to express shame on camera, Hershey's expression of shame is so small and drippy that the sequence misses its punch. We can see that Cameron is attracted to stardom (or what he thinks is stardom—he has seen Nina in a dog-food commercial), but what attracts Nina to him? Is she flattered by his fixation on her? Or does his being hunted by the police constitute stardom in her eyes—the attraction of danger? Or is she excited by the physical risks he takes, or touched by the sense of terror he communicates? I have a feeling that these possibilities are supposed to keep us off balance, constantly revising our interpretation, but all that really comes across is that Nina "falls in love" with Lucky, and there's no tension in their tender scenes together. The tension in the movie is between O'Toole and Railsback; the romantic scenes are dead spaces, in which even the camerawork goes flooey. There are other failures. The whole conception of Cross's finding in Cameron the madness he needs disintegrates when Cross shoots the sequence that is supposed to show this madness: the action, involving Lucky dancing on the wing of a plane, takes too long to get started, and it doesn't seem mad—only awkward and silly.

Even if a line such as "I *am* the movies" were made to sparkle, it would still, like many of the lines and situations that do sparkle, cast too familiar a glow. The clever bits are often drawn from the stockpile of movie gags and anecdotes. And there are scenes—such as the crowd on the beach applauding the bombing and strafing, then seeing the bloodshed and becoming hysterical, thinking that live ammunition has been used, then laughing as the mutilated corpses get up, and applauding again—that have a secondhand surreal irony, even though they work. (The crowd's hysteria is extraordinarily effective, because the audience in the theatre is also momentarily confused by the illusion of real blood.) The rowdiness saves this film from its stale ideas, which are often on a par with Sam's "magical madhouse." There's also a more central flaw. When Rush and Marcus prepared the script, which is based on the 1970 novel by Paul Brodeur, they created different characters while retaining some of the situations and paraphrasing bits of the dialogue. Marcus did an amazing job of turning serious reality-and-illusion convolutions into a game we could all play. The book provided the controlling metaphor, however, and the subjects of paranoia and moviemaking are not linked in the way they would have been if the story had originated with a moviemaker and a screenwriter rather than in the imagination of a New York novelist. Cameron brings his suffering into the world of moviemaking. The suspense in the picture comes from his fear that he is trapped—that if the police don't get him the crazy Eli Cross will. He feels sure that Cross means to kill him at the end of the three days, when he is to recapitulate the stunt of the Duesenberg going off the bridge. Cameron has it all wrong, of course. Cross is the one who said, "That's your point of view. Should we stop and ask the bird what his was?" And it's Cross who frees him from his paranoid delusion. But a movie set is not where you go to get your paranoia cured— it's where you get it inflated. Ask Richard Rush—a big, commanding figure— who had a heart attack last October, following the decision of Melvin Simon Productions (which financed this project after he had spent six years being turned down by the major studios) not to include the film in its distribution arrangements with Twentieth Century-Fox, leaving Rush to spend almost a year trying to get the best picture he has ever made into theatres. (After it ran to enthusiastic audiences in Seattle and became a hit in Los Angeles, Fox took it on, a few weeks ago, and it is now going to open in New York. Finally shot in 1978 and completed in 1979, *The Stunt Man* was first announced as a 1971 release.) Moviemaking is a seedbed of paranoia. On the set, directors—with their feelers out, intuiting what everyone is thinking—are the paranoid kings of backbiting kingdoms. They have to be paranoid to survive, and it makes them look twenty years older than they are. Once when I was at a large party in Los Angeles, a famous director suddenly screamed from across an adjoining room at me and another guest, "I know you're talking about me!" He was right. Working from observation, Peter O'Toole has put the paranoia in Eli Cross, and there's truth in this great caricature, up until the moment when Cross turns benign, like your friendly neighborhood shrink. What's left out of the story line is the suspiciousness and terror and calculation that gnaw away at directors and turn them into bedevilled stunt men.

.   .   .   .   .

Those Lips, Those Eyes—one more boy's-coming-of-age movie—has no nerve center. During the credits, Frank Langella, as the song-and-dance man Harry Crystal, who is the leading performer of a summer-stock theatre that's doing a season in Cleveland in 1951, makes up his face, and the film is already listless. Thomas Hulce (he was the freshman in *Animal House* who got the mayor's daughter drunk and didn't know what to do next) plays Artie, a local pre-med student who signs on with the theatre as prop boy; Artie is an earnest gawker—he oozes stage-struckness. The way Hulce's eyes line up gives him a quizzical expression (like Teresa Wright's when she was an ingénue), and he smiles when he's in repose, as if youth were a state of harmless amusement. We get the story from Artie's point of view (he grows up to be a playwright, just like the Cleveland boy David Shaber, who grew up and wrote this semi-autobiographical script), but the camera picks up the traces of stage stylization in Hulce's acting, and he seems to be a junior manikin, with a painted, crescent-moon grin. The camera keeps scrutinizing that stiff little face; we can't seem to get away from it. Who cares if innocent Artie gets laid? We don't. Only Harry Crystal does. Harry protects Artie when he bungles his backstage duties, sets up a date for him with the dancer of his dreams (Glynnis O'Connor), adroitly maneuvers Artie's parents out of the way, and lends him his room for the First Sexual Experience. Why is Harry pimping for the prop boy? It gets to be embarrassing: you expect Harry to be there in the room, leaning over Artie and coaching him. But apparently Harry is just meant to be a great guy—a second-rater but a man who recognizes that Artie has the same love of the theatre that he has.

This maudlin film asks us to love and pity Harry because even a performer as limited as he is can have a true dedication to the theatre. Maybe we could accept some of this if Harry sang the rousing numbers in *The Red Mill* and *The Desert Song* and *The Vagabond King* and *Rose Marie* with hammy gusto. It shouldn't be hard to do Rudolf Friml and Victor Herbert with a forced ebullience that would give a lift to the open-air summer audience and enrapture a naïve kid like Artie and still let us know that the performer would never make it to the big time. But there isn't any lift. The director, Michael Pressman, doesn't give corn its due: why put on scenes from warhorse operettas (which aren't convincing as a total season for 1951) if not to demonstrate that even in parodied form they still have some ridiculous surefire appeal? This picture wears its love of theatre like a shroud. (If we perk up at the musical numbers, it's only because they come after scenes of Artie with his family, having arguments with his father, who wants him to pay more attention to his pre-med courses.) The special pleading for the heroism of the untalented could be self-serving.

Frank Langella doesn't have it in him to be the robust, good-hearted vulgarian that this picture appears to call for; stridency and inspirational bombast are not in his range, and when he tries to sing operetta he has no projection. He's barely a crooner: what comes out is something like Mel Tormé's velvet fog. Even his soft-shoe is too soft. Langella was extraordinary when he played romantic torment in Kleist's *The Prince of Homburg*, and the depleted emotions of his hero in *The Eccentricities of a Nightingale* were delicately modulated, as a foil to Blythe Danner's passion—it was a superb job of partnering. With his boneless finesse, Langella has the calm center of exhausted nobility. He has a gift for interiorized, smothered emotion, and he can play ironic, seductive roles with the smoothness of a Lubitsch actor. But put his six feet three inches in a Mountie's uniform, with a hat flat across his forehead hiding his thick mop of dark hair, and his mouth open in song, and he doesn't give anything to the audience out there. He's wilted and defenseless, as if he thought that that was the form that second-rateness took.

This movie is every bit as tacky and enervated as the productions that are being staged. The camerawork is brutal to both Hulce and Langella, and there's a scene in which the camera seems to violate Glynnis O'Connor—she strips for no apparent reason except to let it ogle her and invite us to touch her. The picture even drags in the decrepit, sentimental old bit of Pop, the stage doorman, who is humiliated by a temperamental star. This time, Pop is Herbert Berghof, and he's a retired Latin scholar—Doc—who takes a job as the theatre's night watchman, and he isn't just humiliated: he's humiliated in front of his granddaughter at the very moment when he is trying to instill in her his own love of the theatrical classics. There are, however, a few performances that can be watched without squirming. Glynnis O'Connor, who looks lovely in her dancing scenes onstage (among the few well-lighted scenes in the movie), speaks in her usual artificial tone of voice, but when she delivers her fatuous lines she creates emotion out of them, and you know you're watching someone who cares about acting. Joseph Maher brings perfectly controlled dry pathos to the part of an aging, alcoholic actor who hopes to get a shot at a radio soap opera in Chicago. And Kevin McCarthy comes through with a shrewd, workmanlike performance as an agent who shows up at the theatre. His eyes dart around as he checks the house and assesses the possibilities of the girls onstage; for a few minutes, he gives substance and weight to the movie.

Since coming-of-age movies are, for obvious reasons, almost always about writers, and since male writers generally see their adolescent selves as ingenuous yokels, people must come away from these movies wondering if all wimpy kids grow up to be writers. The summer at the theatre is supposed to bring Artie to understand his true vocation. (Harry tells him, "If you quit now, you're going to have an ache in your heart the rest of your life.") On the evidence of this script, a pretty good case could be made that he should have listened to his family and gone to medical school. Of course, if you live in Cleveland you may figure that a logy mind can do less damage in a writer.

September 29, 1980

The Man Who Made

Howard Hughes Sing and

The Iron-Butterfly Mom

*J*ean Renoir instinctively understood what he had in common with characters very different from himself, and when his people are at their most ludicrous—when they are self-pitying or infuriatingly contentious—he puts us inside their skins, so we're laughing at ourselves. Asked to explain how it was that he didn't separate his characters into the good ones and the bad ones, Renoir's answer was always "Because everyone has his reasons," and in his best films we don't need those reasons explained—we intuit them. The young American director Jonathan Demme has some of this same gift, and his lyrical comedy *Melvin and Howard*, which opened the New York Film Festival on September 26th, is an almost flawless act of sympathetic imagination. Demme and the writer Bo Goldman have entered into the soul of American blue-collar suckerdom and brought us close enough to see that the people on the screen are us. Demme and Goldman have taken for their hero a chucklehead who is hooked on TV game shows and for their heroine his wife, who when she's off on her own and needs to work turns go-go dancer. And they have made us understand how it was that when something big—something legendary—touched these lives, nobody could believe it.

The lawyers and judges and jurors who were involved in the 1976–78 legal proceedings over the Howard Hughes will known as the Mormon will looked at Melvin Dummar, raked over his life, and couldn't believe that Hughes (who died in April, 1976) would have included Dummar among his beneficiaries. If you've seen Melvin Dummar on television, you may have observed that he's very touching—he looks like a more fair-haired Andy Kaufman as Latka Gravas in the TV series "Taxi," and he has that square, engaging naïveté that is so thoroughgoing it seems like a put-on. Dummar does, in fact, have links to TV: he is the representative debt-ridden American for whom game shows were created. He won a prize on "Truth or Consequences" but was unsuccessful on "The Dating Game"; he once appeared on "Let's Make a Deal" wearing a string of oranges around his neck and a hat shaped like an orange, and another time in the same hat but with a duck on top with a sign that said "Quacking up for a deal." Actually, Dummar was on "Let's Make a Deal" four times within a period of five years (which is probably a record); in the hearings on the will, an attorney said that this was a violation of federal law, and it was used against him to indicate that since "theatrics and lying" were a way of life for him, he could have faked the will and invented the story that he gave to account for the bequest—the story of how one night around Christmas of 1967 or early January of 1968 he had found Hughes in the desert and given him a ride. Even Dummar's dreams were turned against him: an attorney grilling his second wife in order to discredit him asked, "Mrs. Dummar, didn't your husband once write a song which he entitled 'A Dream Becomes Reality,' with this as one of the lines—'A beggar becomes a king'?" And, of course, the attorney had a point: the Hughes bequest did seem just like another one of Dummar's dreams, though it probably wasn't. The new nonfiction detective story *High Stakes*, by Harold Rhoden, makes a very spiky and convincing argument for the authenticity of the Mormon will, which the whole country laughed at because of the inclusion of Melvin Dummar, who seemed like a pudgy hick. (Johnny Carson got a lot of mileage out of Melvin Dummar jokes; for a while he was the national chump.) Even the many eminent institutions that were also named as beneficiaries didn't put up much of a fight for the will. Maybe their officers couldn't believe Melvin Dummar belonged among the hallowed names. More likely, these officers, knowing that the scary, powerful Summa Corporation, which controlled Hughes' wealth, would not relinquish this fortune without a costly battle in the courts which Summa, with the Hughes resources, could prolong into infinity, decided that it was wiser simply to string along with the general attitude in the media that a will in which Melvin Dummar was a beneficiary had to be a forgery. (The will, dated March, 1968, which would have effectively dissolved the Summa Corporation, left one-quarter of Hughes' estate to medical research, one-eighth to four universities, and the remainder to be divided into sixteen parcels, among beneficiaries such as the Mormon Church, the Boy Scouts, orphans, Hughes' ex-wife, relatives, business associates, and Dummar, whose one-sixteenth would have amounted to over a hundred and fifty million dollars.)

But what if the meeting between Melvin Dummar and Howard Hughes took place just as Dummar said it did? What might have caused Hughes to remember Melvin a few months later and put him in his will? That's what *Melvin and Howard* tells us. By their own imaginative leap, Demme and Goldman make us understand what Howard Hughes might have seen in Melvin Dummar that the lawyers and reporters didn't see. Paul Le Mat (he was the disarming, spacy young hero in Demme's *Citizens Band*) is such an easygoing, non-egocentric actor that he disappears inside the role of big, beefy Melvin—a sometime milkman, sometime worker at a magnesium plant, sometime gas-station operator, and hopeful song-writer. Driving along the California-Nevada interstate at night in his pickup truck, Melvin has a bovine boyishness about him. He keeps himself in good cheer in the desert by singing "Santa's Souped-Up Sleigh"; the lyrics are his own, set to a tune he bought by mail order for seventy dollars, and when he sings—ostentatiously keeping time—you feel there's not a thing in that noggin but the words of the song. Jason Robards plays Howard Hughes, who hits a snag while racing his motorcycle in the desert and is flung into the air. He is lying in the freezing darkness when Melvin spots him—a bony old man in beat-out clothes, with a dirty beard and straggly long gray hair. When Melvin helps him into the front seat of the truck, next to him, he's doubled over in pain, and even as Melvin is wrapping him up to warm him there's a malevolent, paranoid gleam in his eyes. Melvin, who takes him for an old wino—a desert rat—is bothered by his mean expression, and in order to cheer him up (and give himself some company) he insists that the old geezer sing his song with him, or get out and walk.

Jason Robards certainly wasn't a beacon to his profession in last year's *Hurricane* or in the recent classic of nincompoopery *Raise the Titanic*, and it may be true that, as he says, he works in movies "to make it possible to work on the stage." But I doubt if he has ever been greater than he is here. This

Hughes is so sure that people are only after his money that he distrusts everyone; he has bribed and corrupted so many high officers in business and government that he believes in nothing but the power of bribery. His thinking processes are gnarled, twisted; he begrudges the world the smallest civility and lives incommunicado from everyone. And here he is singing "Santa's Souped-Up Sleigh" while sneering at its cornball idiocy and looking over disgustedly, in disbelief, at the pleasure that this dumb bunny next to him takes in hearing his song. In recent years, Robards' Yankee suavity has occasionally been reminiscent of Walter Huston: his Ben Bradlee in *All the President's Men* recalled Huston in *Dodsworth*, and here, when his Howard Hughes responds to Melvin's amiable prodding and begins to enjoy himself on a simple level and sings "Bye, Bye, Blackbird," he's as memorable as the famous record of Huston singing "September Song." His eyes are an old man's eyes—faded into the past, shiny and glazed by recollections—yet intense. You feel that his grungy anger has melted away, that he has been healed. He and Melvin talk about how the desert, after rain, smells of greasewood and sage, and at dawn, just as they approach the lights of Las Vegas, where Hughes gets out, they smile at each other with a fraternal understanding that's a cockeyed, spooky miracle.

In an interview in the *Times* last year, Jason Robards pointed out that Robards was Hughes' middle name and that both of them had Loomises among their relatives. "They couldn't have cast anyone else as Howard Hughes," he said. "I figured I didn't have to do any preparation for the part. It's all built in genetically." What's built in genetically may be the way Jason Robards responds to an acting challenge: the son of an actor father and an actor all his life, he goes for broke in a way that never suggests recklessness. He just casually transports himself to new dimensions (that maybe nobody else has ever been in), as if he had been breathing that air all his life. Robards isn't on the screen for long, but Hughes suffuses the movie. You know he's there without your even thinking about him; he might almost be looking down on Melvin, watching what's happening to him. And this is what the picture is about. The moviemakers have understood the position that Howard Hughes has arrived at in American mythology, and they have used the encounter in the desert to confer a moment of glory on Melvin Dummar. Eight years later, when Melvin finds himself named in the will and realizes that the old coot who said he was Howard Hughes *was* Howard Hughes, he is awed—it's like being touched by God. When reporters, neighbors, and the curious and the crazy gather at his gas station, he hides in a tree and peers out at the crowd in terror.

Most of the movie is about Melvin's life during those eight years—the life that will look so makeshift and shoddy when it's examined in a courtroom. Later in the morning after the encounter in the desert, Melvin's truck is repossessed, and his wife, Lynda (Mary Steenburgen), packs her things and takes their little daughter and goes off to live with another man, pausing only to murmur a regretful goodbye to the sleeping Melvin. They get a divorce, then remarry when she's hugely pregnant, but this marriage doesn't last long. Lynda can't stand Melvin's buying things that they never get to keep, and he can't stop kidding himself that his expensive, installment-plan purchases are somehow practical—that they're investments. So they never have anything—finally not even each other.

Mary Steenburgen was oddly tremulous in *Goin' South*, and though in *Time After Time* she was very sweet in an out-of-it way—a stoned cupcake—she didn't have the quickness or the pearly aura that she has here. Her Lynda Dummar has a soft mouth and a tantalizing slender wiggliness, and she talks directly to whomever she's talking to—she addresses them with her eyes and her mouth, and when they speak she listens, watching their faces. When she listens, she's the kind of woman a man wants to tell more to. Mary Steenburgen makes Lynda the go-go dancer so appealing that you realize she's the dream Melvin attained and then couldn't hang on to. Melvin is a hard worker, though, and he believes in family life. When Lynda leaves him, he's appalled by her exhibiting herself in strip joints; he keeps charging in and making scenes. Lynda is hurt by his attitude; she loves to dance, and she doesn't think there's anything lewd about what she's doing. In a way, she's right: Lynda could shimmy and shake forever and she still wouldn't be a hardened pro. Her movements are sexy but with a tipsy charm and purity. When her boss bawls her out because of a commotion that Melvin has just caused, she quits on the spot, whips off the flimsy costume that belongs to the boss, throws it in his face, and walks through the place naked, and she does it without making an event of it—it's her body. Melvin's second wife, Bonnie (Pamela Reed, who was Belle Starr in *The Long Riders*), isn't a romantic dream, like Lynda. She's a down-to-earth woman with a couple of kids who propositions him with a solid offer—marriage and her cousin's gas station in Utah, in a package deal. She makes the offer almost hungrily. Promising him a good marriage and a good business, she's like a sexual entrepreneur who feels she can use his untapped abilities and turn him into a success.

This is a comedy without a speck of sitcom aggression: the characters are slightly loony the way we all are sometimes (and it seldom involves coming up with cappers or with straight lines that somebody else can cap). When the people on the screen do unexpected things, they're not weirdos; their eccentricity is just an offshoot of the normal, and Demme suggests that maybe these people who grew up in motor homes and trailers in Nevada and California and Utah seem eccentric because they didn't learn the "normal," accepted ways of doing things. When Lynda is broke and takes her daughter, Darcy (the lovely, serious-faced Elizabeth Cheshire), to the bus station in Reno to send her to Melvin, she's frantic. Her misery about sending the child away is all mixed up with her anxiety about the child's having something to eat on the trip, and she's in a rush to put a sandwich together. She has bought French bread and bologna, and she takes over a table and borrows a knife from the man at the lunch counter so she can cut the bread; she salvages lettuce and tomatoes from the leftovers on someone's plate, and sends Darcy back to the counter to get some mustard and then back again to get some ketchup. The unperturbed counterman (played by the real Melvin Dummar) finds nothing unusual in this, and asks, "Is everything all right?" There's no sarcasm in his tone; he seems to understand what she's going through, and he wants to be helpful. She says, "Everything's just fine, thank you very much." She has dominated everyone's attention—she has practically taken over the station—yet the goofiness isn't forced; it's almost like found humor. It's a little like a throwaway moment in a Michael Ritchie film or a slapstick fracas out of Preston Sturges, but there are more unspoken crosscurrents—and richer ones—in Demme's scenes. While you're responding to the dithering confusion Lynda is causing in the bus depot, you're absorbing the emotions between mother and child. Darcy is often very grownup around her mother, as if she knew that Lynda is a bit of a moonbeam and needs looking after. But at the depot Darcy herself is so excited she becomes part of the confusion. Later, during Melvin and Lynda's remarriage ceremony in a Las Vegas "wedding chapel," Darcy is so impressed and elated that her whole face sparkles; she's like an imp Madonna. Throughout the movie, the children—Lynda's or Bonnie's, and sometimes all of them together—are part of an ongoing subtext: they're never commented on, and they never do anything cute or make a move that doesn't seem "true."

When Jonathan Demme does a thriller like *Last Embrace*, he seems an empty-headed director with a little hand-me-down craft, but in *Melvin and Howard* he shows perhaps a finer understanding of lower-middle-class life than any other American director. This picture suggests what it might have been like if Jean Renoir had directed a Preston Sturges comedy. Demme's style is so expressive that he draws you into the lives of the characters, and you're hardly aware of the technical means by which he accomplishes this— the prodigious crane and tracking shots that he has worked out with his cinematographer, Tak Fujimoto, and the fluid, mellow colors that probably owe a lot to Toby Rafelson's production design. The comedy doesn't stick out; it's part of the fluidity. And if you respond to this movie as I did, you'll hardly be aware (until you think it over afterward) that it has no plot, in the ordinary sense. (This could handicap it, though, in movie markets; the pitfall that a picture like this presents is that there's not a hard-sell scene in it. It's a soft shimmer of a movie, and the very people whom it's about and who might love it if they gave it a chance may not be tempted to see it.) There are a couple of flaws: the sequence of Melvin taking the will to the Mormon Church in Salt Lake City is so fast and cryptic it seems almost like shorthand, and if you've forgotten the stories that filled the papers a few years ago you may not understand what's going on; and the following sequence, of Melvin hiding from the crowd, doesn't have quite the clarity or the dramatic fullness that it needs. And there is a small lapse of taste: a shot too many of the blond

Mrs. Worth (Charlene Holt), one of Melvin's milk-route customers—she lifts her head heavenward and mugs silly ecstasy at the prospect of his returning the next day, for another carnal visit. The dialogue is as near perfection as script dialogue gets—it's always funny, without any cackling. Bo Goldman, who is in his late forties, shared writing credits on *One Flew Over the Cuck-oo's Nest* and *The Rose*, but this is his only unshared credit. (After spending a day with the real Melvin Dummar, Goldman decided he wanted to write the script; then he stayed with Dummar for a month and "got to love him," and came to know the two wives and Dummar's friends and relatives and neighbors.) The people in the movie—the large cast includes Charles Napier, John Glover, Gloria Grahame, Dabney Coleman, Michael J. Pollard, Martine Beswick, Susan Peretz, Naida Reynolds, Herbie Faye, and Robert Wentz—all seem scrubby and rumpled and believable; you feel that if you hung around Anaheim or L.A. or Reno you'd run into them. Maybe if you had been at the Sex Kat Klub at the right time, you'd have seen the dancer next to Lynda who was strutting her stuff with a broken arm in a big plaster cast.

Melvin and Howard has the same beautiful, dippy warmth as its characters. Paul Le Mat's Melvin, who barely opens his mouth when he talks, opens it wide when he sings. His proudest moment is probably the hit he makes at the dairy's Christmas party when he grins confidently as he sings a ballad about the gripes of a milkman. (The words, like the words of "Santa's Souped-Up Sleigh," are by the real Melvin Dummar.) Le Mat's Melvin often has a childlike look of bewilderment that he seems to be covering up by his beaming optimism. He's very gentle; he threatens physical violence only once—when he thinks that the assistant manager of the dairy (Jack Kehoe) is trying to rook him out of the big color TV set he has won as Milkman of the Month. Watching a game show, "Easy Street," on that set, he's like an armchair quarterback, telling the contestants which doors to choose to win the prizes. When Darcy is bored by it, he tries to justify his obsession by explaining how educational these shows are, but she isn't conned—she goes out to play.

Demme stages a segment of "Easy Street" (modelled on "Let's Make a Deal") which opens up the theme of the movie by giving us a view of game shows that transcends satire. Lynda, who has been selected as a contestant, appears in an aquamarine dress with tassels and an old-fashioned bellhop's hat, and when she does a tap dance that's as slow as a clog dance the audience starts to laugh. But she keeps going, and though she has more movement in her waving arms than in her tapping feet, she's irresistible. It's the triumph of adorable pluckiness (and the uninhibited use of her beautiful figure) over technique. The host of "Easy Street" (Robert Ridgely) combines malicious charity with provocative encouragement, and the enthusiastic applause confirms the notion that every TV audience loves someone who tries sincerely. In Ritchie's *Smile*, it was plain that the teen-age beauty contestants were not nearly as vacuous as they were made to appear (and made themselves appear), and here it's evident that Lynda the winner, jumping up and down like a darling frisky puppy, is putting on the excitement that is wanted of her. She's just like the pretty women you've seen on TV making fools of themselves, except that you know her; you know the desperation that went into choosing that tawdry dress and that's behind the eagerness to play the game—to squeal and act gaga and kiss everybody. The host personifies the game show, as if he were personally giving all the prizes. He's a pygmy metaphor for Howard Hughes. The game show is the illusion that sustains Melvin: that if you pick the right door, what's behind it is happiness.

Shortly after the probate trial on the Mormon will, the judge who had presided died of cancer; at his funeral service one of the speakers said that on his deathbed the judge told him that he hoped to meet Howard Hughes in the next world—that he had a question he wanted to ask him. The movie shows us a triumphant Melvin Dummar: he knows the answer. He also knows he'll never see the money. (Maybe Howard Hughes was the naïve one, if he thought that he could smash the monster corporation he had created.) Melvin Dummar was touched by a legend. Howard Hughes came to respect him, and so do we.

$$\cdot \qquad \cdot \qquad \cdot \qquad \cdot$$

*Y*ou know you're in for it when you see the solemn white titles against a black background—and in silence. Is it going to be Robert Bresson cauterizing your funny bone? When the discreet classical music starts—a piano, first just one hand and then the other, on Pachelbel's Canon in D—you know it's going to reek of quality, and that it's going to be an attempt at the austere manner of *Kramer vs. Kramer* and *Scenes from a Marriage*. Movie stars who become directors sometimes seem to choose their material as a penance for the frivolous good times they've given us. Paul Newman made *Rachel, Rachel*, and now Robert Redford has made *Ordinary People*, which is full of autumn leaves and wintry emotions. It's an academic exercise in catharsis; it's earnest, it means to improve people, and it lasts a lifetime. The story is about the Jarretts, a Protestant family living in an imposing brick house in Lake Forest, a wealthy suburb of Chicago. Conrad (Timothy Hutton), a high-school student, has the shakes, and dark circles around his eyes, because he can't sleep, and we soon learn that he has only recently emerged from a psychiatric hospital, where he spent four months and had electric-shock treatment, following a suicide attempt. His mild, ineffectual father, Calvin (Donald Sutherland), who is a successful tax lawyer, is worried about him but can make only inane, formal attempts to reach him, and his control-freak mother, Beth (Mary Tyler Moore), whose chief interest is golf, expresses little feeling for him beyond polite aversion. It boils down to Strother Martin's sick joke in *Cool Hand Luke*: "What we've got here is a failure to communicate." There is so little communication in this family that the three Jarretts sit in virtual silence at the perfectly set dinner table in the perfectly boring big dining room; it's a suburban variant of American Gothic. From time to time, Calvin, with a nervous tic of a dimpling smile—it seems to get stuck somewhere in his cheek muscles—tries to make contact with his son, and urges him to see the psychiatrist recommended by the hospital.

Conrad begins to have sessions with this psychiatrist, Dr. Berger (Judd Hirsch), whose office is pleasantly grubby, cluttered, and warmly inviting. Dr. Berger is not a monosyllabic Freudian who waits for the patient to bring up what's bugging him (or the movie would last *many* lifetimes). He's a free-method activist who grapples with the problems; he talks to Conrad, he prods and yells and emotes. And he's the model of what this uptight Protestant kid would be if he were cured: Jewish. (But then why do so many Jews go to shrinks? Ah, that's a different story.) With Dr. Berger shouting "Feel!" at him, Conrad soon begins to have breakthroughs: he learns what you knew as soon as you heard that he had an older brother who was accidentally drowned when they were out sailing together on Lake Michigan—his mother, who loved the brother, blames Conrad, and he feels guilty because he survived. (You knew because it's the standard TV-style explanation; you're consistently ahead of the storytelling, the way you almost always are when you watch a prestigious TV movie—which this really is.) Moving along on the road to recovery, Conrad starts speaking up and expressing his feelings at home, becomes more outgoing, and begins to date a pretty girl (Elizabeth McGovern) who has a deep, purring voice and a funny, understanding manner. But the loosening of his emotional tensions opens up a can of worms in the family. His seeing a psychiatrist makes Beth rigid with disapproval, and when Calvin, talking to a friend at a party, mentions that the boy is going to a doctor, Beth's face twists with anger. (This is the kind of movie in which the mother keeps the dead boy's room intact—a shrine that probably has its own cleaning lady.) Calvin, who realizes the cruelty of his wife's rejection of their son, goes to see Dr. Berger in order to explain what Conrad is up against at home, and after hedging and fumbling he finally comes out with it and says that he guesses he came to talk about himself. At this point, the movie cuts away. And it's at this point, if you had any doubts before, that you know the movie is going to be a cheat.

The way *Ordinary People* is structured, if Conrad's brother hadn't been accidentally drowned everything in the family would have been hunky-dory, neat and happy, and there wouldn't be a picture. Obviously, the film means to get at something much deeper and more widespread: it means to get at the harm that repression causes, and to suggest that orderly patterns of polite living can make it almost impossible for people to express their feelings except by an explosion, like Conrad's attempted suicide. But every time *Ordinary People* comes close to anything messy or dirty or sexual it pulls back or cuts away. What is Calvin's relationship with Beth based on, anyway? (It's not likely that she turns into a hot pixie at night: there are military-looking stripes on her bathrobe.) How did Beth's love for the son who was drowned—a love that, in the one flashback glimpse we get of it, appears to have been flirtatious—affect her and her husband? Did it make Conrad hate his brother? There's a nasty, almost conscious incestuousness lurking in Beth and never brought to the surface, and even at his most neurotic Conrad is still a "nice boy." (There are no drugs in this picture, and no teen sex; he meets his girl at choir practice.) The movie is just as sanitized as the fantasy of upper-middle-class life it sets out to expose. And it's just as empty and orderly: Calvin has the possibility of becoming a decent, whole person, because he is willing to open himself to Dr. Berger, but Beth, who rejects Calvin's plea that she also go, is too proud to admit to any weakness or need; shaking uncontrollably at the thought of her life collapsing, she still rejects help, and she is doomed to freeze-dry.

As this Wasp witch, whose face is so tense you expect it to crack, Mary Tyler Moore also seems to be doing penance for having given audiences a good time. Her idea of serious acting seems to be playing a woman who has a mastectomy (*First You Cry*, on TV), a suicidal, bedridden quadriplegic (*Whose Life Is It, Anyway?*, on Broadway), and this self-deceiving woman who cares more for appearances than for her husband and son. Are fine comediennes still to be called courageous for giving performances as locked in dreariness as Carol Burnett's were when she went through her overage-bachelor-woman pregnancy in *The Tenth Month* and lost her son in *Friendly Fire*? As Beth, Mary Tyler Moore holds her pinched seriousness aloft like a torch. The fault isn't just in her acting; it's also in the writing and in the directing. She has been made into a voodoo doll stuck full of pins. This movie is *Craig's Wife* all over again: Beth is the compulsively neat, dedicated-to-appearances, unloving Harriet Craig, the perfect wife. But this time as a mother. She is so completely Harriet Craig that I didn't believe it for an instant when she left the house at the end. Even within its own terms, the film goes wrong here. The impersonal, ice-palace house is what Beth is married to—the house *is* Beth. It's not for living, it's for show, and it's her proof that everything is just as it should be. Beth would have stayed in her house, like Harriet Craig, and the men would have left. What are they going to do with it, anyway? Invite Dr. Berger in to mess it up and make it homey?

Ordinary People delivers on the promise of that silent opening—a certificate of solemnity. The pace is unhurried, and as a director Redford doesn't like to raise his voice any more than Beth does. Like many other actor-directors, he doesn't reach for anything but acting effects. The cinematographer, John Bailey, lights the images well enough (though the only lighting that's at all arresting is in the high-school swimming-pool scenes), but *Ordinary People* has that respectable, pictorial, dated look that movies get when the director has a proficient team of craftsmen but doesn't really think in visual terms. Redford shows taste and tact with most of the actors, and there are well-observed moments. Yet every nuance seems carefully put in place, and the conversations are stagy, because there's nothing in the shots except exactly what we're supposed to react to, just as there is nothing in Beth's character or in Calvin's except what's needed to fit a diagram of suburban suffocation. Redford's work is best in the light, funny scenes, when Conrad gets a chance at byplay with kids his own age. Alvin Sargent, who wrote the script, which is based on the popular 1976 novel by Judith Guest, wrote some bits of sharp repartee for Conrad. Mostly, though, the dialogue is intelligent in an over-modulated, point-making way, and often it's psychobabble in full bloom. (Calvin to Beth: "I don't know who you are. . . . I don't know if I love you anymore, and I don't know what I'm going to do without that." Beth's only response is to look stricken. Who wouldn't be stricken listening to this crap?) The movie is not above shamelessness: surely we could have been spared the symbolic broken dish and the information that this monstrous woman wouldn't even let her sons have a pet? And when Conrad tries to hug his mother, she sits as straight as a plank of wood, with her eyes wide open in the timeworn manner of actresses demonstrating frigidity. In general, the more emotional the scenes are, the worse they play.

Casting Timothy Hutton, the nineteen-year-old son of the late Jim Hutton, as Mary Tyler Moore's son was astute; he matches her physically, in a very convincing way. (And casting the beautiful Meg Mundy as Beth's mother was also a shrewd decision.) Hutton appears to be phenomenally talented whenever he has a chance at a light or ironic bit, and he has strangely effective moments, as in a scene when a girl (played by Dinah Manoff) whom he wants to talk to leaves him and his eyes look miserable and haze over. But he loses conviction at times, and he has an awkwardly staged scene when he has to accept his father's love and put his head on his father's shoulder. (Sutherland doesn't seem to know what to do with that head resting on him; he isn't allowed to grab the boy and hold him, the way Dr. Berger does when the promiscuous kid hugs *him*.) Sutherland, who slides into stillness and passivity almost too easily, gives a rather graceful performance, considering that Calvin isn't a character—he's just a blob created to be tyrannized by Beth. Sutherland has only one scene that's really all his: in Dr. Berger's office, when Calvin doesn't quite know what he wants to say, Sutherland uses his wonderful long hands to express more than words could. Judd Hirsch's role has the juiciness of burlesque, and Hirsch uses his terrific comedy timing; he gets laughs and manages to pick up the pace, but he's just doing wise, warm Jewish shtick. According to this movie, if Wasps can just learn to express their emotions they'll be all right. The point of view seems predicated on the post–Second World War Hollywood idea that Wasps don't know how to suffer. If you want suffering, get Jews or Italians, because when Wasps suffer, it doesn't show on the screen. (Hollywood Jews and Italians know how to act at dinner tables, too: they scream and quarrel.)

Why is this tragic view of the death of the Protestant family ethic drawing crowds? Maybe because the movie is essentially a simpleminded, old-fashioned tearjerker, in a conventional style. People weep for Beth, who can't change—who can't let herself change. We are given to understand that she would like to come out of her shell but she can't. She's trapped in the pride and discipline and privacy that she was trained to believe in. She was *bred* not to say what's on her mind. And the movie, which treats her, finally, with sympathy yet holds out no hope for her, makes her seem rather gallant. She seems the last standard-bearer for the Wasp culture that the film indicts. With its do-gooders' religion, *Ordinary People* says that the willingness to accept psychiatry divides people into the savable and the doomed. Yet maybe because the film's banal style speaks to the audience in aesthetically conservative terms, this movie about the hell that uptight people live in somehow turns into a nosegay for Wasp repression. Beth will go down with the ship: she will never "communicate."

October 13, 1980

The Frog Who Turned Into a Prince

The Prince Who Turned Into a Frog

*T*he *Elephant Man* is a very pleasurable surprise. Though I had seen *Eraserhead*, which is the only other feature directed by David Lynch, and had thought him a true original, I wasn't prepared for the strength he would bring out of understatement. It might be expected that the material—the life of John Merrick, the grievously eminent Victorian who is sometimes said to have been the ugliest man who ever lived—would push Lynch into the kind of morbid masochism that was displayed in the various versions of *The Hunchback of Notre Dame* and *The Phantom of the Opera*. But this young director (he's thirty-four) has extraordinary taste; it's not the kind of taste that enervates artists—it's closer to grace. The movie shows us what the monster feels about himself and what his view of the world is and what he sees when he looks out of the single rectangular slit in his hood (which suggests an elephant's eye). He must see everything framed, as on a screen, and the movie gives us this sense of framed imagery—of action marked off, with curtains drawn over the surrounding material. (The stitching around the slit gives it depth, and at one point, when the hood is hanging on the wall, the camera moves right into the dark opening.) You may find yourself so absorbed that your time sense changes and you begin to examine the images with something of the same wonder that John Merrick (John Hurt) shows when he looks at the spire of St. Philip, Stepney, from his window at the London Hospital, where he finds refuge.

The Elephant Man has the power and some of the dream logic of a silent film, yet there are also wrenching, pulsating sounds—the hissing steam and the pounding of the start of the industrial age. It's Dickensian London, with perhaps a glimpse of the processes that gave rise to Cubism. Coming from an art-school background, Lynch has rediscovered what the European avant-garde film artists of the twenties and early thirties, many of whom also came from a painting and design background, were up to, and he has combined this with an experimental approach to sound. In Merrick's fantasy life, his beautiful young mother is trampled by elephants when she is carrying him in her womb, and the sounds of those great beasts as they attack her in his dreams are the hellish sounds of industrial London, whose machines will produce their own monstrous growths. *The Elephant Man* isn't as daringly irrational as *Eraserhead*, which pulls you inside grubby, wormy states of anxiety, but it pulls you into a serene, contemplative amazement. Lynch holds you in scenes with almost no action: Merrick may be alone on the screen preening, or fondling the brushes and buffers in his gentleman's dressing case, or just laying them out in an orderly pattern and waltzing around them, like a swell, and you feel fixated, in a trance.

When Frederick Treves (Anthony Hopkins), the doctor who is to become Merrick's friend, first tracks him down in the illegal, hidden sideshow where he's being exhibited as the Elephant Man, Treves goes through what seem to be endless slum passageways and alleys into an abyss—the darkness where the monster huddles. Finally, he sees the pathetic deformed creature, but *we* don't. We see only Treves' reaction, and his tears falling. The grace in Lynch's work comes from care and thought: this is a film about the exhibition and exploitation of a freak, and he must have been determined not to be an exploiter himself. The monster is covered or shadowed from us in the early sequences and we see only parts of him, a little at a time. Lynch builds up our interest in seeing more in a way that seems very natural. When we're ready to see him clearly, we do. By then, we have become so sympathetic that there's no disgust about seeing his full deformity. John Hurt has had the screen long enough to make us respond to his wheezing, groaning sounds and his terrified movements, so we don't see merely the deformations, we see the helpless person locked in the repulsive flesh. Even before Merrick begins to speak to Treves and to recite poetry and to reveal his romantic sensibility, we have become his protectors. He's a large lumplike mass at first, but as we get to know him, and respond to his helplessness, he begins to seem very slight— almost doll-like. There's nothing frightening about him, and he's not repellent, either. His misshapen body and the knobby protuberances on his forehead suggest a work of art—an Archipenko or one of Picasso's bulging distortions.

The only horror is in what we experience on his behalf. When a young nurse sees him and screams, it's *his* recoil we respond to. There is a remarkable sequence after Merrick has been kidnapped from the hospital by his London exploiter and taken to be exhibited again, this time on the Continent. Too sick to stand and in despair, Merrick doesn't gratify the ticket buyers, and he is beaten so brutally that the other fairground freaks decide to free him. The giant strong man breaks the lock of the cage next to the baboons where Merrick has been put and lifts him out in his arms, and there is a dreamlike procession of the freaks in the woods along a riverbank as they help him to escape. They buy him his passage back to England, and a small group of them take him to the ship. (We're apprehensive then, because he's going to be alone.) He arrives in London by train, and as he makes his way slowly and painfully through the station his cloaked, hooded figure attracts the attention of a puzzled boy, who demands to know why he's wrapped up as he is and pelts him with a peashooter. Other kids follow him and taunt him; with only the eye slit on one side, when he clumsily tries to move faster to get away he inadvertently knocks down a little girl. People begin to chase him, and he rushes down a flight of stairs; on the landing, someone tears off his hood and he runs down more stairs and staggers into a urinal. A mob comes in after him, backing him against a wall; he moans that he is not an animal and collapses. This whole sequence is saved from being a cheap ecstasy of masochism by the fairy-tale design of the shots and the lighting. Using black-and-white Panavision, the veteran cinematographer Freddie Francis does lighting here that recalls his expressive work in *Sons and Lovers* and *Room at the Top* and *Saturday Night and Sunday Morning*. The smoke that softens everything is like J. M. W. Turner clouds, but carrying poison. With the help of the production designer, Stuart Craig, Lynch and Francis use the grays to set a tone of emotional reserve yet make the whites and the sooty blacks, which bleed out of their contour lines, seem very passionate (the way they are in the Londoner Bill Brandt's photographs). The imagery is never naturalistic, and Lynch never pulls out all the stops.

Every time the director does something risky and new or reinterprets something very old, you know you're watching real moviemaking. Though the sound isn't nearly as inventive as it was in *Eraserhead*, whenever it's hyperbolic, like the noise of the big gongs that wake Merrick on his first night at the hospital, it has a disturbing excitement. And Samuel Barber's "Adagio for Strings" on the track has an elegiac lyricism—stately, but mellow, too. Lynch is least successful with the conventional melodramatic scenes. When the night porter at the hospital invades Merrick's room with gawkers, and two whores are shoved onto his bed, we want to climb the wall along with Merrick, and not just out of empathy: the staging is crude. And almost all the scenes of the drunken villain, Bytes (Freddie Jones), the exploiter and kidnapper, seem long, probably because you can read his standard evil piggy expressions a mile away. The scenes of Anne Bancroft as Mrs. Kendal, the actress whose visits to Merrick turn him into a celebrity (which leads to his being taken up by London society), feel obligatory. The first time she's close to Merrick, Mrs. Kendal shows a flicker of disgust that she covers with her actressy poise—that part is good. But after that we need to read her feelings in her eyes, and all we register is her smiley, warm mouth; she's gracious in a great-lady way that doesn't provide any clue to why she becomes involved. The dialogue in the script, by Christopher DeVore and Eric Bergren, with the later collaboration of Lynch, is no more than serviceable, and it's less than that in Bancroft's role; she's used like a guest star, and though she's more toned down than in other recent appearances, she seems to have dropped in from another era. Hannah Gordon, who plays Mrs. Treves, has the clearer, better part: when Treves brings Merrick to tea and presents him to his wife, Merrick is so overwhelmed at meeting a beautiful woman that he snuffles and weeps. And she, of course, weeps, too. (There's no sun in this tale of a terrible enchantment, and a tear shed for Merrick is a jewel.)

John Gielgud is in strapping form as the head of the hospital, and Wendy Hiller, as the chief nurse, matches him in vinegary elegance, syllable for syllable, pause for pause. John Hurt and Anthony Hopkins—both specialists in masochism—might have leaked so much emotion that the film would slip its sprockets. But Hopkins comes through with an unexpectedly crisp, highly varied performance—the kind you respect an actor for. He lets Hurt (was ever actor better named?) have a monopoly on our sympathy, and Hurt, using his twisted lips and his eyes, but mostly his voice and his posture and movements, makes of Merrick an astonishingly sweet-souled gentleman of his era. If he were not encased in loathsome flesh, we could never believe in such delicate, saintly humility. But the film makes us understand that in a time when ugliness was thought to come from within, Merrick had to become a dandy of the soul in order to feel human. Once he's out of his cloak and into a suit, he has a soft, sidling walk, askew but airy. He's only in his twenties (he died at twenty-seven), and his wish to be good is childlike and a little cracked, but his kindness seems to come from a mystic simplicity. There's no irony in the film when he becomes a society figure—an oddity and a pet to be pampered. We see his sheer delight in being accepted among people with nice manners; his fawning gratitude is from the heart. He isn't concerned with Treves' problems of conscience about whether he, too, is exploiting Merrick's condition. Merrick knows that Treves has brought him from agony to peace. The director doesn't stray from the Victorian framework he constructs; nothing is interpreted (not even the recurrent mother-being-raped-by-elephants dream), and so nothing is sentimentalized in a modern manner.

This is not the usual movie—in which the story supports the images and holds everything together. Lynch's visual scheme is so imaginative that it transcends the by now well-known story, and scene by scene you don't know what to expect. You're seeing something new—subconscious material stirring within the format of a conventional narrative. There is perhaps nothing as eerily, baldly erotic as that moment in *Eraserhead* when two lovers deliquesce into their bed—disappearing in the fluid, with only the woman's hair left floating on top. But there is something indefinably erotic going on here; it's submerged in the film's rhythm and in the director's whole way of seeing. And wherever you look there are inexplicably satisfying images: a little barrel-chested mutt bulldog waddles across a London street with its tail stretched straight out, like a swagger stick; at the medical college, when Treves, assuming a matter-of-fact tone, presents Merrick in all his glorious deformity to the assembled doctors, a man with a big furry beard turns on the light at the start of the presentation and turns it off at the close—a silly detail to remember, but it's part of the texture, like the carriage horse that suggests a phantom, and the illumination on the cobblestones that makes them look like fish scales, and the night scene on the Continent that might be a painting, except that dawn comes up. In Merrick's dream of the trampling elephant feet, the camera swerves and swoops across the bodies of the great beasts in strange panning movements that suggest the way Merrick, who must sleep sitting up with his head on his raised knees (because of its weight), would dream, with his head wobbling and jerking. And in perhaps the most elusive series of effects, when Merrick realizes his lifelong ambition of going to the theatre and sees a Drury Lane performance of the pantomime "Puss in Boots," it becomes a fantasy of magical transformations, with ducks and a lion and fairies flying on wires and people who seem to be on horseback, except that the horses' legs are their own, and an ogre behind bars and swans—deliriously snooty cardboard swans. You can't be sure what you're seeing: it's like disconnected memories of the earliest stories you were told. The creatures—animal, human, birds, spirits—are all mixed up together, and the bits of glitter that fall on them have the dreamlike quality of the overturned world in the glass ball that fell from Kane's hand. In this sequence, too, there is a suggestion of the wobbling movement of the heavy head. Late that night, when Merrick, in his fresh nightshirt, smooths his clean white bedsheets—it's like another form of preening—his body seems weightless. He is ready to leave it.

. . . . .

*A*t the beginning of Woody Allen's *Stardust Memories*, there is a Bergman-esque nightmare sequence, silent except for the sound of ticking. Woody Allen is on a stalled train, and as he looks around he sees big-nosed misery on the other faces; his fellow-passengers are self-conscious grotesques who might have been photographed by Diane Arbus. Peering out the window, he can see that on the next track there's another stalled train that is headed in the same direction, and it's full of swinging, beautiful people living it up and having a ball.

He motions to the conductor that he's on the wrong train and tries to get out, but he's sealed in. This visual metaphor has almost the same meaning as the Groucho epigram that was quoted twice in *Annie Hall*: "I wouldn't want to belong to any club that would have me for a member." The clubs from which Groucho was excluded were, of course, the gentiles' clubs, and he was expressing his chagrin at being lumped with the other Jews. (Excluded from a California beach club, Groucho wrote the organization, "Since my daughter is only half Jewish, could she go in the water up to her waist?") *Stardust Memories* might be described as an obsessional pastiche. It is modelled on Fellini's *8½*, and the bleached-out black-and-white cinematography suggests a dupe of a dupe of *8½*, with some allusions to the clown's pasty despair at the start of Bergman's *The Naked Night*. The theme recalls Preston Sturges' *Sullivan's Travels*, which is about an acclaimed director who doesn't want to go on making popular comedies—he wants to be stark, tragic, and realistic.

Woody Allen calls himself Sandy Bates this time, but there's only the merest wisp of a pretext that he is playing a character; this is the most undisguised of his dodgy mock-autobiographical fantasies. The setting is the Hotel Stardust, a resort on the New Jersey seashore, where a woman film critic (played by Helen Hanft) conducts weekend seminars; for a fee, the guests spend a weekend looking at the work of a filmmaker and discussing it with him—and they also get to press his flesh. This weekend, Sandy Bates is the celebrity-in-residence; he runs his new picture as well as clips from his comedies, and the discussions are intercut with flashbacks, hallucinations, and fragmentary encounters. The actors slip in and out of the films and his life. Feeling besieged, he goes through a vague sort of crisis, possibly brought on by the seminar guests. Each of them wants something from him—he is asked to appear at a benefit for cancer, to give some personal article to an auction, to sign a petition, to read a script, to answer an imbecilic question. And these pushy fans who treat him in such an overfamiliar way are gross or big-nosed and have funny Jewish names. They're turned into their noses; they leer into the lens, shoving their snouts at Sandy Bates. They chide him (indulgently) for his recent seriousness, and he complains, "I don't want to make funny movies anymore. They can't force me to. I look around the world and all I see is human suffering."

In *Stardust Memories*, Woody Allen degrades the people who respond to his work and presents himself as their victim. He seems to feel that they want him to heal them; the film suggests a *Miss Lonelyhearts* written without irony. (Maybe Sandy Bates means he sees human suffering when he looks around his apartment: his walls are decorated with blowups of news photographs, such as the famous one of the execution in a Saigon street during the Tet offensive, and they change like mood music. Is this evidence of Sandy Bates's morbidity, or is it how he proves that he's politically and socially with it? Is there any way it can't be a joke? *What* is going on in this movie?) Woody Allen has often been cruel to himself in physical terms—making himself look smaller, scrawnier, ugly. Now he's doing it to his fans. People who, viewed differently, might look striking or mysterious have their features distorted by the camera lens and by Felliniesque makeup; they become fat-lipped freaks wearing outsize thick goggles. (They could serve as illustrations for the old saw that Jews are like other people, only more so.) People whose attitudes, viewed differently, might seem friendly or, at worst, overenthusiastic and excited are turned into morons. Throughout *Stardust Memories*, Sandy is superior to all those who talk about his work; if they like his comedies, it's for freakish reasons, and he shows them up as poseurs and phonies, and if they don't like his serious work, it's because they're too stupid to understand it. He anticipates almost anything that you might say about *Stardust Memories* and ridicules you for it. Finally, you may feel you're being told that you have no right to *any* reaction to Woody Allen's movies. He is not just the victim here, he's the torturer. (A friend of mine called the picture *Sullivan's Travels Meets the P.L.O.*)

The hostility of the standup comic toward his night-club audience is often considered self-evident, but the hostility of a movie director toward the public that idolizes him doesn't have the same logic behind it, and it's almost unheard of. Woody Allen has somehow combined the two, and his hostility takes a special form. He's trying to stake out his claim to be an artist like Fellini or Bergman—to be accepted in the serious, gentile artists' club. And he sees his public as Jews trying to shove him back down in the Jewish clowns' club. Great artists' admirers are supposed to keep their distance. *His* admirers feel they know him and can approach him; they feel he belongs to them— and he sees them as his murderers.

Conceivably, a comedy could be made about an artist who thinks that those who like his work are grotesque and those who don't are stupid. This misanthrope would have to be the butt of the comedy, though; his pain would have to be funny—like the pain that Portnoy felt about his life's being a Jewish joke. But Woody Allen doesn't show the ability to step back from himself (as he did when he was making comedies); even the notion of doing this particular film in black-and-white is tied up with his not being able to step back. He sees himself only from the inside, and he asks us to *suffer* for the pain he feels about his success. At times, he sets up scenes as if he recognized that this pain is absurd, but he can't achieve—or doesn't want to achieve—the objective tone that would make us laugh. He brings in characters who seem designed for a payoff—an old school chum who complains that he isn't rich and famous like Sandy, an actress who once played Sandy's mother in a film and has now undergone cosmetic surgery and thinks she has become a beauty—but he stages their scenes in what appears to be a deliberately off-key, quavering tone, so that everything turns uncomfortable, morose, icky. And whether it's because of Woody Allen's desire to show us his loss of faith in these gags, or because of the cinematographer Gordon Willis's penchant for dark abstractions, they are shot at such a distance that the purpose of the scenes becomes opaque. (The actress-mother is seen in distant, cruel silhouette.)

The film has a single moment of comic rapport: Sandy visits his tough, lively married sister (played by Anne DeSalvo), and they take relish in a shared bitchy laugh about their mother. Yet even this visit begins with an aggressively rancid scene making fun of the sister's loud, uncouth friends—particularly a fat woman who was raped the night before; inexplicably, she wears a T-shirt with the word "Sexy" across her huge bosom. And the purpose of the visit seems to be to burlesque Sandy's relatives. The furnishings of the sister's apartment and the corpulent idiocy of her husband, stuffing his face while pumping on an Exercycle, shriek of bad taste. (The writhing wallpaper in her bedroom suggests something dreamed up for a decorator's Halloween party.) The only concession to vitality in the movie (besides the sister) is in the great jazz recordings used as the score, though in this atmosphere the music sounds like Fellini Dixieland.

Starting with the two trains, there are a number of potentially funny situations, but they don't come out funny. You're not sure how to react: the gags are strained—they seem poisoned by the director's self-pity. You can't laugh at the nightmarish melancholy of those dark, pimply train passengers, or at the ugliness of the seminar guests and the sister's pals. And though Woody Allen's attitudes may have a lot in common with those of Diane Arbus, you can't respond as you would to her photographs. The deep malignity in her work gives those photographs an undeniable punch. Woody Allen assembles people and makes them grotesque, but he uses them in such a casual way that he trivializes the ugliness he puts in front of us. There's no power in the images; he trivializes even his own malignity by his half-joking manner. And he doesn't appear to see any comedy in the fact that the only undemanding, unpushy characters in the movie—the three women in Sandy's life—are all gentile. These women are also indifferent to his work; at least, they don't offer opinions of it. They don't have enough independent existence for us to be sure what they're supposed to represent, and what attracts them to him—if not his films and his fame—isn't made apparent. But we can see what attracts him to them: they're the only women on the landscape in "quiet good taste," the only ones with hair that doesn't look like plaster of Paris or frizzed wire. Charlotte Rampling, who is posed in closeup after closeup—a ship's figurehead, like Anouk Aimée in 8½—suggests a decaying goddess. She seems to be used just for her physiognomy—for her bony chest and wide mouth (its corners run right into her cheekbones). Marie-Christine Barrault is used for her matronly-milkmaid-goddess look and the beautiful big teeth that can turn threatening. Jessica Harper is used for her wide brow and perverse, waifish grin. The first two are like toys that Sandy Bates has lost interest in; Harper is a possibility glimpsed which he doesn't care enough about to pursue.

The Jewish self-hatred that spills out in this movie could be a great subject, but all it does is spill out. The ostensible subject is the beleaguered artist and what the public demands of him. In a *Newsweek* cover story in 1978, Woody Allen was quoted: "When you do comedy you're not sitting at the grown-ups' table, you're sitting at the children's table." From the tone of this film, you would think that vulgarians were putting guns to Woody Allen's head and forcing him to make comedies. Considering the many respectful, indeed laudatory reviews he got for *Interiors*, which, he says, even "turned a little profit," and considering the astonishing success of *Manhattan*, in which he tried to be both Ingmar Bergman and Charlie Chaplin—a wet mixture if ever there was one—his contempt for the public seems somewhat precipitate.

Woody Allen, who used to play a walking inferiority complex, made the whole country more aware of the feelings of those who knew they could never match the images of Wasp perfection that saturated their lives. He played the brainy, insecure little guy, the urban misfit who quaked at the thought of a fight, because physically he could never measure up to the big strong silent men of the myths—the gentile beefcake. Big strong men know that they can't live up to the myths, either. Allen, by bringing his neurotic terror of just about everything out front, seemed to speak for them, too. In the forties and fifties, when Bob Hope played coward heroes the cowardice didn't have any political or sexual resonance, but in the late sixties and the seventies, when Woody Allen displayed his panic he seemed to incarnate the whole anti-macho mood of the time. In the sloppy, hairy counterculture era, Americans no longer tried to conform to a look that only a minority of them could ever hope to approximate. Woody Allen helped to make people feel more relaxed about how they looked and how they really felt about using their fists, and about their sexual terrors and everything else that made them anxious. He became a new national hero. College kids looked up to him and wanted to be like him.

That's why it seems such a horrible betrayal when he demonstrates that despite his fame he still hates the way he looks, and that he wanted to be one of *them*—the stuffy macho Wasps—all along. There were moments of betrayal in his other films, such as the peculiar jokiness of his using actors smaller than he as his romantic rivals (the Hollywood doper played by Paul Simon in *Annie Hall*, and Jeremiah, played by Wallace Shawn, in *Manhattan*). But people in the audience could blot out the puzzling scenes of *Annie Hall* and *Manhattan*. In *Stardust Memories*—awful title!—he throws so much at you that you can't blink it away. If Woody Allen were angry with himself for still harboring childish macho dreams, that would be understandable, but he's angry with the public, with us—as if *we* were forcing him to embody the Jewish joke, the loser, the deprived outsider forever. Comedy doesn't belong at the children's table, but whining does.

One of the distinctions that is generally made between a "commercial" artist and a "pure" one is that the former is obsessed with how the audience will react, while the latter doesn't worry about the audience but tries to work things out to satisfy his inner voice. That Woody Allen should try to become a "pure" artist by commenting on his audience seems a sign that he's playing genius. In *Manhattan*, he reworked too much of *Annie Hall*; it was clear that he needed an infusion of new material. In *Stardust Memories*, we get more of the same thoughts over and over—it's like watching a loop. The material is fractured and the scenes are very short, but there was not a single one that I was sorry to see end. *Stardust Memories* doesn't seem like a movie, or even like a filmed essay; it's nothing. You see right through it to the man who has lost the desire to play a character: he has become the man on the couch. He thinks he has penetrated to the core of what life is, and it's all rotten. No doubt he feels that this is the lousy truth; actually, it's just the lousy truth of how he feels. But we've all felt like that at times; he hasn't discovered anything that needs to be shared with the world.

In *Manhattan*, Woody Allen began to use his own face more naturally than he had before on the screen; he didn't turn into a caricature anymore—it was a naked face, sometimes too naked. He is even more relaxed in *Stardust Memories*, and in the absence of other characters you may get fed up with his nakedness and, as his depression enters into you, begin to think about what's in his head. I referred to Woody Allen's recent films as dodgy because I don't think anybody knows how we're supposed to react to the protagonist's metaphysical head cold—his carrying on about death and the shallowness of his friends. He keeps shifting: at one point in a movie he seems to be its moral center, at another point he's a sniper who turns petty grievances into moral issues, and at other times he's the frailest, weakest person around, trying to manipulate people in terms of his needs. In *Annie Hall*, in *Manhattan*, and now in *Stardust Memories*, the protagonist's high moral tone is often out of scale with what he's indignant about and he just sounds like a crank, but we can't tell when Woody Allen means him to sound like one and when Woody Allen really is one.

No movie star (not even Mel Brooks) can ever have been more explicit on the screen about his Jewishness than Woody Allen, and he was especially so in his Academy Award–winning romantic comedy, *Annie Hall*—the neurotic's version of *Abie's Irish Rose* and the TV series "Bridget Loves Bernie." The hero, Alvy Singer, announced that he was paranoid about being Jewish, and at dinner with Annie's Midwestern Wasp family he had a flash and saw himself through their eyes as a Hassidic rabbi—not just the outsider but the weirdly funny outsider, too ridiculous to be threatening. What's apparent in all his movies is that for him Jewishness means his own kind of schlumpiness, awkwardness, hesitancy. For Woody Allen, being Jewish is like being a fish on a hook; in *Annie Hall* he twists and squirms. And when Alvy sits at that dull Wasp dinner and the screen divides and he sees his own family at dinner, quarrelling and shouting hysterically, the Jews are too heavily overdone for comedy. Here, as almost everywhere else in Woody Allen's films, Jews have no dignity. That's just about how he defines them and why he's humiliated by them.

There was self-love as well as self-hatred involved in *Annie Hall*, however: Alvy was very quick to decide that almost everyone connected with show business (except for him) was a sellout. Though the story, which turned into a conflict between East Coast and West Coast, faded before it worked itself out, that fading became part of the meaning: relationships fail, and we're not quite sure why. Diane Keaton's Annie was full of thoughts that wilted as she tried to express them, and her lyrical, apologetic kookiness gave the film softness, elusiveness. She was fluttery and unsure about everything, yet she went her own way, leaving Alvy to continue his love affair with death—an affair that he seemed to think represented integrity and high seriousness. What made the movie run down and dribble away was that while Woody Allen showed us what a guilt-ridden, self-absorbed killjoy Alvy Singer was, always judging everyone, he (and not just Alvy) seemed bewildered that Annie wearied of Alvy's obsessions and preferred to move on and maybe even have some fun. By the end, Alvy and the story had disappeared; there was nothing left but Woody Allen's sadness.

At the opening of *Manhattan*, Woody Allen's Isaac Davis spoke about the corruption of the city's inhabitants in what came across as a satirical commentary; the audience howled. Then that commentary turned out to be the point of view of the picture. But the audience was right to howl: Allen based his case for general moral decay on the weaknesses (not even cruelties) of two or three selfish, confused people. You could indict Paradise on charges like that. In *Annie Hall*, he gave us an L.A. full of decadent pleasure lovers, and his *Manhattan* was also full of naughty, self-centered types: he contrasted their lack of faith with the trusting, understanding heart of a loyal child— played by Mariel Hemingway. (What man in his forties but Woody Allen could pass off a predilection for teen-agers as a quest for true values?) It was clear that he thought we all ran around being rotten and chic, and had to come to terms with our shallowness in order to be saved. (At least he gave us a *big* child to lead us.) Woody Allen the moralist has restated his imponderablle questions about man's destiny so often that in *Stardust Memories* even he sounds tired of them; he tosses them out unemotionally—it's his ascetic reflex. He may be ready to become a Catholic convert. If Woody Allen finds success very upsetting and wishes the public would go away, this picture should help him stop worrying.

October 27, 1980

Dizzy, Dizzy, Dizzy

Private Benjamin is one of the few current movies with an ad that's a real come-on: Goldie Hawn looking bedraggled in an Army helmet, with her lower lip pulled down in the pout of a sad sack who feels abused. The ad is also an accurate representation of the movie's appeal. Goldie Hawn plays a spoiled honey bunch—Judy Benjamin, a rich blond Jewish girl from Philadelphia who has been wasting her intelligence. On the night of Judy's second wedding (her first marriage lasted only six months), the lawyer groom (Albert Brooks) dies of a heart attack while he's exerting himself on top of her on the bathroom floor, having spent himself earlier that evening when he pulled her into the back of a car. (They never get to use the nuptial bed.) Her brain fogged over in confusion, Judy lets a recruiting officer (Harry Dean Stanton) con her with the promise that the Army—the new Army, with its swank new facilities—will take care of everything, and she finds herself scrubbing latrines in Biloxi, Mississippi. Actually, the Army does even more for her than the recruiter promised. It used to be said that the Army would make a man out of you, and in early movies mollycoddled young prigs were whipped into shape and became rugged he-men, leaders, heroes. This hasn't been said much lately, but it's back now in feminist drag. The Army makes a real woman out of the bratty Judy Benjamin. The he-men may have got medals; Judy has her first orgasms.

The script of this women's-liberation service comedy goes from one formula to the next. It's a reworking of generations of male service comedies, with a reverse Cinderella theme: the madcap princess learns to respect the underprivileged members of her ethnically balanced group of recruits and becomes a strong, independent human being. The plot is contingent on the moviemakers' shameless willingness to present Judy as the product of a crassly materialistic Jewish background. And despite the film's feminist veneer, Judy the soldier gets what she wants by manipulation and the shrewd use of sexual blackmail—which we're meant to find adorable. Yet for almost two-thirds of its length the picture is moderately amusing. The director, Howard Zieff, refurbishes stale material with smart camera angles, fuzzy, offbeat timing, and touches so small they're not even gags—they're like the fast flashes in commercials. He holds our attention by casting bit parts with actors who look as if they're going to do something strange, though they don't get to do anything at all, and charms us with a Turkish officer who says some Turkish gobbledygook and then comes back and says it again. The cutting in the basic-training sequences is crisp and often close to inspired—an extra frame or two and viewers might cringe (which I found myself doing during the wargames sequences). Albert Brooks disappears fast, but he makes the bridegroom schmucky yet alive and warm, because everything he does is odd. (Sam Wanamaker and Barbara Barrie, who play Judy's complacent father and neurasthenic mother, have no idiosyncrasies and are dead throughout.)

Zieff appears to be a good director for Goldie Hawn, because almost everything she does here has an infectious, frothy charm. Even if this material was patched together as a showcase for her (she's the executive producer), she had to spin her character out of herself, because it's not in the writing. She gets laughs out of ancient routines about a tenderfoot going through the rigors of basic training; when she runs, she holds her hands out limply in front of her chest, like a bunny rabbit holding up two paws. And she knows enough to recede into the Army group (which includes Toni Kalem, Mary Kay Place, and P. J. Soles) during a spontaneous celebration dance after her side has won the war games. (A black sergeant, played by Hal Williams, who joins in—discreetly dancing with the black Damita Jo Freeman—is the only man in the movie who isn't savaged.) There isn't anything Goldie Hawn can do, though, to redeem dumb service-comedy pranks, like Judy putting blue dye in the shower head of the recruits' captain (Eileen Brennan, in a role that seems to have been conceived by a collection of bickering psychopaths; it requires her to produce a mean slow grin at regular intervals and change her sexual orientation from sequence to sequence).

This picture might have been repugnant with a more militant-looking star. But Goldie Hawn has her smudged, infant sweetness and her little baby belly. When she's fouling up, she's a darling dogface, and when she's stand- ing proud and tall in her élite paratroop-corps uniform, she's still Goldie Hawn of the blue goo-goo eyes and the big, fizzy smile and the limp, straggly curls that always make her look as if she'd been left out in the rain. She finds new, much softer variations of the squeally mannerisms she perfected on the "Laugh-In" shows, and she has a light tone with lines like her unhappy com- ment to the groom (soon to be a corpse) when he grabs her in the bath- room, "Yale, it's not real romantic to make love in a sink." (Her voice expresses weary incredulity.) Her likableness sustains the picture until the plot packs her off to Europe in pursuit of a real dish—a French-Jewish gyne- cologist, whom Armand Assante plays with lowered lids and a heavy accent (like an impersonator's caricature of Charles Boyer) and a wardrobe that looks like a spread in *Gentlemen's Quarterly*. This doctor is a soft nuzzler at Judy's neck. Assante lays on the Gallic sleepy-eyed sexual assurance by the bucketful, yet it doesn't come across as funny. Did the writers (Nancy Mey- ers, Charles Shyer, and Harvey Miller) mean it to? This dreamboat who turns out to be a heel is almost as baffling as Eileen Brennan's growling, butch cap- tain, and everything slumps once he appears. When we realize that the prince is a thickheaded chauvinist who will turn Judy into a subservient wife, as use- less and neurotic as her mindless mother, the picture seems to be stuck in a revolving door. Judy's having to get liberated all over again is bizarre, bizarre. (For the purposes of the plot, she's made out to be a very slow learner.) Yet even here, when at the very last minute Judy pulls out of her wedding cere- mony, Goldie Hawn gets a semi-laugh by the way she inflects "Not so fast" (instead of "I will"). Goldie Hawn demonstrates what an accomplished co- medienne she is—she carries *Private Benjamin* on her back. She's caught in one particularly dumb gambit, though: in order to please the Frenchman, Judy wears her hair Mercurochrome red, in a Cleopatra cut. The material is so thin—it's just Daffy Duck–TV sitcom—that Goldie Hawn can't afford a disfig- uring hairdo. For feminism this phony, she needs every physical asset she can muster and all her honey-bunch wiles.

At the end, Judy the princess who became the sad sack who became the fine soldier is the fairy princess turning down the castle, and as she walks alone down a tree-lined lane in her long, diaphanous wedding gown, there is the sound of military music and her step becomes more firm. Is it really back to the Army for Judy Benjamin? Is male domination so inevitable that she can escape it only by accepting military authoritarianism? This movie, with its message—unmarried womanhood is the only kind of womanhood—is cuckoo.

.   .   .   .   .

Watching Bette Midler in *Divine Madness*, which was filmed on three successive nights at specially arranged performances at the Pasadena Civic Auditorium, you don't know where her energy and spirit come from. She goes from one mood to another in triple time (like a Betty Hutton with brains)—as if she's so alive that all these emotions just spurt out. In *The Rose*, she was probably able to give her passionate, skilled performance by drawing from the same source that Streisand drew from in *Funny Girl*: these "untrained" artists had invented their own training—they had been treating each song they sang as an encapsulated, highly emotional story. Midler—a comedienne who sings—and Streisand are very different, though. When Streisand sings, her command of the audience is in her regal stillness; she distills her own emotions. You feel that she doesn't need the audience—that she could close her eyes and sing with the same magnetic power. Streisand's voice is her instrument; Midler's audience is her instrument. She plays on us and we bring her to life, or at least she makes us feel that we do.

Midler holds you by her changes. She moves like a flighty, mincing Mick Jagger, with a high-heeled, tippy-toed prance and a furious jiggle, and even when her feet don't move, her features do. Everything about her soft and curvy short-waisted body is contradictory: she has narrow hips, slim legs, full breasts, plump upper arms, and slender, expressive hands. When she talks to the audience, telling jokes about a trip to Europe, she shakes like a rowdy burlesque queen, and her toothy smiles are radiantly lewd. When she sings, she's an emotional whirligig, spinning from a cackle to a torchy moan so fast that we're floored by the convictions she brings to each—she can turn gleaming-eyed parody to pure emotion. Midler gives a song a workout, going at it again and again, and topping one big finish with another. Along the way, she may swing it, wail it, shout it, rock it, and throw in some scat, gospel, funk, and punk. She's a bosomy clown who flirts, then weeps, and then clowns again while keeping the passionate, tragic tone. Singing "Stay with Me," which is the climax of her first set of songs, she's suddenly startlingly beautiful; the camera angles on her suggest posters Lautrec didn't get to do. The film critic Michael Sragow wrote that "her face resembles the masks of comedy and tragedy melted into one"—there is an exciting Expressionist bleariness about her.

Except for a prologue skit, in which the house manager gives numbskull instructions to the ushers, *Divine Madness* is essentially a one-woman show: Bette Midler is alone on the stage with her backup trio, the Harlettes. Probably the greatest of all recorded-performance films is the 1979 *Richard Pryor Live in Concert*—when we watch that film we can't account for Pryor's gift, and everything he does seems to be for the first time. Bette Midler mystifies us, too. A crazed, sunny effervescence takes over her face—her demon is a dirty imp. Like Craig Russell, she seems to have a whole troupe of people inside; there's a spooky echo-chamber effect. But *Divine Madness* doesn't have the unity of the Pryor film, and it doesn't get a performance rhythm going, as that did. The separate numbers, with their costume changes, break it up, and Midler's entrances, such as her arrival in a sequined mermaid's tail and a power-driven wheelchair as Delores DeLago, the Toast of Chicago, seem better calculated for the stage than for the camera.

Bette Midler's pneumatic body is very important to her effects. (She's such a tiny Big Mama.) She looks great when she wears a revealing short, spangly dress with thin shoulder straps, and she has a puffed-up physical alertness in the forties swimsuit she wears for "Boogie Woogie Bugle Boy." (It would be even better if she weren't wearing a ribbon that says "Miss Community Chest"; she has gone way past this tired camp.) She has a triumphant moment in a witty enveloping costume that makes her a bride from the front and a groom from the back, for "Chapel of Love," and she's also lighted resplendently during this number. The director, Michael Ritchie, and the cinematographer, William A. Fraker, do discreet, handsome work; they don't try to hide her performance sweat—they let us see that she can be fleetingly beautiful in many different ways, and that her willingness to be grotesque is part of what makes that possible. She has the ability to change glitz to shimmer. *Divine Madness* shows us a great entertainer, though it's not stirring, like *The Rose*, where we could see the dramatic reasons for the incontinent changes of feeling. Here Midler seems to be dipping into a cornucopia—Santa's bag of presents—and she brings the contrasting emotions out so fast that they're somewhat devalued; the meanings crowd each other.

But the only major weakness is that after the first set the song numbers go downhill, and the film gets to be too much. It would have been better with the last quarter lopped off, starting with Midler's mime—a boozing bag lady wearing rainbow-colored rags and carrying an umbrella, who falls asleep on a bench. Some numbers begin poorly and then get better, but once she comes on with that soulful umbrella the jig is up. The bag lady, who is trying to capture the bird of happiness, shows us her longings and her need for fantasy. We've been taking these longings for granted from the start; now Bette Midler lays them out, and all this vulnerability is pretty grim. (It's blobby, like Red Skelton's mime.) The show takes a nose dive with "Rain" and a Kurt Weillish "Ready to Begin Again"—it's inspirational, in the worst sense—and a badly staged "Do You Want to Dance?" Though she almost picks things up at

the very end with the gospel sound of "I Shall Be Released," the sodden banality of that damn bag lady lingers in the air. Bette Midler, who is maybe
better at bawdiness than any other woman entertainer alive, doesn't need to
push her range into show-biz sincerity (which she destroys in Delores DeLago's rendition of "My Way"). And something else goes wrong in this last
quarter of the show: she's swathed in tattered clothing and she loses her
physicality. We need to see Bette Midler's body in movement. When she tries
to be still and make it just on her singing, her act dies. It's not that she's a bad
singer but that her voice alone isn't very distinctive—it lacks personality. The
joy she communicates is in the feeling she gives you that she needs to move
and bounce and take those quick trotting steps—just as she needs to sing and
grin and tell dirty jokes.

．　　　．　　　．　　　．　　　．

Used Cars has a wonderful, energetic heartlessness. It's an American tall-tale
movie in a Pop Art form, with a theme similar to that of *Volpone*. Remember
the convict's advice that Nelson Algren quoted? "Never play cards with a man
called Doc. Never eat at a place called Mom's. Never sleep with a woman
whose troubles are worse than your own." This movie adds "Never buy a
used car from a dealer whose slogan is 'Trust us.' " Its premise is that honesty
doesn't exist. If you develop a liking for some of the characters, it's not because they're free of avarice but because of their style of avarice. Jack Warden
plays twin brothers—the amiable codger Luke Fuchs and the vicious cut-
throat Roy L. Fuchs—who run rival used-car lots across the street from each
other in the booming Southwest. Luke has a bad heart, and every time he
thinks of his skunky brother it gets worse; the only thing that keeps his business going is Rudy Russo. This fast-talking supersalesman, played by Kurt
Russell, is so rambunctiously, ingeniously crooked that he's a standout—a
star in the world of the mendacious. He's slick and sleazy—a vulgarian
through and through. Kurt Russell was sensationally effective when he
starred in the TV film *Elvis* early in 1979; here he goes further. His leap into
satire blots away the ten Disney pictures he appeared in, between the ages of
fourteen and twenty-four. His Rudy has an authentic loudmouth uncouthness; when he's momentarily stumped, his tongue seems to thicken helplessly. He's a son of a bitch, but not a bad guy. The film pits this crass, ferociously
ambitious hero against the sneaky Roy L. They're feuding cartoon animals,
both using dirty tricks. And when they land in court, the judge (Al Lewis)
looks as if long, long ago he smelled something very rotten; it confirmed
what he had suspected and he never let himself forget it.

The movie has a flow of visual-slapstick details and off-color verbal nuances that aren't ever punched up or commented on; they just keep flashing
by. You see from the corner of an eye that the Mexican, Manuel (Alfonso
Arau), who sells Rudy two hundred and fifty used cars (some of them taxis),

conducts his illicit business out of his home in an old airplane that sits in the desert surrounded by cactus. The story line is built of small, wild frauds and jack-in-the-box jokes; they're all interconnected, and, amazingly, every one of them pays off. The film's super-hip use of corn is a home-grown surrealism that the director, Robert Zemeckis, and his co-writer and producer, Bob Gale (they were both born in 1951), have developed out of earlier American slap-stick routines. The intricacy of the gag patterns is all theirs, and so is the way in which the clusters of gags come together—the momentum creates the illusion of being out of control. Zemeckis and Gale are compulsive jugglers, adding more and more balls. But this isn't simple gag comedy with kickers; the comedy is also in the characters, who keep kicking all the time. *Everybody* in the movie is funny—even Toby, Luke's dog. (Actually, you laugh more when the jokes involve Toby than you do the rest of the time, because whenever Toby is part of the chicanery on the lot, there's a cut to his trick and there isn't much else going on in the frame.) The whizzing plot mechanism may make some people feel that they've never been invited aboard—that the picture is speeding ahead without them. And it's vulgarly funny—which may repel some from boarding. Others have said they find it too cruel: there is a sequence in which Roy L. hires a demolition-derby driver to go across the street, pose as a customer, and take Luke for a ride so scary he'll have a heart attack, and Roy L.—he thinks—will inherit Luke's lot. When Luke staggers back into his office in his death throes, the scene might appear unconscionably prolonged if you weren't reacting to the jokes ricocheting off his stagger. Maybe it's just the timing in that sequence that throws some people off; the audience has no problem laughing when Rudy and his pals conceal Luke's death by burying him on the lot, sitting up in a 1959 Edsel.

The action is so fast that at times it's like an adolescent stunt, carried out convulsively—a fit. Everything is staged for motion; there isn't a static thought in this movie. The jokes aren't scattershot: *Used Cars* has the crazy consistency of a picture like *Bringing Up Baby* or *Shampoo*. The bluffs and the scams all play on the theme of trust (just as everything does in Melville's *The Confidence-Man*). It's easy to see why Steven Spielberg, who sponsored Zemeckis and Gale, was drawn to their manic bravura: their moviemaking is a giant version of the toys he set in motion in *Close Encounters*. Spielberg was executive producer of their first feature, the 1978 *I Wanna Hold Your Hand*, and his picture *1941* was made from their screenplay, with John Milius as executive producer; both Spielberg and Milius were executive producers on *Used Cars*. All three of these Zemeckis-Gale projects have been commercial disappointments, and a friend of mine who couldn't stand *1941* said it was like having your head inside a pinball machine for two hours. I know what he meant: *1941* shows you talent without sensibility. And that's also why *Used Cars* seems adolescent, and maybe even pre-human. Like *1941*, it has a carnival atmosphere, and yes, there is something of a pinball machine about it. In both cases, the moviemakers start with a comic premise and take it as far as they can, expanding it with a soaring madness that seems to bring a metallic sheen to the images. What this way of working doesn't allow for is humanistic considerations; such considerations have rarely figured in farce, but Americans may have become touchy. When you see any version of *Volpone* on the stage or the screen, you're not likely to be offended by what it says about human greed, deception, mean-spiritedness. You think of the greed *Volpone* delights in as satiric distortion. But it can rub you wrong to see a used-car lot where everyone swindles everyone else; you may think you're seeing a metaphor of American life rather than a slapstick exaggeration.

Cold-bloodedness shouldn't need to be defended; you can't have pratfalls without it, and the sense of fun in Zemeckis and Gale's hyperbolic slapstick does more for us than pitting virtuous characters against the swindlers would. (It would be demeaning if every movie had to be "balanced," like a political discussion on TV, or like the Marx Brothers pictures made at M-G-M, which, at Irving Thalberg's insistence, were given a supposedly sane crooner and ingénue to balance the insane comedy.) In the context of *Used Cars*, anyone trying to be sane or virtuous would come across as a goosey dimwit, like poor Gloria Jean in *Never Give a Sucker an Even Break*. Zemeckis and Gale's movie is really a more restless and visually high-spirited version of the W. C. Fields comedies.

This picture is entirely made up of comic turns, and at its best there isn't a sincere emotion in it. Rudy's burly sidekick, Jeff, played by Gerrit Graham (he was Beef in *Phantom of the Paradise*), believes in omens, and not just in a small way—he believes totally in omens, and so he lives in spaced-out terror. Most of the time, he looks like a dodo bird in shock, and the gorgeous bimbos he generally has at his side are like feathered trophies. Luke's shell-shocked mechanic, Jim, whose standards of honesty are set by how things are done at Luke's lot, is played by Frank McRae. Given the workaday world in which Jim functions as an honest man, he can't help being funny. David L. Lander and Michael McKean (who's like an American Dudley Moore) play Freddie and Eddie, a pair of electronic wizards who help Rudy and Jeff cut into a Presidential address with their used-car commercials; Freddie and Eddie are like twin brothers, too, and they speak in a doubletalk jargon that suggests the language of robots. The film slides a bit when Rudy falls in love with Luke's long-estranged blond daughter, Barbara Fuchs, because Barbara seems too dainty and too easily duped. Though Deborah Harmon, who plays the part, has a good, eccentric voice and gives her lines little twists, her role doesn't have the hot-ziggety verve to match up with Kurt Russell's. The movie needed to go all the way; it shouldn't have pulled back into this pallid conventionality. (When Rudy says "Trust me" to Barbara, he actually means it.) The film recovers a bit, though. By the end, Barbara, who has appeared in time to take over her father's lot, is wising up, and she becomes a gyp artist, snookering a little old lady with a painted-over taxi. In the big finale, when, in order to keep Roy L. from grabbing the business away from Barbara, two hundred and fifty teen-age student drivers race Manuel's two hundred and fifty jalopies across the prairie, and Rudy jumps from car to car, like the hero of a Western jumping from horse to horse to stop the heroine's runaway coach, the picture adds up the way whoppers told by magnificent liars do.

Surprisingly, the cast works together more smoothly than the group that Spielberg assembled for *1941* did. And the gags interlock even more symmetrically. *1941* had a choppy beginning; it seemed to start with the story already under way, and Spielberg overdid some of the broad, cartoon aspects—several of the performers seemed to be carrying placards telling you what was wacko about them. But the U.S.O. jitterbug number is one of the greatest pieces of film choreography I've ever seen, and the film overall is an amazing, orgiastic comedy, with the pop culture of an era compacted into a day and a night. Its commercial failure in this country didn't make much sense to me. It was accused of gigantism, and it did seem huge, though part of what was so disarmingly fresh about it was the miniature re-creation of Hollywood Boulevard at night in 1941, with little floodlights illuminating the toy cars tootling around the corners and toy planes flying so low they were buzzing through the streets.

Spielberg and Zemeckis & Gale share a mania for comic invention, and there's the feeling of a playroom about their work. That has been true of the acknowledged masters of slapstick, though. Why hasn't *Used Cars* (which received some enthusiastic reviews) done better? The only big reason I can come up with is that maybe you have to be hooked on filmmaking to respond to it, because the jokes run all through and there aren't slowdowns or pauses for laughs. I loved the film, but I didn't laugh out loud a lot, because I was too busy looking at it. I've never seen another movie with the same kind of ravishing, bright Pop lighting, and the cinematographer, Donald M. Morgan, turns the used-car lot at night into a cityscape on the far side of the moon. The movie could be used for a film-school demonstration of dynamic composition and production design (even the clothes are photogenic and funny—Rudy and Jeff dress like natty astro-cowboys, in jeans and iridescent satin shirts). And the editing is by one of the modern masters, Michael Kahn. Maybe the failure is that of the moviemakers, who are so absorbed with their playthings that they fail to draw the audience in. But it could also be that *Used Cars* is so elegantly made and so continuously funny that audiences don't respond the way they would if the jokes were clumsily signalled. You have to bring something to this party. Rudy isn't just a creative sleazo. Why does he work for Luke, whose business is failing, rather than for the get-up-and-go Roy L.? For the challenge, of course. He's selling cars now, but he's still young: he's selling cars only until he can come up with the rest of the sixty thousand dollars it will take to buy the nomination for state senator. He's an American dreamer; he wants to go where the big bucks are. *Used Cars* is a classic screwball fantasy—a shaggy celebration of American ingenuity. Trust me.

November 10, 1980

The Civilization of the Rump

*I*n the series of fifteen full-length movies that Jean-Luc Godard made in eight years—from *Breathless*, in 1959, through *Weekend*, at the end of 1967—he burned away the fat of conventional moviemaking. His films were fine-drawn, quick, lyrical. After a twelve-year stretch of polemical movies and experiments with film and video, he made *Every Man for Himself*. This 1979 picture, which he calls his "second first film," has opened here and has been widely hailed as a return to his great, innovative work of the sixties. It's wonderful to feel the pull of Godard's images again, to feel the rhythmic assurance. There was a special, anarchic sensuousness in the hasty, jerky flow of a Godard film. And there still is. In *Every Man for Himself*, he demonstrates his nonchalant mastery; he can still impose his own way of seeing on you. But the movie may also make you feel empty. More than the fat has been burned out of *Every Man for Himself*: the juice is gone, too.

The film is about money and people selling themselves—their minds or their bodies. The setting is a nameless Swiss city, where the lives of the three main characters are loosely intertwined. Paul Godard (Jacques Dutronc), a video filmmaker who works in television, has left his wife and daughter. Now he is distressed because Denise (Nathalie Baye), a colleague at the video center, is leaving *him*. Isabelle (Isabelle Huppert), a practical-minded prostitute, has only a marginal relation to the two others: she has plied her trade with Paul for a night, and she meets Denise when she arranges to rent the flat Denise is giving up. These characters (and the people around them) have lost hope, are without direction, and don't take pleasure in anything. Sex has become an aberrant, mechanical way to connect, and work yields no satisfaction. They go through the motions of living and searching, but they're dead—and they don't deserve to live. We might almost be back in the world of Antonioni, except that Godard has a gagster's temperament.

His philosophical shorthand jokes give the film a dry whimsicality. The camera may suddenly have a lapse of attention and wander off from the ineffectual principal characters (ineffectuality is a rule of life here) to follow the more entertaining movements of a passerby. Or Godard will toss a joke into the background of a scene: two young motorcyclists yell "Choose!" to the pretty girl with them; one of the men slaps her face, hard, and between slaps the battered girl refuses, crying, "Your turn to choose." Godard may also locate his flip jokes in the relation between image and sound. All through the movie people keep asking, "What's that music?" The gag itself is used as a refrain. At the beginning, Paul is in his hotel apartment; the voice of an operatic soprano that comes from the suite next door irritates the hell out of him, and he bangs on the wall. Then when he leaves, the voice goes with him, like a Fury. But Godard doesn't bring off his old tricks with the surreal snap they once had; he doesn't seem as sensitive as he once did—the shadings are coarser, heavier. Sometimes the jokes are like clever, dispirited imitations of Godard's wit. How can anything be really funny when the people on the screen are so drab, so emotionally atrophied?

As Paul Godard, Jacques Dutronc never smiles; he's glumly dejected in a chic way. His hair swings across his forehead and onto his big specs. (He must see everything through elephant grass.) You don't notice that he has eyes—they're anonymous—and his voice says that he doesn't feel a thing. Nathalie Baye's Denise is less dislikable, maybe because her glumness seems to run deeper. When Denise, who is in emotional flight, is seen going to the mountains on her bicycle, with her dark hair streaming behind her, she's tantalizing, and you want to see her more closely, yet when you do her anxious uncertainty makes her opaque, null, and you don't have any particular reaction to her attempt to find a new way to live. Isabelle the prostitute takes up much of the second half of the picture, and any picture that features Isabelle Huppert is likely to be somewhat numbing. (Right now, if you want to go to the movies she's hard to avoid, though it's worth the effort.) Huppert is never completely *there*, but she isn't any other place, either. She drags her feet across the screen, her voice is placid and toneless, and her face is closed—not enigmatic, just closed. She hardly changes expression; she just gives you a little glimmer of something that is so small and wan no camera yet invented could turn it into an emotion. You feel that she expects the audience to find magic in her matter-of-fact passivity while she remains uninvolved—a visitor on the set. Godard does ritual homage to the delicacy of her features by posing her in a still-life with flowers and in a window that serves as a portrait frame, but it's not her face that gets the attention. In Godard's 1965 *Pierrot le Fou*, Belmondo says, "After Athens, after the Renaissance, we are entering the civilization of the rump." Prophetic words, and Godard does his bit to usher it in with Huppert. Though her pale, freckled face and her light-reddish hair make her seem fragile at the top, she's sturdy from the waist down, and he gets a lot of action out of her round, plump, adolescent-looking bottom. It's licked, spanked, and violated; there are times when you could swear that it pouts as eloquently as her face. And when Huppert isn't onscreen a dairymaid shoves her bare behind in the impervious faces of some cows.

Every Man for Himself lacks the friction that came from the multiple ideas and points of view in Godard's sixties films. He's still employing his provisional, trying-it-on style, but his thinking is absolutist, and the satirical bits have nothing to bounce off. It's all a statement of the same melancholy theme. Paul is corrupted, and so he mopes and displays malaise, like a mannequin. Godard's films were always full of mannequins—they acted out their dreams, strutting and posing and having a good time; they got so far into their dreams you couldn't tell if they were the real thing or not. You don't think at all about the limp, burnt-out Paul Godard. Who would want to know more about him? You can see what he is: he's the spirit of selling out. At the end, Paul Godard has been struck by a car; the driver speeds off, and though Paul's estranged wife and his daughter are among the onlookers, no one comes to his aid. He is left to die in the street, or perhaps to live—nobody bothers to find out. And this isn't a joke, it isn't irony—it's simply Godard (who was in a near-fatal accident some years ago) accusing us of deserting him. When he was making ascetic revolutionary tracts, audiences gave up on him, other filmmakers wearied of being denounced by him, and the press gradually lost interest in him. And so there we all are—the onlookers, who do nothing to help him. He's saying, "You're all hit-and-run drivers." His political extremism has been replaced by a broader extremism—total contempt, shaded by masochism. This film says that we don't care about him, nobody cares about anybody, and he has given up on us. It's Every Man for Himself.

One of the blessings of Godard's sixties films was the absence of psychology: the characters did what they did, and the films didn't ask why. Suddenly we're confronted with a Godard movie in which the hero is named Godard (and Paul, after Jean-Luc's father), and in which he is unwanted by the woman he wants, is suffering moral rot, and is left to die alone. It's a masochistic film about rejection: Godard can't think of any reason for these people *not* to reject his surrogate. Both women in the movie have at least the will to go on and try something different, whereas Paul is at the end of his rope. Godard is saying, "This is what people are, this is what life is, there's nowhere for Paul to go." The car that hits him seems providential.

What made Godard's impulsive style so sharply exciting in the sixties was that his films were of the moment yet kept that moment fresh. He was the master of digressions that would spontaneously connect in a way that made you laugh while your head was spinning. Having got rid of the impedimenta of conventional storytelling, he brought fiction and documentary together, along with essays, parodies, love lyrics, dances, and questions—endless aesthetic and political questions that threw you happily off balance. His way of incorporating the topical, the transient, and the accidental subverted your schoolbook ideas of drama, and he tweaked your empathic involvement with his characters by offhand changes of tone. Neatness was never his goal; nothing was developed systematically. When he showed us the new consumer culture and urban anonymity, he also had an eye for the pop fun of this new soullessness; he understood how seductive amorality in the young can be. His films were more contemporary than anyone else's; they were full of the signs of the future which were all around us but which we hadn't quite become conscious of. Godard let us see the scary comedy of dissociation: the billboards and brand names and news events and revolutionary heroes that had all become part of the comic-strip look of the environment. *Every Man for Himself* does have some of the flavor of here and now, but though the picture wanders all over the place, it never comes together; it has no center. If it were possible to have lyricism without emotion, that might describe the film's style. Godard shows no love for his characters and none for his principal actors.

This is the only one of Godard's non-didactic pictures on which his name doesn't appear as writer or co-writer; the credit goes to Jean-Claude Carrière, who has often been Buñuel's scenarist, and Annie-Marie Miéville, who has worked with Godard before, and who co-edited this film with him. (Godard has said that the ideas were suggested by some of the writings of Charles Bukowski, who also did the English subtitles, along with Barbet Schroeder and Jean-Pierre Gorin; the three must have had a good time with the dialogue, which is translated in tough-guy slang.) Godard has explained his not having a writing credit by saying that he isn't a good scriptwriter, but when have his scripts been written? He developed his own distinctive mix of narration, monologues, and interviews partly to take the place of prepared dialogue. Here the narration (which is all in women's voices) isn't up to his standard. Mostly, it labors the themes of what we're seeing; reading from her journal, Denise apostrophizes "that thing in each man which silently screams: 'I am not a machine,' " and she offers abstract, damp thoughts about work and boredom and movement. Actually, the film was developed from a videotape, used like an artist's sketch for a painting; this may be why Godard's credit reads "A film composed by Jean-Luc Godard." My guess about why his name isn't among the writers is that in some roundabout way he's expressing his scorn of scripts and scripted films—a scorn that perhaps he alone among directors is fully entitled to, and not even he on this film.

This is the only time I have ever felt that the smattering of narrative in a Godard film wasn't enough; there's so little going on in *Every Man for Himself* that you want more drama. The movie features that old standby, the prostitute as metaphor, though Godard himself said in an interview that "the whore's trade . . . brings more money to dried-up scriptwriters and producers than to pimps." His follow-up remark was "I myself am only a whore fighting against the pimps of cinema." When Isabelle holds out on her pimp, she is pulled into the back of his Mercedes and made to repeat after him, "No one is independent, not the whore, not the secretary, not the bourgeoise, not the duchess, not the maid, not the tennis champion, not the schoolgirl, not the farm girl." And we supply "Not the filmmaker." (There's a big difference between selling yourself and not being independent, but they've been merged here.) Godard had already used up this prostitute metaphor. It was central in *My Life to Live*, and it was better there. When Anna Karina represented the whore, we could believe that she kept an area of feeling to herself; with Isabelle Huppert, there is no one under the makeup. Godard returned to the theme in *Two or Three Things I Know About Her*, and it figured to a lesser extent in several of his other films. This time, he makes it more explicit and all-inclusive than ever before. He's saying "Everything is for sale." It's simplistic cynicism, like that of the barroom pundit who tells you, "Every man has his price." We are supposed to accept it as a basic truth of capitalist society that, like everyone else, Paul has sold himself and that this has infected his consciousness. He says, "I make movies to keep myself busy. If I had the strength, I'd do nothing." Who can believe that the actual Godard would rather do nothing? He doesn't make the movies of someone who'd rather do nothing. He wants to make movies, all right, but he also wants to get back at us. It's apparent from this film that he feels mistreated, neglected, and, as he said recently on a Dick Cavett show, "pushed away."

The look of *Every Man for Himself* isn't inhuman, though what it's saying is; that's its poignancy. Godard shows us the soft shadings of what might have been. During moments of degradation, he cuts outside to a sunset, or to traffic that sparkles the way it does when you look through a windshield in the rain and everything is crystalline. The light is similar to the light in Godard's sixties movies, but with a pearly radiance; the faces and colors have a tempered edge. He doesn't use his old comic-strip boldness; he's willing to let things blend. It could be that he wants to break our hearts. The countryside is plushy in an almost banal, rhapsodic way.

Godard tries something new—an analytic stop-motion technique that freezes an action into a series of stills. Every now and then, a scene or part of one (beginning with Denise on her bicycle, during the titles) is decomposed in this way, and an ordinary action is turned into something formal, extravagant, even frightening. The effect is like that of Muybridge's studies of motion in the late nineteenth century; Godard appears to be reinvestigating the start of movies, looking at the images that constitute a movement. (This may have some relationship to his accident and the injuries to his own body.) Like the devices that Godard employed in the past to keep moviemaking in the viewer's consciousness, this one makes you more aware of the formal properties of a film. And it also has a rapt quality, like freeze-frame endings when they were new. (I dread to think how others may employ it—it could get really bad.) It's effective here partly because there's so little dramatic excitement that the film holds us largely by its graphic power anyway. We experience Godard's search for greater graphic meaning in the images as his way of controlling time and slowing life down—of saying that maybe things have been rushing by so fast that he's been missing something. (He's almost *escaping* to this stop-motion.) His editing rhythm is so subtle that these stills don't seem to slow the film itself down, except in one sequence, when Paul and Denise are grappling physically and the double emotion revealed is too obvious— fighting/embracing. The sequence has a line of signpost dialogue—Paul says, "We can't seem to touch without bruising"—which carries the obviousness even further. You feel Godard is trying to pull something complex out of the scene that isn't there; when this grappling was shown on the Cavett show, it was reassuring to hear Godard say he wasn't pleased with it.

The alienation in *Every Man for Himself* has a "commercial" aspect, which is new in Godard's work: almost all the audience laughter comes from sex jokes and the deadpan attitudes toward weird sex. Godard startles the audience by the raw gutter language that Paul uses when he talks about how he'd like to make it with his eleven- or twelve-year-old daughter and when he's talking directly with her. (It's like some crazy literary form of exhibitionism.) And Godard tickles the audience by showing Isabelle dropping her panties and lifting her behind for inspection while she looks blankly detached. Bought sex is treated as gadgetry: a businessman who wants an orgy sits at his desk and, like an inventor arranging a mechanical hookup, tells the three other participants what to do; when they are all linked fore and aft, he says, "The image is O.K., let's do the sound," and he tells them what cries to produce and when. The sex scenes are demonstrations of how joylessly corrupt everyone is; Godard appears to be a catatonic moralist and a giggling pander in the same film. His intentions don't fuse into wit—they stay separate. It could be that he's too despairing to be really funny. Even the somewhat dubious poetry—when he slows down the action into stills—seems a gesture of despair. I got the feeling that Godard doesn't believe in anything anymore; he wants to make movies, but maybe he doesn't really believe in movies anymore, either. Maybe he has given up caring what they're about; it could be that the sex scenes are there to sell the picture—that self-contempt and contempt for the public have come into play, and that along with the experimenting he is doing some conscious whoring.

November 24, 1980

Religious Pulp, or The Incredible Hulk

As Jake La Motta, the former middleweight boxing champ, in *Raging Bull*, Robert De Niro wears scar tissue and a big, bent nose that deform his face. It's a miracle that he didn't grow them—he grew everything else. He developed a thick-muscled neck and a fighter's body, and for the scenes of the broken, drunken La Motta he put on so much weight that he seems to have sunk in the fat with hardly a trace of himself left. What De Niro does in this picture isn't acting, exactly. I'm not sure what it is. Though it may at some level be awesome, it definitely isn't pleasurable. De Niro seems to have emptied himself out to become the part he's playing and then not got enough material to refill himself with: his La Motta is a swollen puppet with only bits and pieces of a character inside, and some semi-religious, semi-abstract concepts of guilt. He has so little expressive spark that what I found myself thinking about wasn't La Motta or the movie but the metamorphosis of De Niro. His appearance—with his head flattened out and widened by fat—is far more shocking than if he were artificially padded. De Niro went from his usual hundred and forty-five pounds to a hundred and sixty for the young fighter, and then up to two hundred and fifteen for La Motta's later days. (No man has ever made a more dramatic demonstration of the aesthetic reasons that people shouldn't get bloated.) And the director, Martin Scorsese, doesn't show us the trim, fast fighter and then let us adjust to his deterioration; he deliberately confronts us with the gross older La Motta right at the start, in a flash-forward.

At first, we may think that we're going to find out what makes Jake La Motta's life special and why a movie is being made about him. But as the picture dives in and out of La Motta's life, with a few minutes of each of his big fights (he won the title in 1949), it becomes clear that Scorsese isn't concerned with how La Motta got where he did, or what, specifically, happened to him. Scorsese gives us exact details of the Bronx Italian neighborhoods of the forties—everything is sharp, realistic, lived-in. But he doesn't give us specific insights into La Motta. Scorsese and De Niro, who together reworked the script (by Paul Schrader and Mardik Martin, based on the book *Raging Bull*, by La Motta with Joseph Carter and Peter Savage), are trying to go deeper into the inarticulate types they have done before; this time they seem to go down to pre-human levels. Their brutish Jake is elemental: he has one thing he can do—fight.

Raging Bull isn't a biographical film about a fighter's rise and fall; it's a biography of the genre of prizefight films. Scorsese loves the visual effects and the powerful melodramatic moments of movies such as *Body and Soul*, *The Set-Up*, and *Golden Boy*. He makes this movie out of remembered high points, leaping from one to another. When Jake is courting the fifteen-year-old platinum-blond Vickie (Cathy Moriarty), he takes her to a miniature-golf course, and their little golf ball rolls into a little wooden church and never comes out. The scene is like one of a series in an old-movie montage showing the path to marriage. But Scorsese just puts in this one step; probably for him it stands for the series. And his neutral attitude toward La Motta is very different from that of forties movies. An idle remark by Vickie—that Jake's opponent in his next match is good-looking—makes Jake so jealous that he goes in and viciously, systematically destroys the kid's face. The movie doesn't throw up its hands in horror; it just looks on. Jake, who enforces long periods of sexual abstinence before his fights, becomes obsessed with the idea that Vickie is cheating on him; you feel that he *wants* to catch her at something. His suspicions lead him to smack her around and to beat up his brother Joey (Joe Pesci), who is his manager, sparring partner, and closest friend. The questions that come to mind (such as why Vickie stays with Jake, or why she leaves when she does, or even whether in fact she *is* unfaithful) clearly aren't germane to Scorsese's interest. Vickie doesn't react much; she accepts Jake's mounting jealousy passively.

Scorsese appears to be trying to purify the characters of forties movies to universalize them. Vickie is an icon—a big, lacquered virgin-doll of the forties. Tall and strong-looking, Cathy Moriarty has a beautiful glassy presence, like Kim Novak in her *Man with the Golden Arm* days, and the same mute sexuality. She recalls other iconographic presences—Jean Harlow, Lana Turner, and the knowing young Gloria Grahame—but she's tougher and more composed. Sitting at the edge of a swimming pool, her Vickie is a *Life* cover girl of the war years. She has sultry eyes and speaks in flat, nasal Bronx tones. It's lucky that Moriarty is big, because when Jake comes at her angrily, like a slob Othello, she looks as if she could take care of herself; there's no pathos. Joe Pesci's Joey is stylized in a different way: he may bring to mind the brother in a movie about a show-biz family. His speech sounds like patter, as if he were doing a routine with Abbott and Costello or the Three Stooges; he has the vocal rhythms of a baggypants comic from burlesque, and though his lines aren't especially funny, his manner is, and the audience responds to him gratefully, because he's so much saner and less monotonous than the Neanderthal Jake. It's Pesci's picture, if it's anybody's, because we can understand why Joey does what he does. Even when he goes out of control and smashes a taxi door repeatedly against a mobster who is caught half in, half out, we know that he's doing what Jake charged him to do. (As the big, gentle mobster, played by Frank Vincent, who's quietly effective, is having his bones broken, voluptuous, forlorn Mascagni music rises. Here, as in much of the movie, Scorsese's excesses verge on self-parody.)

Scorsese is also trying to purify forties style by using the conventions in new ways. If you look at forties movies now, the clichés (which bored people at the time) may seem like fun, and it's easy to see why Scorsese is drawn to them. But when he reproduces them, he reproduces the mechanical quality they once had, and the fun goes out of them. The cardinal rule of forties-studio style was that the scenes had to be shaped to pay off. Scorsese isn't interested in payoffs; it's something else—a modernist effect that's like a gray-out. Early on, when Jake's first wife is frying a steak for him and he complains that she's overcooking it, she hollers and picks up the steak as if she were going to throw it at him, but instead she puts it on his plate. The violence in the scene is right on the surface (she doesn't hold anything back), yet nothing comes of it, and shortly after that she disappears from the movie. We don't get the explosion we expect, but we feel the violence. Scorsese shows us Jake—snorting to himself, and with his belly hanging out—going to see Vickie to get his World Middleweight Championship belt so he can hock the jewels from it, and the scene withers away. Yet we remember his banging on the belt to pry the jewels loose. Scorsese's continuity with forties movies is in the texture—the studio artificiality that he makes sensuous, thick, viscous; there are layers of rage and animosity in almost every sequence.

Raging Bull isn't just a biography of a genre; it's also about movies and about violence, it's about gritty visual rhythm, it's about Brando, it's about the two *Godfather* pictures—it's about Scorsese and De Niro's trying to top what they've done and what everybody else has done. When De Niro and Liza Minnelli began to argue in Scorsese's *New York, New York*, you knew they were going to go from yelling to hitting, because they had no other way to escalate the tension. Here we get more of these actors' battles; they're between Jake and Joey, and between Jake and Vickie. Listening to Jake and Joey go at each other, like the macho clowns in Cassavetes movies, I know I'm supposed to be responding to a powerful, ironic realism, but I just feel trapped. Jake says, "You dumb f—k," and Joey says, "You dumb f—k," and they repeat it and repeat it. And I think, What am I doing here watching these two dumb f—ks? When Scorsese did *Mean Streets*, *Alice Doesn't Live Here Anymore*, and *Taxi Driver*, the scenes built through language and incident, and other characters turned up. But when he works with two actors and pushes for raw intensity, the actors repeat their vapid profanities, goading each other to dredge up some hostility and some variations and twists. And we keep looking at the same faces—Jake and Joey, or Jake and Vickie. (They're the only people around for most of this movie.) You can feel the director sweating for greatness, but there's nothing *under* the scenes—no subtext, only this actor's version of tension. Basically, the movie is these dialogue bouts and Jake's fights in the ring.

The fights are fast and gory and are shot very close in. We're not put in the position of spectators; we're put in the ring, with our heads right up against the heads of the two fighters who are hammering away at each other, with slow-motion eruptions of blood and sweat splashing us. We're meant to see the fists coming as they see them, and feel the blows as they do; the action is speeded up and slowed down to give us these sensations, and the sound of the punches is amplified, while other noises are blotted out. These aren't fights, really; they're cropped, staccato ordeals. The punches are a steady series of explosions—a drummer doing death rolls. The pounding immediacy is grandiloquent—almost abstract.

The picture seems to be saying that in order to become champ, Jake La Motta had to be mean, obsessive, crazy. But you can't be sure, and the way the story is told Jake's life pattern doesn't make much sense. When he loses the title and gives up fighting, he opens a night club, where he's the m.c. and the comic, clowning around with the customers. I had no idea where this cheesy jokester came from: there was certainly no earlier suggestion that Jake had a gift of gab. And there is nothing to prepare us for the poster announcing that he's giving readings from Paddy Chayefsky, Shakespeare, Rod Serling, Budd Schulberg, and Tennessee Williams; we're in a different movie. At the end, before going onstage for his public reading, Jake recites Brando's back-of-the-taxi speech from *On the Waterfront* while looking in his dressing-room mirror. Scorsese is trying to outdo everything great, even the scene of De Niro talking to himself in the mirror in *Taxi Driver*. What does it mean to have La Motta deliver this lament that he could have been a contender instead of a bum when it's perfectly clear that La Motta is both a champ *and* a bum? (Is it a deliberate mockery of the simplicity of Schulberg's conception?) The whole picture has been made looking in a mirror, self-consciously. It takes a while to grasp that La Motta is being used as *the* fighter, a representative tormented man in a killer's body. He's a repulsive, threatening figure who seems intended to be all that and yet to have an element of greatness. He's a doomed strong man—doomed by his love for his wife and by his ability to fight. It's all metaphors: the animal man attempting to escape his destiny. When Jake, in jail on a morals charge, bangs his head and his fists against the stone walls of his cell and, sobbing in frustration, cries out, "Why? Why? Why? It's so f—king stupid! I'm not an animal," it's the ultimate metaphor for the whole film.

The tragedy in Scorsese's struggles with the material in both *New York, New York* and *Raging Bull* is that he *is* a great director when he doesn't press so hard at it, when he doesn't suffer so much. He's got moviemaking and the Church mixed up together; he's trying to be the saint of cinema. And he turns Jake's life into a ritual of suffering. In the middle of a fight, Jake is sponged by the men in his corner, and he has been injured so much that the water is dark: they're washing him in his own blood. Scorsese is out to demonstrate that he can have for his hero a brutish hardhead, a man with no redeeming social graces, and make you respect him. He must have been drawn to La Motta's story by its sheer plug-ugliness: here was a fighter who didn't even look graceful in the ring—he crouched and slugged. And Scorsese goes to cartoon lengths to establish that Jake is a bad guy: Jake actually threatens to kill and eat a neighbor's dog. Scorsese doesn't want us to *like* Jake, because he wants us to respond on a higher level—to Jake's energy and his pain. He wants us to respect Jake despite everything we see him do. We're supposed to believe in his *integrity*. The Mafia bosses force Jake to throw a fight before they'll let him have a chance at the title. He throws the fight by just standing still and taking the blows; afterward, he weeps. It's a fall from grace: he has given up the only thing that counts. We're supposed to think, Jake may be a pig, but he *fights*. Scorsese appears to see Jake as having some kind of loony glory. But if you respond, possibly it's not to La Motta's integrity but to De Niro's; he buries the clichés that lesser actors might revel in, and is left with nothing to anchor his performance. He does some amazing things, though. In the ring taking punches, Jake seems to be crying, "Crucify me! Crucify me!"

With anyone but De Niro in the role, the picture would probably be a joke. But De Niro gives you a sense of terrible pain that is *relieved* when he's in the ring. The film's brutality doesn't seem exploitative; it's mystical.

The magazine *Film Comment* has a feature, "Guilty Pleasures," which it runs intermittently: movie people list the works they wouldn't try to defend on aesthetic grounds but have enjoyed inordinately. When Scorsese offered some of his favorites in 1978, a thread ran through many of his selections. He says, "*Play Dirty* isn't a sadistic film, but it's mean. The characters have no redeeming social value, which I love." Of *Always Leave Them Laughing*, he says, "I admire the guts it took for Berle to make this autobiographical film about a completely dislikable guy." Of the hero of *I Walk Alone*, he says, "He has only one way to deal with his problems: brute force." Of *Dark of the Sun*, he says, "The sense of the film is overwhelmingly violent; there's no consideration for anything else. The answer to everything is 'kill.' " Scorsese likes movies that aren't covered in sentimental frosting—that put the surliness and killing and meanness right up front. But *Raging Bull* has the air of saying something important, which is just what he loved those cheapo pictures for not having. By making a movie that is *all* guilty pleasures, he has forged a new sentimentality. *Raging Bull* is about a character he loves too much; it's about everything he loves too much. It's the kind of movie that many men must fantasize about: their macho worst-dream movie.

Scorsese is saying that he accepts totally, that he makes no moral judgment. I think that by the last fight we're not supposed to care whether Jake wins or loses—we're supposed to want to be in there, slugging. Even the black-and-white is macho: it has something of the flashy, tabloid look of the original *Naked City* movie. But it's so hyper that you're aware of the art, which kills the tabloid effect. We don't get to see the different styles of La Motta's opponents: Scorsese doesn't care about the rhythm and balance of fighters' bodies. There's no dancing for these fighters, and very little boxing. What Scorsese concentrates on is punishment given and received. He turns the lowdown effects he likes into highbrow flash reeking of religious symbolism. You're aware of the camera positions and of the images held for admiration; you're conscious of the pop and hiss of the newsmen's cameras and the amplified sound of the blows—the sound of pain. Scorsese wants his B-movie seaminess and spiritual meaning, too. He wants a disreputable, lowlife protagonist; then he suggests that this man is close to God, because he is God's animal.

By removing the specifics or blurring them, Scorsese doesn't produce universals—he produces banality. What we get is full of capitals: A Man Fights, A Man Loses Everything, A Man Bangs His Head Against the Wall. Scorsese is putting his unmediated obsessions on the screen, trying to turn raw, pulp power into art by removing it from the particulars of observation and narrative. He loses the lowlife entertainment values of prizefight films; he aestheticizes pulp and kills it. *Raging Bull* is tabloid grand opera. Jake is the

Brute Life Force, and the picture ends as he experiences A Surge of Energy. It's a Felliniesque ending: Life Goes On. The picture is overripe, ready for canonization. An end title supplies a handy Biblical quote.

December 8, 1980

Poses

While watching the three-hour-and-thirty-nine-minute *Heaven's Gate*, I thought it was easy to see what to cut. But when I tried afterward to think of what to *keep*, my mind went blank. The writer-director Michael Cimino uses a garbled version of the Johnson County war as his subject. In Johnson County, Wyoming, in 1892, the Stock Growers Association tried to drive new settlers out of the state. The cattlemen claimed that settlers were stealing their cattle, and when they couldn't get the alleged rustlers convicted in the courts they hired mercenaries to hang them or shoot them. Only two people are known to have been killed as a result of the conflict, but the movie turns the events into a shoot-'em-up holocaust, in which the helpless poor are destroyed. And, by implication, will always be destroyed. Cimino might have taken his perspective on American history from one of Gore Vidal's smiling TV chats with David Susskind, who is always profoundly impressed when Vidal explains that since the banks and big business secretly run everything, the American political system is a farce. The conception is a complete downer; there's practically no one left alive at the end—only the marshal, Kris Kristofferson, who seems groggy from the effort to act, anyway. (When he speaks, his eyes are far away; he seems to be trying to read a teleprompter across the river.) Vilmos Zsigmond's soft, golden cinematography is extraordinary, but, with all the dust and smoke and mist and fog, after a while the pictorial effects turn into a beautiful blur. The movie is so unreal—so distant and vaporous—that its message of hopelessness leaves no impression. It just drifts by.

I've seen a lot of worse movies—though perhaps none with such a woozy, morose mixture of visual virtuosity, overarching ambition, and slovenly writing. I think that Cimino did have a vision, but you don't have to be a clear thinker to be a visionary. (It may help if you're not.) The vistas and the crowd scenes are huge, as in a David Lean epic, but not so static or literal-minded. Cimino's is a different sort of madness—he goes for mood, atmosphere, movement. There's so much background action (horses galloping, peasants trudging) that you can't hear the dialogue up front that might help you to understand what's going on; Cimino is big on hubbub. The settlers are bizarrely homogeneous: a whole community from some Bulgarian village seems to have moved to Johnson County, and another whole community from the Ukraine. The immigrants' languages and customs are intact, along with their choral groups; the women, in white babushkas, are bent low pulling a plow. Isabelle Huppert appears, strips, and rushes outdoors; she's a little woodland nymph gambolling about. She's also the madam of the local whorehouse and a fearless fighter for the rights of the poor. It's a Sigmund Romberg operetta that turns into a Dovzhenko movie, with a little help from Bertolt Brecht. Yet even when everybody is riding around hysterically and shells are bursting, the movie seems to be in a fugue state. The bloody actions don't build to any narrative purpose; it's like a movie made by a cataleptic, who can't remember that Huppert doesn't have to tell Kristofferson that the leader of the mercenaries, Christopher Walken, wants her to be his wife, because she already told him, a few scenes back. As a plutocrat who knows how immoral the Association's policies are but is too weak not to go along with them, John Hurt wanders through, tossing his russet locks, addressing cultivated ironic thoughts to the clouds, and giving a performance that is so masochistically rotten that Charles Laughton in his Heaven/Hell must be weeping in envy. In just about every sequence in which Hurt appears, he flaunts his drunken misery by taking swigs from a dainty silver flask that wouldn't hold enough to make a sparrow tipsy. There are bits from all over in *Heaven's Gate*. It's a movie addict's vision of the class struggle—a composite. The spirit is late-sixties, as if Cimino had just become alienated. His romanticism is as movie-ish as his alienation. There's even a revival of the scene of the stalwart man (Kristofferson) bravely trying to down the terrible pie that the loving woman (Huppert) has baked for him.

Some great movies have been made by hustlers who were also dreamers; what has tripped up Cimino this time is that he is innocent in a way that is indistinguishable from ignorance. In a position of power after his *The Deer Hunter* won the Academy Award, he inflated a Western script he'd written years before, turning it into an elegy for the downtrodden—and exposed a fan's sensibility. It's very like the dislocated, floating sensibility that Zeffirelli revealed in the 1979 *The Champ*. Doing his remake of the 1931 American film that had touched him deeply when he saw it as a child in Italy, Zeffirelli directed as if he had never met a human being. His modern American prizefight milieu was full of hearty peasants clustering in courtyards and forming patterns for the camera. And, playing the ex-wife of a dese-dem-dose prizefighter—a woman who had walked out on her husband and infant son and become a fashion consultant—Faye Dunaway was dressed like a dowager empress; when she m.c.'d a fashion show and recited the descriptions of the gowns, the buyers yelled "Bravo!," as if she were Pavarotti, and when she spoke to her child she felt him up with her voice and nuzzled his neck amorously. This sort of insanity has always been endemic in movies. Cimino's hearty peasants have their simple, earthy pleasures—a cockfight, spitting on each other, brawling. When it comes down to it, they're just funny foreigners. They don't even discuss organizing to protect themselves against the mercenaries; it takes a Harvard man (Kristofferson) to show them how to fight. Yet Cimino might have got by with all the snobbishness and the bathos (Zeffirelli did) if he had just used a little street wisdom and told a story. *Heaven's Gate* is no worse a movie than *Star Trek* or *The Black Hole* or *Raise the Titanic*. I'd say the performances in these four films are about on the same level (though maybe more convulsing in *Raise the Titanic*). What makes Cimino's picture truly intolerable is that he got caught up in the visual possibilities and lost sight of basics. You can't make out what's going on or who is in love with whom or where people who are old friends could possibly have met or what this little French mouse Huppert is doing scampering through the picture.

The day after the first disastrous press screenings, United Artists made the announcement that at Cimino's request *Heaven's Gate* in its present form was being withdrawn. It could be said that the press had been waiting to ambush Cimino. His public remarks over the past couple of years since *The Deer Hunter* had invited it, and so had the cost of *Heaven's Gate*, which swelled to somewhere between thirty-six million and fifty million dollars, depending on whether the interest and other expenses are included. And it's easier to jump on a picture like this one than on, say, *Star Trek*, which is so impersonal that there's no one in particular to blame. But *Heaven's Gate* is a numbing shambles. It's a movie you want to deface; you want to draw mustaches on it, because there's no observation in it, no hint of anything resembling direct knowledge—or even intuition—of what people are about. It's the work of a poseur who got caught out. This poseur does have an eye, though; he may not be able to think straight but he's a movie director.

· · · · ·

The Idolmaker is of no special importance, but it's likable. A first feature by the director Taylor Hackford, it has verve and snap, despite a rickety script. The central character—a young songwriter from the Bronx, Vincent Vacarri (Ray Sharkey)—is searching for a singer with "the right look" for the bobby-soxers. It's 1959, and Vinnie, who knows that the look is more important than the voice, has the instinct, the brashness, and the energy to take a dissolute, baby-faced saxophone player from a juke joint and turn him into a rock idol, and then he saturates the country with publicity and pre-sells another idol before the public even hears his voice. As this ingenious, fast-talking hype artist, Sharkey shows his talent for manics. He takes a quick hard look around him and sizes up a situation; he's light on his feet and sharp-faced, with a lower lip that sticks out like a teaspoon when he smiles. Training his protégés to be heartthrobs, Vinnie moves like a flyweight symphony conductor, and when they're onstage performing in front of squealing audiences he's still going through the gestures backstage. He's a combination of conductor, ventriloquist, and double. Vinnie is so aroused by the crowd that he can't control himself: he thinks he's the one being applauded. These doubling scenes are peculiarly resonant slapstick—especially a concert in Rochester, with the baby-face, Tommy Dee, gesticulating in white, and Vinnie in dark clothes making the same gestures behind the curtain and preening with pleasure as the kids express their adoration of Tommy's swivelling hips. Vinnie flying high all alone is a paradoxical image—it has a little of Buster Keaton's detachment. But the script veers between muckraking parody and sloshy melodrama, and poor Sharkey is caught in the middle.

Vinnie hasn't been named Vacarri for nothing: the script, by Edward Di Lorenzo, which was suggested by the life of the rock impresario Bob Marcucci, keeps telling us that Vinnie's vicarious successes can never be fulfilling. So Vinnie must be despondent and take it out on his protégés in dictatorial behavior. He must quarrel with his girl (a dreary, smirky performance by Tovah Feldshuh). He must be beaten and then come back humbled and wiser. And how do we know he has come to terms with his own talent? Earlier, he tried to turn others into what he thought he couldn't be; now he himself performs—he sings a ballad in the maudlin, naked-sincerity style of Barry Manilow. And when Vinnie sings, the film curdles: if you're hip enough to enjoy the satire of such late-fifties pop phenomena as Marcucci's celebrated creations Frankie Avalon and Fabian, you're too hip for this.

Before this sour, self-righteous finish, there's a lot of comedy in *The Idol-maker*. The director takes genuine satirical pleasure in the lewd puckishness of Paul Land as the scummy lowlife Tommy Dee (whose singing suggests Frankie Avalon). Land (who had never acted before) plays the gangling Tommy Dee as a man whose hand is never far from his crotch. A boozing pill-head, Tommy Dee has a great dumb-sickie look when he's in front of an audience; he's morally deficient—a natural degenerate. Land has a furtive comic spark that makes this mind-blown lecher a *believable* caricature. And the director takes another kind of satirical pleasure in the fruity innocence of Peter Gallagher as Caesare (the Fabian take-off). This second idol is born when Vinnie is sitting in an Italian restaurant and the busboy at his table drops a tray; Vinnie yells, and then, looking up, sees a frightened swarthy boy whose eyes and mouth are impossibly—foolishly—large. The kid, who looks like a Sicilian shepherd, is only sixteen. Sliding into Italian and speaking solemnly, with a princely, Old World manner, Vinnie persuades the boy's tough old bird of a grandmother to turn the kid over to him for training. The obedient youth works doggedly at his lessons, and Vinnie remakes him. Soon Caesare's skin is lusciously smooth, he dimples deliciously, his eyes look as sweet and safe as Robby Benson's, his thick hair is brushed up in a pomaded pompadour that scoops down in a curly hunk in the middle of his forehead, and he has the nelly, virginal look of a Donny Osmond.

In the movie's big scene, this terrified dreamboat faces his first audience;

it's as if he were being fed to the mob. We still don't know if he can sing, and before he gets a chance to show what he can do the screaming bobby-soxers break through the guards and mob him, tear his clothes half off, and chase him as he runs offstage. He goes back on, with a reinforced phalanx of guards to protect him, and he sings, leaping and doing splits and whipping his arms high in the air like Engelbert Humperdinck; we see him being turned on by the excitement of turning on the audience, and, with a teasing gleam in his eyes, he goes beyond what Vinnie has taught him and shakes his shoulders to work up the girls. At this point, the people in the movie house were cheering and applauding the galvanic silliness of his triumph. It's after this, when Caesare is eager to perform more and Vinnie, the crazy despot, won't let him, that the movie loses its hold. There's also something more subtle that works against the structure of the film: Paul Land's Tommy Dee and Peter Gallagher's Caesare have more vivid personalities than their supposed creator. Ray Sharkey seems perfect for a character who's always on the jump, and he has the externals down pat, but his live-wire Vinnie doesn't seem to exist inside—there's no fibre supporting the performance. Vinnie has less on the ball than the others.

Onstage, both Tommy Dee and Caesare get the glazed, neutered look of teen-age pinups. (It gives the film a creepy authenticity.) Taylor Hackford doesn't try to score points off their spoiled look or off the pop styles. The rock songs (by Jeff Barry) are of the basic tacky variety, with lyrics such as "I been up, I been down . . . I been in, I been out" and "Come on, Baby, ooh-wee, Baby, ooh-wee." When these songs are acted out with flamboyant gestures, they suggest nursery rhymes for berserk adolescents. Hackford doesn't work up an indignant head of steam about unscrupulous promoters who exploit teen-agers' sexual fantasies—he sees the comedy in it. The staging of the numbers is impudent in a relaxed, not-too-large-scale way; more imagination than money has gone into such scenes as Caesare's concert in Memphis, where he has the Reverend James Cleveland Choir behind him and he's lighted up like a première at Grauman's Chinese. The songs give the film a beat and it moves along. (The only time it's too pokey is when Vinnie goes to see his estranged father; Sharkey has too much moisture in the eyes, too many tortured twists of the mouth.) Hackford gets us past the awful scenes of Vinnie victimizing Caesare and past Vinnie's stupid blackmail threat against a fan magazine, and other fuddy plot devices. And he lets us enjoy the good bits without lingering on them. Near the start, when Vinnie assesses girls' reactions to dark men singers versus blond, and concludes that it's the dark ones who get to them, a blank-eyed, jiggling blond twerp (the actor is named Jimmy Carter) sums up all the bobbing, finger-snapping fellows with aging little-boy faces and names no one can remember. Later, when Vinnie takes Tommy Dee to Rochester, the disc jockey (Kenneth O'Brien), who wants his payola before putting Tommy's record on the air, looks as if he were putrefying before our eyes. Tommy's backup singers have the syrupy sound and the happy, frazzled look that backup singers in a comedy should have, and, all the way through, the costumes (by Rita Riggs) are evocative and funny without ever being grotesque. (In the first flush of success, Vinnie wears a straw hat reminiscent of Murray the K.) A few regrets: When Tommy Dee goes against Vinnie's advice and takes a job in a TV series—a Western—I wish we could have seen him on the box. What a cowboy this fey freak would be! And when Vinnie, at the end, begins his sincere song, it's too bad that the picture can't satirize his little voice—the meaningful croak that is wrenched from his gut. But Hackford comes through with something that's unexpectedly charming: the swooning girls are treated affectionately. They're very young, and the pampered boys with hairless chests who sing to them are, to be exact, living dolls.

·   ·   ·   ·   ·

*I*n *Resurrection*, Ellen Burstyn, a Los Angeles woman, is in a car accident with her blue-collar husband, who is killed. She dies on the operating table— but only for a moment. She has an "out of body" experience and sees her friends and relatives who have died looking happy and beckoning to her. Then she returns. Told that she will never be able to walk again, she's in a truck on the way back to her father's farm in Kansas when she encounters a piercing-eyed old desert rat (Richard Farnsworth, looking like a magical eccentric out of Mark Twain). He operates the Last Chance, a service station that also exhibits curiosities such as a two-headed snake called Gemini; after showing her the snake he reaches into the truck and puts his hand on her head. Soon she is able to cure herself and to heal others through the power of love. The picture is even and smoothly tasteful—a vat of nondenominational caramel custard. The director, Daniel Petrie, does some very polished, fluid work, but you're always aware of the planning and calculation. Mysticism doesn't come easy to him. The cinematography (by Mario Tosi) is maybe too clear and burnished, too awesomely American. Maurice Jarre's strings keep twanging the message "God is love." And the script, by Lewis John Carlino, which attempts to combine holistic healing and feminism, is an amazing fusion of old corn and modern cant.

Carlino was commissioned to write the script for Burstyn, and he has shaped it to her—or perhaps to how she sees herself. As Edna, the healer, Ellen Burstyn is a practical, uneducated woman who is sensual, radiant, and full of wholesome humor. She bestrides the movie, glowing with love. Shirley MacLaine said she'd have killed for the role, and, watching Burstyn, I think maybe she did kill for it—metaphorically speaking. Your eyes don't go to her because she's doing anything of interest but because she has got you collared. In one scene, when she's trying to get feeling back into her paralyzed legs, she talks to her big toe, and I thought, Of course, she's always talking to her big toe—she's barely aware of the other actors, whom she's giving all this love to. Burstyn's simulation of beatific ordinariness is a little frightening. I don't trust an expression on her face. When she smiles, it doesn't disturb the rest of her features; she still looks as if she had a grudge against someone. At times, I felt I could see an angry hanging judge behind the glow.

On the farm, Edna befriends a dog, Clancy, who has been whipped and had his spirit destroyed by her gnarled, taciturn father (Roberts Blossom), and Clancy becomes her devoted friend. (He's like a witch's familiar.) She and Clancy understand each other, because when she was a young girl her father forced her to have an abortion, which made her barren. There is a great deal of "supportive" sisterly understanding among the farm women—and some of the performers (Lois Smith, particularly) give the homespun, inspirational mood a little texture. What can you do with an uncured ham, though? As Edna's Grandma Pearl, Eva Le Gallienne combines the worst elocutionary phoniness of Ethel Barrymore with the darlingness of Helen Hayes to produce the fakiest old sweetheart in modern movies. She wrinkles her nose and lifts her head so she can look out of her half-blind eyes, and she spouts homilies as if she'd lived her whole life onstage. When she and Burstyn hug, you wonder whose talons will gouge deeper. There's also a sub-Eugene O'Neill love affair between Edna and tall, skinny Cal (Sam Shepard), whom she heals after he has been stabbed in a drunken fight. At first, Cal, the hell-raising son of a fundamentalist minister, seems a smart rebel against his father's fanaticism. (Shepard brings the role his rawboned grace and shiny, coyote's eyes. At times, he's like a dangerous, macho Montgomery Clift, at other times like an Ivy League dropout hippie, and you're aware of Burstyn trying to act young to match up with him—she talks baby talk.) But Cal becomes withdrawn and impotent when he sees Edna healing others. Then he turns into a raving nut, and since she refuses to claim that her powers come from God, he decides that they must come from the Devil, and he arrives at her healing rites with a gun. She and Clancy go off into the desert, where she replaces the old miracle man at the Last Chance. The old man doesn't die—he goes to Machu Picchu. There's a streak of countercultural chic in all this.

Resurrection is like an imitation primitive painting. Edna wakes up one day with this awe-inspiring gift, and she's such a down-to-earth woman she isn't fazed by it. Somehow, the movie flattens everything out, so there's no exaltation. You always get the feeling that it's cutting ahead, pushing you forward, yet it never reaches any emotional peaks. The movie is all about uplift, but it never takes off. Maybe that's what happens when a tasteful director thinks he can be intelligently smarmy. The picture is shaped for a star's conception of herself as a larger-than-life Everywoman. It's a newfangled vanity production—a role written to show off Ellen Burstyn's wholesomeness. (I bet she wouldn't have wanted to be wholesome if she'd attained stardom earlier.)

Why doesn't Edna use her gift to help suffering people instead of running off to the desert? There's no point in questioning any of this; there's all that white light to tell you it's beyond reason. In one scene, when Edna's powers are being tested at a scientific institute, she climbs into bed with a twisted crippled woman and embraces her, taking the woman's sickness into herself; the woman's body straightens. The whiteness in the background suggests a halo, although it might be just a squash court. What actress wouldn't kill for this role? Benji would probably have killed to play Clancy.

December 22, 1980

The Funnies

*T*here are no forebears or influences that would help to explain Shelley Duvall's acting; she doesn't seem to owe anything to anyone. She's an original who has her own limpid way of doing things—a simplicity that isn't marred by conventional acting technique, but that by now she has adapted to a wide range of characters. In the new Robert Altman film, *Popeye*, from Jules Feiffer's screenplay, in which she plays Olive Oyl, she sings in a small, wavering voice, and she hits tones that are so flat yet so true that they are transcendently comic. Her dancing has the grave gentleness of the Laurel & Hardy soft-shoe numbers, though she doesn't move anything like either of them. She's Olive Oyl of the long neck and stringbean body and the clodhoppers, and at the same time she has a high-fashion beauty. The screwed-tight hair twisted into a cruller at the neck seems just what Olive needs to set off her smooth, rounded forehead. She curls her long legs around each other—entwining them in the rubber-legged positions of the cartoon figure—and it seems the most natural thing for her to do.

Olive lives in Sweethaven, a tumbledown seacoast Dogpatch, and she's the local belle. When she's teased about getting engaged to the domineering, wide-as-a-barn Captain Bluto, the most hated and feared man in town, she gets the desperate, trapped expression of a girl who knows that she has made a terrible mistake, and, trying to find a virtue in Bluto (who snorts like a bull and looks as if he'd be more comfortable on all fours), she answers, "He's large." And the plaintive defensiveness—the sense of hopelessness—she brings to those words is so pure that you may feel a catch in your throat while you're smiling. When Popeye, the squinting sailor, searching the seven seas for the pappy who ditched him when he was an infant, arrives at Sweethaven, he moves into the boarding house run by the Oyl family. Olive is very uppity to Popeye and to everyone else; she holds her head high on her tube of a neck and sniffs like a duchess. "Persnickety" is the word for Olive, but there are delicate shades of stubbornness and confusion in her face, and sometimes a frightened look in her eyes. Shelley Duvall takes the funny-page drawing of Olive Oyl and breathes her own spirit into it. Possibly she can do this so simply because she accepts herself as a cartoon to start with, and, working from that, goes way past it. So far past it that we begin to find chic in her soft, floppy white collars and her droopy, elongated skirts.

Robin Williams, who plays Popeye, has been given Popeye's bulging forearms, and he has mastered the cartoon figure: the one-eyed squint that comes from talking with a corncob pipe in the mouth; the gruff, raspy voice; the personal patois, with "t" and "k" transposed; the shoulder-first swagger walk; the dancing acrobatics; the speedy round-the-world punch that requires winding up the wrist. He's wonderful at all this mimicry. His cropped carrot-colored hair makes him look like a little kid, and his one blue eye is startlingly bright. He does prodigious work. But he never gets beyond the cartoon, never gives it anything of himself. And so he recedes, is swallowed up in the crowded background. Popeye is always muttering to himself, and these asides—second thoughts and cranky qualifications—become a buzzing in our ears. When he finally gets to sing "I Yam What I Yam," it's in a betting casino, and he has to dart among the customers, dodging traffic. He's always doing something, but it doesn't come to much. He seems locked in those arms.

Part of the reason Shelley Duvall takes over is that she's an oasis of stillness (until the end, when she adds to the commotion). At times, when she stands at a tilt, or just listens, she has the preternatural quiet of Buster Keaton. And it may be an homage or it may be just an accident that she has been given a scene of trying on hats that recalls Keaton's great headgear scene in *Steamboat Bill, Jr.* Duvall may be the closest thing we've ever come to a female Buster Keaton; her eccentric grace is like his—it seems to come from the inside out. And the exaggerated sensitivity in her face might be called an equivalent of his mask of isolation. But *Popeye* is far from a silent movie.

Sometimes the components of a picture seem miraculously right and you go to it expecting a magical interaction. That's the case with *Popeye*. But it comes off a little like some of the Jacques Tati comedies, where you can see the intelligence and skill that went into the gags yet you don't hear yourself laughing. Altman may have been trying too hard, taking the task of creating a live-action musical version of a comic strip (the screenplay is based on Elzie Segar's *Thimble Theatre*) too literally. He was probably reaching for something beyond the written scenes—trying to create a whole comic environment. Altman has to introduce an element of risk on top of the risks that all directors take. Whether this is interpreted as a form of hubris or as part of what makes him an artist or as what keeps him from falling asleep on the set (and it's probably all three), it's Altman's way of directing. Most of the commercially successful movies with actors in roles based on comic-strip characters (such as *Skippy* in 1931, *Blondie* in 1938, and *Superman* in 1978) have been content to deliver the simple catch phrases and repetitive situations that the strips were famous for. Altman tries for much more: the two-dimensional look and the jumbled, congested Krazy Kat feeling of some of the early strips.

Nobody has ever brought this off in a talking picture—not with the degree of stylization that Altman attempts—and when you look at *Popeye* some of the reasons suggest themselves. There used to be animated cartoons in which birds and animals would spoof movie stars—a chicken might be Mae West. Cartoon figures playing movie stars have it all over movie stars playing cartoon figures. In cartoons, the creatures can do anything; their bodies don't get in the way and can't be hurt. But when you watch the actors in *Popeye* doing cartoon stunts, you're aware of gravity and how difficult what they're doing is. When you see an actor lifted up and put on a hot stove, the literalness is dumb and oddly unpleasant. Maybe certain kinds of jokes—especially the ones involving transformations and mayhem, and the ones that derive from the absence of gravity—need the shift in imagination that we make at a cartoon. Some of the most complicated feats of reproducing comic-strip effects in *Popeye*—such as Olive's brother, Castor Oyl, being slammed so hard in the boxing ring that he flies out above the crowd, like a missile, and Popeye, when hit by Bluto, spinning like a corkscrew down through the boardwalk—are eerily unfunny.

Sweethaven (which was constructed on the island of Malta) is a funky cuckoo-land whose people, all crabby obsessives, are as warped as its architecture and its economy. The light that bounces off the grayish buildings has an odd, enamelled quality, and the houses all seem to have been built crook-backed or to have buckled. It's a ramshackle, depressed town, with catwalks and chimneys and ladders and a red-light district—everything weather-beaten and tottering. Sweethaven is so flimsy it seems booby-trapped; you expect it to fly apart or come tumbling down. (Yet when Bluto, in a rage, smashes the Oyls' house, it isn't nearly as funny as the Big Bad Wolf blowing a house down.) Popeye, the outsider, arrives, and even before he finds lodging he's stung a couple of times by the roving tax collector, who demands money in the name of Bluto's boss, the Commodore, the town's unseen tyrant. No one makes Popeye feel welcome—the local citizens scurry away from him. The people of Sweethaven are living quirks; they might have bought their peculiarities at a novelty shop. A long, skinny man keeps hiding behind a pole; there's a man chasing his hat who keeps kicking it ahead of him, and another whose head, when pressed down, sinks into his shoulders like a turtle's. The film has virtuoso bits of business, such as four men moving a piano over a rotting rope bridge. (This gag, which does work, isn't from cartoons; it's out of Laurel & Hardy.) But there are also glimpses of sometimes indecipherable activity at the side of the frame, and there are a lot of dissociated voice-overs—a constant squawking. Some of the remarks we catch are classic griping (Olive's "Not since I was a child have we had a sharp knife in this house"); others seem to be commenting on the action—they're like wise-cracks overheard from the row behind you, and with expletives that would never have been allowed in the funny pages. At first, we anticipate that we'll get to know the grouchy people of Sweethaven, especially the Oyls and Wimpy the moocher (Paul Dooley), but they have no real roles—they just keep the background busy—and the looseness of all this activity is so distracting that the foreground gags don't come off. Sometimes the foreground gags don't come off even when there isn't anything going on around them. There is a painful scene when Olive first shows Popeye his room and the bed collapses, the picture falls from the wall, and the doorknob falls off. You don't laugh, you just stare. It may be that Altman, despite the complex, random-looking incidents he is famous for, doesn't know how to shape and pace basic slapstick. He never does anything stale, and it may be that he can't stomach the thought of clicking out a scene like this one, which has been done a million times. And possibly he thinks he'll get something more exciting by just tossing it off. But slapstick done imperfectly may come across as laborious, and that's what happens in a lot of *Popeye*.

Altman's attempt to reproduce a full comic-strip lowlife environment seems to work against him in all sorts of ways. When Popeye first climbs through the streets of Sweethaven, singing a song, the editing seems peculiarly bad; his song is broken up by shifts in the camera position. Altman must be trying for the jostling, patchwork mood of comics—perhaps even for the slap impact of comic-strip frames—but the patchwork jumble doesn't develop its own rhythm, and we can't find our way into the film. The editing throws us in and pulls us out; we feel as if we're being dunked in cold water. Sweethaven is just a small fishing village, yet when the man-mountain Bluto (Paul L. Smith, who was the head guard in *Midnight Express*) goes to see the Commodore we have no idea where the Commodore's boat is. The boxing ring features a big plaster statue of the champ, Oxblood Oxheart, and when Popeye defeats him the statue falls; it's an abrasive, overpowering shot. I could never get the hang of the editors' thought processes. There's a dinner scene at the Oyls' when they and their boarders are sitting around the table and all their tics seem to intermesh and they've finished the food before Popeye can get a bite. Or is it that there was so little food that nobody got to eat more than a morsel? The double-time movements suggest something funny, but we can't quite tell what's going on.

The picture seems overcomplicated, cluttered, and the familiar Popeye phrases and situations barely emerge. Adults lose the fun of recognition of the ritual lines—they're just throwaways here. And kids aren't likely to come out chanting Wimpy's semi-immortal "I'd gladly pay you Tuesday for a hamburger today"; they may barely register it. With all the muttering and the wordplay and the tricky mispronunciations, to kids the film may seem to be in a foreign language. It's hard to know what Feiffer and Altman intended it to mean to modern children (or adults), because the story doesn't build, or even follow through. Popeye doesn't look for his pappy; he just seems to kill time. And he doesn't punch out the oppressors and become accepted by the people of Sweethaven. (That would give his "I Yam What I Yam" a kick it doesn't have.) Somehow, the oppressed-people theme gets mislaid, and we wind up with boats chasing each other and the principal characters wading around in a cove fighting an octopus and doing a lot of yelling and screaming. This Popeye doesn't even like spinach, which seems sheer perversity on the moviemakers' part—it was the huge cans of spinach that swelled those bulging forearms. (Sometimes they were even shaped like cans.) Now we don't know what the source of Popeye's superhuman strength is. The audience isn't allowed the gratification of the climactic moments in the Fleischers' *Popeye* animated cartoon series; Altman seems almost embarrassed by the conventions. He's trying to do this literal version of the *Popeye* comic strip and at the same time he doesn't want it to add up to *Popeye*. He'd rather it didn't add up.

The picture has lovely moments in the middle section, though. Running away from her engagement party, Olive Oyl meets Popeye on the dock, staring out to sea. They both have their guard down, and they begin to talk. Then they discover the foundling, Swee'Pea, and, enchanted at having a child, they instantly become a loving couple. The movie seems to calm down. The cartoon limits are relaxed, and the audience gets a chance to laugh and show its approval, because the infant (Altman's grandson, Wesley Ivan Hurt) is a blissfully quiet charmer with a faintly lopsided smile that seems in readiness for a corncob pipe. And Olive, proudly infatuated with Popeye, twirling herself around a lamppost as she sings "He Needs Me," seems to be wafted to Heaven. Her goofy duckling-swan lyricism has its own form of weightlessness. If the remainder of the film had concentrated on these three and the shades of feeling that develop when she sings "Stay with Me" and he sings "Sail with Me," it might have been a moonshine classic, even with the deadly slapstick and the ragged editing and the spatial jumble. But when Ray Walston shows up, as Popeye's pappy, and Swee'Pea is kidnapped, the freshness goes out.

There have been oddly tentative songs (by Harry Nilsson) all along, and they've been tolerable, because at least they're not slick. And then, suddenly, there's Walston. Physically, he matches up with Robin Williams; with his muscles and squint and pipe, he's almost a mirror image—that has aged. But Walston's dry rasping is much louder than Robin Williams', and when he sings he bawls out the songs with a rambunctious Broadway pizzazz that cheapens everything. There's no innocence in his performance; it's the Broadway curse—unfelt rhythms, and everything for effect. It's bad enough when he sings "It's Not Easy Being Me"; when he goes on and on with a gravelly, tantrummy number called "Children," the picture begins to hurt your head. Olive Oyl, abducted by Bluto and trapped in a ship's funnel, keeps shrieking for Popeye—and if ever there was a scene that called for perfect timing and cutting, this is it. But her shrieks aren't modulated in terms of the shots that precede them; they're just noise—it could be *any* director's movie. And Altman commits a grandfatherly crime. In the middle of the movie, the audience can't get enough of Swee'Pea—his every expression is greeted with a happy "Aah." But then after he's kidnapped, when Popeye is thinking about him longingly and singing a song, there's Vaseline on the lens and we get a doting reprise of all Swee'Pea's wonderful expressions. This time nobody "Aah"s.

Popeye is a *thing*, though. You don't get much pleasure from it, but you can't quite dismiss it. It rattles in your memory. Would the film have come together better if it had been simpler—without so much "environment"? Maybe—if Robin Williams had broken through, if he had felt free enough to make the role his own. But how could he feel free, starring in his first film with his face all screwed up and using only one eye? Even if the picture had been more quiet and simple, there might still be a sizable part of the public that wouldn't be too crazy about the stylized format. It's my impression that girls weren't waiting at the newsstands to buy the latest issues of comic books, the way boys were. Whether it's something about the comic-strip form itself or whether it was just the subject matter, girls didn't seem to get as hooked as boys did. And you don't hear women talking about what comic books meant to them, either—not to anything like the degree that men do. Women might be happier if Robin Williams had used both eyes and just squinted a little now and then. And this isn't a putdown of women as romantic fools: An actor's face can give us more than an impersonation of a cartoon. Two-dimensionality is tiresome.

.   .   .   .   .

Flash Gordon is like a fairy tale set in a discothèque in the clouds. Up there, the arch-fiend—Emperor Ming the Merciless (Max von Sydow), the Ruler of the Universe—is costumed as if for a space-age presentation of *The Mikado*. His clothes are stiff, like the shell of a crustacean. All that is visible of him is his bald, gaunt death's-head and his spidery fingers, working, working. Ming is jaded, though, and so he takes "power pills" to feel more potent and amuses himself by toying with Earth. He sends us quakes and zigzagging streaks of lightning, and when he wearies of such childish sport he pokes our moon out of orbit, so it will hit us and blow us up. On Earth, only Dr. Zarkov (Topol), a scientist with a fevered brain, perceives the danger, and he's so overwrought that no one believes him. Determined to save Earth, he kidnaps Flash Gordon (Sam J. Jones), quarterback for the New York Jets, and Dale Arden (Melody Anderson), a travel agent, to help him work the controls of his rocket ship, and blasts off. The three Earthlings have barely crash-landed at Ming's palace in Mongo (their arrival is reminiscent of the tacky enchantment of the landing in Méliès' *A Trip to the Moon*) when Ming decides that Dale Arden has the freshness to restore him. He's probably right. Melody Anderson's Dale recalls Jean Rogers, who played the role in the 1936 and 1938 serials, and was considered the sexiest heroine of the genre. Melody Anderson has been made a brunette, and, with eyes like the painted eyes of a doll and a mouth that's slightly askew, she's all the cuddly Miss Rheingolds rolled into one.

There are no hidden themes in this comedy fantasy; everything is on the luscious surface. In order to save Earth, the good-hearted herculean hunk Flash Gordon and the ebullient Dr. Zarkov must stir up the oppressed people of Mongo to overthrow Ming. And they wouldn't be heroes if they didn't save Dale Arden from Ming's spidery clutches. Ming's daughter, Princess Aura (Ornella Muti), has a yen for Flash, but that's not a problem: Flash isn't such a block that he's averse to a little dallying with Aura before he's reunited with Dale. Directed by Mike Hodges (the Englishman who did *Get Carter*, *Pulp*, and the dismal *Terminal Man*), and produced by Dino De Laurentiis, this film is a piece of comic-strip bravura. The script, by Lorenzo Semple, Jr., from Michael Allin's adaptation of the funny-page characters created by Alex Raymond, uses the basic plot of the 1936 serial, starring Buster Crabbe, and is clearly inspired by that serial, which is considered the most expensive one ever made and was possibly also the most popular. Danilo Donati, the Italian designer long associated with Federico Fellini, takes those posh old effects to Halloween haute couture. He did the production designs, the sets, and the costumes, and Donati is not known as an ascetic. *Flash Gordon* doesn't look like other space fantasies; the hardware is closer to Méliès than to *2001*. The music of the rock group Queen is on the track, and the shots are like the comic-strip frames enlarged by Lichtenstein, with the addition of crude, bright skyscapes. The whole movie is painterly; it's flooded with the primary colors of comic strips—blue, and especially red at its most blazing. Donati and the cinematographer, Gil Taylor, make the colors so ripely intense that they're near-psychedelic. When Flash and Dale are dozing in Zarkov's rocket, on their way to Mongo, the burning-red trim on their clothes binds them together. The tiny, voluptuous Princess Aura wiggles and slinks through her father's palace wearing a shimmering scarlet jump suit; she's a flaming nympho. This goddess of lust is the apotheosis of Cobra Woman herself—Maria Montez. When Princess Aura pledges her love to her handsome fiancé, Prince Barin (Timothy Dalton), he says, "Lying bitch," admiringly, in tribute to her polymorphous perversity. No woman with such hot-tomato lip gloss could be faithful. (At times, when she slithered by, I thought I heard moans of distress: she has a figure that could make men suffer.)

Mongo is inhabited by many variations on the human species, and they're all on dress parade—slimy reptile men in the swamps, pet dwarfs on leashes, Gilbert and Sullivan mock-Oriental robots, mask-faced Storm Troopers who are reminiscent of Darth Vader, a row of androids monitoring Mongo's computers. (When one android collapses, the others fall like dominoes.) And one of the moons of Mongo is inhabited by hawk men, whose leader, Prince Vultan (Brian Blessed, grinning to show all his teeth, and hairy as a bear), is enlisted in the revolt against Ming. When Vultan and his fliers are winging through the air, they suggest the flying monkeys in *The Wizard of Oz*. There are also villains who deliquesce like the Wicked Witch, and other reminders that Mongo is like Oz in space. But Timothy Dalton's dashing, enthusiastic Prince Barin of Arboria wears the green tunic of Robin Hood, and his woodland moon, where his men are a companionable band, suggests Sherwood Forest. Arboria has a dark macho rite, though. Prince Barin and Flash are pitted against each other in a fairy-tale form of Russian roulette. They take turns putting a hand into the crevices of a gnarled tree trunk, risking the fatal bite of the resident monster. This sequence, which evokes the illustrations in old books of children's stories, is much scarier than the futuristic torments.

Max von Sydow's Ming has such crazy eyes and he flexes his fingers so fiendishly that he deserves funnier lines and dirtier deeds. He has a fine funny-page moment when he's impaled on the spike end of a little snug-nosed rocket, but he doesn't get enough opportunity to show off his soft, deep voice. Von Sydow brings a playful metallic sheen to everything he does; he has the Fu Manchu look of Charles Middleton in the serials, but with more hauteur. Middleton wore high, stiff collars that framed his shaved head; von Sydow's collars have circular, standup backs so high that his head seems to be resting against a gigantic gong. (Somehow, the effect of this performance is to make von Sydow seem more human: even he wants to have fun sometimes.) Ornella Muti manages to make Princess Aura teasingly funny throughout; this actress doesn't seem any more concerned about what people think of her than a cat would be; she's tickled by the good luck of looking completely carnal. She's a perfect little emblem of camp. The playwright John Osborne (who was the villain in Hodges' *Get Carter*) appears as an Arborian priest, and Mariangela Melato turns up—a brunette here, like the other women—as the wicked Kala, of Ming's secret police. Jones' Flash has blondness enough for the movie, and though his eyes aren't exactly soulful (they seem innocently empty), he's physically entertaining. There's bulk to this fellow—there's so much of him that it's surprising how fast he moves in a series of football skirmishes with Ming's guards. (With Dale Arden as cheerleader whipping him up to glory, this is the film's most all-out-parody sequence.) In the thirties, when Buster Crabbe played the role, Flash was a Yale man, a fencing champion, and a celebrated polo player—i.e., a gent. That would get too close to James Bond terrain, though, and it's more fun to have him a wide-eyed jock, with huge hands, and hair on his chest and in his armpits. It's golden, of course.

Flash Gordon is simply out to give you a good time. It has some of the knowing, pleasurable giddiness of the fast-moving Bonds, and the same sort of saving-the-world plot, though with less emphasis on it. (There are sequences when the moviemakers are so caught up in the round-the-clock adventures on the moons of Mongo that they seem to forget about the timetable for the destruction of Earth.) The director gets right into comic-strip sensibility and pacing. Mike Hodges' work is very assured and clean; he puts the actors where they'll have the most immediate dramatic impact, and he has a flair for the constant shifts of angle in the comics. There wasn't a single slow scene that I wanted to be done with; there was always design to take in. The moviemakers might have paid more attention to tidiness; a fantasy is more satisfying if it all fits together, and this one has dangling ends. When Flash is lowered in a cage into the swamp, there's somebody with him whom he seems to know but who's a stranger to us. And when Ming orders Zarkov's dangerously active brain emptied, we watch on a small screen as his education and experiences are removed, right back to his birth. A few minutes later, Zarkov, as intellectually frenzied as ever, explains that he fended off the emptying techniques by reciting Shakespeare and the Beatles to himself. But we *saw* him emptied. Goofs like these (the result of cuts in the footage, I assume, or of changes in the script) destroy some of the childish pleasure to be had from a Pop fairy tale. And, maybe because not enough seems at stake—it isn't just that the timetable for blowing up Earth seems vague but that saving it doesn't seem such a big deal—the ending lacks punch. Happily, the actors revel in the Pop mindlessness—who wouldn't? When Ming has had Flash drugged and entombed, Princess Aura looks at the sleeping beauty and gives him his awakening kiss. When Dale Arden and Princess Aura are sore at each other, they have a pillow fight—with delicate satin pillows on a harem-sized bed. When Ming tries to win Flash over to his side, he offers him a moon of his own.

January 5, 1981

Sensory Deprivation

Sneaking out of a movie that was heavy when it needed to effervesce or one that was sluggish when it needed to be quick, I have sometimes thought, If the studios are going to put together hopelessly mismatched talents, why don't they just go all the way to lunacy? Why not Alexandro Jodorowsky and Bernard Slade? John Milius and Edward Albee? (*A Delicate Balance*, perhaps.) Sam Peckinpah and Ntozake Shange? Stanley Kubrick and Sam Shepard? (Kubrick and *anybody!*) But I never came up with a misalliance as grotesquely inspired as Ken Russell and Paddy Chayefsky. These two wildly different hyperbolic talents—Russell, with his show-biz–Catholic glitz mysticism, and Chayefsky, with his show-biz–Jewish ponderousness—collaborated (at swords' points) on *Altered States*. I wish I could say that this impossible collaboration is a weird success—that Chayefsky's turgidity is leavened by Russell's craziness. But *Altered States* isn't really enjoyable. It's a bellicose head horror movie, probably the most aggressively silly picture since *The Exorcist*, and argumentative in the worst Chayefsky manner—the dialogue is written like a series of position papers.

The picture deals with the efforts of a psycho-physiologist, Eddie Jessup (William Hurt), who has lost his belief in God, to find the source and meaning of life, by immersing himself in an isolation tank and ingesting a brew of blood and sacred mushrooms. Russell does try to free the movie from Chayefsky's blather by using it *as* blather. Eddie's rant about the religious visions of the schizophrenics that he works with is disposed of by having him come on like a hot-air artist when he first meets Emily (Blair Brown), the behavioral anthropologist whom he marries. Eddie seems to be showing off his obsession with his field to turn Emily on, and as the talk keeps going without a pause or a missed beat while they flirt, while they fornicate, and while they fight, it becomes a parody of academia. It's as if Eddie's and Emily's minds didn't know what their bodies were up to. Russell keeps Eddie and Emily and the two other principal characters—Eddie's bearded research assistant, Arthur (Bob Balaban), and Mason (Charles Haid), an endocrinologist, also bearded—whizzing through their lines, talking at the same time or addressing someone who does anything but pay attention. Sometimes you feel that Russell has ordered up staircases and platforms just so the actors can heave chunks of dialogue at each other. You appreciate that he's trying to spare you the misery of hearing the words declaimed straight. (At one point, Eddie sputters out his academic credentials and his publication record of two papers a year.) But no matter how hopped up the delivery is you can't help feeling that you're in a lecture hall and the characters should all have pointers. After Eddie and Emily have separated and she has returned from a year in Africa with their two small daughters, he comes to see her, violently agitated, and lets out a torrent of words about his latest experiments, shouting that he wants her to look at his data; she thoughtfully summarizes what he has just said and reformulates it. You don't know who's more fouled up—the people on the screen or the writer and the director.

Working with Chayefsky material, Russell at least isn't in danger of trashing real people. You don't sit, as you do at other Russell films, thinking, Does he really imagine that *this* was what Valentino (or Tchaikovsky or Liszt or Gaudier-Brzeska) was about, or what anybody's about? Russell doesn't seem to have the ability to create believable representations of human behavior; he's such an eccentric filmmaker that he has invented his own kind of film—a hectic, stilted sort of picture in which he clomps from one scene to the next. Russell's images often have great energy, so that a film of his can be like a bash. But he has never been a director for flow or seductive rhythm; his pictures are disconnected, and are probably the worst edited of any big director's. In *Altered States*, the psychedelic visions come at you like choppy slide shows. There's also a gaping discrepancy between what you see and how the characters on the screen react to it. Part of the film—the most amusing part—shows the tall, blond Eddie regressing genetically and turning into a short hairy ape-man with jagged teeth. This dirty, blood-lusting creature bursts out of the isolation tank and goes on a rampage, clobbering the night watchmen in the Harvard lab, leaping over cars, being attacked by a pack of dogs, and running to the zoo, where he socks a wild sheep, tears at it, and sates himself on its flesh. Somehow, this busy night of his doesn't even make the papers. (Is Boston *that* blasé?) Russell has his one poetic image in this sequence: in the morning, at the zoo, where the hairy primal man fell asleep, Eddie's long, smooth, white body is curled up peacefully near the sheep's bloody carcass.

The same director who can give us this fairy-tale metamorphosis can be totally flat-footed a minute later. Near the end, Eddie apparently succeeds in traveling genetically back to the beginning of life, and the force he releases is too much for the isolation tank. (His first tank, in New York, is quite pretty, and we can seen his head through a glass porthole; this second one, at Harvard, looks like a big air-conditioner.) Suddenly, there are bursts of apocalyptic light, roaring sounds, thunderclaps, and the collapsing lab is flooded, with Arthur knocked unconscious, and then Mason knocked out, too; a steaming, phosphorescent river seems to be rising, and Emily goes back in time through bubbles and brimstone to reach Eddie. The force of her love saves him from disintegration, and he fights the elements to return to *now*. The attraction of the film is in its psychedelic sound-and-light shows, and this sequence (though the effects are your basic crashes, thwacks, and splats) is the Big One. What are we to make of the subsequent scene with the characters comfortably ensconced in a quiet apartment? While Eddie sleeps it off, Emily imparts the most amazingly anti-climactic information to Mason: she tells him how much she loves Eddie. This is topped by the arrival of Arthur, who comes in complaining that it has taken him three hours to mop up the lab. (Give him four hours and he'd swab out Long Island Sound.)

Appearing in movies for the first time, the artful young stage actor William Hurt brings nuances to his revved-up mad-scientist role by acting slightly withdrawn and inhuman. His Eddie has a cool, quivering untrustworthiness. Hurt is onscreen almost all the time, and he doesn't have a calm moment. But he doesn't act a gibbering hysteric: Eddie is uptight, taut—he's never calm *inside*. Hurt holds back just enough; he makes Eddie the kind of cunning maniac who's always watching to see how people react to his mania. He's neurasthenic, charismatic, and ready to try anything. (The role is probably patterned on Dr. John Lilly, and maybe also on Dirk Bogarde's professor in the 1963 English film *The Mind Benders*.) Inside the first tank, Eddie's face is enigmatic, remote, and the play of light on the water gives him the suggestion of a furtive, private smile. He's a starry-eyed Puritan sneaking some plea-sure. Hurt has almost inconceivably sappy lines: when he isn't talking about his search for the original consciousness, he's muttering about the pain he and Emily inflict on each other or using such choice phrases as "this mean-ingless horror, life." (It's the Ingmar Bergman side of Chayefsky coming out.) Hurt is also handicapped by post-synchronization, which destroys some of the slyness and intimacy of his performance. Still, you can believe that Eddie would try to find the Truth About Life by delving into his own brain, because he has so little feeling for anything outside. He's the right Dr. Jekyll for the hallucinogenic late sixties, when the picture starts. (The hairy Hyde part is taken over by the short, agile Miguel Godreau.)

The references to Timothy Leary just make you uncomfortable, though; this is a movie without a generation. It's effective only on a crude horror-pic-ture level. Some of the scenes of partial Jekyll-and-Hyde transformations are fun—especially Eddie's nonchalance when he's in bed with a lovely young student and he sees his body spontaneously regressing to an anthropoid stage. These old tricks are good tricks. When the primal man breaks out of the air-conditioner tank, all we see at first are his two hairy arms—it's an an-cient horror-movie device (all those lids of tombs rising) and as pleasurably scary as ever, though the technique is more assaultive. While this monster hides from the watchmen and they search for him, the suspense is intensified by the blasting, dissonant music of John Corigliano, which is designed to drive you up the theatre walls. (It's the kind of music you can't easily separate from the sound effects; you may just back up against your seat.) After the primal man had popped out of the box, I thought of the missed opportuni-ties: Eddie didn't have to travel back so far so fast. If he had just taken his time, there could have been cameo roles for famous actors to pop out as his-torical figures—Eddie could have been Jack Nicholson as de Sade, Ricky Schroder as the Dauphin—any Dauphin, Paul Simon as King Tut, John Belu-shi as Nero. The film could have used a few more people. Charles Haid's lik-ably burly, gruff Mason doesn't have much to do (except, for no apparent reason, burning up a bit of Eddie's evidence of his time travels), and there doesn't seem to be anybody around to notice Eddie's charisma except Arthur, whose servitude is rather endearing. Balaban plays this eternal assistant as a happy, grungy mole, who in his one burst of excitement reveals himself to be slightly madder than his master.

Paddy Chayefsky is not the right author for a psychedelic mindblower; you expect the picture not to add up, but you expect its not adding up to have some kick, and *Altered States* has a dismal, tired humanistic ending. All along, Eddie doesn't seem to give a damn about Emily; during their first night together he has visions of Christ and crucifixions—not a promising start. It's she who proposes, coming to him with the news that she got the Harvard job, and since they'll both be there, they should get married. He assents, un-enthusiastically. The next time we see them, two kids and several years later, they're splitting, and he's off to Mexico to take part in the mushroom ritual of the Toltecs. The Indian ceremony, complete with a sinister beady-eyed priest who beckons to Eddie when it's time for his soul "to return to the first soul," is enjoyable low camp, but in Eddie's subsequent hallucination the film seems to get its own point twisted. There's a lot of fancy stuff with dwarf witch doctors prancing about and a snake coiling around Eddie's neck and strangling him. The flashing images reminded me of the surreal dream ballet that Eugene Loring staged for Fred Astaire and Lucille Bremer (in the mythical South American country of *Yolanda and the Thief*)—not one of my dream favorites. There's also a lizard, and Emily is there, naked, and the lizard changes into her—they are one. When Eddie comes out of his vision, we see that while he was tripping, he actually stomped a lizard, leaving it a bloody mess. Surely this suggests some hostile feelings toward Emily—to put it gently? But at the end it's this woman's love for him and his love for her and the children (whom he'd been totally oblivious of) that are strong enough to bring him back from the primal ooze. (Love enables him to "reconstitute" himself.) Why is it that although Eddie's trips look horrible to us, Eddie isn't at all disturbed, except, maybe, by that bloody lizard? After his night on the town of beating the watchmen and fighting off dogs and devouring the sheep, Eddie says it was the most supremely satisfying time of his life. He's exhilarated by the damnedest things. We would respond better to his sense of scientific accomplishment if there were some accompanying revulsion at what he has experienced of his genetic heritage. How could Emily's—or anyone's—love bring him back when he's so euphoric?

Emily is a drag on the movie anyway. This is no reflection on Blair Brown's talent, though about all of it she gets to exhibit here is the beautiful dimple in her lower back. The role is that of the faithful worrier, but in a less-sane-than-usual variation. After Emily has dutifully listened to Eddie's tapes and gone through his data, she knows he was the ape-monster who beat the lab watchmen (almost killing one of them), and she's terrified. So what does this young mother of two do? She phones Eddie and asks him to come over and spend the night with her. What possesses moviemakers to put in a scene like this—and then not even follow through on our fears? (They even manage to lose track of the children, so that we keep wondering where they are.) And what possesses Chayefsky to combine science fiction and the horror film and end with a humanistic sermon? When Eddie regains consciousness after he has gone all the way back to the ooze and flooding waters, he says he has the answer now. He was in the final pit—and it was nothingness. Hell, I had that vision when I was twelve years old and the dentist gave me gas; all it did was make me careful not to let anybody put me in an altered state again. How can you have a sci-fi movie that says, "Let's explore what's beyond," and then comes up with nothingness, particularly after the film has had its hero pulled out of his tank trickling blood from his mouth and explaining that it's from a goat he was eating "back then"? We put up with all the guff about the genetic trail back to the primal unity because we want an entertaining fantasy, and then Paddy Chayefsky gives us the lesson he thinks is good for us: Stay home and love your wife and kids. Consciousness-altering is Chayefsky's metaphor for selfishness—Eddie thought he was growing when he was really shrinking, when he was isolating himself from everyone. People go to the movie for mushroom-head trips, and Chayefsky poisons them with his homiletic profundities. He should have gone into dentistry.

·　　·　　·　　·　　·

*H*eidi (Amy Irving) and Paul (Richard Dreyfuss) are two of six finalists in an international piano competition being held in San Francisco. When they fall in love, will Heidi, who is rich, sure of herself, and only twenty-one, throw the contest to Paul, who is poor, distraught because of the financial strain he has caused his dying father, and almost thirty? And if Heidi doesn't, and she wins, will she lose Paul? The reason that *The Competition*, directed by Joel Oliansky, from his own screenplay (based on a story he conceived with the producer, William Sackheim), may sound like a segment of a daytime soap opera is that it is set up in terms of the problem it raises: Can a man love a woman who has a greater talent than his (in his own field)? The four other contestants—a young girl from the Soviet Union who has a nervous collapse when her coach defects, a suave black expatriate, a robotic prune with a little mustache and no personality, and a Bronx-Italian hustler who tries to attract the attention of the press by pretending that he has climbed up from the ghetto streets—are used to pad out Heidi's and Paul's romantic problem to feature length. With a little more padding, the movie could have been a TV mini-series, allowing a separate episode to each competitor. There is nothing in the way these young pianists are conceived that goes beyond TV differentiation. The older figures, such as Paul's frozen-faced mother, who accuses him of wrecking his father's health, and the angry, screeching mother of the Bronx boy, behave strictly "in character." They're no longer human beings—they're just parents.

Still, there's a certain amount of gimmicky vitality in the problem material, which is carefully loaded so that Heidi has everything going for her and Paul has everything going against him. And cultural values—such as the ones to be found in the struggles of two piano prodigies—generally give a movie an extra dimension of high-strung hamminess. But Oliansky's epigrams about art and life don't have the succulence to be first-class howlers, in the grand manner of *Specter of the Rose*; they're stunted, pathetic little howlers, and Lee Remick, who, as Heidi's famous teacher (a sort of Wasp Rosina Lhévinne), has to deliver most of these nuggets, grits her teeth on them, and stares so blindly that she seems to be in shock. Straight-backed and tense, Lee Remick is all wired up to give a performance, and, with nobody to play against, she comes out sounding incomprehensibly weird. Describing the competition medal to Heidi, she says, "It will turn your tits a lovely shade of puce." It's no wonder that before she hurls a line into the void she plants her feet firmly, like a kid about to recite "The boy stood on the burning deck."

Between them, Amy Irving and Richard Dreyfuss have acquired enough bad acting habits for a different kind of competition. Amy Irving's voice suggests that she's in a thick muggy haze, and she drawls affectedly, as if she enjoyed slopping the words around in her mouth before parting with them. Just a few years ago, she expressed emotion very simply; now her great almond eyes implore us to watch her, and she's got a bad case of the tremblies—her lower lip has a suffering life of its own. At the competition finals, when she mimes the physical excitement of a pianist performing a showy Prokofiev concerto, all her force seems concentrated, and she looks as if she actually could produce the music we hear. But when she tries to be quaveringly sincere she comes across as a princessy witch. Dreyfuss is limply self-conscious, and he has lost any semblance of spontaneity. He scrunches up his face, claps his hand to the back of his neck, and turns away; he chokes back tears and breathes so heavily that his mouth puckers and his nostrils flare. He never eases up: it's all twinges of agony and indecision. Trying to act a sensitive musician under a terrible strain, he comes across as a throbbing, shuddering wreck. (Has he been deliberately made sallow—grief and humility in the skin tone?) Dreyfuss has been prominent in movies only since 1973, yet every single thing he does is a familiar mannerism. And Amy Irving is so determined to be feminine and sweet that there's something squishy about her. What a pair of counterfeit lovers—each listens to the sound of his own endearments and gives himself an ovation.

As the silver-haired maestro of the symphony orchestra that performs with the finalists, Sam Wanamaker tucks the picture in his vest pocket and struts away with it. Generally, Wanamaker appears in emotional roles and chews the scenery ravenously; this time he gives a polished old pro's performance. He plays the eminent, temperamental conductor as a vain man who holds his head so that the public can get the benefit of his strong-chinned, handsome profile; he's an arrogant lecher who's still a world-class musician and a reasonably decent fellow. There's an element of satire in his looking so much like Leonard Bernstein, but the satire goes deeper than that: Wanamaker shows up Amy Irving and Richard Dreyfuss by not tearing himself apart in anguish over whether we'll like him.

The moviemakers must have been desperate for suspense: as each of the six performs his sonata or concerto, the camera hovers so close to the keyboard that we begin to fear for the musician and to expect some horrible, disqualifying booboo. Six red herrings in a row. And what of the problem that has been so carefully set up: Could the impoverished Paul be happy tagging along with a well-heeled woman who is a greater pianist and has an assured future of concert bookings? It turns out that Paul's fear that he might become miserable and impotent was just a momentary, needless anxiety that was unworthy of him. Perish the aberrant thought.

January 19, 1981

Victims

*I*n Thomas Hardy's novels, an action or an object or an element in the landscape will suddenly be charged with almost unbearable dramatic tension. These moments, with their mixture of the painful and the beautiful which essayists refer to as Hardy's plangency, don't seem to be structured. They don't arrive like the prepared climaxes of plays; they appear to just happen. Virginia Woolf wrote that with a "quickening of power which we cannot foretell, nor he, it seems, control, a single scene breaks off from the rest." And we respond to this scene "as if it existed alone and for all time." Of course, we feel that way because it's a perfect fusion of the intuitive and the planned. The scene has the quality of inevitability which makes its arrival an impeccable surprise. Hardy's fated coincidences come at exactly the moment when they're most needed.

The looseness of Hardy's novels, the way emotions flare up, and the headlong force of his characters suggest that he should be one of the most adaptable to the screen of all major novelists, and D. W. Griffith swiped from Hardy as freely as he swiped from Dickens. But while Dickens has often been successfully adapted to the screen, Hardy never has been. (The closest to the spirit of his work that anyone has ever got is probably Griffith's steal from *Tess of the D'Urbervilles* in *Way Down East* when Lillian Gish, who has been seduced by a rake, cradles her dead baby in her arms.) Dickens can be dramatized by reproducing the labyrinthine plots and the knobby characters, with their distinctive modes of addressing each other. Hardy's plots are simple, and his dialogue is mostly just functional. His characters live for us because of their turbulent thoughts and feelings, and because of the irrational power of sex (and sexual aversion) to blast their hopes and tie their lives in knots. And because they live in a universe that seems to be in a diabolical conspiracy against them. In short, because of their inner conflicts—just what movies have the most difficulty with.

For a reader, the shock of *Tess of the D'Urbervilles*, which was published in 1891, is in its refusal to let Tess be simply a woman at the mercy of men, society, and nature: she's also at the mercy of her own passions, her pride, and her sense of shame. She's a strong character—strong enough to fight against the ingrained conviction of the Englishmen of her day that a girl who had been seduced was forever defiled, that she had lost the purity necessary for marriage. The new Roman Polanski film *Tess* was made in English, and though it was shot in France, it simulates the Wessex of the novel well enough to fool Americans (and maybe even the British). Polanski treats the novel with the utmost fidelity and respect (much of the dialogue is verbatim), the movie is authentically detailed—and there is virtually nothing of Hardy in it. (I mean, of course, nothing of *my* Hardy; the film may be an accurate representation of Polanski's Hardy, and perhaps of some other people's.) In the movie, Tess (Nastassia Kinski) is strictly a victim of men and social conventions. The film takes a sympathetic, feminist position toward her—sympathetic, I think, in a narrow and demeaning sense. Because if what happens to Tess is all the fault of men, she is reduced as a character. This Tess isn't a protagonist; she is merely a hapless, frail creature, buffeted by circumstances. Hardy wasn't beating his breast, proclaiming how guilty men were for the fate of women (he saw the characters in the round). The movie is a sustained feat of male breast-beating, a costume version of *An Unmarried Woman*—only it goes back to *An Unmarried Mother*.

Tess is textured and smooth and even, with lateral compositions subtly flowing into each other. The sequences are beautifully structured, and the craftsmanship is hypnotic. You don't want to leave, but you're watching nothing. Those quickening moments that, when you're reading the book, may make you feel that your heart will stop pass by without a ripple; the movie just keeps going, quietly, steadily. There's a visual passion in Hardy when he describes the countryside. The earth turns and you can feel the terror that every living creature is subject to. Polanski's tastefully cropped compositions and unvaried pacing make nature proper. The picture is tame, it's artistic—a series of leisurely Barbizon School landscapes. In Hardy, when the characters blurt out more than they should or some chance incident causes them to do something unaccountably wrongheaded, you can feel the danger building, and you're shaken by it. There's no danger in this picture; it's serene.

Nastassia Kinski, who was seventeen when the movie was shot, is a lovely child-woman, and she gives a delicate, meticulous performance. She doesn't do anything jarring; she may even be a little too sensitive—she's far from a robust English country girl. English is not her native language; she manages something close (I assume) to the correct West Country sounds, but in a small, uninflected schoolgirl voice. And her mouth is not the mouth of someone who grew up speaking English; she has a spooky resemblance to the young Ingrid Bergman, and her mouth forms words in a similar foreign way. Bergman, though, had her deep, emotionally expressive voice, right from the start. Kinski is a doll-like, *jeune fille* Bergman, a soft gamine. This Tess never grows up; when she's a rich man's fancy woman, she's still a child. It's a problem similar to the one that Sissy Spacek (who is in her thirties) had in *Coal Miner's Daughter*. Spacek's shy, naughty smiles were enchanting when she was supposed to be a thirteen-year-old, but when she was supposed to be a grown woman she looked like a kid dressed up in her mother's clothes and wig. Kinski isn't rooted in the earth of any country; she's a hothouse flower—a fairy-tale waif, with puffy, slightly parted lips as an emblem of the carnal world. And, as sometimes happens when an actress speaks in a language that isn't her own, her body doesn't express what her words say; this makes her seem withdrawn, passive, even a trace bovine—which could also be appealing to modern audiences.

Nastassia Kinski's Tess is so pure a sufferer that men who might take a poke at their wives without remorse can get teary-eyed about her. Her immaturity fits Polanski's romantic view of victimization. The story hasn't been dramatized (it's far less dramatic than the book)—it has been orchestrated. The two men in Tess's life—Alec (Leigh Lawson), who "takes advantage" of her, and Angel Clare (Peter Firth), the parson's son, who cannot forgive her for having been taken advantage of—are very well played, but their individual scenes blur. Everything is subdued, blended. I remember discussions with school friends about these two men—talking about Tess's physical anger at poor Alec, talking about the priggish, snobby Angel. The movie is so refined that these men don't have clear enough features for them to be argued about. They are merely the men who do Tess wrong and can never make up for it, though each, in his own way, tries. The early scene in which Parson Tringham (Tony Church) explains to Jack Durbeyfield (John Collin) that he is really Sir John D'Urberville has the boisterousness and anger and all those complicated mixed emotions that the picture loses whenever sweet, languishing Tess is the focal point. The marginal characters—the drunken Durbeyfield especially—are more alive than the central ones. It's a remarkably fine cast; Dairyman Crick and the dairymaids are wonderful. It's Nastassia Kinski, beautiful as she is, and affecting, too, who has the least energy and the least strength.

Hardy's account is raw and sexual; Polanski's movie is lush, ripe, settled. When you watch sweet Nastassia, you almost forget that Tess is a killer—in more than one sense, and including the literal one. Tess kills the man who took her virginity—not because he's a bad fellow (he has never meant her any harm, and he has been supporting her and her mother and brothers and sisters) but because she doesn't love him and she does love someone else. She kills him self-righteously, and the movie makes us feel that she's a tender, innocent, wronged creature. Reading Hardy, you see Tess's indomitability in a complex, frightening light. You can't help being upset by the novel; it's all morally open for you to puzzle over. And you can't help being appalled by the irrational acts committed in the name of love. But Polanski, who has been such a wizard at perversity, and whose specialty was characters in a double bind, goes soft. He doesn't show us Tess's furious, vengeful act—stabbing the man who penetrated her. The next scenes drift right past it without the emotional ante being raised. Polanski's *Tess* is Hardy's *Tess of the D'Urbervilles* under sedation. The film has a penitential attitude toward the suffering that men inflict on women. This *Tess* becomes a tribute to women's dear weakness.

·　　·　　·　　·　　·

A new epic film by Kurosawa is an international event, especially when it's the only film he has made in Japan in ten years, after he had just about given up hope of ever working there again. On top of that, many people consider the film—*Kagemusha* (*The Shadow Warrior*)—a masterpiece, and so I haven't been surprised to receive calls and letters asking why I hadn't reviewed it yet. The answer is, Because I didn't much like it. I thought it mechanistic yet baffling, and I shoved it to the back of my mind. On the surface, *Kagemusha*, which is set during the wars of the clans in sixteenth-century Japan (the period just before the country was unified), seems to be about the ruler's responsibility for the survival of the clan, about the foolishness of rulers who provoke unnecessary battles, and possibly also about the nobility and grace of the samurai who sacrifice their lives for the clan. That is, it seems to be about essentially the same subjects that John Ford treated in Westerns, such as *Fort Apache* (1948), and that other American directors have taken up in military epics, such as *The Charge of the Light Brigade* (1936). But the film is distanced, and Kurosawa doesn't appear to be much interested in the leaders as characters. *Kagemusha* is something of a contradiction: a movie about immobility.

At the opening, a static triptych composition (like a three-panel Japanese screen) is held for about five minutes. Sitting on a platform in the center panel is the head of the Takeda clan, the warlord Shingen, known as The Mountain; his younger brother (who has sometimes "doubled" for him) sits slightly lower on one side; and on the other, sitting farther down, is a thieving peasant who has been condemned to death but whose life will be spared because he looks so much like Shingen that he can be useful as a new double. It's a formal, slightly wacko scene: a conversation among three seated men who look identical and are identically bearded and robed. (The scene is so stiff that at first I thought all three must be the same actor, but though Shingen and the thief are both played by Tatsuya Nakadai, the brother is played by Tsutomu Yamazaki.) Shortly after this, Shingen, who is the most powerful of three warlords fighting for control of the country and has almost achieved his goal, is mortally wounded, at night, by a sniper. Before dying, Shingen orders the leaders of the Takeda clan to conceal his death for three years, so that the clan won't fall apart and be open to attack.

We're primed for the look-alike peasant to develop will and inner strength as he takes the warlord's place, but we're let down. The thief is more heated in the first scene, when he challenges Shingen's morality—suggesting that Shingen is simply a bigger thief—than he ever is again. Having set up this promising *Prisoner of Zenda* bit of hokum, Kurosawa doesn't show us the transformation of the ignorant, mangy thief into a leader, except in a very special sense. Shingen's effectiveness as a ruler appears to have depended almost completely upon his mountainlike immovability. When a castle belonging to the clan has been attacked and the clan must do battle, the shadow warrior doesn't lead the soldiers; he sits on a campstool on a hill overlooking the battlefield. (He could be a movie director, except that he's wearing the helmet of a war god—a huge winged helmet that's like a great metal butterfly.) The soldiers can look up and see him sitting perfectly still; this is supposed to give his men courage and demoralize the enemy. (And it works: an enemy general, seeing him there in all his majesty, sounds retreat. Ah, yes, we say, the illusion of power defeats the enemy. But do we believe it? It's a schoolmaster's fable.) We are told that sitting still is the most difficult thing to do. But it doesn't look so hard to us—and the idea that impassivity is what made Shingen a great ruler seems a little folksy. Shingen's brother talks about the torture—the inner pain—of playing a double and giving up one's identity. But the shadow warrior doesn't show much in the way of inner conflict. He lives secluded in Shingen's stronghold, surrounded by vassals and servants who know his true identity, and, apart from the relationship he forms with Shingen's small grandson (they play together), he's alone, idling away the three years.

In *Kagemusha*, as long as people don't make any moves they're in great shape, but as soon as they budge they bring chaos down on themselves. The static opening triptych is followed by a startling kinetic sequence: the camera sweeps along with the running figure of a messenger, who rushes down a mountain, hopping lightly in a zigzag over the bodies of hundreds of exhausted, resting soldiers, and causing a stir behind him as he passes. The film veers between immobility and danger. Shingen was wounded because he left his protected position to hear a flute song, and, near the end of the third year, the shadow warrior is exposed as an impostor when he tries to ride Shingen's horse and is thrown. And when Shingen's son, who has been passed over in the line of succession, leaves his own terrain and goes to fight on enemy soil, he brings on the destruction of the three echelons of the Takeda army. ("The mountain has moved," the enemy leader says gleefully, as he prepares to pounce.)

Is Kurosawa suggesting that all rulers are shadow warriors—that their power is in the appearance of implacable strength? Seventy when he made this film, Kurosawa had been boycotted by the Japanese production companies—because of his independence or because of his irresponsibility, depending on whom you ask—and he had lost years in failed efforts to raise money for two previous projects. During four years of trying to get financing for *Kagemusha*, he made hundreds of drawings and gouaches of the costumes and action, "to leave something behind of my ideas." Then Francis Ford Coppola and George Lucas persuaded Twentieth Century-Fox to put up one and a half million dollars for world distribution rights outside Japan, and the Toho Company agreed to back the film (which, at a cost of six and a half million dollars, is the most expensive picture ever made in Japan). All this bears a relation to the detached tone of the film, which appears to be a parable about not getting involved Maybe the reason it doesn't have a clear narrative line is that the incidents are meant to represent a theory of history—the alternation of peace and war, seen as a natural process (and so, hopeless). Kurosawa seems to be saying that you're safe as long as you sit tight, but sooner or later you're impelled to do something rash. You stick your head up and it's cut off. He seems to be saying that wisdom dictates caution, security, stasis, but to be alive is to be subject to impulse, to chaos. The only enduring stillness is the stillness of death. Warfare is treated dispassionately; the pomp and pageantry are cheerless. There's a touch of Bresson in this film; Bresson has always been seventy.

The modernity of Kurosawa's earlier samurai films (especially *The Seven Samurai*) was in their pulse and jagged immediacy. The shocks were never trivial; when we were plunged under the horses' hooves we weren't outraged—the violence had something to do with the brute importance of life. This film has no reminders of that kind of barbaric power. The style is ceremonial rather than dramatic; it's not battle that Kurosawa is interested in here but formations in battle regalia. It's the flags, the swords, the sun—and the horses. This film is about mobilization for war and war's aftermath; the absence of the battles themselves seems part of the film's pattern. In a recent interview in the *Times*, Kurosawa said, "I am more relaxed and move more slowly, and this is reflected in my technique. I set up the camera, step back, and watch the action flow by." The action doesn't exactly flow by, though. I'm not sure how much of what goes on in *Kagemusha* is related to a change in Kurosawa's perception and how much is unintentional. The film doesn't seem contemplative—just uninvolving and spiritless. The narrative line is woozy, and the big showpiece sequences, such as the runner leaping—almost flying—over the soldiers' bodies, don't appear to grow out of the narrative; the narrative appears to be shaped to encompass the showpieces. There are some engrossing scenes: the sniper trying to prove he hit Shingen by reënacting how he did it (he shot through a triangular opening in the wall, and by means of triangular calculation); the shadow warrior looking into a giant urn and seeing the mummified Shingen in full armor staring back at him. And there are bizarre scenes, such as the one with a few men on a lake in a tiny rowboat, with this giant urn covered in blue cloth; it's the biggest urn you've ever seen, but onlookers supposedly aren't going to guess there's a body inside. (It's like the setup for a Laurel & Hardy routine: how are the men going to pitch the urn overboard without tipping the boat?)

Probably, Kurosawa doesn't want us to be concerned about the fortunes of the Takeda clan. The hothead son who brings the clan to ruin is treated as a fact of nature, and when the soldiers lie dead on the shores of a reddening river we don't seem to be meant to feel any rage at his suicidal folly. And since we have no strong feelings about any individual Takeda warriors, we have no reason to care who wins the climactic battle. Yet this Battle of Naga-shino is the symbolic end of the elegant rituals of samurai warfare. When the Takeda armies—the lancers with the heraldic reds that signify fire, the infan-try with the greens that signify the forest, and the cavalry with the blacks that signify wind—go forth in battle array, we don't see swordsmanship, we hear gunfire. These armored knights are easily and efficiently mowed down. This was the historical event that started Kurosawa on the film: the late-sixteenth-century battle in which on one side no one died, while the other side was wiped out. Even if you take a very long view of history, it is a battle with a special horror. But we aren't made to feel that horror. In this movie, Ku-rosawa sees war as part of the turmoil of life, and he asks us simply to ob-serve what he shows us. Perhaps he thinks that this way the horror will reach us at a deeper level. But he's also in love with the aesthetics of warfare—he's a schoolboy setting up armies of perfect little soldiers and smiling at the pat-terns he has devised. These two sets of feelings may have neutralized *Kage-musha*—put it at a remove and made it somewhat abstract.

Visually, the movie is without depth or shading, and often the composi-tions seem cramped; possibly the chalky, off-key look was by choice, but, if so, I'm not sure what dictated it. This is Kurosawa's first period film in color, and he has used color in an eerily unrealistic, painterly way. Soldiers march in psychedelic orange light. When Shingen returns to his shadow in a dream, the imagery suggests the work of twentieth-century painters: it's visionary and smeary—Kokoschka or Nolde, flattened out on a Sony TV. When the clans prepare for battle, we get a splendid fashion show of sixteenth-century fabrics and uniforms and armor; there are visual reminders of Kurosawa's *Throne of Blood*, and mounted soldiers out of Piero della Francesca. With all the cos-tumed marching men and the horses and the banners and standards, the film has pomp and flourishes. But the grandeur is undercut by melancholy. Noth-ing heartening is meant to come of these military parades. There are magical, misty shots looking out of a castle onto fogged-over mountains and water, and at one point Shingen's spirit takes the form of a rainbow-like bar of light. There are lots of flat vertical compositions full of people going up to the top of the frame so that they form a mountain-triangle; in other scenes, soldiers slide down hills. In one virtuoso formal shot, the empty frame is filled by cir-cling soldiers—for all we know, they could be lining up for a high-school-commencement photograph. It's not just that we might be watching from another planet that gets to be wearing; it's that even the most conceptually daring scenes lack internal excitement—they feel static. They even look static; the intricately designed fabrics have more life than the geometric composi-tions. A good score might have helped to give the sequences some tension, but the Western-style music is emotional in a vacuous, slurry way; it gets be-tween you and the movie—rubs you wrong. (This is a recurrent problem with Japanese movies. Remember the *Rashomon* music that sounded like Ravel's "Bolero"?) The dialogue scenes, which are largely exposition, are frequently played in a fixed frame—a vise, like a stage—and some of the acting in them is really bad. There's a likable grizzled old lord—the Fire General, who wears flame-colored kimonos—but the younger and skinnier the lords are, the more they seem to resort to eye-rolling and arm-waving.

The film is fixated on mountains, triangles, threesies. Shingen's garden has a pyramid hill; the shadow warrior has three guards hidden behind a sliding wall. There are three bumpkin enemy spies who keep turning up and tumbling over themselves, like John Ford's lovable Irishmen; they're trying to find out if Shingen is really still alive or is being impersonated. And there are even three tests that confront the shadow warrior when he first takes over for Shingen: with Shingen's grandson, with Shingen's concubines, with Shingen's horse. The first he passes, the second he avoids, the third he avoids until he becomes emboldened by his success at demoralizing the enemy, and the animal proves his downfall. Shingen's horse cannot be taken in by a look-alike. The movie seems to shift into a different dimension whenever there are horses in the images. After battle, the men die like puppets; it's the horses who suffer. (They suffer so convincingly that I was distracted by the question of how these effects were obtained.) When the Takeda clan is smashed, wounded horses are lying in the mud. A few struggle to get up (in slow motion), arching their long necks in agony and falling again; one of them is on its back, kicking the air in the effort to right itself; another strains against the bit—a detail out of *Guernica*. The horses are the film's visual emblems of kinesis, war, chaos. In a way, it's as if only the horses could die, because only the horses were fully alive—the horses and the shadow warrior.

Kagemusha is a mixture of formality, impenetrability, and disfiguring sentimentality. The central character is pathetic, and Kurosawa seems to embrace his pathos. After the shadow warrior has been thrown from the horse and is exposed, his humility knows no bounds. Inexplicably, Shingen's brother and the other lords of the clan, who appreciate the service he has done them, won't let him say goodbye to the child he has come to love; men of the clan pelt him with mud and rocks, and he is driven out into the rain in thin rags. He isn't resentful: he feels he failed them all. From then on, the movie is like a feudal *Stella Dallas*, with the heartbroken peasant standing in the crowd at Shingen's official funeral and staring from behind a bamboo fence at the child he loves. Loyal to the clan forever, he follows the Takeda warriors when the disinherited son's reckless actions force them into battle. When they fight, he's there wandering around the battlefield, hiding in tall grass, looking on, wanting to be one of them. He has aged (fast), but, even frail and doddering, he needs to prove his bravery. When the Takeda soldiers are slaughtered, he goes among the corpses and picks up a lance, and is shot by the enemy. But he keeps going, walking into the river. The drowned soldiers have let fall the Takeda battle flag; he sees it and tries to retrieve it. The powerful Takeda clan has been annihilated, and he dies reaching for the clan's flag, which floats by him, eluding him forever. There's a pukey warmth in the film's attitude toward this eternal humble victim, and his is the only courage that is celebrated. We aren't meant to care about any of the other characters; they're essentially figures in a design. But we're expected to empathize with the shadow warrior—he's that old crock the common man.

February 2, 1981

Abel Gance

*A*bel Gance's art is the art of frenzy, tumult, climax. He dashes toward melodramatic peaks and goes over the top. The result is overwhelmingly literary, highfalutin, romantic, and foolish. His corn is purple—and it makes you gasp with pleasure because he achieves his effects by the most innovative means. He's like an avant-garde De Mille. Gance has a nineteenth-century theatrical sensibility, but he's also obsessed with the most avant-garde film techniques, and he uses these advanced methods to overpower you emotionally. When he succeeds, you're conscious of the humor of your situation—you applaud, you cheer, because the exhilaration of his technique freshens the stale, trashy ideas, gives them a grand lunacy.

In Gance's greatest film, *Napoléon*, which had its première at the Paris Opéra in 1927, and was presented at Radio City Music Hall in a reconstructed version at the end of January and the beginning of February, Napoleon (Albert Dieudonné) is a Man of Destiny. Before that, when he's still a boy (Vladimir Roudenko), he's a Boy of Destiny. In the opening section, a fortress-like military school is in the distance, while in the foreground the courageous twelve-year-old Napoleon commands his outnumbered troops in a snowball fight. The camera seems to encompass miles of landscape, yet there's so much activity within the shots, and the movement of the boys is so quick and darting and funny, that the effect is of your eyes clearing—of everything becoming bright. Gance cuts from the long shots to closeups, and adds superimpositions, and then the cutting becomes fast and rhythmic, with Napoleon's face flashing by in one frame of every four, and you realize that the principal purpose of this jazzy blinking is to give you a feeling for speed and movement—and for the possibilities of the medium. Gance doesn't dawdle; he starts off with pinwheels, sparks, madness.

Back in 1927, a lot of people must have got off the carrousel right there, saying, "It spins too fast, it makes me dizzy—and it's stupid." And maybe when Francis Ford Coppola, who served as impresario for the New York showings, opens the film more widely, some new people will. Years ago, when I was managing theatres, each time I ran an Abel Gance picture there were intelligent, highly educated people who would patiently explain to me how freakishly moldy the ideas were. I would impatiently respond that they weren't allowing themselves the goofy rapture they might feel if they could just give over for a little while. I said that Gance's technique transcended his ideas—that there was a fever in his work which came out of love of the medium itself, and that this love was the real subject of his movies. (I didn't convince anybody.) The problem for these people wasn't that Gance was avant-garde—it was that he was avant-garde and old-fashioned. This is a mixture that some moviegoers just can't swallow.

Napoléon was originally made as a six-hour silent film, in color (the prints were tinted and toned by a dye process), and with sections designed to be run on a triple-width screen, by a process called Polyvision. Gance intended this work—thought to have been twenty-six or twenty-eight reels—to be shown in two-hour chunks on three successive nights. But even at the 1927 Paris opening (under the title *Napoléon vu par Abel Gance*) it was, instead, abridged and run in one night. The six-hour original played briefly, on a three-night basis, in eight European cities; then the film was chopped down into so many different versions (some of them reëdited by Gance himself) that it took the English filmmaker and film historian Kevin Brownlow years to assemble this new, relatively complete version. He estimates that twenty to forty minutes of footage are still missing; and a subplot of about fifteen minutes has been cut for the new American opening. At Radio City, where the film was run at twenty-four frames per second (it was originally run at approximately twenty frames per second), it lasted about four hours. (There's a simulation of the original color for an instant at the very end.) Gance actually intended his six-hour movie, which ends with the young Napoleon leading his army in Italy, to be just the first (*Première Époque: Bonaparte*) in a cycle of six Napoleonic films.

*T*he opening "Youth of Napoleon" section includes the revenge of Napoleon's enemies—the boys who have lost the fight in the snow. The subtitles tell us that both the masters and the pupils feel an antipathy to this proud, fierce child, and that his only consolation is his pet eagle; after the fight his enemies let the eagle out of its cage, and the bird flies into the night. Not knowing which boys are responsible, Napoleon goes from bed to bed, systematically challenging every one of them; he takes on the whole dormitory.

The brawl turns into a pillow fight (the ancestor of the celebrated lyric, feathery sequence in Vigo's *Zero for Conduct*), and as he fights them all and the feathers start to fly the screen divides into four separate shots, then into six, then into nine. And with all nine images in motion the screen becomes a fantasia of boys, pillows, feathers. There's so much movement that the separate images dissolve in the whirling mass. The fight is broken up by the masters, who punish only Napoleon, sending him to spend the night outdoors; he has fought with honor, though, and as he huddles alone in the cold his eagle returns to him. The audience applauds the gaudy, romantic inevitability of the bird's return. (The eagle will be Napoleon's totem throughout the picture.) This early section has a charm that is reminiscent of Mack Sennett and Chaplin, and even the small touches are likable. During the snow fight, a scullion who admires Napoleon's courage warns him that his enemies are putting rocks in their snowballs. After the pillow fight, a stinky little boy (one of the two who let the eagle out) lies snug in his bed; he snores, and a bit of down puffs out of his mouth.

*G*ance works directly on our senses. When images that are no more than a few frames long are intercut repeatedly in a fixed pattern, there's a flickering, blinding effect, like a strobe. And when he divides the screen into multiple images, so that we see seething forms, he's obviously trying to affect us at a subconscious level. I think Gance always meant to be a prophet showing mankind the Way, but he's a prophet only in terms of movie techniques. As a thinker, he is essentially a fantasist, a mythmaker enslaved by his own schoolboy gush.

It's amusing to see the boy Napoleon treated as a Genius, but in the next sections—Napoleon and the French Revolution, and then the Italian Campaign—when the young man Napoleon is treated as the embodiment of the French Revolution, you know you're in the grip of a crazy. There are certain subjects that pose special hazards for great moviemakers, and they are just the ones that attract them the most: the Promethean conquerors, the mad kings, the Men of Destiny, the visionaries. The imaginative moviemaker knows that there are no limits to what is possible in the movie medium, and belief in his own omnipotence rises in him like sap. Imperial moviemakers can't settle for less than the imperial subjects that have no clearly defined limits. (It's no accident that Welles wanted to do *Heart of Darkness* or that Kubrick wanted to do a *Napoleon*.) The trap of these subjects is not merely that they grow to excessive length, that they become misshapen, or are unfinished because funds run out, or that they get mutilated, but that the moviemaker, who begins with a sense of holy mission, winds up not knowing what he meant to say, and the scale of his epic makes the utopian humanistic message he settles for look puny. There's an incoherence that seems almost integral to visionary epics: the bravura techniques have everything to do with exploring the medium, but they have nothing to do with the filmmaker's "statement" about pacifism or revolution or tolerance or a world nation. There's a kind of Pyrrhic poetry about Coppola's having put up more than a quarter of a million dollars to reopen this film in Radio City Music Hall, and with his father, Carmine Coppola, in the pit, conducting the sixty-piece American Symphony Orchestra. Back around 1920, it was D. W. Griffith who arranged for the American opening of Gance's 1919 film *J'Accuse*.

Gance's life has been a tragedy of waste. When *Napoléon* opened, he was only in his mid-thirties, and he has spent the rest of his life (he is ninety-one now) mainly on commercial subjects and unfulfilled grand projects. This cannot be completely blamed on tightfisted, shortsighted businessmen. The fact is that most of Gance's epic ideas reek of nineteenth-century grandiloquence. He isn't rounded (as, say, Renoir was). His films are superb in glimpses or in sequences, but they're not unified by simple emotion, as Griffith's epics were. They're held together by obsession, by fervor. When Gance tries for simple, ordinary feelings, he's usually at his worst. It isn't that he treats the simple moments as filler and pays little attention to them but that he makes something kitschy and embarrassing of them. He layers them with obvious ironies, whole-hog patriotism, facetiousness. For him, common experience is comic relief. In *Napoléon*, during the Terror two government clerks try to save people they like from the guillotine by chewing and swallowing their dossiers, but one of them keeps gagging. Josephine's son (about twelve) sits in a room where Napoleon is courting his mother, and the kid enjoys every minute of it. (That'll be the day!) When Napoleon marries Josephine, the wedding ceremony is comically brief. (Napoleon is a man in a hurry.)

What Gance offers us is not merely a Napoleon without politics; his is a divine Napoleon. Gance's Man of Destiny has a mesmeric gaze. When Napoleon meets with any opposition, Dieudonné's eyes light up like the eyes of the kids in *Village of the Damned*. The power of Napoleon's gaze was famous, but this is a horror-film comedy routine. When he turns his piercing stare on them, rioting crowds back away, and even unruly generals do his bidding. Others don't need to be glared at: characters such as Fleuri (Nicolas Koline), the admiring scullion who later becomes an innkeeper, and his daughter, Violine (the lovely, teen-age Annabella), turn up from time to time, so they can symbolize the good common people and worship Napoleon from afar.

There is no doubt that Gance takes a mystical view of his hero. When Napoleon attacks the British, and the messy battle goes on for seventy-two hours and ends in hand-to-hand combat in rain and mud, a subtitle announces: "He is in the thick of fire. He is in his element." (Some of the night fighting scenes were originally in blue, others in red.) Everything is explained by "fate." Before Napoleon and Josephine have met, he is a young officer in the street outside a fortune-teller's shop, while she is inside being told that she will be a queen. Gance is shameless: everything is foretold, ordained, or revealed in a hideous presentiment. It's clear that Gance conceived of his huge cycle of films as a glorification of Genius. His hyperbolic romanticism knows no bounds: in one scene Napoleon stands alone on a peak overlooking the ocean, and a subtitle tells us that Ocean is his friend and they meet as equals. When Gance tries to "humanize" this hero, he shows him embarrassed and fumbling in his courtship of Josephine. We come away from a Griffith epic, such as *Intolerance*, or even *Orphans of the Storm* (which is also set in the French Revolution), with a feeling for the characters, and a sense of pleasure in the whole story, and memories of small, surprising moments. We come away from *Napoléon* exulting in Gance's extraordinary inventiveness and spirit. In the same sense that his Napoleon is the Revolution, Gance is the film we have been watching.

*H*e can be a great show. When Napoleon is in Corsica, with a price on his head, he takes down the French flag, which he believes the Corsicans are unworthy of; he jumps from a building onto a horse and, clutching the flag, rides away to escape a large group of horsemen pursuing him. Suddenly we're in a Western chase, but in this Western the camera is more interested in the movement of the horses' legs than in the possibility that the posse might catch up to the hero. (For some of the inserts, Gance strapped the camera to the back of a horse.) Pursued all the way to the sea, Napoleon hops into a dinghy and unfurls the tricolor for a sail. It's a piece of flamboyance that makes one laugh and applaud. What follows is even higher on the hog: A sirocco comes up, and the little boat is flung about in the splashing waves—and we're flung about, too. Gance built an underwater camera, which, he said, he placed at the level of the waves, so the image would not be "that seen by a person looking at the waves, but rather that of one wave seen by another." This storm at sea is intercut with the political storm at the National Convention in Paris, with Danton orating and Robespierre crushing the Girondists. In order to produce a parallel sense of vertigo from the waves of the surging crowd, Gance mounted the camera on a pendulum, which swung over the extras' heads. It's a freak sequence: a forced metaphorical connection between two phenomena, and an essentially verbal metaphor besides. It's obvious and hokey, yet the effect is smashingly modern, with the swaying camera whipping us right into the movement of the crowd, and back and forth, in ever quicker shots. And then the two storms are superimposed. What we admire is, of course, Gance's zingy virtuosity.

In the first Gance picture I ever saw, his 1936 sound film *Un Grand Amour de Beethoven*, released here as *The Life and Loves of Beethoven*, the sequence of Beethoven going deaf was invested with so much passion that it was almost painful. Beethoven (the magnificent, plug-ugly Harry Baur) couldn't understand what was happening to him. Charging outside, with his big blunt face stricken, he could see the bells ringing, see the blacksmith at work, see the noisy washerwomen. But he couldn't hear anything—and we shared the silence with him. Then we heard a sudden pealing of bells, and all the other sounds that he was henceforth denied. The sequence was so emotionally devastating that when he swung a clenched fist at the camera as he died, his anger seemed completely just. Gance's 1922 *La Roue* has a comparable passage about the onset of its railwayman-protagonist's blindness. (The Russian giants of the twenties studied a print of Gance's original thirty-two-reel version, and this film's lightning-fast montages of engines and pistons, rails and wheels, were probably a chief influence on Russian montage.) Gance's 1937 sound remake of his anti-war film *J'Accuse* ends with a sequence so overpowering that it obliterates the rest of the film. In this finale, the war dead rise to confront the living; the mutilated, the crippled get up and march toward us. In George Romero's 1968 *Night of the Living Dead*, the onslaught of the dead is used for a gruesome horror effect; in Gance it's a nightmare miracle, and awesome. The soldiers just keep marching toward us—a vast army of the dead filling the screen.

Gance is a master of a certain kind of theatrical rhetoric; he must think in tropes. In *Napoléon*, at the climactic moments the eagle appears. It lights on the topmost part of a ship carrying Napoleon, it settles on a pole in the camp where he's sleeping after his victory over the English at Toulon, and, at the end, the eagle spreads its wings across the three screens.

All through *Napoléon*, you can see why Gance had to invent the Polyvision wide-screen process (which was the predecessor of Cinerama and Cinema-Scope). Whenever there's a mob onscreen, the action seems to be pushing against the sides of the frame. That square frame is like a straitjacket to Gance: you feel that he can't accept it and work within it—that he *has* to push it wider. I never got this sense of confinement from Griffith (who often used a flexible frame—blacking out the top and bottom for a proportionately wider image, or blacking out the sides for a narrow vertical image) or from Eisenstein or the other Russians. Gance needs a wider canvas because he just naturally tries to encompass more than the square can hold. Though he has a dazzling compositional sense, the halls with crowds seated or jumping to their feet look compressed and static. When, at the climax, Napoleon addresses his army in Italy and the screen opens up to triptych width, the squeezed look disappears and Gance's compositional style seems, at last, fulfilled. (At Radio City, three synchronized projectors were used, though something like this effect can—and probably will—be accomplished by putting the triple-width section on 70-mm. film.) Napoleon reviews his troops, and we see the whole damned army stretched out over the landscape. It's like a photographic map—the country is laid out in front of us. We see the encampments, the tents, the troops, and Napoleon himself, high on a peak, addressing them. And there is an effect that suggests 3-D (which Gance also experimented with while making this picture): several horses and riders cross in front of the vista and seem to ride right into the theatre. This concluding section is a triumph: the three images are sometimes one continuous panoramic view; at other times the center panel is complemented by the wings in a contrapuntal effect, or all three are different. And the extravagance is compounded by two, sometimes three, sets of superimpositions. (There were also three earlier, brief uses of the triptych width in *Napoléon*, but apparently Gance, despairing because it didn't seem that anyone would ever be interested in the footage, destroyed it.) Gance, the visionary who reached out to bring more and more into his frames (some scenes have as many as six thousand extras), must have felt a strong temperamental affinity with Napoleon, the visionary conqueror. Gance—he appears here, with gold loops in his ears, in full-screen closeups, as the handsome, lordly Saint-Just—has often been described as looking like an eagle.

*O*ne of the reasons that *Napoléon* failed with the public may be that Gance works on such a large scale that he uses his performers for their physiognomies—their look—rather than for any contribution they might make to the film as actors. We see them in luminous, expressive closeups—faces abstracted from the action—and we see them in long shots. But there is little of the middle distance, where we might get to know the characters they're playing. We don't find out what the Revolution is about or what Danton and Robespierre stand for. The kind of mind that thinks in tropes doesn't dramatize particulars. The crowds at the National Convention don't represent anything to us—they're just people milling around. They're illustrations of history. When Antonin Artaud, who plays Marat, appears, the Radio City audience applauds him for who he is; his acting wouldn't call up any cheers. Artaud gives a hyperactive, bulging-eyed performance (though he was gentle and superbly modulated in Dreyer's 1928 *The Passion of Joan of Arc*). The thin, elegant Pierre Batcheff (he was the cyclist in the Buñuel-Dali 1928 *Un Chien Andalou*) plays Josephine's lover, General Hoche; he has almost nothing to do, but he does make you wonder why Josephine tosses him over for Nappy, who is still just an intense, glowering little nerd. Dieudonné (he looks like Rod Stewart on a stormy day) has presence, but he seems much older than Napoleon was at this time (all of twenty-six), and, with his pale eyes and thin, dark-lipsticked mouth, he's rather off-putting. This Napoleon may be fire and eagle and all, but we never get a sense of the man, or of the tactician, either. All we know is that his will is steely, his military plans are brilliant, he loves his mother, and he's on a divine mission—he's going to spread the French Revolution to other countries by conquering them. Gance doesn't seem to notice anything odd about the idea of bringing self-respect to people by defeating them in war.

There is a truly disingenuous sequence: Gance attempts to purify Napoleon's plans by a supernatural device. After the rush-rush wedding and a hurried night with his bride, Napoleon, at dawn, heads for Italy. (He allows himself only three months for its conquest.) But on the way, just after taking leave of Josephine, he stops at the empty Convention hall. It is inhabited by the phantoms of the guillotined Revolutionary leaders—Danton and the others. These dead speak to him: They tell him that the Revolution cannot prosper without a strong leader, and they ask him to be that leader. They tell him that the Revolution will die if it doesn't expand beyond France, and that he must spread it. And he solemnly promises these apparitions that he will liberate oppressed peoples and create a united Fatherland. (He was racing off to "liberate" Italy anyway, so it's rather funny that he reacts as if the dead had just laid this burden on him.)

*J*osephine (Gina Manès), who carries a lapdog, is a tough, worldly tart. Her brutal nature may perhaps show too clearly on the outside—she has a hard jaw, as if she'd been chewing on things too long. When Napoleon's face is in the center panel, with a globe of the world on a side panel, and then Josephine's face, in all its leering glitter, is superimposed on that globe, we are supposed to see that his pure dream of a universal state is being corrupted. She is the temptress who comes between him and his Destiny. The film ends with Napoleon still triumphant, though there are mystic forebodings of defeats to come. The strange thing about the structure is that, as everything has been set up, Napoleon should win out over his enemies. There is so little sense of political or military reality in this film that the only way Napoleon's defeats can be prefigured is by mystic hints and Josephine's enigmatic, dirty smile. It's as if Christ were done in by Eve.

*A*t Radio City, *Napoléon* had the right setting and a great audience. I had seen the triptych section set up with three projectors and three little screens in the auditorium of the San Francisco Museum of Art in the forties, and the group of us there were wild-eyed with excitement about what we saw. We were only the lunatic fringe, though. At Radio City, there were as many people in the audience as there were on the screen, and for a spectacle film designed to work on mass emotions a big screen and a crowd make an enormous difference. During the two-storms sequence, you could feel a third storm—waves of audience response. It's inspiriting to be in a large audience so knowledgeable about movies that it reacts with surprise and excitement to each unusual technical device, and with enjoyment to the romantic flourishes. In the twenties and thirties, people were rebelling against the nineteenth-century sentiments expressed here (and talkies had brought in a new realism), and in the forties if the film had played to a large crowd it might have appeared obscene. But the picture's flowery pannationalism just seems a curiosity and a camp now. This could be the time for Gance, because there are so many more people now who recognize what he was doing technically. It could even be the right time for Gance the size freak, because after the years of TV and tiny art houses you begin to feel how much size matters. The score that Carmine Coppola conducted—and composed, with some acknowledged borrowings from Berlioz and others—helped the film enormously; over the years, I have seen *Napoléon* in several versions, and it never moved as fluently as it did with this music. I've never heard the score that Honegger wrote for the 1927 opening, or the new score that Carl Davis prepared for the London showings last year, but this one has pulse and spirit. (It's an incredible workout for the orchestra, and for the conductor, who must be close to seventy—four hours of almost continuous playing.) There was only one spot where I thought the synchronization of the score and the images failed: the organ interlude during the Battle of Toulon episode. An organ doesn't have the right sound for battle, or for councils of war, either. And even after Napoleon called for "Order, calm, silence" the organist was rushing on excitedly.

*I*f a huge, hip audience can do wonders for a film, it can also expose blunders: when Charlotte Corday comes to murder Marat, she is ushered into the room where he is soaking in his bathtub; a curtain is drawn (as if we were at a theatrical performance), and then it's pulled back after he has been stabbed. Stage and screen conventions have got confused here, and the audience broke into laughter. (Marat's death is staged as a "living picture"—an exact re-creation of the famous painting.)

After the Terror, the subtitles inform us, there is a reaction of joy, and people celebrate at balls. The one that Napoleon goes to is the Victims' Ball, attended by those who have narrowly escaped the guillotine or lost relatives to it. Gance has shown a fine eye for beautiful women throughout, but suddenly he seems to have shifted centuries, because the sparkling-eyed beauties at this party carry on like flappers at a twenties artists' ball. The men are properly costumed, but the women are in the kind of dresses that go with cloches. Two of them sit in a swing high above the crowd, wearing only little wisps of clothing; others dance, bare-legged and bare-bottomed, with, here and there, a breast exposed. (This jazzy revel is reminiscent of the cubistic Charleston montage in Lubitsch's 1926 *So This Is Paris*, except there are no black musicians.) Watching this twenties orgy during the French Revolution, I thought it might have been Gance's gesture toward his backers—an obligatory scene, like the car chases that have been forced on Hollywood directors in recent years. But then I remembered (and found) a still of a shindig from Gance's 1935 *Lucrezia Borgia*, starring Edwige Feuillère, which I'd saved because the garlanded maidens dancing semi-nude had such a howling thirties look. Maybe Gance goes into little time warps.

Napoléon is full of aesthetic contradictions, and seeing it with an audience that enjoys them adds to the picture's freshness. When you watch a Gance film, you're seeing a film made by a man who was born in the nineteenth century (in 1889) and who mastered a twentieth-century art while remaining a romantic dandy of the past. Gance is still ahead of most film artists, yet he has always been behind movie audiences. He's a double anachronism, a living time warp. This man, who sold his first scripts in 1909, once wrote a play for Sarah Bernhardt, and his thinking (if his later movies, such as the 1964 *Cyrano et D'Artagnan*, accurately express it) hasn't changed. But he's such a passionate wizard that in his hands the old declamatory conventions sometimes become iconographic right before your eyes. There are masters whose technique is invisible (Renoir, De Sica, Satyajit Ray), so that what you respond to is the stories and the people. And there are masters of bravura, such as Gance and Welles, who often seem wildly "cinematic" because they are essentially theatrical. This isn't a negative observation: it may be that they love movies so much because they loved the theatre.

February 16, 1981

The Itch to Act

*I*n *Fort Apache, the Bronx*, Paul Newman throws himself into the role of Murphy, a veteran of eighteen years on the New York police force, and he stays in character. There's no star self-protectiveness, no holding back; there's an elasticity—a snap—in what he does. In recent years, I've hardly ever seen an American star show such physical eagerness to act. It's as if Newman had better sight than the performers around him: chuckling happily, he waits for the nugget of a scene to come along so he can pounce on it. He plays the over-the-hill Murphy gleefully, licking his chops. He has fun with who he is in a scene; he dances, he shuffles. There's a beautiful hamminess about his work: he's scratching an itch and getting a huge kick out of it.

Newman enjoys bringing out the animal shrewdness of the kind of man who clowns around with the fellows and plays dumb. In the 1977 *Slap Shot*, he demonstrated that he could do broad, cartoon comedy as part of a character. Here he uses a broad style more subtly, as just a surface element of Murphy's character—what Murphy shows to the boys. Newman doesn't make a big thing of Murphy's horseplay and banter; they're simply how men learn to get along on the job, in bars—everywhere. (And Newman seems to enjoy working with the other actors; the horseplay is sincere.) But Murphy is very different with a woman he respects: the hidden ideals, the real feelings come through. Paul Newman is an honest actor: he doesn't stoop to play an ordinary cop—he plays the ordinary Murphy as a man as sensitive, as confused, and as intelligent as he himself. Assigned to a patrol car in the rotting Forty-first Precinct, in the South Bronx—the most shattered, crime-ridden section of the city—Murphy doesn't know whether his efforts to deal with muggers, arsonists, pimps, and dealers have any permanent results, but he believes in his work just the same. The role of his young partner, Corelli, played by Ken Wahl, is just sketched, and Wahl gave a much stronger performance in his first film, the 1979 *The Wanderers*, but, with his loose-limbed, slightly raw-boned tall frame and his smiling, dark-haired good looks, he matches up well with the trim, compact, silver-haired Newman. Wahl has a little trouble with his New York accent—his upper lip seems to get in his way—but he has an easygoing, up-front quality that makes Corelli immediately likable. Without deceiving themselves that they're making any big difference, Murphy and Corelli do the best they can to protect the people in the area. In the movie's view, it's a Sisyphean task.

At the start, as we see the desolate South Bronx, with Manhattan in the distance, we hear exotic Spanish music and drums—it's a musical sick joke. And the opening sequence is hair-raising: A tall, sinuous, stoned-out-of-her-mind hooker (Pam Grier), with dark skin and hair dyed yellow, weaves her way over to a parked patrol car; she's so wasted she moves and talks in slow motion. Grinning lasciviously at the two rookie cops—one black, one white—sitting inside eating their breakfast, she propositions them in a whispery, seductive voice, then pulls out a gun and, as a train goes by, shoots them in the face. She wanders off, and in a few seconds the patrol car is surrounded by vandals, who rob the corpses and then disappear. That's our welcome to the South Bronx; it's also the crime that sets the plot in motion. And throughout the movie each time Pam Grier's angel-dusted hooker appears, making snaky movements with her tongue, she gives us a feeling of obscene terror—she's a death machine. Yet we understand why nobody pays much attention to her: she's so slowed-down she seems harmless—just one more psycho junkie, the kind who look as if they couldn't make it across the street on their own power.

Based on the accounts of two policemen, Thomas Mulhearn and Pete Tessitore, who were assigned to the precinct in the sixties, when the police station was known as Fort Apache (arsonists have been so busy that the station is now called Little House on the Prairie), the movie is an attempt to show urban crisis in extremis. (Half of the buildings in the Forty-first Precinct have been gutted or have crumbled.) The scriptwriter, Heywood Gould, was probably trying for something like the comedy-in-the-midst-of-chaos feeling of Altman's 1970 *M*A*S*H* and for some of the pungent, jangling tone of

Lumet's 1975 *Dog Day Afternoon*, but the movie comes out closer to . . . *And Justice for All*. A lot of the dialogue is written as street vaudeville—as colorful, tough talk, with the information about the characters worked into pretend-casual exchanges (where it drops like a weight). A different director might have used this script for a visceral comedy of horror—a picture in which all the things that seemed random and meaningless were revealed to be connected, and were still utterly senseless. But the storytelling is lax—some essential dramatic intuition seems to be missing. The work of the director, Daniel Petrie (he did *Sybil* and *Eleanor and Franklin* for TV, and his movies include *Lifeguard*, *The Betsy*, and *Resurrection*), is, as usual, benign, courteous; he allows people their dignity. But Petrie, though he makes movies, is not a moviemaker. He doesn't have a moviemaker's vision; in *Fort Apache, the Bronx*, he doesn't create the sense of place that would make the violent actions seem organic (the way they did in Carol Reed's *The Third Man*, or in Martin Scorsese's *Mean Streets*). There's an idea behind the movie's bleached, bluish look (you wouldn't be surprised to see mushrooms growing out of the walls), but there isn't enough atmospheric tension for the humor to function as a release. Petrie doesn't seem to know where the suspense should be, or where the wormy fear should be, either. The picture is sprinkled with small, surefire-charm touches: when the people of the community march on the station to protest some arrests, there's a shot of the community's stray dogs running along. Petrie shoots this stuff, but he's too much of a gent to get a real laugh out of it. He glides over the action, evening things out, shooting on the Bronx hellhole locations as if he were making a travelogue.

The scenes don't play off each other. The pasty-faced cops at the station just stand around delivering wisecracks, and looking unshaven. (The whole movie suffers from five-o'clock shadow.) Ed Asner, who plays Captain Connolly, the new commanding officer of the precinct, comes down so hard on his lines that he sticks out the way George Kennedy sometimes does; you dread it every time he starts to speak. (Each speech sounds like six or seven of his TV shows rolled into one.) Asner is impaled on a tired device in the plotting: Captain Connolly thinks he can improve things by insisting that the officers abide by the letter of the law, that they "go by the book." This cliché movie conflict—the martinet (Asner) versus the experienced officer (Newman) who bends the rules to make them more reasonable—doesn't open anything out to us. It just gets in the way of our understanding what the officers do for the community, and how the sordidness eats away at them, destroying some of them, such as Officer Morgan (Danny Aiello), who happens to see a Puerto Rican boy on a rooftop necking with a girl and, full of anger (and feeling the power of his uniform), throws the boy off the roof. The plot centers on the reaction of Murphy, who witnesses this totally gratuitous murder. But the movie feels amorphous. Though the incidents are all intricately linked to this murder (and there's some tricky symmetrical patterning), they seem to dangle uncertainly. One thread of the plot involves Hernando (Miguel Piñero, with an Afro), a strutting drug dealer, but if you bat an eye and miss his buddy's looking down from a window and seeing Murphy's car in the street, you won't know why Hernando maliciously gives the Hispanic nurse (Rachel Ticotin) whom Murphy is dating an overdose. Newman and Rachel Ticotin are a very agreeable team; they communicate the feeling that Murphy and the nurse find sanctuary when they're together—there's an ease between them. She has a curly mouth, like the young Bacall; it's too bad that she has to use that mouth to speak some fancy, literary lines—"People pass you and they're laughing, only you think they're screaming." She explains that she takes drugs to get the misery of the hospital and the streets out of her mind; it's for a "vacation"—"a few hours floating on a raft in the Caribbean." In the words of Frank Nugent, "Odets, where is thy sting?"

There's a psychological vacuum right at the center of the conception. The murdered boy didn't offer Morgan any provocation; the only preparation for the murder is Morgan's having acted like a nasty villain earlier, by dropping racist remarks. And this may be why the movie doesn't come together: If we don't see that deep in his bones every cop up there in the rubble and garbage of the South Bronx must at some point have wanted to fling the junkies and pimps and muggers off a roof, the act has no resonance. Only if the others had felt the same murderous impulse, and realized that even an innocent teen-age boy could fill them with hate, would Morgan's carrying out the impulse give the film real power. If the reason that the other cops who witnessed the murder (Murphy and Corelli and Morgan's partner) wouldn't testify against him was that each of them recognized that he himself had felt the same insanity, there'd be something much larger at stake than the familiar cops' code of not ratting on each other. Suppose that Morgan weren't a sadistic racist but a relatively decent guy, like Murphy or Corelli, who suddenly felt his gorge rising—maybe because a scared Puerto Rican kid tried to show off by cursing him . . . But *Fort Apache, the Bronx* doesn't go that far. Of course, if the picture were stronger—and better—it would probably offend more pressure groups than it does now.

As it has been made, it's a drama of conscience—Murphy's conscience. Murphy is the standard liberal protagonist: the man of honor who has to stand up and denounce the racist Morgan, even if that means being a stoolie. There's a limitation built into Newman's role. Murphy the decent cop lacks the capacity for doing what Morgan did, or even for recognizing it as a possibility in himself. A screenwriter who understood something about heroic roles might have made Murphy and Morgan one character—or, at least, spiritual brothers. This picture has no center, because Murphy is morally superior to Morgan. *Fort Apache, the Bronx* has many of the ingredients for a shocking, memorable movie, but it's earnest where it needs to have some of the sick-joke surrealism of its inferno locale. The picture is about the grisly ugliness of what a policeman in the slums has to contend with, yet the point of the picture is that Murphy's faith in the police is undermined by Morgan's action. Murphy can't understand how a cop could do such a horrible thing; for

Fort Apache, the Bronx to be a really good movie he would have to under-stand all too well.

Newman could have played it that way. You feel he's aching to go much further than the movie lets him. Newman is blissfully happy in roles where he can look foolish, and he brings a sure instinct to "ordinary" men. He gives detailed performances—full of little tricks (like Murphy's lounging around with both a cigarette and a toothpick in his mouth, or getting a psycho to surrender a knife by turning his police hat around, popping his eyes, wag-gling his hips, and slackening his jaw so his face wobbles like a moron's). It takes a long time for an actor to develop the assurance that Newman has, yet there's still a bloom on everything he does. It's the movie that pulls him back to niceness and nobility. It's the movie—not Newman—that's afraid to get into the muck. He's suspended, in a near-great performance. Unfortunately, it's the only performance in the movie, except for Pam Grier's, and her Satan Lady is so scary that when you see her you tense up for more terror than you get. The picture is a mess, with glimmerings of talent. There's a beautiful, un-derstated scene of Murphy dragging the dead nurse back and forth, trying to revive her, and saying "Murphy, Murphy," as if it were she talking to him. (Did the same person who conceived this scene think up the shot of the pooches running to the demonstration?)

There are a lot of things wrong with *Fort Apache, the Bronx*, but the charges made in leaflets handed out in front of theatres—that it is exploitative and stereotypes blacks and Puerto Ricans as "savages, criminals, and degener-ates"—seem way off the beam. The movie is clearly an expression of disgust at racism. It may not go very deep; it may be inept. But shallowness and clumsiness aren't the same as exploitation.

February 23, 1981

Tramont's Mirror

Women à la Mode

*T*he tone of *All Night Long*, starring Gene Hackman and Barbra Strei-sand, is slapstick irony. The film is an idiosyncratic, fairy-tale comedy about people giving up the phony obligations they have accumulated and trying to find a way to do what they enjoy. It's the story of a middle-aged dropout who doesn't consciously drop out; his reflexes make the decision for him. Hackman's George Dupler is a Los Angeles business executive who after twenty-one years with a company suddenly goes ape, punches a higher executive who has been jabbering corporate doubletalk, and hurls a chair through the glass sheath of the building. The company gets him out of the way by demoting him to the job of night manager of one of its twenty-four-hour Ultra Save drugstores. These stores are vast, computerized sleaze centers, where you can buy almost anything—pills, toys, candy, liquor, stockings, pillows, and gadgetry. And at night they attract shoplifters, robbers, and crazies of all kinds. So George enters the squalid Los Angeles night world, and once he has fallen from respectability he spirals down, down. But he also begins to put himself together as a different man. By the end of the movie, he is doing what he always wanted to do (to work with his hands, and be an inventor), and he has broken with his wife (Diane Ladd) and taken up with Cheryl (Streisand), the wife of one of his wife's in-laws—a deliriously seductive blonde who likes to think she's turning men on.

The director, Jean-Claude Tramont, a Belgian who has worked in American television but whose only other feature film is the French-made 1977 *Focal Point*, with Annie Girardot and Jacques Dutronc, is a sophisticated jokester. There may be a suggestion of Lubitsch and of Max Ophuls in his approach, and there is more than a suggestion of Tati, and because he is working here with the scriptwriter W. D. (Rick) Richter the free-floating gags sometimes recall other Richter gags, especially the ones in *Slither*. When I saw the picture, a young man a few rows ahead of me laughed at almost everything Hackman did; others laughed hardly at all. A new comic sensibility in films takes a while to adjust to, and Tramont's slapstick is very distinctive. He doesn't point up the jokes; he just keeps planting them. The outgoing night manager gives George a gun and talks to him about the scum he'll have to deal with—"and things like that," he says, referring to a blank-faced kid barrelling down the aisle toward them. The kid comes up, and it's George's eighteen-year-old housepainter son (Dennis Quaid), who has come to see his father. When George goes to an extended-family party, the conversation is all introductions and explanations of how each is related to somebody or other. George looks for a loft to rent in an old factory building, and the elderly landlady takes him into a studio where an Oriental sits painting the standard view of Mt. Fuji. As George and the landlady walk through, the camera, following them, reveals that behind the painter there are rows of Orientals, all sitting there painting the same view of Mt. Fuji. When the landlady asks him what he wants the space for and he explains that he's an inventor, she says, "You got your work cut out for you, 'cause nothing they got now gets the job done."

Hackman, whose specialty has been believable, lived-in characters, gives one of his most likable performances. He does the kind of comic acting that rings true on every note, yet he's never predictable. Hackman has bags under his eyes, and his face has caved in a bit; maybe that's why when he lights up, it really means something. He does the damnedest, strangest bits, and you think, Of course, that's exactly what George Dupler would do. George is particularly funny in his scenes with his muscular, inarticulate son, who grunts like a comic-strip barbarian; to George this hulk sitting across the table from him is the result of some sort of genetic prank. Hackman and Quaid act with so much rapport that you can feel the father-son bond, whether they're fighting or just glaring at each other. And, in George's domestic scenes, when he tries to get some sleep during the days so he can face his fluorescent nights he's as groggy and ground down as W. C. Fields was in *It's a Gift*, when his days were given over to hating his family because they could sleep nights and he could never sleep. The attraction that Hackman has often had for people in the audience is (as he himself has pointed out) that they can say, "I know who that guy is," and it really works for him in this role—the only full-scale comedy part he has had on the screen.

But we don't know who Streisand is. She doesn't use her rapid-fire New York vocal rhythms in this movie, and a subdued Streisand doesn't seem quite Streisand. She's a West Coast flake this time, and she stays in character as soft-spoken Cheryl, who dresses in gauzy, clinging outfits—crushed-polyester lavender velours. Cheryl's what-a-dish-I-am walk makes people giggle; she moves mincingly—a knock-kneed, pigeon-toed floozy. She's intuitive, cuddly, and more than a little gaga—the sort of woman who sets the table with pleated colored paper napkins standing, fan-shaped, in glasses—and her cooking rivals that of Shelley Duvall in *3 Women*. (Cheryl serves George her special creamed tuna on toast—the creaming from an undiluted can of mushroom soup.) Cheryl has been playing the dumb, loving, obedient wife to her macho fireman husband (Kevin Dobson) for so long that even though she hates her life she's terrified of losing the security, scared of how she will live without her things. There were times when I couldn't tell whether Streisand was uncomfortable with the confused, frightened character she was playing or trying to indicate Cheryl's discomfort with herself. It's a Marilyn Monroe flower-child, crazy-lady role, and there was a certain amount of discomfort in it for us when Monroe did it, too—but a different kind of discomfort. The character came out of Monroe; with Streisand it isn't clear what it comes out of. She's a thin-faced, waiflike question mark walking through the movie, and you can't quite grasp why George Dupler, who is very bright, would respond to Cheryl's bleached-blond tackiness. Annie Girardot turns up in a guest bit (she teaches French to George's wife); when her eyes connect with Hackman's, there's a flash of something more substantial than the goofing around between him and Streisand.

All Night Long is spare yet romantic. It's a worldly-wise comedy of manners in which the people are isolated—are left on their own. When George quits his job at the Ultra Save and the employees salute him, I was surprised at how sorry I felt that we wouldn't see more of these people and their lunar world; I had become attached to it. (There is a beautiful slapstick scene of two executives from Ultra Save's corporate headquarters being chased through the store by a toy helicopter.) And when George drops in on Cheryl at a time when he knows that her husband will be home and razzes him, it's apparent that Cheryl enjoys the danger of the situation—there's a sexual thrill in it. There are a lot of feelings buzzing in this sequence; it's knowing without being offensive. Tramont views people's mixed emotions with formal, almost austere bemusement. Folly pleases him. (If Stendhal's Count Mosca had left Parma and gone to Los Angeles, he might have observed life there much the way Tramont does.) There's a perverse little game going on: If you expect something to happen, it doesn't—even when Cheryl's enraged husband picks up a cake, he doesn't throw it. The film is punctuated with unforced bits of comedy—some are no more than a gesture of Hackman's or his way with a line of dialogue. And the first of George's inventions that we see is fairly startling: a mirror that doesn't reverse the image—that shows you yourself as other people see you.

Conceptually, the movie is a little lazy—it's too pleased with the idea of free spirits rebelling against stuffy jerks; the incident of George turning in a fire alarm in order to get Cheryl's husband out of the way recalls the carefree madness of empty-headed heroes in thirties screwball comedies. But when George is in his loft and you hear José Padilla's "La Violetera"—the poignant *cuplé* from Chaplin's *City Lights*—Tramont's elegant spareness comes into its own. (Apparently, he had used Chaplin music, orchestrated and conducted by Georges Delerue, for the whole soundtrack, but the executives at Universal insisted on removing some of it; they also insisted on some cuts in the film.) "La Violetera" completes the tone of *All Night Long*. You can hear the sound of the violin bow against the strings, and it's an intimate sound. You understand that what you're seeing is a comic lament—a what-if picture with a delicate, faint chill. It's a romance about how romance passes.

·   ·   ·   ·   ·

*T*he lovely, toothy Helen Morse is the heroine of the 1976 Australian movie *Caddie*, which has just opened here. She's Caddie, a young suburban housewife who in 1925 leaves her cruel, philandering husband, taking their two small children with her. Directed by Donald Crombie, from Joan Long's adaptation of a woman's pseudonymous autobiography, the picture, which is set in Sydney, shows us the penniless Caddie going to work as a barmaid in a rowdy workingmen's pub, just barely surviving during the rough years of the Depression, and then taking a job in a pub where she has to handle illegal betting. *Caddie* is moderately absorbing. There are reminders of the very recent past: Men and women don't drink together. The bars are for men, and they're convivial gathering places (though brawls often break out). Women who want a drink must go to the women's parlor—a back room where morose, down-at-the-heels women (some of them battered) sit alone at tables, and where cackling, gap-toothed crones insult each other and get into fights.

The soft-color period evocations are visually pleasing, the barmaids wear their flapper clothes with real élan (they have John Held, Jr., silhouettes), and the ruddy-faced men at the bar are so well lighted and directed that each extra seems to have a cameo role.

The picture often has the charm of photographs of the past, but that's all it has. It doesn't dramatize Caddie's life; it treats her as if she were the subject of a documentary. We're meant to think her chipper and courageous when she stands her ground and says "How dare you!" to the many lowlifes she encounters, but we never learn anything of how she feels. And every time we get interested in someone who crosses Caddie's path—the snappy barmaid Josie (Jacki Weaver), the bookie Ted (Jack Thompson), the shy peddler Sonny (Drew Forsythe)—and some interaction seems possible, the character promptly drops out of the picture, never to return.

Caddie's story is presented as a precursor of women's liberation: Caddie has the courage to leave her husband, and years later, when Caddie's former best girl friend—who had had an affair with Caddie's husband—turns up, a bruised wreck, in the women's parlor, she says she envies Caddie. (That's almost the only dramatic contour in this movie.) But Caddie attracts men by her classy, aloof manner. Even when she is on welfare or is suffering from malnutrition, she's still standoffish. And the man she likes is a perfectly boring gentleman: a tall, romantic Greek (Takis Emmanuel), who is like Hollywood's Spanish gallants of the silent era—he aches with fidelity. The least convincing character in the movie, he represents Caddie's only chance for happiness—a chance she loses, because she can't take her children out of the country without their father's consent.

The more we see of the noble-souled Greek, the more we long for the return of Jack Thompson's brash, flippant Ted, whom Caddie threw over, because he was a heel. (When Ted told Caddie that he loved her, she said, "Maybe you only think so," and he replied, "What's the diff?") Thompson gives the film a burst of energy. In *Agatha*, Helen Morse had a comparable live-wire quality—she was dimply Evelyn, the woman Agatha met at the spa. Here, she gives a beautifully modulated lifeless performance, which is undoubtedly just what the director had in mind. And she has received several festival awards for it. Her Caddie is a completely controlled person, who keeps her ladylike distance. She's the female equivalent of the Englishman who dresses for dinner in the jungle. When the picture came to an end, with a few titles explaining what happened in the remainder of Caddie's life, the audience, quiet and respectful up to that point, made a good-natured squawk, because there was no dramatic resolution. Caddie just stays on her treadmill. The audience has every reason to think, Why was a movie made about her?

The day after I saw *Caddie*, I happened to be talking with a visiting Australian dignitary who has been involved in the renaissance of his country's film industry, and I asked him why this picture was so enormously successful at home. He laughed, and asked if I knew that James Ivory's 1979 film *The*

Europeans had been an astounding success in Australia. Then he said, "Australians don't like confrontation; they like nostalgia and mood pieces. They want a slice of life, set retrospectively. For Australians, the most important things happen far away—in England or America. Typically, in Australian films the central character has no idea what he wants to do, and is easily diverted. The films say, 'You won't change events, events will change you.' " I told him that in American terms *Caddie* just didn't get anywhere, and he replied, "If you said to the director of *Caddie*, 'But it's got no point of view,' he'd probably answer, 'Who'd be interested in *my* point of view?' "

.   .   .   .   .

*I*t was reported in the press that Joel Schumacher, the director of *The Incredible Shrinking Woman*, wanted to make the whole picture look like Necco wafers—and he brought it off: the film's synthetic pastels evoke a dreamlike, leisure-suit existence. The 1957 *The Incredible Shrinking Man*, based on Richard Matheson's novel, was science fiction; the new film—a light, satirical fantasy starring Lily Tomlin—retains only a few of Matheson's incidents, and they're not meant to be scary. The film is an idyll of consumerism; the style is Necco Deco—a sort of plastic lyricism. There are no organic colors: everything in the suburban development where Pat lives, with her husband (Charles Grodin), their two children, and a big, fluffy white dog, has a muted artificiality. Walls and clothes are turquoise or lavender, peach or pink, tangerine or pale mint green; people look as if they'd learned how to dress by looking at food wrappers. And there are no natural textures or rough edges. Everything is smooth and clean—junk food, junk clothes, polystyrene furniture. Pat herself has a calm, soft radiance: she loves her pastel paradise. She smiles at the commotion her affable, bratty children make, banging toys around and spraying each other with household cleansers. She smiles at her worrywart husband, an advertising man who prepares campaigns for new products, which he tries out on her. Things are always being spilled or splashed on her, and she just keeps smiling. In the midst of all the hundreds of household upsets, she is tranquil. The whole family is a little benumbed—like the people in TV commercials who don't react to anything that doesn't roll on or come in an aerosol can or make the floors shine. Everyone seems to be on automatic pilot.

Even after Pat starts to shrink (and learns that it is because of exposure to the chemicals in the products that the family delights in, plus a flu shot, the tap water, the smog, birth-control pills, and maybe some sort of predisposition or "imbalance"), she tries to see the bright side of things. There's a surreal normality about her. She goes on valiantly shopping and cooking, even when she has to climb up to the sink, and she tries not to make a fuss about it when she's so little that her head is smaller than the balls on her ball-fringed drapes. The charm of *Shrinking Woman* is in the out-of-whack rhythm of Pat's happy family life and in the insidious, candy-colored suburban blandness of this apocalypse. It's in brief, unstressed scenes: the kids go to bed, and Pat sings them the lullaby they request—"I wish I was a little bar of soap"; Pat is examined at the Institute for the Study of Unexplained Phenomena and as she leaves a woman can be heard crying and screaming from inside a big box that's being carried in; the teeny Pat, a celebrity because of her mysterious ailment, sits in a doll house with typewriter and tape recorder, working on her memoirs, and listens to a loud, booming playback.

The picture loses much of its stylized originality when it sets up a good-guys-versus-bad-guys conflict in order to give us a rooting interest in the outcome. Pat is kidnapped by a super-conglomerate called the Organization for World Management, which wants to make a serum from her blood, so that it can shrink whole populations and control them. But even when the picture turns into a gimcrack farce it's offhand and likable. Pat, imprisoned in a hamster's cage, finds a friend in a zonked lab technician (Mark Blankfield, of the TV comedy series "Fridays"), and she becomes the beloved of a gorilla named Sidney (played by Rick Baker, who designed and constructed the Sidney suit and then worked inside it, as he did with the 1976 King Kong suit). Sidney, who has red hair on his head, knows sign language, and seems to understand English, too, gives the picture a boost of foolishness. (It should be a great movie for kids; it's full of toys.)

Schumacher and the scriptwriter, Jane Wagner, have tried to avoid the preachiness implicit in the chemical-pollution theme, but their pulling back makes the film almost as self-conscious as it would have been if they'd gone ahead and punched out their message. (Neither would have been necessary if the film's ante hadn't been raised by introducing the conflict with the super-conglomerate.) As the film is structured, Pat feels she should tell people why she is shrinking and warn them, but her husband, at the instigation of his boss (Ned Beatty), urges her not to create a crisis of confidence in American products. And so when she's on the Mike Douglas TV show she passes up her big chance to alert the public, and when she finally speaks out to a crowd in her shopping center all she says is, "You don't need me to tell you what's wrong with the world," though it's clear that they do need her to tell them— they haven't any idea why she is shrinking, or (from the way they look) that there *is* anything wrong with the world. (Pat didn't, at the start.) It's a case of damned if you do and damned if you don't. Now, in not letting Pat make an out-and-out attack on the promiscuous use of chemicals, the movie suggests that Pat, the smiling housewife, is a masochist who just goes from one cage to another.

The visual style of *Shrinking Woman* is somewhat reminiscent of Woody Allen's *Sleeper* (on which Schumacher worked as costume designer), though this is a grubbier production—a mixture of the bizarre and the amateurish. The sound is frazzled, and some of the scenes near the beginning are blurry around the edges—they seem deliberately (yet inexplicably) overfiltered. The special effects are often miscalculated: when the wee Pat has a conversation, the people she's supposed to be talking to sometimes look at her in the wrong spot. But it's an amiable sloppy film. Jane Wagner provides a lot of quietly aberrant wordplay, and Schumacher's vision of the banality of slow death by chemicals is satirical in an odd, unstable way. And Lily Tomlin shows a new, wistful charm. Pat's determined efforts to cope with her household duties when she's so small that each task involves complicated logistical problems are funny because they grow out of her cheerful, accepting character. (That's why her line "You don't need me to tell you what's wrong with the world" sticks out; it isn't Pat talking—Lily Tomlin has taken her place.) Actually, Tomlin has been doing a warmup for this role for years—whenever she has played Edith Ann, the five-and-a-half-year-old girl in the oversize rocker. But Edith Ann has the gleaming eyes of most Tomlin characters; she's a child witch. Pat is probably the closest thing to an ingénue that Lily Tomlin has ever played, and she's more spontaneous in this role than she has been on the screen before. In *Shrinking Woman*, when she does a brief turn as Ernestine, the prune-faced power-freak telephone operator, whom she used to play on the TV "Laugh-In" shows, and when she does several not so brief turns as Judith Beasley, Pat's next-door neighbor, who sells a line of cosmetics, she slips back into clever—sometimes fiendish—caricature. (She has done all this before.) But Pat is a fresh creation—a sweetly loony happy housewife in a pretty-poison dream world. It's a surprisingly free performance. You feel that Lily Tomlin is inside the character; there's nobody inside Ernestine or Judith Beasley.

·　　·　　·　　·　　·

*L*ily Tomlin looks much more angular in *Nine to Five*. Her deadpan straight-shooter performance, with the character's feelings coming out in precise, venomous inflections, is like an extended version of one of her TV skits; still, it is shaded enough to give some comic distinction to this piece of strong-arm whimsy, directed by Colin Higgins, from a script by Patricia Resnick that he reworked. Lily Tomlin plays a smart, efficient office worker who is passed over for promotion while men she has trained move up, and at times you could swear that you saw the clicking of her mind in her slitted eyes. (They glitter in one brief scene, and there's genuine wit in the sparks she gives off.) The picture is shaped as a feminist revenge fantasy: Tomlin and two co-workers—Dolly Parton (in her film début) and Jane Fonda—each with a complaint against the lecherous, petty-tyrant boss, Mr. Hart (Dabney Coleman), kidnap him, get the business humming, and institute reforms, such as equal pay for equal work, flexible hours, hiring the handicapped, and providing day-care services. Tomlin confirms herself as a star whenever she gets some material; she has a wickedly sure instinct for playing to the camera—she's the only one of the three who connects directly with the audience. Dolly Parton is a little out of it, but her dolliness is very winning; she has a big, sunny smile, and she's unpretentious, like a down-home, unthreatening version of Mae West. It's easy to forget that Jane Fonda is around; this must be the first time that she has ever got lost in the woodwork. (And this film is a production by IPC—the company formed by Fonda and Bruce Gilbert—which also produced *Coming Home* and *The China Syndrome*.) She plays a prim, mousy deserted housewife who arrives for her first day at work in a stiff little hat, a shapeless print suit, a blouse that ties in a big bow at the neck, and a carnation on her lapel, and it's not much fun watching her get politicized all over again. (Three productions, three losses of innocence.) It seems inconceivable that Jane Fonda should have become a humorless actress.

Colin Higgins is a young fossil who gets laughs by setting up flaccid, hand-me-down gags as if they were hilarious; maybe he really thinks they are. Like *Silver Streak*, which he wrote, and *Foul Play*, which he wrote and directed, *Nine to Five* seems a back number—his movies are as anachronistic as Jane Fonda's wallflower costume. Yet this picture, which opened at Christmas, is a huge hit, and—a sitcom to start with—it's being used as the basis for a new TV series. The Broadway audience I saw it with enjoyed it—men even cheered the militant feminist statements. When the black and Puerto Rican men in the Broadway audience applauded Goldie Hawn in the anti-male *Private Benjamin*, I assumed that they identified with her misery in basic training; she was going through what they had gone through. And at *Nine to Five* I assume that the men laughing are identifying with the underdog heroines in their fight against the boss. But this is a leering, doddering movie; it has almost none of the humor of *Private Benjamin* (although this one, too, features a sisterhood pot party). Higgins moves the camera from one parking place to the next. *Nine to Five* looks so bad (especially the yellow meringue interiors, and that's most of the picture) that when I checked the credits it wasn't to find out the name of the cinematographer but to see if there was one.

The idea behind the film seems to be to use a slick-package movie as a vehicle for progressive ideas. There's a well-conceived credit sequence, showing morning in a big city, with women rushing to their office jobs, while Dolly Parton sings the title song (which she wrote) in her mellow country voice. But then the film starts to push and grab, and the three women turn into bungling sillies who run around chasing a cadaver (which they think is Mr. Hart). Cast in the Charles Grodin–Bruce Dern role, Dabney Coleman adds a dash of Paul Lynde's foul-minded relish. Yet as if it weren't enough for Mr. Hart to be a pompous, stupid loafer, he has also been made a big-time embezzler—which would seem to require cunning, and close attention to the business. And Mr. Hart—a small-fry division manager—lives on an estate that Kirk Kerkorian wouldn't be ashamed of. Higgins doesn't worry about comic logic: when Jane Fonda is defeated by a Xerox machine, it's not enough that she is made to look a ninny—the Xerox machine defeats her by doing things Xerox machines can't do.

The film's technique infects its ideas. For example, Dolly Parton's less than subtle wardrobe serves a double purpose: she gets laughs just on the basis of how curvy she looks, yet she can point out how humiliating it is that the boss keeps trying to peer down her cleavage (and his twerpy maneuvers also get laughs). In the guise of feminism, Dolly Parton is used just the way the frilly, bosomy blondes of the fifties were. At the pot party, each of the heroines has a fantasy of murdering Mr. Hart. In Tomlin's, she's Snow White, and, with a couple of dotty, chirping little birdies and other animated creatures looking on, she twinkles—in complicity with us—as she opens a ring and drops poison into Hart's coffee. This sequence is Higgins' moment of glory: it's fanciful without bludgeoning us. (He does have some facility.) But the two other murders are grimly unfunny (except for a couple of the expressions on Dabney Coleman's face when Parton is raping him). Higgins directs them as if they were uproarious, though, and damned if the audience doesn't laugh. Higgins has the new gift of Midas: a relentlessly confident laughtrack sensibility. The way he writes and directs comedy, the audience is primed by the idea that something is going to be funny; the jokes don't have punch lines—the laughs are in the setups. There are chuckles even when Parton fantasizes killing Mr. Hart by smothering him in her bosom—one of the more weirdly suggestive effects in the history of movies. Higgins uses the form of black comedy without the content. The women don't actually kill Hart—that might make audiences dislike them. Instead, everything is jockeyed into place so that they can torture him and still be innocuously likable.

The line that gets the biggest laugh (and was used in the TV commercials) comes in an office scene of Dolly Parton telling off the boss; she says that if he doesn't stop making advances to her she's going to "turn him from a rooster to a hen with one shot." Didn't any of the feminists involved in this project register that a castrated rooster is a capon, not a hen, and that this joke represents the most insulting and sexist view of women?

March 9, 1981

Love, War, and

Custodial Services

As Albin, the female-impersonator star of a gay night-club revue who is the central character of the 1979 *La Cage aux Folles* and the new *La Cage aux Folles II*, Michel Serrault doesn't make the mistake of acting like a woman—he acts Albin like a transvestite's idea of a woman, going beyond impersonation into convoluted areas of sex confusion. Albin (whose stage name is ZaZa) is always primping; he is obsessed with how he looks, and is terrified of aging—that is, of no longer being loved. He's a heavyset middle-aged man trying to be a sex goddess in chiffon; he thinks he's ravishing when he's wigged and made up and dressed in the trailing kind of women's clothes that women don't wear. Holding his head at what he thinks is a distinguished angle, he enters a room like a dowager in full sail—he glides and swivels and sways.

Albin is grotesque, but he's not aware of it. He's acutely anxious, though, when he tries to pass as a manly man. The first film has an inspired moment when Albin, wearing a man's suit, sits in a chair attempting to look like a regular guy—and doesn't know what to do with his hands. You can laugh at his horror-stricken embarrassment, because Serrault admits you into an intimacy with the character; you're laughing at Albin's plight from both the inside and the outside. His is a special kind of vain, simpering pathos that never makes you want to cry—he's too absurd for tears. Serrault's feat—Albin's inability to look like other men—seems all the more remarkable to those who are familiar with his performances in heterosexual roles. In *Get Out Your Handkerchiefs,* Serrault was the neighbor who came in to complain about the noise and later paired off with the boy prodigy's mother. Back in 1957, Serrault was one of the two stars of the Sacha Guitry comedy *Assassins et Voleurs*, released in this country as *Lovers and Thieves*. The other was Jean Poiret, who wrote the play *La Cage aux Folles*. Serrault and Poiret were teamed as Albin and Renato when it opened in Paris in 1973; it kept going until 1979.

The first *Cage* was a filmed version of the stage farce, and, with Albin and Renato's plushy living quarters (above their Saint-Tropez night club) constantly being invaded by the straight world, the stage mechanics were still visible. There was also a gaping hole in the structure. The film begins with a dumb joke: while Albin is onstage performing, Renato (played by Ugo Tognazzi), his mate of over twenty years, receives a handsome young man, and we are led to assume that Renato is cheating on Albin, until it's revealed that the boy is Renato's son (the result of a brief heterosexual indiscretion). And, whether for the sake of this joke or just from thoughtlessness, the movie leaves out the maternal relationship between Albin and his lover's son. We're *told* that Albin has been like a mother to the boy, and the plot hinges on Albin's determination to be accepted as the boy's mother by the family the boy is marrying into, but they never have a scene alone together, and the boy shows neither affection nor aversion to him. Yet, with all its forced effects and clumsiness, the film had the two characters—the foolish Albin and Renato, the loving husband, fed up with Albin's silly self-delusions yet protective of him. Tognazzi's Renato, with a touch of makeup and a suggestion of a corset in his posture, and mannerisms such as wetting a pinky on his tongue and using it to smooth an eyebrow, is almost as vain as Albin, though his being able to "pass" is part of what he's vain about. It isn't hard to understand why the picture has become possibly the highest-grossing foreign film on record in this country: this extraordinary couple mirrors the pressures of heterosexual marriage in an exaggerated form that everyone can laugh at. Apparently, a lot of people have gone back to see it several times—the way their children went back to see *The Graduate* over and over—because it puts them in a cheery mood. Even people who might feel threatened by young homosexuals, perceiving them as a danger to the continuity of their own families, feel safe with elderly homosexuals. And gay activists haven't been obstreperous about the film, since it deals—affectionately—with the transvestites of gay night-club life, who can hardly be considered representative homosexuals.

The opening titles of *Cage II* invite you to see old friends again (the way the Bing Crosby and Bob Hope *Road* pictures did), and the film makes good on the invitation. Like the first picture, this one is a vaudeville show about love, vanity, lunacy. *Cage II* isn't as original as the first, but it gives the two actors more range. Although the thriller plot (a spy plants a capsule of microfilm on Albin, and from then on spies and government agents pursue him) is no more than a pretext to get Albin and Renato out of their stage-set apartment, it's serviceable. Directed (as was the first) by Édouard Molinaro, this one is much smoother. The camera isn't just a recording instrument for entrances and exits; it moves around, covering the lovers' masquerades as they travel to Italy to hide at Renato's mother's farm. And at each point along the way we see the straight world's reactions to Albin. (The Italians to whom Albin is presented as Renato's wife are afraid to move a muscle in their faces.)

When Albin pretends to be a window-washer, he doesn't just put on a workman's cap and blue denim overalls—he dresses up in them, and he's pure sissy. We can laugh without malice, because even though it's apparent that Albin doesn't seem right in any guise, we can tell how much he enjoys the dressing up. He's happy in his make-believe roles: in a sequence in Italy, Albin, dressed as a peasant woman, toils in the fields among the women, and he looks youthful and radiantly fulfilled—he really believes that he is one of them. He's like a diva who has triumphed in the role of a peasant heroine. Albin doesn't see what we can see: wherever he is and however he's dressed, he's so far into his fantasy that he looks like no one else.

As the chief of the government agents, Marcel Bozzuffi shows only the most minuscule of reactions to Albin: his double takes are no more than teeny movements in the eyes. Bozzuffi's performance isn't just a parody of deadpan acting—it's also the polar opposite of Serrault's effusiveness. If there's anyone whom Serrault's Albin recalls, it's Alice Brady in her plump and squealing society-matron roles; the same sort of uncontrollable shrill yelps come rippling out of Albin, and these falsetto screeches seem to keep the movie going. The only character who suffers from the change in format is the black manservant (Benny Luke), who has a vision of himself as a dainty maid, and maybe as a Southern belle, too; he belongs to the stage-farce world of the first picture, where his prancing in and out was used as a running joke. He has almost nothing to do this time—only a few walk-ons—but he gets laughs just by showing up in his dinky spandex hot pants, with little lacy aprons. He's a human valentine.

La Cage aux Folles II has nothing to do with the art of movies, but it has a great deal to do with the craft and art of acting, and the pleasures of farce. Serrault gives a superb comic performance—his Albin is a wildly fanciful creation. There's a grandeur about Albin's inability to see himself as he is. And maybe it's only in this exaggerated form that a movie about the ridiculousness and the tenderness of married love can be widely accepted now. At the end, after Albin has been kidnapped by the spies, Renato, who is nearby with the police, can't think of anything but his beloved Albin. And, suddenly, forgetting the danger, each starts running toward the other, and they meet between the two armed groups like lovers in an opera. One of the policemen watching their embrace is weeping. "It's beautiful," he says.

.   .   .   .   .

The Dogs of War is a swift and intelligent demonstration of how the conventions of action movies can be adapted and given new meaning. There is no romanticism about "soldiers of fortune"; the central figures—the leader, Christopher Walken, and his key men, Tom Berenger, Paul Freeman, and Jean-François Stevenin—are mercenaries. We aren't asked to like them, and Walken kills a spy (set on him by his own employer, who doesn't trust him) in such a horrifying way that we really couldn't like him. But we do want to watch him. Without anything being made explicit, the film indicates that it's more than money that impels these mercenaries to fight. They are men from several countries who, having been in wars, and having felt the excitement and ruthlessness of fighting and the power of weaponry, can't settle down to peacetime occupations. They want the highs, the camaraderie, the professionalism and pride. It's a form of craziness, but, having seen combat, they have had something burned out of them; they feel trapped in safe jobs, released in action.

The casting of Walken in the lead gives this picture the fuse it needs; without him—with some stalwart, tough-looking actor—it might seem just a crisp example of an action film. But Walken, with his pale, flat-faced mask of pain and his lithe movements, suggests a restless anger. His eyes look spooked, like a cat's, and you feel he'd be cold to the touch. There's something gnawing away at Walken's Jamie Shannon, and it's going to devour him or explode. Walken convinces you that there is nothing besides fighting left in Shannon's life. That doesn't mean that Shannon doesn't care whom he fights for. The instincts that make him a responsible leader who takes care of his men are at work all the time. This is a tough-minded movie that gives you the underside of the loner myth, but it isn't completely cynical. Even mercenaries have their discriminations—though when they make a moral choice, it may be less out of idealism than out of disgust at corruption. At the end, what Shannon does is believable, because of Walken's anger and those glaring eyes.

Freely adapted from a best-seller by Frederick Forsyth, this movie shows Shannon on a reconnaissance mission to Zangaro, a small, decaying West African country, run by an Idi Amin–Papa Doc–style despot—President Kimba. A British company that is interested in Zangaro's platinum can't get the mining rights from Kimba, so it sends an emissary (Hugh Millais) to hire Shannon to determine how strong Kimba's government is and whether a coup can be staged, so that the company can install its own, handpicked dictator. This is the first feature film by John Irvin, an English documentarian and TV director. (*Tinker, Tailor, Soldier, Spy* is his best-known work here.) Irvin does everything allusively and almost silently in this preliminary section, which was actually shot in Belize, formerly British Honduras. With Jack Cardiff as his cinematographer, Irvin shows us the eerie disorder in the bright sunshine as Shannon, claiming to be a nature photographer, saunters along the dirt streets of this crummy little police state, where soldiers loiter around fully armed. The squalor and the brutality are palpable. So is Shannon's arrogance. It's a paranoid landscape, with an increasingly paranoid visitor. The impassive Shannon, with his feline sense of danger, loathes everything about the place, with a few exceptions: North (the skillful Colin Blakely), a boozing TV journalist he meets in the hotel bar, who has come to Zangaro in the hope of interviewing President Kimba; Gabrielle (Maggie Scott), the hotel manager's beautiful and well-educated daughter; and Dr. Okoye (Winston Ntshona), who was once a political opponent of Kimba's and has been imprisoned since Kimba took over. Shannon makes the kind of outsider's mistake that can be fatal in a country like Zangaro: Trying to get a picture of the military installations, he photographs Gabrielle in front of the Army garrison and, when he's arrested and beaten, says he was just taking a picture of a pretty girl. Upon hearing that, the soldiers go to work on him with chains, because Gabrielle is Kimba's mistress. They throw him into prison, and that's how he meets Dr. Okoye, who tends his wounds.

Shannon is deported, and we don't see Zangaro again until he goes back with a boatload of men and munitions. Most of the movie is spent on his recruiting his team, getting provisioned, training the men. The choice of details seems almost random, but the taut, abbreviated scenes are kept hopping, and there is certainly never too much of anything. The picture appears to be edited for tension and rhythm and the crackle of dialogue; the moviemakers are rather cavalier about slashing through explanations, but in terms of the full effect their choices are sound. The raid on Zangaro—at night—is very brief, but it's the psychological culmination of months of planning. During the attack, Walken and Berenger each carry an incredible new toy—the XM-18, a portable rocket launcher (about the size of a Thompson submachine gun, with a drum)—and they yell like happy demons as they fire off gas, smoke, and high-impact missiles. Irvin has studied a master: some of the most feral images are almost direct quotations from Peckinpah's *The Wild Bunch*.

The Dogs of War isn't pulpy. Maybe the traditions in which John Irvin was trained have saved him from the crude tricks that have cheapened the action genres. There is one element of excessive refinement about the film: the dialogue is recorded very softly. That would be fine if you saw the film in a quiet theatre or at home on television, but, seeing it in a big Broadway house, I missed a lot of the lines. The ones I heard (from the script by Gary DeVore and George Malko) made me regret the ones I lost.

. . . . .

Eyewitness has something big going for it: the audience's eagerness to sit back and enjoy a swank, glossy murder mystery—a movie with the kind of torrid menace that inspired Ran Blake's music on the Arista record *Film Noir*. And there's the promise of excitement in a contemporary, New York City movie that stars two smart, young, stage-trained performers: William Hurt, who made his screen début in *Altered States* as the hero with a case of high-intellectual jitters, and the tall, striking Sigourney Weaver, who was the executive officer (in bikini panties) of the spaceship in *Alien* and plays a television newscaster here. There's also the promise of fresh, whimsical slapstick in the collaboration of the director Peter Yates and the writer Steve Tesich, who worked together on the 1979 comedy *Breaking Away*. But *Eyewitness* bogs down in a tangle of plot. Yates and Tesich are trying to do something complicated: a new, more meaningful version of a forties melodrama—one that will celebrate America's ethnic diversity while demonstrating the unlimited possibilities of people misunderstanding each other. But they don't know how to adapt and modernize forties-thriller conventions. And so something berserk happens: Sigourney Weaver, Irene Worth, and Christopher Plummer, who are all playing Jews, play them like Nazis. They're intense, drawn, haggard, rich, and highly cultured, and when they're all together at a musicale in the stately town house of Weaver's parents—with Weaver at the piano, Worth (as her mother) on the cello, Albert Paulsen (as her father) on the violin, and the slimy-suave Israeli, Plummer, with his skin a color that doesn't exist in nature, standing by to make a fund-raising speech—they're a stiff and sinister bunch. From the conspiratorial look of things, they and their friends might have gathered for a Black Mass.

Weaver's parents—Russian Jews who speak with heavy accents—are so rich and cultured that they consider themselves disgraced by their daughter's career in television. Presumably, it's too vulgar for people of their aristocratic background. (I've not heard of these Jews who came out of the Soviet Union rich and aristocratic; the ones I know of are running candy stores or restaurants in Coney Island, or driving cabs out of it.) Just about no one is believable in this movie—not the prowling Amazonic sabra who is some sort of warriorlike accomplice of Plummer's, and certainly not Plummer, the distinguished Israeli, who is also a fanatic Zionist, involved in clandestine operations with Weaver's parents. (That musicale group has all kinds of questionable implications, which Yates and Tesich appear to be unaware of.)

By training, temperament, and spectacular good looks, Sigourney Weaver seems a natural for stardom in this era; she's scaled to be a modern heroine. But what can she do in the role of Tony Sokolow, which shows her revelling in her work, enjoying every minute of it, and then has her announce that she's going to do what her parents want—quit her job and marry the man of their choice? Yates and Tesich have put an eighties woman into a claptrap forties-movie situation. When Tony makes that announcement, the movie dries up and blows away. I recently saw Sigourney Weaver on the stage (in Christopher Durang's *Beyond Therapy*), where she was slender yet strapping and you were aware of her joints—she seemed lucky to have so much body to act with, and you could feel her physical pleasure in the funny lines she got to deliver. Here, in her newscaster scenes, she begins confidently, but then the writing wipes her out. The cinematographer doesn't do well by her, either—she becomes pale and rather remote; even her wavy thundercloud of hair gets squashed. (Some of her speeches appear to be looped, and this may help to account for the remoteness.)

Hurt manages to remain appealing—a triumph in the circumstances. He's playing Daryll, an Irish-American former Marine, decorated in Vietnam, who works as night janitor in a Manhattan office building where a Vietnamese merchant is murdered. Daryll, who has fallen in love with Tony on TV, meets her when she comes to film a news item about the murder. He talks a blue streak, because he's afraid that if he stops talking she'll turn away and he'll never get another chance. He pretends to know something about the murder—he suggests that he may have been an eyewitness—in order to pique her interest. This flirtatious improvisation of his makes the two of them targets for the killers, for those who seek to avenge the killing, for the police, and—it begins to seem—for every passerby. What's entertaining is the flirtation itself. Hurt, who can be funniest when he's most fervent, has the come-on lines, and he inflects them for all they're worth, and quite a bit more. Daryll speaks with a withdrawn, rhapsodic earnestness that's hip and comic. He makes mock-naïve declarations of love to Tony: he says exactly what he feels, yet his awareness of how batty his words must sound gives them an edge—a slight suggestion of a put-on. She is, naturally (just about her only chance at a natural emotion here), thrown off balance.

It's clear what Tesich is getting at in having his hero work as a night janitor (the job must be a first for a Hollywood hero): a lot of intelligent and well-educated Americans work at blue-collar and custodial jobs, because these jobs don't infringe on their lives. Some do it only while they're college students (as Tesich did, working as a night janitor in an office building, like Daryll); others do it so that they can keep their minds free to write or paint, or just to enjoy a freedom from responsibility which isn't possible in professional fields or in business—or because they get into the routine of an undemanding job and just stay in it. Tesich (a Serb, who emigrated from

Yugoslavia when he was thirteen) is saying that in this country people doing menial work don't necessarily feel that it's degrading or that they are menials. He's saying that Daryll is simple in terms of his needs, yet he's intelligent and competent, and has enough sense of his own worth not to be concerned about class barriers. Daryll watches Tony on television so intently (it's like Zen concentration) that he makes you accept the idea that he's completely and unalterably in love with her. If the audience didn't go along with this far-out romantic premise, there wouldn't really be any movie. But as Hurt plays Daryll, you feel that he has the strength and the flukey intensity to bring his fantasy off. And Daryll's winning Tony is halfway plausible, because Hurt and Weaver look great together: whatever the social differences, nature is on their side—they match up.

Still, about midway, I thought, I wish Tesich would get over his love affair with America, or at least stop trying to authenticate the American dream. I think the intention is to present Daryll's love for Tony as an absurdist romance that can come true in America, but the film's thriller aspects aren't absurdist—they're just plain unconvincing. There are frequent eavesdropping scenes and lurking-about scenes—cuts to a couple of Vietnamese thugs overhearing what Daryll is saying to Tony, or misconstruing what they see him doing, or following somebody in a car and boding ill. These inserts are so silly I wondered if they could have been meant as a running gag; whether intended to be comic or serious, they've gone wrong. When Daryll and Tony are in his apartment at night, and his closest friend (James Woods), who had a grudge against the murdered man, is in the street below spying on them, Woods needs a light for his cigarette; he bums one from a man whom the flame reveals to be Plummer, who is also there spying. Surely this is meant to make us laugh, and it does, somewhat, but there's no tension to release—it's just a casual laugh. Even the menacing set pieces (such as Daryll at work being trapped in a trash compactor) don't build suspense and then release it—they just dribble away. There's an essential innocence in Yates's and Tesich's attempt to provide motivation for the murder and the subsequent events: they are all somehow linked to fund-raising to get Jews out of the Soviet Union. (I never got it to add up, exactly.) Innocence may be too kind a word. I could have done without such keys to Daryll's harmoniousness as the information that he has a special rapport with children and animals, who will do anything he wants. Are Yates and Tesich trying to make a holistic thriller? If they needed to prepare for Daryll's way with horses in the final, riding-academy sequence (a true bummer; it looks like unedited footage), they could have planted the information that he was experienced with horses instead of making him one of nature's noblemen. The pieces of the movie don't fit together in tone: this noble janitor is elsewhere given a tinny, smartass double-entendre speech in which he offers to buff Tony's floors.

The film has some saving grace notes. Though the dialogue is just functional (and lumpy) a lot of the time, when it's funny it's often marvellous.

What works best is something that is never supposed to work: the literary flourishes that most good directors would immediately cut. Yates must have had the instinct to recognize that these rather florid riffs would give the film a special charm. I would have been happier without Daryll's account of what happened at his first dance; it didn't do a thing for his character, it reeked of creative-writing courses, and it echoed Brando's story in *Last Tango* about going on a date with cow dung all over his shoes. But Kenneth McMillan, as Hurt's paraplegic father, brings off a soul-baring speech about marriage and love with the kind of juicy mastery that makes you want to applaud. It interrupts the action, but it's more fun than what it's interrupting. There is a series of cynical, griping conversations between a team of police lieutenants (Morgan Freeman and Steven Hill); these exchanges are high points. And, as Daryll's old girlfriend, Pamela Reed, with her bright brown eyes and her seemingly limitless energy, plays a scene in which she is so avid to get things off her chest that her words develop a rhythmic charge, peak, and keep going. (It's an aesthetic disgrace that the camera is too close to her and she also sounds too loud.) With the possible exception of the police lieutenants' conversations, none of these speeches would work in a good thriller, but we clutch at them here. They have punch, and we know where we are when we hear them. They locate us in a world of actors scoring in character bits. (Several of the actors seem to be brought on just for the sake of these numbers; McMillan is *carried* on. Playwrights who can't fit these showoff speeches into one play often save them for the next.)

Eyewitness is moderately enjoyable to watch, but when you think about it, it gets weirder and worse. There's a level of common sense missing. Trying to be Russian Jewish enough, Irene Worth talks as if she were shifting potatoes around in her cheeks; her face is gnarled from all this guttural exertion. (A scene in which she wraps her tongue around the words "This is so painful" could be the low point in her career.) Trying to be sleek and exotic (as befits an Israeli diplomat!), Christopher Plummer speaks in silken cadences and acts like a homosexual courtier of the last century. Nobody ever seems to do the next logical thing in this movie: When Daryll finds the body, we expect him to call the police; instead, we see him riding home on his motorcycle. When Tony is attacked on the street by the two Vietnamese, she never considers notifying the authorities. *Eyewitness* has such elaborate thematic patterns that even Daryll's dog is misunderstood—first by us (we think he's murderous when he's only romping) and later by Daryll. But the moviemakers miss out on the simple things: Daryll comes home after a full work shift and doesn't take the dog out—doesn't even worry about it. The dog never goes out.

March 23, 1981

Chance/Fate

*B*urt Lancaster started out, back in the 1946 *The Killers*, as a great specimen of hunkus Americanus. In Louis Malle's new comedy, *Atlantic City*, from a script by John Guare, Lancaster uses his big, strong body so expressively that if this were a stage performance the audience would probably give him a standing ovation. I don't see how he could be any better. He plays Lou, an old-timer who tries to keep up appearances; he irons his one good silk tie before going outside. Still dreaming of the good old days, when he was a flunky and bodyguard for big-time racketeers, Lou scrounges for a living as a numbers runner, making his rounds of Atlantic City's black slums and picking up bets of fifty cents or a dollar. He also takes handouts—and abuse—from Grace (Kate Reid), the widow of a mobster he used to work for. She has an apartment in the same building where he has a small, seedy room; she stays in bed, pampering herself, while he shops and cooks for her and walks her dog—a tiny poodle, which he hates. Grace is a hypochondriac and complainer, and she razzes him mercilessly; he accepts her reproaches, though he snarls to himself in weary resentment. You sense that he barely hears her anymore; Lou's thoughts are elsewhere. When he's in his room and looks out the window, across the airshaft, he can see into the apartment where Sally (Susan Sarandon) lives; hiding to the side, he watches her nightly ablutions when she comes home from her waitress work at the Oyster Bar in the Resorts International casino. She puts a tape of *Norma* on her cassette-player, cuts lemons in half, and rubs the juice onto her upper body. Excited, Lou hurries down to Grace's apartment, puts a record on, and crawls into bed with her.

Lancaster's acting in *The Killers* wasn't at all bad, but his physical presence was so powerful in the busy years that followed that he became a caricature of an action star. Sometimes he was a satiric caricature (as in the 1952 *The Crimson Pirate*), and sometimes he was an impressive, highly sexual man of action (as in the 1953 *From Here to Eternity*), but in his many attempts to extend his range beyond action roles—in *Come Back, Little Sheba* (1952), *The Rose Tattoo* (1955), *The Rainmaker* (1956), *Separate Tables* (1958), *The Devil's Disciple* (1959), *The Young Savages* (1961), *Judgment at Nuremberg* (1961), *Birdman of Alcatraz* (1962), *A Child Is Waiting* (1963), and, most notably, in *Sweet Smell of Success* (1956)—you could often see him straining for seriousness, and it shrivelled him. (When Lancaster put on a pair of specs, he looked as if he'd been bled by leeches.) Probably no other major star took so many chances, and a couple of times—as the prince in Visconti's *The Leopard* (1963), and as the patriarch in Bertolucci's *1900* (1976)—he came through with a new weight of emotion. In those pictures, he seemed able to use his bull-like physicality with a new dignity and awareness. He was more physical than ever, but physical in the way that Anna Magnani (with whom he was teamed in *The Rose Tattoo*) was—battered, larger than life, vain, naked. In shallow action roles, he played bloody but unbowed; when he was working with Visconti or Bertolucci, he wasn't afraid to be bloody and bowed. And that's how he is here, but more so, because this time he isn't playing a strong man brought down by age and social changes: he's a man who was never anything much—he was always a little too soft inside—and Grace won't let him forget it.

Though I have a better time in the theatre at John Guare's plays than I do at the plays of any other contemporary American, I would not have guessed that his charmed, warped world and his dialogue, which is full of imagery, could be so successfully brought to the screen. In a Guare play, the structure isn't articulated. There's nothing to hold the bright pieces together but his nerve and his instincts; when they're in high gear, the play has the excitement of discovery—which you don't get in "well-crafted" plays. You're not stuck with the usual dramatic apparatus—the expository dialogue and the wire-pulling to get the characters into the planned situations. Instead, you get gags, which prove to be the explanations. *Anything* may turn up in a Guare play. In Joseph Papp's Public Theatre production of Guare's *Marco Polo Sings a Solo*, set on an Arctic island in 1999, Anne Jackson, who played Joel Grey's mother, revealed that her son was the first person in history to have only one parent: she was a transsexual, she explained, and had conceived him with semen saved from before her sex-change operation. In the same play, another character talked about Chekhov's *The Three Sisters*: "Those poor girls, all the time trying to get to Moscow. The town they lived in was only forty-eight miles from Moscow. In 1999 that town is probably part of greater downtown Moscow. They were in Moscow all the time." Guare's vaudeville jokes subvert traditional conceptions of drama. Anyone who has ever been embarrassed for the actors who had to fling a prop dead bird around the stage in *The Sea Gull* or *The Wild Duck* would have appreciated Anne Jackson's aside to the audience apropos of some similar props: "I don't know much about symbols, but I'd say that when frozen flamingos fall out of the sky, good times are not in store." In a foreword to the published version of his play *The House of Blue Leaves*, Guare wrote that what had got him out of a creative cul-de-sac was watching Olivier perform on successive nights in Strindberg's *The Dance of Death* and Feydeau's *A Flea in Her Ear*. In his imagination, they blended, he said, and became one play, and he asked himself why Strindberg and Feydeau shouldn't get married, or at least live together.

I have resorted to quoting from *Marco Polo* because I would like to suggest Guare's comic style without uncorking *Atlantic City*. Let me just indicate how the jokes function: Lou reminisces about the glories of this resort town in the days when there were real songs, like "Flat Foot Floogie with the Floy Floy," and he adds, "The Atlantic Ocean was something then." You laugh in recognition that for him life has lost its savor. Guare's one-liners are more deeply zany than we're accustomed to. His characters sound as if they had all invented themselves and their life histories right on the spot. And Guare has a way of shaping a funny line of dialogue so it goes loop-the-loop into pathos. Sometimes I think that his is the only kind of theatrical pathos that's really enjoyable; it erupts suddenly, when a character's invention can't go any further and he's left with truth. But it's still part of a gag. Kate Reid's Grace, lying amid boxes of chocolate and rose satin quilted covers, may remind the lucky few who saw Guare's most intense and macabre play, *Bosoms and Neglect*, of her performance as the bedridden, blind, and cancerous old Irish mother, Henny. (When Henny is in the hospital for surgery, her son visits a woman he picked up in Rizzoli's—a blond bibliophile who tries to seduce him with her first editions. He describes his mother's torments, and she cries, "I suddenly have this image of being blind. Oh God. Never to be able to browse.") Guare was one of the three writers who worked with Miloš Forman on the 1971 *Taking Off*, but the film's sensibility was Forman's. *Atlantic City* is a collaboration much like that of Elia Kazan and Tennessee Williams on, say, *Baby Doll*. Louis Malle has entered into Guare's way of seeing—a mixture of observation, flights of invention, satire, perversity, anecdote, fable. And depth of feeling—what Lancaster, in the finest performance he has ever given (with the possible exception of his work in *1900*), brings to the film. And he brings it to the jokes.

Near the beginning of the film, one of the vast, curvy old Baghdad-by-the-sea buildings that date from Atlantic City's days as a resort community is dynamited; this rock-candy relic is making way for the new hotel-casinos, which have been shooting up since New Jersey legalized gambling there, in 1976. (It was chosen partly because it's on an island and can be closed off from the mainland.) Malle's Atlantic City is very different from the seedy, decrepit one in which Bob Rafelson shot *The King of Marvin Gardens*, in 1972. The destruction and construction that go on in all cities are accelerated in the new Atlantic City; it suggests a giant movie lot, where sets are built and struck. This spa that became a racketeers' paradise during Prohibition and is now on its chaotic way to becoming Vegas with a beach is an improbable place; it gives a hallucinatory texture to the characters' lives. And it's the ideal real place for a Guare comedy—everything arriving and departing in one fell swoop. Atlantic City is the film's controlling metaphor. Malle and Guare must have let the city itself set the motifs: demolition and construction; decay and renewal; water, baths, ablutions; luck. The city says so much on its own that the moviemakers don't have to press down for meanings; if anything, they need to hold back (and they do).

When the rambling pleasure palace crumbles, the film takes up the story of another relic—Lou. The movie is a lyric farce, in which Lou and Sally, and Grace also, realize their dreams, through a series of accidents and several varieties of chicanery. Sally has been training to become a croupier, under the tutelage of the Frenchman (Michel Piccoli) who gave her the Elizabeth Harwood tape of *Norma*. Her plans are disrupted when her wormy husband (Robert Joy) hitchhikes into town with her pale, sweetly zonked younger sister Chrissie (Hollis McLaren), who is hugely pregnant by him. They turn up, scuzzy from the road and with their packs on their backs, at the sleek casino where Sally works. Sally's husband expects her to let them crash at her place until he can dispose of a bundle of cocaine that he stole in Philadelphia. Once he arrives, nobody in the movie seems to have any principles or to have heard of honesty. (Chrissie doesn't even believe in gravity.) Lou—through a fluke—gets hold of the money from the cocaine, and starts behaving like the sport he has always wanted to be. He spreads the wealth around and squires Sally to an expensive restaurant; she's eager to learn more about the world, and, little as he knows, he's a fount of knowledge compared with her.

The role of the ignorant Sally, a back-country girl from Saskatchewan who hopes to work her way to Monte Carlo, is essentially that of Gabrielle in *The Petrified Forest*, and, for once, Susan Sarandon's googly-eyed, slightly stupefied look seems perfect. She doesn't rattle off her lines in her usual manner; she seems to respond to the freshness and lilt of the dialogue. In Malle's last film, *Pretty Baby*, she was mysteriously beautiful when she was posing nude for photographs, but she gave an inexplicably petulant and vapid performance; she did so much ruminating she was cowlike. Susan Sarandon has sometimes come through in strange circumstances, though; the permutations of her rattle provided the sprightliest moments of *The Other Side of Midnight*. Maybe she seems so skillful here because this is the best part she's ever had on the screen. Her double takes are very delicate; she keeps you tuned in to her feelings all the time. Sally's expression is frazzled yet affectionate when she looks at her Hare Krishna–ite little sister. Hollis McLaren (she was the half-mad girl in *Outrageous!*) brings a winsome dippiness to the role of gullible Chrissie, a flower child born into the wrong era. Simplicity like Chrissie's seems almost soothing, but not if you're her sister and don't know what to do with her. What can you do with a pregnant angel?

When I see a Guare play, I almost always feel astonished; I never know where he's going until he gets there. Then everything ties together. He seems to have an intuitive game plan. That's how this film works, too. It takes Malle a little while to set up the crisscrossing of the ten or twelve major characters, but once he does you can begin to respond to the interior, poetic logic that holds this movie together. By the second half, *Atlantic City* is operating by its own laws in its own world, and it has a lovely fizziness. Everything goes wrong and comes out right. It's no accident that Guare said Feydeau had helped him out of a cul-de-sac. We get the pleasure of seeing everything sorted out, as it is in a classic farce, except that the perfect pairings, the slippers that fit, the kindnesses rewarded have the dadaist quality of having been plucked out of the air.

The casting is superb, and each time a performer reappears you look forward to what he's going to do this time. There are just a few minor disappointments. Acting in English, Piccoli doesn't have his usual nuanced control (he overemphasizes his lines), but he certainly knows how to play a practiced European lecher; in one scene he circles around Sally, like a weary dancer. A murder sequence in a hydraulic parking structure is perhaps too tricky; it looks as if it was a bitch to shoot and edit. But there are almost constant small pleasures, such as Lou's meeting an old pal, Buddy (Sean Sullivan), who has become a washroom attendant, and swapping stories, and a hospital sequence, in which Robert Goulet, on behalf of Resorts International, presents the casino's check for a quarter of a million dollars to the Atlantic City Medical Center, the Frank Sinatra Wing, and sings to an audience of patients brought down to the lobby to make the presentation a media event. (It's like an epic-size Bill Murray routine.) One sequence appears to drift, but then has a great conclusion: Sally and Lou go to the house that she plans to share with nine other croupiers-in-training. (Each of the ten is studying to deal a different game—baccarat, blackjack, and so on.) Sally takes Lou to the room she needs to paint, and when they're alone he tells her that he watches her at night. She is moved and he can see that she is going to let him make love to her. He pushes her blouse down from her shoulders and looks at her ripe young flesh, and his watery eyes are full of reverence and regret.

This picture has just about everything that *Pretty Baby*, which was also made in this country, and in English, lacked. Every line of dialogue in *Pretty Baby* was stiff. It was clear that the person who made the film was a director, but it was hard to believe that he'd ever worked with actors before. In *Atlantic City*, Louis Malle is in full control and at his ease, and his collaboration with John Guare produces a rich, original comic tone. Sometimes the most pleasurable movies seem very slight, because they don't wham you on the noggin. Malle's skill shows in the way he keeps this picture in its frame of reference, and gives it its own look. Visually, it's extraordinary, though in a way that doesn't hit you on the noggin, either. The lighting is vivid but muted and indirect. A whole room may be in focus, yet with very little light—no more than the modulated light you see on cloudy days. The cinematographer, Richard Ciupka, is a young Québécois (the film was financed partly by Canadian funds); his work here suggests Storaro—it's like studio lighting but softer. The whole city seems to be in deep focus; you're sharply aware of old and new, age and youth. The ocean breezes are chilling to Lou; he's bundled up as he makes his rounds. But by the end he enjoys looking at the ocean again. The movie is a prankish wish-fulfillment fantasy about prosperity: what it does to cities, what it can do for people. There's a closing image of a massive building—the wrecking ball keeps pounding it, and it keeps refusing to yield. When you leave the theatre, you may feel light-headed, as if there were no problems in the world that couldn't be solved.

．　　　．　　　．　　　．

*I*n James M. Cain's novel *The Postman Always Rings Twice*, Cora and Frank take her husband, the greasy Nick, who likes to sing opera, up into the mountains, where they plan to kill him and send the car crashing down with him inside. Nick, who has had too much to drink, gets out of the car to be sick, discovers that there's a fine echo, and lets out some high notes. Frank, the narrator of the novel, who is sitting in the back seat, tells him it's time to get going. Nick climbs into the car but shoves his face out the window and lets go with one last note. And Frank reports, "I braced my feet, and while he still had his chin on the window sill I brought down the wrench. His head cracked, and I felt it crush. He crumpled up and curled on the seat like a cat on a sofa. It seemed a year before he was still. Then Cora, she gave a funny kind of gulp that ended in a moan. Because here came the echo of his voice. It took the high note, like he did, and swelled, and stopped, and waited." The new version of the story, directed by Bob Rafelson, from David Mamet's adaptation, re-creates this murder scene faithfully but leaves out Nick's echo. That's a pretty fair indication of Rafelson's and Mamet's judgment.

Cain (who was briefly the managing editor of *The New Yorker*) is more famous for two short passages of dialogue in this novel—his first—than for anything else. The reader knows all that is necessary about Frank when Frank describes Cora: "She had a sulky look to her, and her lips stuck out in a way that made me want to mash them in for her." A few pages later, he does, and her response is "Bite me! Bite me!" He reports, "I bit her. I sunk my teeth into her lips so deep I could feel the blood spurt into my mouth. It was running down her neck when I carried her upstairs." The second passage comes just after they've killed Nick, when they're preparing the "accident." Frank reports, "I began to fool with her blouse, to bust the buttons, so she would look banged up. She was looking at me, and her eyes didn't look blue, they looked black. I could feel her breath coming fast. Then it stopped, and she leaned real close to me." She says, "Rip me! Rip me!" and he obligingly tears her clothes open, punches her to make her look bruised, and they're both so excited that they have sex, a few feet from Nick's corpse. The movie re-creates these incidents also but omits "Bite me! Bite me!" "Rip me! Rip me!"

There's almost a death wish about this adaptation: Rafelson takes the granddaddy of hot tabloid novels and treats it with dedication and concern—even going to all the trouble and expense of setting it in 1934, the year that the book was published—but he leaves out the most memorable parts. Was he afraid that people would laugh at them now? I don't think they would—not if the director made the scenes tense and tawdry. And if he can't *The Postman* isn't the right property for him. Were Rafelson and Mamet scared off by

Edmund Wilson's derision of the dead man's echo as "Hollywood"? Maybe Mamet—a Pinterite who pares away and wants austerity—considered it "shtick." But Cain's raw flamboyance is the essence of this story; take it out and *The Postman* is flabby, third-rate Hemingway or just a variation on Sidney Howard's *They Knew What They Wanted.* Wilson also said, of Cain's novels, "They are a kind of Devil's parody of the movies. Mr. Cain is the *âme damnée* of Hollywood. All the things that have been excluded by the Catholic censorship: sex, debauchery, unpunished crime, sacrilege against the Church—Mr. Cain has let them loose in these stories with a gusto as of pent-up ferocity that the reader cannot but share. What a pity that it is impossible for such a writer to create and produce his own pictures!" If even Edmund Wilson admitted that he shared the excitement, I think Rafelson might have trusted that movie audiences wouldn't be too sophisticated for it.

This picture isn't a cloddish disgrace; you can see the taste and craftsmanship that have gone into it. It's overcontrolled, though, and methodical in its pacing. It's wrongheaded. Rafelson seems drawn to make art; the images are overscaled, and he has too much at stake in each frame. This story didn't need to be set back in time: the period detail makes it look studied and accurate, when what's wanted is impulsiveness and haste. The book is written in the American tough-guy vernacular ("I had to have her, if I hung for it. I had her"). Rafelson's detached, meditative tone is about as far from this vernacular as you can get. The camera stays at a chilling distance and never heats up. The cinematographer was Sven Nykvist, and the dark-blue tones and the lighting make the South California setting look Swedish; the atmosphere is damp and rainy. The words that would describe this movie are at the opposite pole from how anyone would describe the book. There's a stunningly beautiful opening shot of Frank (Jack Nicholson) hitchhiking at night; the tony visuals outclass the characters right from the start.

Nicholson appears to be working very seriously, yet he doesn't come up with anything fresh, and he doesn't seem to know how to do anything simply. As Frank, he does a run-through of his overdeliberate sly, malevolent expressions from *The Shining* while still lobotomized from *Cuckoo's Nest.* He's even still doing that crazy thing with his eyes—looking up into the lids as if he were trying to locate his brains. (His performance could have been given by a Nicholson impersonator.) Nicholson's face is becoming a Kabuki mask: it's those triangular eyebrows and the hair receding on both sides of his head and the stylized, leeringly evil expressions. At times, he recalls Elisha Cook, Jr.,'s blank-faced criminals, and there's something about the way he holds his upper lip open that is startlingly like Arthur Kennedy. Nicholson has a difficult and underwritten role: the Frank of the book is a twenty-four-year-old kid, a stud who has been bumming around; he had never been in any serious trouble until he developed this passionate hunger for Cora, and she likes him because he is young (like her) and clean. Nicholson, who's going on forty-four and looks older, has to account for what he's been doing, and the movie's solution is to make Frank an ex-convict. But he looks so mean and burned-out that we don't fear for him when Cora suggests that he can have her only by killing her husband. Actually, Frank, with his surly cock-of-the-walk virility, seems almost as sexually repellent as the genial slob Nick (John Colicos, who gives a very shrewd, unsentimental performance as an Old World Greek). The kind of rough banging that Cora (Jessica Lange) gets from Frank doesn't seem that different from what she probably gets from Nick. Frank never bothers to shave for her, and he's almost as greasy as Nick. (She doesn't get much of a break.) Nicholson's Frank sets a nasty mood; he's such a scowling son of Satan that you wonder why Nick would ever trust him enough to hire him to work in the service station next to the roadside café that he and Cora run.

Jessica Lange has a beautiful camera face that is still relatively new to the public; she has been in only three pictures—*King Kong, How to Beat the High Cost of Living*, and *All That Jazz*, where she was swathed in gauze. (She seemed to be playing Our Lady of the Oxygen Tent.) Rafelson and Mamet don't develop Cora's character—they put her through changes instead. And, whether it's lack of training or of feeling, there are times when you can almost read in Jessica Lange's eyes, "Am I getting by with this? Is it all right?" But she's still the best reason for seeing this *Postman*. She has a great, expressive body. Though she seemed slender and willowy in *King Kong* and *The High Cost of Living*, here she looks good-sized—muscular but rounded, and with strong flanks. She stands and walks with her rump out proudly, and it dominates the movie. You have no trouble believing that Frank has to grab her. With her short, curly blond hair, a Japanese silk wrapper pulled tight, and a lewd, speculative smile, she's both seraphic and steamy. Her closeups are sometimes unusually revealing when she's almost still, but she also has startling moments—like her agonized expression when she hears the crunch of Nick's skull. Rafelson directs Jessica Lange very skillfully in many scenes; she's wonderful when she tries to fight off Frank's first assault and then snarls, "All right, c'mon," challenging him to show her what he can do. If there's something missing—if she never quite catches fire—it's probably because of the way the film has been distanced.

The story is about how Frank and Cora's animal passion turns into love, and the movie needs to be propelled by a growing intensity in their sex scenes and then by the jeopardy these lovers are in. But the first sex, on the table in the café kitchen, is the hottest, so things go downhill. What should be the high point—sex by the corpse—is just a few flashes. And even in the kitchen the lust is empty. There's a lot of grappling, but the sex doesn't make much sense—Cora seems to have a terrific orgasm as soon as Frank's dirty hand starts crawling up her thigh. There was a lot of pre-release publicity about how the film was going to show what had to be left out of the 1946 version, with John Garfield and Lana Turner, but there were also strange statements by Rafelson that he was going to shoot the film as an X and then cut it as an R. Why? For his own diversion? If he did it that way, he probably couldn't compensate for what he had to take out: these sex scenes are a mess—quick cuts with no erotic feeling.

The film never develops momentum, because pivotal scenes aren't clear. Cora makes an early, abortive attempt to kill Nick by hitting him on the head while he's in the bathtub, but a cat steps in the fuse box, the lights go out, and Cora panics. We don't understand (except from the book) that the lights went out before she could drown him; we're given no clue that that was what she was going to do, so we're not keyed up—we're just confused. After Nick's death, the courthouse scenes are too abrupt, the dialogue deteriorates, and the movie becomes aimless. One episode is completely off in tone: Anjelica Huston, in dominatrix bangs, turns up as a lion tamer with a Ruritanian accent; she plays odalisque to Nicholson, who, dropping the character of Frank altogether, plays pasha. During this second half, we lose confidence that the moviemakers know where they're going. Cain's story has the reader in a state of apprehensive excitement; it just keeps coming. But Rafelson tries to purify the material, to essentialize it. Why else hire Mamet to provide sparse, Pinteresque dialogue that leaves out the juice? (Mamet's silences are really silent.) Rafelson lays on effects that are supposed to stand for the characters' erotic heat; all that happens is that the atmosphere becomes dissociated from the action. With all that elegant cinematography, the film has no images that stay in the mind the way Cain's descriptions do.

There is one change that I think betrays the whole scheme of the story, and is offensive to boot. In the book, when Cora and Frank are arrested for murder (nobody is fooled by their accident story) their lawyer is a man named Katz. This is Frank's description of him: "He was a little guy, about forty years old, with a leathery face and a black moustache, and the first thing he did when he came in was take out a bag of Bull Durham smoking tobacco and a pack of brown papers and roll himself a cigarette." Katz makes a hundred-dollar bet with the prosecutor that he can get Cora and Frank off, and he does, by working out a deal with the two insurance companies involved in the case. Cora and Frank are freed and collect ten thousand dollars in insurance. And Katz gets his trophy—a check for a hundred dollars, which he has no intention of cashing. He plans to frame it and put it up over his desk. In the movie, Katz is played by Michael Lerner, who livens things up by his finely shaded performance, but he's a big, heavyset man who also has a great hooked nose, and there's no bet—he gets Cora and Frank off and takes the ten thousand as his fee. He's a smart Jew who is interested only in the money. Rafelson and Mamet don't seem to know a good story when it's right in their hands, so they cheapen it. The whole point of Cain's *The Postman Always Rings Twice* is that Cora and Frank are doomed; they're small fry who, in the long run, can't get away with anything. They're so small they can be saved—for the moment—by a wager, a jest. Katz knows what they are: greedy killers. He probably understands even the sexual insanity that drove them to murder.

(Everybody who looks at them understands.) He doesn't want their dirty money; he won something that means more to him. Rafelson and Mamet's alteration puts Katz on the same level as Cora and Frank. The moviemakers use Cain's story to carry meanings that are far less gallant than his.

Everything about the picture suggests that Rafelson and Mamet disdain James M. Cain's sleazy primitivism as a storyteller: they don't want "doom" hovering over their characters, they don't want their picture to have a vulgar charge. To paraphrase Orwell, it takes intellectuals to be this dumb. The movie seems twice the length of the novel, yet it never gets to the point. Rafelson and Mamet leave out the final twist of fate that the dead man's echo prefigured: in this version, the postman only rings once.

April 6, 1981

Boorman's Plunge

John Boorman is an intoxicated moviemaker, with a wonderful kind of zeal—a greed to encompass more and more and more in his pictures. His action scenes are rarely comprehensible. He can't get any suspense going. He doesn't seem to understand the first thing about melodrama. He has no particular affection for humor. And his skills are eccentric and his ideas ponderously woozy. But I don't know of any other director who puts such a burnish on his obsessions. Moviemaking is clearly the first of them, with mythology a close second. I would never have imagined that I could enjoy a retelling of the Arthurian legends which was soaked in Jung and scored to themes from Carl Orff's "Carmina Burana" and Wagner, but Boorman's *Excalibur* has its own kind of crazy integrity. At first, I couldn't quite believe what I was seeing: a serious, R-rated fairy tale. Boorman had been trying to get this project financed for the past decade, and he'd been mulling it over for much longer than that. No doubt he got the go-ahead because of the success of *Star Wars*, which is essentially the Arthurian story set in "a galaxy far, far away," but he has done the legends straight. Children may be enthusiastic about *Excalibur*, but it hasn't been made as a family movie, and though Excalibur is clearly The Force, symbolized in the magic sword, which is effective only when used for good purposes, Boorman doesn't linger on that. He doesn't bring a comic-strip sensibility to the material, and he doesn't make the narrative easy to understand, in the manner of the Hollywood *Knights of the Round Table*

(1953), with Robert Taylor as Lancelot and Ava Gardner as the Queen. What Boorman has in mind is probably closer to *The Seventh Seal*.

He just plunges into the Dark Ages, smiting us with raging battles, balls of flame, mists of dragon's breath, knights with horns and tusks jutting out of their armored heads, and battle-axes that hack off limbs, which seem to ricochet off the armor. He sails through the Arthurian stories, from Arthur's conception and birth to his death, without pausing even for the awesome, triumphant moment when the boy Arthur pulls the sword from the stone where his dying father had placed it. This scene is staged with townspeople gathered, some saying that his pulling out the sword means he's the King, some saying that it doesn't and he isn't, and with all this clutter and dissension there's no tingle at seeing the visualization of one of the high points of fairy lore. Something in Boorman must rebel at the thought of a dramatic climax. The film is almost all action, with very little at stake for us, because we hardly have a chance to meet the characters before they're off and running. The hackings aren't any more upsetting than the hackings in *Monty Python and the Holy Grail*; in fact, the ones in *Monty Python* may have been more disturbing, because they were funny and gruesome at the same time. In *Excalibur*, they're neither. You don't see the limbs or heads that are lopped off; you see the red-stained armor. The hackings are part of the visual texture, along with the spiked elbows and the jutting metal earmuffs that look as if they could kill a stag at bay.

The imagery is impassioned, and it has a hypnotic quality. You feel that there's something going on under the narrative; you're very much aware of shine and glitter, of hair and skin—the imagery has a tactile life of its own. Boorman doesn't bother with episodes that don't stir him; there's no dull connective tissue. The film is like Flaubert's more exotic fantasies—one lush, enraptured scene after another. The images are crystal-clear, gold-tinted, jewelled; it's a stained-glass movie. But, of course, the Flaubert exotica—such as *Salammbô*, which, as Francis Steegmuller writes, covers a great literary canvas with "the colors of violence and physical suffering, and above all with the color of blood"—are the ones that many readers find too rich.

The dialogue in *Excalibur* is near-atrocious; written by Rospo Pallenberg and Boorman, it reveals what Boorman thinks he's doing. He thinks he's showing us the primal harmony of man and the magic forces of earth and air, and then man's loss of magic, which passes into the unconscious. Jung believed that his investigations carried on the work of Merlin and the alchemists, and Merlin (Nicol Williamson) is the presiding spirit of this movie—its resident pundit and ironic relief. He's presented as the peacemaker: he counsels first Uther Pendragon (Gabriel Byrne) and then Uther's son, Arthur (Nigel Terry), against violence, and makes deals with them, granting them magical favors in exchange for their behaving peaceably. Wearing a silver skullcap with an encrusted jewel—a third eye—in the middle of his forehead (the cap could be a leftover from Max von Sydow's Ming the Merciless headgear in *Flash Gordon*), Merlin is both seer and jester. He's always threatening to disappear for an aeon or two, or for eternity, but he keeps showing up to tell us how despondent he is about men's brutality and his own ineffectuality. He's a soft touch—he does favors that he knows he shouldn't, and they have fatal consequences. He's also a real talker, Mercutio-style, and he informs us of the meaning of what we're seeing. "The one God comes to drive out the many gods," he announces, thus presaging the ascendancy of Christianity, and soon King Arthur dispatches his knights on the quest for the Holy Grail. Merlin's speeches are wisdom droppings. Nicol Williamson toys with them; he uses a lilt and his deepest basso growl, but he's better off when he gets to do Gaelic incantations and we can just enjoy his vocal purring. It's as sensual as a love aria sung in a language that we don't know a word of.

Boorman's last two movies—*Zardoz* and *Exorcist II: The Heretic*—were also attempts at mythmaking, and we might have considered them classics if we hadn't known English. If we'd been able to imagine that the words were as lyrical and hallucinogenic as the images, we might have acclaimed Boorman instead of falling on the floor laughing (as a friend assures me he did when he saw *Zardoz*) or throwing things at the screen (which happened at some theatres showing *The Heretic*). Boorman is telling the Arthurian legends straight, all right—as straight as he can ever do anything. One of the great things about modern movies which distinguish them from the pictures that used to be made by the studio factories is that the artists' nuttiness comes out now. If they're mediocrities, their nutty movies can be much worse than the movies that used to be patched and smoothed. But if they're giants, their work may have a virtuoso looniness all its own. Boorman is a giant. But he's a sensualist with images and a pedant with words. It isn't enough for him just to present an immensely complicated series of legends; he also tries to build in a Jungian interpretation, so that the movie, adapted from Sir Thomas Malory's *Le Morte d'Arthur*, will demonstrate what man lost when he gained modern consciousness—how he has never been "whole" since, and all that jazz. Boorman's self-seriousness gets in the way of his artistry. In *The Heretic*, the dialogue and how it was directed were ruinous; Richard Burton's recitatives were theological gibberish. Merlin's fanciful remarks are far more entertaining, though the central role that Boorman gives him takes time and emphasis away from Arthur and his knights.

Boorman appears to have got so caught up in his theory of the lost magical Oneness that he leaves a gaping hole in the middle of the Arthurian stories. When Arthur has become a man of peace and his kingdom (roughly, Europe) is flourishing and his court at Camelot is the center of culture, where's the chivalry? We get only a few glimpses of Camelot in long shot, and when we're inside, the knights look bored. (There was more even to the Kennedy Administration—they gave a few good parties.) We don't experience the realization of the paradisiacal dream, and so we're not horrified by its collapse. But the Arthurian stories support Boorman's visual style much more gracefully than his last two films did. I loved watching *The Heretic*, but I couldn't recommend it to anyone without starting to grin shamefacedly. *Excalibur* is much simpler: it spans three generations—first Uther and his feuding with the other Celtic lords, then Arthur's reign, and, finally, the challenge to Arthur's power by his demonic son, Mordred. The movie might have been clearer still if the knights had had their names embroidered on their chain mail or painted on their foreheads. (Who is to say that this wasn't sixth-century practice?) Since the actors are almost all new to movies, it takes a while to sort the knights out.

The actors become more attractive and much more impressive as they age and we get to know them better. This is particularly true of Nigel Terry's Arthur and of Perceval (played by Paul Geoffrey)—undistinguished youths who grow shaggy beards and develop presence and depth. (When Paul Geoffrey, who gives perhaps the most affecting performance, is bearded, he resembles Francis Ford Coppola.) Boorman seems to be caught in a bind, though. He can visualize what the men were doing in the sixth century— jousting, riding, and, no doubt, polishing their armor. (Lancelot's has such a silvery-white gleam that he can't have had time for much else.) But what were the women up to? Nothing but mischief, apparently, and Boorman can't seem to get them matched to the same century as the men. How do you get pretty women to look like barbarians? Boorman's Guenevere (Cherie Lunghi) is a hot chick with a mop of gorgeously dishevelled curly dark hair; she's like the young Susan Hayward wearing a Pre-Raphaelite gown to a disco joint. The Lady of the Lake floating in the water might be Bo Derek. And as the treacherous Morgana (who in Hollywood versions used to be called Morgan le Fay) Helen Mirren is such a slinky witch that she looks as if she were practicing to play opposite Snow White in gay-bar theatricals. (Nobody in the movie seems to have any fun except Merlin and Morgana when they're huddled together talking about potions and spells. There's a conspiratorial intimacy between them; he's like a master cook imparting the secrets of the kitchen to a guileful apprentice.)

Somehow—maybe by sheer force of will—Boorman keeps the women's scenes from collapsing into camp. He needs the women; they're essential to the stories, because they're the source of evil. The Arthurian legends, like the stories of Helen of Troy and of Adam and Eve, are repositories of a peculiarly male mythology: woman the temptress causes man to fall from grace, to fight and kill. Yet though Boorman is in love with images and the whole movie has an erotic sheen, the adultery that shakes the kingdom is almost chaste. When hot little Guenevere follows Lancelot (Nicholas Clay) into the forest and chums up with him, they look so innocent, curled up together naked, like babes in the wood, that you can't accept the idea that this trivial frolic destroys the Golden Age of Camelot and brings starvation and pestilence on the land. The effect is altogether disproportionate to the cause, and you feel that something is off, that something is missing. No matter how this adultery was presented, it might be difficult for modern audiences to accept it as earth-shaking, but Boorman makes it just about impossible. What's off, I think, is the scale of the characters.

The film's Germanic-Byzantine-Celtic style often suggests Fritz Lang's *Siegfried* and *Kriemhild's Revenge*, which were also serious dream-world epics. There's no problem of disproportion between action and consequences in Lang's movies, though, because the characters are scaled heroically. Boorman is telling magical, heroic tales about men and women as large as gods, but he has populated the screen with the kids next door: they're not big enough in spirit, in aspirations, in dreams, or in passions for the myths built on their adventures. The stories are of characters who are sorcerers or part phantom, part man, or who assume different guises. Arthur is himself born of magic: Uther persuades Merlin to transform him into the likeness of the husband of the dancer Igrayne (Katrine Boorman), so that he can sleep with her. Arthur's son, Mordred (Robert Addie), is conceived through a similar magical deception, concocted by Morgana, who is Arthur's half sister as well as the mother of his son. When Mordred is fully grown, he wears golden spiked armor and, on his head, a gold gargoyle mask that his own sneering mouth completes. This apparition of evil comes closer to mythological scale than Arthur or Lancelot or Guenevere or any of the others do.

Love and lust are so human that they're easy to forgive; the picture doesn't seem to have a real issue. You think, Is that what the Arthurian legends come down to—not gods, just these little people with their warts? Boorman denies us the elation that we expect to experience at the end of a heroic story. He has made the characters so small that the myths themselves shrink in his telling. The picture gives us a different kind of elation, though. The Dark Ages section, with its armored brutes—they're like crustaceans tearing each other apart—is a thrilling piece of moviemaking. The second and third sections don't have the same concentration, but they do have shots—such as the one of the aged Arthur and his aged knights riding through a Klimt-like grove of flowering trees—with the mystic ambience of silent-movie fairy tales. If *Excalibur* is a lamebrainstorm of a movie, it's at least a genuine storm. There's a stubborn, freakish discipline in the way Boorman refuses to hold the iridescent images for the extra beat that would make an audience exclaim at their beauty. Even when there's an effect that might make the audience's flesh tingle—like the scene on a hill when the knights stand in the ring that will soon become the emblem of their fellowship—Boorman barely waits for you to take it in. Where Fritz Lang would let you bask in the imagery, Boorman has so much he wants to do that he hurries you past. Was there really an iron snout protruding from someone's face armor? Those slimy creatures that crowded around Merlin as he rested in the shadowy foliage—were they his familiars? And when his eyes turned that dark, evil red, what tricks was he up to? Which were the knights hanging on the tree, where Morgana had trapped them? The picture moves along so inexorably, with lances going through chests in barbaric, orange-amber landscapes, that there isn't time to absorb all the components of the shots. When Merlin leads Morgana down into some dank rotten place—a grotto in the netherworld—the set could almost be an homage to Fritz Lang and his great designers. Boorman's cinematographer, Alex Thomson, his production designer, Anthony Pratt, and Trevor Jones, who prepared the score and conducted it, must have given him their fealty as well as their talent, because, amazingly, he does this kind of spectacle on the (relative) cheap. Using the Irish landscape and the Ardmore Studios, near Dublin, he is able to do for ten million dollars what would probably cost at least twice that if it was attempted here. At times, I was aware that there weren't quite as many extras as we're used to seeing, and there's a little joke near the end: the dragon's breath comes out of the old hag Morgana, and Arthur, who is leading his handful of surviving knights in a battle with Mordred's men, says, "In this fog, they won't know how few of us there are." It sounds like a reproach to the production manager.

Boorman's medieval battles don't have the same kind of impact as the great battle in the mud in Welles' *Falstaff*; every shot in the *Falstaff* battle scenes registers in your mind and helps to build the sequence. Boorman doesn't build. *Excalibur* is all images flashing by—ravishing images—and though we can't retain them, we drink them in. Each, in some weird way, seems to be on its own. This may help to explain the film's hypnotic effect: the events keep gliding into each other. We miss the dramatic intensity that we expect the stories to have, but there's always something to look at. The images keep coming, and the cadences are bizarrely even. Every now and then, there's an inchoate swelling—as in the royal-wedding sequence, where the sensuousness of metal and flesh makes you feel that something might be about to explode. Boorman sets an aestheticized mood, and by quivering, wiredrawn control he sustains it. At times, he's doing something close to free-associating visually. It's as if he were guiding us down a magic corridor and kept parting the curtains in front of us.

April 20, 1981

Safes and Snouts

Thief is all highfalutin hype. It's a great big trailer for itself—pounding music, lights reflected on cars, big-time crooks. It's the underworld movies of the forties and fifties made volcanic and abstract and existential. There's so much of the rainy-night-in-the-neon-city school of cinematography that the picture is close to being a parody of *film noir*; there's even a vertical pan down a building in an alley, moving from fire escape to fire escape and on to the wet street below. Then we get to see the thief, Frank (James Caan), at his trade; he's a pro, of course, who works with the latest precision tools. And while he's drilling open a safe, Tangerine Dream's synthesized electronic music is trying to out-throb Giorgio Moroder. This is the first theatrical feature by the writer-director Michael Mann. (He was the "creator" of the TV series "Vega$" and a sometime writer of "Starsky and Hutch" before making his reputation with the Emmy-winning TV movie *The Jericho Mile*.) Mann has set *Thief* in Chicago and designed it like a choo-choo train to the box office. He seems determined to outdo *The French Connection* and *Midnight Express*, but in his own classier, more ascetic way, and with Ideas.

At the film's center is this smart operator Frank, who's a thief with a dream—the American dream. He wants to take his bundle and retire, marry, have a nice house, and raise a family. He was an orphan, you see, and he wants to give other kids what he never had. But the System is against him. I don't think there's a trace of invention in this movie—anything that isn't derived from simpler, quieter, better movies or from noisy hits. I take it back. There is one: Frank carries in his wallet a carefully folded, worn piece of paper—a collage of his future which he made in prison. It shows the things in life that he cares about: he has cut out *Family Circle*-type pictures of a suburban split-level house and a wife and a baby, and at the side there's a snapshot of an old safecracker who was his cellmate and was like a father to him—the old man, who's suffering from angina, is still in prison, and is afraid he'll die there.

Frank proposes to Jessie (Tuesday Weld), a dazed, frizzed-out cashier at the Belden Deli, and they join hands across the collage. Mann could have cut his characters and situations out of *Family Circle*, too. There's a grotesque scene in which Frank and Jessie (she can't have children) go to an adoption agency for a baby. They're rejected, and Frank explodes at the injustice of his prison record's being held against him. (Couldn't somebody explain to Michael Mann that there aren't babies available for people without prison records, either?) In case we haven't been won over already, the old safecracker is played by Willie Nelson, long braids and all. A movie with a dying Willie Nelson is as shameless as a kiddie-matinée movie with a crippled boy whose dog is run over: when Nelson's face crinkles in a beatific smile, his eyes show pain. And he dies on the day he is to be released from prison. At the end, when Frank has learned that he can never escape the life of crime, he takes out the picture of his future, crumples it up, and throws it away. Michael Mann assumes the mannerisms of hardboiled realism; he's anti-pathos while going for pathos.

We're supposed to be fixated on Frank's professional expertise and his equipment—his electromagnetic drill and his custom-made eight-thousand-degree thermal lance—and also on his huge profits, his Cadillacs, and his eight-hundred-dollar suits. And then we're supposed to see that he's tough only on the outside. He spent eleven years in Joliet for stealing forty dollars when he was twenty; the sentence was extended because he killed another inmate, but we get the idea—Frank never had a chance. Everything is loaded so that we'll think, What a raw deal—the whole world is against him. Mann has set up one of the tiredest of plots: Though Frank seems to be stashing away huge chunks of money and has almost half a million in cash, he decides that he has to make one last big haul before he'll have enough to raise his dream family on. And so this loner agrees to work just this once, or maybe twice, with "the Mob," whose head is the unctuous, smiling Leo, played by Robert Prosky. (Anybody who would trust a man who's always smiling can never have been to the movies.) Frank is denied the father he needs, and acquires Leo, the father nobody needs.

Thief is the only film I've ever seen in which the pulsating suspense music lifts the roof of your head off when there isn't much action on the screen but stops when something is about to happen. This isn't accidental; nothing in *Thief* is. Everything in it is shaped for a big purpose. The cinematography (by Donald Thorin) goes beyond slickness to exhibitionism: at night the puddles in the street are a poisonous brew of purples and greens; Frank's activities are shrouded in cold metallic blues; and the glittering diamonds he steals and Chicago's glittering skyline practically become the laughter of the gods. When Frank's helper (James Belushi) is murdered at the car lot Frank owns, the patterns of light reflected on chrome are the focus of attention. (Michael Mann seems to have got a dose of Robert Bresson via Paul Schrader.) Everything about the movie is showy in the way that reviewers on TV like to call "searing." This film's ambitions are epitomized in a scene at a California beach—a long, meaningful shot of waves. Mann turns music into suspense noise, and it keeps starting up to jolt you; it's on-and-off music, and some people in the audience are so zapped by the beat that they can't sit still. He makes sure you won't relax, by tossing in quick images that interrupt what you're watching, and by the use of flash-forward sound—letting you hear the dialogue and noises of the next location before you get to it. At one point, when Frank and his wife-to-be leave a night club, the music from inside becomes louder as they step outside—it's shouting the film's importance. During the two robberies, there are so many closeups of machinery that you're being told you're witnessing technological marvels. I'm not really avid to learn how to crack a safe, but if I were and thought there was real craftsmanship involved I think I might be miffed to see that in the second robbery (which is in L.A.) Frank has such powerful equipment that he simply burns through the side of the safe; he makes his own opening. (This is a highly photogenic way to crack a safe—a lot of sparks fly.)

Thief isn't really about heists; the opening, with its *Rififi*-like concentration on a robbery, is essentially just an attention-grabber. *Thief* is meant to be—hang on to your hat—a parable of the death of the American dream. Except for the underlings, who don't count, everyone in it is corrupt: the mobsters; the fences; the sadistic cops, who are on the take; the judges, who can be fixed. Everyone except Frank. Safecracking is the work he does, but he's a hard laborer and he's pure—he's spiritually cleansed by his dedication to his craft. He's the only one in the movie who tries to make a connection with the dream of a normal life. So he gets a wife who isn't a wife. (She carries a banner that says "burnt-out," and she has no womb.) He gets a child that isn't his own. (Leo, who has made the arrangements, calls it "a rented child.") Even Frank's house isn't quite his own. (Leo holds the paper on it.) Why do Frank and Jessie take their newly rented child to a Chinese restaurant? It's so we can see what a mockery of the American family they are: they don't think to name the baby until a Chinese waiter tells them they should.

This is one of the new, spangly existential movies about alienation (like *Raging Bull* and *The Postman Always Rings Twice*), in which the heroes are made so limited or stupid that the director has no way to enter them and aims straight for pyrotechnics. The less that is going on, the more stylish the movie has to become. In *Thief*, Mann needs to keep pouring on the false urgency of that damn loud music because there isn't any real danger in Frank's heists: the police are never about to break in—we're just watching a workman using fancy tools. We get the snazzy cinematography and the overheated sound not because the characters or situations are bravura but because the filmmaker thinks his ideas are bravura.

The title *Thief* is a paradox (the hardworking Frank is a man of integrity); the title is also anonymous, pristine, abstract. (Mann has trumped Walter Hill's foray into anonymity, *The Driver*, by eliminating even the frill of "the.") James Caan is almost the definition of a "gritty" actor—rough skin, jabbing movements, nervous tics, nervous sweat. Mr. Volatility. Caan shows you that he's holding back his anger but is ready to explode at the slightest frustration. When he's riled in *Thief*, he grips his gun in both hands and holds it out in front of him—he means business. He's the right actor for Michael Mann, who belongs to the pressure-cooker school of filmmaking, because he's a clenched-jaw, pressure-cooker actor. Caan isn't bad in featured parts (as in *The Godfather*) or in co-starring roles (like his Billy Rose in *Funny Lady*), but when he's the only star he seems dull, and I begin to feel that I don't care whether he's a good actor or not—I just don't want to watch him. He's skillful at conveying the prickly feelings of his heroes, but he makes those heroes too easy to read; there's nothing special inside them, and nothing hidden. (The critic Kathy Huffhines, writing in the Boston *Real Paper*, nailed it, I think, when she said, "You look at De Niro in a film and think, 'Something's eating him.' You look at Caan and think, 'He's eating something . . . pizza?' ") Caan isn't anybody in particular—he's a generic inarticulate strong sufferer. Which fits Mann's conception: Frank is a cipher—a symbolic "stranger."

Frank is initially presented as smart: in the four years since he got out of prison, he has used the safecracking skills his old cellmate taught him and parlayed his thefts into a network of businesses, including the big car lot and a bar. He seems to know exactly what he's doing, and how to handle the people he deals with. Then Frank turns into a clod (like the heroes of *Raging Bull* and *The Postman Always Rings Twice*), the better to express an inarticulate despair. *Thief* is designed like a sales pitch, and what it's selling is nihilism. Frank's collage is a simple man's existential diagram of what he wants; it demonstrates that he's a decent man, still clinging to human values and hoping for the normal pleasures of life. When he crumples it and throws it away, it's because he realizes that he has never really left prison, that he has to go through life on the same terms that enabled him to survive in Joliet—by "gettin' to where nothin' means nothin'." The film sets up an improbable character in a series of rigged situations and then leaps to universal despairing conclusions. Michael Mann's pitch is that you're free only when you don't care about life and have nothing to lose. And so Frank explodes: he kills his enemies and blows everything up—the split-level house, the bar, the fleet of cars at the car lot. He's getting back to freedom—the freedom of numb indifference.

Thief is hyper-animated by this conception of existential tragedy. Mann revels in the nihilistic destruction. I hated this movie from beginning to end—it's a movie on the make, a high-minded hustle. Near the finish, when Frank, in outrage at everything that has happened to him, bangs his head against a mirror, he's just like La Motta in *Raging Bull* battering his head against the stone prison wall and the Frank of *The Postman* lowering his head and sobbing. They're all protesting man's destiny. Why would a director who's a pretty fair technician come on so strong with all this big-time crime and even bigger-time Nothingness? If the movie is about anything, it's about Mann's attempt to give the audience a rush of excitement and have a hit, and at the same time be acclaimed a cinematic poet of despair. *Thief* is full of symbolic figures and situations, each with its own provenance. Oozing sincerity, Willie Nelson is so "real" here it's hard to look at him. Tuesday Weld steps in from another world, with a faint shudder; over the years she has become an emblem of loss. Frank himself is the hard-luck hero of thousands of movies taken to a fantasy realm. He's the outsider, a loner in pain—the embodiment of a macho mystique. He's too good and too honorable for this rotten world, and so at the end he must disappear into the shadows. Is grandiloquent masochism so appealing to men that they'll buy this cosmic drizzle? (I think it's unlikely that many women will.) It's the fantasy of being the best of men—the toughest and the most anguished.

.   .   .   .   .

*I*n *The Howling*, when people turn into werewolves they transform on camera: you see the stages they go through—growing fur and fangs, their chests expanding and their teeth yellowing—and you see each long snout shoot out of the face like a locomotive. It's a funny, elegant effect; the characters turn into what look like huge toy wolves, and there are clever inserts of wolflike legs, and paws with switchblade talons. (At the start, the title is clawed in, letter by letter, with a ripping sound, as if the screen itself were being slashed.) *The Howling* doesn't take itself seriously; unlike horror movies such as John Carpenter's *Halloween* and David Cronenberg's *The Brood*, it's consciously trashy. At most horror movies, audiences laugh at some of the conventions; even kids in the audience know more than the characters up there, who go into the houses they shouldn't or enter the rooms they've been warned against or take a walk alone in the dark forest for the sole purpose of getting killed. (Remember those fools wandering about searching for the cat in *Alien?*) In *The Howling*, the director, Joe Dante, and John Sayles, who rewrote the Terence H. Winkless script, based on the novel by Gary Brandner, give the conventions a nudge over into self-parody and set up the laughs. The picture isn't afraid of being silly—which is its chief charm.

This werewolves-in-California movie is strewn with references to wolves and werewolf lore, horror-film memorabilia (some of it live—actors such as Kenneth Tobey, who survived *The Thing*), and a clip from the cartoon *The Big Bad Wolf*. It's a very casual movie—a tossed-together mixture of three kinds of material. A scene may be a sendup of TV: a diligently serious L.A. anchorman, Bill Neill (Christopher Stone), delivers the news, but as the camera angle changes we realize he isn't on television, he's in the men's room at the station, practicing. A scene may be a satirical bit about "self-discovery" cults: Dr. George Waggner (Patrick Macnee), the station's plump, bland English psychiatrist, goes into his TV spiel like a snake-oil salesman, babbling on about the beast inside us. Or a scene may be a scary episode: Karen White (Dee Wallace), the pretty blonde of the news team, sets up a date with a psychopathic killer on the loose; the police who are supposed to be tailing her lose her, and she's alone with the maniac in a booth at a porno parlor. When he faces her, what she sees sends her into shock and she can't remember it. This is the incident that cranks up the plot. Karen is such a wreck afterward that Dr. Waggner insists that she take time off at his woodland clinic, The Colony, up the coast in Mendocino, and stodgy Bill Neill, who is her husband, drives up with her. In the car, she says, "I hope these people aren't too weird," and the film cuts to the venerable John Carradine, in the light of a campfire, his eyes crossed as he yelps at the moon. Later that night, Karen, lying in bed with Bill, hears howling outside their cottage; she takes a flashlight and goes out to investigate. The audience laughs, affectionately; the affection is for the genre, the clichés, and the filmmakers' impishness.

Dante and Sayles haven't the temperament—or the skills, either—to attempt what Hitchcock could do and what Brian De Palma can do: make the comedy intensify the scariness, and vice versa. In *The Howling*, the gags are mostly asides and inoffensively smartass pranks—except for the basic joke, which runs through the whole movie, and relates to the title and the slang meaning of "wolf calls." The spoofy erotic tone is closer, in some ways, to

Love at First Bite than to the werewolf films of the past, but *The Howling* isn't as farcical (or as aggressively funny) as *First Bite*, and it retains the horror-movie status that *First Bite* chucked away. Though Sayles writes funny skit dialogue, he doesn't offer much in the way of characterization, and the story is vaporous. There are compensations: you're entertained continuously, and since there are no real characters, you can enjoy the transformations and deaths without a morbid pang. But that pang is what gives horror movies their power. When horror is parodied, as it is here, there are no mysterious anxieties set up in the audience; we don't feel the queasy, childish dread that is part of the dirty kick of the genre. *The Howling* leaves almost no imprint. It's very inventive, but—except for the makeup effects, created by Rob Bottin—it isn't really imaginative. Joe Dante doesn't appear to have the nightmarrish quirkiness of a horror director—the cruelty of a Mario Bava or the spooky lyricism of a Franju. There are no scenes that you can't shake off. Dante may be too sane to make a real shocker: he'd rather kid the characters than work up your fear about what's going to happen to them. So the end of this film, which takes place on television and should have a sensational charge, has almost none. It's supposed to be ironic that the television viewers don't take what they see seriously, but the irony goes flat, because we haven't been taking the characters seriously, either.

There are no embarrassments in the cast, and besides Macnee, who plays the charlatan psychiatrist as an amiable weakling, there are other performers who bring a strong, aberrant personality to their parts. Dick Miller, who was in Roger Corman's *The Little Shop of Horrors*, is the enthusiastic bookshop owner who starts to gab the minute a customer comes in. Elisabeth Brooks, who plays Marsha, the fiery slut of The Colony, seems to be made up to emphasize her resemblance to Barbara Steele in Mario Bava's 1960 *Black Sunday*, but she has a lusty, man-eater presence that's all her own. And Kevin McCarthy, in the role of the general manager of the TV station, who delivers the editorials, is awesomely self-satisfied; he catches the exact tone of TV-pundit inauthenticity. There are startling images, such as a view of Carradine (so thin he's stylized by nature) in which his demented head is like an Eskimo carving. But there's also a sizable amount of flat-footedness. Dante doesn't have the grace to give us the illusion of spotting a copy of Allen Ginsberg's *Howl* for ourselves—he shoves it at us by not having anything else going on in the shot. He doesn't appear to know how to shape a sequence dramatically—how to make it count. As a director, he seems a mixture—in just about equal parts—of talent, amateurishness, style, and flake. Not a bad mixture, but it doesn't give him much control over what he gets. The picture is too long, probably, in terms of effectiveness, though its length and variety make it satisfying; you don't come out hungry for a movie.

Homage is paid to George Waggner, who directed the 1941 *The Wolf Man*, by giving his name to the Patrick Macnee character, and at least half a dozen other characters are named for horror-film directors. (I wish that these inside-joke homages added to the movie in some way, but I'm afraid they're just arcane bits for film freaks.) Roger Corman, for whom Dante, Sayles, Bottin, and the editor, Mark Goldblatt, all worked together on the 1978 *Piranha*, turns up waiting outside a phone booth. John Sayles appears as an attendant at the morgue, when it is discovered that the corpse of the psychopath who set the story in motion has walked away; the police who shot him didn't know that only a silver bullet would do the job. For all its goofing off, *The Howling* observes the rules of the game, and it's infinitely better than many horror films that take themselves more seriously. It includes clips from *The Wolf Man* with Claude Rains talking to poor, sad, wolfy Lon Chaney, Jr., and with Maria Ouspenskaya, in her thick accent (and with the emotions and vocal rhythms that were the same for every role she played, and gave each of her utterances a ponderous importance), delivering herself of these words: "Even the man who is pure in heart and says his prayers by night may become a wolf when the wolfbane blooms and the moon is full and bright." *The Howling* doesn't just take gems like that from the treasure trove of camp; it also replenishes the stock. The dialogue often sets off little bugle calls: when Karen first tells Bill about the sound she has heard outside their cottage, he tells her that it must have been a dog, and she replies, "Not like any dog I ever heard." And there's a visual nifty that horror movies of the future are almost sure to quote: a man and a woman turn into werewolves as they couple—baring their fangs, slavering and moaning, clawing, and biting each other. And howling.

May 4, 1981

Waddlers and Bikers

Caveman has a funky buoyancy. Its humor is the sort of indecorous silliness that still delights people when they see the casual Paramount comedies of the thirties. The characters are prehistoric men and women who wear rough, shaggy pelts and have not yet learned to walk erect; these stupes stoop—they waddle bent over. The rear-up position does wonders for Lana (Barbara Bach), who wears the skimpiest and tightest of bushy-tailed fur briefs; when she moves, her twitchy bottom is a whirligig. Beautiful Lana beds down with the tribal leader, Tonda, a squatty man-mountain (played by John Matuszak, a defensive tackle for the Oakland Raiders, and about three hundred pounds of muscle). All the men in the tribe ogle Lana, and one of them, a peewee named Atouk (Ringo Starr, bearded), is so lecherously in love with her that he devises a strategy for taking her away from Tonda. His plan fails, and Tonda throws him out of the tribe. Little Atouk is still determined; forced to use his brain if he means to prevail over Tonda's brawn, he leaps from discovery to discovery. He learns to stand upright, and, grasping the value of coöperation, he teaches the other misfits who have joined him to stand upright, too. In one great day, he discovers fire and then cooking, and that night he and his group, sitting around the first campfire, discover musical instruments. In about ten seconds, they're chanting and singing, and thirty seconds later they have moved on to syncopation, and Atouk has become a rock drummer.

In *Caveman*, the origins of man and the origins of slapstick are one and the same. Mankind evolves because of Atouk's efforts to get into Lana's furry hip-huggers. The basic, old jokes of burlesque are made older—are made prehistoric. It's as if we were in on their creation, and this gives them an extra lift. The characters have a wide range of grunts, and they speak in what sounds like gibberish but isn't, because what they say is perfectly intelligible. Carl Gottlieb, who directed, and Rudy DeLuca, who co-authored the script with him, devised a fifteen-word language that's indebted about equally to comicstrip balloonese and Yiddish, and it seems to take care of the characters' conversational needs. (The noun "bo-bo" means man, friend, human being; the interjection "Aieee!" means Help!, Save me!, Mayday!; the adjective "fech" means bad, no good, ugly.)

The fifteen words are not the only means of communication, though. Ringo Starr talks with his big, droopy eyes, and he goes beyond that—he thinks with his eyes. Best of all, maybe, is the way he shrugs with his eyes, like Belmondo. It's hardly a bolt from the blue that Ringo Starr has crackerjack timing, but, unexpectedly, Gottlieb, making his début as a movie director, gets crack timing from the whole cast and never lets a routine go on too long. (That's just about the highest compliment any moviemaker can be paid at the moment.) Gottlieb, who earned his chance to direct by having been co-writer on three films that together have earned more than three hundred million dollars in rentals (*Jaws*, *Jaws II*, *The Jerk*), was himself a comedy actor in the San Francisco group The Committee, and he shows a veteran entertainer's gift for pacing and a gift for something even rarer—blithely moronic monkeyshines. As Lana, Barbara Bach (the Russian-spy heroine of one of the best Bonds, *The Spy Who Loved Me*, and, arguably, the most delectable of all the Bond women) treats her own lusciousness as comic. Her body language says, "Whatever you have to go through to get me, I'm worth it." (What was it Frank Sinatra said to Rita Hayworth when she turned him down in *Pal Joey*? Something like "If you knew what you were missing, you'd cut your throat." Atouk has a pretty fair idea of what he's missing.) Matuszak, who made an impressive screen début in *North Dallas Forty* (he was the terrifying bearded giant O.W., who psyched himself up for the big game), brings more than his physique to the role of Tonda. He plays stupid with a hairy-furry vengeance— Bluto unleashed. He and Ringo are perfectly matched Goliath and David adversaries: it's not just that Matuszak is a spectacular embodiment of bluster and brawn and that as Tonda he seems to live in the frames of a comic strip, it's also that Ringo represents a modern consciousness. He has just about infallible rapport with the audience; each subdued gesture, each self-deprecating expression tells us that he's one of us—that he doesn't give himself points for anything. And he holds the movie together.

Made in rocky Mexican landscapes and in the Churubusco Studios, in Mexico City, the picture has Mexican bit players and a supporting cast of some of the best knockabout comedians in the business: Avery Schreiber's spongy-cushion clown's face keeps peeping out from Tonda's entourage. Dennis Quaid, who was the malcontent in *Breaking Away* and Gene Hackman's meaty, inarticulate son in *All Night Long*, is Atouk's pal, Lar; Quaid has an open-faced, deadhead style—he's just the right stooge for gags like Ringo's helping him by squishing a mega-insect that has settled on him. Shelley Long, a wispy, wide-eyed blonde from the Second City troupe, is like a buttercup with a steel-trap mind; she plays Tala, who adores Atouk and tries to get him to take his eyes off Lana. And the great, angelically gaga Jack Gilford is Tala's blind father—an archetypal fud who keeps wandering off and bumping into angry dinosaurs.

These critters—there are four of them—are charmers, each with its own foolish innocence, and each a star. The pot-gutted Howling Lizard is seen at night baying at the moon and at sunrise cock-a-doodle-dooing. The Pterodactyl is a huge flying reptile who seems to drop in for a guest appearance. The Big Horned Lizard has eyes that stick out like a frog's, and they wiggle and roll as he cogitates; when Atouk throws a melon at him, it's impaled on the single, rhinoceroslike horn in the middle of his face, and the critter crosses his bulging eyes and stares at it helplessly. The Big Horned Lizard is the ding-a-ling of the troupe; the Tyrannosaurus Rex is the sweet patootie. He has two vestigial appendages, like an infant's arms, and when he is distressed, ecstatic, or just plain drowsy, this winsome beast wrings his poor, dinky hands. Created by highly sophisticated animation techniques, all four are domesticated, parody versions of the scary monsters in sci-fi horror films—they're pets. (The score, by Lalo Shifrin, contributes satiric allusions to the use of Ravel's "Bolero" in *10*, and to films such as *The Bridge on the River Kwai* and *2001*.)

Caveman never cuts loose and goes wild in the way that the first Cheech and Chong movie, *Up in Smoke*, did; it just goes bopping along. It's a little mild: it doesn't have the dirt or meanness or malice to make you explode with laughter; it suffers a bit from good intentions and sweetness of spirit. (There's no visual lyricism to redeem that sweetness.) You grin, though, or chuckle, and who would guess that an original, consistently enjoyable comedy would be lurking behind an ad campaign that recalls nothing more inspiring than *The Flintstones*. There is a running gag I could have done without (an Oriental who uses modern English words). That's the only bummer that comes to mind. The movie is full of sight gags that might have been dismal if Gottlieb's pacing weren't right on the nose: gags such as Tonda picking up huge rocks to throw, losing his balance and going backward or forward with them, or a set-piece sequence in which Tonda and his men try to carry an immense dinosaur egg up a hill and are forced down and then up the hill behind them. Gottlieb is a generous director: the people on the screen look wonderful, despite their matted pelts. Ringo's beard is lustrous, Barbara Bach justifies his goatishness, Shelley Long is delicate and bubbly. Jack Gilford doesn't have enough to do, but he's magically likable—he is perhaps the most rapt of comedians. (I wish that W. C. Fields had lived to confront him.) And when Tonda finally straightens up, his girth is mythological—he's Homeric. If you've been searching for a comedy you can enjoy along with your children, this is the one.

·　　·　　·　　·　　·

*G*eorge A. Romero's *Knightriders* is a sixties wheeler, with different headgear. Now the motorcyclists wear medieval-looking helmets with plumes, and they joust on their bikes at the Renaissance tournaments that they stage. They're a travelling community, held together by a neo-Arthurian code that their king, Billy, administers, and this code is supposed to keep them safe from the hucksterism of the outside world. Romero has been called a master by a lot of enthusiasts. They may think that there's more to *Knightriders* and his previous film, the 1979 *Dawn of the Dead*, which is being double-billed with it, than there is. They may think that a picture like *Dawn of the Dead* can't be for real—that its amateurishness and tedium are distanced by irony. Bad acting can be taken as part of a new, affectless stance, a new hipness. College students who bamboozle their friends and teachers with their knowledge of the intricacies of the schlock culture of underground head comix have been known to say that the picture's lack of sophistication was intentional, and so was its lack of feeling. And that people were tired of passion; they'd had it. Slovenliness, passivity—this was the real critique of American culture.

In *Dawn of the Dead*, the recently deceased rise from their graves; they're insatiably hungry, and they cannibalize the living, chomping on anyone they can grab. The chomped, in turn, become ghouls. This idea had already served Romero as the subject of his 1968 *Night of the Living Dead*, a cheaply made, gray and grainy, truly frightening movie, but this time he did it in shining, comic-book color, on an epic scale, and with a foursquare carnival approach. The ghouls can be stopped only if their brains are destroyed. So the four central characters, who hole up in a suburban shopping mall and are besieged there, use the resources of the sporting-goods store to blast away at the ghouls' brains, and for most of the film's two hours and six minutes the audience watches as, one by one, heads splatter and drip in bright, gory reds. The obviousness of the shock effects, the banality of everything about the movie, and its sheer stupefying repetitiveness give the audience a giggly kick. (There's also a good joke involved: one of the four asks why ghouls keep arriving at the mall, and another theorizes, "It's a kind of instinct. . . . This was an important place in their lives.") You're supposed to need a strong stomach to sit through the picture, but since you watch glaringly fake bloody splatterings over and over again, you begin to laugh with relief that you're not being emotionally challenged or even affected; it's just a gross-out. The George Romero of *Dawn of the Dead* is as literal-minded about horror as Russ Meyer is about breasts. (Meyer, too, had a period of acclaim. It could be that there are a lot of dumb people around pretending to be smart people acting dumb.)

In *Knightriders*, Romero passes from underground head comix to true-romance comics. Possibly, he had in mind both the big M-G-M *Ivanhoe* (1952) and Tom Laughlin's *Billy Jack* (1971), with its mystical man-of-action hero. Romero's King Billy (Ed Harris) has fear-struck eyes, thinning pale-blond hair, and looks drained and neurasthenic. He seems meant to be a Wasp Christ figure, or at least a Wasp with a Christ complex: he's a screaming hysteric exhorting his flock, telling his people that the code he administers is "the truth." If I read the picture right, Romero wants us to see that Billy has become too fanatic and masochistic to be an effective king, but that the code itself brings serenity to the members of the community and keeps them from selling out. In the course of the movie (it runs two hours and twenty-six minutes), the community breaks apart. Billy calls the defiant cynic, the black-bearded Morgan (Tom Savini), and the others who leave "stray sheep" and calmly waits for their return, using the free time to scourge his flesh. And after a few days of experiencing the low materialistic sleaziness of American society the stray sheep come varooming back, and the community is reunited. *Knightriders* is a devout, male flower child's counterculture movie: King Billy and his wan queen (Amy Ingersoll), whose face is always pinched from worrying about him, sit on their thrones, wearing their crowns (spiritually, Billy's is a crown of thorns, we're told) and presiding over bikers' contests that are far more noble and "real" than the cash customers realize.

If there's an emotional appeal in the movie, it's probably in the sunny, well-meant scenes of the racially and sexually integrated barnstorming group as a community. As with most modern American evangelical groups, nothing is difficult and there's no question of faith being tested—if there were, it would be multiple-choice. Salvation is a cinch: turning up is confirmation of faith. And evil is easily defined. The picture has a core of very crude, easy social satire, and an even cruder social message. The outside world is represented by predatory sexual slobs and media sharks and by the obnoxious loudmouth rubes who come to the fairs for the daredevil feats and the crashes. (A beer-swiller with rabbity teeth, who says that the jousts are a fake, is played by the horror novelist Stephen King, who is collaborating on two future Romero projects.) During a long jousting sequence, the crosscutting contrasts the anxieties of Billy's subjects, who realize the risks the knights are taking, with the glee of the people in the stands, who are gorging on hot dogs and danger but don't really understand the rituals of the jousts. I didn't, either. Romero doesn't seem to know how to stage the action so that you can see who the bikers are or what's at stake. He keeps his stunt men in motion—whirring by, crashing, flying through the air. But there's no film craft, no kinetic drama in the hurtling bodies; it's just an exhibition of stunt work. Most of the time, we don't even see the weapons hit the riders and unseat them, and the way that the contests are photographed, there's no physical grace in the knights' athleticism. What the movie comes down to is the romance of taking risks—of endangering your life as a pure demonstration of skill and courage.

Since the community (and the picture, too) is selling thrills and spills, and staging one whomping crash after another, it's more than disingenuous—it's weird—for Romero to ridicule the people in the stands who love the excitement and are applauding the action. This contempt for outsiders is demonstrated throughout the movie: Julie (Patricia Tallman), a teen-ager who joins the community when she falls in love with Alan, the Lancelot figure (Gary Lahti), has a swinish big father who beats her frightened little mother. In the community, men and women cherish each other; the chivalric code takes care of that. And, of course, we're supposed to see that there's no sexual discrimination in the group, since there's a woman knight. (She is, however, a lesbian!) Romero makes a point of showing us that everybody is accepted in the community—too much of a point. The scenes about Pippin (Warner Shook), who announces the contests on the loudspeaker system, being gay seem to be in the wrong movie. In *Knightriders*, the acceptance of Pippin can only be self-congratulatory and patronizing. Like the artisans and the knights' ladies, Pippin is part of the community yet has no voice in its affairs; everyone is under the protection of the knights—whatever that means in the eighties. There's some kind of schoolboy madness floating around in this stratified subculture, with its mixture of permissiveness and kingly authority.

Knightriders can be seen as a parable of Romero's romantic conception of his own development. It's hard to avoid this interpretation when Morgan, the pleasure-loving black sheep of the fold—the reformed sinner who, unlike the colorless Billy, has some life in him—becomes the balanced, responsible new king. Savini is a swashbuckling brute of a man, a smaller version of the bearded, six-foot-four Romero. And this king selects Angie, the top grease monkey and his longtime girlfriend (played by Christine Forrest, who recently became Romero's wife), to be his queen. Romero has his own counter-Hollywood filmmaking community; it breaks up and then regathers for the next project. He still makes his films in the Pittsburgh area (though this one cost roughly $3,700,000, about thirty-three times the cost of *Night of the Living Dead*, and the stunt work was done by the same crew that appeared in *Hooper*, *Smokey and the Bandit*, and *Every Which Way but Loose*). But even though what Romero is trying to be romantic about is probably at least partly himself and his way of life, he doesn't have a gift for romanticism, or for irony, either.

Camelot, in this movie, means being together, belonging to something, and the members of this dress-up commune say they get "a spiritual fix" out of their life with King Billy, but the medieval conceit doesn't take hold of your imagination, and you can't believe that it has taken hold of theirs. Late in the movie, when the teen-ager Julie is deposited back at her parents' home by Alan-Lancelot, and she says she doesn't understand why, you feel she has a legitimate gripe. The two of them appear to get along fine, and they even look alike, but suddenly he seems to remember that it's Lancelot's destiny to love the queen. Romero wants to have things both ways. He builds up a horrifying moment: a motorcycle goes out of control and hurtles toward the stands, and a young mother, trying to save her baby, is smashed by it. Later, the incident is casually disposed of by having someone remark that the woman wasn't hurt. (The whole movie is about the courage of the crashing bikers, but nobody ever gets hurt except for a pretty, symbolic wound on Billy.) Toward the end, when Billy—who becomes more appealing when he stops screaming—gives up the throne, is at peace with himself, and is about to ascend to Heaven, or wherever deranged saints and martyrs go, the audience was audibly angry at the flossy mystical stuff Romero was trying to pull. He's even got an Indian medicine man on a bike following Billy's bike—a sort of deathly escort to the next world? When a writer-director as literal as Romero goes poetic, the audience is, I think, emotionally right in refusing to go along with him. I was at the Los Angeles opening of *Dawn of the Dead*, where, in introducing his film, Romero said, "Someone told me this was schlock disguised as art. I didn't think it was disguised." Romero enthusiasts are now talking as if *Dawn of the Dead* were art disguised as schlock, and in *Knightriders* Romero himself is trying to save our souls. We should all go jousting.

Knightriders isn't offensive; it's simpleminded, though, and inept. Near the start, Billy, refusing to pay off a crooked cop, accompanies one of the group to jail; the others discuss ways of getting the two of them out, but we never learn who actually springs them or how. The fine-boned, shaven-headed black actor Brother Blue, who plays Merlin, has rings on his fingers, butterflies painted on his pate, his face, and a palm, and an owl perched on his shoulder, but he never gets to do any magic. Ken Hixon plays the community's lawyer, Steve, who has one foot in the community and one out; there are possibilities with a character like this, but Romero doesn't think up anything for his characters to do. And what he gives them to say isn't dialogue—it's just filler to carry the movie from point A to point B. (The tinny sound recording doesn't help.) *Knightriders*, with its medieval costumes, is pulp—

quaint puritan pulp. In Romero's permissive, multiracial community, there's love—men and women walk arm in arm, or lie together in verdant fields. When outsiders arrive, there's revolting, lewd sex—a naked fat, giggly woman and her fat, drunken lover pigging out on pizza.

May 18, 1981

Sad Songs

*N*ear the beginning of *This Is Elvis*, the nineteen-year-old rockabilly singer Elvis Presley has a ducktail pompadour, long sideburns, and a young, hot redneck swagger; his lids are heavy and his expression is provocative—smoldering, teasing. It's the mid-fifties, and he gives country music and Negro rhythm-and-blues songs a lightning-bright attack and a frenzied fast beat. You can see his eagerness to shock people and deliver the message: good times, pleasure. His lip curls in a half grin as he gyrates; his sexual energy is like laughter busting out because it can't be held in anymore. He enjoys the impudence; it's part of the music—the new part, what's going to get a generation jumping. By the end of the picture, in 1977, the heavyset, forty-two-year-old celebrity-god Elvis Presley is a gulping, slurring crooner, faltering on the lyrics of "Are You Lonesome Tonight?" He wears studded jumpsuits that rival Liberace's splendor, and waves fingers with rings the size of doorknobs. His head has blown up more than his body; he looks like Nero, and he sweats so much that his face seems to be melting away. There's no assault or danger or exuberance in his overmiked wailing; he might be just another Las Vegas entertainer singing "My Way" and coming on sincere and humble, if it weren't for the dissolving face that recalls De Palma's pop-culture horror movie *Phantom of the Paradise*.

This Is Elvis is a pop-culture horror movie of a different kind. We witness the transformation of a young whirlwind performer into a bloated druggie with dead eyes, yet the middle-aged audiences at Presley's latter-day appearances are even more hysterically excited than the young crowds at his early ones. What, exactly, are they shrieking for? It can't be his bored glissandos; it must be that they're excited simply to be in the presence of this sick, liquefying idol. After almost a decade of making movies and recording, Presley gave up his highly lucrative movie career in 1968, because he knew it was a betrayal of his music. (He starred in thirty-one movies, which ranged from mediocre to putrid, and just about in that order.) He wanted to get into contact with live audiences again—he wanted to feel good again. And he came back with some startling TV specials: his energy was explosive, and his voice seemed richer and more passionate. He'd grown up. But he was so big a name that live performances meant Las Vegas, Madison Square Garden, the Cow Palace, the Houston Astrodome. By the time he started touring, in 1970, the Beatles and the Rolling Stones and Vietnam had changed the music scene. He was still the king, but what he stood for was nostalgia for the fifties. He got, basically, his old audience, grown sentimental. He was caught: after all the years of Colonel Tom Parker's management, he was programmed to sell himself out.

There's another layer of horror in this movie: the people who assembled it—the executive producer, David L. Wolper, and Malcolm Leo and Andrew Solt, who are credited with having written, produced, and directed it, and Colonel Parker, who is credited as technical adviser—don't give any indication that they're aware of a difference between the music of the young Elvis and the bland, throbbing tearjerkers that come out of the bloated Elvis; one of the many narrators assures us that whatever Elvis did to himself, his voice was never affected. The movie packagers' attitude toward him is much like that of three of his bodyguards, who, after being fired, wrote a book exposing him as a bad-tempered pillhead; two of them are interviewed in the movie, and they see him as a man who had it made, who had everything *they* wanted in the palm of his hand, and so they can't understand why he couldn't just be happy. That is basically the "mystery" that Leo and Solt offer up: Why wasn't Elvis Presley happy with his success? What they show us— when they stick to footage of Elvis himself—is the raw material for a movie about a singer with a superabundance of restless American energy who lost his way and couldn't, or at least didn't, find a route back. (Maybe Elvis had become so rich and famous that there was no route back.) But we have to fill in the gaps and piece together this story for ourselves. The movie doesn't deal with Elvis the artist. Leo and Solt don't give any hint of the effort that the young perfectionist craftsman put into a song to make it his, or of the dozens of takes he did before he was satisfied with a record. And they don't show the process by which the music was watered down and Elvis became Colonel Parker's cheesecake movie star, who made as much as thirty-five million dollars a year and was contemptuous of everyone, including himself.

The movie is a monstrosity. Whenever someone announces the creation of a new form—the nonfiction novel or the docudrama or Ralph Bakshi's innovative animation (which means tracing live action) or, as in the case of *This Is Elvis*, "the first theatrical movie to tell a story by blending existing footage with historically accurate re-creations"—watch your wallet. The announcement may signify that con artist and artist coexist in the same body and are playing devious games with each other or that, as in the cases of Bakshi and of Leo and Solt, something really scuzzy is going on. *This Is Elvis* is Elvis Presley and four other guys thrown in to impersonate Elvis at periods of his life that weren't recorded on film, and the voice of a fifth guy, to impersonate Elvis as a narrator; and there are actors impersonating members of the Presley family and other people who figured in his life, and actors supplying voices for those actors in the narration.

The material that Leo and Solt have written and directed—mostly Presley's childhood and teens—seems insultingly dumb. What the actors and voices dish up is a batch of inanities, generalities, and—arguably—fabrications. It doesn't add to the powerful images of Elvis himself (seen in films, concert footage, TV kinescopes, newsreels, and home movies). It takes away. And maybe that's what it's meant to do. I'm not suggesting that what is clearly lumpy and inept is actually Machiavellian; what I mean is that the purpose of the "re-creations" is to make Elvis Presley seem an ordinary boy. When the film cuts from the two young Elvis impersonators to the real Elvis, at nineteen, singing to a crowd, there's a charge in his face and body, and there's something blanked out from us—sealed off. This isn't the later version of the innocuous kids we've been watching. The re-creations try to turn Presley into much less than he was, so that movie audiences will more readily identify with him. They deny Elvis his singularity, his drive, and his tragedy.

He's too strong for them, though. There's an authentic mystery about him: when we see footage from his early Hollywood movies, he's only a kid of twenty-one or two, yet he has the zonked eyes of his later years and he seems to be alive only from the waist down. He walks through his starring roles with his face somnolent and masked; you don't have a clue to what he's thinking. (He was a terrible actor. He must have understood that he would never amount to diddly in these crum-bum movies, and been resentful and bored.) At twenty-three, he was inducted into the Army, and the newsreel footage of him being given a G.I. haircut and during the two years of his service (1958 to 1960) shows him more open-faced than at any other time. The sneering, Greek-statue look he had in his movies disappears; he's leaner, and his smile is boyish. But as soon as he's out of the Army and resumes his movie career, the surly overripeness is back. The mixture in Elvis—part artist, part exhibitionist, part good ol' boy, part romantic kid, part unknown—could have fused only in pop culture, and it didn't fuse for long. (Presley's romanticism is creepy and gothic: his Priscilla, whom he met—and presumably fell in love with—when she was fourteen and he was twenty-four, looks to be his twin. He arranged for her to be brought to live at his mansion and to be educated, and he married her when she turned twenty-one; his actual twin, a boy, died at birth.)

In his seventies performances, wearing huge stiff collars on his bulging neck, and wide, glass-encrusted belts on the heavy, tight-fitting matador outfits that seem designed to swelter him (were they a penance for his flabbiness or a mad attempt to copy Mick Jagger?), he often seems cynical and slugged. The road—the party that never stops—could destroy anybody. Why did he do it? He was obscenely rich and in bad physical condition, and droning out the same songs over and over must have intensified his weariness. It may be that he felt so empty that the hysteria of the crowds was the only thing he could respond to. Maybe they excited him on about the same nostalgic level that he excited them on: they magnetized each other.

Almost everything that Leo and Solt have done to the raw footage makes you cringe. They've even got the man singing "And now the end is near" when he's melting away. But Presley is the star in his life that he never was in his Hollywood movies. He commands the screen, as powerful an image of the artist who loses faith in the audience as Brando. Some people have it all—greatness is in their reach. And they piss it away. It's overwhelming to see a life spread out on film—especially the life of someone who peaked a couple years after finishing high school, when he still had the look of a white-trash schoolboy sheik. Presley showed the strength to peak again when he quit Hollywood, and then just slid. *This Is Elvis* is hair-raising because of what Elvis turns into: joyless stardom gives him the look of a mutant.

•   •   •   •   •

*S*hot and directed by James Szalapski, *Heartworn Highways* is an informal documentary about performers such as Guy Clark, David Allan Coe, Townes Van Zandt, and Steve Young—part of the seventies "outlaw" generation of country music (outlaw because it wasn't sanctioned by the recording companies in Nashville). Szalapski is an attentive and scrupulous cinematographer; he loves his subjects, and the imagery is so warm and finely detailed that I had a hard time believing I was seeing a blowup from 16-mm. But in this first film he isn't yet a director—not fully, anyway. He shot most of the footage in six weeks around Christmas of 1975, and then spent three or four years, off and on, trying to get the movie distributed. It's fairly clear that during the (underfinanced) shooting he caught whatever he could; he couldn't plan a structure, and he probably wasn't looking for anything as vulgar as a hook or an angle. Which is too bad, because although there's very little in the film that isn't friendly or funny or really soul-stirring, it has no unifying energy. Watching it is like being carted off to a good party by people who told you where they were taking you so casually that the names of the people who were going to be there didn't sink in. You don't know how you got there or who the hosts are, and you never quite catch the last names of the assorted celebrities telling tall tales and singing lovely sad songs. (You're not even sure what the occasion is.) Szalapski's group of artists apparently know each other very well, but except for David Allan Coe, who has a star tattooed on his neck, and his name emblazoned on his glitter-cowboy outfit in at least three places, and wears earrings, and a belt buckle the size of a wagon wheel, I couldn't figure out who the people were until the end titles, when everyone is clearly identified. Since this is a group that was more or less spawned by hippiedom and is outside the Nashville orbit, most of the performers dress so inconspicuously they could be taken for college instructors; so I was puzzled by Coe's flash. Was it a put-on, because he was on his way to perform at Tennessee State Penitentiary and, as a former prison inmate, wanted to make it clear to the guards that he didn't mean to be detained? (Afterward, I learned that he had a hit album in 1974 called *The Mysterious Rhinestone Cowboy*, and a follow-up album called *The Mysterious Rhinestone Cowboy Rides Again as the Longhaired Redneck.*)

Among the many kinds of disservice that *March of Time* and the educational documentaries of several decades back did us, one is still taking its toll: the narrators in those days were so officious that later documentarians turned against any form of explanation, by voice or subtitle. It became almost a mark of "class" not to explain anything, and, ever since, audiences have had to puzzle their way through films such as Fred Wiseman's *Essene* trying to figure out simple, basic things. Instead of devising inoffensive—and maybe even entertaining—ways of clarifying material, filmmakers have swung to the position that any clarification by words would be an intrusion on their art, and this solipsistic position has been cutting them off from the viewer's need to know what he's looking at. Many of us must have had the experience of watching a documentary presentation in some bewilderment and then, in the discussion afterward, listening to the documentarian tell the audience all sorts of fascinating stories—just what might have fired our interest in his picture if he'd had the wit to work some of it in.

Heartworn Highways is so personal and appealing that I wish Szalapski had gone further into informality. The performers are very relaxed, talking to the camera at home (*somebody's* home) or at a gathering or at some hangout that appears to have a connection with the music. Why not ask them to introduce themselves and tell us where they are and maybe where they perform and for what sorts of audiences? Or if Szalapski didn't recognize that he had a problem until he'd finished shooting, it might not have been so terrible to bring himself into the movie by introducing the episodes with a few words of voice-over or some titles telling us where he encountered each performer and who each was. I was puzzled but amused by the bridges Szalapski tossed in: when a man sings about Jack Daniel's we get a quick montage inside the Jack Daniel's bottling plant; when Steve Young sings about wanting to be free on the Alabama highway, we get a brief montage of vehicles, congestion, and an overturned semi; and when the Charlie Daniels Band is getting ready for a concert, there's a speeded-up short comedy of the seats being filled. (The only real dead spot is a montage of houses and trucks while the Daniels Band performs the dull, jiggling "Texas.") Were these montages included because Szalapski had the footage and didn't want to waste it, or did he really go out specially to shoot these sequences because he thought he should illustrate the songs? There's something so natural and easygoing about the hustling humor of country people in the South—did it rub off on Szalapski, or is he being earnest?

A lot of documentarians have argued that verbal information is extraneous and leaving it out makes you concentrate totally on the images (and, in this case, the songs), which speak for themselves. But after you've seen *Heartworn Highways* it's hard to remember the music, because you were so dislocated when you saw it that you didn't know who and what you were seeing. At one point, inside a tavern, a middle-aged woman with a nondescript voice but real conviction sings "Let's Go All the Way," and you think, Why has this particular woman been photographed? The only answer I could come up with was, Because Szalapski shot the footage and figured it would show that everybody in this part of the country sings. Then I realized I didn't actually know what part of the country it was. The film seems to move around Tennessee and Texas, and I thought I recognized part of North Carolina, too. (Is this music, which attempts to return to the earlier traditions of workingmen's country songs, somehow tied up with—white—masculine values, and is that why there are no major women performers in the picture?)

If I linger over this messy movie, it's because there are so many questions it leaves you with, and because there are wonderful things in it, such as an image of car lights serpentining on a highway under a full moon. Szalapski understands that Southerners have different facial contours from Northerners. Larry Jon Wilson, seen recording "Ohoopee River Bottomland," has a face that looks like a bag of boiled potatoes, and it's wonderful; the pouches on his cheeks make him look like Santa Claus—he's a Toby jug carrying a guitar. (I guess I said *boiled* potatoes because Szalapski has lighted him so tenderly that he's knobby but not rough—you're almost touching him, and the camerawork on his hands is as delicate as his playing.) There's an incredible image of a seventy-nine-year-old black man, "Walkin' Blacksmith" Washington, his red eyes weeping as he listens to Townes Van Zandt sing "Waitin' Around to Die." And there's a marvellous jokey fable told, as a preamble to a song, by a man who I afterward learned was Gamble Rogers, a troubadour who travels the coffee-house circuit and is known as "the poet laureate of St. Augustine, Florida." He keeps his shaggy anecdote going, and we begin to realize how linguistically polished it is and what a baroque structure it has. Just before singing, he explains that he told the story so you'd know where his art comes from. (His song is the salute to Jack Daniel's—"Black Label Blues.")

The best evidence that Szalapski has directing talent is in his rapport with the performers (he makes it look so easy that we take it for granted) and in his feeling for diversity. He understands that we're interested not only in Guy Clark's beautiful, mournful voice but also in his dignified manner and his humility (he's like a Quaker pacifist) and in how they relate to his music, and we're interested in Van Zandt's accomplished prankishness as he gives us a tour of his property and disappears in a rabbit hole, and in Coe's strange, pungent lyricism in a song with the words "I've got nowhere to run," which he sings at the state penitentiary, and in his Beau-Brummell-of-the-underdogs act, and in his reminiscence of a prison shower when he was eighteen, which is like a white variant of a Richard Pryor routine—the kind of story that sounds insanely true. There are a lot of different poses in this movie, but underneath them all there's that po'-boy humor and grungy, rapturous melancholy that makes the South a land of spellbinders.

June 1, 1981

Whipped

---

*T*he marketing executives are the new high priests of the movie business. It's natural. They're handling important sums of money. And they dispense the money dramatically, in big campaigns that flood out over the country. It's not unusual for more to be spent on marketing a picture than on making it, and this could become commonplace. (Everybody takes it for granted that more is spent selling soap than manufacturing it.) Right now, the easier a project looks to market, the easier it is to finance. And the scope of what these priests think they can sell becomes narrower all the time. Except for the occasional prestige picture that offers middle-class group therapy (*Ordinary People, The Four Seasons*), it's all fantasy. There isn't a human being on the screen. Having lost the habitual moviegoers, the studio heads have no confidence that if they approve projects they like, an audience will be attracted; they're trapped by empirical evidence to the contrary. And so they listen to the marketing men, with their priestly jargon—"normatives," "skewed," "bimodal audience." The mysterious phrases are soothing to the worried studio heads. And when the new geniuses are given what they want—comic-strip pulp or slobby horror—they swing into action heroically. Daggers menace us in TV commercials, magazines, and newspapers, and *sometimes* the slob movies do become hits. But if you boil out the feathers what it comes down to is: When there's a flop, the marketing men cluck their tongues and say, "Well, boys, the picture just didn't have it." When there's a hit, the marketing men pound their chests like King Kong and say, "Boy, did we know how to sell it!"

These marketing divisions are a relatively new development. (In earlier years, there were two much smaller departments—advertising and sales.) Their growing power isn't in any special effectiveness in selling pictures; it's in their ability to keep pictures that don't lend themselves to an eye-popping thirty-second commercial from being made or, if they're made, from being heard of. In the new Hollywood wisdom, anything to do with people's lives belongs on TV. (As a result, television now makes contact with us in ways that movies no longer do.)

Like poor relations, the print media are the residual legatees of the huge marketing campaigns for pictures. The thinking is that anything associated with a big new hit will become a hot ticket. So magazine editors, ever eager to increase their newsstand sales, prepare their cover stories. Alan Alda, publicizing *The Four Seasons*, is the perfect cover boy for the women's magazines; if his film makes money, the writers and editors will feel they guessed right. I can't think of a single occasion when a small movie that really needed help got a slick-magazine cover, no matter how much the in-house critic liked it. The magazines try to ride on a hit picture's tail wind.

This month, God knows how many publications are featuring *Raiders of the Lost Ark*, a collaboration between George Lucas and Steven Spielberg—both still very young (Lucas is thirty-seven, Spielberg only thirty-three), and each responsible for some of the very top box-office successes in the history of movies. If anybody has a chance to turn movies around, it would seem to be these two (or Coppola). But *Raiders* is a machine-tooled adventure in the pulp-esoterica spirit of Edgar Rice Burroughs; it appears that Lucas and Spielberg think just like the marketing division. According to modern movie legend, Lucas, who had watched the serials of the thirties and forties on television in the fifties, has long cherished the idea of a hocus-pocus series "following the exploits of an adventurer/archeologist, Indiana Jones," but he got more interested in his other idea—*Star Wars*—and put *Raiders* aside, for later. Over the years, he worked up the story idea with Philip Kaufman—the first picture was to be set in 1936, in order to take advantage of Hitler's well-known interest in the occult—and in 1977 he offered it to Spielberg to direct. Spielberg, who was then finishing *Close Encounters* and was committed to making *1941*, agreed to do it after that, and Lawrence Kasdan, who had done the rewrite on *The Empire Strikes Back*, prepared the screenplay.

A Lucasfilm, financed by Paramount, *Raiders* is an old-fashioned cliff-hanger produced with incredible sophistication of means. The images have an unreal clarity: the camera shows us more than we could possibly take in if we were there on the spot. And the hero—Indy Jones (Harrison Ford), the daredevil archeologist, whose weapon is a bullwhip—makes the kind of bright-eyed entrance that's so intensely dramatic it's funny. Spielberg—a master showman—can stage a movie cliché so that it has Fred Astaire's choreographic snap to it. He transcends the clichés by sensational, whiplash editing. But Spielberg's technique may be too much for the genre: the opening sequence, set in South America, with Indy Jones entering a forbidden temple and fending off traps, snares, poisoned darts, tarantulas, stone doors with metal teeth, and the biggest damn boulder you've ever seen, is so thrill-packed you don't have time to breathe—or to enjoy yourself much, either. It's an encyclopedia of high spots from the old serials, run through at top speed and edited like a great trailer—for flash. It's like a hit number in a musical which is so terrific you don't want the show to go on—you just want to see that number again. When the action moves to Indy back home lecturing to an archeology class, you know that Spielberg, having gone sky-high at the start, must have at least seventeen other climaxes to come, and that the movie isn't going to be an adventure but a competition—Spielberg versus Spielberg. Even if he could keep topping his own showmanship (and he can't), he'd still be the loser, because the audience is fresher at the start. The central story is the search for the Ark of the Covenant (a chest holding the broken stone tablets of the Ten Commandments). Hitler, we're told, means to use its invincible powers to lay waste opposing armies and proclaim himself the Messiah. Indy, working for the United States government, races to find the Ark ahead of his arch-enemy, the suave, amoral Belloq (Paul Freeman), who is in cahoots with the Nazis. And the picture races along with Indy.

Kinesthetically, the film gets to you. It gets your heart thumping. But there's no exhilaration in this dumb, motor excitement. The best of the satirical pulp-adventure movies—the 1939 *Gunga Din* (with a plot lifted from *The Front Page*)—was carefree: there was fresh air between the thrills and the gags, there was time for digressions and for the pleasure of seeing actors you knew horsing around. The picture made you feel good, as if you were singing along with it. In the past, Spielberg has demonstrated a talent for just that kind of elating silliness, and he has a lot of it going here, especially with Harrison Ford, who does mammoth double takes, recoiling in disbelief. But *Raiders* is so professional and so anxious to keep moving that it steps on its own jokes. You can almost feel Lucas and Spielberg whipping the editor to clip things sharper—to move ahead. (I say the two, rather than just Spielberg, because this picture gets dangerously close to cancelling itself out, in a way that recalls *More American Graffiti*, which Lucas also produced.) The effect of the obsessive pace is that the picture seems locked in. Our eyes never have a second just to linger on a face or on an image of planes coming out of the clouds. The frames fit into each other, dovetailing so tight that sometimes it seems as if the sheer technology had taken over. It's all smart zap—a movie-maker's self-reflexive feat.

Yet it isn't beautifully made—not like Spielberg's other pictures, anyway. He has always been a conventional director, but he could do conventional material better than just about anybody else around, and he did it with a gleeful spirit. There's a gag here that shows the true Spielberg touch—slapstick so precise that it seems inspired: Indy flips a date into the air, meaning to catch it in his mouth, like a peanut; in that instant, his Egyptian friend, Sallah (John Rhys-Davies), registering that the date is poisoned, grabs it in mid-air, leaving Indy with his mouth open. It's so quick it's a visual haiku. Yet in the very next shot Spielberg blows what should be the capper: when Sallah shows Indy that a pet who stole a date from the dish lies dead, the timing is slightly off, and Spielberg fails to give the pet its due. It's an unfeeling shot, when it could have been a beautiful little sick joke. Spielberg rushes; he cuts corners and takes the edge off plot points. I've never seen him settle for approximations before or just throw effects at you, hoping that some of them will stick.

The moviemaking team appears to have forgotten the basic thing about cliff-hangers: we had a week to mull over how the hero was going to be saved from the trap he'd got himself into—we enjoyed testing our ingenuity against the moviemaker's. There's no room for speculation here, and Spielberg even loses track of what we want to see in a scene; he rides right over the dramatic possibilities. Does the film reproduce the plot holes of the serials deliberately, or does it stumble into them? (Why is the Well of Souls, where the Ark is buried, so exposed that it could hardly have escaped discovery before? Why isn't Indy's dig at least over the next ridge from Belloq's, so we can believe that Belloq doesn't spot it until the crucial moment? Why are we shown scenes that prepare us for Belloq to have a change of heart when he doesn't? And so on.) John Williams' pounding score could be the music from any old Tarzan movie, though with a fuller orchestra and at ten times the volume. Like just about everything else in the picture that misses, the klunky music can be said to be intentional—to represent fidelity to the genre. Yet, with the manicured wide-screen images and the scale of this production, klunkiness sticks out in a way that it didn't in the serials, which were usually all of a piece. Parody can be a true form of homage, but these moviemakers aren't aiming at parody—they're trying to reinstate a form that they just can't help parodying. So the script doesn't seem worked out. There was something else basic about cliff-hangers: our longing to know who the real evil power behind all the crimes was. This mystery has been eliminated, without any other kind of suspense replacing it. (Why *not* allow Belloq to change sides? His pangs of conscience are rather elegant.)

The actors are mostly just bodies carrying pieces of plot around. They sound as if they were ordered to read their dialogue on the run—all except Paul Freeman, who has the luck to play a character torn in different directions. He manages to make the ambiguous Belloq a little laid back. (At one point, when Freeman begins to speak, a fly walks into his mouth and he goes right on and delivers his lines. What a trouper!) The character of Sallah is defined completely by the word "friend," and the film continues the process of turning Nazism into comic-book mythology—the Nazis are fiendish clowns. The heroine, Marion Ravenwood (Karen Allen), who is the daughter of a famous archeologist, and so the possessor of a medallion—the headpiece to the Staff of Ra—that Indy needs in order to find the Ark, is fearless, resourceful, and as perky as all get-out. She hops around conking people on the head—she's playing Sabu in *The Thief of Bagdad*. At the same time, we're supposed to take her for a woman with a past: Indy—somehow we know that that's really for Independence, not Indiana—loved her but left her ten years before, and she's been running a dive in Nepal. Yet even when she's wearing a hideous long dress with a bustle, or clinging satin, she struts as if she were chipper little Shirley Temple trying to walk like a soldier. I liked Karen Allen in the strip-poker scene in *The Wanderers*, and her first moment here—sitting with a man who looks like Brendan Behan and drinking him under the table—isn't bad, either, but the filmmakers seem to have a fix on tomboy gumption. There's no space for sex. When Marion and Indy finally kiss, the music rises with such a clatter and shriek you think the theatre has been nuked. The people in *Raiders* reminded me of a friend's saying that her five-year-old niece, who was sitting back watching the Mandrell Sisters on TV, suddenly got up, put her face right up against the screen, squinted, and asked, "Are those puppets?"

Indy tries to keep the Ark from falling into the wrong hands because he's the intrepid archeologist hero who goes after treasures; to him the Nazis are no different from the half-naked tribesmen shooting poisoned darts in South America—it's all in the day's adventure. The holy artifact itself is just a MacGuffin, and a dull one at that—one more super death machine that could enable Hitler to win the war. And when the Ark must do its mystic tricks it sprouts poltergeists that recall the impish flying saucers of *Close Encounters* without living up to them. There's nothing at stake in *Raiders*—no revelation, and no surge of feeling at the end. (The Ark is disposed of in a sour, open-ended modernist way.) The thrills are fully consumed while you're seeing this movie, and it's totally over when it's over. It's a workout. You feel as if you'd been to the desert digs: at the end your mind is blank, yet you're parched, you're puffing hard—you want relief.

What's at stake is outside the movie: it's how the picture will do at box offices worldwide. And maybe the anxiety about grosses is what has emptied the film of emotion. When Marion kisses Sallah a grateful goodbye, you're surprised by the show of affection: they barely seemed to have met. Despite its daring surface, *Raiders* is timid moviemaking: the film seems terrified of not giving audiences enough thrills to keep them happy. It's an amalgam of Lucas's follies—plot for its own sake, dissociated from character or drama; the affectless heroine, who's a tougher version of Carrie Fisher's spunky Princess Leia in *Star Wars*—and effects that Spielberg the youthful magician has already dazzled us with. I kept wondering if it was the drubbing that the press had given Spielberg on *1941* (where he was trying new things) that made him so cautious. He seems to have accepted the Lucas pulp-repulped format as a safety net. It's not right for him. The movie comes alive in the kinetic comedy: in the lowdown, rowdy slapstick, when the Nazi sadist Toht, played by Ronald Lacey, picks the medallion up out of the fire, drops it from his blistering hand, and runs out screaming; and in the balletic slapstick, when Marion is the prisoner of the Nazis and Toht arrives and takes out a metal apparatus that Marion—and we—think is an instrument of torture but turns out to be a coat hanger. But Spielberg fumbles a lot of his action sequences, such as the ones on a tramp steamer and a U-boat, and even the early chase, in which Marion disappears. And some of the episodes are simply tired: a fight between Indy and a huge, sadistic German wrestler; a sequence with Indy jumping on a moving Nazi truck that's full of soldiers, chucking them off one by one, and ramming other cars in the convoy, to the accompaniment of soul-grinding music. Seeing *Raiders* is like being put through a Cuisinart—something has been done to us, but not to our benefit.

It's a shocker when the big-time directors provide a rationale for the marketing division—when they say, as Spielberg does, that "the real movie-lovers are still children." And there's no doubt he means that in a congratulatory sense. The whole collapsing industry is being inspired by old Saturday-afternoon serials, and the three biggest American moviemakers are hooked on technological playthings and techniques.

Behind *Raiders* is the soft-spoken George Lucas, who says things like "I'm really doing it so I can enjoy it. Because I just want to see this movie." I believe him. I wish I didn't. I wish I thought he talked that way just as a come-on for *Raiders*, because if Lucas, who is considered one of the most honorable people who have ever headed a production company, weren't hooked on the crap of his childhood—if he brought his resources to bear on some projects with human beings in them—there's no imagining the result. (There might be miracles.) I don't think the deterrent to his producing movies with human characters is just financial risk. Lucas, who keeps a tight rein on budgets, probably wouldn't stand to lose too much of his own or other people's money. The bigger deterrent may be Lucas's temperament and tastes. It's not surprising that he takes pride in the fine toys that *Star Wars* generated, and controls their manufacture carefully; essentially, George Lucas is in the toy business.

·   ·   ·   ·   ·

Cattle Annie and Little Britches is based on the lives of two adolescent girls in the late nineteenth century who became infatuated with the Western outlaw heroes they had read about in Ned Buntline's stories and left their homes to join them. The outlaws that the girls find are a mangy, demoralized bunch—the remnants of the Doolin-Dalton gang, led by the aging Bill Doolin (Burt Lancaster). The fiercely strong Annie (Amanda Plummer), who's about sixteen, shames the men and inspires them—almost catastrophically—to try to become what she had imagined them to be, and the younger, softer Jenny (Diane Lane) finds a father figure in Doolin, who calls her Little Britches. There is everything here to make a classic comedy-Western except a script to give the potentially rich material shape and a dramatic center. The cinematography, by Larry Pizer, is vivid: the colors are strikingly crisp and intense. (His work here reminded me how much I'd liked his startling reds in Karel Reisz's *Isadora* and his wild, acid-rock palette in *Phantom of the Paradise*.) The cast is convincingly grubby and hirsute; as the surly Bill Dalton, Scott Glenn, in long sideburns and a mustache, has almost no resemblance to the man in *Urban Cowboy* with the fish-net T-shirt. Lamont Johnson's directing has the clean intelligence that he gets a chance to demonstrate on TV more often than in movies; Johnson has a warm, honest touch and, an actor himself, he knows how to hold actors down. As the beady-eyed U.S. marshal, who's determined to nail Doolin, Rod Steiger is probably more contained than he has been in years. The last time I saw him—doing his padre number in *The Amityville Horror*— his spiritual agony was enough to shatter the camera lens.

David Eyre and Robert Ward, who wrote the script, from Ward's book, may be writers—the dialogue and most of the incidents have a neat, dry humor—but they're not screenwriters. The movie dribbles along pleasantly from scene to scene, and though it doesn't falter, it has no impetus; it's "nice" when it should be explosively, painfully funny. Through Doolin's efforts to live up to the girls' vision of him, he's carted off in a cage to an Oklahoma jail, where he waits to be hanged. The girls wangle their way in disguised as newsboys, and, with the help of the gang, Doolin gets out and rides off to safety with his men. The girls are triumphant, though they can't get away from the marshal and are sent back East, to spend two years in a Massachusetts reformatory. It's a wonderful, partly true story, which you can savor even if you have to pull it together for yourself. You don't find out what brought the girls together, or what their earlier lives were—what the fantasy played off—but there are some remarkable performances—Lancaster's and Diane Lane's, and, especially, the unheralded, prodigious screen début of Amanda Plummer. (Actually, everything about this picture is unheralded. It was finished over a year ago, but nobody wanted to release it, because a couple of other Westerns had failed. It wasn't really released: it was just dropped into a Broadway theatre for a week, to plug up a hole before *Outland* arrived.) As Bill Doolin, Lancaster (who made this film before *Atlantic City*) is a gent surrounded by louts—a charmer. When he talks to his gang, he uses the lithe movements and the rhythmic, courtly delivery that his Crimson Pirate of 1952 had when he told his boys to gather 'round. The great thing about Lancaster is that you can see the face of a stubborn, difficult man—a man who isn't easy to get along with. He has so much determination that charm doesn't diminish him. In his scenes with Diane Lane, the child actress who appeared in New York in several of Andrei Serban's stage productions and who, single-handed, made the film *A Little Romance* almost worth seeing, Lancaster has an easy tenderness that is never overdone, and she is completely inside Jenny's childish dependency. And when he's by himself, naked, soaking at the hot springs (where the marshal traps him), he's a magnificent, sagging old buffalo. Lancaster looks happy in this movie and still looks tough: it's an unbeatable combination.

Young Amanda Plummer gives a scarily brilliant performance: her Annie could teach Lucas and Spielberg a few things about tomboy gumption. Annie is scrawny, a guttersnipe showoff and dreamer, but there's also a woman there, with a spark of womanly greatness. When Annie saves the gang from a posse by stampeding a herd of cattle and stands among the running beasts with her arms outstretched, if your mind clicks to the tableau in *Women in Love*, with Glenda Jackson poised, dancing in front of a herd of swaying bullocks, Amanda Plummer doesn't suffer from the comparison. Whatever this young actress does here she does in character—whether it's the exaltation as she stands among the cattle or the resolve she shows when the outlaws seem cowardly. Her gaze is steely—implacable. She could burn holes in you with those eyes. Even her romance with one of the outlaws, played by John Savage, is fully felt—on her side, at least. No doubt the director guided this young actress, but her spirit is so distinctive it has to be all hers. It takes a few minutes to adjust to her face and voice, because you can see both of her parents (Tammy Grimes and Christopher Plummer) in her and you can certainly hear her mother's inflections, which have never seemed to belong to any country or class but only to the theatre, and to oddity. The daughter uses those inflections with a special vehemence: Annie is a taut young girl whose hoarse voice gives her raw emotions away. The only other actress I've ever seen make a movie début this excitingly, weirdly lyric was Katharine Hepburn.

June 15, 1981

Hey, Torquemada

As Nero in Mel Brooks's *History of the World—Part I*, Dom DeLuise is so greedy and sated that his eyelids droop from the weight of the food in his stomach; wreathed in fat, burping from indigestion, he goes on eating. DeLuise has always been funny in a distinctive, angelic, slightly hallucinated way. Even as the Polish assassin in *The End* (where he was so creatively crazy that he seemed to be inventing a new type of dementia right before your eyes), he was still well meaning. Not here: this Nero is rotten through and through, and DeLuise embraces rottenness with blissful abandon. It gives him a new dimension: he's funny in a great tradition of shameless low comedy. So is the movie. Structurally, *History*—a series of bawdy sketches—is a jamboree, a shambles. It's a floating burlesque show that travels from one era to the next, lampooning the specialties of each age—its particular infamies. Brooks is the writer, the director, and the star. His staging is often flaccid and disorderly, and he has never quite mastered the technique for building a film sequence, so even when he and the dozens of other comics in the cast are racing about, the movie often feels static. It's powered by its performers, though, and their way with a joke. It's an all-out assault on taste and taboo, and it made me laugh a lot.

Once the film gets past the Stone Age, Brooks is the star of each section: he's Moses, he's Comicus (a standup philosopher who performs for Nero), he's Torquemada, and he's Louis XVI, as well as a royal servant who doubles for Louis. We get more of the maniac side of Brooks than ever before, and it's enough to give this picture a charge of pure energy. I wish that he had selected less familiar periods of history. Rome has already been worked over (*A Funny Thing Happened on the Way to the Forum*, *Roman Scandals*, *The Boys from Syracuse*, *O.K. Nero!*), and so has French court life (most recently in Richard Lester's *The Three Musketeers*, which had a chess game much like the one here). I'd rather see Brooks as an Etruscan, or maybe a Mayan, or he could have been an ancient Persian miniaturist, or a Shaker, or one of those anonymous artisans we're always hearing about who worked on the cathedral at Chartres. But he still finds plenty to do in Rome—which is full of tradesmen's signs that take you back to your first puzzlement over Roman numerals, and the use of V for U. All through the movie, there are graceful painted vistas, by the special-effects wizard Albert J. Whitlock.

History is about show business through the ages, and some of the routines are golden shtick: a vestal virgin says to a group of men, "Walk this way," whereupon each of the men imitates her sweet-young-thing saunter. (In *Young Frankenstein*, it was Igor's humpbacked slouch that was copied.) More specifically, the film is a parody of the Broadway-Hollywood approach to the squirmy "offensive" subjects: religion, the poor, and minorities—Jews, blacks, women, and homosexuals. The deluxe, tanned vestal virgins at Nero's court (courtesy of Hugh Hefner: they're actually *Playboy* playmates and models) are dressed in low-cut gowns, and every one of them has her bosoms squished together; they're riper versions of the Goldwyn Girls in *Roman Scandals*—what moviemakers used to call "pulchritude." Brooks may take a special delight in this kind of throwback; he may be saying that this aspect of show biz doesn't really change. He also revels in old theatrical effeminacy: Howard Morris is Nero's mincing court spokesman, Andreas Voutsinas is a fop hairdresser, and so on. They're exaggeratedly nelly, but they're not very funny, unless you find nelliness itself a howl—as burlesque patrons used to, and as Brooks probably still does.

Brooks doesn't modulate his material; he tends to keep everything at a manic pitch. Luckily, some of the comics he has rounded up preserve their own unruffled timing. When Beatrice Arthur, as a clerk at the unemployment office in Rome, questions the people in line, her unhurried, deep, ringing voice shrivels them. And there are quiet bits by Henny Youngman as a Roman chemist, by Jonathan Cecil as a bewildered popinjay at the court of Louis XVI, and many others. It's a great variety show: there are gags and routines by such people as Paul Mazursky, Ron Carey, Sid Caesar, Spike Milligan, Jackie Mason, Fritz Feld, Jack Riley, Ron Clark, John Myhers, Jack Carter, Jan Murray, Pat McCormick, John Hillerman, Charlie Callas, John Gavin, Ronny Graham as Oedipus, Cloris Leachman as Madame de Farge, and Madeline Kahn as Nero's wife, the gum-chewing Empress Nympho, who has a voice that could shatter brass. Even Harvey Korman, who always seems to lose his bearings in Brooks's films, has a good bit when—as the prissy Count de Monet—he bashes his hand against a door, in anger at mispronouncing his own name. There are just two casting choices that stand out as mistakes: Shecky Greene as the lovelorn warrior Marcus Vindictus, the only man Nympho (a smart lady) rejects; Greene, who seems to have taken off the weight that Dom De-Luise gained, lets you see him trying to act funny. And Mary-Margaret Humes as the vestal-virgin ingénue, Miriam, has been handed too many toothy closeups, and she's a romper—when she's pleased about something, she jumps up and down. At first, you think somebody is going to do a number on her; Groucho certainly would have.

Sometimes the casting is on the nose: for example, John Hurt as Jesus presiding over the Last Supper. But Brooks must have laughed so hard at the idea that he didn't develop it; the people in the audience who aren't familiar with Hurt's previous roles (as a supreme sufferer) have no way to share the joke. The whole, brief Last Supper sequence is inspired, though. And so is the best-edited and best-sustained part of the picture—the Spanish Inquisition as a big musical number, with Brooks as a dancing, singing Torquemada in a red-devil cassock, and with lyrics such as "Hey, Torquemada, what d'ya say?" "I just got back from the auto-da-fé." This sequence has a pedigree: the Inquisition was done as a musical number in the Harold Prince production of Leonard Bernstein's *Candide*—remember Sondheim and Latouche's lyrics "What a day, what a day for an auto-da-fé"?

When I saw *History*, there were hisses and walkouts during this number, and the film has been attacked as a disgrace by reviewers in the press and on TV. I bet nobody hissed or walked out on *Candide*. When Prince and Bernstein do it, it's culture; when Brooks does it, there's a chorus of voices saying, "He has gone too far this time." Earlier in the film, the dancer Gregory Hines, who makes a breezy film début as Comicus' Ethiopian pal, Josephus, tries to convince the slavers who are sending him to the circus to be eaten by lions that he's not a Christian but a Jew. With his loose-limbed body—his legs seem to be on hinges—he does a mock-Jewish dance, and then a shim-sham, and the racial humor didn't appear to bother the audience. But during the Inquisition, when nuns toss off their habits, and a giant torture wheel to which pious Jews are attached is spun in a game of chance, there were mutterings of disapproval. Yet it's Brooks's audacity—his treating cruelty and pain as a crazy joke, and doing it in a low-comedy context—that gives *History* the kick that was missing from his last few films. The Inquisition is presented as a paranoid fantasy, with Jews as the only victims, and when Torquemada whacks the knees of gray-bearded old men imprisoned in stocks—using them as a xylophone—you may gasp. But either you get stuck thinking about the "bad taste" or you let yourself laugh at the obscenity in the humor, as you do at Buñuel's perverse dirty jokes. The offensive material is a springboard to a less sentimental kind of comedy.

If Mel Brooks doesn't go "too far," he's nowhere—he's mild and mushy. It's his maniacal, exuberant compulsion to flaunt show-biz Jewishness that makes him an uncontrollable original. At his best, he is to being Jewish what Richard Pryor is to being black: wildly in love with the joke of it, obsessed and inspired by the joke of it. What *History* needs is *more* musical numbers with the show-biz surreal satire of the Inquisition section; it's the kind of satire that makes the Marx Brothers' *Duck Soup* a classic farce. Brooks goes wrong when he pulls back to innocuous lovability—when he has Gregory Hines say to him, "You're the first white man I even *considered* liking." (Now, if that had been "the first Jew . . .") Hines' dancing—the movie could have used more of it—deserves better than a suck-up line.

When Brooks has a hot streak on a TV talk show, you can see his mental processes at work, and amazing things just pop out of his mouth. He can't get that rhythm going on the screen with prepared gags. Some movie directors can give their material that surprise. Altman has often done it, and in *Hi, Mom!* De Palma did it, with a highly inflammatory race-relations subject. But Brooks isn't a great director—far from it. He's a great personality, though, and he moves wonderfully; his dancing in his Torquemada robes is right up there with Groucho's lope. Wearing a little mustache and with his lips puckered, Brooks as Louis XVI bears a startling resemblance to Chaplin in his *Monsieur Verdoux* period. I kept waiting for him to do something with this resemblance, but he didn't. Was he unaware of it? Lecherous Louis did, however, make me understand why women at the French court wore those panniers that puffed out the sides of their skirts; we see those ballooning bottoms through his eyes. (Brooks may be wasting his talent by not appearing in other directors' movies while he's preparing his own.) As a director-star, he has the chance to go on pushing out the boundaries of screen comedy, because, despite the disapproving voices in the press and on TV, he can probably get away with it. Like Pryor, he's a cutie.

．　　．　　．　　．　　．

Outland has a great look. The setting is Io, a volcanic moon of Jupiter, which the League of Industrial Nations has franchised to an Earth-based company, Con-Amalgamate, and the metal frontier city that Con-Am has constructed is like the offspring of a gigantic pipe organ and an oil rig. The miners sleep in layered cubicles; their living quarters are an erector-set honeycomb—functionalism divorced from all civility. At work in the titanium mine, the men wear space suits with headgear that resembles a deep-sea diver's, but with a string of lights inside circling the visors—like the lights around an actress's mirror. To relax, the miners, and the other people on Io (the administrators, the maintenance workers, the corps of prostitutes, and others who provide support services), go to the leisure club—a big bar that features erotic entertainment. Writhing, dancing, and maybe copulating couples—a man and a woman, two women—perform in blue-green laser spotlights. The film aims for realistic sci-fi: the future is conceived as a continuation of capitalist exploitation in space, and the staging of the action sequences accentuates the sealed-in, claustrophobic boredom of life on Io. The workers (who sign on for a year) are meant to be just like ordinary Americans of the present—the kind who might have worked on the Alaska pipeline.

O'Niel (Sean Connery), the new federal district marshal, whose job it is to keep law and order among the two thousand people on Io, learns that a high proportion of the miners are going berserk and killing themselves or attacking others. Through the use of his computers and his TV monitors, O'Niel quickly sorts out the facts: Sheppard (Peter Boyle), who runs the mining operation on Io for Con-Am, is selling the workers amphetamines that keep them speeding for ten or eleven months, until they become psychotic. That's how Sheppard has been able to raise productivity and ingratiate himself with the top management. When O'Niel interrupts this operation by destroying a shipment of the drug, Sheppard sends for hired killers, and, just as in *High Noon*, the one lone good man finds he has to fight by himself.

This isn't a Western situation, though, where the local people are indebted to the lawman who has protected them but are afraid to aid him in a fight against professional gunmen; it's an existential *High Noon*. *Outland* is set in a morally grimy future: nobody else in the lunar company town cares what happens. O'Niel fights to prove something to himself. What, exactly, isn't clear. Sean Connery isn't afraid to open himself to the camera—he lets you read every shade of feeling that O'Niel hides from the other characters. He gives the movie the illusion of a central human presence. (Without him, it would be junk metal.) But when the camera moves in, expectantly, for O'Niel's big soliloquy—the moment when he will explain why he must fight—Peter Hyams, who wrote and directed *Outland*, has no words to put in O'Niel's mouth. Probably, Hyams is afraid that if the hero stood up against Sheppard's hirelings because he believed that the law meant something, or even out of disgust over the cruelty of the drug traffic, *Outland* might be jeered at as naïve and optimistic. But in using the structure of *High Noon*, with its preachy predictability, and then denying the hero's actions any heroic meaning, he deadens everything—even the spectacular chases through the tubular sets and the murderous grappling of bodies in space. The chases seem to be prolonged for their own sweet sake.

The miners come to Io because they need the high wages for their families on Earth. Yet Hyams expects us to believe that the marshal can't arouse them (or their union leaders) to indignation about the way they're being exploited by amphetamines—or even to anger about the gruesome deaths of their buddies. Hyams is like a guy who saw *High Noon* and didn't get it. It's insane that the workers refuse to help O'Niel—that they don't mind being killed off. The picture would have had much more point if it had jettisoned the Western-in-space idea and had one of the miners as the hero who discovers how the company is speeding them to death.

Outland is full of missed opportunities. O'Niel watches what's going on all over the town on his wall of television monitors, and he can deduce who the drug pushers are because he has a computer that sorts out the names of Sheppard's henchmen for him. Astonishingly, Sheppard—the general manager—doesn't have any monitors on which he can watch what O'Niel is up to. It might have been fun if he had—if he and O'Niel followed each other's moves until, maybe, they were just sitting at their sets staring at each other. As Hyams lays it out, it's too simple—only O'Niel has technical resources. All the imagination seems to have gone into the sets and costumes and chases. When the hired killers arrive on the space shuttle and stalk O'Niel, his only ally is a sour, snappish, elderly woman doctor, who's probably a boozer. (Frances Sternhagen does wonders with the role, and when this lanky doctor races desperately through long passageways to help O'Niel, she's surprisingly graceful.) Meanwhile, the miners, who know that O'Niel is being stalked, lounge around in their bar, and Sheppard, the murderer of dozens of their fellow-workers, sits among them, accepted. This cockeyed setup might have had at least a little point if there had been some TV monitors in the bar and if practically everybody on Io were clustered there to watch the big shootout—and perhaps lay odds on the outcome.

Hyams isn't one for touches, though. He has an eye for staging action, and he uses the stunning industrial-nightmare sets (designed by Philip Harrison) for a lot of feverish fast tracking. But he proceeds in an almost painfully straightforward way, even though it doesn't take him where he needs to end up. In *High Noon*, the gunslingers were the enemy; here the hit men are merely Sheppard's employees. So when O'Niel dispatches them the story still feels incomplete. We're supposed to know that Sheppard is finished—we've heard a Con-Am boss telling him that if these killers didn't take care of his problem the next group would be coming for *him*. But when O'Niel is content to give Sheppard a wallop on the jaw, justice doesn't seem to have been done. The climactic actions of the film involve O'Niel fighting nonentities.

The casting is very convincing, though the characters are purely functional. Except for Connery and Frances Sternhagen, only one of the actors—James B. Sikking, who plays Montone, O'Niel's sergeant—makes a strong impression. You can belive that Montone has been on Io awhile; he's like a cop who has been going through the same routine for a long, boring stretch. His lines are no better than anybody else's, though. The stuff Hyams lets people say! O'Niel's wife (Kika Markham) leaves him a videotaped goodbye: "I just can't take it anymore. . . . Paulie . . . is a child and he's never set foot on Earth.

Never. . . . Don't you see, he deserves a childhood." It's obvious that O'Niel loses his wife and son so that we can appreciate the sacrifice he makes in order to face the challenge of fighting evil, but who could work up feelings of sympathy for the loss of a wife who talks like that? She's the Ghost of Rotten Movies Past.

Outland recalls another hermetic sci-fi film—the somewhat more spirited *Alien* (which was also produced by the Alan Ladd, Jr., team). *Outland* doesn't have the leavening of freakishness that *Alien* did, but it, too, features an element of the repugnant, and it has a comparable grinding unpleasantness. Both these films belong to a new subgenre: Jacobean sci-fi. The deaths are the high spots and are as powerfully upsetting as the moviemakers dare to make them. In *Outland*, people who walk into a depressurized air lock without their space gear die like puffed pigs—their heads and bodies swell and explode, leaving a mess of splattered blood and intestines. And for those who want something more conventional, a deranged worker slashes a naked prostitute. The picture is horrifying yet somber, and the barrage of sounds coming from all directions intensifies the pressure—we can't escape the clanging metal or the footsteps or Jerry Goldsmith's score, which is on top of it all. This could be the Dolby movie of the year. During O'Niel's last fight, the noise rises to a Götterdämmerung level. At the end, Hyams has a note dedicating this film to his two young sons; he may be perfectly sincere.

June 29, 1981

Good News

*D*ragonslayer draws us into the mysterious world that it creates. Though it gives visual form to the monsters in our imagination—we see the fire-breathing dragon that must be slain; we even see its horrible progeny—the movie never appears to be literal-minded. Rather, it invites us to enter the murky darkness where dragons live. Scaly, winged, huge—the beautiful, grotesque monster that we see is more mysterious, probably, than any we could have imagined for ourselves. We never have enough of this dragon, and it always looks different, depending on how near or far away it is, and whether it's rearing up on its hind legs with its head so close it fills the screen or soaring like a gigantic bat. Even when we're looking right at it, we don't quite believe what we see. The producer, Hal Barwood, and the director, Matthew

Robbins, who wrote the picture together, met at the U.S.C. film school and worked as a scriptwriting team; they were credited on *The Sugarland Express* (1974), *The Bingo Long Traveling All-Stars & Motor Kings* (1976), and *Mac-Arthur* (1977) before they produced and directed their first picture, *Corvette Summer*, in 1978. The skills Robbins showed then, in his handling of the actors and his placement of the camera, flower in *Dragonslayer*. It's a night bloom.

In Britain, during the Dark Ages—roughly the sixth century—a delegation from the remote kingdom of Urland arrives at the castle of an ancient sorcerer, Ulrich (Ralph Richardson), perhaps the only sorcerer left who can call forth the elements and command streaks of lightning. A youth named Valerian (Caitlin Clarke) speaks for the group and pleads with Ulrich to help them. A dragon has been ravaging Urland, and in order to appease it the King offers it human sacrifices. Twice a year, he holds a lottery in which the names of all the virgins in his kingdom are entered; the unlucky winner is tied to a tree outside the dragon's lair. Though Ulrich has foreseen his own death, he agrees to go with the visitors. But Tyrian (John Hallam), a black-bearded emissary from the King of Urland, arrives to prevent any interference with the lottery, which has kept the dragon peaceful. Tyrian challenges old Ulrich to a test of his magic, and Ulrich appears to be slain. There is no one left to help the Urlanders except Galen (Peter MacNicol), Ulrich's apprentice.

Galen knows a few tricks, he has learned a few spells, and he has inherited Ulrich's amulet, but he's far from certain of his powers. Bravely, he goes forth to face the dragon, who becomes enraged by this boy magician's paltry efforts to destroy him. The King (Peter Eyre), terrified, puts Galen in a dungeon, and the King's naïve daughter, Princess Elspeth (Chloe Salaman), is distressed when Galen tells her that through bribery her father has been keeping her name out of the lottery. She helps Galen escape, and Valerian (a girl disguised from birth as a boy, to protect her from the lottery) and her father, the blacksmith (Emrys James), hide him from the King. Valerian gathers scales that the dragon has shed and makes Galen a fireproof shield, while the blacksmith prepares him a lance for his next onslaught against the dragon.

Galen stands up to danger, but he is of this world; he's just a kid who's in over his head. Ulrich and the dragon are the two great antagonists in this movie. Ralph Richardson, who has been otherworldly for some years now and moves so airily that he barely seems to touch earth, is ideally cast. Richardson recites spells in Latin while mixing a witches' brew, and he puts on his wizard's squashed hat at a rakish angle, like W. C. Fields with his con man's topper. (They both had a go at playing Dickens' Micawber.) When Richardson was younger (he was born in 1902), he was typecast as a quiet, civilized Englishman who concealed his suffering under a bland exterior—as in *South Riding* (1938) and *The Fallen Idol* (1948). And even when he became an outsize figure—the powerful, rigid father in the impressive *The Heiress* (1949) or the penny-pinching father in the great *Long Day's Journey Into*

Night (1962)—he still gave himself over to the roles. But in recent years he has become so powerfully eccentric a presence that the roles appear to be subsumed; he plays his parts with perfect control and yet enlarges them by his stare of astonishment, his imperiousness, and his wraithlike, distracted manner. He transcends the roles, makes them greater by the force of his mischievous indomitability. *Dragonslayer* is perhaps the only film in which Richardson shows the full, magnificent balminess that has marked his recent stage appearances. His Ulrich is like a batty, drunken old Shakespearean actor; his Latin spells have a poignant lilt—they could be elegies.

Playing in Shakespeare must have been the unifying experience for the cast of American and British actors. They speak plainly, in cadences that don't sound quite contemporary and that we can easily accept as sixth-century English. Peter MacNicol and Caitlin Clarke are both stage-trained Americans making their screen débuts. MacNicol has a flickering resemblance to Mark Hamill (it's the modelling around the mouth); Clarke has an intelligent, sensual grace, and she looks like a miniature Harriet Andersson. The brusque manner that Valerian developed when she was dressed as a boy lingers on, agreeably. She and Galen suggest a pair of Shakespeare's charmed lovers lost in an Ingmar Bergman forest. They have the right mixture of courage and callowness to set off the terrors of the older characters, especially those of the irascible, frightened King. Peter Eyre is what many a king in many a tale of enchantment was meant to be—a worried, loving daddy cloaked in arrogance.

The cinematography (by Derek Vanlint) is very active, very dramatic. When Galen goes inside the cavernous lair, it's like entering Hell—the fires burning in stagnant water are sinister. And the lyrical, lunging camera movements thrust us into Galen's position. We're down inside the luxuriant romantic dangers of a fairy tale. The dragon breathes flames at him, and you think, Of course—something this majestic would have to breathe fire. I've never seen a movie monster that was as evilly voluptuous when it moved as this one; it seems to walk on its wings. The dragon's reptilian sliminess is jewelled, and when it discovers that Galen has killed its young and cries out, it's horror crying in horror. The production designer, Elliot Scott, and the special-effects supervisor, Brian Johnson, and the editor, Tony Lawson, all seem to understand that the film has one purpose: to be magical. Like Barwood and Robbins, they're all sorcerers' apprentices. So is Alex North, whose Mahler-esque score is a beauty. The opening music recalls the deep bass sounds of the mother spaceship in *Close Encounters* when it answered the five-note theme of the Earthlings; this may be Barwood and Robbins' salute to their friend Spielberg, and also a link between the mythology of the past and of the future. When the dragon belches smoke or shakes the earth, the sound editors work the voices and sounds into the fabric of the music. At times, the music and the fiery dragon seem one. The beast is angered when a Christian monk who has stationed himself outside its lair addresses it as "Lucifer, a Fire Loosed from Hell," and it instantly—almost casually—breathes out and incinerates him.

Dragonslayer recalls reading a fairy tale that has the mixture of happiness and trauma to set your imagination whirling. It's true that almost everything in the film echoed in my memory: it all comes from movies. But it has been transformed and made new; in the terms the picture sets, it is almost completely successful. There are a few inexplicable details: How has the one giant dragon produced young? Is it hermaphroditic? Or, as its relation to its infants makes more likely, female? (But why sacrifice virgins to a female?) And, of course, people in the audience are bound to wonder why the scared girls don't set about losing their virginity pronto. Also, I was uncomfortable for a moment during the last lottery when Valerian's shouts from the crowd were crude—as if she were ready to kill the winner herself. But Barwood and Robbins aren't afraid to linger on suggestive images (such as a white horse rearing up in fear at the approach of the dragon); the allusive imagery and the music gradually enfold you. There's a second of acute magical suspense when the ambient sounds die away and all you hear is the dragon's intake of air before it expels fire; the camera looks down on the victim from the dragon's point of view and then there's a startling cut to the flames and the face of the dragon. By the time there is a moment of abhorrence—when you see the foul dragonettes munching on a human body—it's the shock that makes the whole vision take hold.

$\cdot$　　$\cdot$　　$\cdot$　　$\cdot$　　$\cdot$

Superman II has an old-fashioned virtue—charm—and a lot of entertaining kinkiness, too. The moviemakers went through heavy, reverent labor preparing the legend in the 1978 *Superman*; Richard Lester, who directed this second film (and who, it has been revealed, also did some work on the first), takes off from the legend. He brings it one light touch after another, and pretty soon the movie has a real spirit—what you wished the first had had. It's patched together, of course: there are corny Metropolis street crowds that must be holdovers from the earlier shooting, the special effects are highly variable in quality, and the whole film—blown up from 35-mm to 70-mm for the big-theatre showings—is grainy and bleached and often poorly framed. But that doesn't seem to matter much. Neither, really, does the fact that the script (credited to some of the same people who worked on the first: Mario Puzo, David Newman, Leslie Newman, and Tom Mankiewicz) cheats by telling you that something central is irreversible and then reversing it. The movie is full of smart gags and good ideas, and Lester stages little incidents (such as the hero being hit by a car: he doesn't get a mark on him, but the car's a wreck) that compensate for the big, klunky ones (like an episode involving terrorists setting an H-bomb in the Eiffel Tower). And Lester has got rid of most of the tedious characters who cluttered up the first film; Valerie Perrine and Jackie Cooper make mere token appearances this time—that's a big improvement right there.

Christopher Reeve, who brings emotional depth to Superman, pulls a switch on the material: Kryptonian that he is, Superman is the only human being in the movie. It's largely his love for Lois Lane and his sense of responsibility toward her (and the whole country) which give this film its jokey yet touching romanticism. By the end, he's no longer a square; he has suffered humiliation and grown up—you come out of the picture thinking about Superman's feelings. And Reeve has become a smoothie: his transitions from Clark Kent to Superman and back are now polished comedy routines. Margot Kidder's Lois Lane is still too cartoony. Her crinkly smile has no warmth, and she's so callously insensitive to Clark Kent—making fun of him for not being Superman—that she seems unworthy of Superman's devotion. (She's also cruelly photographed at times, with emphasis on her angular face, her pallor, and smudged charcoal eyes.) But Kidder and Reeve work well as a team, and they look blissed out together when they fly.

The originality of the movie is in its villains: Gene Hackman's bald, insidious Lex Luthor and the three Kryptonian traitors who in the first film were imprisoned for eternity in a Phantom Zone and now, through an accident, are released. Lester stages a series of perverse comic incidents with these arch-fiends in their black, high-punk jumpsuits; each has powers equal to Superman's and all three are just naturally vicious. Terence Stamp's General Zod (who becomes ruler of the United States) is a vain psychopath with a fish-eyed stare of boredom, Jack O'Halloran's Non is a hulking, moronic brute, and Sarah Douglas's Ursa is a sadistic tease. These three open their lips as if to pout and they blow up a storm that sends people and cars crashing; you may feel a shiver of helplessness—you wonder what could stop them. Ursa is just about the heroine of the film—not because she does anything admirable but because she does her dirty deeds with such blasé nonchalance, and the merest flick of a malicious smile. There's no way for Ursa's character to develop, but Sarah Douglas has style, and the kind of face cameras worship. The presence of this monochromatic rotten trio liberates Hackman, who is free to be a chiseller, a shyster clown. Whenever Hackman gets the chance to do comedy—whether it's his blind-man bit in *Young Frankenstein* or his starring role earlier this year as the inventor in *All Night Long*—he grows in vitality. His eyes sparkle when he tries to trick Superman or tries to wheedle a present from Zod (just a small one: Australia). He's a juicy comedian who loves to be a bad guy, and Richard Lester shows real affection for Hackman's snivelling and bargaining. Lester is in his element on *Superman II*—it's full of sneaky details. In the midst of chaos, people examine their bashed cars, shaking their heads over each scratch. The picture grows faster and quirkier as it moves along. It's more sheer fun to see than anything else around.

.   .   .   .

I'd always wondered what kind of person would think up fraternity-initiation rites; when I first watched Bill Murray on "Saturday Night Live," in 1976, I said "That kind." He seemed like something out of a swamp—cold-blooded yet sweaty. Was he a wimp trying to be a bully—was his obnoxiousness a wimp's revenge? He seemed the shiftiest of comics, and I didn't see how the smug, dislikable aspects of his personality could resolve in a comic persona. Yet the more I saw of him the funnier he became. He's a master of show-business insincerity. His shifty aspects haven't resolved; they may be his essence. Part of him is always in hiding, and there's a wild strain loose inside the doughy handsomeness which saves him from predictability. He looks capable of anything, yet he isn't threatening: he'd just do something crazy. Murray seems enormously likable now—the more so, maybe, because he has been wearing his suave put-on expressions so long that he has no way to be straight without appearing even phonier. In the eminently forgettable *Meatballs*, where he played big brother to a gooey-eyed kid with a crush on him, he avoided embarrassing himself (and us) by somehow contriving to look above the kid's head, offscreen—anywhere but at that moist, adoring face. *Meatballs*, directed by Ivan Reitman, was a hit with the kiddies and subteens. *Stripes*, the new Bill Murray comedy, also directed by Reitman, doesn't have a sentimental hook, and it's a much funnier movie, though anyone who stumbles into it without having seen Murray on TV may be floored—he's not someone you fall in love with at first sight.

In *Stripes*, Murray plays a wreck of a hipster who has screwed up his life and is in terrible physical condition. He's presented as a benign sort of nihilist who's too tired to care about anything, and he looks ungainly and lumpish. Having nothing better to do, he decides, on a whim, to enlist in the Army to get back in shape, and he cons his buddy, played by Harold Ramis, into joining up, too. The picture is not an aesthetic object; it's just a flimsy, thrown-together service comedy about smart misfits trying to do things their own way in the Army. But it has a lot of snappy lines (the script is by Len Blum, Dan Goldberg, and Ramis), Reitman keeps things hopping (it's untidy but it doesn't lag), and the performers are a wily bunch—they're professional flakes. John Candy, the big-blob charmer from the Second City, plays another recruit, and you keep spotting other Second City people—such as Joseph P. Flaherty, as a border guard spouting Slavic gibberish. But you can't take your eyes off Murray, because even when he's in an Army barracks he's never completely in the situation—he's slightly withdrawn, watching everyone else. (If you look away from him, you may miss out on information about one of the other characters.) Murray has feelers out in all directions. He's so anxiously aware of everything going on around him that you almost feel he's watching you.

Stripes doesn't follow through on the idea of hipsters versus the military mind. When Murray, who assumes leadership of the recruits right from the start, has his big confrontation scene with the new platoon's drill sergeant (Warren Oates), it's a dud. The picture doesn't follow through on anything, not even on the characters—a wild-eyed recruit (Conrad Dunn) introduces himself by saying that people call him Psycho, and there's no payoff; a Hispanic recruit in a bandanna (Antone Pagan) looks promising but never has a scene to play. Meanwhile, a Peeping Tom captain (John Larroquette) has too many scenes; any of him would be too many. The story comes to a natural end with the recruits' commencement exercises; afterward, when the platoon is whipping around Europe, the action is standard farce. Yet even when the plot goes all over the place the performers carry on as if they were doing something really spiffy, and the funny lines keep coming. Bill Murray is like a bomb ticking, and he keeps erupting with smartass remarks. At the same time, he's the supreme practitioner of going with the flow; he is never surprised. It's a rare comic who acts superior to the people around him and is still funny. Maybe Murray's know-it-all hipness isn't offensive because it seems compulsive and it just gets him into trouble. And because he's in direct contact with the audience. Or should be. But I doubt if the people who appreciated the message of *Private Benjamin* are going to laugh at a trivial service comedy in which nobody learns a lesson and nobody's character is improved. The moviemakers may have innocently blundered: they're still operating in the post-counterculture comedy terms of the late seventies—the recruits here don't believe in anything at the beginning of the film or at the end, either. This may be a silly, dated view—a remnant of stoned alienation—but it's a useful premise for a comedy. And could Bill Murray believe in anything? I wouldn't want to be within fifty yards of anything he believed in.

July 13, 1981

Portrait of the Artist
as a Young Gadgeteer

At forty, Brian De Palma has more than twenty years of moviemaking behind him, and he has been growing better and better. Each time a new film of his opens, everything he has done before seems to have been preparation for it. With *Blow Out*, starring John Travolta and Nancy Allen, which he wrote and directed, he has made his biggest leap yet. If you know De Palma's movies, you have seen earlier sketches of many of the characters and scenes here, but they served more limited—often satirical—purposes. *Blow Out* isn't a comedy or a film of the macabre; it involves the assassination of the most popular candidate for the Presidency, so it might be called a political thriller, but it isn't really a genre film. For the first time, De Palma goes inside his central character—Travolta as Jack, a sound-effects specialist. And he stays inside. He has become so proficient in the techniques of suspense that he can use what he knows more expressively. You don't see set pieces in *Blow Out*—it flows, and everything that happens seems to go right to your head. It's hallucinatory, and it has a dreamlike clarity and inevitability, but you'll never make the mistake of thinking that it's only a dream. Compared with *Blow Out*, even the good pictures that have opened this year look dowdy. I think De Palma has sprung to the place that Altman achieved with films such as *McCabe & Mrs. Miller* and *Nashville* and that Coppola reached with the two *Godfather* movies—that is, to the place where genre is transcended and what we're moved by is an artist's vision. And Travolta, who appeared to have lost his way after *Saturday Night Fever*, makes his own leap—right back to the top, where he belongs. Playing an adult (his first), and an intelligent one, he has a vibrating physical sensitivity like that of the very young Brando.

Jack, the sound-effects man, who works for an exploitation moviemaker in Philadelphia, is outside the city one night recording the natural rustling sounds. He picks up the talk of a pair of lovers and the hooting of an owl, and then the quiet is broken by the noise of a car speeding across a bridge, a shot, a blowout, and the crash of the car to the water below. He jumps into the river and swims to the car; the driver—a man—is clearly dead, but a girl (Nancy Allen) trapped inside is crying for help. Jack dives down for a rock, smashes a window, pulls her out, and takes her to a hospital. By the time she has been treated, and the body of the driver—the governor, who was planning to run for President—has been brought in, the hospital has filled with police and government officials. Jack's account of the shot before the blowout is brushed aside, and he is given a high-pressure lecture by the dead man's aide (John McMartin). He's told to forget that the girl was in the car; it's better to have the governor die alone—it protects his family from embarrassment. Jack instinctively objects to this coverup but goes along with it. The girl, Sally, who is sedated and can barely stand, is determined to get away from the hospital; the aide smuggles both her and Jack out, and Jack takes her to a motel. Later, when he matches his tape to the pictures taken by Manny Karp (Dennis Franz), a photographer who also witnessed the crash, he has strong evidence that the governor's death wasn't an accident. The pictures, though, make it appear that the governor was alone in the car; there's no trace of Sally.

Blow Out is a variation on Antonioni's *Blow-Up* (1966), and the core idea probably comes from the compound joke in De Palma's 1968 film *Greetings*: A young man tries to show his girlfriend enlarged photographs that he claims reveal figures on the "grassy knoll," and he announces, "This will break the Kennedy case wide open." Bored, she says, "I saw *Blow-Up*—I know how this comes out. It's all blurry—you can't tell a thing." But there's nothing blurry in this new film. It's also a variation on Coppola's *The Conver-*

sation (1974), and it connects almost subliminally with recent political events—with Chappaquiddick and with Nelson Rockefeller's death. And as the film proceeds, and the murderous zealot Burke (John Lithgow) appears, it also ties in with the "clandestine operations" and "dirty tricks" of the Nixon years. It's a Watergate movie and on paper it might seem to be just a political melodrama, but it has an intensity that makes it unlike any other political film. If you're in a vehicle that's skidding into a snowbank or a guardrail, your senses are awakened, and in the second before you hit you're acutely, almost languorously aware of everything going on around you—it's the trancelike effect sometimes achieved on the screen by slow motion. De Palma keeps our senses heightened that way all through *Blow Out*; the entire movie has the rapt intensity that he got in the slow-motion sequences in *The Fury* (1978). Only now De Palma can do it at normal speed.

This is where all that preparation comes in. There are rooms seen from above—an overhead shot of Jack surrounded by equipment, another of Manny Karp sprawled on his bed—that recall De Palma's use of overhead shots in *Get to Know Your Rabbit* (1972). He goes even further with the split-screen techniques he used in *Dressed to Kill* (1980); now he even uses dissolves into the split screen—it's like a twinkle in your thought processes. And the circling camera that he practiced with in *Obsession* (1976) is joined by circling sound, and Jack—who takes refuge in circuitry—is in the middle. De Palma has been learning how to make every move of the camera signify just what he wants it to, and now he has that knowledge at his fingertips. The pyrotechnics and the whirlybird camera are no longer saying "Look at me"; they give the film authority. When that hooting owl fills the side of the screen and his head spins around, you're already in such a keyed-up, exalted state that he might be in the seat next to you. The cinematographer, Vilmos Zsigmond, working with his own team of assistants, does night scenes that look like paintings on black velvet so lush you could walk into them, and surreally clear daylight vistas of the city—you see buildings a mile away as if they were in a crystal ball in your hand. The colors are deep, and not tropical, exactly, but fired up, torrid. *Blow Out* looks a lot like *The Fury*; it has that heat, but with greater depth and definition. It's sleek and it glows orange, like the coils of a heater or molten glass—as if the light were coming from behind the screen or as if the screen itself were plugged in. And because the story centers on sounds there is great care for silence. It's a movie made by perfectionists (the editor is De Palma's longtime associate Paul Hirsch, and the production design is by Paul Sylbert), yet it isn't at all fussy. De Palma's good, loose writing gives him just what he needs (it doesn't hobble him, like some of the writing in *The Fury*), and having Zsigmond at his side must have helped free him to get right in there with the characters.

De Palma has been accused of being a puppeteer, and doing the actors' work for them. (Sometimes he may have had to.) But that certainly isn't the case here. Travolta and Nancy Allen are radiant performers, and he lets their radiance have its full effect; he lets them do the work of acting, too. Travolta played opposite Nancy Allen in De Palma's *Carrie* (1976), and they seemed right as a team; when they act together, they give out the same amount of energy—they're equally vivid. In *Blow Out*, as soon as Jack and Sally speak to each other you feel a bond between them, even though he's bright and soft-spoken and she looks like a dumb-bunny piece of fluff. In the early scenes, in the hospital and the motel, when the blond, curly-headed Sally entreats Jack to help her, she's a stoned doll with a hoarse, sleepy-little-girl voice, like Bette Midler in *The Rose*—part helpless, part enjoying playing helpless. When Sally is fully conscious, we can see that she uses the cuddly-blonde act for the people she deals with, and we can sense the thinking behind it. But then her eyes cloud over with misery when she knows she has done wrong. Nancy Allen takes what used to be a good-bad-girl stereotype and gives it a flirty irides-cence that makes Jack smile the same way we in the audience are smiling. She balances depth and shallowness, caution and heedlessness, so that Sally is always teetering—conning or being conned, and sometimes both. Nancy Allen gives the film its soul; Travolta gives it gravity and weight and passion.

Jack is a man whose talents backfire. He thinks he can do more with technology than he can; he doesn't allow for the human weirdnesses that snarl things up. A few years earlier, he had worked for the Police Department, but that ended after a horrible accident. He had wired an undercover police officer who was trying to break a crime ring, but the officer sweated, the bat-tery burned him, and, when he tried to rip it off, the gangster he hoped to trap hanged him by the wire. Yet the only way Jack thinks that he can get the information about the governor's death to the public involves wiring Sally. (You can almost hear him saying, "Please, God, let it work this time.") Sally, who accepts corruption without a second thought, is charmed by Jack be-cause he gives it a second thought. (She probably doesn't guess how much thought he does give it.) And he's drawn to Sally because she lives so easily in the corrupt world. He's encased in technology, and he thinks his machines can expose a murder. He thinks he can use them to get to the heart of the matter, but he uses them as a shield. And not only is his paranoia justified but things are much worse than he imagines—his paranoia is inadequate.

Travolta—twenty-seven now—finally has a role that allows him to dis-card his teen-age strutting and his slobby accents. Now it seems clear that he was so slack-jawed and weak in last year's *Urban Cowboy* because he couldn't draw upon his own emotional experience—the ignorant-kid role was conceived so callowly that it emasculated him as an actor. As Jack, he seems taller and lankier. He has a moment in the flashback about his police work when he sees the officer hanging by the wire. He cries out, takes a few steps away, and then turns and looks again. He barely does anything—yet it's the kind of screen acting that made generations of filmgoers revere Brando in *On the Waterfront*: it's the willingness to go emotionally naked and the con-trol to do it in character. (And, along with that, the understanding of desolation.) Travolta's body is always in character in this movie; when Jack is alone and intent on what he's doing, we feel his commitment to the orderly world of neatly labelled tapes—his hands are precise and graceful. Recording the wind in the trees just before the crash of the governor's car, Jack points his long, thin mike as if he were a conductor with a baton calling forth the sounds of the night; when he first listens to the tape, he waves a pencil in the direction from which each sound came. You can believe that Jack is dedicated to his craft, because Travolta is a listener. His face lights up when he hears Sally's little-girl cooing; his face closes when he hears the complaints of his boss, Sam (Peter Boyden), who makes sleazo "blood" films—he rejects the sound.

At the end, Jack's feelings of grief and loss suggest that he has learned the limits of technology; it's like coming out of the cocoon of adolescence. *Blow Out* is the first movie in which De Palma has stripped away the cackle and the glee; this time he's not inviting you to laugh along with him. He's playing it straight, and asking you—trusting you—to respond. In *The Fury*, he tried to draw you into the characters' emotions by a fantasy framework; in *Blow Out*, he locates the fantasy material inside the characters' heads. There was true vitality in the hyperbolic, teasing perversity of his previous movies, but this one is emotionally richer and more rounded. And his rhythms are more hypnotic than ever. It's easy to imagine De Palma standing very still and wielding a baton, because the images and sounds are orchestrated.

Seeing this film is like experiencing the body of De Palma's work and seeing it in a new way. Genre techniques are circuitry; in going beyond genre, De Palma is taking some terrifying first steps. He is investing his work with a different kind of meaning. His relation to the terror in *Carrie* or *Dressed to Kill* could be gleeful because it was Pop and he could ride it out; now he's in it. When we see Jack surrounded by all the machinery that he tries to control things with, De Palma seems to be giving it a last, long, wistful look. It's as if he'd finally understood what technique is for. This is the first film he has made about the things that really matter to him. *Blow Out* begins with a joke; by the end, the joke has been turned inside out. In a way, the movie is about accomplishing the one task set for the sound-effects man at the start: he has found a better scream. It's a great movie.

* * * * *

*W*hen John Gielgud was young, he looked like a tortured aesthete; he was lean and gaunt-faced and literally a highbrow—you couldn't imagine him playing a part like Hobson, the valet in *Arthur*, who is close kin to P. G. Wodehouse's Jeeves. Though Gielgud entered movies in 1924, he has rarely appeared in screen comedies, so his skill here has an element of surprise—he may be the most poised and confident funnyman you'll ever see. Gielgud can steal a scene by simply wearing a hat; it's so crisply angled that you can't take your eyes off him—you want to applaud that perfect hat. Gielgud has become more robust with the years, and he uses his hypercultivated tones—his speech is a form of trilling—as a supreme joke. As Hobson, he appears to be amused by his own astringency, his jowls, and the pursed mouth with which he can administer rebukes. Even when Gielgud gives the driest of dry inflections to his lines, his voice mellows them out. (For true dryness, you'd have to sit through *The Legend of the Lone Ranger* to hear another great comedian, Jason Robards, as President Ulysses S. Grant, rasp out at the end, "Who is that masked man?")

Arthur, written and directed by Steve Gordon, is about a drunken millionaire playboy; it harks back to the screwball comedies of the thirties, but its attitudes are vaguely contemporary. In the thirties, Arthur, the New York playboy (Dudley Moore), would have straightened out once he fell in love with the working-girl heroine. But in this movie Arthur's childishness is endearing—it has saved him from the vices of hypocrisy and practicality—and Linda, the working girl (Liza Minnelli), loves him for it. There is no need for Arthur to grow up: Hobson has been his nanny all his life, and Linda is eager to take over. The rich, virtuous bore (Jill Eikenberry) whom Arthur's family decrees he must marry—or lose his fortune—is the one who wants to get him off the bottle and straighten him out. (You can't be sure whether the picture is pre-Freudian or post-Freudian or just anti-Freud.) Considering that Arthur—a top-hatted lush who's forever making whoopee—is a very thin comic construct, Moore does an amazing amount with the role. Arthur has a mad sparkle in his eyes and there's always something bubbling inside him; the booze just adds to his natural fizz. You don't want him to sober up, because he's such an amiable, funny drunk, chortling happily at his own nonsense. He picks up a hooker named Gloria (Anne DeSalvo), takes her to the Plaza, and introduces her to his relatives there as Princess Gloria, from a domain so tiny that "they've recently had the whole country carpeted." He even laughs in his sleep—he's telling jokes in his dreams.

The picture doesn't make the mistake of letting Arthur renounce his seven hundred and fifty million dollars. (We would all have gone home feeling empty-handed.) But it makes a lot of other mistakes. Disrupted weddings at which everybody waits until the prospective bride or groom cancels the festivities are among the least salvageable of old-movie rituals, and the one here goes on so long it had me whimpering. This is Steve Gordon's first time out as a movie director; he has the imagination to make giddy light comedies, but his pacing is ragged, he has a pretty feeble sense of structure, and he's a long way from being able to do with images what he can do with words. Still, the film has a friendly spirit, and, with some help from the young cinematographer Fred Schuler, it squeaks by; the city looks elegant even when the staging suggests a waxworks museum. Gordon plays a television-comedy trick: For the sake of a laugh line, he deceives us at first; he lets us think that Hobson despises Arthur. Then we discover that they are beatifically devoted to each other. (That's really the romance in the movie.) But Gordon also has inspired bits: There's a scene of Hobson ill, propped up stiffly in bed, wearing a cowboy hat and cradling a basketball. He's like an ancient Egyptian prepared for the next world. And there are low-comedy bits that are very satisfying: When Arthur goes to see Linda in Queens, he stumbles into the wrong building and gets involved in the marital mess of two complete strangers. (The episode is more entertaining than what happens when he finds the right building.) There are also spots where you can perceive a comic idea that doesn't quite work: Barney Martin, the Mr. Cellophane of the Broadway show *Chicago*, who plays Linda's father and looks like a baggypants-comedian version of her, has a gentle quality that promises more humor than he gets to deliver.

A larger idea that doesn't work is the casting of Liza Minnelli. Moore and Gielgud bounce off each other like Bertie Wooster and Jeeves; they have a common ground. But when Minnelli turns up she doesn't bounce off anybody, and there's no common ground under the three of them. Gordon doesn't seem to know how to write for women. Geraldine Fitzgerald, who plays Arthur's grandmother, has scenes that I don't think anybody could get by with, and the zest she gives them goes peculiarly wrong. (She had similar problems in the forties when she played heroines: her intensity didn't quite seem to belong to her roles then, either, and for a time she was rather like the intellectuals' Joan Crawford.) I haven't a clue to what Linda is supposed to be, and I doubt if Minnelli had much of a clue. It would have helped if Linda had had her share of the good lines, and if at our first sight of her she had done something so irresistibly charming that we were smitten at the same instant that Arthur was. But he becomes infatuated with her when he spots her shoplifting (a device that is somewhat short on enchantment), and he adores the rather shrill aplomb with which she attempts to outwit a store detective. There's no question but that Liza Minnelli is dedicated, talented, vital. But she's stylized—she's like a series of photographs of theatrical poses. (Gielgud is stylized, too, but he modulates; Minnelli has no small emotions.) She is said to be known in France as *"la petite Piaf américaine"*; if so, the French have got it wrong—she's the big American Piaf. Holding a stage by herself has enlarged her socko presence, and when she needs to be appealing she's electrifying: her gamine eyes pop open as if she'd just seen a ghost. Linda is supposed to be the one girl for Arthur, but even Princess Gloria, in her red stretch pants, has more going on with him. You feel Arthur would be better off marrying Hobson.

•　　　•　　　•　　　•　　　•

Zorro, the Gay Blade is a joyously silly farce—a satire of the impracticality of swashbuckling heroes. George Hamilton, who has turned into a wonderful, slinky farceur, puts on a mock-Spanish accent and a magnificent leer of self-satisfaction, and Donovan Scott, as his plump, teddy-bear servant, Paco, brings off routines that I've been seeing all my life and that never worked before. (He's like a more innocent Roy Kinnear.) The picture must have been an actors' holiday: Ron Leibman, Brenda Vaccaro (doing a Madeline Kahn), and many of the other performers haven't looked this alive in years. The script, by Hal Dresner, is crammed with vintage jokes and a fair number of débutants; it's the kind of farce at which you laugh so hard that when something misfires it's just a little rest. The director, Peter Medak, parodies all those films that featured peons in outsize headgear, starting with Eisenstein's pictorial essays on the nobility of wearing a sombrero; Medak dispenses with the faces and just gives you a sea of hats.

July 27, 1981

Dunaway Assoluta

*F*aye Dunaway gives a startling, ferocious performance in *Mommie Dearest*. It's deeper than an impersonation; she turns herself into Joan Crawford, all right, but she's more Faye Dunaway than ever. She digs into herself and gets inside "Joan Crawford" in a way that only another torn, driven actress could. (She may have created a new form of *folie à deux*.) With her icy features, her nervous affectations, her honeyed emotionalism, Dunaway has been a vividly neurotic star; she has always seemed to be racing—breathless and flustered—right on the edge of collapse. In *Mommie Dearest*, she slows herself down in order to incarnate the bulldozer styles in neurosis of an earlier movie era; her Joan Crawford is more deliberate and calculating—and much stronger—than other Dunaway characters. As Joan the martinet, a fanatical believer in discipline, cleanliness, order, Dunaway lets loose with a fury that she may not have known was in her. She goes over the top, discovers higher peaks waiting, and shoots over them, too. Has any movie queen ever gone this far before? Alone and self-mesmerized, she plays the entire film on emotion. Her performance is extravagant—it's operatic and full of primal anger; she's grabbing the world by the short hairs. Maybe Dunaway had to get into this hard-nosed Crawford drag—the mannish shoulders, the popping eyes and angry mouth—before she could yell this loud. Her back is stiff, her voice is thick with barely suppressed rage, and her diction has become ridiculously cultured. This congealed-syrup voice is the only voice Joan has got. She's a very scary, sinewy woman; wearing a silver lamé gown fitted at the waist, she looks like a high priestess with breastplates. In a scene in the sterile Crawford mansion, Joan is on her hands and knees vigorously scrubbing her own shrine. She's proving her right to be a star the only way she knows—by compulsive, punishing work. She has to scrub the floor because the maids don't get it clean enough; if they did, they wouldn't be maids.

The film includes the nocturnal rampages that were the most talked-about episodes in the book by her adopted daughter, Christina Crawford, on which the movie is based. In one, Joan, prowling through her children's closets, finds a flaw—an expensive little frock on a wire hanger—and goes out of her head. In another, Joan responds to the news that she's finished at M-G-M by systematically cutting down her rose garden; she's wearing a sequin-top evening gown as she chops away at a tree. Dunaway brings off these camp horror scenes—howling "No wire hangers!" and weeping while inflecting "Tina, bring me the axe" with the beyond-the-crypt chest tones of a basso profundo—but she also invests the part with so much power and suffering that these scenes transcend camp. The destruction orgy that follows her discovery of the wire hanger may recall the gothic flamboyance of *What Ever Happened to Baby Jane?*, and her smeary cold cream gives her the white face of a Kabuki demon. Yet she's so wrecked, so piteous—and so driven—that she isn't funny. You can't help laughing at the movie, but you can't laugh at her. When she beats Tina with the offending wire hanger, or whomps her with a can of Old Dutch Cleanser, the horror isn't ridiculous, because you feel her tension and madness; you feel the strength of her need to smash this child, who isn't the malleable doll she fantasized when she bought her. (Movie stars were pioneer customers in the blond-blue-eyed-baby traffic.) Dunaway doesn't hold back: when Joan abuses Christina, you know that the child represents all the disappointments and disorder in Joan's life.

Dunaway gets at the mania for precision and order which often comes with age—it's almost always part of the running battle between parents and children, and sometimes goes as far as weird geometrical obsessions about where things should be. And for an aging star trying to deal with the pressures of the business world—someone who has labored to develop competence and needs order so that she can function—precise arrangements can be the only peace that's attainable. (It's too bad that the film doesn't provide any specific allusions to her early life, so that we could visualize the squalor she has climbed out of.) There's an aesthetic involved in Joan's rejection of wire hangers: when everything is symmetrical and expensive, she knows where she is—she can feel that she lives in harmony, unthreatened. There's no *mess*. Order is beauty to her, and the satisfaction she takes in it keeps her going. She's providing her kids with the perfection she yearned for, and they don't appreciate it. So she blows sky-high and shows them real disorder—the mess they deserve.

Dunaway has only one sequence that's merely camp (and it's an entertaining lowdown number): after the death of Joan's last husband—Alfred

Steele, of Pepsi-Cola—when she lets the company board of directors know that she's not going to be pushed around, she belts out, "Don't f—k with me, fellas. This ain't my first time at the rodeo." She's like a rowdy female impersonator, savoring the jolt she gives the fellas—and the audience. It's a release the audience needs.

The Joan Crawford of this movie has the insecurities of an aging beauty and the strident aggressiveness of a two-fisted butch lesbian. It's an overheated, horrifying combination. And she's both mother and father to her adopted kids; actually, she is so authoritarian that she's neither mother nor father—she's a demented androgyne. There is nothing appealingly soft in this boss-lady bawling out instructions, so it's flabbergasting to see the rapport that the normally smooth Dunaway feels with this tough, crazy grotesque. It's one star speaking for another, saying that the business devours your sanity and your femininity. The picture sets up Crawford as Lady Macbeth of Hollywood. In a pre-title sequence, she is awakened by an alarm clock; it's 4 A.M. She unstraps her facial mask while getting out of bed, scrubs her face and arms briskly (she could be sandpapering herself), and plunges her face into ice to tighten the skin. There's anger mixed with a sense of duty in the determination of her movements as, wordlessly, she puts on garments from her perfect closets and walks through the chaste halls and into a waiting limousine, where she studies her script—*The Ice Follies of 1939*—and autographs photos on a special tray-desk. Not a second is wasted: everything she does is purposeful. She appears to be overzealous, inhuman. But Dunaway takes this star-machine Joan Crawford and shows you that she isn't evil or inhuman—she's frighteningly human.

Dunaway goes at the role with such magnificent loony empathy that her posture and movements and the way she runs recall Crawford's self-consciousness, and sometimes when her movements are most like Crawford's they're also quite crazy. Beyond your horror for the child whom Joan tries to subjugate, you're involved in Joan's need to enforce her perverted idea of discipline. The little girl (Mara Hobel) who plays the child Christina has a prematurely wise face; she's like a pixie dwarf. And in the scene with this creepy, narcissistic child sitting at the mirror pretending to be her creepy, narcissistic mother, only to have her mother pounce on her and, as punishment, hack off her golden curls, the mother and the daughter are both so hysterically upset and the mother is so unrelenting, cropping more and more of the hair, as if to root it out, that the nightmarish collision of temperaments begins to suggest a great subject: the horrible misunderstandings between all parents and children—their need to "correct" us, our need to spite them, our raw nerves that they can pinch, theirs that we can press down. Diana Scarwid, who takes over from Mara Hobel when Tina is about thirteen, holds you by letting you watch Tina's secret thoughts. The adolescent Tina is a fresh-faced yet hidden person—she has to be hidden to survive. She's not docile—she's careful and cagey. But every once in a while she forgets herself and speaks her mind, and she's in real trouble. Scarwid has good low tones in her voice which suggest the ordeals Tina has been through, and she brings the role a twinkle, a gleam of rude humor, that seems to sustain Tina through her mother's most fiendish persecutions. On the occasion when it deserts her, and she raises her voice and talks back to her mother, Joan tries to choke her; Tina is rescued by a writer from *Redbook* (played in a believable, I've-seen-everything way by Jocelyn Brando) who's in the house doing a puff piece on the star's home life. Nobody is really in a position to help the children: Joan wouldn't put up with anybody strong enough to fight her. Her secretary-companion, Carol Ann (Rutanya Alda), who sees Tina's misery, is a wan, pinched acolyte. When she prays for Joan to win the Academy Award (for *Mildred Pierce*), there's a good possibility that she's really saying, "O God, save us from what we'll have to go through if they don't give it to her."

The best that can be said about the movie itself is that it doesn't seem to get in the way of its star. Mostly, it's bare and uninhabited. Produced by Frank Yablans and directed by Frank Perry, from a script they patched together (which was also worked on at various times by Tracy Hotchner and by Robert Getchell), it takes place in limbo. There's no illusion of any life going on around the action, which is staged right up front; you can practically hear the camera motor crank up for each shot, and when a crowd gathers, it seems to number eleven at the most. The film is a jumbled scrapbook of Crawford's life from her middle years to the end, with continuity that's slightly berserk. After the pre-title morning ritual, which goes on until Joan comes out of the makeup room at the studio and is ready to present herself to be photographed (this is the only sequence that's ingenious in visual terms), the film cuts back to her at home. Right after she wins the Academy Award, the film cuts to her wire-hanger fit, as if it were later that night. (Does the picture mean to suggest that she's so far gone that nothing can appease her? Or is there no relationship between the two sequences?) Some of the most promising episodes aren't shaped. The one in which the grown-up Tina, who has become an actress and is appearing in a soap opera, becomes ill and is hospitalized and the elderly, drunken Joan fills in for her is just a limp, squashy mess. There's an unexplained, tatty little scene with Tina accepting an award on Joan's behalf while Joan lies in bed weepy-eyed, watching the ceremony on TV. And Alfred Steele is presented as if he were a butter-and-egg salesman from Topeka rather than the head of an international corporation; Joan seems to lead him by a nose ring. And did the movie go through a budgetary crisis? Joan forces Al to spend excessive amounts of company money on a huge apartment that is to be their showplace, and then we never get to see the finished thing. There's too much of a beginning to some of Scarwid's scenes— we're almost watching her prepare for them. And Perry violates her performance with shots of the adolescent Tina necking which feature flashes of her white panties. But he doesn't intrude on Dunaway—he gives her long takes so she can go into her arias, and she sustains them. She becomes as grim and harsh as the actual Joan Crawford was—in her films of the forties and fifties, especially, when her falseness was so regal and heavy that you couldn't cut through it. You didn't feel the presence of anything else underneath. In the obit that George Cukor wrote, he said, "Whatever she did, she did whole-heartedly." Strenuously, rather; she was incapable of lightness, of delicacy. In a scene in which Joan is rehearsing for *Mildred Pierce*, Dunaway looks like her, but you're aware of an enormous difference: this is *Mildred Pierce* with a real actress in the part.

The emotional violence in this film is potent; you can't get it out of your mind. There are probably people in the audience saying to themselves, "If Joan Crawford had adopted me, I would have known how to handle her"— and forgetting how they fought with their own parents. And there are proba-bly others to echo the sentiments of Larry Rivers, who got up after a screen-ing of *Mommie Dearest* and said, "You know what I just realized—I *am* Joan Crawford." Somehow, the movie is balanced: you see both sides. There's no question that Joan is guilty of battering her child, but Tina isn't exactly inno-cent—she has to test Joan in order to get her bearings in the world. The sur-prise of the movie is that you can watch Joan's killer instinct at work and still not hate her. When the little Tina deliberately interrupts her mother's session with a handsome stud, you know what the session means to Joan, because you've seen her preparing for him, preening herself and anxiously checking out the leg she then casually displays to him. You've seen her jogging, work-ing out: she has constructed herself almost mechanically—a post-industrial Venus. She wants to be perfect, like her spotless mansion. Her assumption of a charitable social role and her generosity to her fans are not just self-serving. She works to provide them with an ideal, and feels generous to those who can never accomplish what she has and yet believe in the ideal. Dunaway sees a grandeur in Joan Crawford, and by the size and severity of the tor-ments she acts out she makes Crawford seem tragic. After Michael Redgrave played the insane ventriloquist in *Dead of Night*, bits of the character's para-noia kept turning up in his other performances; it could be hair-raising if Faye Dunaway were to have trouble shaking off the gorgon Joan.

.　　.　　.　　.　　.

*F*or the movie version of John Fowles' *The French Lieutenant's Woman* to set our imaginations buzzing, the one essential is that the distraught heroine, Sarah Woodruff, who keeps a vigil on the stone jetty of an English seacoast village in 1867 and, motionless, looks out to the gray sea, must be alluringly mysterious. If she isn't, there's no story, because the novel—a pastiche—is (among other things) a meditation on the romantic mystery women and sen-sual madwomen of Victorian fiction. It's Fowles' rather charming conceit that if this mysterious cloaked siren, with her haunted face and wild, free-floating hair, happened to stray into the ambience of the Pre-Raphaelites she would seem to belong there—she would be a free and independent New Woman. We never really get into the movie, because, as Sarah, Meryl Streep gives an immaculate, technically accomplished performance, but she isn't mysterious. She's pallid and rather glacial. When she ensnares the aristocratic Charles Smithson (Jeremy Irons) and tells him her two different versions of her relations with the French lieutenant and how she became an outcast, there's no passion, and not even any special stress, in her accounts, and so they have no weight in the movie. Meryl Streep's technique doesn't add up to anything. We're not fascinated by Sarah; she's so distanced from us that all we can do is observe how meticulous Streep—and everything else about the movie—is. Harold Pinter, the famed compressor who did the adaptation, has emptied out the story, and the director, Karel Reisz, has scrupulously filled in the space with "art": every vocal inflection is exact, the period settings seem flawless, and the cinematographer Freddie Francis's camera movements and muted colors are superbly elegant. The result is overblown spareness, with remnants of subplots and clues that lead nowhere. It's all so controlled that everything seems to be happening punctually, yet it's bewildering. If you want to know what's going on between Sarah and Charles, you have to go back to the book (which isn't all equivocation).

The movie may be getting so much attention because it represents the height of a certain kind of refinement. (There's certainly nothing funky going on.) This sort of restrained, calibrated moviemaking wears its cultural credentials right up front, like a house done in impeccable Swedish modern. Pinter's script is almost as frugal with emotion as his script for *The Last Tycoon* was. The anemia of the book is fairly amusing, since it's part of Fowles' game to drain the blood out of Hardy's novels and scrutinize what's left. But Pinter proceeds to drain out Fowles' playfulness, and even the devices that link the characters and tie the plot together. An example: Charles' enterprising man-servant, Sam, is a variation on Dickens' Sam Weller, and he plays a crucial role in the fate of Sarah and Charles. In the movie, you see Sam (Hilton McRae) sneaking a look at a sealed letter that Charles receives and spying on him and hinting of blackmail, but nothing follows from any of this. In the book, Sam decides not to deliver a letter that Charles gives him to take to Sarah—it's the letter in which Charles avows his love for her, tells her that he will extricate himself from his engagement, and declares his honorable intentions. He orders Sam to take it to her at the hotel in Exeter where he has left her—and where, he assumes, she will wait for him. Sam finds it more expedient to ingratiate himself with the about-to-be-jilted girl's wealthy merchant family, and is rewarded with a job in the family's department store, while Sarah, not expecting any word from Charles and not receiving any, leaves for London, and Charles, who ruins himself to break his engagement, can't find her. In the movie, Charles just tells Sarah that he'll be back, and she slips away before the appointed time. The melodrama is gone. Moviegoers are left vaguely wondering: Does the penniless Sarah disappear because she's a hysteric and a professional victim? Or has she suddenly snapped out of her doomy, repressed state? Or shucked off her feelings for Charles? Or gone off to "find herself"? Since she's not especially fascinating, it's hardly an urgent issue. You don't know what happened and you don't care.

Pinter won't let us have the fun of the book's plot—the particulars by which poor honorable, snobbish Charles, an advanced thinker yet a fool, loses his expectations of a title and a fortune, and his good name as well, all for the sake of a mysterious siren who stirs his passion. The movie is exceedingly literary, yet it doesn't offer the pleasures (minor though they are) of the book. Fowles provided a compound ending—diverting in different ways. Pinter provides no ending. He interpolates bits of a parallel modern story about the actors who are making a movie of Fowles' book, and simply cuts away from the story of Sarah and Charles, leaving their futures dangling. The movie thus acquires an undeveloped theme—the relation of actors to the characters they play—and the movie can also be said to be an exercise in adaptation and to be about "levels" of something or other, though Pinter may never have done anything as bland and ordinary as the parallel story, and the viewer's relation to the characters is tepid throughout.

Still, there are lovely moments, and a few have magical overtones. When Charles goes to break his engagement, he sees that his fiancée, Ernestina, played by Lynsey Baxter, is practicing her archery; he flinches, recognizing that he's to be her next target—and we laugh at his discomfiture. Lynsey Baxter gives a sweetly funny performance; she brings just the right daintiness and triviality to her role, and she has the mouth of a comedienne—it turns up at the sides, like a crescent moon lying down. Physically, she and Charles match up as cartoons of the privileged: the pampered *jeune fille* and the condescending pipsqueak. Jeremy Irons is tall and has an uppity nose and a long, pointed chin, with a slight overbite in between; in his elaborately layered hiking outfits and his broad-brimmed hats, he's an upper-class scarecrow. Irons has—or uses—a very closed face and an expressionless, lacklustre stare; he doesn't make much contact with us except when he smiles (and that happens rarely). He has just one scene when Charles comes alive: heated up after playing court tennis with his lawyer, and all pent up besides, he suddenly tells the lawyer, in no uncertain terms, what he wants done. It's an unexpectedly strong moment; it arrives like a gift.

There's also a jazzy little *frisson* that comes out of the interpolated material: the actress Patience Collier, who has appeared in the nineteenth-century scenes as Sarah's mean-spirited, puritanical employer, Mrs. Poulteney, is suddenly glimpsed, looking sporty in chic modern clothes, at a cast get-together for Sunday lunch. Meryl Streep has a few moments that register: there's one in which Sarah Woodruff dramatizes herself, sketching her own vision of her grief, and there's another, toward the end, when, in the middle of a scene that is being played for the cameras, Sarah suddenly loses her accent and metamorphoses into the American actress playing her. The idea of the actress "going out of character" (and pulling the actor playing Charles out, too) is more showy than what is done with it, but in a picture that's as much of a frost as this one you're grateful even for tricky ideas.

Most of *The French Lieutenant's Woman* might be taking place in a glass case, and Streep seems to be examining her performance while she gives it. If Reisz and Pinter and Streep are doing this deliberately, it's an almost unforgivable mistake in judgment—what could be the point of showing us actors who don't fully get into their roles? Moviegoers have no urgent need to see more uncommitted acting. When the learned Sarah says, "I am a remarkable person," you may want to make some small, coarse sound of derision. In the modern scenes, as the American actress, Streep has a promising spark—she often seems about to giggle. But all she's given to do is a demonstration of how casual the actress is about an affair, and she wears a short, straight hairdo—the most disfiguring star coiffure since Mia Farrow's thick wig in *The Great Gatsby*. *The French Lieutenant's Woman* isn't infuriating; it doesn't have enough power for that. It's just ostentatious, about its own supposed intelligence. It's pedantic.

· · · · ·

So Fine is the first film directed by the comedy writer Andrew Bergman, and he and his cinematographer James A. Contner seem to have only one thought: to get a reaction from us. I sat way back in my seat, trying to escape the pinkish faces of the actors, which Bergman and Contner keep shoving at us. The film is a visual insult: crudely lighted and framed, and jumping out at you. Jack Warden is Jack Fine, a Seventh Avenue dress manufacturer in debt to the mob; his most frequent line is "Holy shit," which he delivers whenever Bergman thinks the movie needs a really big laugh. Richard Kiel is the mobster who has Fine's son, Bobby (Ryan O'Neal), kidnapped from his teaching job at a college, so he can bring some new ideas into his father's business. The central gimmick is that Bobby splits a pair of jeans and stuffs see-through plastic into the cheeks, and that this turns into a fashion craze. Ryan O'Neal moves well; he has a light comedian's physical ease. But he's given frantic, tired gags, and he just revamps his tight-mouthed professorial priss from *What's Up, Doc?* The lovely, tiny Italian blonde Mariangela Melato appears as the mobster's wife, and in her deep voice she garbles her English charmingly; she's an erotic imp—she looks a bit like Harpo Marx, and she's always flying, like Carole Lombard in a hurricane. She brings the movie its only real freshness. Irving Metzman, who plays Jack Fine's accountant, gives likable readings to his few lines—he's one of the few people in the movie who don't yell all the time. Bruce Millholland, who is seventy-eight (back in 1930 he was the original author of the play that became *Twentieth Century*, when Hecht and MacArthur reworked it), is cast as Sir Alec, the world's greatest poet. His role is potentially the film's most original parody idea, but Bergman doesn't know how to give timing and polish to his own jokes. This picture works too hard at being funny to be a simple embarrassment, yet movie audiences are now made up of TV watchers, who are trained to laugh on signal. *So Fine* keeps punching out signals—it could be a hit.

October 12, 1981

Three Pairs

Something has gone wrong with Robert De Niro's acting. In the 1974 *Godfather II*, when he was quiet and almost expressionless he was so intense that he seemed in danger of imploding. Now, in *True Confessions*, when he's quiet and almost expressionless there's no intensity—there's nothing. He could be a potato, except that he's thoroughly absorbed in the process of do-ing nothing. It may be that De Niro took up an intellectual puzzle in 1976 on the set of *The Last Tycoon*: How do you act without doing anything? In *True Confessions*, he has carried it so far that he's not in the movie. The movie isn't in the movie, either. Ulu Grosbard, who directed, may have got hold of a variant of that puzzle: How do you make a movie that stands still?

There's thriller material in *True Confessions*—the investigation of the late-forties murder of a pretty twenty-one-year-old hooker whose body was cut in two and dumped in a vacant lot—but it's relegated to the background. In the foreground, Robert Duvall plays Tom Spellacy, an L.A. police detective in the homicide division, who finds evidence linking the dead girl to his brother, Monsignor Desmond Spellacy (De Niro), a rising young clerical power broker who is chancellor of the Los Angeles archdiocese, and to Jack Amsterdam (Charles Durning), a big-shot builder who has been putting up parochial schools and playgrounds. The background and the foreground, which never quite mesh, have a carefully polished, deliberately obscene sur-face of Irish self-hatred; the idea is to take the lovable Irish brothers of thirties films—James Cagney and Pat O'Brien (and sometimes Spencer Tracy) are the prototypes—and turn them inside out. The characters in a thirties movie of-ten used a recurrent slang phrase that was always good for a chuckle; here the characters speak in phrases that become clichés and are recycled from scene to scene—to demonstrate that they have nothing to say to each other. In this movie, the character who does an Irish jig at his daughter's wedding reception isn't a jolly, tipsy leprechaun; it's the cancer-riddled whoremonger Jack Amsterdam, who has bought his way to an audience with the Pope.

Grosbard and the writers—John Gregory Dunne, who wrote the 1977 novel that the film is based on, and his wife, Joan Didion, who collaborated with him on the script—have put a damper on the narrative. After a hushed prologue, the titles come on over shots of Des performing the Amsterdam nuptials in a giant cathedral, and the images are inert, as if the director meant to throw us into a funk right from the start. Because of the framing device of the prologue, with the forties story as a flashback, you know that the picture isn't heading anywhere you want to go. And all the way through, Grosbard dulls out the material. *True Confessions* carries hardboiled detective fiction to a virtually abstract level. It's apparent that Tom doesn't care about solving the murder case, because when he goes to an abandoned porno-movie studio and finds an ant-infested restaurant take-out container with remnants of the food that was also found in the dead girl's stomach, he tosses it back to the ants. He and the movie are after something bigger than who killed the girl or why: the corruption at the top, which for Tom seems to revolve around his brother. Tom doesn't find evidence that could convict the big, bloated Amsterdam for the girl's murder, but he brings him down anyway, and Des with him—wrecks their reputations, "exposes" them. As Tom and the movie see it, the eminent cleric and the respected businessman are contaminated, and Tom, who is repelled by their hypocrisy, has to knock them off their thrones.

This is a very odd movie: it attempts to be both a *Chinatown* and an Irish *Godfather*. The details of the general corruption in the precinct and the archdiocese are laid on, one scummy detail after another; you can just about see a hand coming out from the side of the screen and pointing. We learn that Tom used to be "on the take" and despises himself for it, and after a while we begin to suspect that he despises his brother even more than himself. But if it's jealousy or resentment that drives him—if he's angry because his brother can order people around and he has to shove them around— nothing is made of it. A scene in which the two brothers go to visit their senile, childish mother, who's still playing little catechism games—the games that Des bought and has gone on playing—suggests the background of their rivalry. But when they're together everything is internalized. Tom is so locked in that we never get to see how he feels about Des, and De Niro's role is so underwritten that Des doesn't particularly react to Tom, or to anything else. De Niro is in his chameleon trance; there's no light in Des's eyes—he seems flaccid, preoccupied, mourning his lost innocence. What we need to know— what the movie is supposed to be about—is what the brothers are mulling over on their silent, troubled walks, alone and together (and still alone).

Scenes begin with an apparent purpose, but at the slightest puff of air they fall apart and blow away. We see Des in the locker room of the golf club changing his shoes—slowly, as if he were contemplating the wasteland of his soul or getting ready to roll over and play dead. A little later, he comes into his room in the cardinal's residence, takes off the shoes, and gets into his slippers. We wait for the revelation as he takes off his sweater and hangs it up. But that's it—end of scene. There's a standard Hollywood gag about beginning screenwriters who write descriptions such as "Phillip Mortimer turns his back to the camera and his face shows all his searing agony." These brothers face the camera, all right, but in spirit they've got their backs to it. (Whenever there was a scene with a window, I found myself looking out.) The only way you can tell that an episode is coming to an end is that soft music starts up. The music, like the whole mood of the film, seems sacramental. When Tom finds the place where the murdered girl was butchered, we half expect some-one to come in behind him and clobber him. Something must be about to happen. But no, he looks at the bloody bathtub and the blood-spattered walls and floors—the music suggests a High Mass—and he goes out. Soon he's taking another stroll.

It's clear that Tom's emotions are bottled up. But what emotions are they? Probably we're meant to think that Tom, who was once Jack the pimp's bagman, is so full of festering shame that he wants to show that Des is a bag-man, too. He wants to explode the corruption. He's a Catholic version of the terrorist who plants bombs promiscuously—whoever is blown up deserves it for being part of a rotten society. (And if babes in arms get it, that's all right, too, because it will add to the guilt of the guilty.) Tom doesn't care if Des and Jack Amsterdam are innocent of the girl's death; as he sees it, they are guilty of everything that's wrong with the world. In the film's most turbulent scene, Tom, not knowing that his brother's big dinner honoring Amsterdam is a way of paying Amsterdam off and getting rid of him, disrupts the festivities and tears the sash with the words "Catholic Layman of the Year" off Amsterdam's beefy chest.

The visual pun of that sash, with its schoolboy overtones, suggests the naïveté under the film's display of corruption. The details that are piled on all relate to prostitution and payoffs. The death of a priest who has a heart attack in a brothel is treated as evidence of the most sordid and scandalous degrada-tion. The physical relations between Amsterdam, a pillar of the community, and the murdered hooker are viewed as proof that the diocese is a sinkhole. Sex—which non-Catholics might see as the Church's binding hold on its members, the biological instrument by which the Church turns them into sin-ners and sets itself up as their only means of achieving absolution and re-demption—is seen completely in Catholic terms. Implicit in the film's conception is the belief that there is a pure Catholicism tucked away some-where, waiting for Des to return to it. This true faith is represented by Bur-gess Meredith, a cantankerous old priest but a man of God; he complains so much about the Church turning into a business that the velvet-gloved tough buzzard of a cardinal (Cyril Cusack) loses patience and packs him off to a parish in the desert, in the middle of nowhere. (No one asks the saintly grouch why he is so innocent of Church history; the film, which endorses his view, appears to have been conceived by a choirboy in shock.)

Tom's intention when he breaks up the dinner can't be to save Des's soul; Tom's clenched, angry face isn't the result of tender brotherly solicitude. But neither Des nor the director ever raises the basic question: Why did Tom set out to destroy his brother? Instead, the film offers the irony that in smashing Des's career Tom actually helped Des find his faith. At the end—many years after the disastrous dinner, years that Des has spent in that same desert parish—Des suggests that he has become a real priest. There's nothing about him that would confirm this, though he does look as if he had been doing a lot more mulling.

For actors it's probably bliss to work with Ulu Grosbard, because he encourages them to take time and space. But on the basis of the four pictures that he has made—*The Subject Was Roses, Who Is Harry Kellerman and Why Is He Saying Those Terrible Things About Me?* (that title is reason enough), *Straight Time*, and this one—he appears to be a serious director who lacks a film sense. He simply has no feeling for the vital energies that propel a movie. Essentially, he makes films by photographing the performances of actors whom he admires. This almost worked in *Straight Time*, because some of the situations and lines were surreally precise and funny, and Dustin Hoffman, playing a paroled robber who would always be a convict at heart, gave a great mean, unyieldingly bitter performance, and Harry Dean Stanton, Gary Busey, and M. Emmet Walsh all had a grip on something new and hip. But even in *Straight Time*, with these actors bringing a jumpy dynamism to their roles, the pacing was a drain; you could enjoy the movie more when you thought back on it than while you were watching it. You don't have even retrospective pleasure with *True Confessions*, because, for all Grosbard's love of acting (and there are times when you feel that he made the picture to show to acting students), several of the key performances don't hold together in the memory. Or if they do, it's for the wrong reasons. (Rose Gregorio's brothelkeeper who has fallen upon hard days is played for gallant pathos. It's actory acting—the kind that acting classes applaud—and Grosbard pins a "First Prize" ribbon on it.)

Robert Duvall is a formidable technician, and as Tom he's up there on the screen tense and glaring—a pair of sunken eyes in a death's-head. But Duvall is working under a considerable handicap: if an actor isn't given the center of his character—if he isn't given any human motivation—what can he build the character on? I've seen Duvall only once when I thought he was really bad—in his screaming and yelling in *Network*. His rip-roaring madness in *Apocalypse Now* was almost too good: there was no higher pitch of madness for the picture to attain—it climaxed out in its first half. But Duvall has a deficiency as a star (it showed in *The Great Santini*, as it does here): we watch the performance objectively, *as* a performance—we don't have any special empathy with him. There's nothing about Tom that would make us hold our breath in fear for him—fear of what he might do next. Duvall is a little dry. We're used to seeing him in roles like that of Dan, the lawyer for the archdiocese, a part that is played expertly and selflessly here by Ed Flanders, wearing an innocuous little mustache. If we can easily visualize Duvall as the recessive Dan, that's not just because the part resembles his role in the two *Godfather* movies—it's because Duvall is in some special sense an anonymous, selfless actor. We perceive a "self" in most stars; we don't in Duvall, nor do we want to. There are roles he can do perhaps better than anyone else and without strain—in *Ike* on television, for example. But you can see the confines of each role he plays; he's not an actor who fills out a part and spills over the edges. Nothing flows out of him. When he plays a short-tempered Irishman like Tom Spellacy, there's nothing in his face *but* anger and tension. Aridity in an American actor is so rare that people may mistake Duvall's control for greatness, but he never gets to the point where technique is subsumed and instinct takes over. He has to slug us to get our attention, and he knows it; he has become a pugnacious actor. As Tom, he's consciously determined to mime craziness, but there's no craziness in him; if we're frightened, it's the ambitious acting that's scaring us.

The movie is in a stupor; you have to put up a struggle to get anything out of it. It keeps jazzing us with deliberately "smutty" talk while telling us that we have fallen into sin. It says "Get thee to the desert." The only performance with any juice in it is Kenneth McMillan's, as Crotty, Tom's partner in the homicide investigation. It's a minor role: the fat, despicable Crotty gives Duvall someone to play off—he's there to inspire disgust in Tom. But McMillan spills over and then some. Crotty isn't a shame-filled, cynical sufferer, like Tom, or a baffled, withdrawn sufferer, like Des—he has sides to his character. Sitting in a Chinese restaurant eating food that tastes delicious to him because he doesn't pay for it, he accepts financial tribute from the restaurant owners and leers with pleasure at his own crooked shenanigans. Shrewd and slovenly, with a dirty-bad-boy twinkle in his watery eyes, he enjoys the profits of chiselling almost as much as he enjoys the feeling of being smart and powerful that chiselling gives him. He's the living image of petty graft—and the only likable character. McMillan is the token human being among all these actors carrying their roles like pallbearers.

.   .   .   .   .

Chariots of Fire, which opened the recent New York Film Festival, tells the story of the courage and the triumph of two young runners who represented Britain in the 1924 Olympics, held in Paris. It's a piece of technological lyricism. The effects calculated to make your spirits soar are the same effects that send you soaring down to the supermarket to buy a six-pack of Miller or Schlitz or Löwenbräu. This film is full to bursting with the impersonal, manufactured, go-to-the-mountains poetry that sells products. The director, Hugh Hudson, doesn't build sequences by internal rhythm, and whether the script (by Colin Welland) was sketchy or Hudson botched scenes and then cut them out, the episodic narrative doesn't make a lot of sense. The picture works, though. It's held together by the glue of simpleminded heroic sentiments, and the audience is there to watch a couple of guys win races.

The two runners—Harold Abrahams (Ben Cross), a wealthy Jewish boy who is a student at Cambridge, and Eric Liddell (Ian Charleson), a divinity student—win because they have something to run for. The unbelievably self-possessed Abrahams runs against anti-Semitic snobbery and prejudices, represented here, rather grandly, by Lindsay Anderson and John Gielgud, as a pair of gargoyles—masters at Cambridge who embody the polite, entrenched bigotry of the educated classes. The devout Liddell runs in an ecstatic state, because "when I run, I can feel His pleasure," and the film is structured so that its big crisis comes when Liddell's qualifying heat is scheduled for a Sunday and he refuses to take part. The film is gimmicky, with too many tricks and lots of dead spots, and the two heroes have no real connection—they barely meet. Abrahams is lucky: he doesn't have to listen to Liddell's right-from-the-heart sermons. We do.

There's one well-staged scene: Abrahams' first date with a young D'Oyly Carte singer-actress, Sybil, who is played by Alice Krige. The scene—supper at a restaurant—feels as if it were shot in one take; the two flirt to perfection, with no break in their excitement. It's the attraction of opposites: Ben Cross (who gives a performance of unusual dignity) has wonderful bones and planes in his long, angular head, and Alice Krige's teasing-cherubim face, under her wide hat, has curly wine-red lips and fresh, full cheeks. Krige may perhaps be doing a little too much with her face, but her cooing, artificial style—a little reminiscent of Joan Greenwood's purring—brightens up the movie, and she's stunning in the early-flapper fashions of the period. (The cinematographer, David Watkin, lights her lovingly.) Maybe this flirty interlude is so tickling because it's just about the only time that the movie isn't making points and congratulating us for responding to its noble perceptions. (Or leaving us bewildered: What is going on in the scene on the grounds of a great estate with Sybil bidding adieu to a handsome young lord? Adieu to what? Why are there so many cuts to the wet-eyed anxieties of Liddell's sister, played by Cheryl Campbell? And after the elaborate fuss about Liddell's not being willing to run on Sunday why is the ploy by which he can run another day skidded over so fast?) The races are generally shot frontally, perhaps with a telephoto lens, so that we see the runners flat on, coming at us, and we don't know who is ahead until the winner hits the finish ribbon. That's when Hudson seems to get interested—at the finish. He's addicted to slow-motion poems of the runners' strain and agony as they collapse.

Produced by David Puttnam, who is widely regarded as the major force in the (coming) revivification of the British film industry, this movie is in love with simple values and synthesized music. Apparently, Abrahams' and Liddell's principal competition—the American runners, played by Dennis Christopher, with his face drawn wire-taut, and Brad Davis, who manages to overact even in a small, almost wordless role—have no goals or beliefs strong enough to sustain them. Abrahams' fight for his dignity as a Jew and Liddell's unswerving faith in God carry the day. It's character that makes the difference between a good runner and a great one, the movie says. Maybe. Character may have something to do with making a good movie, too. I hope *Chariots of Fire* wasn't dedicated, like Liddell's sprinting, to the glory of God, because it looks as if it were thrown together in desperation in the cutting room. It's retrograde moviemaking, presented with fake bravura. *Chariots of Fire* has a mildewed high moral tone, and it takes you back; it's probably the best Australian film ever made in England.

．　　　．　　　．　　　．　　　．

Rich and Famous features those two great underpopulated bodies Jacqueline Bisset and Candice Bergen. They can't dip into themselves and bring out characters; they're simply art objects rattling off lines, and they rattle incessantly in this remake of the 1943 film *Old Acquaintance*, which starred Bette Davis and Miriam Hopkins. The picture spans about twenty years in the lives of two writers, pals from their college days. Bisset is the tense "modern" artist—blocked, perpetually dissatisfied, self-conscious, hard-drinking. Bergen is the gusher—as a housewife and mother she writes a roman à clef about her Malibu Colony neighbors and then she just keeps pouring out her fantasies and getting richer and richer. When the two women are about forty, Bisset, who has attained literary eminence—she has published one novel and writes small essays for *The New York Review of Books* and *The Atlantic*—is in New York for a few days, staying at the Algonquin, and a young man of twenty-two (Hart Bochner) is in her room interviewing her for *Rolling Stone*. She gets a phone call, and while she's on the phone he stands facing her with his back to the camera, and the focus is held snugly on his bluejeaned rear. (Are we in the audience supposed to be turned on *for* her?) Shortly afterward, an eighteen-year-old boy with an assured grin picks her up on Fifth Avenue, and when he's in her room he strips (wordlessly) with the knowingness of a hot young hustler, slow music is heard, and poor distinguished, sex-starved Bisset can't resist his smooth young flesh. She begins to kiss his abdomen passionately, gratefully. It's gruesomely silly: the tone of the film has shifted from *Old Acquaintance* and *The Turning Point* to *The Roman Spring of American Gigolo*. This picture might have been *made* by young hustlers.

The *Rolling Stone* fellow, who stays at the Chelsea, delights Bisset's soul by quoting T. S. Eliot on what D. H. Lawrence said, and soon she decides she loves him. Her old pal Bergen, who stays at the Waldorf, encourages her to marry him. (Bergen is meant to be ridiculous, but with an understanding heart. As well as a powerful collarbone—from being yoked to her typewriter?) This picture keeps trying to be savvy. In 1969, Bisset, making a speech in the course of being honored at U.C.L.A., refers to "a dear old man, James M. Cain"; that night, after a party in Malibu, she listens to Bergen reading her drivel aloud and then angrily spouts off. Sample: "In Paris, in France, they had a guy who was, for the record, both homosexual and a Jew, who wrote a seven-volume book they continue to refer to as a masterpiece, who was such nitroglycerine in the head he had to hide out in a cork-lined room or he'd a gone up in shrapnel."

It's a hopelessly demented movie. Bisset doesn't seem to have any notion of how puffed up her lines are; she reads them all straight and all with the same intonations. If she doesn't know that the picture is a comedy, this may be because Gerald Ayres, who wrote the script, seems to mean everything she says. Her character is intended to be fearfully intelligent, and so the bland Bisset is unvaryingly intense, and her English accent sounds heavier than usual—maybe because in playing an intellectual she wants to be clipped and precise. Bergen is much the livelier, but her caricature of a shallow bitch is too busy. When Bergen's husband leaves her after fifteen years, you see her attempting to be comically hysterical. Candice Bergen was surprisingly funny in her rather small role in *Starting Over* (she gave the film its only surprises), but she's trying too hard here. Overdressed, in the manner of a younger, American version of Barbara Cartland, she heaves in sight like a ship in full sail. She's a good sport rather than an actress, though she probably does as much for the role as anybody could.

Rich and Famous isn't camp, exactly; it's more like a homosexual fantasy. Bisset's affairs, with their masochistic overtones, are creepy, because they don't seem like what a woman would get into. And Bergen is used almost as if she were a big, goosey female impersonator. Directed by George Cukor, this movie has an unflagging pace, but it's full of scenes that don't play, and often you can't even tell what tone was hoped for. (When Bergen, on "The Merv Griffin Show" to plug a book, is asked what she tells her fourteen-year-old-daughter when the girl thinks about boys, she says, "I tell her to go ride a horse," and she smirks as if she had been very clever.) Just about everything that's said or done is at least slightly off. This movie wants to be about what Bergen's best-sellers are about: celebrity sex. But it admires the Bisset character's highfalutin literacy. It's a tawdry self-parody.

October 26, 1981

Childhood of the Dead

*T*here are three million abandoned children in Brazil—swarms of scavenging, thieving street kids. Unwanted—many of them children of prostitutes or unmarried mothers—they're born into vagrancy; turned loose by parents who can't feed them or send them to school, they learn to pick pockets and grab purses and hustle. It's their only way of surviving. In the Brazilian movie *Pixote* (pronounced roughly "pee-*shoat*"), a judge has been murdered on a street in São Paulo, and the police have to take some action, so they routinely round up dozens of these kids, including the ten-year-old Pixote (Portuguese slang for Peewee), and throw them in a reformatory. There, behind rotting walls, Pixote (Fernando Ramos da Silva) watches as several of the larger boys gang-rape a kid not much older than he is. He sees boys beaten and killed, and he learns to say nothing when the guards and officials come around and ask questions. A bully spits in his milk and he drinks it down, because if he doesn't he'll be in trouble with one group or another. He stares as if he weren't there—his round eyes go dead, and his truculent baby face is indifferent. But he's a little camera taking it all in, and he's quick—he learns how to maneuver.

A group of boys, including Pixote, break out, and he and three others stick together like a family; they snatch enough purses and wallets to make their way to Rio de Janeiro and begin dealing cocaine. Outsmarted by the adult criminals, the kids buy an aging, drunken prostitute from a pimp and go into business with her: she brings men home and they rob them, at gunpoint. When you see children who are treated as an urban infestation—who *are* an urban infestation—you recognize the enormous difference between countries where kids get an education and countries where large numbers of them don't. (The slum children who were recruited to act in this movie can't read or write.) As the director, Hector Babenco, sees it, there's something essential missing in Pixote: no one has ever made him feel that his life had any value. He's a snub-nosed infant asserting his wants, and when they're denied his mouth turns down and he changes into a baby gangster—a runt Scarface. He kills innocently, in the sense that he doesn't understand the enormity of the crime.

When the boys are on the grayish beach in Rio, Babenco isn't doing travel-poster shots of Sugar Loaf. *Pixote* has its own look—a very distinctive pinkish glow, as if the film stock were infused with the colors of dawn—and there are lovely pale-salmon tones and grays and browns. The incidents don't appear to be set up for the camera—things just seem to be happening and every image is expressive. (Well, maybe not every one: when the whore brings an American back to her fleabag, he's such a crude, swag-bellied gringo that the picture seems, fleetingly, to be pandering to audience hostility.) What goes on in this movie is different from what goes on in American movies. The imagination at work is both romantic and anti-romantic, and the mixture has the intensity that reaches back at least as far as *Don Quixote*. (Babenco, who wrote the script with Jorge Duran, from the novel *Infância dos Mortos*, by José Louzeiro, may have chosen the film title for its ironic echo of Quixote.) Brazil is steeped in poverty and paganism and Christianity and Pop; starving teen-age transvestites—Indian and Negro—put on wigs and call themselves Marilyn. Babenco's imagery is realistic, but his point of view is shockingly lyrical. South American writers, such as Gabriel García Márquez, seem to be in perfect, poetic control of madness, and Babenco has some of this gift, too.

South American artists have to have it, in order to express the texture of everyday insanity. In Colombia a few years ago, I saw soldiers stationed on street corners who wore gold spiked helmets and carried machine guns; they didn't look down as a shrivelled little girl of perhaps eight, bent over parallel to the pavement from the weight of a huge bundle of wood on her back, passed by at their feet. The little girl, who will undoubtedly be deformed, walked past buildings with enormous billboards advertising American action movies; Yul Brynner, Burt Lancaster, and other stars are giant deities looming over the cities.

When Pixote and his pals mug somebody, the camera pulls back so that we have a view of the whole area: we get the social picture, and we see them dart in, score, and run off. It's fast teamwork, like a football scrimmage; each mugging has its own choreographic plan. But most of the incidents in the film aren't so distinctly shaped. They're loose and sometimes a little blobby. (When the kids and the whore, Sueli, lock one of her customers in the trunk of his car and drive off to celebrate—they park, turn up the car radio, and dance—we're distracted by wondering what's happening to the poor guy in the trunk. In other scenes, we wonder what happens to the fresh corpses.) Throughout the film, though, even when the acting is minimal there are no wrong notes in it. (Babenco says that the children themselves "guided" him, and came up with ideas that changed perhaps forty per cent of the script.) And the lighting is extraordinary: in the second half, and particularly after Sueli appears, the tones shift from the pastels to bright pinks and reds, and at night a boy's Afro acquires an orange aureole from the light reflected from neon signs. But Babenco doesn't build the film rhythmically, and you don't feel the dramatic intensification that you do when a structure is beautifully worked out. (There's a particularly confusing episode in which the guards pack some of the boys into a van and send them to a prison.) *Pixote* doesn't have the purity of *Shoeshine* or the surgical precision of *Los Olvidados*. It's effective cumulatively, and, because of the strength of feeling that Babenco has put into it, it becomes more and more devastating. Babenco is only a first-generation South American (his parents—Russian and Polish Jews—left Europe in the mid-thirties and went to Argentina), but he's not afraid to be florid, and his excesses are some of his finest moments.

At its best, *Pixote* isn't a political film, except in the larger sense in which films such as Vigo's *Zero for Conduct* and Jean Genet's *Un Chant D'Amour* are political films. I think *Pixote* has some relation to those two pictures—certainly it shares their feeling for the ecstatic—and it may also relate to several Fellini movies. It has a fairly obvious thesis: when you see the handsome Babenco in the prologue and then meet Pixote, the child resembles the director so startlingly that it's almost as if Babenco were saying, "This could have happened to me or to you or to anybody who was deprived of minimal care and affection." The film is too pat and predictable when the kids start being destroyed by their contact with adults. And it's too clever when Pixote sits on Sueli's bed staring at the TV, then at Sueli and one of his pals going at it, and back at the TV; you register that the kids are making another attempt—a grotesque attempt—to construct the family they never had. Babenco is wildly ambitious, in the manner of gifted young artists: he's attempting to be a poet while making points for us to process. But the richer characters—Lilica (Jorge Julião), a seventeen-year-old transvestite homosexual, and the whore Sueli (Marília Pera)—transcend the demonstration. Jorge Julião, who hasn't acted before, and Marília Pera, who is a leading Brazilian stage actress, give such full performances that they take the picture to the ecstatic levels that Babenco hoped for.

The swanlike Lilica, who has a classic transvestite look, is in terror of his next birthday. (In Brazil, children under eighteen can't be prosecuted for criminal acts; they're merely sent to reform schools, like the one we've seen.) Lilica is a soft creature, flamingly nelly—an imitation of a young girl without parody. Emotionally, he's the most courageous kid of the bunch. The brutality he has seen inflicted on others hasn't made him callous; it has deepened his understanding and made him more loving. Pixote's soul hasn't been awakened; Lilica seems all soul. He's like a male version of the Giulietta Masina character in *Nights of Cabiria*, except that he's smarter and funnier, and much younger. He suffers romantic tragedies, but he doesn't go long without falling in love again.

Sueli is the whoriest whore imaginable. When we first see her, she has just given herself an abortion; she's feverish and full of hate. Pixote is frightened by the sight of the bloody fetus, and she cruelly, vindictively forces him to understand what it is. In the scenes with her, as she begins to have a swell time with the kids, dancing and drinking and coupling, the movie achieves a raw, garish splendor. Sueli is alive in the most brutal sense. When Pixote, who has accidentally killed one of the other kids while trying to help him, vomits, she takes him in her arms and consoles him. He puts his mouth to her breast and hangs on, suckling. He won't let go. What he's doing is perhaps too overtly Oedipal and symbolic, but it's an amazing scene, because of Sueli's violent response. She's repelled by his attempt to become her child; she pulls him off her and throws him out. This sick, broken-down streetwalker may have cradled him in her arms for a minute, but she doesn't want the burden of this child any more than she wanted the fetus she threw in the waste can.

After I saw *Pixote*, I had an opportunity to speak with Babenco, and since the street kids in the movie are all boys, I asked, "What of the girls?" His answer was "Their lives are ten thousand times as bad." I was left wondering whether his two women characters—a treacherous drug dealer, Debora, also aging, who kills one of the four boys, and Sueli, who takes Lilica's young lover away from him and destroys the remnants of the family—are supposed to be an indication of how poisoned the girls' lives are, or are part of a melodramatic myth. The film is apparently non-judgmental, but at a deeper level it's judgmental as hell.

No matter what act of horror Sueli has participated in, she's elated—

ready for a high time. She takes a savage's delight in the spoils. She may suddenly weep, even as she's dancing, but the tears are strictly for herself. Sueli needs Pixote and the other kids to make a party out of the horror of her life; horror *is* her party, and after some gullible john has been robbed she dances as if at a tribal celebration. She's a mother who thrusts children away or takes them as lovers. Babenco must have intended her to be the opposite of what he intended the children to be. (The kids do horrible things, but they don't rejoice in them.) Lilica's is the most sexual presence in the movie; he represents tenderness, love. Sueli represents annihilation—and the uglier her deeds are, the more hauntingly beautiful she becomes. (That's where Babenco shows class, and a genuine feeling for the mythic.) Marília Pera, who appeared in the first of Babenco's two earlier features, is best known as a comedienne. Playing Sueli must have been a deliverance for her; dusky and aquiline-faced, she has an Anna Magnani–like presence—horrifying and great. Babenco is too didactic about Pixote's blank slate; the sociological component of this film doesn't get at much that we don't know, and what the camera is going to find in most of the boys' faces has been predetermined. But Marília Pera's face registers the immediacy of the moment. Her Sueli is like a raging sun; when the inexpressive kids revolve around her and feel they own her, it's almost as if she were their only chance to learn what can be in a face.

It's not the boys' innocence that the movie seems to be about but their innocence in relation to the camera. Pixote sits still and the camera gets nothing from his impassive face; we may halfway accept Babenco's notion that he's so young that there's nothing written on it yet, and that his impassivity is his survival technique. But isn't it really that he's a blank because he's not an actor? Sueli darts around and the camera picks up everything she feels. The picture comes to life with Sueli, because she's the whore spawned out of men's darkest imagining, in the way that Medea and Clytemnestra and Lady Macbeth and Jocasta and Euripides' fierce Helen of Troy were spawned, and because the actress is so sharply and completely there.

The picture isn't quite great, maybe because you can see it struggling to be, and the end (a lyric, ironic switch on the *Vitelloni* ending) is awfully portentous, with the rejected Pixote, gun in pocket, kicking a can as he walks down the railroad tracks—a baby bandit on his way. You know it's supposed to make you think. But what I thought about was a male fantasy of barbaric, rejecting females, and an actress whose display of passion wiped the little non-actor kids off the screen. *Pixote* is good enough to touch greatness; it restores your excitement about the confusing pleasures that movies can give.

$$\cdot \qquad \cdot \qquad \cdot \qquad \cdot \qquad \cdot$$

*M*ichael Crichton directs like a technocrat. This ties in with a small problem he has with his scripts: he can't write people. His new film, *Looker* (it's his fourth), gives the impression of having never been touched by human hands;

it's a shiny, cold job of engineering that manages to turn even Dorian Harewood, as a Los Angeles police lieutenant, into a piece of furniture. The plot is pseudoscientific piffle about the machinations of the head of a conglomerate, played by the now completely white-haired James Coburn in the desiccated-amoral-old-bastard manner of John Huston. This old rascal's laboratories at Digital Matrix are developing computer-generated images to make hypnotic TV commercials for political as well as economic use. To the rescue of civilization as we know it comes Albert Finney, like a lame tortoise. Finney gives what looks to be the laziest performance by a star ever recorded on film. Boredom seems to have seeped into his muscles and cells; he's sinking under the weight of it, and the only part of him still alert is his wiry hair. He plays an eminent plastic surgeon who has "perfected" several women models according to mathematically exact specifications supplied by Coburn's lab; his highest point of animation comes when he selects Vivaldi for the day's accompaniment to his tiny incisions. (There can't be much choice: he could hardly use "Kitten on the Keys" or Terry Riley's "In C.") He's the target of a murderous thug who is so characterless that if he didn't wear a thick brush mustache we'd have no way of recognizing him from one scene to the next. With no people around, *Looker* is as empty as Crichton's *Coma* would have been without Geneviève Bujold.

The picture begins promisingly, with a couple of the models who have been worked on by the doc coming to mystifying violent ends. But Crichton's iciness is effective only when he's ingenious; he isn't, here. The plot explanations seem to be babble. It isn't clear why Coburn's evil scheme requires models to be surgically perfected in order to be the basis for computer images, especially since the hypnotic effect of the images is achieved only with the models' eyes. And we never learn why the girls are then marked for destruction. For that matter, we don't find out in what way Coburn's elaborate technology is more effective than simple subliminal messages. Thinking about this movie could give you frostbite of the brain. Susan Dey is the pertly pretty heroine, who poses another riddle. We're told that she, like the others, has been physically perfected, down to the shadow of a millimetre, but she has a highly visible individual feature—a friendly little wart on her belly that should set off alarm systems or topple the towers at Digital Matrix.

At the end, it comes as quite a surprise that Doc Finney is meant to have a sexual interest in this charmingly blemished beauty. So *that's* why he was trudging around trying to keep his eyes open. (He'd need electric shock to consummate the union.) When the man with the mustache shoots hypnotic flashes at Finney that are meant to numb him, you think, What a waste of special effects. Couldn't Crichton, with his medical background, invent an excuse for the doc's thick torpor—make him a sufferer from narcolepsy, at the least? This is the film that should have been called *Coma*. What's worst about it may be the exact, knowing readings that the actors give their computer-generated (or close to it) dialogue. So much care has gone into this dumb, hollow thing, and all it does is sell a few impressively constructed semi-nude models. In the big climax, people stalk each other amid computer-generated images just like the men and humanoids stalking each other in Crichton's *Westworld*; it's a little early in his career for a recap. He tries to tone up the purpose of *Looker* by providing a cautionary statistic and then having a disembodied voice repeat it at the end. It sinks in, all right: one and a half years of an average American's time is spent watching commercials. But there is no qualitative difference between this affectless, impersonal film and a commercial. There was no reason for Finney to rouse himself. One and a half years plus ninety-three minutes.

·   ·   ·   ·   ·

*J*ohn Belushi is a reactor: he includes his own appreciative response right in with his jokes. In *Continental Divide*, there's nothing left for Blair Brown, who plays opposite him, to do. Hell, even with his being both comic and straight man, there's hardly anything for Belushi to do. The waddling bopper of "Saturday Night Live," whose greatest weapon was surprise—we never knew what he'd do next—is trying to be a romantic hero, and so the grossness and bellowing are gone. Now he's—well, winsome. And predictable. The script is a Lawrence Kasdan original, and you can see why actors love Kasdan's work: there's a single plot thread, so they're onscreen practically all the time, with almost no subsidiary characters and no action to cut away to. There's no subtext, either—just nothingness, with this tidy, old-fashioned structure laid on top of it.

Belushi plays a muckraking Chicago reporter so famous that everyone on the streets knows him. (And so they would, if he appeared on TV often enough or did beer commercials.) Blair Brown is a saintly ornithologist who lives on a mountaintop in Colorado studying the American bald eagle. (She seems consecrated to this task, as if it were to be her complete life's work.) Kasdan has them meet when the reporter, in danger of being murdered by crooks he has exposed, is sent up to her cabin to interview her. He is smitten. Then Kasdan is at an impasse: how can he get these two together in marriage without taking either away from a dedicated endeavor at one particular site? Kasdan is working with the formula of the genre typified by the Tracy-Hepburn *Woman of the Year* (a generally dismal picture, in which she was an unfeeling careerist and he was Mr. Fatherly Understanding). But Kasdan has eliminated all the conflicting interests and the psychological impediments to a happy marriage, leaving the physical separation as the only obstacle. There's nothing left for the movie to be about except how the hero and heroine can conquer space. And at the end the picture fudges even this—somehow or other they're going to, without anyone's telling us how. But before that we wait and wait as the director, Michael Apted, tries to create a little texture out of the void. He manages a wisp of embellishment for incidents such as Belushi, the city hotshot, becoming a helpless tenderfoot in the ornithologist's rough environment, and even getting mauled by a mountain lion, and Blair Brown taking him up to the mountains to show him the continental divide, the "oldest church in America." This meant-to-be-awe-inspiring moment fizzles, because the cinematography, which is crisp in Chicago, is lifeless and rather blurry in the Rockies. The characters' mild quandary drags on and on. What the movie never even whispers (because it would be bad sexual politics) is the simple fact that neither of these people cares enough about the other to give up anything. *Continental Divide* could be called *Endless Like*.

·   ·   ·   ·   ·

Body Heat, which Kasdan both wrote and directed, is a forties pastiche that verges on camp but takes itself straight. It's an unusually controlled film, especially considering that this is Kasdan's first time out as a director. It's clear that he accomplished exactly what he set out to do, but planned silliness may be the most ominous kind; it could mean that he's silly. He has devised a style that is a catalogue of *noir* clichés—Deco titles, flames and a heat wave, ceiling fans, tinkling wind chimes, old tunes, chicanery in muted voices, a weak man and a femme fatale in white, and insinuating hotted-up dialogue that it would be fun to hoot at if only the hushed, sleepwalking manner of the film didn't make you cringe or yawn. Kasdan has modern characters talking jive talk as if they'd been boning up on Chandler novels, and he doesn't seem to know whether he wants laughs or not. It's like listening to Mae West deliver her bawdy innuendos in a sincere tone. And the talk has an echo-chamber effect: if you know the movies that it's modelled on, such as *The Postman Always Rings Twice*, when Kasdan's seductress describes her husband as "small and mean . . . and weak," you wait for "and Greek." Eventually, the terse, racy metaphors patterned on the Bogart-Bacall exchanges dwindle away. The hardboiled double-entendre dialogue that was developed in the thirties and forties as a joke—a way of kidding the restrictions on sexual language and behavior—is ludicrous in a contemporary film with four-letter words and naked lovers; if Kasdan's lovers had gone on using their gaudy patter when they were clawing at each other, the picture might have been a great camp comedy.

Back in 1966, when Jacques Demy made what was his idea of a Hollywood musical, *The Young Girls of Rochefort*, he didn't really understand the mechanisms of American musicals—what made them move. He produced a strange, stilted movie with dancing that was static. I don't think Larry Kasdan "gets" *film noir*, either; those dark, twisted thrillers enjoyed their own malice, and the turns of the plot created a weblike atmosphere, and there was a reason for all those seedy, malignant characters in the background—they made the stars shine. Yes, the visual style was calculated, even deterministic, but there was a little motor inside the picture.

Body Heat, like *Continental Divide*, leaves out just about everything that made its genre watchable. Kasdan has found an actress (Kathleen Turner) who is tall and has a lovely voice. But he poses her as if she were a hot number, and she works on her smolder with such diligence that if she has any sensuality in her it's completely blocked. In general, the most embarrassing thing a performer can do is to act more sexy than he or she appears to be, and Kasdan has led Turner into this trap, but she's so remote that she isn't even embarrassing. She lures a lawyer (William Hurt) who's a chump to murder her rich husband (Richard Crenna), as if she were following the marks on the floor made by the actresses who preceded her. If we felt that this siren enjoyed her perversity and control—as Barbara Stanwyck did in *Double Indemnity*—there'd be some humor, at least, in her ensnarement of the lawyer. Or if she had Stanwyck's smeary mouth and cheap, teasing way of rubbing against her fall guy, there'd be the suggestion of zingy, nasty sex. But what she's hiding never peeps through. She's groomed and cultivated, like Lauren Bacall in a fool's reverie. And maybe because Hurt's role doesn't call for much range or any bravura, he gives his least entertaining screen performance yet. I never thought that I'd compare anyone unfavorably with Fred MacMurray, but MacMurray in *Double Indemnity* made a better chump. Hurt does some small clever things, but he's too tight and held in. We don't see ourselves in him; we did in MacMurray. And we certainly don't see ourselves in Turner—she's like nothing human.

The actors in the few minor roles are considerably livelier, and one, Mickey Rourke, who plays Teddy, a professional arsonist, has an awareness of danger that almost makes you feel you're at a real movie. Teddy moves warily, and when he talks about how to set a fire he's hunched over, leaning in close as if he were sharing state secrets with you—he delivers his lines in a diplomatic pouch. When Ted Danson, who plays the assistant district attorney, unexpectedly takes a little leap and does a few tap steps, it's like a shot of oxygen. People praise Kasdan for his sense of structure, but it's really just formula, and when you're sitting there watching the femme fatale and her prey you feel as if you're looking at a void. The lovers sweat constantly—lavishly. But it might as well be dew. Kasdan's formal style doesn't allow for passion; if his actors had any he'd have to stamp it out.

November 9, 1981

The Swamp

*T*he ironically titled *Southern Comfort* draws you into the eerily beautiful Louisiana bayou country and then has you running for your life in circles—a classic nightmare situation. The green-gray marshlands are a maze, with moss-bearded cypresses that rise up out of the stagnant water and reflect themselves. Everything about this terrain is mucky and primordial, and the director, Walter Hill, tests himself and his cinematographer, Andrew Laszlo: this is a movie with one set—it all takes place in the bayous (and in a bayou village), and it's almost all in the same color range. The look is Barbizon School, slightly distorted by the locale itself, which is just naturally kinky. And right near the beginning Ry Cooder's guitar music is pretty yet just a little intimidating; it's out of your control.

A National Guard squad of nine—a motley group of civilians doing weekend service, along with one experienced man, a sergeant—is sent into the area on overnight training maneuvers, with dummy ammunition. When the Guardsmen are all together, at the start, bitching and joking, the movie has a crackling liveliness, and the men are feeling sporty and high when they see three little canoes that belong to Cajun hunters and trappers. They've come to a body of water that isn't on their map, and they don't want to slog through the mud and retrace their steps, so they appropriate the canoes, leaving a note saying that the boats will be returned—though chances are that the Cajuns can't read English. The Cajuns come back and see the Guardsmen paddling off, and they're incensed. The Guardsmen shout at them to read the note, and then one of them, a prankish yokel playing soldier, moronically turns his machine gun on the gesticulating men and fires a salvo of blanks; the Cajuns return the fire with a real bullet, and the sergeant is struck in the head.

From then on, the Guardsmen are toyed with, hunted down, ambushed. *Southern Comfort* is about their different responses to the challenge. Set in the winter of 1973, it's a contemporary film in the genre of *The Lost Patrol*. It's also a survival-game movie—a variation on *The Most Dangerous Game* and *Deliverance* in which almost defenseless men who manage to lose their compass in the water, along with their map and their radio, become the prey of hunters. And watching the dissension among the squad as some of them

turn vengeful or go mad and one after another is picked off is rather like seeing Agatha Christie's *Ten Little Indians* set outdoors in a Deep South version
of Vietnam. At the end, hardly anyone is left alive.

Hill uses the locale for its paranoia-inducing strangeness (it's like a landscape dreamed up by Max Ernst), and he uses the men to demonstrate what
he thinks it takes to survive. The squad may suggest the ethnically balanced
platoons in Second World War movies, but in those movies the men were an
ethnic composite in order to affirm that members of various races and reli-
gions were united in the war effort. Hill uses a mixed group so that he can
show how the more rational and intelligent are endangered by the actions of
the hotheads and crazies. He pulls you into the morass that his characters are
in; you feel that the world—this bog they're in—is physically against them.
(The film's setting is supposed to be Louisiana's Atchafalaya Basin, an eight-
hundred-thousand-acre swampland, but because of problems of road access
to the Basin it was shot in the Caddo Lake region of Louisiana and eastern
Texas.)

The main roles are played by Keith Carradine, as a likable, educated fellow who works in his father's bank in Baton Rouge, and Powers Boothe, as a
Texan who has just moved to Louisiana—a man who grew up among rednecks but studied and became a chemical engineer, and is disgusted by the
ignorance and folly of the redneck clowns in the squad, who are risking his
life. Carradine and Boothe could not be more different, in terms of presence
and what makes them attractive. Carradine is blond, slender, relaxed—he
really is "easy." Boothe is sullen, a brooder with a dark, heavy spirit. As the
Reverend Jim Jones in the TV film *The Guyana Tragedy* and as the anti-union
loner and fink in the abominable TV series "Skag," Boothe showed his acting
skill, and he also showed that he knows how to use a dead stare and a slight
curl of the lips to woo the audience. He stands out: his heavy-lidded, sensual
presence, his "haunted" look, and his potential for violence make you think
"star." His lumpen facial planes recall Elvis Presley; his cheeks look swollen,
as if from spiritual toothache. It's a smoldering, cocksure camera face, and it
prepares us for more than Boothe gets to do in *Southern Comfort*. So does
the script: the moviemakers give him a strong will and the name "Hardin"
(male writers will be boys); they set him up as the outsider, the mystery man,
and he announces that he means to fight his way out—that he means to live.
We're led to expect something explosive. Then they don't supply the scene
he needs, the scene that the whole movie appears to be leading up to. We
feel somewhat cheated.

The rapport between Carradine and Boothe isn't overdone—the two
bond instinctively, helping each other out. The sequence in which they take
refuge in a Cajun village that is having a celebration, with a feast and dancing,
is a shift in tempo and style that's a wonderful extension of the paranoid-
nightmare atmosphere. Trying to escape the Cajun killers who are after them,
the two men enter this communal gathering without knowing the rules, and

they look to the Cajun faces, which won't show an expression—won't give them their bearings. This sequence is edited to Cajun dance music, with frequent cuts to the great moonface of a man singing in an unintelligible French patois, and you get the feeling of a closed folk society; these two invaders have no more clue to interpreting it than if they were from Mars.

As an action director, Walter Hill has a dazzling competence. *Southern Comfort* comes across with such immediacy that it had a near-hypnotic hold on me and I felt startled—brought up short—when it ended. The picture is limited by its structure, though, and by its ideas. Hill's previous film, the 1980 *The Long Riders*, which was about Jesse and Frank James and the Cole Younger gang, had the look of loving, reverent authenticity; it was like a series of daguerreotypes examined closely. But Hill, who means to go beyond motivation and to reveal what a man is by how he handles himself in action, didn't help the audience understand why the sets of brothers had become robbers, or why they hated the railroads, or why they had become folk heroes; nothing was built up to, not even the Northfield Raid that smashed the outlaw bands. *The Long Riders* had everything it needed to be a great Western except that the center of the picture, the mythic framework that would have supplied the tension, was missing; to put it crudely, the film had no angle on the outlaws—it had no hook. And so Hill's extraordinary taste and craftsmanship came across as consciously elegiac and a shade dull. The picture didn't have the unifying visceral force of Hill's 1979 *The Warriors*, which was all hook. *Southern Comfort* is all hook, too. This picture is visceral, or it isn't anything, because the characters don't have the depth to stay with you.

Movies with a neat "classic" structure are always a problem: they look too set up. This movie is built like a trap; it's an infernal machine that closes in on the characters, who are designed to be trapped. Each character seems to shed his anonymity and be given an identity just before he's picked off. But we're not sure why Hill is making the movie—except to make a movie. It's an intense experience if you're drawn in—you may find it darkly magical, perhaps even threatening—yet afterward you're likely to keep thinking of ways it could have been better. This may be partly because the start is so good that it raises your expectations and then there's a sag in the middle, and also because the end *does* bring you up short—by a few frames, at least. It's too fast; it's abrupt, and you're left slightly dazed.

Hill was, of course, making a Vietnam parable, and that limited him, because it meant that the Guardsmen have to die ingloriously. In structure, *Southern Comfort* is very similar to *The Warriors*—in each, a group of men tries to make it home through the territory of hostile natives. But in *The Warriors* the group was heroic, and it suffered few losses. Here we're put in the position of watching buffoons and psychotics get themselves killed. In *The Warriors*, which was made in raw comic-book frames, the conception ruled out characterization in the usual sense. Here we want more of it than we get. The picture doesn't cry out "Parable!" and chances are that people seeing it will be too engrossed in the smashingly edited atrocities even to think about the Vietnam analogy until they get out of the theatre. But having that in his mind must have determined how Hill planned the situations, and how the scriptwriters—Michael Kane and then Hill and his producer, David Giler—conceived the characters. The movie says a fair amount about how confused the American soldiers must have been in that paddy-field terrain, and about how, unable to distinguish friend from foe, they began to see everyone as an enemy. But it doesn't say anything about the policies that sent them there. They didn't get themselves into the mess, like the men in the movie. And that's where the movie may rub you wrong: the provocation that the Guardsmen give the Cajuns isn't commensurate with the Cajuns' brutal revenge. You can believe it when Hardin says, "They must be hunting us just for the fun of it." You can believe that the Cajuns might want to teach these jokers a lesson, but not that they'd also kill them off. In order to put together a gripping action film with an absurdist tone, the moviemakers bring on a series of punishments that are way out of proportion. The Cajuns destroy the Guardsmen in retaliation for a fool's prank—that's a long way from what happened to the American soldiers in Vietnam.

Southern Comfort has a fine bunch of actors, but a few weeks after seeing it I don't have a very clear memory of the individual performances, except for T. K. Carter as the snappy, live-wire dope dealer and Carlos Brown as the high-school teacher who goes berserk, while more than a year and a half after seeing *The Long Riders*, which made me grumble and shift about restlessly, I have exact impressions of the deep humor of David Carradine's performance as the mangy, melancholy Cole, and of Pamela Reed's performance as the brazen-faced Belle Starr, of Fran Ryan, James Whitmore, Jr., and red-haired Amy Stryker—and, of course, of the bloodied outlaw families escaping from the disaster at Northfield. *Southern Comfort* is a much better movie, but you don't take as much away with you. Hill works here like a modest Peckinpah. The traps are sprung, the brutalities are consummated, but he doesn't try for the flamboyant high notes of some of his other movies. He's not driven, like Peckinpah.

The limitation of *Southern Comfort* is that Hill works inside an action-movie format that belongs to the studio-factory era. And his ideas—his macho-existential version of the survival of the fittest, by which he means the cool and intelligent—belong to that format. There's nothing underneath his characters' macho masks. Each person is sketched in a few bold strokes—just enough to give us a stake in what's going on. Peckinpah's films are full of exacerbated human emotions—bursts of rancor and shame, great quantities of disgust, and sometimes even greater quantities of affection. He fills the old forms to overflowing or bursts them. Hill accepts the conventions and doesn't bring them new meaning—merely ideas. He aestheticizes action, with techniques adapted from Peckinpah and Arthur Penn and the early masters of the genre. Hill is himself a new master, but, partly because there were so many good, shallow action films made in the studio period, a movie like *Southern Comfort* no longer seems enough.

The action film is a terrible vehicle in which to try to probe anything political, because it has to deliver shocks on schedule. And it colors anything political by its own brand of action politics. The viewer gets the feeling that the world is irredeemably violent: in a Clint Eastwood film, Eastwood can't go into a diner and ask for a glass of water without someone's picking a fight with him. Action movies say that the world is always threatening your manhood every minute of the day. In the forties, action directors used the anti-Nazi theme for hollow and sadistic violence; in the late sixties and early seventies, they used the anti–Vietnam War theme the same way (and we became the Nazis). In recent years, action directors have been using "survival." In other eras, the wilderness was sentimentalized as innocent. Now even nature is malevolent, and Walter Hill presents us with the world as swamp where vengeful, sneaky Arcadians slaughter vengeful idiot Guardsmen, and where the passport to survival is a college education—i.e., superior intelligence, demonstrated in faster, more powerful action. The idea that a man is defined in action (essentially, by how good a fighter he is) comes out of a boys'-book world divided into the brave and the cowardly. It's an aesthetic and moral standard that had a romantic charm in the days when Gary Cooper was young. *Southern Comfort* is a beautiful and affecting piece of moviemaking. It's also horse manure.

· · · · ·

Ticket to Heaven has a hot dramatic subject. On a trip to San Francisco, the hero, David (Nick Mancuso), a young Toronto schoolteacher, a liberal nonbeliever from a Jewish background, is sucked into a religious cult that worships its Oriental founder. The film calls this sect Heavenly Children, and these Children refer to the founder as Father. At the beginning, David is somewhat depressed and at loose ends, because the woman he has been living with has broken things off, but he's a big, handsome fellow with a bruiser's strong jaw. Mancuso suggests a dark, young Burt Lancaster; he has that overcast intensity. And at first, after David is tricked into spending a few days at the group's farm camp, all he wants is to get out. But once he opens up and talks about his life, as he sits with the group around the campfire, they've got him, and he starts going to pieces. Deprived of sleep, of food, and of any solitude for reflection, he gradually shrinks into a despairing masochist. Lancaster disappears: tormented, David looks more like Anthony Hopkins. Soon he has shrunk down to a smiling child-zombie panhandler, part of a team selling flowers on the streets. It's a plausible metamorphosis: David's independent spirit is visibly drained away, and he becomes passive and obedient—a pod person. His greatest excitement is joining with the others in the chant "Bring in the money! Stay awake! Smash out Satan!"

Maybe because this is the Canadian director Ralph L. Thomas's first theatrical feature, and his background is in journalism and documentary, the film is somewhat tentative—it's careful. Thomas sets things up without any frills (or much texture), and we have time to think about the way that David's forcible conversion parodies conversions to the established, more reputable faiths and about how this cult takes off from the counterculture movement. It uses the idealism of the disaffected remnants of the counterculture, and the confessional, therapeutic "sharing" of the human-potential movement, and the tax benefits of being a church. The Children are building an ideal world; they don't have to give it any thought—all the answers are in Father's book. If anyone has any doubts, that proves he's weak, and the group hammers away at him until he's strong again. David is told that "a questioning mind is Satan's mind." Although the movie doesn't make it explicit, it seems fairly clear that these clean-cut Heavenly Children lose all desire for sex. Even if they had the time or energy or privacy for sexual encounters, the enthusiastic voices always raised in song would douse any impulse toward pleasure; at dawn the whole cheery group is warbling "When the Red, Red Robin Comes Bob, Bob, Bobbin' Along."

The strapping, handsome David becomes so passive that the center of the movie doesn't hold; he turns into just one more mindlessly conformist saintly fool. Though this structural weakness is built into the material, an actor more experienced than Mancuso might have been so varied—so unusual—at the start that we would have had an acute sense of loss each time we saw him glassy-eyed. But Mancuso doesn't endow David with a great deal of personality to start with (and, possibly, those most accessible to cults don't have very distinctive personalities). Fortunately, the movie, which is based on Josh Freed's 1978 newspaper series and his 1980 book *Moonwebs*, has provided a secondary hero, Larry (Saul Rubinek), who has been David's friend from childhood. Larry goes to the cult's retreat in the woods—it's really a psychotherapeutic concentration camp—in an effort to get to David and talk with him. If at first we empathized with David and then pulled back as we saw him surrender his mind, now we get a look at the Heavenly Children through Larry's bright, brimming eyes that register double takes. Larry—a would-be standup comic who holds down a job as an accountant but performs wherever he can—is small and dark, with a wry, affectionate manner. The author Josh Freed helped rescue a friend from the Moonies, and movie stand-ins for authors are generally the worst roles, but Rubinek makes Larry more vivid than David ever is. Larry has a schlumpy kind of simplicity: you can believe that he'll do his damnedest to rescue David. He also rescues the movie, by lightening its tone—he's warm and funny when he's trying to put on the group leaders. After he has seen enough, he sneaks away and goes to David's family and friends and old girlfriend back in Toronto, and they all get together on a kidnap plot. Gentle little Larry is at his funniest when he's carrying out this clandestine operation, and his eyes spark with amazement that he's actually involved in a criminal act. It's as if he'd suddenly found himself at an orgy.

But after the kidnapping, when the abductors are holed up with David in an Oakland apartment, the de-programmer (R. H. Thomson), a tall, imperious figure, stalks in and upstages everybody else. And though we could see and understand David's conversion (and mutation), the de-programmer's methods seem bullying and arbitrary. The director, who, with Anne Cameron, adapted the Josh Freed book, doesn't do enough to clarify the steps in this process (if it is a process, rather than just hit or miss). The relatives and friends (Larry among them) hang around helplessly, cowering when they hear sirens outside, because they know that the cult will have filed kidnapping charges, and the police may get to them before David can be persuaded not to go back. Everybody seems passive now except the arrogant de-programmer. If the others reacted to his lordly manner, we might know how to react. Why aren't they puzzled about what he's doing? *We* are. The dramatic logic of the film requires that we see the beginning, at least, of the re-formation of David's character, and surely the high point needs to be the moment of breakthrough. But it isn't clear how this hotshot expert means to get to him, or how, in fact, he does. Potentially, the story has everything: the horror of the destruction of a man's mind and his personality, and then the illegal actions that are the only means available to those who want to help restore him. It's all here, only it's in rather slack form. *Ticket to Heaven* could have used a better script and more taut direction, but a good subject does a lot for a movie—you don't feel humiliated by it.

.   .   .   .   .

*R*eturning to the screen after a twenty-year retirement, James Cagney, who was born in 1899, has the faint, satisfied smile of an old tiger, and it's a pleasure to look at him. As New York Police Commissioner Waldo, he gives *Ragtime* something: a tartness, some tension and dignity—he doesn't go soft. Actually, none of the performers disgrace themselves; it's the moviemakers who flub everything in sight. E. L. Doctorow's novel *Ragtime* was already a movie, an extravaganza about the cardboard cutouts in our minds—figures from the movies, newsreels, the popular press, dreams, and history, all tossed together. Doctorow played virtuoso games with this mixture—games that depended on the reader's having roughly the same store of imagery in his head that the author did. He drew you into the many stories, and the complex narrative—all that plot!—had a rush to it. *Ragtime* was a near-perfect entertainment for the people who read hardcover books, but it wasn't surprising that the book didn't travel well, and had "disappointing" sales in the mass-market paperback editions: to enjoy the novel you really needed a mind stuffed with images of Admiral Peary and Stanford White and Emma Goldman and Harry Houdini and the *Our Gang* comedies, and enough knowledge of the period just before the First World War to appreciate the joke of the conversation between J. P. Morgan and Henry Ford and the anecdote of Freud having a fainting fit after taking a boat ride with Jung. The book was superficial yet dense, with marvelous details that whizzed right by, and Doctorow's way of slipping invented characters in among the cutouts and having them interact made for a giddy, kinetic synthesis of fact and fiction. Reading the book really was like seeing a movie; the book had a movie-inspired way of perceiving—it's how we look at the past now, with the historical figures and the actors who played them all jumbled, and scandalous items from *Time* and *Newsweek* replacing the battles and dates. (And we no longer expect—or want—to separate things out.) *Ragtime* was an elegant gagster's book, and the character of the poor immigrant Tateh, who lives on the lower East Side and works at his display cart cutting out silhouette portraits of passersby, and then moves on to selling the flip-page "movie books" he makes, and goes from that to designing magic lanterns, and eventually takes the title of Baron and becomes the producer of the ethnically mixed *Our Gang* comedies, was Doctorow's American artist. He was also Doctorow: the people in his movie book are also seen in silhouette.

In 1975, the year *Ragtime* was published, it was announced that Robert Altman was going to direct the film version and that Doctorow was writing the script; how they meant to go about it wasn't explained, but if anybody could do *Ragtime* it was Altman, because he has the nerve and the genius to try things that nobody else would think of. He's a showman with a sense of fun, and he's as obsessed as Doctorow with large casts and chance meetings and nostalgia for what should have happened. It was clear that he was deeply excited by the book and eager to tackle it: when his 1976 movie *Buffalo Bill and the Indians* came out, there he was, tossing historical and fictional figures together, in the spirit of *Ragtime*, and working on a huge canvas with stars in cameos flitting in and out. But he didn't bring it off, and, ironically, his deep involvement with *Ragtime*—which helped to wreck *Buffalo Bill*—cost him the chance to film *Ragtime*, because the producer Dino De Laurentiis, who had bought the rights to the book, had also financed *Buffalo Bill*.

There is probably no American novel that would be more difficult for a European director to adapt to the screen than this one, which depends on the kind of background that we soak up unconsciously over the years—that's a steady buzz in our heads. De Laurentiis made, I think, a calamitous mistake when he turned the project over to the Czech Miloš Forman, who had already demonstrated almost total incomprehension of the American habitat in his grossly energetic *Hair*—so much that his hippies, who were meant to be charming, were abrasively smug. And everything that should have been flowing was chopped up—overedited. (Forman didn't appear to understand that the great achievement of the hippies was that they loosened up the middle classes; he had them shocking rich stiffs who lived in a style that might have come out of editorial denunciations in Pravda.) But there's no reason to think that the Italian De Laurentiis would have recognized the difficulties Forman was bound to get into. Forman simply didn't have the storehouse of associations to make a *Ragtime*. (Could anyone besides Altman get the humor across? Possibly Spielberg—he has the playfulness. But he wouldn't spark the connections that Altman might make.) Forman chose Michael Weller, his writer on *Hair*, to prepare a new script, and they worked together to produce this graceless piece of prose.

The movie *Ragtime* isn't a splashy comedy, isn't full of tricky juxtapositions, doesn't have an impudent slapstick vision, isn't a pop epic, or even a satiric fling. I'm not sure what it is. It's limp—it always seems to be aiming about halfway to Doctorow's effects. Is it possible that Miloš Forman thinks that if he doesn't go for razzle-dazzle what is left will be "truth"? If so, he started from the wrong book. I don't know what people who haven't read it can make of the movie; first there's a chunk of time with one group of characters in New York and then there's a shift, without any transitional guidance, over to another group, in New Rochelle, and then to different characters in New York. And many of the actors are more famous than the people they're playing. Norman Mailer turns up as the expansive, contented Stanford White and has a couple of scenes before he's killed off; there may be just a *few* people in the audience who won't know who Stanford White is, and the movie doesn't identify him, or explain why he and the other gents he's dining with are wearing laurel wreaths. The film goes to great pains to re-create the rooftop theatre of the old Madison Square Garden, where White was shot during the opening performance of the musical *Mamzelle Champagne* (a few flashes of Twyla Tharp's choreography here), and we don't even get a good look around. (Forman is not—to put it courteously—strongly visual. His extras are generally posed frozen-faced in a row in the background—they look exactly like extras.) Pat O'Brien, who has aged extraordinarily gracefully, has the bit role of a lawyer, and Donald O'Connor seems to be enjoying himself in his scene as Evelyn Nesbit's dance instructor; he's heavier now but moves well and has an air of professional calm—like Cagney, he seems amused at how little is asked of him.

The film might have been turned into an earnest, socially conscious drama about race relations, because Doctorow does have his liberal nice-guyism, and the book features a black piano player, Coalhouse Walker, who suffers nobly for a principle and who is the weakest and least believable thing in it. (Fortunately, Doctorow's vivacity overwhelms his sentimental side.) And Forman has, in fact, put Coalhouse Walker (Howard E. Rollins, Jr.) pretty much at the center. But the movie isn't even socially conscious, because Coalhouse Walker (Doctorow's tribute to Kleist's Michael Kohlhaas) is now so totally, aberrantly unbelievable that there's no social milieu that could account for him. This guerrilla Coalhouse has the sugar-sweet smile of a Johnny Mathis, and when he gathers a band of urban guerrillas and sets off bombs, we don't know on what conceivable basis he could have recruited them.

The movie reduces the number of characters considerably but leaves in allusions to some of the discards, in the form of simulated and actual newsreel footage. The story never quite expands, yet what's left of it doesn't quite fit together, either; the editing here seems even more unplanned than in *Hair*. A lot of talented actors come across as dead. As Mother, Mary Steenburgen is directed to be so uncertain of what she's going to say that she pauses before each soft, gentle utterance, yet the payoff—the fact that she's morally right and iron-willed, and her blustering husband (James Olson, in a totally charmless role and a performance to match) always gives in—dribbles away. Brad Dourif is Younger Brother—a role that might seem ideal for him, since in the book Younger Brother is strange, likable, and probably totally crazy. But in the movie his full weirdness doesn't emerge. As Willie Conklin, the racist rowdy from the firehouse who causes all the trouble for the musician, Kenneth McMillan seems unsinkable, even though Forman keeps him stripped down to his long underwear. Does Forman think that an actor like McMillan needs a low-comedy prop in order to be low? This actor is also deprived of the climactic scene we're led to expect: we're told that Willie is going to be delivered to Coalhouse's justice, and then nothing happens. But the performer who is treated the worst is the lovely young Elizabeth McGovern, who plays Evelyn Nesbit. Forman appears to see Evelyn as some sort of open-mouthed retard. The actress is photographed so that her cheeks look stupidly full, and Evelyn is not merely dim-witted, self-centered, and venal—she's also such a crude little peasant that when she's interrupted in the middle of naked lovemaking with Younger Brother she proceeds to discuss a business deal with a couple of lawyers without having the instinct to cover herself. Younger Brother makes a move to cover her breasts, but the cloth falls and she ignores it and goes on talking. The focus of the scene is on Elizabeth McGovern's torso. And we sit there uncomfortably, knowing that Forman could make his small, ponderous point just as easily by framing the image so that only her shoulders were visible—it would be perfectly clear that she was naked below the frame. When an actress is left exposed this way, it's the director who's crude.

November 23, 1981

The Devil in the Flesh

*T*he people in Fred Schepisi's *The Devil's Playground* are like sculptured figures that glow with their own light. You're not aware of surfaces, of skin. You're aware of the substance of the flesh. The Marist Brothers at the

Catholic seminary around which most of the film is set seem to be looking into themselves, puzzled and deeply disappointed by their own physicality. And the pubescent boys gaze with thunderstruck eyes at the eruptions of their bodies. The movie is always on the borderline of comedy, because they have all—monks and seminarians alike—been taught that "an undisciplined mind is the Devil's playground," yet they can't get their minds off their bodies. They can't control the urges that the Church's teachings say they must control. They're in a losing battle with their flesh.

Schepisi is odd man out—the artist in the Australian film renaissance, which is otherwise a celebration of the work of intelligent, slightly impersonal craftsmen. That may be why it took him five years to complete this semi-autobiographical first feature (it's set in the fifties) and why it has taken another five years for the film to get a New York opening. (*The Devil's Playground* was finished in 1976; Schepisi's second picture, the 1978 *The Chant of Jimmie Blacksmith*—a masterwork—opened here in 1980.) *The Devil's Playground* treads a delicate tightrope; there has probably never been a film that treats priestly shame—amounting to agony in some cases—with such understanding. Most of the monks have genuine affection for the boys they teach, and sympathy for the plight of little kids bewildered by their erections. And the monks are acutely aware of each other's concealed torments. They're tolerant of the drinking of Brother Victor (Nick Tate), who goes into the city wearing civvies, picks up two women and flirts and teases right up to the verge of actual sex, and then just barely makes his escape, gasping to the younger monk waiting for him, "They nearly had me." And when Brother Francine (Arthur Dignam), the most agonized of all, and the most repressive with the students, instructing them that "Your body is your worst enemy," has been drinking wine with the other brothers, he suddenly lets out a torrent of rage and self-disgust and shouts, "The body won't be denied." The men in the room with him look away, look inward; they are aware of each other's miseries, but each is thinking, Why has this horrible thing—sexuality—been inflicted on me? They remain very still, yet they're pulsing, like the figures in Rodin's *The Burghers of Calais*.

Schepisi's passion is expressed visually—in his thematic use of water imagery, in the voluptuous shifting of dark and light, in the matte green of the monks' billiard table, and in the deep green of the huge, overhanging trees on the seminary grounds and the paradisal trees in the countryside, with twisted, mossy limbs. His use of color eroticizes the environment. Outside the seminary, the greens and the aquas are tense, acid, and at a family picnic there are bright pinks and reds that look electrified next to the greens and the blues. Trees and grass have a special vibrancy—they, too, seem to glow with their own light.

Schepisi is a rarity—an artist whose sense of justice and proportion is as highly developed as his sensual aesthetic. He's sane and balanced in his treatment of the characters. At the center of the story is the cheerful thirteen-year-old Tom (Simon Burke), whose pigeon-toed front teeth give him the grin of a friendly child-satyr. Tom thinks he has a calling to the religious life (as Schepisi did at thirteen), but he's the joke of the seminary, because, as the monks observe, he has a constant erection. (A very old monk gently tries to dissuade him from his vocation.) For Tom, sexuality is a source of pleasures he can't resist. For the sallow, fanatic Brother Francine, it's an agonizing burden that threatens him. On a trip to the city, he sneaks off to a public swimming pool and gapes at exposed flesh—at men's hairy underbellies, at women's breasts slightly askew in their wet bathing suits—and his huge dark eyes bulge with shame for his voyeurism and his lust. The most intense eroticism in the film is in a dream that tortures Brother Francine: underwater, naked, his face in shock, expressionless, and his eyes wide open, staring, he is surrounded by beautiful naked nymphs—all of them for his pleasure, except that he's incapable of feeling pleasure even in a dream. Arthur Dignam brings a self-dramatizing fervor to the role: Brother Francine, isolated with his fantasies, is contemptuous of the lesser suffering of the other monks. This mortified zealot, whose emotions are a tangle, has the richest (and most sepulchral) voice in the film.

The sound of *The Devil's Playground* is a comic cantata: the boys' voices are in various stages of changing, and the kids are as surprised as we are by the spooky, quavering tones that come out of them. The monks' voices are educated, modulated—avuncular. But in some cases (such as Brother Victor), the rough, slangy Australian vulgate comes through. And in the case of Father Marshall—played by the Australian novelist Thomas Keneally, from whose book Schepisi adapted *Jimmie Blacksmith*—an Irish lilt can be heard. The bald and bewhiskered Father Marshall, a missionary who officiates at the boys' three-day retreat, is a heightened version of the other monks. A friendly leprechaun, he goes out of his way to ease the boys' fears. (He gives Tom a vial of holy water from Lourdes so that he can put a drop of it on his tongue—to help him with his bed-wetting.) But when Father Marshall delivers a sermon it's pure fundamentalist hellfire and damnation, holding up to the boys images such as a fiery worm consuming their entrails for eternity, and real terror hovers in the air. The combination of dogmatic teachings and the onset of puberty drives some of the boys more than a little crazy: three of them become involved in secret purification rites, and their leader, thinking he's ready to walk on water, is drowned.

Schepisi wrote himself a beautiful script: it's all theme and variations, yet nothing seems forced. Instructed that they must not talk during their retreat, the boys awkwardly dispose themselves on the shore of a lake. The silence is oppressive to them—it feels false and silly—and Tom tosses a pebble into the water. Others toss pebbles—a whole volley of pebbles—and then a fat boy slips in, with a big, thudding splash, and the tension is broken and they all laugh together. Almost every incident in the film gives us, like this one, an intuitive perception of how the boys' impulses are thwarted and how the kids consciously or unconsciously fight back. The monks are simply the boys at a more advanced stage of repression and guilt; locked in by their feelings of unworthiness, they're on permanent retreat.

Perhaps Tom's encounter with a young girl is a shade too idyllic. And when he was visiting with her and with his family I was a little confused about where they all were. And perhaps the old monk who counsels Tom against striving for priestly celibacy and perfection is too kindly; it might be better if he didn't mutter "It's unnatural"—Schepisi needn't tell us what he's showing us. But there are few flaws, and they're piddling ones. I don't really see how this movie could be much better. Schepisi is a great filmmaker, with his own softly rhythmed style. The full, widescreen images glide by; the cadences are elusive—like Scott Fitzgerald's prose rhythms. Schepisi's two features, this one and *Jimmie Blacksmith*, are not like the work of any other director. In this first film, even the way that the music comes in on scenes and rises up during the underwater dream is very personal. I had the feeling that everything in the film was breathing. When a director so clearly knows what he's doing, you can sit back and smile with pleasure. The details are satisfying: the way the boys ignore the crabbing of the seminary cook; the suave righteousness with which the head of the school refuses to give Tom the address of a friend he wants to write to who has been expelled; the crew-neck sweater that Brother Victor wears on his flirtatious foray into town—just clerical enough for him to feel a little safe. The film gives you the impression that Schepisi has got the whole thing right. He must have freed himself very thoroughly: this isn't an anti-Catholic movie. Far from it. Schepisi loves these tormented comedians. But he looks at them with humorous pagan eyes.

.   .   .   .   .

On Golden Pond is an unbelievably literal-minded movie. It opens with images of sunset on a lake, and we hear the cry of a loon; there are views of two loons in the water and closeups of flowers. Katharine Hepburn and Henry Fonda, arriving at their summer house in Maine, get out of a car, and it's a stage entrance, with both of them so busily in character that I felt a slight throb in the temple—a foreboding. When Hepburn, fluttering girlishly and listening with poetically cocked head, announced, "The loons, the loons. They're welcoming us back," and Fonda, crotchety as could be, let us know that he was too deaf to hear what she was carrying on about, I knew what I was in for. *On Golden Pond* is the kind of uplifting experience that traffics heavily in rather basic symbols: the gold light on the pond stands for the sunset of life; the loons, whom Hepburn refers to as a husband and wife, represent Ethel and Norman Thayer (Hepburn and Fonda). Do you dig it? Do you have the stomach for it? Directed by Mark Rydell, from Ernest Thompson's adaptation of his own 1978 play, the movie is a doddering valentine in which popsy Norman, who's having his eightieth birthday, and mopsy Ethel, who's nearing her seventieth, crack jokes, weather domestic crises, and show us the strength of solid Yankee values. Or is it "good American stock," or Hepburn's pedigreed cheekbones? Fonda is seventy-seven, and Hepburn is seventy-five, and the media have been turning them into monuments. This film is a rather indecently premature memorial service.

Surely the only way to show respect for elderly performers is to hold them to the same standards that they were held to when they were younger, and it's almost impossible for Hepburn and Fonda to do anything resembling a creditable job of acting in a vehicle like *On Golden Pond*. It comes out of the Theatre of Safety. It's shaped so that it seems to be getting at the problems of old age (Norman's eyes and ears are failing, his memory is spotty, and his body is becoming more and more unreliable), but then Norman's crankiness is made to seem sly—a form of one-upmanship. He's meant to be a lovable curmudgeon. And he and Ethel are such an adoring, lovey-dovey old pair that there are no recriminations and just one regret—and that is taken care of in the course of the film. It concerns their child—their daughter, Chelsea (Jane Fonda), now forty-two, and still bitter and resentful because she has never felt that she could please her father or that he cared about her.

Ernest Thompson takes a roundabout route to the rapprochement of father and daughter. Chelsea, whose first marriage failed, arrives for her father's birthday, bringing her new lover, Bill (Dabney Coleman, bearded), a Los Angeles dentist, and his thirteen-year-old son, Billy (Doug McKeon), an unhappy little tough, whom she and Bill park with the Thayers for a month while they vacation in Europe. Wouldn't Billy be happier in a summer camp, with kids his own age? Oh, but then we couldn't be faced with the gruesome prospect of watching canny old Norman reclaim the boy—get his mind off chasing girls and onto fishing and diving and other outdoor sports—and change him into an ideal, tenderhearted kid. Somehow, the affection that springs up between the old man and Billy makes it possible for Chelsea, on her return, to gain self-respect by doing the backflip dive that she was afraid to do as a young girl, and to talk—talk "meaningfully," that is—to her father for the first time. Naturally, the picture ends with Norman and Ethel saying their annual goodbye to the lake; there are more shots of the sunset on the water, and Mr. and Mrs. Loon, whose baby has learned to fly and has gone off on its own, come round to say goodbye to Norman and Ethel.

This isn't material for actors, no matter what their age. It's material for milking tears from an audience. Hepburn and Fonda are playing America's aged sweethearts—A Married Couple for All Seasons. Norman and Ethel are more in love than on the day they were married; he is a retired professor (apparently without any anxieties about inflation or other money worries), and they have always lived graciously. It's no accident that the publicity sketch showing Henry Fonda, in a fishing hat, and the smiling faces of Hepburn, Jane Fonda, and Doug McKeon looks like a knockoff of a Norman Rockwell *Saturday Evening Post* cover. That's the world that the film tries to evoke. But the sketch has a sickly, creepy quality, and so does the movie. Henry Fonda appears to give an honest performance, but his clean-old-man role is conceived so grotesquely that I found it impossible to like Norman—and our liking him is the linchpin of the whole enterprise. Hepburn is a special case: she's heady, as if exhilarated by her own acting. She overdoes Ethel's being entranced with nature, and she horribly overdoes Ethel's devotion to Norman, so that it calls attention to Ethel's own wonderfulness. Ethel is meant to be a capable, down-to-earth woman, but Hepburn leaps about weightlessly— she never comes close to touching the ground. She has become a Kate Hepburn windup doll—chipper and lyrical, floating in the stratosphere, and, God knows, spunky. Her star turn is a parody of the great Hepburn performances—it's all pirouettes.

The director has not done himself proud. Listening to the dialogue is like being at a bad play: you can count out the beats in the pauses. And some of the shots go on a few frames too long, so that you see the actors' false emotions freezing and the people look the way they do in the sketch. Doug McKeon is stiff, as if he had played Billy a thousand times already and were bored past showing any emotion. And Rydell has the actors hitting some very strange notes. In the only scene that Billy has alone with his father, Bill threatens to send him back to his mother if he doesn't behave, and there is such ugly menace in his tone that I had the vagrant thought that Chelsea was making another big mistake in her life—that Bill, the bearded dentist who talks L.A. psychodrivel, was some sort of weirdo con man. There certainly seems to be something suspicious about him when he has a conversation with Norman and his face switches expressions crazy-fast—he's like a speed freak trying on attitudes. It turns out that Bill is meant to be a charming fellow and the right husband for Chelsea—it's only Mark Rydell who has taken leave of his senses. In extenuation of Dabney Coleman's performance, it should be pointed out that Norman mocks Bill so cruelly and so sneakily that it might be difficult for any actor to know how to read Bill's lines.

As the playwright has set things up, Norman, who has the bulk of the one-liners, gets laughs by jokes about his own enfeeblement and then gets more laughs by being on top of the situations and zapping people who think he's feeble. We're meant to enjoy the way he picks on people and makes them feel foolish, and we're also asked to weep (and people around me certainly *were* weeping) for his frailty, for his courage, for the beauty of his love affair with his wife of forty-eight years. The author is both ruthless and shameless—a real winning combination. He even gives Norman a bit of an angina attack onstage (sorry about that—on camera). The fakery at the core of the material is that Norman is a mean old son of a bitch to his daughter and to just about everyone else except his wife and Billy. Yet we're asked to dote on him, and Chelsea is made out to be a neurotic mess for not having responded to his true loving nature. Chelsea is a terrible role, and Jane Fonda plays it so tensely that she's like an actress in a soap opera telegraphing her psychiatric miseries. (In a lakeside scene, in a bikini, she looks spectacular, yet she keeps her body held in so tight that you can't believe she's breathing.) Ethel, who is so understanding with her husband, is starchy and impatient with her daughter, telling her, "All you can do is be disagreeable about the past. What's the point? . . . Life marches by, Chelsea. I suggest you get on with it." That's not a mother talking—it's a headmistress. Yet we're supposed to applaud Ethel's no-nonsense stoicism. Ernest Thompson works the audience for any approval he can wring out of it.

Some sections of the press are doing backflips of their own. What is going on when *Time*, in a reverential cover story on this movie and Hepburn and Fonda, uses terms such as "breeding" and gets right down to lineage: "Both their families were established in the colonies by the 18th century, and the pedigree shows in the two who took up acting"? Hepburn and Fonda have not, then, merely "ascended to proud new peaks"; they are Our Betters. I don't think this snobbery should be blamed on the Reagans. I think it's a worshipfulness (and maybe envy) that overcomes some people when they look at Hepburn's imperial bones. They feel she must belong to a superior race. (Henry Fonda is let in on a pass, because he has played so many great liberals.)

There's a moment, after Norman and Billy have become buddies and are out fishing together, when the movie gives us a quick-flash reminder that the subject is mortality: Billy hauls in a dead loon and then, in his new, reformed manner, asks Norman, man to man, if he's afraid of dying. The movie is like a striptease without nudity. It's a death tease; nobody dies—the only corpse is that loon, and it isn't even one of Norman and Ethel's beloved loons. All the talk about death and dying is really very cozy, because Norman is demonstrated to be such a tough old bird that he can still outwit everybody around. And there can be few people in the world as snugly protected in their old age as he is, with a selfless wife dedicated to his care. Even the symbols—the golden-sunset years, the pair of loons—are soothing. This twaddle is a pacifier—it's a regression to the movies with cute and wise old codgers.

December 7, 1981

Dreamers

Pennies from Heaven is the most emotional movie musical I've ever seen. It's a stylized mythology of the Depression which uses the popular songs of the period as expressions of people's deepest longings—for sex, for romance, for money, for a high good time. When the characters can't say how they feel, they evoke the songs: they open their mouths, and the voices on hit records of the thirties come out of them. And as they lip-sync the lyrics their obsessed eyes are burning bright. Their souls are in those voices, and they see themselves dancing just like the stars in movie musicals.

Visually, the film is a tarnished romance. The sets are stylized—not just the sets for the dance numbers but also the Chicago streets and stores, the movie houses, the diners and dives, which are designed in bold, formal compositions, for a heightened melancholy. This is our communal vision of the Depression, based on images handed down to us: motionless streets and buildings, with lonely figures in clear, cold light. The film actually re-creates paintings and photographs that are essences of America. There's a breathtaking re-creation of Edward Hopper's *Nighthawks* coffee shop, and its held for just the right length of time. There's Hopper's interior of a movie house with a woman usher leaning against the wall, and there are bleary faces and purplish red-light-district scenes by Reginald Marsh, and thirties photographs of desolation, such as a dark flivver parked in front of a plain white clapboard house. These images blend in and breathe with the other shots. The whole movie seems a distillation of that forlorn, heavily shadowed period, while the songs express people's most fervent shallow hopes. When the hero, Arthur, a sheet-music salesman, a big talker just smart enough to get himself into trouble, goes on his selling trips, from Chicago to Galena, in 1934, the land is flat and deserted, with almost nothing moving but his little car chugging along the road.

As Arthur, Steve Martin has light-brown hair cut short, and when he calls up a song he has an expression of eagerness and awe that transforms him. You forget Steve Martin the TV entertainer, with his zany catch phrases and his disconnected nonchalance. Steve Martin seems to have forgotten him, too. He has a wild-eyed intensity here that draws you right into Arthur's desperation and his lies. Arthur believes the words of the songs, and he tries to get to the dream world they describe. At home in Chicago, he pleads with his wife for a little sex: he mimes a love song—"I'll Never Have to Dream Again"—and Connee Boswell's voice comes out of him. It's our first exposure to the film's device, and though we're meant to laugh or grin, Connee Boswell is saying something for Arthur that his petite and pie-faced wife, Joan (Jessica Harper), refuses to hear, and the mixture of comedy and poignancy is affecting in a somewhat delirious way. Joan cringes at Arthur's touch; she thinks his attempts to make love to her are evidence of a horrible, sullying perversion. Then, in the little town of Galena, when he's in a music store trying to get an order, a shy schoolteacher, Eileen (Bernadette Peters), walks in; Arthur mimes Bing Crosby singing "Did You Ever See a Dream Walking?" and Eileen dances to the music, and the two of them form romantic, thirties-movie-star silhouettes in his mind. Eileen is pale and gentle, a brown-eyed blonde with soft curls—tendrils, really. She looks malleable, like the young Janet Gaynor. Eileen lives in a song world, too, and she's eager to believe Arthur's lie that he isn't married. She also has a spicy, wanton side; she turns into a Kewpie doll when she mimes Helen Kane's boop-boop-a-doops in "I Want to Be Bad." She has everything that Arthur wants, except money. As the story develops, it's so familiar it's archetypal; it's a manic-depressive libretto. Alfred Kazin has written about the passion of "a period—the thirties—that has had no rival since for widespread pain and sudden hope." That's what this black-humor musical, which Dennis Potter adapted from his six-segment BBC mini-series, is about.

The lip-syncing idea works wonderfully; it's in the dialogue interludes that the movie gets off on the wrong foot. Most of these scenes need to be played faster—to be snappier and more hyperbolic, with little curlicues of irony in the performances to point things up. For example, we see a gigantic billboard showing Carole Lombard with a huge black eye in Faith Baldwin's *Love Before Breakfast*. (It's the same billboard poster that appears in a famous photograph by Walker Evans, taken in Atlanta in 1936.) A little while later, with the Lombard poster looking on, a love-starved man grabs a blind girl, and when we next see her, dead, she has a black eye. The director, Herbert Ross, plays it straight, and so instead of being bizarrely, horribly funny it's peculiar. Black humor played too slow *is* peculiar; it may seem that the misery level is rising awfully high. Ross's deliberate pace makes the film's tone uncertain. Sometimes he doesn't go all the way with a shocking joke, or he muffles it, so the audience doesn't get the release of laughter. There's so little movement during the dialogue that the characters seem numbed out, and the audience's confidence in the film is strained—the discomfort of some of the viewers is palpable. I think our emotions get jammed up. Yet the scenes in themselves—even those that are awkwardly paced and almost static—still have a rapt, gripping quality. And even when a scene cries out for a spin, a further twist of artifice, the actors carry the day. Bernadette Peters has ironic curlicues built in, and her exaggerated Queens diction (which is certainly eccentric for an Illinois girl) gives her her own cheeping-chicky sound.

Besides Arthur and Joan and that heavenly angel cake Eileen, there are two other major characters. Vernel Bagneris (the director and star of the long-running show *One Mo' Time*) plays a homeless, stuttering street musician and beggar, the Accordion Man, whom Arthur picks up on the road, and it's Bagneris who mimes the title song. The version he lip-syncs isn't the happy-go-lucky Crosby version from the totally unrelated 1936 film that was also called *Pennies from Heaven*; it's that of Arthur Tracy, which is much darker and much more potent. The sorrow of the Depression and the hoping beyond hope are concentrated in this song and in the Accordion Man himself. Arthur Tracy's wrenching voice—it has tears and anguish in it—comes pouring out of the stuttering simpleton, and, as if the song had freed him, the Accordion Man dances, sensually, easily. With a photo-collage of the Depression behind him and a shower of shimmering gold raining down on him, he stretches and struts. I never thought I'd go around with the song

"Pennies from Heaven" pulsating in my skull, but the combination of Arthur Tracy and Vernel Bagneris is voluptuously masochistic. Popular singers in the thirties brought out the meaning of a lyric as fully as possible, and the original recordings, which are used here, have the true sound of the period. (The bridges between these old arrangements and the dances—and the dance sequences themselves—are said to have been orchestrated "using antique recording equipment" to preserve the thirties sound; however it was accomplished, the result is worth the effort.) Where the movie misses is in the timing of the contrapuntal gags: after the Accordion Man has had his shimmering-gold epiphany, Arthur, feeling like a real sport, hands him a quarter. Ross somehow buries the connection, the shock. Everything in the material is double-edged; it's conceived in terms of extremes—the melodrama and the pathos on one side and the dream world on the other. Normal life is excluded. But the director keeps trying to sneak it back in; he treats the piled-on sentimental gloom tenderly, as if it were meant to be real life. (Would he be this afraid of the cruel jokes in *The Threepenny Opera*?)

The other major character—almost as much transformed as Steve Martin—is Christopher Walken, with dark, slicked-down hair. As Tom the pimp, who puts Eileen on the street, he has the patent-leather lounge-lizard look of a silent-movie wolf, and his scenes play like greasy magic. In his first movie musical, Walken, who used to dance on Broadway, has more heat and athletic energy than he has shown in his straight acting roles. He has never been quite all there on the screen; he has looked drained or packed in ice. (That's what made him so effective as the chief mercenary in *The Dogs of War*—that, and the tense way he walked in New York, like an animal pacing a cage.) Here, there's sensuality in his cartooned apathy, and when he first spots Eileen his eyeballs seem to pop out on springs. In a mock striptease in a saloon, he shows how powerfully built he is, and he's a real hoofer. He takes the screen in a way he never has before—by force, and with lewd amusement, particularly when he bares a grotesque valentine tattoo on his chest.

There hasn't been this much tap dancing in a movie musical in many years. Arthur does a derby-and-plaid-suit vaudeville routine with two other salesmen, who are played by Tommy Rall (best known to moviegoers as Ann Miller's partner in the 1953 *Kiss Me, Kate*) and spaghetti-legged Robert Fitch (best known to theatregoers as the original Rooster in *Annie*). It's a fast, showy number—to the Dorsey Brothers Orchestra's playing and the Boswell Sisters' singing "It's the Girl"—and the three men have wonderful frilly gestures as they curve and sway to imitate femininity, and use their hands to model their dream girls' shapes in the air. Steve Martin doesn't slow his celebrated partners down; he's spectacular—he really is Steve (Happy Feet) Martin. In the film's most startling sequence, set inside the Hopper movie theatre with the weary blond usher, Arthur and Eileen sit watching *Follow the Fleet*. Arthur is transfixed, and as Astaire sings "Let's Face the Music and Dance" Arthur begins singing, too. He goes up on the stage, and Eileen joins him—

two tiny, sharply edged figures in deep, rich color against the huge black-and-white screen images of Astaire and Rogers dancing, and they really seem to be there. They dance along with the stars on the screen, and then the two minuscule figures shift into black-and-white, and take over. Arthur is in tails, Eileen in a copy of Ginger's glittering gown with its loose fur cowl. And a chorus line of men in tails appears, tapping, like the men in *Top Hat*. It makes you gasp. Do Steve Martin and Bernadette Peters really dare to put themselves in Astaire and Rogers' place? Yet they carry it off. You may still be gasping when Arthur and Eileen leave the theatre (the exterior is a Reginald Marsh) and hear newsboys shouting the headlines. The police are looking for Arthur.

Herbert Ross has never shown much audacity in his other screen work, and when a director has been as successful as Ross has been with bland muck (*The Sunshine Boys, The Turning Point, The Goodbye Girl*), and has even been honored for it, it certainly takes something special to make him plunge in. Ross didn't go in far enough, but this is still quite a plunge. Dennis Potter's idea—obvious, yet strange, and with a pungency—provided the chance of a lifetime; Ross's collaborators must have felt it, too, and possibly they came up with ideas he couldn't resist. He had a superlative team. The production designer was Ken Adam, who designed the eight most imaginative James Bond pictures and also *Dr. Strangelove, Barry Lyndon,* and *The Seven-Per-Cent Solution*. The film's greatest splendors are those re-created visions—particularly the coffee shop with Arthur and Eileen as nighthawks, and Jimmy's Diner, which has a sliding glass wall, so that the Accordion Man can slip out into the rain to dance. Among its more obvious splendors is an Art Deco Chicago bank in which Arthur, who has tried to get a loan to open his own music shop and been turned down, dreams that he's deluged with money: to the music of "Yes, Yes!," performed by Sam Browne and the Carlyle Cousins, he and the banker (the matchless Jay Garner) and a batch of chorines perform in a dance montage that suggests the harebrained variations of Busby Berkeley montages.

The choreographer, Danny Daniels, does each number in a different theatrical style, and he palpably loves the styles that he reworks, especially the lowdown, off-color ones, like Walken's "dirty" sandwich dance—he's wedged between two blowzy whores. With the exception of a few routines with chorus girls as Rockette-style automatons, Daniels' choreography isn't simply dance—it's gag comedy, in which each dancer has his own comic personality. The dances are funny, amazing, and beautiful all at once. There are no problems of pacing here (except that a few numbers are too short and feel truncated). Several of them are just about perfection. And with teasers—comedy bits that prick the imagination. Bernadette Peters has a big production number ("Love Is Good For Anything That Ails You") that's like a dance of deliverance. Her classroom is transformed into something palatial and white, with children tapping on the tops of miniature grand pianos, and with her in silver and white, shimmying down the center aisle. (All the costumes are by Bob Mackie.) And when Arthur dreams of himself as a happy man, settled down with both Joan and Eileen, the three of them mouth "Life Is Just a Bowl of Cherries," like a radio trio. It's an indication of the depth of Jessica Harper's performance as the little witch Joan, shrivelled by repression and hatred, that it takes a second to recognize her as the pretty brunette in the trio.

The cinematographer, Gordon Willis, provides the lighting to carry out Ken Adam's visual ideas, and it's different from anything that I can remember Willis's ever doing before. The movie is about ordinary experience in a blazing, heightened form, and Willis keeps the level of visual intensity phenomenally high. At times, the color recalls the vivid, saturated tones in the 1954 *A Star Is Born*: the images are lustrous, and are often focussed on the pinpoint of light in the dreamer-characters' eyes when they envisage the pleasures celebrated in the songs. Eileen's eyes switch on and off, and so do the Accordion Man's; Arthur is possessed by the dream—his eyes are always on. My eyes were always on, too: even when I wanted to close up the pauses between the actors' lines, there was never a second when I wasn't fascinated by what was happening on the screen.

Despite its use of Brechtian devices, *Pennies from Heaven* doesn't allow you to distance yourself. You're thrust into the characters' emotional extremes; you're right in front of the light that's shining from their eyes. And you see the hell they go through for sex and money. Arthur, the common man with an itch, will do just about anything. When he blurts out something about his wife to Eileen, he covers his traces blubbering about how horribly she died in an accident, and then uses the invented tragedy to soften up Eileen so he can hop on top of her. He's a bastard, but you're not alienated from him; the songs lead him by the nose. As it turns out, the one character whose dream comes true is the pinched and proper Joan, who has dreamed of taking revenge on Arthur for his sexual demands on her.

There are cruel, rude awakenings; maybe they should be more heartlessly tonic, more bracing. But they do give you a pang. When Eileen is happily dreaming away in her classroom, seeing it as a tap dancers' paradise, with the children tapping and playing musical instruments, the principal comes in, enraged by the noise that the kids are making, and he takes a ruler and smacks the hands of a fat boy—a boy who has been proudly blowing on a tuba in her dream. The injustice to the boy—the humiliation—is one of those wrongs that some people are singled out for. The boy is fat, Arthur is horny, Eileen is gullible, the Accordion Man is inarticulate. This double-edged movie supplies a simple, basic rationale for popular entertainment. It says that though dreamers may be punished for having been carried away, they've had some glorious dreams. But it also says that the emotions of the songs can't be realized in life.

There's something new going on—something thrilling—when the characters in a musical are archetypes yet are intensely alive. This is the first big musical that M-G-M has produced on its lot in over a decade. The star, Steve Martin, doesn't flatter the audience for being hip; he gives an almost incredibly controlled performance, and Bernadette Peters is mysteriously right in every nuance. Herbert Ross and Ken Adam and Danny Daniels and Gordon Willis and Bob Mackie and the whole cast worked at their highest capacities—perhaps were even inspired to exceed them. They all took chances. Do you remember what Wagner said to the audience after the première of *Götterdämmerung*? "Now you have seen what we can do. Now want it! And if you do, we will achieve an art." I am not comparing *Pennies from Heaven* with *Götterdämmerung*. But this picture shows that the talent to make great movie musicals is out there, waiting.

.   .   .   .   .   .

Reds represents an enormous amount of dedication and intelligence. It's absorbing, and you feel good will toward it. But it's rather a sad movie, because it isn't really very good. You can see that Warren Beatty, who was the producer, the director, and the co-writer (with the British dramatist Trevor Griffiths), and is also the star, is deeply involved with the material—the American journalist John Reed's participation in the Bolshevik Revolution—but the movie keeps backing away from its subject. It's possible that Beatty, who had been thinking about the possibility of doing a film on Reed for about ten years before he began discussions with Griffiths, in 1976, got so far into the material and changed his thinking so many times that he lost the clarity needed to dramatize it. The excitement that he must once have seen in Reed's life leaked out. The film is tentative, full of doubts and second thoughts and fifteenth thoughts; directors often grow past their most long-cherished projects.

There's clear evidence of what's missing: In order to brief the audience on what the Greenwich Village bohemians of the 1915–20 period were all about—how the stimulus came from a combination of new ideas about art and sex and politics—Beatty includes documentary footage of survivors from that era. Some thirty-two contemporaries, associates, or acquaintances of John Reed and his wife, Louise Bryant, speak to an offscreen interviewer and give us quick impressions of Reed and Bryant and those times. These "witnesses," who are in their eighties and nineties, include such people as Rebecca West, Henry Miller, Roger Baldwin, Dora Russell, Scott Nearing, Hamilton Fish, George Seldes, Will Durant, and Arthur Mayer. What works against the movie is that they are all much peppier and more vital than the actors. These witnesses had an exhilarating youth, and even now, crumbling before our eyes, they're still enjoying themselves. (Several have died since Beatty interviewed them. Regrettably, in the movie they're all robbed of identity—probably out of fear that names at the bottom of the screen might suggest a TV news show.) Most of them are spirited talkers, for whom words and ideas have the excitement of wonderful, sensuous toys. You can't believe that Beatty as Reed and Diane Keaton as Louise Bryant belong to the same generation as the witnesses; when these two drop a bit of political information, their voices go dead, as if they didn't expect anyone to be listening. Beatty could be reciting from a manual, and Keaton might be dubbed—the words don't seem related to anything going on in her head.

Yet part of what makes *Reds* absorbing is Beatty's struggle to get inside the reckless revolutionary who was perhaps the best first-person, eyewitness journalist this country has ever had, and who, in 1920, less than two years after writing his classic of romantic reporting, *Ten Days That Shook the World*, and a few days before his thirty-third birthday, died in Moscow, of typhus and a stroke. (In Godard's *Breathless*, a celebrity movie director is asked what his ambition is, and he answers, "To become immortal, and then to die.") It's often remarked that Reed is the only American buried in the Kremlin (though he isn't). What is less often noted is that the powers inside the Kremlin proceeded to alter subsequent editions of his book, and, as the film indicates, that he had the evidence for disillusionment before he died, although he couldn't bring himself to abandon the cause that had brought him fame and given his life purpose. *Reds* isn't about the folly of a handsome, gifted Harvard man who sacrificed himself to bring about a system that turned out to be a repressive, dictatorial one; it's about a man who died for an ideal. That, in actors' terms, is an almost holy subject.

Reed's life hasn't been dramatized, exactly; candles have been lighted and then nervously snuffed out. As a producer, Warren Beatty is not nearly as rigorous with himself as, in all likelihood, he would be with another director or another writer. With others, he would have insisted on the clarity about characters and situations which made *Bonnie and Clyde* and *Shampoo* sharp and to the point. He would never have permitted the three-hour-and-twenty-minute length of *Reds*. It's because of the way *Reds* wavers and searches for what it's trying to say that it needs the length. Yet wavering and wobbling are somehow integral to Beatty's anxious—almost yearning—approach.

The script is an honorable try at an impossible task: clarifying the various aspects of an undefined epic theme. The principal structural weakness is, I think, that the writers didn't work out a scrutable character for Louise Bryant. *Reds* is conceived as a love story set against a background of bohemian living and revolutionary fervor, and so the two roles are of almost equal importance. But somewhere inside *Reds* the idea may be floating around that a man who gets caught up in inciting workers to Communist revolution is relatively clearheaded (even if events prove him shortsighted and foolish), while a pretty woman can't be a revolutionary—only the consort of revolutionaries. Louise Bryant is presented as a tiresome, pettishly hostile woman—dissatisfied because she isn't taken seriously but not giving anyone reason to take her seriously. She complains because Reed spends too much time at the events he writes magazine articles about, and with workers' groups, and in bull sessions with his Greenwich Village cronies (Maureen Stapleton as

Emma Goldman, Max Wright as Floyd Dell, Edward Herrmann as Max East-man, and many others). Even in 1916, when she and Reed are part of the Provincetown Players—sometimes called the happiest group of bohemians ever to inhabit the American scene—neither appears to be having much fun. Louise is a combination of a giddy dilettante, a groupie, and a driven woman (she has a lot of Catherine in *Jules and Jim* in her), and she's always griping or storming off somewhere. Reed seems to spend the entire movie trying to placate her, and his close friend Eugene O'Neill (Jack Nicholson) is in love with her, yet we're never shown what either of them sees in her. (She's Cath-erine without the magic.) And we never learn what is crucial, and what might have given Diane Keaton a clue to how to play the part: Is Bryant's jealousy of Reed that of an untalented woman or a talented one? It takes Keaton a long time to get any kind of bearings; at the start her nervous speech patterns are anachronistic—she seems to be playing a premature post-hippie neurotic.

Beatty and Griffiths probably didn't feel free to invent a character for Louise Bryant; they tried to stay close to what is known about her. But by the second half they give up on the messy currents of sexual politics and have her set off on a (fictitious) dangerous journey to go to Reed, who has been imprisoned in Finland. She stows away in New York on a freighter bound for Norway, goes through a terrible storm, and then begins a long trek across the icy tundra, on and on, painfully making her way across snowy wilds and wastes in scenes that seem to belong to a different picture (something Zhiva-gooey). And then the film embraces her, because she's doing what a woman is supposed to do—go through any hardships to be with her man—and, of course, she finds herself by giving up everything for love. This resolution of her character doesn't develop out of what we saw in the first half—it's a deni-al that there was any point or value in her thrashing about, presumably trying to figure out what independence might mean for a woman, and getting hag-gard from the strain.

Beatty gives a very touching performance—it's also too touching. If he was concerned about playing a character so much younger than he is, he needn't have been; he's great to look at, he is unquestionably a star, and he's remarkably subtle in the way he tunes in to whoever is in a scene with him. But he's still presenting himself (as he did on a much simpler level in *Heaven Can Wait*) as bewildered, shaggy, eager. He makes himself appealing by shy stammering and graceful gaucherie that emphasizes his height. In his room in Moscow, he keeps bumping his head on the chandelier, or just remembering in time not to. Beatty is a showman who aims to please the audience. He plays so much on what the audience responds to in him—the all-American combination of innocence and earnestness—that he's in danger of turning into Li'l Abner. When, as Reed, he brings a Christmas present to Louise, it's a puppy *gift-wrapped in a box*; he's petting the audience, tugging at its sleeve—taking out insurance on the movie, by making it inoffensive. And maybe that's why he says his lines about economic democracy with so little conviction—he doesn't expect you to be interested in any of that. As Reed, he doesn't let his energy come through, and the role needs it. John Reed was notoriously boyish, but he was also a spellbinder and a bit of a rake and a forceful writer, with an ear for fine adjectives. We don't get to see that side of him. Louise is the aggressor, and he's so timid that their only believable coming together is during the high they both experience in Russia while the actual revolution is taking place. And, of course, this simultaneous historical and personal climax is too movieish; it's the Big O, all right.

The politics aren't central to the relationship between Reed and Bryant; we don't know what is, exactly. The political discussions are like footnotes in search of a thesis. The script provides a pretty fair cram course in the opposition of some American groups to the First World War, in the split of the American Socialist Party, and in the steamroller tactics of the Russian leaders, especially Zinoviev (the novelist Jerzy Kosinski), but most of this impinges on the story only by taking Reed away from playing house with Bryant. Her distress has been given no weight; she's essentially in the position of the little movie wife crying, "Please don't go up to break the sound barrier tonight, dear." And finally she actually says that if he goes to Russia again "I'm not sure I'll be here when you get back." (It's not the film's proudest moment.)

The picture, with its daring subject—the romantic life of an American Communist—is extremely traditional, and in movies traditional means derivative. The visual rhetoric is often simply too familiar to stir the feelings it's meant to, and the comic devices (Reed ineptly trying to cook dinner and burning it, for example) may have you staring blindly at the screen. In technique, *Reds* is the least radical, the least innovative epic you can imagine. It's in expensively ritzy big-historical-movie taste; the palette is beautiful but so limited that you ache for some bright color. (The reds are too subtle even to be felt as red.) The film doesn't look posed; it has movement, and there are fine shots of the Russian railway stations and of streets with beacons—shots that are sensitive to Constructivist values. But the images don't connect up dramatically, and the cinematographer, Vittorio Storaro, who's a master of rich interiors, can't do much for the Reeds' rather drab living quarters in the Village, in Provincetown, and in Croton-on-Hudson.

The same instinctive showmanship that robs Beatty's performance of force robs the movie of content. Whatever he started out to make the picture for, he has replaced it with stale gags and bits of business that he thinks will work with an audience. He must have been so concerned to provide the film with distraction and comedy relief that by the time he finished, that was just about all that was left. The short, disjointed scenes fade out or hurtle against each other and don't seem to get anywhere. And gags that worked for Beatty before—such as telling a joke that nobody laughs at, a routine that played well because it went against the grain of *Bonnie and Clyde* and *McCabe & Mrs. Miller*—become the grain of this picture.

Beatty has his strengths. He keeps the actors close to us—he has a feeling for intimacy. And he knows how to use actors. He has a trained instinct, and he doesn't let them get away with fakery. The jitters and freak exhilaration of Jack Nicholson's recent performances are gone. He isn't just throwing off sparks here. His mannerisms have been straitjacketed, except for the bare minimum—the lurking malevolence, the eyes rolling back, one leering high-flying eyebrow. As O'Neill, Nicholson gives matters some consideration. He sinks down into himself and plays a quiet, deeply bitter man, who makes each word count. Though he manages the O'Neill mustache and the dark-eyed, taciturn stare and the famous "tragic handsomeness," I'm not sure that he's convincing as O'Neill. (Nicholson's own personality is very strong.) But he holds you as Nicholson the sly; he has the art of making almost any line sound dirty. And, maybe because of Beatty's respect for him as an actor, Nicholson's scenes are carefully shaped, and self-contained, like set pieces in a play. I found the film's conception of O'Neill embarrassing, but Nicholson is perversely enjoyable—this O'Neill gets to express contempt for American intellectuals when their eyes shine with Communist faith, and he gets to tell Louise off. (Something Reed never does.)

Gene Hackman (who was Beatty's brother in *Bonnie and Clyde* and also worked with him earlier, in *Lilith*) appears, unbilled in the ads, in the small part of a magazine editor; he's too good for his role—he has such audience rapport that he jumps out from the screen. Beatty directs Kosinski (who looks like a demonic eagle) so that his Zinoviev is a totally rational, understandable bureaucrat-villain. Zinoviev, who isn't interested in anyone's personal problems, is a foil for Reed; he provides a full-blown example of the ruthlessness that Reed shows only in his brief organizing period. And Beatty subdues the loud overactor Paul Sorvino, who gives a believable, muted performance as Louis Fraina, the Italian-born spokesman of the Communist faction that Reed's group is at odds with. (The secret seems to be the soft Italian accent; it gives Sorvino an Old World dignity.) None of the performances are bad (with the one crucial exception), and many of them—such as Roger Sloman's as Lenin and Dolph Sweet's as Big Bill Haywood (one of the other Americans buried at the Kremlin)—are too brief.

The best is Maureen Stapleton's Emma Goldman. When I heard that Stapleton was playing Emma, I groaned, thinking how ethnically wrong she would be. What I forgot was that she is (on occasion) a great actress: she doesn't need the Russian Yiddish inflections. When her Emma talks about how the new revolutionary government is jailing radicals and shooting dissenters—when she talks about anything—her simple concentration on the act of communicating what she's saying to the person she's talking to makes you listen intently. There's purity in her acting, and warmth. And she gives Emma just the right edge of asperity; this Emma Goldman is not a woman who believes in wasting her time. (The one insight that we get into Louise Bryant is in a dialogue exchange with Emma late in the film; Emma, apologizing to her, says, "I was wrong about you," and Louise says, "So was I.") Diane Keaton, who makes an enormous effort to deal with her hopeless role, is much more secure with Stapleton—and even with Nicholson—than she is in her improvisatory-style scenes with Beatty.

The movie could have used a little grunge—Louise coming home to find her husband romping around the house with a naked woman, for example. As it is, Reed is such a fine, courtly fellow, bringing home flowers (lilies, yet), that we can't believe he has affairs, and Louise's jealous anger makes no sense. And we could have used the details of the Finns' arresting Reed—he was carrying diamonds worth roughly fourteen thousand dollars and fifteen hundred dollars in currency, which the Comintern leaders had entrusted to him, to help foster Communism in America. But the absence of grunge is part of the film's slightly unworldly appeal. The pragmatic Emma Goldman has the courage to say what Reed can't: "The dream that we had . . . is dying." She lays out the facts and says that the system "cannot work." He says, "It's just the beginning," and Beatty does some of the best acting he has ever done in these scenes, when Reed, who is near death, has to believe. Beatty uses his eyes for very convincing pain when he's playing lost and hurting. Near the end, there's an almost great moment when Reed is on a train that's attacked by counter-revolutionary forces, and a Red Army caisson rolls out of the train and goes after them, and he chases after it as fast as he can. At the start of the film, he has been in Mexico, racing after one of Pancho Villa's wagons and climbing aboard. Now, wracked by illness and doubts, he's still running toward the revolution. It would truly be a great moment if the logistics of the scene didn't have to be puzzled out.

Reds is like the reverse of a Graham Greene novel: it's about the beauty of an American idealist's good intentions. And its saving grace is the beauty (and surprise) of Warren Beatty's solemn high intentions. In an almost childlike way, he vindicates the old Communist Left: the picture says that promises that couldn't be kept are not the same as promises broken.

December 21, 1981

Flag Nag

When Arthur Penn goes wrong, he goes laboriously, painfully wrong, and the moments of talent that stick out are so jarring that they seem to make things even worse. *Four Friends*, his first film since *The Missouri Breaks*, in 1976, is way out of tune and so miscalculated in its rhythms that some of us sit there squirming. The actors are dim—they're colorless and rather lost. But they don't come up with flamboyant howlers. They don't need to. Penn somehow manages to have them do relatively small things that are so off they erupt in your head: when the meant-to-be-vibrant young heroine (Jodi Thelen) speaks up in her tweety-bird voice and delivers a line such as "I'm so tired of being young," the words carry a ball and chain of significance; when an aristocratic rotter (played by James Leo Herlihy) arches an eyebrow, it's like a cannon going off.

Four Friends was probably inspired by the Ettore Scola film *We All Loved Each Other So Much*, which opened here in 1977, and which is also about the friendship of three men and the woman each of them loves at some time—a friendship that for Scola spans postwar Italian social history and for Penn spans the American social changes of the sixties. Scola, whose raffish, slapstick melancholy may in fact have been influenced by Penn's mingling of tones in the 1967 *Bonnie and Clyde*, takes his four characters from youth to middle age. Penn takes his from adolescence to maturity. The script is a semi-autobiographical account by Steve Tesich of the arrival in this country of a Yugoslavian working-class boy, Danilo, who comes with a big, heavy symbolic trunk—it seems to be full of solid values. The story of Danilo's growing to manhood in the America he loves is—although Tesich would probably disagree—deeply conservative. Danilo and the heroine may be opposed to the Vietnam War and may take all the correct anti-Establishment positions, but they're also always learning life's important lessons. An immigrant himself, Steve Tesich trumpets the values that each immigrant generation has trumpeted. There's a wholesome, beefy moralism in his writing which goes right back to the behavior of stalwart movie heroes of the past. And Arthur Penn, who in *Bonnie and Clyde* and *Alice's Restaurant* helped define the counterculture, and was even smug about it in *Little Big Man*, tries to make Tesich's vision express his own feelings. It's no wonder we writhe in our seats: their two sensibilities don't mesh.

In East Chicago, Indiana, in his last year of high school, Danilo (Craig Wasson), a steelworker's son, and his closest friends—a tall Wasp, Tom (Jim Metzler), and a short, pudgy Jewish boy, David (Michael Huddleston)—are all, to varying degrees, in love with Jodi Thelen's Georgia. Whenever she's in Danilo's thoughts (he is the most smitten), the soundtrack apprises us of the fact by supplying Ray Charles singing "Georgia on My Mind"—a great version of a great song that does not deserve to be used so promiscuously, and as if the Georgia in the title meant no more than Irene or Sweet Sue. The film's Georgia is so naturally sensual that when she performs on her clarinet in the school orchestra—it's Dvořák's *"New World" Symphony*—she has to get up and wiggle her hips to the music. (No high-school orchestra that I've ever heard would arouse this much erotic intensity.) *Four Friends* combines the worst of the Freudianism and self-pity of the William Inge–Elia Kazan *Splendor in the Grass* with the worst of the big immigrant theme of Kazan's *America America*. Georgia, a would-be dancer who, at sixteen, sees herself as an artist and a free spirit, and says that Isadora Duncan's soul is in her, loves Danilo and wants to have her first sex experience with him. But Danilo, who writes poetry, is too frightened to leap at the chance, and she, offended, makes do with Tom. Danilo goes off to study at Northwestern, and David goes into his father's mortuary business. When, some three years later, Georgia becomes pregnant and Tom, who isn't interested in marriage, goes off to war, she marries the obliging David. At the wedding, Danilo tells her she'll never dance, and he goes back to college, where he has acquired a chin beard like Solzhenitsyn's and a rich, crippled roommate, Louie Carnahan (Reed Birney).

In order to accommodate a whole catalogue of symbolic events of the sixties—everything from a race riot to the landing on the moon—the plot bounces along exhaustingly. The enfeebled roommate, who's into astronomy, talks about stars colliding "as if to embrace," and dreams of making it with a woman before he dies. When the restless Georgia becomes fed up with her middle-class existence, she takes off, at Christmastime, leaving the baby behind with the ever-obliging David. She goes to Northwestern to see Danilo; he isn't there (he's back in East Chicago, asking his father's blessing for his coming marriage to Louie's sister Adrienne), but she sees the bedridden Louie, and, sizing up the situation, she undresses and gives him a Christmas present. When Louie is put in the ambulance that will take him to the airport for a trip home, he's happily singing "Georgia on My Mind." In *Breaking Away*, which Tesich also wrote, the director, Peter Yates, lightened Tesich's humor, but Penn, trying for a large-scale social vision, brings out its hearty bouquet.

Louie and Adrienne's parents are played by James Leo Herlihy and Lois Smith, and a creepier, more decadent pair you've never seen. In the film's flossiest sequence, set on the Carnahan estate on Long Island, the wedding celebration comes to a violent, tragic end, and the shocked Danilo goes to work driving a taxi in New York City. Meanwhile, Georgia has come to the city and become a hippie. Danilo finds her dancing barefoot in the street, in water from a fire hydrant. He tells her, "I wake up in the morning loving you. I go through the day loving you. I go to sleep loving you." But she says, "Not now. . . . I don't know." So Danilo goes back to the steel mills, dragging his trunk and searching for his honest roots. And pretty soon we get crosscutting between Danilo in a full beard folk-dancing in the sunshine with his immigrant-worker friends and Georgia and her soul-sick druggie-hippie pals at a strobe-lighted psychedelic revel that features acid and a suicide in flames. It's health versus sickness, life versus death. And the movie carefully spells out which side it's on.

Although Danilo is against the Vietnam War, when he sees a flag being burned at a Don't Fight in Vietnam rally he's upset. Danilo-Tesich believes in a proper respect. *Four Friends* views the American sixties as a sturdy burgher from central Europe might: these kids don't appreciate their freedom; they have a lot of growing up to do. There's something disgusting in the obviousness of the stern Old World steelworker father who doesn't want his son to go to college and the careworn mother who's always slaving over a hot stove. I haven't seen a mother this old and careworn in an American movie in decades. What is she doing, huddled over in misery all the time? She has only one son and one husband—how much agony can the cooking be? And there's Georgia, who has to learn her lesson—has to accept the responsibility of being a mother and has to mature enough to appreciate the vitality that Danilo represents. At the end, Danilo prepares for his new life: he makes a ritual of burning his symbolic trunk, and he and Georgia and her child stand firmly facing the future, along with Tom, who has acquired an Oriental wife and her two children, and David, who has also found himself the right woman. This foursquare optimism is much harder to take than cynicism or disillusion, because we're supposed to learn from it, and what we're supposed to learn is how lucky we are to be Americans. We'd have to be terrible fools not to know that. And we'd have to be moral idiots not to be disturbed by what is entailed in our good fortune. There's a flag-waving underlayer to this picture's love affair with America the melting pot; Tesich is the screenwriter as national cheerleader. When the three high-school boys are out in the streets playing woodwind and horns and serenading Georgia, they're like *The Spirit of '76*.

At the end, when Danilo tells his hardworking father (Miklos Simon) that he has never seen him smile, the father chuckles and tries to oblige; he has to screw up his face to do it, and it's a cockeyed grin. I think it may be the only genuinely funny thing in the movie, and it seems to be there as an iconic seal of confidence in the future. Mostly, we get detestable fake epiphanies: when Danilo has been shot (not fatally) and is in the hospital, his father mutters "America!" He's saying to his son, "That's what happens when you run around with Americans"—as if Danilo's getting hurt were proof of some kind of national degeneracy. And then we hear "The Star-Spangled Banner," faintly, ironically. Who is it who's making this comment? Is it actually Arthur Penn—is he backing up the father's fatuousness? This love-hate confusion inflates the importance of the film. It's all one great big ambivalent message. Doesn't Penn understand that in *Bonnie and Clyde* he intuitively celebrated the country, and that when he sets out to do it consciously here he merely falsifies it? Lois Smith has a peerless example of the indefinably sad, indefinably symbolic Lois Smith scene, in which she says, "The excess of all this is a little staggering." Then she lets out a yelping sound that's like the grandmommy of a scream. Arthur Penn shouldn't let anyone in this movie use the word "excess."

· · · · ·

*A*n immense amount of skill and planning must have gone into making *My Dinner with André*, which is like a mad tea party or a mad, modern Platonic dialogue about the meaning of life. It flows smoothly and easily, creating the illusion that we are simply listening in on the dinnertime conversation of the playwright Wallace Shawn and the former avant-garde theatre director André Gregory. But it has a beautiful structure, and the two men have turned themselves into perfect foils. The premise of the movie is that they haven't seen each other since 1975, when André, after directing a play of Wally's at the Public Theatre, dropped out—took off on a spiritual quest for "reality," which led him around the world. Actually, they taped their conversations two or three times a week for three months, and then Shawn worked for a year shaping the material into a script; though they're playing comic distillations of aspects of themselves, they had to learn their lines and rehearse with the director, Louis Malle.

Wally persuades André to tell him what he has been up to, and the thin, ascetic, hawklike André, who's like the sum of all the crackpot glittery-eyed charmers in the world, pours out the record of his preternatural experiences. He just keeps going, in wave after impassioned wave, describing astonishing, preposterous adventures in the Polish forests, where he worked with Jerzy Grotowski's students (and during a group trance discovered he could hold his hand in a flame); in India and Tibet and in the Sahara, where he and a Buddhist ate sand; in the Findhorn colony in Scotland, where he talked to plants and made them grow; and even in Montauk, where he was buried alive in a death-and-rebirth ceremony. André is the kind of person who becomes ecstatically involved in every system of ideas that isn't grounded in anything and who is at the site of every imaginary volcano. Wally the imp gets a glazed expression and has a rough time keeping his eyes open. When he's more alert, his face registers total incomprehension and disbelief, and when André says that reading *The Little Prince* made him weep, Wally squints, stupefied. He throws in an occasional skeptical dart, and then, when he begins to talk, he plays warthog to André's soaring flights of mysticism. He claims that he feels no need for anything more than the satisfactions of the everyday, and he offers the grubbiest of small comforts as proof of the fullness of his life.

We see André from Wally's point of view, and we're put in the position of feeling, as Wally does, that André is talking ethereal gibberish. But there's a suave, hypnotic urgency in the theatricality of André's diction and manner, in the rapidity of his speech, even in the movement of his pointed long jaw. (It's a bit reminiscent of John Carradine's.) He's an aging man of the theatre—all profile, and with handsome long, flat ears, and long fingers that are constantly in motion, accompanying his words. He still has a full head of hair. (The much younger Wally is wide-faced and bald.) André's outpourings are those of the men and women of the theatre who became dissatisfied with the limits of stage performance and began to delve into para-theatrical cults. What André acts out for us is the questing that has torn so much of the modern theatre apart. And though he says that he feels he has squandered his life, you get the strong impression that he's still ready to take up the journey and head for the newest, most exotic hallucination.

Wally, the pragmatist and sensualist, may stand for our common sense and our comforts, but André, with his cadenced mumbo-jumbo and his love of being outrageous and the bemused, faraway gleam in his eyes, is the star and the hero. He's the more deeply funny of the two, and no doubt Wallace Shawn planned it that way. It's an amazing performance that André Gregory puts on, and we could not have the illusion of simply listening to a man pouring out the story of a willed (and thoroughly enjoyed) madness if Louis Malle didn't have the art to be self-effacing. Possibly, Shawn didn't need to turn himself into a Sancho Panza cartoon; he might have made a stronger case for the richness of everyday life. But his theatrical instinct was probably sound: he plays the earthly clown to André's fool of God. This is a bizarre and surprisingly entertaining satirical comedy—the story of the search beyond theatre turned into theatre, or, at least, into a movie.

·　　·　　·　　·　　·

*I*f movies were given grades for neatness, *Absence of Malice* would go to the head of the class. This trim, well-paced newspaper melodrama is remarkably lucid and easy to follow. A federal strike force in Miami investigating the disappearance (and presumed murder) of a union leader decides to stir things up by putting pressure on Michael Gallagher (Paul Newman), an honest small-scale liquor wholesaler, whose dead father was a Mafia leader and whose uncle is now the top man in the organization. The thinking of the federal agents is that the uncle either ordered the "disappearance" or knows who did, and that if Gallagher is put in enough of a bind he will find out what they want to know in order to clear himself. And so the head of the strike force (Bob Balaban) arranges to leak the false information that Gallagher is being investigated for involvement in the union leader's disappearance. Megan Carter (Sally Field) is the eager-beaver reporter who snaps up the story and spreads it on the front page. The longshoremen's union immediately refuses to let its men handle Gallagher's goods, and his business is shut down. The movie tells the story of how Gallagher turns the methods of the authorities and the newspaperwoman against them.

Paul Newman is leaner than ever, and, by contrast with his body, his large, silvery head has become more imposing—he's majestic, without losing his cockiness. In *Absence of Malice*, as in *Slap Shot* and *Fort Apache, the Bronx*, he seems to have transcended age. This may be because all his senses are quickened by the desire to act: there's nothing stale or brackish about Paul Newman's acting these days—it's bilge-free. The role of Gallagher needs a strong star face, because the character's emotions aren't written. Newman takes this parched construct—an intelligent, decent, and loyal man—and invigorates it by his swift movements. Gallagher is a man of few words. (The script is rather frugal.) Newman suggests a man who has lived by himself for so long that he has lost the habit of small talk, and his angry reserve gives the role some depth. Newman's Gallagher isn't someone you'd want to cross. This is a sly, compact performance, and in the one scene where Gallagher blows up, throws Megan on the floor, and hisses his rage right into her ear, Newman shows that his emotional force is stronger than ever, more concentrated. Newman hasn't turned himself into a mini-industry. He's a canny actor, and when he gets a real scene (in *Fort Apache*, walking the dead nurse and trying to bring her back to life, or, here, his explosion at the reporter's callousness, which has caused the suicide of Gallagher's close friend, Teresa, an achingly helpless, frightened woman, played by Melinda Dillon), he has the freshness in him to reach for and to achieve emotions that he has never attempted before—not on the screen, at least.

The directing, by Sydney Pollack, is controlled and efficient; he does a tight and tidy job. But there's a problem with the conception of Megan. The plot requires that she be basically insensitive and shallow, and she seems to be the kind of careerist who rises in the world because of her convenient dumb ruthlessness. And Sally Field's Megan, with her puckered, disappointed face, is the right type. Yet the movie also wants to cook up a bittersweet romance between Megan and Gallagher. So it softens her, and Sally Field tries to be appealing, and the film loses its assured tone in her scenes. It also isn't clear whether Gallagher is genuinely attracted to her or is manipulating her. (The director may have been afraid of making him a son of a bitch.) Megan's pathetic grapplings with journalistic ethics—with conscience and "responsibility"—might have had a satirical edge, but Pollack directs them as though they were serious and honest. If I hadn't seen Sally Field's work in the two-part TV movie *Sybil*, I would think from her performance here that she was a puny actress with no range. Having seen what she can do, I assume that there's courage in her staying with Megan's small soul and her tired expression and little-girl voice. But there's something off in the performance: Sally Field is skillful here, but she isn't interesting. Paul Newman can't help diminishing her. He gives you the feeling of a man thinking—you can see from the glint in his eyes that there's something going on—and she has nothing under the tacky surface. The writing doesn't help. The script, by Kurt Luedtke, a former newspaperman, is crisply plotted, but he doesn't write scenes to reveal anything more in the characters than the plot requires.

The film's neatness is a limitation, not a virtue. It's moderately entertaining, but it leaves no residue—except for Melinda Dillon's scenes, which violate the film's tidy functionalism and, momentarily, give it a crazy humanity. Melinda Dillon takes us so far inside Teresa that she has no protective covering—she's transparent, and we understand perfectly why Gallagher cherishes his long friendship with her. Teresa's scene at dawn, when a newsboy delivers the papers carrying the story that Megan has written about her, and she does a leaping little walk from one patch of lawn to the next, gathering the papers so her neighbors won't read it, has a touch of wobbly poetic terror. Melinda Dillon's work here and in *Slap Shot* and in the early part of *F.I.S.T.* adds up to something marvellously inventive. She may be that rarest of critters—an actress who thinks out completely new characters.

The opposite of her kind of acting is Bob Balaban's performance. He must think that he's doing Captain Queeg. He has devised an attention-getting nervous shtick—he spins his hands around while playing with rubber bands—and he never gives it a rest. Those rubber bands are the only character he's got; he carries functionalism so far that his acting is a joke. But the other minor roles are played with a high degree of professionalism and personality. Pollack likes actors—there's a scene or two in which attention is focussed in turn on Barry Primus, Luther Adler, Josef Sommer, Wilford Brimley, Don Hood, and John Harkins. Part of what makes *Absence of Malice* so much like a smart, modest melodrama of the thirties or the forties is Pollack's use of these performers as character types. (It's like the Warners stock company.) The whole picture is in the American-movie tradition of entertaining muckraking. In order to give the plot symmetry, Gallagher takes a sweet revenge that is morally questionable—and is also not available to most people whose names are dirtied in the press. And I doubt that people who are out to get even are as calm and well-balanced as Newman's Gallagher; he gives revenge class, so we can all enjoy it. It's the fantasy of getting even that people whose names never appear in the papers could still share in when Carol Burnett won her libel suit against the *National Enquirer*.

There have been indignant mutterings that this film represents an attack on the press; actually, it represents a fairly straightforward querying of journalistic practices. And why not? (It may be that some members of the press just don't like to see one of their own treated as a pain.) The only thing that's the matter with this material as a movie subject is that, with the exception of Newman's intensity and Dillon's scenes and a few of the character bits, you could get it all by reading an article; it might easily be an essay-question test in ethics, and, in fact, will probably be used that way in journalism courses. And very likely the students trying to puzzle out whether Megan is doing anything morally wrong will think in the same abstract terms that she uses, and will forget the words that Gallagher, bewildered by what she has done to Teresa, says to her: "Couldn't you see what it was to her? Couldn't you stop scribbling for a second and just put down your goddam ball-point pen? Didn't you *see* her?"

January 4, 1982

Shoot the Moon

*T*here wasn't a single scene in the English director Alan Parker's first three feature films (*Bugsy Malone*, *Midnight Express*, *Fame*) that I thought rang true; there isn't a scene in his new picture *Shoot the Moon*, that I think rings false. I'm a little afraid to say how good I think *Shoot the Moon* is—I don't want to set up the kind of bad magic that might cause people to say they were led to expect so much that they were disappointed. But I'm even more afraid that I can't come near doing this picture justice. The characters in *Shoot the Moon*, which was written by Bo Goldman, aren't taken from the movies, or from books, either. They're torn—bleeding—from inside Bo Goldman and Alan Parker and the two stars, Diane Keaton and Albert Finney, and others in the cast.

Diane Keaton is Faith Dunlap, and Finney is her husband, George. The Dunlaps have been married about fifteen years and have four school-age daughters. George is a nonfiction writer who's had a rough time, whipping up free-lance articles to meet the bills. But now he has become reputable, and they are doing better financially and are comfortable in their big old house in Marin County, across the bay from San Francisco. Their relationship has been poisoned, though. Faith knows all George's weaknesses and failures, and her knowledge eats away at his confidence. "You always remember the wrong things," he tells her. So he's having an affair, and feeling so rotten about it that he sobs when he's alone. And though he tries to keep the affair secret from Faith, she learns about it and is devastated. She can't look at him; her anxious eyes turn away. When he says, "You look really pretty," she can't stop herself from saying, "You seem surprised." Her angry misery is almost like a debauch; it makes her appear sodden. When she's with him, her face sinks—it's the dead weight of her sense of loss. At a book-awards ceremony in San Francisco, she overhears photographers who have taken pictures of the two of them decide on the caption "George Dunlap and friend." She blurts out, "I'm not his friend. I'm his wife." The movie begins on the eve of the day when she drives him out of the house, and it covers the next months of separation.

Their oldest daughter, the thirteen-year-old Sherry (Dana Hill), who has known about her father's adultery, feels that it's treachery to her and to the whole family. She can't forgive him, and after he has moved out she refuses to talk with him or to go along when he drives the younger girls to school or takes them away for the weekend. She shuts him out of her life, and the bond he feels with her is so strong that this is even more intolerable to him than being shut out of his own home. The other girls are sunshiny, but Sherry's face goes slack, and she looks burned out, like her mother. Faith, though, can look young and animated when she isn't with George; the years just fall away when she smiles her ravishing, clown's smile. Sherry's mood doesn't lift. She has had the most love and the most pain. She's the embodiment of what went wrong between her parents, and she's always there.

The movie isn't labored, like Ingmar Bergman's *Scenes from a Marriage*. It's essentially the story of the husband and father as supplicant for re-admission into the family, but it touches on things without seeming to address them directly. It's like a person with many sides. There are gags that pay off and keep on paying off—they turn into motifs. And sometimes the lines of dialogue that seem funny or ironic go through a variation or two and become lyrical. Parker has caught the essence of Bo Goldman's melancholic tone in the theme music—"Don't Blame Me," picked out on the piano with one finger. That, too, is turned into a joke and then has its original tone restored. There's an amazingly risky sequence, set in the restaurant of a Northern California inn, where George and Faith meet by chance and have a rowdy spat that's played off against screwball-comedy circumstances, with an elderly, quavering-voiced woman singer using the theme song in a hopeless attempt to drown out their shouting, and a man at the next table taking exception to their loud use of vulgar language. Many of the scenes have details that touch off very personal feelings: George pulling down the note pad that hangs on a string in his car to write excuses for his children's being late to school; one of the girls leaning toward *The Wizard of Oz* on the TV and chanting the Wicked Witch's threats slightly ahead of Margaret Hamilton. In this movie, the people have resources; they try things out. They take a step forward, and then maybe they move back. The tension that George feels with Faith is gone when he's with his perfectly shallow new lover (Karen Allen). She tells him, "You're my friend, George. I like you. I love you. And if you don't come through I'll find somebody else." She means it; she's adaptable.

The kids had a real presence in Bo Goldman's script for *Melvin and Howard* (his other screen credits include co-writing *One Flew Over the Cuckoo's Nest* and *The Rose*), and they have an even stronger one here. The family has been close in the loose, Northern California manner; the kids talk as freely as the parents do, and they're at ease, the way the house is. The girls have moments of imitating their high-and-mighty and short-tempered parents and then dissolving in giggles; they bitch each other heartlessly and then do something in perfect unison. When they squeal and carry on as they watch their parents on TV at the book awards, you know that this movie was written from observation and directed that way, too. The interaction of the four girls with each other and with their parents and the interaction of the girls with each parent's new lover are part of the substance of the movie. Alan Parker has four children, and Bo Goldman is the father of six; that may be the bond that made *Shoot the Moon* possible. This movie isn't just about marriage; it's about the family that is created, and how that whole family reacts to the knotted, disintegrating relationship of the parents. The children's world—a world of fragmented, displaced understanding—overlaps that of the adults and comments on it. And the texture of domestic scenes with bright, sensitive kids squabbling and testing keeps the film in balance. Bo Goldman has too much theatrical richness in his writing to make an audience suffer. He lets people be the entertainers that they are in life.

The four girls are inventive—they slip in and out of roles. Instinctive vaudevillians, they're always onstage. And whenever they're around, the movie is a variety show. Faith is sensitive to the comedy and drama of her family—she's constantly soothing and adjusting, and helping the seven-year-old get equal billing. When the morose, separated George takes the three younger kids out, he works so conscientiously to keep them happy that he sounds completely false; they feel his strain and try to humor him. When they're with him and his new lady, they try to play their parts, to keep tension to a minimum. (The comedy here is in how transparently they assume these roles.) And the sign of Sherry's confusion is her insistence on bringing up just the things nobody wants to have brought up, on forcing her parents into bad scenes. Yet she is never a pain. She keeps the atmosphere raw, and rawness is what makes this movie get to you.

Albert Finney, who has been sleepwalking in his recent movie appearances, is awake and trying out his reflexes. There's a profound difference in Finney; this is not a performance one might have expected from him. He uses all the impacted sloth and rage that show in the sag and weight of his big, handsome face. Locked out, George looks stunned, as if he'd been hit over the head—you can see the emotions fermenting in him that he himself isn't conscious of. He doesn't know that he's going to explode when he does. In a sequence in which he goes to the house doggedly determined to give Sherry her birthday present, Faith tells him that Sherry won't see him, and bolts the door. All he knows is that he has to get to Sherry. He kicks at the door and then he suddenly smashes a glass panel, sticks his arm in and pushes the bolt, rushes upstairs, grabs the child and spanks her, brutally. Sherry reaches for a scissors and holds him off with it. And then they huddle together, sobbing, and he, unforgiven, caresses her, pleading for a chance. It's one of the saddest, greatest love scenes ever put on film; you feel you've lived it, or lived something so close to its emotional core that you know everything each of them is going through. When George leaves, in disgrace, he trudges out carrying the present; then, a few paces away from the lighted house, he suddenly breaks into a run. Both as a character and as an actor, Finney seems startled and appalled by what has been let loose in him. His scenes seem to be happening right in front of us—you watch him with the apprehensiveness that you might feel at a live telecast. Keaton is Faith, but Finney seems both George and Finney. He's an actor possessed by a great role—pulled into it kicking and screaming, by his own guts.

Diane Keaton may be a star without vanity: she's so completely challenged by the role of Faith that all she cares about is getting the character right. Faith's eyes are squinched and you can see the crow's-feet; at times her face is bloated from depression, and she has the crumbling-plaster look of an old woman. Keaton is tall but not big, yet she gives you a feeling of size—of being planted and rooted, while George is buffeted about. He doesn't know how he was cast loose or what he's doing at sea. He has done it to himself and he can't figure out why. Throughout the movie, he's looking for a dock—he's reaching out to his wife. But Faith is unyielding; she doesn't want more pain. Very few young American movie actresses have the strength and the instinct for the toughest dramatic roles—intelligent, sophisticated heroines. Jane Fonda did, around the time that she appeared in *Klute* and *They Shoot Horses, Don't They?*, but that was more than ten years ago. There hasn't been anybody else until now. Diane Keaton acts on a different plane from that of her previous film roles; she brings the character a full measure of dread and awareness, and does it in a special, intuitive way that's right for screen acting. Nothing looks rehearsed, yet it's all fully created. She has a scene alone in the house in the early days of the separation—soaking in a tub, smoking a joint and singing faintly (a Beatles song—"If I Fell"), getting out to answer the phone, and then just standing listlessly, wiping off her smudged eyeliner. It's worthy of a Jean Rhys heroine; her eyes are infinitely sad—she's cracking, and you can sense the cold, windy remnants of passion that are cracking her. But this scene is a lull between wars. Faith is rarely alone: she still has her life around her—she has the kids and the house. (And that house, with its serene view, is itself a presence; it's upsetting when George smashes the door.) Faith can ignore George and start having a good time with a rather simple new fellow (Peter Weller)—a workman-contractor who puts up a tennis court for her in the grove next to the house. But George can't ignore her, because she's still holding so much of his life—the kids, the house, all the instinctive adaptations they had made to each other. George can't take anything for granted anymore.

Alan Parker and Bo Goldman circle around the characters, observing their moves and gestures toward each other; the movie is about the processes of adaptation. That's why that sequence at the inn is so funny and satisfying. In *Melvin and Howard*, it was a great moment when Howard Hughes got past his contempt for Melvin and they spoke together about the smell of the desert after the rain, and finally were friends and so close that they didn't need to talk. In *Shoot the Moon*, the only time that George and Faith reconnect is in their drunken dinner at the inn when they start eating out of the same plate and yell at each other, and then they wind up in bed together. What a relief it is for George—for a few hours he can live on instinct again.

This film may recall Irvin Kershner's 1970 *Loving*—a story of separating that had a high level of manic pain. But the wife in that (played with great delicacy by Eva Marie Saint) wasn't the powerhouse that Faith is. Faith doesn't back down when she and George fight, and her angry silence is much stronger than George's desperate chatter—Faith has no guilt. *Shoot the Moon* may also call up memories of *Long Day's Journey Into Night*, in the theatre or on the screen. But in that, too, the husband held the power. George is powerless. He has an extraordinary reconciliation scene with Sherry: she runs away from her mother on the night of a party celebrating the completion of the tennis court, and comes to find him, and they talk together on a pier, sitting quietly, with George's brown cardigan pulled around them both to keep out the chill. But when he takes Sherry back home and sees Faith and her lover and their guests and the strings of festive lights on the tennis court, he's filled with a balky, despairing rage—you can almost see his blood vessels engorging. He has been stripped of too much of his life; throughout the film he has been losing emotional control, breaking down—he can't adapt.

Alan Parker doesn't try to rush things or to prove himself. His energy doesn't come all the way through to the surface, as an American director's might; it stays under, and it's evenly distributed. George becomes resentful of any sign of change in Faith's or the children's lives, but the film doesn't over-emote—it looks at him and at the others very steadily. It's a measure of the quality of Parker's direction that no one in the picture asks for the audience's sympathy. When George is self-pitying, as he is in a sequence of visiting the ruins of Jack London's house and telling his kids what a great author London was and how someone set fire to the house the night before the great author was supposed to move in, his maudlin tone is played off against the girls' questions and remarks about London's marriages and children; they all project their own feelings onto the Londons—it becomes a comedy routine. This is an unapologetically grown-up movie. Though Alan Parker doesn't do anything innovative in technique, it's a modern movie in terms of its consciousness, and in its assumption that the members of the movie audience, like the readers of modern fiction, share in that consciousness.

Probably Parker couldn't have brought it all off with such subtlety and discretion if he hadn't had the collaborators who were with him on his other features—the producer Alan Marshall, the cinematographer Michael Seresin, the production designer Geoffrey Kirkland, and the editor Gerry Hambling. They must have helped free him to devote his full attention to the cast. He directs the actors superbly. Diane Keaton and Albert Finney give the kind of performances that in the theatre become legendary, and, in its smaller dimensions, Dana Hill's Sherry is perhaps equally fine. And the three child actresses—Viveka Davis as Jill, Tracey Gold as Marianne, and Tina Yothers as Molly—are a convincing group of sisters and the very best kind of running gag. Even George Murdock, who has a single appearance as Faith's dying father, is remarkable—the old man has a clear head. Parker has created a completely believable family and environment (the picture was all shot on location), and he has done it in the wet days and foggy light of a country and a culture that aren't his own. And he has given us a movie about separating that is perhaps the most revealing American movie of the era. *Shoot the Moon* assumes the intelligence of the audience, as *Bonnie and Clyde* did; it assumes that people don't need to have basic emotions labelled or explained to them. When you see *Shoot the Moon*, you recognize yourself in it. If there's a key to the movie, it's in one simple dialogue exchange. It comes at the inn when George and Faith are in bed, lying next to each other after making love. She talks about how much she used to love him and then:

FAITH: Just now for an instant there—I don't know—you made me laugh, George—you were kind.

GEORGE: You're right, I'm not kind anymore.

FAITH: Me neither.

GEORGE: You're kind to strangers.

FAITH: Strangers are easy.

January 18, 1982

Melted Ice Cream

*T*here are easily recognizable danger signals:

When a director announces that the movie he is working on is "ahead of its time," you can guess that he's in deep trouble, because what he's saying is that the public won't know enough to appreciate what he has done.

When a director announces that he is becoming a film "composer," you know he's saying that he doesn't have much in the way of a story or characters.

When a director says that his movie is about "fantasy and reality," you suspect he's carrying on in the ringmaster tradition of Fellini.

When a director starts talking about his "revolutionary" video-film technology, you squirm, because you're not sure you understand what he's saying, and the parts you do understand make you squirm even more.

Put it all together and it spells Francis Ford Coppola's *One from the Heart*.

This movie isn't from the heart, or from the head, either; it's from the lab. It's all tricked out with dissolves and scrim effects and superimpositions, and even aural superimpositions—there's a song track, with Crystal Gayle and the growler, Tom Waits, telling us the meaning of what we're seeing, and wailing words of wisdom. *One from the Heart* is like a jewelled version of a film student's experimental pastiche—the kind set in a magical junk yard; there's nothing under the devices but a hope of distilling the essences of movie romance. And so even when Coppola hits on something eerily charming, such as an image of Nastassia Kinski as a Las Vegas showgirl wriggling for the customers' delectation inside a huge, neon-outlined Martini glass, he doesn't tie it in to anything. It's there simply because Coppola thought of it and was able to do it. You get the feeling that the movie grew by accretion—that he didn't think out the character relationships but simply piled visual ideas and comedy bits on top of the small story he started with until the movie became so jewel-encrusted that the story practically disappeared from sight and the movie turned into something like a poet's salute to the banal silver screen.

Coppola and his studio resources are always present in this film, in the same way that Fellini has become the star of his movies. And people in the audience at Radio City Music Hall, where the film had two sold-out previews on January 15th, applauded the swooping-in and pulling-back camera movements and the special effects and the pretty, painted scenery representing Las Vegas, just as audiences at stage plays sometimes applaud the set or the costumes. Visually, the film has the kind of stylization sometimes seen in the dance numbers of M-G-M Technicolor musicals of the forties and fifties—a deliberately artificial glow. It is studded with references to other movies, and the whole thing might be regarded as a giddy, unimpassioned variation on Scorsese's *New York, New York*, which was set in the forties and employed a stylized, studio look though the actors talked in a semi-improvisatory, seventies-psychodrama manner. *One from the Heart* takes place in a studio-made Las Vegas, heavy on the neon and painted skies, and is set in a timeless present, with casual, throwaway dialogue.

When a director becomes the star of his movie—when his devices are chuckled over and applauded—the audience is, in a sense, applauding its own knowingness. And because it's a knowing audience it expects a lot. The chuckles are anticipatory, eager. They don't last as long as *One from the Heart* does, because eventually the audience realizes that there is nothing—literally nothing—happening except pretty images gliding into each other, and you can hear people saying to each other, "It's a pastry chef's movie," and "I didn't know Coppola had become such a ding-a-ling."

It's easier to get by with an empty hat in the context of Vietnam than it is in a metaphorical Las Vegas. In this fantasyland, Hank (Frederic Forrest), the stick-in-the-mud hero, is a partner in a junk-yard business called Reality Wrecking, and the heroine, Frannie (Teri Garr), who has been Hank's roommate for the past five years, works at the Paradise Travel Agency—but she has never been anywhere. It's the Fourth of July—Independence Day—and Frannie, bored with Hank, walks out on him. The holiday is treated like Mardi Gras, with crowds dancing through the street that the art director, Dean Tavoularis, has designed. All that day and night, the film crosscuts between Hank and Frannie, or they physically crisscross or go past each other, as Hank becomes involved with the showgirl and Frannie takes up with a singing and piano-playing Latin waiter (Raul Julia). Hank has a partner and confidant, played by Harry Dean Stanton, who looks tan and wiry and shows glimmers of a subversive sanity. Frannie has as her partner and confidante Lainie Kazan, whose décolletage is overpowering, but who has a frantic, funny routine talking about the horrors she goes through on dates as she dashes off to another one. Essentially, that's the cast and the story. These six flit about on the street set; everything seems to be happening on a large stage—as, in fact, it is. All we're asked to care about is whether Hank, who's in love with Frannie, will win her back. Or, rather, this story being negligible, what we're asked to respond to is Coppola's confectionery artistry.

Some artists become Jesus freaks; movie artists are more likely to become technology freaks. In interviews, Coppola has talked about directing from inside a trailer while watching the set on video equipment. This movie feels like something directed from a trailer. It's cold and mechanized; it's at a remove from its own action. The two main characters are always talking to each other through glass or when the other isn't there; Coppola seems more fascinated by reflections of the actors than by the actors themselves. And the video editing techniques that he uses seem to destroy the dramatic definition of the scenes; everything runs together—the movie is like melted ice cream. When the Mardi Gras crowds are milling about in the street, there's no excitement; the kind of energy that can be built into a sequence by conventional editing methods has been replaced by bland fluidity. The technique is self-cancelling. The most virtuoso effects—the ones that should reverberate with all the romance of the movie past—liquefy and are gone. Afterward, even your own thoughts seem to come to you by remote control, and a day later the picture is as blurry in the mind as the memory of a psychedelic light show.

Some directors have begun to use video as a tool—for keeping track of the continuity and for other subsidiary functions—but Coppola has got to the point of talking as if the video equipment itself would direct his movies. It's almost as if he'd got beyond directing—as if he has to make it more of a game by complicating it and putting technology between the film and himself. The most you can say about *One from the Heart* is that it's pretty, because, even at its loveliest, the imagery isn't expressive. The effects don't have any emotional meaning in terms of the characters, and so they don't mean anything to us, either. When people are frolicking in the street, people in the audience are whispering that it's a Dr Pepper commercial. Coppola has found a way to shrivel movie magic. *One from the Heart* is like a visualization of Warhol's "Everything is pretty."

Looking pale-eyed, Frederic Forrest is onscreen too much for the little he's given to do, such as a half grin of dumb pleasure when Frannie talks about how when they met she didn't expect to like him. Mostly, Hank mopes, and chases after Frannie, calling her name plaintively. And in the sequence in which he demonstrates his love for her by singing a song "from the heart" he's so maudlin you'd think it would confirm her in her decision to split. Forrest has been lighted by the cinematographer, Vittorio Storaro, who also shot *Last Tango in Paris*, as if he were Brando in that picture. At home, with part of his face in the shadow, he looks like a serious, deeply exhausted man—a Roman emperor in his last days—until he opens his mouth and talks like a sheepish dumb slob. Teri Garr is nippy and speedier. From her first movie roles, she has seemed to be a likable funnyface—a cartoon of herself; she's certainly not like anybody else. She's so slender here that she seems weightless, and she wears perhaps the wispiest wardrobe ever assembled for a movie heroine—she's always slipping in and out of her teddies or some other bit of gossamer, and when she dresses up for conquest she puts on a sleeveless, practically dressless red dress and spike heels. Dancing a brief tango with Raul Julia, she puts her spikes down very firmly, like a confident, hot pony. But she's spiritually weightless, too, and Hank's suffering when he loses her seems overscaled. The people in this movie are charming but not interesting.

Nastassia Kinski seems intended to be the spirit of something—of Vegas, perhaps, or of romance itself. (I would love to have a tape of Coppola explaining the role to her.) She's not only a Vegas showgirl; she's also a Fellini-esque circus girl—an acrobat. Her scenes are the least enjoyable (because she has no personality), but they're not painful, because she is very diffident and very lovely—a sad young vamp, slightly worn. The childlike dewiness that carried her through other roles is gone; Coppola has put a veneer of lacquer on her, and she smiles her big, empty smile as if she were visiting from another planet. She poses and cavorts on the hood of Hank's car and walks a high wire in his—yes—magical junk yard (which recalls Syberberg's set in *Our Hitler*). Her dialogue is flossy babble in which this junk yard reminds her of the Taj Mahal, but her blasé innocence protects her—flat-voiced, she seems to be saying lines that she learned without finding out what they meant.

The sets and the story suggest that we're going to see a musical, and that is how the film was described in advance publicity, but the nearest it comes is in its allusions to *Saturday Night Fever* and *Flying Down to Rio* and other musicals. There are no singers or dancers in the cast. I think that Coppola thinks it's a musical—or, at least, a "musical play" or a "fable with music," as he has also called it—because of the way the scenes slide into each other. It could be popular with kids who grow up addicted to video games, and they could use it to get high on, the way others have used *Fantasia*. But, except for the grace of the images and the amusing edge to the acting, it's like *South Pacific* without the music, and Coppola must have felt that this didn't quite do the job. Hence the song track, which, like the narration in *Apocalypse Now*, seems designed to plug up the holes. The bellyaching songs (Waits wrote them) become as draggy as Richard Baskin's songs in *Welcome to L.A.* And when you can understand the lyrics, that's when it's worst.

The set does have a wonderful grandiloquence, like a child's vision of a world's fair of the past, or something from one of those static English fantasies, such as *Stairway to Heaven*. But Coppola hasn't figured out what to do with it—maybe because there's no particular reason (except the metaphorical one) for the story to be set in Vegas. The original script, by Armyan Bernstein, was set in Chicago, and when Coppola rewrote it he didn't do anything to tie the characters in to the changed locale. There's nothing under the tutti-frutti sweetness of the surface (except, perhaps, boredom and impatience). If the movie is slight and evanescent, it's because Coppola has begun to think of art as invention—he has begun to think like Edison, or Preston Tucker, the automotive-design genius whom he frequently talks about. The climax of the film comes, really, in the end title that proclaims "Filmed entirely on the stages of Zoetrope Studios." Coppola has become so entranced by technical feats that he no longer thinks like a writer or a director. A man who can say, with the seriousness of a hypnotist, that new movie technology is "going to make the Industrial Revolution look like a small, out-of-town tryout" seems to have lost the sense of proportion that's needed for shaping a movie. The artist has been consumed by the technology. T. S. Eliot's "I can connect nothing with nothing" has become a boast.

.   .   .   .   .

Jack Nicholson may still have plenty of surprises in him. In the unheralded *The Border*, filmed largely on location in El Paso, Texas, by Tony Richardson, Nicholson plays a United States border patrolman whose job it is to shove Mexicans back to their side of the Rio Grande, and he gives a modulated, controlled performance, without any cutting up. Except for his brief appearance in *Reds*, this is the first real job of acting that he has done in years. The film also marks a change in the work of Tony Richardson: he has a major, muckraking subject, and he works to serve the material. Over the years, he has developed a considerable body of skills, and this may be the most unobtrusively intelligent directing he has ever done for the screen. It's a solid, impressive movie.

Charlie, the patrolman, hates his work; it fills him with disgust, because most of the patrolmen are in cahoots with the American businesses that hire wetbacks, and the patrolmen make their money—their big money—by closing their eyes to vans full of workers earmarked for their business partners. It's an ugly, corrupt life—persecuting enough Mexicans to keep the government bureaus happy while functioning as slave dealers. The trade sickens Charlie, but he gets caught up in it by the social-climbing idiocies of his wife, played by Valerie Perrine. When he was an Immigration investigator in the Los Angeles area, he had felt worthless and wanted to return to the Forest Service. But his wife talked him into transferring to the Border Patrol in Texas, because she had friends there, and now she and the wives of the other slave dealers belong to a Southwestern parody of upper-middle-class society: they shop for tight, bright clothes and decorate their gaudy dream houses, and the men wear expensive boots and cowboy hats and slap each other's backs at the barbecue parties held on the patios near the swimming pools. Charlie doesn't have the stomach for this camaraderie. If the loaded vans are discovered by any stray honest patrolmen, Charlie's pals may protect themselves by jailing the passengers or getting them killed.

Back in 1933, the picture *I Cover the Waterfront* caused a great stir by showing that when the captain of a ship smuggling Chinese illegals into California ports spotted a Coast Guard vessel heading toward him, he sank his human cargo—chained to go down swiftly. With any luck, *The Border* will cause a fuss, too, because it lays out—very graphically—the essential irrationality of government policies, and the cruelty that develops out of them. Working from a script by Deric Washburn, Walon Green, and David Freeman, and with the cinematographers Ric Waite and Vilmos Zsigmond, Richardson is able to encompass so much in the wide-screen frame that he shows how the whole corrupt mess works.

Charlie is a little like the hero of Kurosawa's *Ikiru*, who knew that he couldn't do anything big to fight the bureaucracy but was determined to have one small accomplishment to leave behind. Charlie is so wasted and fed up that he tries to do one simple, decent thing—he wants to feel good about something. Among the Mexicans living in an encampment on their side of the Rio Grande and waiting to make the trip over, he spots a round-faced young madonna, who has come from a village devastated by an earthquake. Played by Elpidia Carrillo, a twenty-year-old Mexican actress who suggests a dark, adolescent Ingrid Bergman, she is clear-eyed and natural—the image of everything unspoiled, and the opposite of Charlie's giggly sexpot wife. She has a beautiful, plump babe in arms and is accompanied by her younger brother. Later, she's in a group Charlie has to round up and arrest, and when she's in the prison camp her baby is stolen from her by thieves (working in collusion with the slave dealers) who arrange for infants to be sold to childless couples. Charlie tries to help her and her brother make it over the border safely in one of the vans, but things go horribly wrong, and she is injured and the boy is shot. Charlie can't help the wounded boy, who dies, but he's determined to restore the girl's baby to her. That's all he hopes to do. He has no designs on the girl; she represents an ideal of what people can be if they're not corrupted, and his belief in that ideal is about all he has left. It gets to the point where the only thing that can give his life any meaning is to reunite the girl and her infant. In order to do it, he has to fight his buddy in the Border Patrol (played by Harvey Keitel) and the boss of the unit (Warren Oates) and he goes through hell.

Tony Richardson handles the large cast with apparent ease. Keitel is subdued and believable. Valerie Perrine, who has been giving disgraceful performances for several years, plays the dumb-tart wife to whiny perfection. And Shannon Wilcox, who plays Keitel's wife, a more confident tart, has a lifetime of teasing in her big smiles and swinging walk. There are also some very scary thugs headed by Jeff Morris.

Nicholson does his damnedest to make this muckraking melodrama work. (Luckily, or maybe through shrewd calculation, he wears dark glasses in much of the picture, so we can't see if he's doing his trademark stunts with his eyeballs.) Charlie is at the center of the story: the corrupted, conscience-ridden, self-hating American wishing he could feel clean again. Maybe Nicholson hasn't yet regained the confidence or zest to be exciting (while staying in character) that he had in, say, *The Last Detail*, where he used his crazy-smart complicity with the audience. But probably that zest would work against the conception of Charlie, who has to be spiritually beat out. The movie might have been disastrous if anyone else had played the part. Nicholson is completely convincing as a man who has been living in dung up to his ears, and so when Charlie feels he has to do something decent before it covers his head, there's nothing sentimental about his need. It's instinctive—like a booze-soaked man's need for a drink of water.

February 1, 1982

The Man Who Understands Women

*P*ersonal Best is a celebration of modern American women's long-legged bodies. It's also a coming-of-age movie that shows what most of us go through—the painful experiences that later on we like to see as comedy. The surprise of this film—written, produced, and directed by the celebrated screenwriter Robert Towne (*The Last Detail*, *Chinatown*, *Shampoo*)—is that most of the story is told non-verbally, and character is revealed in movement. This is perhaps the first directing début by a writer that buries motivation and minimizes the importance of words. Towne may have had to cut a couple of strings off his fiddle, but he plays a great lush, romantic tune. He bears down only on sensory experience, and he uses the actors, who are in fact athletes, as dancers. He presents a physical world that few of us know much about—the world of women athletes—and when he shows the adolescent Chris Cahill (Mariel Hemingway) preparing for the start of a race by hammering a block into the ground it's like Melville doing a how-to chapter. This is a very smart and super-subtle movie, in which the authenticity of the details draws us in (as it does in Melville); Towne cares enough to get them right, and he cares about the physical world in a reverent, fanatic way. When he shows Chris and the other heroine arm-wrestling, he concentrates on their throbbing veins and their sinews and how the muscles play off one another. He breaks down athletic events into specific details; you watch the athletes' calves or some other part of them, and you get an exact sense of how their bodies work—it's sensual and sexual, and it's informative, too. This film celebrates women's bodies without turning them into objects; it turns them into bodies. There's an undercurrent of flabbergasted awe. Everything in the movie is physically charged.

Perhaps consciously, perhaps instinctively, Towne has used the basic schema of growing up: of self-love, of discovering and exploring your own body and then moving through narcissism to friendship with someone of the same sex—a friendship that is tinged with homosexuality or is combined with it, and in which the friend serves as guide and teacher—and then moving to love of the other sex. And he has so deeply imagined it within the setting of sports competition that it's as if the whole physical world were the embodiment of coming of age sexually. Towne's cameras make love to women the way the hero did in *Shampoo*: you can feel the warmth going out to them. The cinematography (by Michael Chapman, with a few scenes by Caleb Deschanel, who filled in when Chapman wasn't available) is soft-colored and generous. The imagery is rapt: you feel involved almost before anything happens. The two heroines—the young Chris and the more experienced Tory Skinner (Patrice Donnelly)—meet at the 1976 Olympic track-and-field trials, where Chris fails to make the team. Tory, who has qualified, helps her and falls in love with her. Over the next three years of preparing for the 1980 Olympics, they live together. Then Tory loses her—first because of the pressures of competition and the interference of the coach (Scott Glenn), and later because Chris falls for a boy. And they're such nice girls that you may feel bad about the misunderstanding between them—you want them to be friends. When Tory is competing against Chris in the 1980 pentathlon trials, the pain of rejection is too much for her, and she loses heart. It's up to Chris then to help Tory.

So little background information is provided that some people may think that Towne doesn't situate the story very well—that he hasn't brought us into it by showing where the characters come from and then developing them. But he doesn't need to. He excludes most of what would go into an ordinary sports film—college life, money problems, and much more about families. He doesn't explain the two heroines; he exults in them, and leaves them to explain themselves physically. When they make love, they are so tender with each other and so beautiful that it would take a very stern puritan to see anything wrong in their behavior. These two warrior women care for each other. They're loving friends, and as the cameras show them Chris and Tory can't be immoral any more than they can be mean or duplicitous—look at how honestly and openly they compete, look at how they stand, how they move. Their lovemaking begins playfully—it's more sensuous than erotic. But when they tease each other there's an erotic element in it. The movie (deliberately) takes a primer approach to sex: it begins with tickling. When Chris picks up a lamp so she can see the naked Tory's scarred knee better, it's a child's lamp in the shape of a pelican. And the same childlike approach is taken to Chris's first heterosexual experience: it's playful and exploratory.

Towne bathes you in his love for the strength and delicacy of women's bodies. You see Chris and Tory through fog, you see them upside down, reflected in water—you see them every which way, and you see every section of their bodies. The movie admires every part of them. There has probably never been a growing-up story presented on the screen so freely and uninhibitedly; even the 1954 Colette film *The Game of Love* (*Le Blé en Herbe*) was more circumspect. There isn't much dialogue, but it has an original, modern ease, and every line works on about four levels. The talk is so casual that sometimes you hardly register a joke until a second or two later, and then you laugh; you hear it after you've heard it. And sometimes the athletes tell jokes that the adolescents in the audience have heard before, and they laugh in recognition; Towne gets us all to laugh at the naturalness of joking. We've seen many movies on the same theme, but *Personal Best* feels unfamiliar, and it's this woozy, hip unfamiliarity that magnetizes us. Towne turns the heavy breathing of the women athletes working out into music; the sounds are sexual, and so are the images of ankles and hamstrings and thighs and crotches. The whole film is a series of open double-entendres. When the two girls arm-wrestle and then make love, there's an electric space heater in the room—the kind of heater that has coils that begin to glow, reach a certain intensity, turn orange and go off, and then start up again. And when the coach talks to Chris about running the hurdles or about anything else, he's also talking to her about Tory. The film orchestrates sexual maneuvers so that you take most of the moves in only partly consciously. You sense the pain that Tory feels when she loses Chris, and the pain that Chris, who is still finding her way, feels because she's hurting Tory. Chris is at that age when you're in a love affair that you don't understand and it's emotionally overwhelming to you.

Mariel Hemingway's Chris hasn't fully grown into her broad-shouldered body; it's the body of a Valkyrie jock while she's still a dear, giggly child with a radiant smile and a little kid's high, squeaky enthusiasm. When Denny (Kenny Moore), a water-polo player, meets her, we know that they're right for each other, because their voices match. (But there is no suggestion that Chris's heterosexual development is in any way morally preferable to her affair with Tory.) With her long, sun-streaked hair and her true-blue eyes, Chris is a beauty. She's also a visual comedy: almost six feet of muscle plus girlishness. The women athletes are all great-looking and all funny, because physically they have advanced so much faster than men's thinking about them has. They razz men flirtatiously, flaunting their own strength; the team clown is Emily Dole (the Throwin' Samoan), a heavyweight shot-putter. (In some sports, women are already hitting the men's records of only a few years ago; Mariel Hemingway worked out for eighteen months in order to be able to stand up next to the women champions who fill the screen.) When Chris and Denny are in the athletes' weight room, she gives him pointers about doing bench presses; while she's leaning over him talking about the weights, he's fixated on her genital area. She's a towering image of strength; when she's out with him and has to wait while he comes around to open the car door for her, she rolls her eyes in impatience, as if to say, "Get a load of this."

Chris the colt is touching because she doesn't know how to use her power, and when she's running, her anxious face, held down, is bobbing with her body. Essentially, the film is Chris's story: in the course of it she becomes a person. At first, her emotional range seems too limited for us to care about her, and she's rather blubbery and inert (like a hulking male jock) up to a particular moment: Denny has seen her to her door and returned to his car, when suddenly she leaps down the stairs, vaults over the fence, and says, "If you're not in a hurry, slow down." Until then, she has been acted upon, and Tory and the coach (who is her bridge to the other sex) and Denny, too, have all been watching her; now she wakes up and starts trusting her own impulses. But though she's the central character, physically Tory represents the film's ideal. When Tory runs, she's all of a piece, and she's thinking more clearly than at any other time. Patrice Donnelly, like most of the cast, hasn't acted before. Willowy yet strong, she's an Olympic hurdler. And when, at the end, Tory competes in the last pentathlon event, the eight-hundred-metre run, she moves like a beautiful machine. You don't see tension; what you see is the kind of transcendence that a great singer or a great dancer feels when every part of him is doing what it should and he's in a state of bliss. When you see her run, she seems to be sailing through the air, and you think, This is what all the training was for—so she could feel this way, and realize her highest physical capacities. That, of course, is what the title refers to. (In this sense, both girls win.) And you also see that the conception of the film is really inseparable from the performers.

Towne is esteemed for writing dialogue that allows actors to speak in their own voices—for adapting the dialogue to the actors, so that it doesn't sound forced or artificial. Here he has devised dialogue that enables the cast of athletes to sound natural. But he has gone beyond that: the movie has developed out of the adolescent gawkiness of Mariel Hemingway and out of the more recessive presence of Patrice Donnelly, who is part Shoshone and has an extraordinary profile—with her helmet of dark hair and her smooth skin, she looks like the women in Tuscan paintings. Her slightly flat nose contrasts with Hemingway's pretty little pug. They're an amazing pair—Donnelly, who has the neck of a goddess and eyes that cloud with suffering, and Hemingway, with her wide cheekbones, who's like a wonderful overgrown pet.

If there was a tipoff to Towne's emotional makeup, it was in the sensuous simplicity of the hairdresser played by Warren Beatty in *Shampoo*. When this hero's girl (Goldie Hawn) caught him with a girl friend of hers and started a chain of accusations, he said, "Well, look, I don't know what I'm apologizing for. I go into an elevator or walk down the street and see a pretty girl, and that's it: it makes my day. I can't help it. I feel like I'm gonna live forever. Maybe it means I don't love them, and maybe it means I don't love you, but nobody's gonna tell me I don't *like* them very much." As Towne explained in interviews, the hero loves women because "they're pretty, they're nice to touch, they smell great, they look great, they feel great." And "there's nothing corrupt or crude about the guy at all—he's very sweet." Only a man who really loves women could have made *Personal Best*.

Towne's feelings come through clearly in the steam-room scenes. If he were directing a bunch of naked men, the scenes would have wild payoff lines—some of his famous kickers. But he's so entranced by the women's beauty and conviviality that the scenes are just there, like stanzas in a love poem; the composition is head on and classical—an Ingres Turkish bath. By an act of imagination, Towne looks at the women with the detached obsessiveness that athletes and dancers often have about their own bodies. In *Carrie*, when De Palma took us into the girls' locker room we were (deliberately) put in the position of a male voyeur, and what we saw was a boy's leering fantasy. When Towne takes us into the steam room, the camera might be one of the girls; he makes you smile or laugh as you recognize that the girls' nudity has the same easygoing quality as their dialogue. When the girls are shown in the high jump, flipping over onto their backs, they can't help being sexy, even though the camera keeps a straight face, and it's this detachment that makes you laugh. The camera never ogles the athletes' bodies. And no one in the movie is ever made to look bad—not even Scott Glenn as the scowling, sour-tempered coach with a Prince Valiant haircut and a teen-age boy's clothes, who taunts a male runner when Chris out-races him, and who does his damnedest to separate Chris and Tory, because their attachment might dull their competitive edge. He brings the team members out farther than they'd let themselves admit they'd like to go. He provokes Chris's hostility and brings out her strength; his victory with her is to get her to tell him to kiss off. Glenn gives the role a tensile ruggedness; this coach provides abuse and takes it—he's much like a movie director.

Towne, who was born and educated in Southern California, may have one of the most purely Southern California sensibilities to reach the screen. After the meets, the men and women athletes get together. These beer-drinking party scenes have the kind of imagery that is exploited in TV commercials and they could be ridiculous, but Towne likes the people who are there—he likes their relaxed, considerate ways. He believes in simplicity and sweetness and in the body. (A lot of people misunderstood *Shampoo*, because they didn't perceive how simple and warmhearted the hero was meant to be, and they thought that at the end, when he was deserted, the film was punishing him for his sexual high jinks.) What Towne is saying in *Personal Best* could be reduced to "A horse's intelligence is in its hooves," and I think he means this in more than a romantic, metaphorical sense. He wants to believe that the beauty that excites him is the same as "character," and that a woman who moves beautifully is beautiful through and through, right to her soul. (When a girl flubs in competition, we can see the emotional confusions that are making her do it.)

Personal Best should be one of the best dating movies of all time, because it pares away all traces of self-consciousness. Nakedness is no big deal for the people on the screen. And you almost can't help feeling the two girls' emotions. It's not just the laughs that have an echo effect. Now that Towne is doing not only the writing but the whole thing, he sets up the movie so that everything resonates—the words, the gestures, the sudden hurt silences, the deep breaths. The slow-motion sequences are like ripples on a pond; bits of dialogue become motifs; and rhythms recur. His women athletes of the late seventies are like the figures you see romping on a Greek vase; you feel joined to them. He has made a dance film, seamless and fluid, about normal life. Watching this movie, you feel that you really can learn something essential about girls from looking at their thighs.

February 22, 1982

Carry Your Own Matches

*E*ighty thousand years ago, on broad primeval plains, Naoh (Everett McGill), the bravest warrior of the spear-carrying Ulam tribe, and two fellow-warriors, Amoukar (Ron Perlman) and Gaw (Nameer El-Kadi), are sent out on the sacred mission of finding fire and bringing it back to the Ulam. The science fantasy *Quest for Fire* is a full-length version of the ape-man prologue to *2001*; it's a heavy dose of Desmond (Naked Ape) Morris in 70-mm., with blaring Dawn of Consciousness music, and as Naoh, Amoukar, and Gaw fight off predatory animals and hideous, apier men you begin to wish you could detect famous actors under all the makeup, the way you could in the Biblical spectaculars. "The Stone Age is this ancient country from which we have all been exiled," the screenwriter, Gérard Brach, has explained. "However, its memory remains in the collective unconscious, in the unconscious of each of us, regardless of race, creed, philosophy or social position. *Quest for Fire* transcends languages and nationalities and speaks to the deepest human experience." It sounds like the ground plan for the U.N.

I'm sure that the film was no end of trouble to make, and that the mucky, scraggly landscapes (of the non-tourist areas of Africa, Scotland, and Canada where it was shot) couldn't have been much fun to work in. But if it weren't for the grisly closeups of confrontations between apelike men and beasts and between ape-men and ape-men, with the music working up a frenzy, the picture might be taken for a put-on. (If it were double-billed with the comedian Carl Gottlieb's *Caveman*, its overblown solemnity might backfire.) Only one pleasant thing happens to the three Ulam on their travels: they encounter Ika (Rae Dawn Chong), of the highly developed mud-people tribe, the Ivaka. When they first see the smooth-skinned, bluish-looking Ika, who wears nothing but body paint, she has been captured by cannibals and is strung up like a deer carcass next to another slender young girl, whose arm has already been chewed off. Rescued by Naoh, Ika scampers after him and his pals, and stays close to them for protection, screaming shrilly at Amou- kar's attempt to jump her from behind, but accepting Naoh. When she runs away to her own village, he follows, and discovers that the Ivaka, who have pottery and the beginnings of a culture, know how to *make* fire. Later, Ika goes with him to the Ulam encampment and shows the Ulam the secret. It's woman the fire-bringer in this very eighties movie—Promethea. Ika brings the Ulam fire like a dowry. She also teaches Naoh the missionary position, and they experience mutually satisfying sex; soon after, he pats her pretty lit- tle swollen tummy and, smiling, looks up at the moon—having presumably figured out the menstrual cycle.

It's almost impossible to guess what the tone of much of this ape-man love story (based on a 1911 French novel, by J. H. Rosny, Sr.) is intended to be. Are we meant to laugh at the gaminess? At the men's werewolf foreheads? (Thick hair sprouts about an inch above their eyebrows.) The director, Jean-Jacques Annaud, seems to be willing for us to laugh but not sure about how to tell us when. He must be aware that Amoukar has been made to look like George Lucas's Chewbacca, and that Amoukar and the foolish Gaw are often like a team of baggypants comics without the pants. But probably Annaud doesn't mean for us to laugh at the credentials of the people involved—An- thony Burgess, who "created" the "special languages," and Desmond Morris, who "created" the "body language and gestures." Surely Anthony Burgess wasn't on the level when he came up with words like "wa wa" and "aga vau"? The cannibals are the Kzamm, and the Neanderthal plunderers with thick body hair, like gorillas, are called the Wagabou. The whole thing sug- gests one of those issues of *National Geographic* that kids used to pore over to see what furry people looked like naked. But the director seems to have aspirations that go beyond the Kubrick prologue and *Star Wars* to some- thing—well, higher.

It's that higher something which appears to be behind the gore and gruesomeness—the wolves and bears attacking and devouring, the ape-men hitting each other with clubs and bones. The picture keeps shoving torn flesh at us, continually demonstrating the bloody violence of our beginnings. The composer, Philippe Sarde, has really let himself go in the Stravinsky and Wag- ner department, and the soundtrack provides a mixture of a heavenly choir and electronic grunts and howls. The dubious *Naked Ape* theory of man's innate violence is implicit in this way of showing human development, and it probably accounts for the film's featuring the spear-carrying Ulam, in their rough animal skins, as our ancestors. This is a new wrinkle in racism: the pic- ture concentrates on the Ulam, who are *potentially* Caucasian. The implica- tion of the title—that Naoh's quest represents the beginning of civilization— is something of a fake, since the relatively peaceful, giggly Ivaka (and perhaps other tribes) know how to make fire and have devised ways of using it when the Ulam are still running around trying to steal it and carry it home.

Jean-Jacques Annaud has his own primitivism: the camera starts a scene from way back and then moves in—almost always in the same way. And he has a makeshift, linear approach to storytelling. He doesn't seem to have discovered crosscutting yet. If, for example, Naoh goes into the cannibals' camp to steal their fire while his buddies try to distract the cannibals and draw them away, the camera stays with Naoh and we don't find out how things are going for the others. Menacing tribes or animals conveniently disappear while we follow the fortunes of another character. What's fun in the movie is the makeup, and the way that the faces of Everett McGill, Ron Perlman, and Nameer El-Kadi are simian and yet attractive. (The sixties have made the ape look seem hip.) Amoukar and Gaw are like companionable monkeys—their brows are furrowed when they're picking nits off each other. And Rae Dawn Chong, with stripes of dark paint across her face that make her look like a lemur, and her blue-clay-dyed nakedness and high-pitched chattering, slithers around amusingly. The makeup on the Kzamm and the Wagabou—who are like nasty, brutish versions of the citizens of *Planet of the Apes*—is entertaining in a giddy, horror-movie way. But the makeup on the animals is much less effective; the elephants draped in shag rugs so that they can simulate mammoths come out looking more like Muppets. And the sequence they're in is a pipsqueak version of the Androcles and the Lion story: the mammoths attack the enemies of the Ulam because Naoh shows his respect for the giant beasts and offers their leader some grassy fodder. The sabres on the sabre-toothed tigers look pretty flimsy, but these big cats are part of the one likable sequence. Pursued by the tigers, the three Ulam warriors climb a weak, spindly tree and hang on at the top among the few branches. Trapped there as it grows dark, they get hungry and nibble a leaf or two; there's a cut to the morning, and the men are still up in the tree, which is denuded.

· · · · ·

When Jack Lemmon puts his finger under his stiff collar and twists his neck—that familiar tic of his which he uses to show that the character he's playing is writhing in discomfort—he puts me in mourning for the lost evening. The Italian actor Ugo Tognazzi often has the same effect on me. It's not that they're bad actors, exactly—it's that they're sweaty, loyal, and hollow. They're actors through and through; they're nothing *but* actors. When they're in realistic roles—as Lemmon is in Costa-Gavras's *Missing* and as Tognazzi is in Bernardo Bertolucci's *Tragedy of a Ridiculous Man*—they're busy being realistic. The more they try to become Everyman, the more actorish they are. They're lightweights—gifted comedians—who get soggy when they try to fill the screen in heavyweight, tragicomic roles. Jack Lemmon is so eager to have depth that he looks on a serious role as a chance for redemption—he goes at it with the wide-eyed-kid enthusiasm of a Jesus freak. Subdued and dolorous as he is in *Missing*, he's still hyperactive, and when he walks down a corridor clutching his stomach the screen oozes boringness.

Set in Chile (the country isn't named but its capital is), *Missing* takes place in 1973, at the time of the military coup against Allende's government. It's a didactic melodrama, based on the actual case of Charles Horman, a young American living in Santiago who disappeared a few days after General Pinochet and his junta took power. Horman's wife (called Beth here, and played by Sissy Spacek) can't find him, and his father, Ed Horman (Lemmon), who is a conservative, Christian Scientist businessman, comes to help in the search. Ed is a Middle-American prig so antagonistic to his son's counterculture way of life that you practically expect him to start yelling "Pinko prevert!" at the distraught wife. Jack Lemmon is playing a variant of the role that Jane Fonda has been playing in films such as *Coming Home* and *The China Syndrome*: he's the naïve, protected, nonpolitical conservative who is radicalized (or, at least, reëducated) by what he learns. For the sake of this demonstration, the actual Ed Horman, a cultivated man who married a painter (Mrs. Horman was at one time president of the National Association of Women Artists) and was a devoted father, is presented as a rigid conformist who believes what the American Embassy officials tell him and thinks that if his son got into trouble it was his own fault. He brushes aside his daughter-in-law's suspicions that they're being stalled and lied to. It's by turning Ed Horman into Costa-Gavras's notion of a Middle-American Everyman that the film hopes to make an impact on the mass audience. Everything in *Missing* is predetermined—it's a Q.E.D. production, laid out to teach us, step by step, as Ed Horman gradually comes to share Beth's views. He has his own Dawn of Consciousness.

According to the film, which hops back and forth between the runaround that Ed and Beth are given and flashbacks to the last days of the son's life, Charles Horman (John Shea) was executed, with American foreknowledge and consent, because "he knew too much." While showing a visiting old friend (Melanie Mayron) around Chile, he had stumbled on information about American involvement in the planning of the coup. *Missing* opens with the statement "This film is based on a true story. The incidents and facts are documented." And, yes, it is *derived* from a true story. But Costa-Gavras's idea of documentation may be closer to surmise than yours or mine. There appears to be considerable doubt about whether American officials did in fact conspire in Charles Horman's execution, and though there is no doubt that the American government tried to prevent Allende's election in 1970, and was actively involved in destabilizing his regime and subsidizing opposition parties and making his life hell, there is a good deal of doubt about whether the American military actually helped stage the coup. But we bear so much guilt for what happened in Chile that perhaps it's almost a fine point—a quibble—whether we actually pulled the triggers.

The Battle of Chile, which interpreted Allende's overthrow in much the same way, is far more manipulative, yet I think it's a great film. *Missing* isn't; it isn't even good. Making his first American movie, Costa-Gavras uses the same approach that American directors have often used when they wanted to teach us something: he has given his accusatory political thriller a soft, warm-and-human center. Ed has to face some bitter truths before he awakens politically. Costa-Gavras, who wrote the script with Donald Stewart and the uncredited John Nichols (it's based on a book by Thomas Hauser), goes so far that he has the American Ambassador in Chile tell the father that there are three thousand American firms doing business there and that he must protect those interests, and has the father reply that they're not *his* interests. It's catechism time.

This approach to an audience is offensive enough when American directors employ it; it's worse when Costa-Gavras does, because his antipathy to Americans appears to be so deep-seated that he can't create American characters. Charles and Beth are so sweet and flower-headed they're like talking kittens, and their apartment has whimsical drawings and messages stuck to the walls—it's like a nursery. Sissy Spacek tries to give her role some spunk, and she brings a twangy homeliness to her resigned acceptance of Ed's fatuity; and John Shea, with his vague, poetic gaze, has a good face for peering out of windows. But Charles Horman, the political journalist and organizer, has been made so dreamily innocent you'd think he was living in Chile because it was the only place where he could have a pet duck and read *The Little Prince* aloud to his wife.

Every detail of the transformation of Ed Horman takes place on schedule: we have to listen to his initial tiresome spatting with Beth so that we can observe each step in the calibrated process of his coming closer to her counterculture values. I like the way Sissy Spacek handles him; most of what she does in the movie seems fresh and natural. But when she puts an arm around Ed, you hear a click in your head: he's beginning to see the light. And because this is the foreground action the only real filmmaking is in the backgrounds. *Missing*, which was shot in Mexico, has texture: it has the anxious, ominous atmosphere of a city under martial law—the sirens, the tanks, the helicopters, the feeling of abnormal silences and of random terror, the scuffles between civilians and soldiers, the stadium where those suspected of left-wing connections are held, sitting in the bleachers. There's a memorable scene with Beth, who has missed the last bus home and is out on the street after curfew, hiding in an alcove behind some iron grillwork, listening to volleys of gunfire, some quite close. Sissy Spacek is stunningly at odds with everything that's going on there in Santiago. She never seems more American than when she's huddled, curled up behind the fence, sleeping. The visual details have something tangible about them; the plot points don't. If the friend played by Melanie Mayron was with Charles Horman when he learned so much about what the American brass was up to, why was she allowed to leave the country? Too many details are left dangling. You may get the impression that Costa-Gavras's only interest in Charles Horman's death is as evidence for conclusions about the general pattern of United States meddling in other countries that he formed years ago. He isn't making the film for himself; he's making it for us—all us Ed Hormans. Those are the gift horses to look in the mouth.

Probably the producers at Universal thought of asking Costa-Gavras to take on the book about Charles Horman because, essentially, he had already done it, in his 1972 *State of Siege*. What he does here is simply a smoother, slowed-down version of a Costa-Gavras film, but I doubt whether even the staccato urgency of his earlier editing style could have enlivened it. It's a tired, emotionally exhausted movie. Maybe if the Jack Lemmon character had been left out and if we had seen Sissy Spacek and her young American friends using resources of pragmatic intelligence they'd never had to draw on before, and trying to figure out how to behave to be effective with the right-wing Chileans . . . But that would be an altogether different movie—you'd have to be interested in what Americans might do in those circumstances.

Costa-Gavras isn't a Communist Party-liner. He did make *The Confession* (1970), an examination of the show trials in Czechoslovakia. His political position appears to be a pro-left hopelessness. He knows there's a difference between the Soviet Union and the United States. (He would hardly be invited to the Soviet Union to make a film critical of its secret maneuvering in other countries.) Yet he appears to hate Americans—or what he perceives as Americans—so deeply that he turns any American characters involved in military, diplomatic, or political life into pasteboard villains. A Greek expatriate who went to Paris when he was nineteen, he sees the United States as the force that drives people to Communism, and he isn't exactly wrong. But he also condescends to people he doesn't understand, and will probably never understand, because he has all the answers already worked out.

Why is *Missing* receiving so much praise? Maybe because it's such a virtuous cornball melodrama about closing the generation gap, and because Lemmon is there exuding all that heartfelt sincerity and learning how misguided he was. Maybe because Costa-Gavras has found a way to make a political indictment of the United States so custardy that it's palatable.

. . . . .

*B*ertolucci's *Tragedy of a Ridiculous Man* is much more sophisticated and more personal, but it's a dopey movie—complex yet undramatic, and centering on Ugo Tognazzi doing his robust-life-force and peasant-cunning number. He does have more energy than anything else in the movie, but, like Lemmon's, it's the kind of actor's energy you want to get away from. Tognazzi can play cuckolds and he can also play the men who do the cuckolding, and he has a talent for yearning sentimentalists. But he doesn't have the fullness to carry a picture—he needs a complementary partner, like Alberto Sordi or Michel Serrault.

As Primo, an ordinary man, he's so empty he might be on a puppet stage. Bertolucci gives him some visual weight, but Tognazzi, trying to be magnificently human, never does anything that seems like what a human being would do. *Tragedy*, which Bertolucci has called "a completely Italian movie," doesn't seem to be happening in Italy, or anywhere else. It isn't a tragedy, and Primo isn't a ridiculous man. What it is is a terrorist fairy tale. Primo, who has risen to become the owner of a big cheese factory, is married to a handsome, educated Frenchwoman (Anouk Aimée) and has a villa and a yacht. When his only son (played by Tognazzi's son Riki) is kidnapped and he receives the ransom terms, he feels that selling his factory is like committing suicide, but he and his wife put up the factory and everything else they have in order to raise the money—a billion lire. Things start getting more complicated, in a paralyzed, logy way. Along about then, I started thinking that it was too bad that the kidnappers hadn't set a time limit; there's no urgency, no tension, and you sense that you're not going to find out what's going on, that it's all metaphorical. Primo has received messages from the left-wing terrorist kidnappers through Laura (Laura Morante), who says she's his son's girl, and through Adelfo (Victor Cavallo), a worker priest who says he's a close friend of the son's, and although Primo actually witnessed the kidnapping, he begins to realize that he hardly knows his son and to wonder if the boy isn't in on it. For no apparent reason, Laura and Adelfo tell him that his son is dead, whereupon he turns practical and figures that he can screw the moneylenders and use the ransom money to recapitalize his factory. But his wife is determined to deliver the money. At the end, you get the feeling that everything is going to work out, but you no longer care.

The viewer doesn't find out who is actually involved in the kidnapping. That may be an accurate reflection of the confusion in modern Italy, but it's maddening in a movie, and for Primo not to ask any of the key questions seems inconsistent with his character—it seems false. If he were truly ridiculous, he might keep trying to solve the mystery and keep failing—which would be *something*. But he remains passive, and we stay outside his situation, observing him in a semi-comatose state, because there's nothing to engage us. This is a movie about a father-son relationship and about the terrible generational split that has developed in Italy, but Bertolucci centers the movie on the father, while he himself still feels like a son. His tone—the film's tone—toward Primo is patronizing. Primo is a grubby, uninteresting man, and we have no clue to what the son is about. (Bertolucci has spoken publicly about the despair of youth, and has said, "From their silence you cannot guess if they are mutely pleading for help or getting ready to pull the trigger on you." The film is less eloquent.)

The ending is optimistic in a relaxed, Marxist way. But it gives one no particular pleasure, because the whole picture is so visually cool and restrained. In Bertolucci's last film, the Freudian *Luna*, the camera moves had become overdeliberate and self-conscious, as if Antonioni had entered into his soul (or his superego). The picture's cold lyricism was melancholy and elegant, but some vital connection seemed to be missing (in the Antonioni way), and though you could extrapolate the Freudian explanations that Bertolucci had worked in, you didn't feel them. He turned Freud into an abstraction, an ideology; even the moon-mother connection didn't come across. The picture seemed alienated from its own subject. In *Tragedy*, with his usual cinematographer, Vittorio Storaro, tied up on *Reds* and *One from the Heart*, he used Carlo Di Palma, who shot several films for Antonioni, and it's as if Bertolucci wanted to be alienated from himself, wanted to cut himself off from the pleasures of his own style.

The setting is Parma, the Parma that we have come to know from his films, but it could be a place we've never seen before and have no wish to see again. Bertolucci is a director with ideas, and there are unusual scenes—Primo watching his kitchen staff dance to a rock-and-roll number and joining in, Primo and his wife clutching each other in bed, aroused by anxiety about their son. But none of the scenes go anywhere. Bertolucci's vision is grayed out here and mediocre at heart. Clearly, he feels the need to try things, to change and grow, but he seems to equate maturing with dullness, with using the colorless Ugo Tognazzi, with a kind of passive acceptance. The film is in no hurry, and there's no feeling of discovery in the acting, no zest in the editing; it's like an old man's movie. If you're going to make a picture about a kidnapping and not let the audience know whether the supposed victim was in on the whole thing, then you've got to involve the audience in the characters of either the conspirators or the people who are expected to pay up or in the kidnapped person—or all three, or just two, as the case may be. You've got to involve us in *something*. But to let it all slip out of your hands, as if to say, "It will all work out anyway, that's how life is," is to remind us that life is also going on outside the theatre.

March 8, 1982

Francesco Rosi

*F*rancesco Rosi is like a great painter who after many years of tangled experiments suddenly arrives at a clearing in the woods and begins to work simply, integrating everything he has learned. Rosi was always brilliant; there was Marxist flash and filigree in his movies and shock cuts and equivocal conspiracies—the kind that "everyone" in the society is in on. He didn't tell simple stories: his films were, as he said, "collections of fragments," and he didn't put them together for you—he selected the pieces, but you had to arrange them in your own mind. He left it to simpler political filmmakers to supply loaded answers; he raised loaded questions, and did it with a jagged buoyancy. In *The Mattei Affair* (1972), an inquiry into the life of Italy's government oil czar, Rosi went *Citizen Kane* one better: it starts with a plane crash, and Mattei's body itself is in bits and pieces, which are collected, like the scrambled parts of a jigsaw puzzle. In *Illustrious Corpses* (1975), his most elliptical and abstract film—a political spectacular on the theme of conspiracy—he opens with the decaying mummies of the powerful men of the past in the catacombs, and then goes aboveground, where he shows monumental institutional architecture dwarfing the people of the city. When characters disappear, they seem to have been swallowed in the conspiracy or lost in the geometrical compositions. Perhaps both: the architecture is an objective correlative of the conspiracy—Fascism in stone. Rosi shows such a majestic, ominous spatial sense in this movie that at times it seems to be an architectural fantasy about a country of the dead. It's a stunning, misshapen, unresolved movie; maybe he had pushed his obsession with power, corruption, and vendettas even further than he could handle. Those who asked questions were killed, until there were no questions left: there was nothing but paranoia. The film ended with a remark (made by a Communist)—"The truth isn't always revolutionary"—that didn't seem to go with what we'd been looking at but that perhaps summed up other things that Rosi was feeling. *Illustrious Corpses* was marvellous at first, while you were waiting for what you never got. By the end, it seemed like a magnificent, stately version of John Boorman's *Point Blank*, and I wondered if there could be such a thing as an artist with no real mind—only this surface intellectuality. Or was Rosi simply a virtuoso filmmaker who lacked the depth of an artist?

The jumpiness of *The Mattei Affair* and the flamboyance of *Illustrious Corpses* disappeared when Rosi made his 1979 version of Carlo Levi's memoir *Christ Stopped at Eboli*; it was straightforward, limpid, exploratory. The crankiness, the rancor were gone, and the work seemed less ambiguous and "intellectual" and more intelligent. The overt concerns that formed the style of the earlier pictures were submerged in *Christ Stopped at Eboli*, and Rosi was willing to let them emerge on their own. And so it had depth—much greater depth than we're used to at the movies. We could feel the pleasure that Rosi took in getting to know the Lucanian village and its people; it was like the best passages of Ann Cornelisen, when all her energy is concentrated on the Lucanian villagers she's writing about—on finding the words to make us see what she sees. And in Rosi's elegiac new film, *Three Brothers*, once again there are no villains, seen or unseen. He respects the perplexities of the three sons of an aging farmer, and he's fair to their differing points of view. Earlier, full of theory, Rosi imposed his vision; now he searches it out—he goes deeper down into himself, and much further into his subject. His images no longer clamor for attention; a more selfless urgency has come into his work. When I saw *Christ Stopped at Eboli*, I was completely absorbed by what I was seeing; despite the truncated rhythms that were the result of the film's having been cut from three and a half hours to two hours (it was financed by RAI, Italian television, as a four-part series), the picture was deeply satisfying. The audience seemed hushed, as if at a concert where the musicians were playing very softly. And it was the kind of music that people who were used to slam-bang movies might not be able to hear. I felt the same way at *Three Brothers*, because, even though the structure is schematic, the film moves on waves of feeling. Maybe it's simply that Rosi, whose earlier work was about the enigmas of power and corruption, has, as he has aged (he was born in 1922), become more interested in the powerless. His investigations centering on famous dead men—*Salvatore Giuliano* (1961), *The Mattei Affair*, *Lucky Luciano* (1973)—culminated in *Illustrious Corpses*. The leap from *Illustrious Corpses* to *Christ Stopped at Eboli* is a leap into observation and simple emotion. (An American distributor has finally bought the rights to the full version of what was released here as *Eboli*, and perhaps he'll also restore its proper title.)

Three Brothers is not as fine a work as *Christ Stopped at Eboli*. It doesn't have anything comparable to Gian Maria Volonte's performance as Carlo Levi, the writer and artist exiled by Mussolini's government to the remote hilltop village of Gagliano—a harsh place past Eboli, the last stop on the train, beyond which (the saying goes) even "Christ did not come." But *Three Brothers* is wonderful enough. It's set in the Apulia region of the South, from which the three brothers emigrated to the cities, and it has the structure of a modern folktale. The picture opens to the sound of heartbeats and with the credits appearing on the side of a building, a giant stone-gray abstraction with dark window hollows, like blind eyes. Stone—endurance—is the film's primary image. When the credits are over, the camera pulls back from the building and we see a garbage-strewn lot, full of rats, and one of them seems to run right up against the camera lens and snap at us, with a horrible ratty sound. From there we move into the huge Institute for the Correction of Minors in Naples, where the middle brother (Vittorio Mezzogiorno)—whose rodent nightmare we've been in—teaches young delinquents and tries to keep them off drugs and out of the hands of the police. This man of about forty is scholarly and devout, a loner, and right after we see him we observe that his profile matches that of his old, peasant-farmer father (Charles Vanel, at the age of eighty-nine). The quiet, slow-moving father sets out from his stone farmhouse, where the living quarters and the granary and the barn are all part of one massive, almost white structure, to go to the nearby town. On his way, he sees his wife chasing a rabbit, which she says she planned to cook for his dinner. She has a flirty smile, and he catches the rabbit and gives it to her, but she lets it go and then disappears. When he arrives in the town, he sends three telegrams: "Your mother is dead. Father."

The gentle, hallucinating old man has eyes that seem to go back before history. They're so old he seems to look inward rather than outward, and, serene in his Southern Italian rural isolation, he feels little need to speak to his three sons when they arrive. The oldest (Philippe Noiret) is about fifty; as the firstborn son, he was given the expensive education, and he's a judge in Rome. He feels it his duty to accept a case involving the terrorist assassination of one of his colleagues, even though his life is being threatened. The youngest (Michele Placido), a hothead, who's about thirty, is an angry, rebellious factory worker in Turin. The judge hasn't brought his nervous wife or his languorous son, and the teacher from Naples is unmarried; each of them arrives alone for the funeral. But the worker has had a rift with his Northerner wife, and, not wanting to leave his eight-year-old daughter with her, has brought the child with him.

The film might be said to be an inquiry into the terrorist chaos of modern Italy: that's the underlayer, and it's always present, even though it comes to the surface only in the judge's nightmares and in conversations in the nearby town and among the brothers. The movie doesn't dramatize what it's actually about; instead, the characters walk through a charged situation. These brothers—expatriates who have left the soil that is still everything to their father—represent modern Italy, with its roots torn up. This is a sociological folktale with the judge trying to defend the basic legal structure of the society, the teacher hoping to prevent his delinquents from turning into full-scale criminals, the young militant defending the right of the workers to improve their condition by strikes and bloodshed. The film is about the violence in the cities, the split between the North and the South, the break between the generations. Yet it's set in the old man's world, where the cycle of nature is what matters. It's as if the three brothers had returned to an earlier age, an ancient, pastoral Italy that had never heard of progress. In their old, shared bedroom, they spend a mostly sleepless night, before the day of the funeral, talking, arguing, falling into dreams and reveries. When the factory worker fantasizes reconciling with his wife in Turin, the city itself is so different from the farmhouse and its courtyard that it's like a moonscape; we *feel* the difference between North and South. The movie is about ideas, yet it's saturated with emotion.

What's distinctive about these last two Rosi films is that so much of the emotion comes from the rhythm of the scenes, from the unhurried ease of his pacing, from the fluid camerawork. I liked the crackle and volatility of Rosi's earlier films, but the smooth, unobtrusive, always moving camera that he uses now is peerless. He was impatient in *The Mattei Affair*; now he's not forcing anything. He takes the time to show you people and places for their own sake. (The judge pays a visit to his old wet nurse: he asks to go into the back to see the fig tree he used to climb, and is dismayed to find what a scrawny little thing it is, while the gnarled, toothless crone, jolly and benign, apologizes for not being able to bend down to pick the snails out of her yard anymore.) Rosi has been working with the same cinematographer, Pasqualino De Santis, since the early sixties, and maybe De Santis is now like a part of him—his right hand. For the little girl (Marta Zoffoli), everything about the farmhouse is a mystery to be explored. The camera, going with her on her tour, seems to do the most exquisite loop-the-loops, in a simple, matter-of-fact way. You don't sit there admiring the filmmaking technique; you don't even sense the planning that has gone into the long, graceful shots. What you see is the subject.

The image of the old father, just walking, has the kind of resonance that most directors never achieve. And when the father is stretched out on one side of his big double bed, wearing his trousers and shirt and vest, while his little granddaughter rests on the other side, the image seems to go back in time; it's like an old photograph. The father's memories of his wedding day in the rain, and of his honeymoon trip to the beach, where his bride lost her ring in the sand, and of how he sifted the sand until he found it (the same ring that the next morning, as the coffin is being carried away, he puts on his own finger)—all this is so rich that it soaks through the conversations the sons are having. The old man has lived his life without ever needing to worry about terrorism, crime, chaos. The sons' thoughts and fantasies all come out of their anxieties; the old man dreams of the good things in his life. The break between the father and the sons is complete. In the North or in the cities, you're running away from death; in the South, on the land, you get back in touch with it. The father has his place in the larger ritual; when the sons come back, they realize that they've lost their place. They're neither here nor there, and they know it.

With so much greatness in it, why is it that *Three Brothers* doesn't quite take? The skeleton of the film may be a little too heavy; you may expect the symbolic characters to be more fully fleshed out than they are. And a film with so many big, serious themes may make you think that something pompous is going on; it's easy to imagine that it must be pedantic or doctrinaire. Actually, its attitudes are very open, and nobody in it speaks for the director or tells us the wise course. (It's only the outline that's rigid.) The chief weakness, I think, is that the picture doesn't have actors who can really embody the conflicts and tensions of the terrorist-ridden country. Vanel is superbly right as the father—his face in the sunlight is primeval, like a lizard or a turtle. And the little girl, with her angelic calm, is everything one could want her to be; when she burrows into the grain, lying in it and playing with it, as her grandmother had played with the sand on the beach, she's a perfect image of innocent sensuality. This little girl, who walks with the old man, holding his hand, is probably intended as a bridge between North and South, and perhaps as the herald of a return to pastoral values. And when she finds an egg and gives it to him she appears to represent the hope for the future. I wish the lovely child weren't loaded with this theoretical hocus-pocus, but it doesn't damage her performance, because she's innocent of the director's lapse of judgment.

It's the actors playing the three brothers who have no fire in them. Philippe Noiret is rueful and reflective as the judge; we can feel his grief about his obligations—it's there in his hangdog expression. Vittorio Mezzogiorno is quietly withdrawn—perhaps too withdrawn and too solemn—as the dedicated teacher leaning against the oak tree near the farmhouse; Mezzogiorno also plays the father as a young man, and he's a little less pallid in that role. As the restless agitator-worker, the handsome Michele Placido is too actorish; he has an amusing but unfortunate resemblance to Harry Hamlin (who's currently featured in *Making Love*), and he lights a few too many cigarettes as he walks around smoldering and being the South with all its frustrations. He's awfully manly, as if consciously shouldering his symbolic burden. We're drawn into the dreams of these characters; we feel an intimacy with them. Yet—and the fault may be partly in the writing and in the directing—it's as if they had nothing in them but the characteristics of an honorable judge, a conscientious teacher-reformer, an explosively angry worker.

When this worker visits an old girlfriend (Sara Tafuri), and when he has the reverie of reconciliation with his wife (Maddalena Crippa), these women are vivid. In using a folktale structure, Rosi and his co-scenarist, Tonino Guerra, may not have noticed that they were symbolizing the old rural Italy (the father) and the chaotic new Italy (the three brothers) in completely masculine terms. Or perhaps they did: some years ago Rosi was asked why women were such minor figures in his movies, and he said that he made films about "power and institutions" and that "women are rarely there." This may be desolating to the women of Italy, but it's a break for the actresses in *Three Brothers*. They're free to create characters, and they're the ones who give the fiery performances. The old girlfriend in the South is passionate but not a fool; she's aware that her old boyfriend doesn't even know why he has come to see her. And the wife makes you feel how sexy her Northern, less expansive nature is to her hot young husband.

Rosi may have wanted the three men to be ordinary, so that they would seem more representative, but this notion never really works. If actors aren't exciting, we don't see ourselves in them—we're less involved, we tend to detach ourselves from them. In this film, we're not satisfied with the brothers, yet we can't quite detach ourselves, either. While you're watching this film, you're enveloped in it; grateful for its intelligence, you sink into it. As with some of the De Sica pictures, small gestures become miraculous, because it seems as if they hadn't been noticed before. And we feel connected to the world on the screen by responding to it. This is the kind of movie that a viewer can fall in love with, even though he's aware of its flaws. Rosi is trying to take a long view and to look at *everything*; that's the problem, and it's also what's wonderful. This is probably what it's like to live in Italy now; the film is a dirge for the whole blasted mess—people talk about what should be done, but nothing seems to mean anything. The talk is just part of the texture of their lives. At dawn on the day of the funeral, the teacher looks down into the courtyard and sees his brothers standing at a distance from each other, sobbing. And he joins in. But they're not necessarily sobbing about their dead mother. She's the excuse, the provocation. They're sobbing about their own confusion.

Rosi has one of the greatest compositional senses in the history of movies; he's able to keep you in a state of emotional exaltation because there isn't a frame that fails to sustain the mood. He's conscious of the weight of a human death; the whole movie is set off by the mother's death. The air is full of life and death—the whirring and the creaking of the pigeons taking off and landing, the humming and clicking of insects. We're led by the camera, and we trust its movement. Something more is always going to be revealed. Rosi is discovering life.

March 22, 1982

Comedians

Diner, written and directed by Barry Levinson, is a wonderful movie. Set in Baltimore, around Christmas of 1959, it's like a comic American version of *I Vitelloni*. A fluctuating group of five or six young men in their early twenties hang out together. They've known each other since high school, and though they're moving in different directions, they still cling to their late-night bull sessions at the Fells Point Diner. Shrevie (Daniel Stern), who has nothing to say to his young wife, ducks out on her, and the others take their dates home, and then they all make a quick dash back to the diner—where, magically, they always seem to have plenty to talk about. They're so relaxed together that they can sound worldly and sharp; they may never sound this quick-witted again. Levinson, who is making his début as a director, has a great ear; he's as sure on the nuances of dialogue and as funny as Paul Mazursky was in *Bob & Carol & Ted & Alice* and *Next Stop, Greenwich Village*. And when Levinson hits the contrasting notes—such as Shrevie's outburst at his affable young wife, Beth (Ellen Barkin), that leaves her emotionally annihilated—there are times when the lyrical intensity of the lines lifts you right out of the situation, transcends it. Conversations may roll on all night at the diner—it's kidding, reassuring patter—but when these boys are out with girls they're nervous, constricted, fraudulent, half crazy. They can't be the same people with women that they are with each other.

Diner is a great period piece—a look at middle-class relations between the sexes just before the sexual revolution. If any men (or women) think they regret the changes, this is the movie they ought to see. Although the trappings have changed, the dynamics are still much the same—except among people who make a real effort not to fall back on them. Set when it is, this film can show those painful dynamics at the last period in our history when people could laugh (albeit uneasily) at the gulf between men and women. It takes place just before this gulf became an issue of sexual politics—before it began to be discussed as a *problem*. (Perhaps that's the real change: the earnest psychiatric language took over.) The most innocent of the group is smiling, coddled Eddie (Steve Guttenberg, in a performance with such perfectly inflected Paul Newman–like grins that it atones for a lot, even his appearances in *The Boys from Brazil* and *Can't Stop the Music*). Eddie lives for football, and the Baltimore Colts, who are about to play the New York Giants, are his passion. He's scheduled to get married on New Year's Eve, but only if his bride-to-be passes a "monster" football-trivia test that he has scheduled for her; she's cramming for it. His rationale is that he wants to be sure they'll be able to communicate after they're married. There's a beautiful, bone-chilling moment when this simple, warm kid asks Shrevie what marriage is really like, and Shrevie, who has just said that he can't hold a five-minute conversation with his wife, thinks it over for a few seconds before telling him, "It's O.K."

The sleaziest and most charismatic figure of the group is Boogie, played by Mickey Rourke, who was the young professional arsonist in *Body Heat*. With luck, Rourke could become a major actor: he has an edge and magnetism, and a sweet, pure smile that surprises you. He seems to be acting to you, and to no one else. There's nothing standard about Rourke—he has an off-kilter look, like Louis Hayward, but with depth. Here, with his hair swept back, he's Boogie the flashy, experienced chaser, the gambler who's in bad trouble with his bookie, the guy who thinks of crooked ploys but can't really carry them out. Boogie works in a beauty parlor in the daytime, sits up till all hours at the diner, and still finds time to chase girls. Though completely unsettled and sweaty from exhaustion, he's ready for anything. He's also the most tender in his dealings with women, and the most gallant. Boogie courts women; he likes them. And you can see what makes him appealing to women; he's charming. But he has no real connection with them except sex.

Fenwick (Kevin Bacon), a smart, self-destructive dropout, is half drunk, half flipped out all through the film. He plays reckless practical jokes that get him and three of the others arrested; he's withdrawn, in a bitter funk. It's not until you see him alone, watching the "College Bowl" TV quiz show and gleefully beating the contestants to the answers, that you realize how consciously he's throwing himself away, and when you see him with his mealy-mouthed brother and discover that his father is the only parent who won't bail his kid out, you get a sense of why he's so screwed up. Fenwick is so infantile that the only girl he goes with is a highly developed eleventh grader.

Kevin Bacon, with his pointed chin, and the look of a mad Mick, keeps Fenwick morose and yet demonic. You can see why the others try to take care of him and shield him. Fenwick will do more for his friends than he'll do for himself; he'll do anything he can think of to help Boogie with his debt—which means trying, failing, getting more drunk.

These are amazing performances—all four of them. You don't need to follow these characters' lives for years to get a sense of what will happen to them. And as Shrevie's young wife, Beth, Ellen Barkin, with her tough wistfulness, does things I've never seen before. Beth is crass and almost lewdly ordinary, yet her bruised, beat-out expressions stay with you. Barkin has a broad face, and at moments her Beth suggests the punchy Brando of *On the Waterfront*, with his slow reaction time. When Shrevie, who works in a store selling TV sets and refrigerators, tells her not to play any of the records in his collection, because she gets them mixed up, you feel that he enjoys putting her down. He's a fetishist about his records. They have been his own private world—what he cared about most—and it's slipping away from him; singing along with the music in his car, he looks utterly lost. (When the gang disintegrates, he'll be the worst off.) Sports, chasing girls, conversation, the early rock music are all linked together for the group at the diner. The movie isn't about sex but the quest for sex, the obsession with making out, which, for Shrevie, at least, has ended in the nothingness of marriage.

Levinson is less successful with the more proper Waspy characters. Timothy Daly, as a graduate student in another city, who has returned to be the best man at Eddie's wedding, is saddled with a beautiful, bland television-producer girlfriend (Kathryn Dowling). Their scenes aren't as well written as the others; they don't have the back-and-forth movement. But there are fully rounded marginal characters—Modell (Paul Reiser), a moocher who's often part of the group, is so funny when he tries to coax Eddie out of half his roast-beef sandwich or tries to bum a ride from him that the two of them seem to have had this bickering relationship since childhood.

Levinson never allows us to think that we know everything there is to know about these characters. They have sides—all of them—that are hidden from us and from each other. Levinson doesn't violate his characters by summing them up—he understands that we never fully understand anybody. Near the beginning, when several members of the group have gone to the Christmas dance at their old high school Boogie discovers that Fenwick has sold his date (whom he really likes) for five dollars; Boogie goes looking for him and finds him in the basement of the building smashing windows. Boogie asks him why he's doing it, and Fenwick says, "Just for a smile." Yes, he's a crazy masochist, but he is also really looking for a smile; he's trying to amuse himself. And Modell the reticent moocher, a dark, persistently self-righteous fellow, with small, suspicious eyes, turns out, at the wedding, to be a hilarious speechmaker. Nobody is merely what he seems. This movie is so beautifully detailed that the parents are as many-sided as their kids. The bride's football exam, with her father there judging the fairness of the scoring, is a perfect piece of loony Americana. So is the wedding, with the Baltimore Colts marching song and the bridesmaids' dresses in the Colts' colors (blue and white), and Beth trying to teach her record-aficionado husband to dance, and just about all the characters we have met gathered together listening to Modell making his toast.

Some twenty-six records are heard during the movie—the singers include Lil Green, Elvis Presley, Bobby Darin, Fats Domino, Sinatra, Jerry Lee Lewis, and Chuck Berry—but I was so caught up in the characters that I barely registered what was playing when. That may be an indication of the kind of talent Levinson has. He isn't thrillingly visual, and there are a few sequences (such as the intermingling of a TV soap opera with a messy real-life situation) in which his idea is a few jumps ahead of his ability to carry it out. But he's a storyteller with fresh stories to tell, and they're all bound together. You have the impression that he lets things take their own shape. His background is as a writer and performer; he wrote for "The Carol Burnett Show" and for Mel Brooks on a couple of movies, and he and a partner, Valerie Curtin, wrote ... And Justice for All. Diner is that rare autobiographical movie that is made by someone who knows how to get the texture right. Levinson likes actors, the way Mazursky does. Boogie, being roughed up and trying to push his assailant away, the kid who wanders around quoting from Sweet Smell of Success—these are scenes that are just about perfectly rendered. Levinson has a great feel for promise. At the diner, the boys are all storytellers, and they take off from each other; their conversations are almost all overlapping jokes that are funny without punch lines. The diner is like a comedy club where the performers and the customers feed each other lines—they're all stars and all part of the audience. The diner is where they go to give their nightly performances, and the actors all get a chance to be comedians.

•　　•　　•　　•　　•

When Chaplin began to talk onscreen, he used a cultivated voice and high-flown words, and became a deeply unfunny man; if he had found the street language to match his lowlife, tramp movements, he might have been something like Richard Pryor, who's all of a piece—a master of lyrical obscenity. Pryor is the only great poet satirist among our comics. His lyricism seems to come out of his thin-skinned nature; he's so empathic he's all wired up. His 1979 film Richard Pryor Live in Concert was a consummation of his years as an entertainer, and then some. He had a lifetime of material at his fingertips, and he seemed to go beyond himself. He personified objects, animals, people, the warring parts of his own body, even thoughts in the heads of men and women—black, white, Oriental—and he seemed to be possessed by the spirits he pulled out of himself. To those of us who thought it was one of the greatest performances we'd ever seen or ever would see, his new one-man show *Richard Pryor Live on the Sunset Strip* may be disappointing yet emotionally stirring. His new routines aren't as fully worked out; Pryor hasn't been doing the stage appearances that he used to do—hasn't, in fact, given any one-man shows since the 1979 film was shot—so these routines haven't been polished and sharpened, and they're not as varied. The material—specially prepared for this film, which was shot at two performances at the Hollywood Palladium—is rather skimpy, and a lot of it is patterned on routines from the first. Pryor doesn't seem as prickly now—he doesn't have the hunted look, or the old sneaky, guilty gleam in his eyes. He says he isn't angry anymore, and he seems to have been strengthened—he's more open. This probably has something to do with the vast public outpouring of affection for him after his near-fatal accident in June, 1980, when (as he acknowledges here) the dope he was freebasing exploded and set him on fire.

Pryor must have realized that millions and millions of people really wished him well, felt grateful for the pleasure he'd given them, and wanted him to live. How does an ornery, suspicious man who brought the language and grievances of the black underclass onto the stage deal with acceptance? (This is not a problem that Lenny Bruce, who brought the backstage language of the tawdriest levels of show business onto the stage, ever had to face.) Pryor doesn't appear sweetened, exactly. Even in the films in which he has played Mr. Nice Guy to children or whites, the stickiness hasn't clung to him; he's shed it. And he's always come clean with the audience. Pryor's best jokes aren't jokes in the usual sense—they're observations that are funny because of how he acts them out and because of his inflections. He constantly surprises us and makes us laugh in recognition. He tells us what we *almost* knew but shoved down, so when we laugh at him we feel a special, giddy freedom. That hasn't changed—he isn't soft in *Sunset Strip*. He tries on some benign racial attitudes and then drops them very fast—that's how you know he's still alive and kicking. He's different, though. You may sense that there has been a deepening of feeling, that there's something richer inside him, something more secure.

At the same time, he's adrift as a performer, because he isn't sure that he's got his act together. And he hasn't. The pressure of a one-man show before a huge crowd and on camera must be just about heart-stopping if you haven't been working in front of big live audiences. And that first film made him a legend; he has the pressure here of an audience expecting history to be made. This film doesn't build the performance rhythm that the 1979 film did; it's very smoothly put together, but in a meaningless way—you don't feel that you're experiencing *Pryor's* rhythms. Is the editing bad, or were the editors trying to stretch the material to this eighty-eight minute length? (Why are there so many cutaways—at just the wrong time—to laughing, dressed-up people in the front rows? You half expect to see a star or two among them. It makes the movie feel canned.) Haskell Wexler headed the camera crew, and the color looks true and clear, and Pryor, in his scarlet suit, black bow tie and shirt, gold shoes, and a snazzy designer belt with a piece hanging straight down, is vividly close to us. But he has trouble getting going. He has hunches—he touches on things and you wait to see what he'll do with them. And most of the time he doesn't do anything with them; they don't develop into routines—he just drops them. Midway, he starts getting into his swing, in a section about his experiences during the filming of parts of *Stir Crazy* in the Arizona State Prison. He goes on to talk about a trip he took to Africa, and it's a scene—he can live it. He turns himself into a rabbit, a bear, a lion, a couple of cheetahs, and a fearful gazelle. You feel his relief when he does the animals; a lot of the time he has been looking for his place on this stage, and now he has something physical to do. But then there's a sudden break. Voices, ostensibly from the audience, can be heard. One of them calls, "Do the Mudbone routine," and, rather wearily, saying that it will be for the last time, Pryor sits on a stool and does the ancient storyteller Mudbone, who in the seventies was considered one of his great creations. And the movie goes thud. This section feels like an interpolation—it doesn't have the crackle of a performer interacting with an audience. It's almost as dead as what happens when Johnny Carson asks an aging celebrity to tell the joke he used to tell that always broke Johnny up. Pryor looks defeated, shot down. The sudden dullness is compounded by his sitting: we're used to seeing him prowling—accompanied, when the spots hit the curtain behind him, by wriggling shadows.

When he picks up his act again, he talks about freebasing, and the feelings he had about his pipe—it talks to him, and he becomes the pipe. We feel as if we were actually listening to his habit talking to him. And he builds up a routine about his wife and his friend Jim Brown telling him what cocaine was doing to him. But "the pipe say, 'Don't listen.' " And then he tells about the hospital and about Jim Brown's visiting him every day. He's a great actor and a great combination of mimic and mime; he's perhaps never more inspired than when he assumes the personality of a rebellious organ of his body or of an inanimate object, such as that pipe—or Jim Brown. This is the high point of the film. When he becomes something or someone, it isn't an imitation; he incarnates the object's soul and guts. But he doesn't have enough material to work up the rhythmic charge he reached before Mudbone. What he has in *Sunset Strip* is the material for a forty-minute classic.

The picture is full of wonderful bits, such as his demonstration of how he loses his voice when he's angry at his wife, and to those unfamiliar with Pryor's infectiousness and truthfulness and his unfettered use of obscenity, and to all those who missed his 1979 film, it may be a revelation. But the greatness of *Richard Pryor Live in Concert* was in the impetus of his performance rhythm—the way he kept going, with all those characters and voices bursting out of him. When he told us about his heart attack, he was, in almost the same instant, the helpless body being double-crossed by its heart, the heart itself, a telephone operator, and Pryor the aloof, dissociated observer.

We registered what a mysteriously original physical comedian he is, and we saw the performance sweat soaking his collarless red silk shirt. (There's no visible sweat this time.)

If he fulfilled his comic genius in *Live in Concert*, here he's sampling the good will the public feels toward him. Audiences want him, they love him, even in bum movies, and he appears to be experiencing a personal fulfillment. But he hasn't yet renewed himself as an artist: it may seem cruel to say so, but even the routine on his self-immolation is a pale copy of his heart attack. In the first film, there was a sense of danger; when he used the word "nigger," it was alive and raw. When he uses it here, it just seems strange. He's up against something very powerful: the audience may have come expecting to see history made, but history now is also just seeing Richard Pryor. He knows that he doesn't have to do anything. All he has to do is stand there and be adored. And he knows there's something the matter with this new situation, but he doesn't know how to deal with it.

.　　　.　　　.　　　.　　　.

Deathtrap felt like one to me. Ira Levin's wisecracking whodunit, which is in its fifth year on Broadway, is a pastiche of murder-mystery tricks. It's the sort of cumbersomely ingenious entertainment that's meant to be played by slick, easy actors; it has to be done frivolously and artificially to compensate for the fact that it's just a machine for making money, cranking its way across the stage. But the director, Sidney Lumet, and the screenwriter, Jay Presson Allen (she's also the executive producer), have decided to make the movie version as realistic as possible. What this comes down to is a very broad, obvious movie that looks like an ugly play and appears to be a vile vision of life. When the central character (Michael Caine), a playwright who had a series of hit thrillers but, more recently, has been having one flop after another, is in his luxurious East Hampton home (a large converted-windmill structure), he talks on the telephone to a former student (Christopher Reeve) whose flawless play *Deathtrap* he means to steal, and, to create movement, Lumet has the camera go with him as he keeps walking in a circle with the phone, while in the background his rich wife (Dyan Cannon) dutifully registers reactions to her husband's wickedness. It has already been planted that she has a bad heart, so we wait for her to keel over. The basic plot twist is out of *Diabolique*, and Ira Levin provides the playwright with a vast collection of medieval murder weapons and instruments of torture and such later devices as Harry Houdini's handcuffs. (This movie is for people who dream of seeing *Sleuth* again—there must be at least one or two of them.) In another scene, Caine, on the porch of the manse, talks with poor Cannon, who must busy herself among the outdoor plants—misting them, or something, with a tiny spray bottle. The movie clanks and klunks. Irene Worth comes running in, as a Dutch psychic who's living in the house next door (which, from the look of this one, must be quite a distance away). And bewilderingly, though the master bedroom is in the tower and the creaking windmill makes quite a ruckus, it has no plot function at all. There's also a bizarre early sequence, before the action settles down in the house: Caine, returning from Manhattan by train, sleeps past the East Hampton station, gets off at Montauk, and takes a taxi home. Maybe Lumet and Mrs. Allen thought we needed an excursion?

This movie grows worse and worse, with each twist and reversal destroying whatever involvement we had before, and at the end the staging and editing are so fast and muddled that you can't be sure what's happening. Except for the shouting, which has become *de rigueur* in a Lumet film, the actors don't disgrace themselves. Caine is a virtuoso at letting us know what his character is thinking. Reeve seems less beefy these days and can look craggy and sinister, though at times his pecs compete with Dyan Cannon's. She's cruelly treated by the camera and doesn't do anything she hasn't done before and better, such as her startled shriek from *Heaven Can Wait*; still, she's in there trying and gets a couple of laughs. And initially Irene Worth is certainly more welcome than she was in *Eyewitness*. But what we should never see in a movie of this type is actors working hard; yet that's all we see, and their acting gave me no pleasure. It's not a kick when the characters who are meant to be homosexual are mincingly vicious and effete. And it's not a kick, at the very start, before Caine gets on the commuter train home, when he's in the theatre where his latest play is collapsing, and the producer (Joe Silver) turns to him and, in full-screen, large-nosed profile, yells, "Putz!" That's the Lumet touch.

April 5, 1982

Rhapsody in Blue

*T*he French romantic thriller *Diva* dashes along with a pell-mell gracefulness, and it doesn't take long to see that the images and visual gags and homages all fit together and reverberate back and forth. It's a glittering toy of a movie, like *Touch of Evil* or *The Stunt Man* or *Zazie dans le Métro*. This one is by a new director, Jean-Jacques Beineix (pronounced simply Ben-ex, with the stress on the second syllable), who understands the pleasures to be had from a picture that doesn't take itself very seriously. Every shot seems designed to delight the audience. Now thirty-five, Beineix has been working as an assistant to other directors for ten years; he begins his own directing career as a Euro-disco entertainer with a fabulous camera technique. The movie doesn't have the purity of conception of those other toys. It isn't quite in their class, and though you may come out of it with some of the same exhilaration, it isn't really memorable. But the images are so smooth yet so tricky and hip that Beineix might be Carol Reed reborn with a Mohawk haircut.

The diva of the title is an awesomely beautiful black American soprano called Cynthia Hawkins (and played by the American Wilhelmenia Fernandez), who inspires a fanatic following, like that of Maria Callas. But the glorious Cynthia has a major eccentricity: she refuses to make recordings, because she wants the public to have the full experience of a singer's presence. Jules, the eighteen-year-old hero (Frédéric Andrei), a skinny young postal messenger in Paris, with an official cap that's too big for his face, is, perhaps, Cynthia's most dedicated fan. He rides his motorbike all the way to Munich and other cities she performs in, and when she gives a concert in Paris he sneaks his Nagra tape machine in and makes a recording—he wants to be able to listen to her at home. Her voice is thrilling in the hushed, expectant atmosphere; her off-the-shoulder satin gown reveals a creamy brown arm, and her lips push out toward us as she articulates the words. Jules' face is full of adoration; a tear collects in one eye and falls, while his hands skillfully regulate the dials. It's at this point that the picture opens, and from there on we follow the chaos that envelops Jules because of this tape and a second tape that he knows nothing about. A barefoot prostitute, running away from two assassins and trying to reach a policewoman to turn over a cassette revealing names and details of a narcotics-and-vice ring, sees the killers coming at her, and, just before being murdered, she drops the tape in the saddlebag of Jules' bike. The wide-eyed music lover Jules is the subject of two intertwined chases. The police and the killers are after him for the prostitute's exposé, and a pair of Chinese record pirates from Taiwan are trying to get his concert tape, so that they can use it to blackmail Cynthia Hawkins into signing with them—they threaten that if she doesn't they'll release the illicit recording.

For a while, Jules innocently goes on about his life. In a music store, he watches a young Vietnamese girl, Alba (played by the fourteen-year-old Thuy An Luu), as she calmly snitches a record and brazens it out with the suspicious clerk. The unfazable Alba is the post-Godardian tootsie—in her short-short skirts and transparent plastic coat, she's a lollipop wrapped in cellophane. Alba appears to have no inner life at all, to be totally—and enchantingly—a creature of surface attitudes, all pose. In the street, outside the store, she tells Jules that the record is a present for a guy who's in his cool phase, and takes him to meet the guy—Gorodish (Richard Bohringer), the most dream-born of the characters (and ultimately, perhaps, the least successful element). When you see this movie, which opened in Paris in March, 1981, and is still running (it has just won some of the top French prizes—Best First Film, and Best Photography, Sound, and Music), you get a clearer sense of what went wrong for Coppola in his *One From the Heart*. Much of what Coppola seemed to be aiming for—the dreamy-disco fun in the detritus of tech commercialism (bashed-in old cars, broken signs, painted skies on billboards)—Beineix had already got onto the screen. And Beineix made it work, because his picture has the baroque characters to go with it—a dozen or so of them—and an amusing enough suspense plot to support it (though the plot is so smart it outsmarts itself in places, and the introduction of a fairy godfather does seem a bit of a cheat). Jules lives in a warehouselike garage and auto graveyard that's reached by a huge car-lift elevator, and Gorodish (he could be thirty-five or forty) lives in a vast bluish space so large Alba skates around in it. Kinetic sculptures slosh water back and forth, and Gorodish works on the waves of a giant jigsaw puzzle of the sea, while piling up Gitanes cigarette boxes, with their wavy blue and white lines. When all hell breaks loose around Jules, Gorodish in his white suit helps him hide out by packing him into his white Citroën and taking him to a lighthouse-castle that's magical in the blue dawn light. Gorodish seems to be a punkers' deus ex machina, wise in the ways of criminals. He knows how to deal with the forces in society, and, effortlessly, he has the wherewithal to do it. The hero of a novel by Delacorta—which, adapted by Beineix and Jean Van Hamme, was the basis of the film—Gorodish is the bemused Mr. Cool. The conception may be all too airily French. Gorodish is a tease of a character—a Zen master of gadgetry—and he's enjoyable. But toward the end, when he takes over, something gets dampened. Gorodish isn't either believably human or high-wire enough to be a creature of fantasy. He's in between.

Jules' garage, with its crippled Rolls-Royce and its posters for events long past, looks much like Frederic Forrest's dream refuge in *One From the Heart*, but there's a sizable difference. Forrest's company was Reality Wrecking, and he wandered through the painted Las Vegas set morosely. Beineix accepts the faddish, constantly changing reality; he didn't build this vision—it isn't a set, it's Paris as he sees it, and he shows the crazy, dissociated pleasures in it. He isn't even saying that this is a condemned playground; he doesn't make any moral judgment—he's having too much fun looking at the players. *Diva* is the human side of *Alphaville*. Even gags, such as Alba in Jules' garage hopscotching on a nude woman painted on the floor, or Gorodish wearing a diver's mask and snorkel as he chops onions, seem to come out of their characters. And conceits, such as Alba sitting on top of Gorodish's refrigerator as if she were Helen Morgan on the piano, or affectations, such as Jules strolling in the Tuileries with Cynthia Hawkins and holding a white umbrella above her head to frame her beauty, seem exactly what these characters would do. Beineix presents people who charm us because they arrange their reality to suit their whims. They're unself-conscious about being self-conscious. Godard showed us people who were turning into cartoons; the people here don't mind being cartoons—they amuse themselves at it. They make their lives scintillate.

When Cynthia listens to Jules' tape of her singing, she realizes she was wrong to be against recording. But in a way she wasn't. If you put on the record of Wilhelmenia Fernandez singing her big number in the movie—the aria from the first act of Catalani's *La Wally*—you may decide that Cynthia Hawkins was right, because without her beauty and the drama of her presence and the charged setting that the movie gives her performance, her voice isn't quite as overwhelmingly glorious. A movie can do for a performer most of what a live stage appearance can do, and then some. (What singer in a solo recital could afford a whole orchestra behind her?) Actually, the entire movie demonstrates the richness that you can get only from movies. If it's about anything, it's about the joy of making them. (At the lighthouse, Alba serves Jules coffee out of a coffeepot that could be a miniature version of the lighthouse itself.)

Diva is a later stage of what Godard was getting at in *Masculine Feminine* and in his other movies about "the children of Marx and Coca-Cola"—except that now Marx is gone and New Wave music and video games have settled in. What Marxists and other puritans have never wanted to allow for is the fun to be had with the material goodies that capitalism produces (such as entertaining movies). Godard knew it, recognized that alienation wasn't all torment, and then somehow blotted it from his mind. (When he became more political, he *wanted* us all to be tormented.) Alba, the wise-child playmate, may be shell-shocked, but she's having a good time. The young actress Thuy An Luu is completely at ease in front of the camera; if that's the result of fundamental indifference (and it may very well be), it works to her great advantage here. Jules is the Jean-Pierre Léaud of Godard's films with a love of music and a sweeter nature; he wears an invisible aureole, but he's still a fan. Cynthia treats him like a lovely pet, and that seems just about right—he's birdlike. (Wilhelmenia Fernandez' American-accented French and her amateurishness as an actress are ingratiating. It's her bad luck, though, to be caught in the only real lapse of judgment in the movie: Cynthia invites Jules to stay with her while she practices, and then proceeds to sing "Ave Maria"—the banality of the choice momentarily strips her of glamour.)

Beineix may not be interested in what's underneath, but he has a great feeling for surfaces. A chase through the Métro and an escape to a pinball-machine and video-game arcade are so ravishing that they're funny, intentionally. The whole high-tech incandescence of the film is played for humor. Beineix takes it for granted that we'll make all sorts of connections between his images and other movies we've seen—Cynthia Hawkins at the start is like Arletty's Garance in *Children of Paradise*; a police informer who works on a boardwalk operating a Wheel of Chance has layer upon layer of movie associations; there's a little salute to Marilyn Monroe in *The Seven Year Itch*; and Welles is in the huge deserted bluish factory where the all-knowing Gorodish arranges a meeting with the villain—it recalls *The Trial*. Welles is everywhere. But Beineix doesn't force connections on us. Everything is deft, flamboyant yet light—Jules takes Cynthia Hawkins' pearly satin gown and flings it around his neck, like a First World War aviator's scarf, as he rides off on a borrowed motorbike. In the factory, Gorodish's tape-recorded voice directs the villain.

Every shot seems to have a shaft of wit. It's Welles romanticized, gift-wrapped. It's a mixture of style and chic hanky-panky, but it's also genuinely sparkling. The camera skids ahead, and you see things you don't expect. Beineix thinks with his eyes.

April 19, 1982

Audience Pleaser

*T*he writer-director Blake Edwards is an ingenious rough-and-tumble farceur, but he's relentless. He keeps hitting you in the same place with the same hammer, and even after you scream that you get it, you get it, he keeps hitting you. There's a built-in exhaustion factor in his pictures: the laughs (mine, anyway) stop long before the plot winds up. His overextended farces turn into frantic epics, with the humor left behind in the first half. Back in his 1965 *The Great Race*, two thousand cream pies went splat. In the last couple of *Pink Panther* films, he staged cliché gags and then repeated them. And in recent years he has devised a bulldozing sort of comedy. Each joke is announced about six times; Edwards is like the train conductors who boom out the name of the next station long before you get to it. He thinks he has to go to the brassiest lengths to reach us and make us react. He plays to the swinishness in the audience; he feeds it. At his new picture, *Victor/Victoria*, the people around me in the Ziegfeld Theatre laughed hardest at the crudest setups and the moldiest, most cynical dumb jokes. The movie isn't all bad. Edwards comes up with some venerable bits of slapstick goofiness, and his sight gags work better here than they did in the last *Pink Panther* films, because they're not central—they're incidental and more casual. Despite the nullity of the songs (by Henry Mancini and Leslie Bricusse), and the deliberate pacing, with the camera lingering on the payoffs, the first half is more amiable than Edwards' recent *10* and *S.O.B.*—it has a yeastiness. But *Victor/Victoria* is an audience pleaser in the worst sense.

The movie began life as a 1933 German film, *Viktor und Viktoria*; the new version is at least the fifth (and, I would bet, the most ponderously Teutonic). The idea resembles that of *Some Like It Hot*, which had a similar cluttered ancestry. In *Some Like It Hot*, Tony Curtis and Jack Lemmon were musicians who hid out from "the mob" by becoming part of a girls' orchestra. *Victor/Victoria* has an extra fillip—the heroine, Julie Andrews, an English

331

singer stranded in Paris in 1934, pretends to be a man so that she can get work as a female impersonator. Yet while *Some Like It Hot* is at its most entertaining when Tony Curtis and Jack Lemmon trip along in high heels, passing as women, *Victor/Victoria* is at its best in the slapstick embellishments of the preparatory sequences; when Julie Andrews finally gets into men's clothes, there's nothing remotely funny about it.

The laughs from the audience are bellybusters, though. Probably the loudest one comes when James Garner, as a big-shot night-club owner from Chicago who's in love with Julie and has covertly made sure that she's really a girl, tweaks her by offering her a cigar, and she, trying to be manly, bravely inhales and chokes. (Some of us groaned at that routine in the thirties and forties; it's such a stupid putdown of women as weak creatures.) And how does Garner ascertain that his beloved is definitely female? He hides in her bathroom, and then sneaks away. This is the picture that has been characterized in the press as "subtle," "stylish," "daring," "delightfully risqué," and "ultra-sophisticated." Edwards fills it with brawls (three or four of them), and there's a musical number, set in a Chicago night spot, in which Lesley Ann Warren, who plays the girlfriend Garner discards when he meets Victoria, leads a row of chorus girls as they gyrate, bent over, presenting their rear ends to the patrons and smacking their own flesh enthusiastically. It's too coarse and frenetic to be satirical; it's possibly the most contemptuous display of women's bodies I've ever seen in a major-studio movie. People at the Ziegfeld were roaring their approval. They were practically rolling in the aisles.

If *Viktor und Viktoria* went through many permutations, surely it was because the idea lent itself to an atmosphere of sexual ambiguity. In the only one of the previous versions that I saw—the 1935 English musical comedy *First a Girl*—the bouncy, long-legged Jessie Matthews was an adorable ingénue, and the idea that she was palming herself off as a man was very funny. In the new version, you don't believe that Julie Andrews could successfully impersonate a woman on the stage. You don't know what she's doing up there. In her first big number, "Le Jazz Hot," she doesn't have her usual cool, prissy tone, and there's none of the singing down to the audience which is her worst fault as an entertainer; she wears heavy eye makeup, and she's more rousing than usual—she puts the song over. But her other major number—a Spanish routine—is listless. And by the second half of the movie her pale face is drawn and tired and she talks seriously, in an all-knowing tone. She wears men's clothes, but she isn't tantalizingly androgynous; she comes across as neuter. She doesn't even seem to be in drag—it's just Julie Andrews in a short haircut. She could be Irene Dunne impersonating David Bowie.

Sometimes Julie Andrews has done well by other directors: she was just right in Arthur Hiller's *The Americanization of Emily*, and she warmed up and appeared to become softer in parts of George Roy Hill's *Hawaii*. But in *Darling Lili*, *The Tamarind Seed*, *10*, *S.O.B.*, and this picture—the five films she has made with Blake Edwards (who is her husband)—she's always a Trapp. Sandy Duncan, who also has clear, piping enunciation and a perky, scrubbed-clean quality, could conceivably play this role, because she has a spark of insanity in her timing, and the possibility of giddiness. But Andrews is too infuriatingly sane and remote to be at the center of a farce. In *Victor/Victoria*, we get no sense of her as an actress or as a person.

Robert Preston, who plays Toddy, an aging homosexual entertainer who likes the destitute Victoria and trains her as a female impersonator, is obliged to deliver Blake Edwards' curdled witticisms—such as "Shame is an unhappy emotion invented by pietists in order to exploit the human race" and (about himself) "There's nothing more inconvenient than an old queen with a head cold." That one, with its buzzword "queen," gets a roar. Preston plays a sentimental stereotype so heartily and likably that he redeems the musty material. This is yet another movie in which a girl's best friend is a homosexual—who can be her best friend because he has no designs on her. Toddy's affection for Victoria is *pure*; since there is no sex involved between them, there is, presumably, no jealousy or competitiveness, either. Toddy is an idealized partner and manager; he's a buddy to confide in, a shoulder to lean on.

Preston, with his thick, curly mane and his broad smile, brings an unholy glee to his work. He has often been the best thing in a movie; he was memorable as Hemingway's Francis Macomber in the key scenes of the 1947 *The Macomber Affair*, and he was great singing "Ya Got Trouble" in the 1962 *The Music Man*. (It wasn't the wrinkled-silk patter style of Rex Harrison; Preston stomped on his lyrics—he gave them an American charge.) He was great again as Steve McQueen's father in Peckinpah's 1972 *Junior Bonner*, and he made *S.O.B.* bearable. He gets such a big kick out of acting that he's like a con man who thinks he's conned you into letting him have a good time. He loves performing. Julie Andrews doesn't; she performs dutifully; and, maybe because she was trained for the stage as a child, she slips into a manipulative manner automatically—in whatever she does she includes the audience response that's wanted. (It's what used to drive some of us crazy when we watched little Margaret O'Brien: she did our reacting for us.) But maybe some of Preston's love of his profession rubbed off on Julie Andrews, because she relaxes in the "You and Me" number she does with him; she comes alive—she comes close to enjoying herself. For a few seconds, she may even be playing on instinct. And in the early part of the movie she also has some conversational rapport with Preston. But when she's supposed to be in love with Garner she gives the most joyless and sexless performance I've seen since her bizarre unpleasantness in *10*, when she demanded to know if Dudley Moore was going to make love to her, in a tone that would clearly render it impossible. In bed with Garner, the grim-faced Victoria lectures him on sexual politics; she tells him (and us) that he shouldn't mind having people take him for a homosexual—being gay or straight is less important than people's other qualities. Her remarks sound very odd coming from the mouth of the woman who took one look at the tall, dark, and handsome—and rich—Garner and confided to Toddy that she'd like to have an affair with him.

Why are homosexual spokesmen celebrating the film? Maybe for the same reason that the young American leftist press celebrated *Reds*. They're hungry to see fantasy versions of themselves on the screen, and, forced to, they'll accept crumbs. Once a movie shows itself to be on their side, it doesn't matter what its content is. They can say, "At least it isn't against us—which is more than we expected from Hollywood." Since it has the right message, that gives them a license to respond to the silliness of the gags, each with a long, long lineage but with some humor still left in it, even when it's executed in a far from masterly way.

Homosexuals used to experience shame; now that has shifted over to pride. The shame was a snare; the pride can be, too. And damned if it doesn't enter into some of Julie Andrews' speeches. The movie has the feeling of gay in-jokes. Its tone is: We know so much that we can have fun. This attitude is (anachronistically) embodied in the character of Toddy—a big open heart and no conflicts. (There is no way an "old queen" in the thirties—he would have grown up in Oscar Wilde's day—could have been so at peace with himself.) Toddy feels no twinges of pain; he isn't even militant—that's left to Victoria. She spouts the new, eighties show-biz enlightenment; he's the all-accepting, fun-loving darling, free of fear. But at the same time that the picture sentimentalizes homosexuality it's full of prejudicial old gags. For example, we're supposed to be charmed by Victoria's feistiness when she socks Richard, Toddy's former partner. Richard, being homosexual, and thinking she's a fellow, is too upset and cowardly to return the blow. (The audience applauds the scene.) At the end, Toddy, replacing Victor/Victoria on the stage in her Spanish number, does a traditional parody of a drag routine. Preston's performing zeal really does seem bigger than questions of sexual orientation, and this is the best-sustained comic routine in the movie. But the point of it appears to be that men are so hopelessly lunky and butch that they fall all over themselves when they try to look like women. Watching the burly Preston, who's wearing a form-fitting señorita costume, people in the audience can be reassured: "Yeah, that's how preposterous men look when they put on women's clothes."

Blake Edwards has a standard, safe approach: the audience is never in doubt about Julie Andrews' straightness or about James Garner's straightness. He doesn't make overtures to her until he has assured himself that she's a woman. (Garner, in a mustache, and acting like a funny, scowly Clark Gable, plays the businesslike bathroom scene very cleverly—he has cartoonishly obsessed eyes.) What the audience is worked up to howl over is his pretending to think Victoria is a man—pretending to be broadminded. The standard sexual clichés are reaffirmed in this movie: Garner takes Andrews to a prizefight and she is sickened; she takes him to the opera—*Madame Butterfly*—where she weeps and he is bored numb. (In both cases, she's the over-emotional one.) Julie Andrews makes a pompous, educational speech about wanting to go on dressing in men's attire because of how much more liberated she is as a man (though her getup isn't that of a man but that of an effeminate homosexual, which would be a far more restricting social role than a woman's). At the end, of course, she gives up her pin-striped suits and her career for her man. At no point does the pretense of being Victor offend her or violate her feelings as a woman; she never even expresses any rage that her performing skills are rejected by managers when she's in her true guise and fawned over when they believe her to be a female impersonator. Edwards doesn't think anything through. But he's careful: he doesn't take any real chances. (That must be what some people mean when they say he's "a professional.") He's at his most confident when he lets Garner's comic bodyguard (Alex Karras) "come out," but he never even raises the possibility that Garner might be attracted by a woman who's boyish. I don't think Edwards means Julie Andrews to be successful at looking like a man. He doesn't want the audience to suspend disbelief for an instant. He just wants to tease and tickle.

This is a movie that stops cold for high-minded speeches about the need for women's liberation while scoring most of its biggest laughs by degrading Lesley Ann Warren. (Edwards uses her so grossly that she's like a drag queen.) She does some inventive, dippy line readings—exaggerated versions of Jean Harlow's nasal petulance in *Dinner at Eight*. She's a comic-strip eccentric, and you feel her sweetness—you want to go on liking her. But Edwards ties tin cans to her tail. He makes her nasty and unfeeling, and turns the movie against her so she's just a screeching floozy—a piece of meat. He doesn't really understand that the magic of an eccentric is inexplicable. He tries to explain everything; he reduces her to rational greed and destroys her. Julie Andrews is always teaching you lessons, and so is he. Edwards attaches a High Church of Hollywood importance to each joke—he keeps you posted on every single nutty thing that he does. And doesn't do: some of the jokes that are announced far in advance don't arrive, but people have already had their laugh at the announcement. When homosexuals were despised, there was a compensatory myth that they had better taste than anybody else. Their enthusiasm for *Victor/Victoria* should help debunk that myth. Maybe they no longer need it.

. . . . . .

*T*here's no American director who gives his movies a tonier buildup than Paul Schrader does. His interviews about his new *Cat People*—cover stories in both *Film Comment* and *American Film*—might make the picture seem mouth-watering to those who hadn't seen his *Blue Collar*, *Hardcore*, and *American Gigolo*. But if you did see that last one you know his trouble: his movies are becoming almost as tony as the interviews. Working with his team—the visual consultant Ferdinando Scarfiotti, the cinematographer John Bailey, and the composer Giorgio Moroder—Schrader is perfecting an apocalyptic swank. When his self-puffery about magic and myth and eroticism and about effecting a marriage between the feeling of Cocteau's *Orpheus* and the style of Bertolucci's *The Conformist* is actually transferred to the screen in *Cat*

People, each shot looks like an album cover for records you don't ever want to play.

While trying to prove himself a heavyweight moralist, Schrader has somehow never mastered the rudiments of directing. He doesn't shape his sequences. In *American Gigolo*, the design was stunning and the camera was always moving, but the characters were enervated and the film felt stagnant, logy; its only energy was in Deborah Harry's singing "Call Me" during the opening credits. And in *Cat People*, from a script by Alan Ormsby that's a to-tal reworking of the much simpler 1942 film, Schrader repeatedly kills your pleasure. Just when a scene begins to hold some interest, he cuts away from it; the crucial things seem to be happening between the scenes. He's trying for a poetic, "legendary" style—which turns out to be humorless, comatose, and obscure. You can fake out interviewers if you're as smart as Schrader is, but he may be falling for his own line of gaudy patter. *Cat People* has all the furnishings for a religious narrative about Eros and Thanatos, but what's go-ing on is that Nastassia Kinski and Malcolm McDowell—the sister and broth-er with black leopards inside them—are jumping out of their skins and leaving little puddles of guck behind. According to the film's newly minted legend, the two of them can have sex only with each other; sex with anyone else releases the beast inside, who devours the lover. The picture is often ludi-crous (especially in the orange-colored primal-dream sequences), yet you don't get to pass the time by laughing, because it's so queasy and so confus-ingly put together that you feel shut out. You're brought into it only by the camera tricks or the special-effects horrors, or, perhaps, the nude scenes, or a strange image—such as the façade of an Art Deco church covered in lights.

Nastassia Kinski's voice has no music; she continues to sound dubbed. Is it simply that she speaks English inexpressively? Or is it from that slightly twisted openmouthed look, as if a toad had just leaped out? She never quite seems to be inside the story, even when she's prowling about in the moon-light, naked and sinuously clumsy, with blood drooling out of her mouth. With the possible exception of McDowell's, the performances are of no inter-est. Even the marvellous, red-haired Annette O'Toole (who is sometimes like Meryl Streep with more grit) isn't well-directed; she's trying too hard to be natural, and she pops out at you. Still, she shows a little freshness—especially when, as a New Orleans zoo worker, she laughs as she sprays water on the elephants, who seem to be laughing, too. She's more vivid than the zoo-keeper hero (John Heard), who spends most of his time smiling to himself. Ruby Dee plays the kind of role we might have thought she'd graduated from some years back—the sinister servant. (This one exchanges troubled, mean-ingful looks with the master, and winds up in prison for reasons that the movie doesn't impart to us.) The dialogue that the actors are given to speak is dead. Eventually, Nastassia, who's in love with the zookeeper, pleads with him—"Kill me. You must free me." He says, "I can't," and you want to yell, "Oh, go ahead and kill her."

May 3, 1982

A Devil Without Fire

*I*stván Szabó's *Mephisto*, the West German–Hungarian co-production
that won the Academy Award for Best Foreign Film, is an indictment of a
morally bankrupt actor, Hendrik Höfgen (played by Klaus Maria Brandauer),
who, because he wants to go on performing, truckles to those in power. At
the start, in Hamburg, in the twenties, Höfgen is a provincial actor furiously
banging his fists against his dressing-room wall because the applause he
hears is not for him; it's for a pretty visiting operetta star from Berlin, who has
just sung the "I'll give my heart" aria from Millöcker's *Dubarry*—which deals
with a milliner's rise to power as the favorite of Louis XV. During the pre-Nazi
period, Höfgen climbs out of his provincial status; he slips into the guise of a
man in the throes of romantic ardor, courts and marries the daughter of an
eminent cultural figure, and within a few years he has risen to stardom in Berlin. (Hendrik Höfgen is based on Gustav Gründgens, who was married during his early years to Thomas Mann's daughter Erika; the movie is loosely
adapted from the 1936 novel *Mephisto*, by her brother Klaus Mann, who is
believed to have been Gründgens' lover.) Höfgen sometimes performs at left-
wing cabarets, and he spouts idealistic "revolutionary" theories about workers' theatre, but when the Nazis come to power and his wife goes abroad he's
afraid to uproot himself; he's afraid that he won't be able to act without the
German language—that without it he'll be nothing.

We observe the stages in Höfgen's Nazification, as he offers to play supporting roles to the bovine, dimpled blond Valkyrie who is the mistress of the
Nazi Prime Minister—the General, a Göring-like figure, played by Rolf Hoppe.
(There's no Hitler in the film's Germany; the situation is meant to be allegori-
cal, and so we don't hear "Heil Hitler!"—just "Heil!") Höfgen accommodates
himself to the wishes of the General and becomes part of the Nazi spectacle
while he tries to protect his own mistress, a dancer who is part black, and his
left-wing and Jewish friends. But he is drawn further and further into the General's coterie, until he is finally the General's favorite actor and lapdog. He
reinterprets classic plays in order to make them politically acceptable, and he
becomes Germany's leading actor and the head of the State Theatre. (Only
he and the General know how powerless he really is.) All these stages in the
damnation of a man who we know from the start is an opportunist are fairly
routine.

The picture has another theme, though, which has fresh possibilities, and it's this theme, I think, that makes the movie peculiarly gripping. Szabó sets up Höfgen as a symbolic actor—a man who has no substance, who is merely the sum of the roles he plays offstage and on. The theatre is his temple, and Nazism, with all its theatricality, is a larger stage. Höfgen lives to perform. A flamboyant actor-director-manager when he's so young that there's still a suggestion of baby fat in his cheeks, he's a whirlwind. There's an element of mystery in the subject of acting, and at the outset Brandauer, who has gleaming cat eyes and a seductive, impish smile, seems a startlingly right choice for the part, because he evokes so many other performers, dozens of them—such as Marius Goring, the young composer in *The Red Shoes*. At times, when Brandauer's Höfgen smiles, there's a flash of a devilish Albert Finney. He appears to be an *enfant terrible*, a baby-faced killer-genius, like the young Orson Welles. Half undressed and dancing orgiastically with his black mistress, Höfgen seems self-hypnotized, admiring his own sensuousness and the flutter of his thigh muscles. He gives the impression of being homosexual, though he has no affairs with men. For his second wife he chooses an actress with no principles—one in good standing with the General. The only woman he really seems to care about is the black dancer (who is played to feline perfection by Karin Boyd, a German stage actress), and there is a strong suggestion of kinkiness in their relationship. The first time we see him visit her, she holds a whip behind her back, and they don't copulate—they dance, he twirls himself into a frenzy, and then she performs fellatio on him. (This film contains many "suggestions." Höfgen's first and second wives appear to have been lovers; at least, they smile very knowingly at each other. And there is also a prodigiously bad woman sculptor who's in high repute with the Nazis; she makes looming, uplifting statues that would have fitted right into a Cecil B. De Mille epic, and she, too, has that soft, carnal smile. Her name is Leni. If this is meant as an allusion to the great moviemaker Riefenstahl, Szabó is grotesquely wide of the mark.)

In the shoptalk of stage and screen directors, one frequently hears about a pure actor (or actress) type—a performer who doesn't exist without roles to play, a sort of neurotic vacuum. Directors (who are often jealous or angry about the power position of stars) say that this empty actor may give you a stunning performance but he's hell to work with, because you never know from one day to the next what attitudes he's trying on or what he'll blow up about. This is a fertile, almost unexplored movie subject, except for the slapstick satirical treatment that actors and actresses used to be given in comedies such as *The Royal Family of Broadway*, *Twentieth Century*, and *Bombshell*. But Szabó goes at it with so much heavy moral condemnation, contrasting Höfgen with anti-Nazi actors who forfeit their lives, that it seems as if the only good actor is a dead actor.

Mephisto unintentionally raises a lot of questions that the director doesn't deal with. It isn't hard to come up with a guess about why he doesn't want his actor to be homosexual: he's probably hoping to make Höfgen a more universal representative of those who collaborate with evil. But he doesn't want to suggest that a collaborator could be "normal" either; the lesbian touches may be there to indicate that Höfgen has sexual problems—that he marries women who don't make much of a demand on him. But why are the glimpses of him as an actor so pedestrian? I never saw the actor that Höfgen is modelled on in a live performance, though I've heard accounts of him on the stage (Gründgens brought his *Faust* to City Center in 1961) and I've seen him in movies—most conspicuously as the black-gloved, leather-coated chief of the underworld in Fritz Lang's *M*. With a bowler hat for a crown, he was cocky and almost comically frightening; he had a powerful presence. Höfgen doesn't; even when we see him onstage as Mephisto, he isn't demonic—he's a lightweight. And we never get to see any of his "reinterpreted" Hamlet. It's a key limitation in Szabó's approach that he fudges the issue of whether Höfgen is really a great actor. Is it because of lack of flair on Szabó's part that Höfgen, who has a meteoric rise in the theatre, shows nothing out of the ordinary in his onstage scenes and that the staging itself is conventional? I have a feeling that Szabó doesn't want Höfgen to be an inspired actor or director, because that might seem to justify his determination to go on working in the German theatre whatever the circumstances. But at the same time I doubt if Szabó does have much theatrical flair. He might be able to fuse this film's two themes if he had the emotional extravagance to evoke the crazed romanticism of a narcissistic star—to make us feel what theatre might mean to Höfgen. But in denying greatness, or even dedicated artistry, to Höfgen he prevents the movie from soaring. He's forever heading off his own subject at the pass.

The revelations of the character are all in the first half, and Brandauer shows his vivacity when Höfgen is being willful and unpredictable. But Höfgen doesn't have the chance to flower as an actor, or even to enjoy himself as an actor; he's never at ease—he knows he shouldn't be doing what he's doing. Midway, he tones down and the film dries up. And when Szabó reaches for a big symbolic effect—the actor dissolving in the glare of spotlights—it doesn't really work. We're too aware of the director's didactic intentions. (A friend told me that he found the last part of *Mephisto* incredibly impressive; he said that Höfgen's thoughts were almost tangible, and he felt as if he could reach out and grab them. Well, of course Höfgen's thoughts are tangible: he speaks them right to the camera, and the subtitles spell them out for us. He tells us how pathetically empty he is.)

This movie has a stern air of rectitude that produces discomfort. Other films by Szabó that I've seen dealt with contemporary experience in Communist Hungary, and in them he brought unusual intelligence (and craftsmanship) to the pickles his people were in. He knows how fuzzy and complicated moral decisions are in a Communist country, and how unexpected the results may be, but when he goes back in time to Nazi Germany (before his birth, in 1938) everything is suddenly black and white. The movie has no generosity. It doesn't ask if, perhaps, Höfgen the symbolic actor has something to give, or even if, possibly, he feels fully alive only when he's on-stage singing or dancing or assuming a false identity that excites him. His desire to perform is treated as careerism, and he is presented as a tantrummy infant with an insatiable greed for attention. That's what the slapstick comedies said, too (though affectionately); Szabó's portentousness prepares us to expect something more revelatory. Szabó (who co-wrote the script, with Péter Dobai) probably means to be condemning a type that he thinks is rampant throughout civilization—the scale of the picture prepares us for a big subject. Originally two hours and forty minutes long, it's an epic, with a multinational cast (the soundtrack of the two-hour-and-sixteen-minute version showing here is in German, with considerable dubbing, though not in the two principal roles—Höfgen and the General). But Szabó builds his case on this one ambitious pipsqueak. Since Höfgen hasn't been allowed to be a great actor, he seems too small for the scale of the attack. It's like *Citizen Kane* with somebody like John Dean at the center.

Actors tend to go on performing, whatever the changes in their country's government, just as most people in any society—Fascist, Communist, or capitalist—make adjustments. We don't condemn Szabó because he made movies in Budapest after the Soviet tanks rolled in. (We might condemn him if he made movies glorifying the Soviet Union for crushing the Hungarian Freedom Fighters.) An actor's wanting to please—wanting to have the pleasure of giving pleasure—is not necessarily as ugly as this movie makes it. Gründgens, who was in fact Göring's protégé, actually *was* able to save some people's lives, and he did not distort the plays he appeared in; he was cleared after the war and went on performing, as popular as he had been during the Nazi period.

To Szabó, actors are unformed—they lack backbone. But if they had it they might be hopeless as actors. Maybe they need a streak of the infantile and of undefined androgynous sexuality. Actors try things out; they don't know in advance what a role will demand of them. Szabó condemns them for it—essentially, he's condemning them for being actors. The picture is out to demonstrate, once again, that the man who compromises is doomed, that his art will suffer, that Fascism destroys the soul. Yet it starts with an actor who we are given to understand has no soul. Everything in the movie is pointed; it's all damning him. But when you leave the theatre you're not sure what the point is. Even when you might want to slap Höfgen, Szabó does all the slapping for you. Eventually, you feel for the guy.

May 17, 1982

Fighters

*R*oger Donaldson's *Smash Palace* is an amazingly accomplished movie to have come out of New Zealand. It's only Donaldson's second feature film, and his first, the 1977 *Sleeping Dogs*, which opened here a few months ago, was also the first movie to be produced in New Zealand in fifteen years. *Smash Palace* (a wonderfully apt title) is a variant of the "separating" movies that have recently been made in this country, but with a more basic male-female conflict. Al Shaw (Bruno Lawrence) is a man's man—a racing-car driver, who met his French-born wife, Jacqui (Anna Jemison), eight years ago, when he was on the European circuit. But soon afterward his father died in New Zealand, and he went home, accompanied by Jacqui, then pregnant, to sell his father's wrecking-yard business, the Smash Palace; instead, he settled into the vast yard—it stretches over acres in an isolated area near a railroad crossing. Except for the pleasure he takes in watching his daughter, Georgie, scooting around in miniature cars, he lives like a single man, puttering with motors, burning up the country roads in the Grand-Prix Formula One Racer he's restoring, and drinking beer with his pals. He has slipped into a male dream existence; he has everything just the way he likes it, except that Jacqui keeps expressing her dissatisfaction. And, up to a point, that's all right, too—her complaining confirms his male way of life.

Bruno Lawrence and Anna Jemison embody this conflict to an uncanny degree: Al is virile, likable, growing bald—he's flesh-and-blood; Jacqui is fine-boned and fastidious. Everything about her is lovely and precise, and it seems exactly right that when she leaves Al she takes a job teaching French. They're the kind of mismatch that isn't apparent during courtship, or even during the first years of marriage; he must have been a dashing daredevil and she glowing, delicate, and seemingly soft. But to anyone looking at them now it's clear that he belongs in this remote corner of New Zealand and she doesn't. In a virtuoso sustained sequence, they charge through the house arguing and hitting each other while Georgie, in her bedroom, tries to blot the sounds out of her consciousness, rhythmically sucking her thumb and rubbing her nose with one hand and snapping a flashlight on and off with the other, and then escaping—she climbs out of her window and huddles with the family dog in the cab of Al's pickup truck. By then, the fighting has entered a different phase, with Al, aroused, pulling off Jacqui's clothes and having a go at her. It's the kind of angry sex that ends an argument but resolves nothing and tends to make a woman furious, because of her feeling that the man's superior strength and his potency are his answer to everything. As Al and Jacqui lie together afterward, exhausted, she tells him what we already know—that she's leaving him. The full force of the scene comes in his not replying.

Donaldson trusts his material; he doesn't force the situation into conventional dramatic revelations. The silences are as expressive as the dialogue, and a great deal of what the movie is about comes across in quick shots of Georgie's face. She's the battleground. Jacqui takes the child with her, of course, and though she knows that the one thing Al loves more than cars is Georgie, she views his attempts to be with the child as irresponsible and obtains a non-molestation order. Georgie is close to her mother, but she has a special rapport with Al—they can't help smiling when they look at each other, they get high on each other. Al goes a little crazy when Jacqui, who now has the upper hand, coolly and self-righteously deprives him of the child.

The movie is like those Warners pictures of the thirties that took their stories from the headlines in the tabloids; it originated in a news item about a child in a gun siege. But after we've come to know Al and Jacqui, what happens seems to flow naturally from their particular blindnesses. Donaldson wrote the script, with Peter Hansard and Bruno Lawrence (who was well known in New Zealand as a jazz and rock musician—he had his own group—long before he took up acting), and the film is conceived with a freshness and depth that you didn't get from the Warners pictures. Jacqui goes to a back-country party, where the raw faces tell life stories that don't connect with hers; there's a scene of Georgie twirling and unbraiding one of her pigtails as she stares fixedly at a TV set, watching all alone as her father wins a race; there's a memorable—desperate—birthday celebration, with party hats made from folded newspaper. And all of it is something to look at. Donaldson, who was born in Australia in 1945, worked as a still photographer before he went into making TV commercials and earned the money to try his first short films; he had several years of directing movies and shows for television before he tackled *Sleeping Dogs*. His intensive experience helps to explain how he could shoot *Smash Palace* in six weeks. It's beautifully photographed, with no empty pictorialism—no pretty pictures for their own sake. The New Zealand light seems different from ours, and the landscapes (the brush and the cluttered, junglelike bush and the steep mountains) are unfamiliar; we're seeing a different part of the world, with a different sort of color, but every frame serves the story. And the partly electronic score has a spare, percussive elegance that points up the desolation of the characters in the open, undeveloped countryside. Donaldson has the kind of neo-neo-realist technique that a viewer is unconscious of; he doesn't tip us to how we're supposed to feel, and he gets us in deep. He himself disappears into the story. Even the easy, dry wit seems to belong to the material, along with the summery light. It's a remarkable piece of work, and the handling of the little girl

(Greer Robson) who plays the seven-year-old Georgie is beyond praise.

This is the sort of movie that engages some of us so fully that it becomes a personal affront if someone says, "Who needs it?" Yet that is exactly the response that some people are bound to have to it, because it's short on the type of entertainment values that they want when they go to the movies. *Smash Palace* represents a high point of a certain kind of realism which these people don't respond to, because they feel it's too much like life. An artist friend I recommended it to was angry at me afterward, and said, "I see it going on all the time; I don't need to see it on the screen." I don't really know how to answer this; maybe there is no answer to people who feel this way—certainly no answer that would change their perceptions. But I think that *Smash Palace* shows us far more than we see going on all the time. It's true that the surface seems almost documentary and that the people are believably real and not unusual, but every detail has been selected to reveal just what we might not perceive if we knew them casually. Everything has been selected to indicate their capacities for cruelty and self-destructiveness, for comedy and tragedy. We literally see an affable, intelligent man driven mad. And not mad in the funny, cuckoo sense but mad in the obsessed way that so many people seem to go during the process of separating. There's a rigorous fidelity to modern experience in this movie, and it's not what you'd see if you lived next door to these people, because, with Donaldson's help, Bruno Lawrence makes Al's emotions transparent. Even when he's deranged—which is when he's convinced that he has resolved his festering conflicts and become logical and he sets out on a carefully planned course of action—we read his thoughts. Though the characters don't have the dimensions or the self-awareness of the couple in *Shoot the Moon*, and though the story is simpler and the tone completely different, a few of the incidents in the two movies are startlingly similar. The rage of fathers deprived of their children—something that few men experienced in the past—is no doubt a key madness of our age.

·　　·　　·　　·　　·

*I*t may not be sufficient reason for adults whose kids don't talk them into it to go see *Annie*, but as the head of the New York City orphanage where Annie lives till the age of ten Carol Burnett is at her most exuberantly macabre. As Miss Hannigan, who hates little girls and loathes her job, she takes off into some other dimension, and maybe she meets Angela Lansbury there. They both have a talent for playing old bats and wearing clothes that are unsuited to any imaginable occasion yet seem howlingly right on them. As Hannigan, Burnett is unleashed—she's wild (the way she has sometimes been on TV). Breathing out a dirty-minded, ironic sort of wrath, as if it were smoke from a dragon's nostrils, she charges into the orphans' dormitory accusingly—"Did I hear singing in here?" If the director, John Huston, did nothing else for the movie (and he doesn't seem to have done much else), he made a contribution by the three words he is reported to have said to her when she was having trouble getting a handle on the role: "Play it soused." She makes Hannigan a glorious man-hungry sot. (At times, she's a bit like Gwen Verdon in *Damn Yankees* gone over the edge and down a few cliffs.) In an alcoholic stupor throughout, Hannigan has inflections that spin around and make her the butt of her own sarcasm. There's dementia in her when she's wriggling at men seductively. Pie-eyed, in ruffles and gathers and a long red necklace that beats a tattoo on her belly, she's both hag and trollop—a fit mate for W. C. Fields' Egbert Sousé up there in pickled heaven.

The comic strip *Little Orphan Annie* was once the most popular strip in American funny papers. The child-Cinderella story of the orphan who in 1933, during the Depression, is taken for a week into the home of the billionaire Daddy Warbucks and proceeds to spread sunshine and to inspire President Roosevelt to create the New Deal cries out for a cockeyed fairy-tale tone. But the movie has the feel of a manufactured romp, and Annie (Aileen Quinn), a ten-year-old with a heart-shaped face and brass lungs, bawls out "Tomorrow" regularly, on schedule. The child is almost frighteningly assured; she's a little freckled, red-haired engine, designed to be cheerful, inspirational, and spunky—a fearless toughie who uses her fists on any boys who mistreat animals. Aileen Quinn has a pleasant enough voice when she does a more subdued reprise of "Tomorrow" at the White House, yet even in her restrained song, "Maybe," when her voice is at its softest and most musical, she's too professional a Broadway babe; there's nothing spontaneous or touching about her. All the little orphans seem to have been trained by Ethel Merman; they belt in unison. And when they dance it's showy leaping about, and the editing breaks it up, making it more hectic. Annie arrives at Daddy Warbucks' mansion, and his household staff dances; the cutting is so choppy that the pump-and-tumble dancing—arms like pistons and stomping feet—turns into commotion.

Most of the things that are the matter with the movie started with the purchase of the rights to the stage musical for the record-shattering price of nine and a half million dollars (about a third of it deferred). From that point on, the picture had to be thought of as a musical that would draw enormous audiences, and any chance for a film that might have had a goofy lyrical quality—might have floated—disappeared. The producer, Ray Stark, believed that the story should be given a grounding in reality, and hired Carol Sobieski to write a script that would make the characters more real. That turns out to mean timeworn, adorable show-business types of real people—even the kids seem to have white whiskers. And the story isn't developed; for example, we never actually see Annie charm Daddy Warbucks. Stark hired Arlene Phillips (*Can't Stop the Music*) to do the choreography—not, perhaps, the best choice for comic, folkloric invention. Every sequence seems to be trying too hard to be upbeat and irresistible, and it's all ungainly. Has there ever been a lyricist as maladroit as Martin Charnin? The songs come out sounding incoherent.

Children from about four to about eleven will probably enjoy the pic-

ture—how often do they get to see a musical that features a little girl conquering all? Annie even serves as matchmaker between Daddy (a smooth,
amused performance by Albert Finney, who models his manner of speech on
Huston's awesome velvet growl) and his personal secretary, Grace (Ann
Reinking), thus fulfilling a child's fantasy of selecting its own parents. Grace
has been made pure and perfect—she seems more nursie than secretary. This
is a waste of Reinking, a dancing bonfire with a low, lusty speaking voice,
who, as she showed in *Movie Movie* and *All That Jazz*, has the kind of presence that carries a thrilling jolt. (She has something like what Barrie Chase
had in her television specials with Fred Astaire, when she seemed to give the
atmosphere an electric charge that rejuvenated Astaire.) Still, it's better to see
Ann Reinking playing prim and dancing to square choreography than not to
see her at all. Other performers get less of a chance than she does: Tim Curry,
who plays Carol Burnett's bunco-artist brother, Rooster, has a great slimy
look and matches up well with her physically but has little to do, and Bernadette Peters, as Rooster's hooker girlfriend, has even less. One little trouper,
Toni Ann Gisondi, with dark bangs and big cheeks, who plays the dimply
youngest orphan, Molly, is a real scene-stealer, though, and the cameraman
and the director must have fallen in love with her eagerness to perform. (At
one point, I was reminded of the famous gag in Woody Allen's *Bananas*—
two Christs on their crosses quarreling over a parking place. Aileen Quinn
and the little Gisondi are like two competing Shirley Temples.) The other
group that may love the movie is the fetishists. It features little-girl panties and
big-girl panties.

What you don't feel in this movie is that Huston was having a good time.
Even with its feeble melodramatic script and in its own terms, it has frequent
possibilities that he doesn't seize. For example, when Grace goes to the orphanage to pick out a child to take to the Warbucks establishment we never
see the moment when her eyes connect with Annie's and she knows that this
is the one she wants. A parody of a thirties radio show is too awkward to be
funny. And when Daddy Warbucks buys out Radio City Music Hall so he can
take Annie to the movies for the first time, he sits there watching Garbo and
Robert Taylor in *Camille* with Grace and Annie and Annie's dog, Sandy, and
we see Daddy enjoying the movie and Grace weeping and Annie dozing, but
we don't see how Sandy reacts. Of course, it would be corny if he were
whimpering, but if the moviemakers had foxed us by showing him doing
something that took us by surprise and made us laugh, that needn't have
been so corny. Skipping over Sandy leaves a gap. The production must have
become such a cumbersome nightmare that the brushwork and the details
were never worked out. There are puzzling lapses in judgment. Did the Warbucks house have to be so cold and ugly? There's nothing there that would
delight a child—you almost expect Annie to say "Let me out of here." And
though it doesn't really matter that *Camille* didn't play the Music Hall—it
wasn't considered family entertainment—and didn't come out until 1937,
was it necessary to crop the top and bottom and show it in wide screen? As it

turns out, it's dangerous to insert a soft-spoken clip like this; the audience may not want to get back to the noisy, Disneyish cavorting and the big numbers that are as abrasive to listen to as the finales of miked Broadway musicals. The picture uses the same Dolby and six-track system as *Apocalypse Now*, and it sounds like *Apocalypse Now*.

．　　　．　　　．　　　．　　　．

*S*ince *Rocky II* was a reprise of *Rocky*, you may wonder what is left for *Rocky III*. Even to ask yourself that suggests an inability to comprehend the shamelessness about repetition and about everything else that made *II* a hit and will very likely make *III* another hit. There are people in the audience who cheer when they're "emotionally clobbered." That's the term that the TV host Phil Donahue used when he was congratulating Sylvester Stallone; Donahue reported enthusiastically that his tough-producer brother-in-law had been emotionally clobbered by the film—and that's just what Stallone as writer, director, and star is trying to do to you. The picture goes beyond wretched excess. Whatever oddball charm and silliness the first movie had is long gone. *Rocky III* starts with the hyped climax of *II* and then just keeps going on that level; it's packaged hysteria. The saintly-sweet Rocky has no greed, no lust, and no mean impulses; he's all heart, and he keeps taking punishment, his face turning into hamburger. He does it either for charity or to prove to himself that he's a real champion. Early in the picture, he gets into the ring with a gigantic and murderous wrestler who's built like a buffalo, but the main challenger he has to fight is Clubber Lang (played by an actor called Mr. T), a vicious brute with a sci-fi Mohawk haircut. Clubber is black, but he's such a disgrace to black people that Rocky's old adversary Apollo Creed (Carl Weathers), who lost the title to Rocky in *II*, trains Rocky for the fight against Clubber. (Weathers, whose physique makes Rocky look like a lump, gives a sensible, unaffected performance.)

Stallone doesn't know a lot about dramatic construction, but he knows how to keep the emotional pressure on the audience; the movie really works you over. You're pummelled by the noise and the rock music and the images of bodies being whammed. The pace is accelerated by a crude, hustling shorthand—montages of Rocky in the ring defending his title against a series of contenders, Rocky doing commercials, Rocky with his family, Rocky's training intercut with Clubber's training, and so on. The first *Rocky* was primitive in a relatively innocent way. This picture is primitive, but it's also shrewd and empty and inept. Backstage before Rocky's world-championship fight with Clubber, the brute hits Rocky's old trainer, Mickey (Burgess Meredith), causing him to have a heart attack, and there's no doctor around. (Don't world champions have their own doctors in attendance, and don't there *have* to be two doctors at ringside, by law?) So Rocky goes into the ring upset and unable to concentrate on the fight; you'd think he'd want to kill Clubber, but no, he just wants to be at Mickey's side. Throughout the match, Rocky's wife, Adrian (Talia Shire), and the other people backstage vaguely fret about getting an ambulance, but they seem paralyzed. Finally, a doctor shows up, and when the fight is over he says to Rocky, "Time is important. We must get him to a hospital immediately." That leads to more fretting, and Mickey, still backstage, expires, with Rocky blubbering over the corpse.

Stallone must see the clean-living Rocky as the nation's great example to youth. Rocky attends a ceremony in his native city, Philadelphia, where a statue of him in boxing trunks and gloves is unveiled, as a tribute to "the Indomitable Spirit of Man"—and he realizes he must live up to it. He's also an ecumenical figure. He and the black Apollo become like brothers. And Mickey has a Jewish funeral service; his having been Jewish is certainly a surprise to the audience (and would surprise Mickey even more, because in the first two pictures he thought he was Irish). But the camera fastens on what's important: how deeply moved Rocky is by the loss of his Jewish friend. This movie features Rocky having a dark night of the soul. You wait for him to get his head screwed on right, so he can win. Stallone sticks to formula, and you can see all the moves coming, but the enthusiasts in the audience—and they appeared to be in a majority—didn't seem to mind. They accepted this horrible masochistic pap as if it were a highly entertaining ritual; they appeared to enjoy the puling sincerity and the taking of physical punishment. Blubber and Clubber. Rocky's brother-in-law, Paulie (Burt Young), makes a pro-forma appearance near the start (it's like an opening number): he recapitulates his jealousy of Rocky; then Rocky gives him sound advice (including an admonition against the use of the swearword "hell"), and he straightens out. And from time to time the loving Adrian is displayed; she's an icon, so heavily made up she looks like a wax prop. After a few more of these movies, will the cheering audiences get the same glazed look?

May 31, 1982

The Pure and the Impure

Steven Spielberg's *E.T. The Extra-Terrestrial* envelops you in the way that his *Close Encounters of the Third Kind* did. It's a dream of a movie—a bliss-out. This sci-fi fantasy has a healthy share of slapstick comedy, yet it's as pure as Carroll Ballard's *The Black Stallion*. Like Ballard, Spielberg respects the conventions of children's stories, and because he does he's able to create the atmosphere for a mythic experience. Essentially, *E.T.* is the story of a ten-year-old boy, Elliott, who feels fatherless and lost because his parents have separated, and who finds a miraculous friend—an alien, inadvertently left on Earth by a visiting spaceship.

If the film seems a continuation of *Close Encounters*, that's partly because it has the sensibility we came to know in that picture, and partly because E.T. himself is like a more corporeal version of the celestial visitors at the end of it. Like *Close Encounters*, *E.T.* is bathed in warmth, and it seems to clear all the bad thoughts out of your head. It reminds you of the goofiest dreams you had as a kid, and rehabilitates them. Spielberg is right there in his films; you can feel his presence and his love of surprises. This phenomenal master craftsman plays high-tech games, but his presence is youthful—it has a just-emerged quality. The Spielberg of *Close Encounters* was a singer with a supple, sweet voice. It couldn't be heard in his last film, the impersonal *Raiders of the Lost Ark*, and we may have been afraid that he'd lost it, but now he has it back, and he's singing more melodiously than we could have hoped for. He's like a boy soprano lilting with joy all through *E.T.*, and we're borne along by his voice.

In Spielberg's movies, parents love their children, and children love their siblings. And suburban living, with its comfortable, uniform houses, is seen as a child's paradise—an environment in which children are protected and their imaginations can flourish. There's a luminous, magical view of Elliott's hilly neighborhood in the early-evening light on Halloween, with the kids in their costumes fanning out over the neatly groomed winding streets as each little group moves from one house to another for trick-or-treat, and E.T., swathed in a sheet and wearing red slippers over his webbed feet, waddles along between Elliott and his teen-age brother, Michael—each of them keeping a firm, protective grip on a gray-green four-digit hand. E.T. isn't just Elliott's friend; he's also Elliott's pet—the film catches the essence of the bond between lonely children and their pets. The sequence may call up memories of the trick-or-treat night in Vincente Minnelli's *Meet Me in St. Louis*, but it's more central here. All the imagery in the film is linked to Halloween, with the spaceship itself as a jack-o'-lantern in the sky, and the child-size space visitors, who have come to gather specimens of Earth's flora, wrapped in cloaks with hoods and looking much like the trick-or-treaters. (The pumpkin spaceship is silent, though when you see it you may hear in your head the five-note theme of the mother ship in *Close Encounters*, and the music that John Williams has written for *E.T.* is dulcet and hushed—it allows for the full score that the movie gets going in your imagination.)

E.T. probably has the best-worked-out script that Spielberg has yet shot, and since it seems an emanation of his childlike, playful side and his love of toys, it would be natural to assume that he wrote it. But maybe it seems such a clear expression of his spirit because its actual writer, Melissa Mathison, could see what he needed more deeply than he could himself, and could devise a complete structure that would hold his feelings in balance. Mathison was one of the scenarists for *The Black Stallion* and is a co-writer of *The Escape Artist*; it probably isn't a coincidence that all three of these films have young-boy heroes who miss their fathers. Writers may be typecast, like actors; having written one movie about a boy, Mathison may have been thought of for another, and yet another. In *E.T.*, she has made Elliott dreamy and a little withdrawn but practical and intelligent. And very probably she intuited the necessity for Elliott, too, to be bereft—especially since Spielberg himself had experienced the separation of his parents. Mathison has a feeling for the emotional sources of fantasy, and although her dialogue isn't always inspired, sometimes it is, and she has an ear for how kids talk. Henry Thomas, who plays Elliott, and Kelly Reno in *The Black Stallion* and Griffin O'Neal as the boy magician in *The Escape Artist* are not Hollywood-movie kids; they all have an unusual—a magical—reserve. They're all in thrall to their fantasies, and the movies take us inside those fantasies while showing us how they help the boys grow up. Elliott (his name begins with an "E" and ends with a "T") is a dutiful, too sober boy who never takes off his invisible thinking cap; the telepathic communication he develops with E.T. eases his cautious, locked-up worries, and he begins to act on his impulses. When E.T. has his first beer and loses his inhibitions, Elliott, at school, gets tipsy, and in biology class when each student is required to chloroform a frog and then dissect it he perceives his frog's resemblance to E.T. and sets it free. (His classmates follow suit.) The means by which Elliott manages to kiss a pretty girl who towers over him by at least a head is a perfectly executed piece of slapstick.

It's no small feat to fuse science fiction and mythology. *E.T.* holds together the way some of George MacDonald's fairy tales (*At the Back of the North Wind*, *The Princess and the Goblin*, *The Princess and Curdie*) do. It's emotionally rounded and complete. The neighborhood kids whose help Elliott needs all come through for him. Even his little sister, Gertie (Drew Barrymore), is determined to keep the secret that E.T. is hidden in Elliott's room. And when Elliott's harried mother (Dee Wallace) rushes around in her kitchen and fails to see E.T.—fails to see him even when she knocks him over—the slapstick helps to domesticate the feeling of enchantment and, at the same time, strengthens it. Adults—as we all know from the children's stories of our own childhoods, or from the books we've read to our children—are too busy and too preoccupied to see the magic that's right there in front of them. Spielberg's mellow, silly jokes reinforce the fantasy structure. One of them—Elliott on his bicycle dropping what look like M&M's to make a trail—seems to come right out of a child's mind. (Viewers with keen eyes may perceive that the candies are actually Reese's Pieces.) Among the costumed children radiating out on Halloween is a tiny Yoda, and the audience laughs in recognition that, yes, this film is part of the fantasy world to which Yoda (the wise gnome of *The Empire Strikes Back*) belongs. And when E.T.—a goblin costumed as a ghost—sees the child dressed as Yoda and turns as if to join him it's funny because it's so unaccountably right.

Henry Thomas (who was the older of Sissy Spacek's two small sons in

Raggedy Man) has a beautiful brainy head with a thick crop of hair; his touching serio-comic solemnity draws us into the mood of the picture. When one of the neighborhood kids makes a fanciful remark about E.T., Elliott reprimands him, rapping out, "This is reality." Dee Wallace as the mother, Peter Coyote as a scientist who from childhood has dreamed the dream that Elliott has realized, and the other adult actors are the supporting cast. Henry Thomas and E.T. (who was designed by one of the authentic wizards of Hollywood, Carlo Rambaldi) are the stars, and Drew Barrymore and Robert Macnaughton, as the teen-ager Michael, are the featured players. Elliott and his brother and sister are all low-key humorists. When Michael first sees E.T., he does a double take that's like a momentary paralysis. Elliott has an honestly puzzled tone when he asks Michael, "How do you explain school to a higher intelligence?" Little Gertie adapts to E.T. very quickly—he may have the skin of a dried fig and a potbelly that just misses the floor, but she talks to him as if he were one of her dolls.

Spielberg changed his usual way of working when he made *E.T.*, and you can feel the difference. The visual energy and graphic strength in his work have always been based on his storyboarding the material—that is, sketching the camera angles in advance, so that the graphic plan was laid out. That way, he knew basically what he was after in each shot and how the shots would fit together; his characteristic brilliantly jagged cutting was largely thought out from the start. On *E.T.*—perhaps because the story is more delicate and he'd be working with child actors for much of the time—he decided to trust his intuition, and the film has a few fuzzy spots but a gentler, more fluid texture. It's less emphatic than his other films; he doesn't use his usual wide-screen format—he isn't out to overpower you. The more reticent shape makes the story seem simpler—plausible. The light always has an apparent source, even when it gives the scenes an other-worldly glow. And from the opening in the dense, vernal woodland that adjoins Elliott's suburb (it's where we first hear E.T.'s frightened sounds), the film has the soft, mysterious inexorability of a classic tale of enchantment. The little shed in back of the house where Elliott tosses in a ball and E.T. sends it back is part of a dreamscape.

The only discordant note is the periodic switch to overdynamic camera angles to show the NASA men and other members of the search party whose arrival frightened off the space visitors and who keep looking for the extraterrestrial left behind. These men are lined up in military-looking groups, and the camera shows us only their stalking or marching bodies—they're faceless, silent, and extremely threatening. Their flashlights in the dark woods could be lethal ray guns, and one of them has a bunch of keys hanging from his belt that keep jangling ominously. The rationale is probably that we're meant to view the men as little E.T. would, or as Elliott would, but most of the time neither E.T. nor Elliott is around when they are. Later in the movie, in the sequences in a room that is used as a hospital, it's clear that when adults are being benevolent in adult terms they may still be experienced by children as enemies. But the frequent intrusive cuts to the uniformed men—in some shots they wear moon-travel gear and head masks—are meant to give us terror vibes. They're abstract figures of evil; even the American-flag insignia on their uniforms is sinister—in modern movie iconology that flag means "bad guys." And this movie doesn't need faceless men; it has its own terror. Maybe Spielberg didn't have enough faith in the fear that is integral to any magical idyll: that it can't last.

When the children get to know E.T., his sounds are almost the best part of the picture. His voice is ancient and otherworldly but friendly, humorous. And this scaly, wrinkled little man with huge, wide-apart, soulful eyes and a jack-in-the-box neck has been so fully created that he's a friend to us, too; when he speaks of his longing to go home the audience becomes as mournful as Elliott. Spielberg has earned the tears that some people in the audience—and not just children—shed. The tears are tokens of gratitude for the spell the picture has put on the audience. Genuinely entrancing movies are almost as rare as extraterrestrial visitors.

. . . . .

As if to offer positive proof of how confounding people can be, Spielberg has also made an anything-for-a-scare movie—*Poltergeist*, a suburban gothic in which the children's paradise turns into a children's hell. Although the writing credits are shared, he wrote the initial story and rewrote the other writers' work on the script, and he produced the picture and supervised the final edit. And although he picked Tobe Hooper to direct, he storyboarded the shots and, it appears, also took over, in considerable part, on the set. Whatever the credits say, he was certainly the guiding intelligence of *Poltergeist*—which isn't a high compliment. There are some amusing possibilities suggested at the outset—they relate to kids and television. The film's biggest disappointment is that these aren't the ones that are followed through. *Poltergeist*, which is about a family besieged by nasty, prankish ghosts (there appear to be multitudes of them), is no more than an entertaining hash designed to spook you. It's *The Exorcist* without morbidity, or, more exactly, it's *The Amityville Horror* done with insouciance and high-toned special effects. There are lots of these, and some are awkwardly reminiscent of effects in *Close Encounters* and *Raiders of the Lost Ark*, but the worst thing about them is that there's no rationale for the forms that the poltergeists take on or for what they do.

At first, Spielberg's skill may get your hopes up—you think everything will come together in some wonderful sneaky-clever way. When you realize that it won't, your whole relationship to the movie changes. You've become the director's target: you're being subjected to thrills, bombarded by them, as you were in *Raiders*. And so, since the director puts you in the position of being a connoisseur of special effects, you sit back and turn bitchy—at least, I do. It doesn't take long for the principle of diminishing returns to set in: after a while your anticipation of a grisly new horror is more fun than what is delivered—ectoplasmic manifestations, spinning rooms and flying objects, gooey stuff that extrudes around closed doors, ambulatory cadavers, and angry, roiling skies and a mean tornado. The spectral effects are so varied that the film turns into a showcase for fancy opticals. And when we get into that jaded mood any effects that actually carry an emotional charge—such as the little boy in the family having nighttime terrors of a gnarled old tree with clawlike moving branches that's outside his bedroom window, or the boy's anxiety about a ghastly stuffed clown doll (its eyes seem to light up)—may be irritants. These effects don't have any clearer connection to the poltergeists than the others do, but they bother some of us because we associate them with our own childhood fears, and so we respond to them on another level than connoisseurship—and it seems almost callous for the movie to toss them in with skeletons popping up and other "Boo!" effects.

If *Poltergeist* succeeds to a degree, it's because of the warmth of the family itself in its tract home, full of toys, in a fast-expanding new subdivision. In *Amityville*, the family was an indifferent—even ludicrous—group; you didn't care what happened to those people. But in *Poltergeist* Diane, the mother (JoBeth Williams), and Steve, the father (Craig T. Nelson), are terrific, groovy people. When the ghostly manifestations start in the kitchen, what happens seems so benign that Diane reacts as if her household objects were staging a vaudeville show for her—she's turned on by it. High and giddy, she's bubbling over when she tells Steve about it, prefacing her description with "Remember when you used to have an open mind?" The oldest of the three kids is a teen-age girl who's so busy with her friends that she's hardly ever around, but the two little ones—Robbie (Oliver Robbins), who's eight or nine, and Carol Anne (Heather O'Rourke), who's about five—are really menaced. It's Carol Anne, who was born in the house, that the spooks are after, and they steal her away, but not far. She can be heard calling out to her mommy from somewhere inside the house. What prevents the situation from being too harrowing is that the film keeps up a cheerful, cartoonlike comic tone (the family dog is a heavy old slobby, snuffling golden retriever); and, besides, you know that Diane and Steve will battle any evil spirits to bring Carol Anne back. These parents love their kids so much that no harm can come to them. JoBeth Williams makes Diane a cool, jazzy mother, and you develop real affection and respect for the blandly handsome Craig T. Nelson as an actor—he brings out something sly and pointed in Steve's intelligence. Steve knows he's beefy—he's a kid in a big, oversize body. They're both kids at heart; the suburbs are a big toy to them—which makes them ideal parents for a Spielberg movie.

Diane and Steve seek help from a doctor of parapsychology, a role played by Beatrice Straight, who bores the audience blind and, in a few of her speeches, brings the picture to a halt, as if she'd put a hex on the director and the editor. But then a psychic is brought in: a little woman named Tangina comes to "cleanse" the house. As played by Zelda Rubinstein, the four-foot-three-inch actress who recently organized the Michael Dunn Memorial Repertory Theatre Company in Los Angeles, this character gives the movie new life, and she makes a large chunk of it work. Tangina has a slightly metallic, childlike voice (it sounds as if it were coming through a megaphone), and she emanates the eerie calm of someone who is used to dealing with tricky, deceiving ghosts. Zelda Rubinstein isn't fazed by having to deliver a speech that's a groaner. She holds the screen like a small Florence Bates; she's so fresh a performer that you want to applaud her exit line. It seems remarkably ungallant—and clumsy—of Spielberg to press on with plot developments that undercut the conviction she has brought to her role, which is about the only solid thing in the picture. If *Poltergeist* doesn't do much more than give people a rousing summer spook show and make money for M-G-M, it should at least bring honor and recognition to this actress and her (nonprofit) theatre group.

You hear bits of Spielberg's voice all through *Poltergeist*, but it isn't a song—it's more like whistling in the dark. *Poltergeist* doesn't have a structure; it has only a situation, and a bunch of flapping loose ends. Spielberg must have had to work much harder on this film than on *E.T.*, because it doesn't tap the sources of magic; it's just a dumb concoction, and every effect has to stand on its own. What's lacking is what *E.T.* has—the emotional roots of the fantasy and what it means to the children. There is nothing about Diane and Steve and their kids that relates in any way to what happens to them. The parents show their love for Carol Anne, but it was never in doubt. Their courage is tested, but that doesn't seem to have any particular meaning for them or for the kids, or any connection to how things turn out. Because Spielberg is a dedicated craftsman and a wit, he can make a much better low-grade, adolescent entertainment than most directors. But he isn't really thinking in this film—he's just throwing ideas and effects at us. If he'd tossed in an earthquake and a batch of giant, mutant ants, they'd make as much sense as anything else in *Poltergeist*.

·   ·   ·   ·   ·

*A*t first, *The Escape Artist* seems to have everything going for it. Directing his first feature, Caleb Deschanel, who made short films (such as *Trains*) and was the cinematographer for *The Black Stallion* and *Being There*, brings a new sensibility to the screen. The quietness of everything draws you in. Deschanel is a patient, courtly director, with a down-home grace; his unstressed humor makes you grin and his feeling for beauty makes you take a deep, clear breath. The script, by Melissa Mathison and Stephen Zito, based on David Wagoner's novel, has some of the qualities of the writing in *E.T.* and of the sleepy-American-city sections of *The Black Stallion*. And as Danny Masters, the teen-age magician, who believes that his dead father was "the greatest escape artist in the world, after Houdini," Griffin O'Neal (Ryan's son and Tatum's brother) is a great-looking gamin daredevil.

The orphaned boy has practiced magic tricks while living with his grandmother; when he thinks he's good enough to be a pro he runs off and goes to see his aunt and uncle (Joan Hackett and Gabriel Dell), who do an act together in vaudeville. The film takes place in a small, rather underpopulated Midwestern city (the exteriors are mostly Cleveland), in an indeterminate time in the past. This is probably a mistake: we feel somewhat dislocated. But in general everything is promising up to the point when Raul Julia comes into the picture. Since Julia, with his Puerto Rican accent, is playing the half-mad son of the crooked Mayor (the senior Desi Arnaz, with his Cuban accent), his entrance suggests a crazy-comedy interlude. But Raul Julia sticks around (though his girlfriend, Teri Garr, comes and goes), and the characters and the story that the director has been carefully building seem to disintegrate. There are lapses in the continuity, and the picture is pushed toward a ready-made, theatre-of-the-absurd melodrama—the kind of instant fantasy that filled *One from the Heart*. It all begins to revolve around a stolen wallet that contains the Mayor's graft money. *The Escape Artist* was made at Zoetrope Studios, under Coppola's aegis, and there were reports in the trade press of test screenings with different running times. It's just about impossible to judge whether the alterations were warranted or whether they wrecked the film— maybe a little of both.

In what's left, almost everything that Griffin O'Neal does gives off sparks of pleasure. He has a naturally pugnacious face; as Danny, he looks like a street urchin who could find his way around back alleys. He's determined and resourceful, yet he's sunny. O'Neal's husky voice helps: his Huck Finn croak goes with his freckles. And, with Deschanel guiding him, O'Neal lets you see the calculations that are going on in Danny's mind, so you actually experience the boy's triumphs and his frights right along with him. (The movie suggests Mark Twain with a solemn face.) O'Neal has a good scene or two with Jackie Coogan, as the owner of a magic shop, and some lovely moments with a girl he courts (Elizabeth Daily) so that he can persuade her to be sawed in half, and Deschanel has given him a stunningly lighted, red-hued vision in which he makes his father levitate under a cloth cover and then disappear. This scene is true magical moviemaking. With the exception of Barry Levinson (*Diner*), Deschanel is probably the most talented new American director to appear since Jack Fisk made his début last year, with *Raggedy Man*, and both he and Fisk are the kind of visually expressive moviemakers whose images linger in the mind even if their narratives go wrong. Still, just about everything that Raul Julia does is unignorably bad. He seems to act from the outside, like a man training to be a matinée idol. Deschanel tries to use this sleazy theatricality as part of the character of the Mayor's son, and he doesn't sentimentalize him—he keeps him a creep to the end. But there's nothing in Raul Julia's face for the camera to register; even his big dark eyes are blanks. (Have you ever seen an actor who's less interested in creating a character? That dead thing he does with his eyes is his way of trying to bring you into cahoots with him; it's like what Johnny Carson does—going deadpan and playing dumb for you while signalling "We're both hip to this.") *The Escape Artist* is so misshapen that it's only intermittently affecting. A boy magician's determination to perform the tricks that his father did—and even the one that may have caused his father's death—has suspense. But a stolen wallet is an insult to the audience. It's as if the movie were yawning at us.

June 14, 1982

The Only Logical Thing to Do

S*tar Trek II: The Wrath of Khan* invites you to have some wonderful callow, dumb fun. The director, Nicholas Meyer, hits just the right amused, slightly self-mocking note in the opening scenes, and the whole picture is played *almost* straight. There are little twists and whirls built into the dialogue, and the cast knows just what to do with them. The same actors who looked flabby and embarrassed in the 1979 *Star Trek—The Motion Picture* turn into a troupe of confident, witty professionals. Even their bodies seem to be toned up. You enjoy being with this group; you enjoy their company.

Nicholas Meyer, the author of several popular novels (among them *The Seven-Per-Cent Solution*, which he also adapted for the screen), has directed only once before—*Time After Time*, in 1979—and he's far from a great moviemaker, but he has an instinct for an eccentric form of yarn-spinning, and, at thirty-six, he seems to know how to spin it right on the screen. The story is credited to Jack B. Sowards and Harve Bennett, and the script to Sowards, yet it isn't hard to detect Meyer's hand (especially when he leaves his signature—at a crucial point he has the hero, William Shatner, echo the words of the hero in *Time After Time*). Shatner has probably never given as polished a performance—not as Captain (now Admiral) Kirk or in the more challenging roles he has played, either. Kirk's fatuity is a joy here. He's the most prim and bureaucratic of all action-adventure heroes, and his complacency has acquired a patina. Shatner has begun to inject a little irony into the character: Kirk, who always has something up his sleeve, is so well satisfied with himself that his composure is positively plummy. Yet with middle age there has come the fleeting awareness that younger officers may find him an unctuous know-it-all. Kirk experiences a few doubts.

His crew is an ethnic joke that over the years has become a monument: Winged Banality. The actors assembled for the TV series (there were seventy-nine episodes on NBC from 1966 to 1969, and then the show went into worldwide syndication) represent the men and women of the Starship Enterprise, patrolling the galaxy for the United Federation of Planets at the end of the twenty-second century, and now at the start of the twenty-third. But they've retained the comic accents and characteristics of second-rate early-twentieth-century vaudevillians. The doctor, "Bones" McCoy, is always nettled about something; the Oriental, Sulu, is smiling, willing, and obliging; the black woman, Uhura, is sensual, efficient, and totally professional; Scotty, the engineer, is, of course, bluff and loyal; the Russian, Chekov, never seems to have got past the language barrier—he's a little pained and fuddled, as if he weren't sure what was expected of him. (Life is one long, bewildered double take for this fellow.) These tatty representative characters—designed, I assume, on the principle that "ordinary" viewers would identify with them—were all slow thinkers, and they thought before they spoke their prairie-flat lines. These were Earth's finest, sent to encounter the weirdest, most threatening forces of the unknown. One member of the crew came from another planet—the logical, half Vulcan Mr. Spock (Leonard Nimoy). And, happily, in *The Wrath of Khan* he has brought into their midst a protégée, a voluptuous half Vulcan called Lieutenant Saavik (Kirstie Alley), who looks enough like Spock to be his daughter, but her puzzling over how Earthlings operate has a good deal more intensity.

The druggy blandness of the TV shows—their stretched-out quality (with "Negative" for "No")—is comforting; it's part of their mild charm. I don't speak as a Trekkie, or even as someone who would watch "Star Trek" at home. But I've had it on when I was unpacking or washing my hair in a hotel room and there was nothing else on the box that wasn't a car chase or a preacher. The only time I've ever actually sat down to watch it was a few weeks ago, when the 1967 episode "Space Seed," to which *The Wrath of Khan* is a sequel, was run. This episode certainly doesn't demand one's full attention, but it was much more impassioned than the ones I had seen, and I was surprised at how closely *The Wrath of Khan* tied in with it. What made "Space Seed" special was the contrast between Khan himself, as played by the fiery, powerfully built Ricardo Montalban, and the pasty Captain Kirk.

Despite all the fuss about the cost of the 1979 *Star Trek* (it was the most expensive movie made in this country up to then, and probably up to now, with the possible exception of *Annie*), the people who worked on it retained the somnolence and the sententiousness of the TV show; they may have been afraid of humor, afraid of the film's becoming campy and offending Trekkies. So they depended on special effects to energize the movie—something that special effects rarely do. A friend called it "a middle-aged dentists' convention in space"; the picture was so pooped out that it has just about totally gone from mind. (We seemed to spend half our time watching the actors in their long johns stare at TV-size monitors, with expressions that they hoped were appropriate to whatever effects were going to be put there, and the other half looking at the effects, which never did quite match up with the faces.) This time, with a different group of moviemakers in charge, the actors carry the story and the effects are secondary—they serve the dramatic situations. Meyer has made the dialogue scenes jazzy without violating the characters, and, using the contrast between Montalban and Shatner as the psychological center, he keeps the movie whipping from one incident to another. It takes your full attention and then some; the editor, William P. Dornisch, whose background is in TV commercials, doesn't believe in wasting time. Even at the end, when you get a small dose of the mystic fundamentalism so dear to the heart of Gene Roddenberry, the L. Ron Hubbard of TV sci-fi, who was the "creator" of the TV series, and the producer of the '79 film, it's double-edged. (The words "to boldly go where no man has gone before" are so incantatory and so familiar from television that the audience laughs in recognition while giving in to the soaring emotion.)

Montalban, who was born in Mexico in 1920, is one of those potentially major actors who never got the roles that might have made them movie stars. He appeared to have everything else—a marvellous camera face, the physique of a trained dancer, talent, a fine voice (he could even sing), warmth, and great charm. Maybe the charm was a drawback—it may have made him seem too likable, a lightweight (though it didn't stop Charles Boyer). In Montalban's first English-language picture, M-G-M's *Fiesta*, in 1947, which featured Esther Williams as a matador, he danced with Cyd Charisse. M-G-M next had him dancing with Charisse and Ann Miller in a Kathryn Grayson–Frank Sinatra film called *The Kissing Bandit*; it was said that the dancing was added after the executives saw the movie—they wanted to give the customers *something*. He kept working—in pictures such as *On an Island with You*, with Charisse and Esther Williams, and *Neptune's Daughter*, and *Sombrero*, starring Vittorio Gassman, and the low-budget *My Man and I*, in which he played a sexy handyman and displayed his pectorals, and *Latin Lovers*, in which he carted Lana Turner around in a tango. He had secondary parts in *Sayonara* and *Hemingway's Adventures of a Young Man*, and in *Cheyenne Autumn*, and he brought conviction to every role that anyone could bring conviction to, but, after almost twenty years in Hollywood, there he was in 1966 in *The Singing Nun*, with Debbie Reynolds, and, with Lana again, in *Madame X*. He seems to have lived a (lucrative) horror story, especially when you think of the TV commercials and his ever-ready smile on "Fantasy Island." It may be that Khan in "Space Seed" was the best big role he had ever got, and that the continuation of the role in *The Wrath of Khan* is the only validation he has ever had of his power to command the big screen.

Montalban is unquestionably a star in *The Wrath of Khan* (and his grand manner seems to send a little electric charge through Shatner). As a graying superman who, when foiled, cries out to Kirk, "From Hell's heart I stab at thee!," Montalban may be the most romantic smoothie of all sci-fi villains. Khan's penchant for quoting Melville, and Milton (which goes back to "Space Seed"), doesn't hurt. And that great chest of Montalban's is reassuring—he looks like an Inca priest—and he's still champing at the bit, eager to act: he plays his villainy to the hilt, smiling grimly as he does the dirty. (He and his blond-barbarian followers are dressed like pirates or a sixties motorcycle gang.) Montalban's performance doesn't show a trace of "Fantasy Island." It's all panache; if he isn't wearing feathers in his hair you see them there anyway. You know how you always want to laugh at the flourishes that punctuate the end of a flamenco dance and the dancers don't let you? Montalban does. His bravado is grandly comic. Khan feels he was born a prince, and in all the years that he was denied his due (because of Kirk, in his thinking) his feelings of rage have grown enormous. They're manias now; nothing can stop him from giving in to them. His words and gestures are one long sigh of relief—he's letting out his hatred. This man, who believes that his search for vengeance is like Ahab's, makes poor pompous Kirk even more self-conscious. Kirk is Khan's white whale, and he knows he can't live up to it—he's not worthy of Khan's wrath.

Star Trek II is, by modern standards, an inexpensive epic; it cost about a fourth of what the 1979 *Star Trek* did; allowing for inflation, that may be closer to a sixth. And there's something rather friendly about an epic that doesn't look wildly, competitively overproduced. (The picture doesn't have to be huge; it's Khan's feelings that are epic and give the film its scale.) The special effects, which were handled by George Lucas's Industrial Light & Magic (the firm also responsible for the effects in the modestly budgeted *E.T.* and *Poltergeist*), are lushly pretty (some are even paradisiac), and Khan's secret weapon—small, slimy armadillo-like creatures that enter the human mind through the ear—is as horrifying as anyone could wish. (Khan himself has a bug in his brain.) Some of the best effects aren't special effects. A rat in space, a funeral with "Amazing Grace" on the bagpipes—though adapted from earlier films, these are the kinds of quirks that a movie like this needs. Such guest performers as Paul Winfield, Judson Scott, and Bibi Besch (who, as Kirk's rediscovered old love, has a couple of the best lines ever to adorn a sci-fi movie) shine in their roles. There are a few disappointments, though. Mr. Spock used to have sleeker sideburns, and his ears aren't as baroque as they once were—they've lost their efflorescent upper curl. Nimoy has lost something else: his juice. Mr. Spock's sacrifice, which is prefigured when he gives the antique collector Kirk a copy of *A Tale of Two Cities*, would be more effective if his deadpan weren't so dried out. He looks as if he were made of ashen putty. The script provides the kind of fluky, showy dialogue that wreathes actors' faces with contentment—DeForest Kelley (prickly Bones) is crisp and positively chic, a cool self-parodist—but Nimoy seems miserable, as if he couldn't bring himself to play these childish games anymore, or didn't want to. Though this mindless entertainment has a lovely darting wit, he doesn't yield to his role. Too bad, because it is the only logical thing to do.

Nicholas Meyer's talent appears to be for pickups: he takes characters—legendary people and pop icons, such as Freud and Sherlock Holmes and Watson and Moriarty in *The Seven-Per-Cent Solution*, and the "Star Trek" crew—and builds on what we already know and feel about them. The associations they have for us work every which way. He couldn't quite bring his idea off with Jack the Ripper and H. G. Wells, in *Time After Time*—Jack the Ripper was too ugly a character, and Malcolm McDowell's shy, flustered Wells didn't fit the Wells of our recollections, and, with much of the picture set in a modern city, Meyer didn't have the control he needed. But he has really done it this time. The movie is endlessly inventive. It's cross-stitched with comedy and make-believe and a special kind of romanticism. Meyer wants you to be carried away by his vision, which is made up of so many impacted levels of reality and fantasy that they can never be separated out. (The theme of the movie is death and rebirth.) He gets the "Star Trek" regulars to loosen up and become more resilient. And they find themselves having fun in the roles they had become rigid in. This is what happens in the story, too: Kirk, who had become stiff from sitting at his administrative post, takes a breather—a three-week cruise on his old starship. He has been on the Enterprise so many times before that he expects to be groggy with boredom. But this trip awakens him. When the previously smug, canny Kirk speaks the line that Malcolm McDowell's Wells spoke in *Time After Time*—"I know nothing"—he means it. He has finally wised up and become likable.

Meyer takes a lot of care in shifting you away from any expectation that the movie is going to dazzle you, and the care he takes is pleasurable. He seems to be admitting that the picture isn't going to be anything but tomfoolery. He asks you to indulge him, and by his jokes and by directing as if he were just drawling he induces you to go along with him. He gets you to relax your defenses, to adapt your rhythms to the film's rhythms. Once you've lowered your guard, Meyer coaxes you to let the characters sneak up on you. He seems to be nudging you sweetly, saying, "Come on, come on," and he gets you to admit that the TV show made you laugh once or twice. Very quickly, you discover that even if you weren't a Trekkie you've been fond of this crew. Even if you hardly ever saw them, they took up lodging in your head; they put down roots there.

It's almost as if Kirk and the whole bunch had been lying in wait for you. Meyer taps the good will you have toward the crew of the Enterprise by showing you the good will they have toward one another. The pieces of the story fit together so beautifully that eventually he has you wrapped up in the foolishness. By the end, all the large, sappy, and satisfying emotions get to you. You're part of the crew, accepting, as they do, that the one whose coffin has landed on a newly created planet will begin a new life. Maybe you don't believe it, exactly, but you feel it, and you feel the power of this kind of thinking to inspire belief. And if the picture doesn't convince you that death can be transcended it does demonstrate that silliness can be. If William Shatner can go beyond himself—if he can give the performance he does in his grief-stricken scenes—who can doubt miracles?

June 28, 1982

Baby, the Rain Must Fall

*R*idley Scott, the director of the futuristic thriller *Blade Runner*, sets up the action with a crawl announcing that the time is early in the twenty-first century, and that a blade runner is a police officer who "retires"—i.e., kills— "replicants," the powerful humanoids manufactured by genetic engineers, if they rebel against their drudgery in the space colonies and show up on Earth. A title informs us that we're in Los Angeles in the year 2019, and then Scott plunges us into a hellish, claustrophobic city that has become a cross between Newark and old Singapore. The skies are polluted, and there's a continual drenching rainfall. The air is so rotten that it's dark outside, yet when we're inside, the brightest lights are on the outside, from the giant searchlights scanning the city and shining in. A huge, squat pyramidal skyscraper (the new architecture appears to be Mayan and Egyptian in inspiration) houses the offices of the Tyrell Corporation, which produces those marvels of energy the replicants, who are faster and stronger than human beings, and even at the top, in the penthouse of Tyrell himself, there's dust hanging in the smoky air. (You may find yourself idly wondering why this bigwig inventor can't produce a humble little replicant to do some dusting.)

The congested-megalopolis sets are extraordinary, and they're lovingly, perhaps obsessively, detailed; this is the future as a black market, made up of scrambled sordid aspects of the past—Chinatown, the Casbah, and Times Square, with an enormous, mesmerizing ad for Coca-Cola, and Art Deco neon signs everywhere, in a blur of languages. *Blade Runner*, which cost thirty million dollars, has its own look, and a visionary sci-fi movie that has its own look can't be ignored—it has its place in film history. But we're always aware of the sets as sets, partly because although the impasto of decay is fascinating, what we see doesn't mean anything to us. (It's 2019 back lot.) Ridley Scott isn't great on mise en scène—we're never sure exactly what part of the city we're in, or where it is in relation to the scene before and the scene after. (Scott seems to be trapped in his own alleyways, without a map.) And we're not caught up in the pulpy suspense plot, which involves the hero, Deckard (Harrison Ford), a former blade runner forced to come back to hunt down four murderous replicants who have blended into the swarming street life. (The term "blade runner" actually comes from the title of a William Burroughs novel, which has no connection with the movie.) It's a very strange tenderloin that Ridley Scott and his associates have concocted; except for Deckard and stray Hari Krishna–ites and porcupine-headed punks, there are few Caucasians (and not many blacks, either). The population seems to be almost entirely ethnic—poor, hustling Asians and assorted foreigners, who are made to seem not quite degenerate, perhaps, but oddly subhuman. They're all selling, dealing, struggling to get along; they never look up—they're intent on what they're involved in, like slot-machine zealots in Vegas. You know that Deckard is a breed apart, because he's the only one you see who reads a newspaper. Nothing much is explained (except in that opening crawl), but we get the vague impression that the more prosperous, clean-cut types have gone off-world to some Scarsdale in space.

Here we are—only forty years from now—in a horrible electronic slum, and *Blade Runner* never asks, "How did this happen?" The picture treats this grimy, retrograde future as a given—a foregone conclusion, which we're not meant to question. The presumption is that man is now fully realized as a spoiler of the earth. The sci-fi movies of the past were often utopian or cautionary; this film seems indifferent, blasé, and maybe, like some of the people in the audience, a little pleased by this view of a medieval future—satisfied in a slightly vengeful way. There's a subject, though, lurking around the comic-strip edges: What does it mean to be human? Tracking down the replicants, who are assumed not to have any feelings, Deckard finds not only that they suffer and passionately want to live but that they are capable of acts of generosity. They have become far more human than the scavenging people left on Earth. Maybe Scott and the scriptwriters (Hampton Fancher and David Peoples), who adapted the 1968 novel *Do Androids Dream of Electric Sheep?*, by the late Philip K. Dick, shied away from this subject because it has sticky, neo-Fascist aspects. But this underlying idea is the only promising one in the movie, and it has a strong visual base: when a manufactured person looks just like a person born of woman—when even the eyes don't tell you which is which—how do you define the difference?

Scott's creepy, oppressive vision requires some sort of overriding idea—something besides spoofy gimmicks, such as having Deckard narrate the movie in the loner-in-the-big-city manner of a Hammett or Chandler private eye. This voice-over, which is said to have been a late addition, sounds ludicrous, and it breaks the visual hold of the material. The dialogue isn't well handled, either. Scott doesn't seem to have a grasp of how to use words as part of the way a movie moves. *Blade Runner* is a suspenseless thriller; it appears to be a victim of its own imaginative use of hardware and miniatures and mattes. At some point, Scott and the others must have decided that the story was unimportant; maybe the booming, lewd and sultry score by Chariots-for-Hire Vangelis that seems to come out of the smoke convinced them that the audience would be moved even if vital parts of the story were trimmed. Vangelis gives the picture so much *film noir* overload that he fights Scott's imagery; he chomps on it, stomps on it, and drowns it.

Blade Runner doesn't engage you directly; it forces passivity on you. It sets you down in this lopsided maze of a city, with its post-human feeling, and keeps you persuaded that something bad is about to happen. Some of the scenes seem to have six subtexts but no text, and no context either. There are suggestions of Nicolas Roeg in the odd, premonitory atmosphere, but Roeg gives promise of something perversely sexual. With Scott, it's just something unpleasant or ugly. The dizzying architectural angles (we always seem to be looking down from perilous heights) and the buglike police cars that lift off in the street and rise straight up in the canyons between the tall buildings and drop down again give us a teasing kind of vertigo. Scott goes much further, though. He uses way-off-kilter angles that produce not nausea, exactly, but a queasiness that prepares us for the feelings of nausea that Deckard is then seen to have. And, perhaps because of the what-is-a-human-being remnant in the story, the picture keeps Deckard—and us—fixated on eyes. (The characters' perambulations include a visit to the eyemaker who supplies the Tyrell genetic engineers with human eyes, and he turns out to be a wizened old Chinese gent—as if eyemaking were an ancient art. Maybe Tyrell picks up some used elbows in Saigon. His methods of operation for creating replicant slaves out of living cell tissue seem as haphazard as bodywork on wrecked cars.) In Nicolas Roeg's films, the characters are drained, and they're left soft and androgynous in an inviting way; Scott squashes his characters, and the dread that he sets up leads you to expect some release, and you know it's not the release you want.

All we've got to hang on to is Deckard, and the moviemakers seem to have decided that his characterization was complete when they signed Harrison Ford for the role. Deckard's bachelor pad is part of a 1924 Frank Lloyd Wright house with a Mayan motif. Apart from that, the only things we learn about him are that he has inexplicably latched on to private-eye lingo, that he was married, and that he's tired of killing replicants—it has begun to sicken him. (The piano in his apartment has dozens of family pictures on it, but they're curiously old-fashioned photos—they seem to go back to the nineteenth century—and we have no idea what happened to all those people.) The film's visual scale makes the sloppy bit of plot about Deckard going from one oddball place to another as he tracks down the four replicants—two men, two women—seem sort of pitiable. But his encounters with the replicant women are sensationally, violently effective. As Zhora, who has found employment as an artificial-snake charmer, Joanna Cassidy has some of the fine torrid sluttiness she had in *The Late Show*. (Nobody is less like a humanoid than Joanna Cassidy; her Zhora wasn't manufactured as an adult—she was formed by bitter experience, and that's what gives her a screen presence.) And, in the one really shocking and magical sequence, Daryl Hannah, as the straw-haired, acrobatic Pris, does a punk variation on Olympia, the doll automaton of *The Tales of Hoffmann*.

The two male replicants give the movie problems. Leon (Brion James, who brings a sweaty wariness and suggestions of depth to the role) has found a factory job at the Tyrell Corporation itself, and his new employers, suspecting that he may be a renegade replicant, give him a highly sophisticated test. It checks his emotional responses by detecting the contractions of the pupils of his eyes as he attempts to deal with questions about his early life. But this replicant-detector test comes at the beginning of the picture, before we have registered that replicants *have* no early life. And it seems utterly pointless, since surely the Tyrell Corporation has photographic records of the models it has produced—and, in fact, when the police order Deckard to find and retire the four he is shown perfectly clear pictures of them. It might have been much cannier to save any testing until later in the movie, when Deckard has doubts about a very beautiful dark-eyed woman—Tyrell's assistant, Rachael, played by Sean Young. Rachael, who has the eyes of an old Murine ad, seems more of a zombie than anyone else in the movie, because the director tries to pose her the way von Sternberg posed Dietrich, but she saves Deckard's life, and even plays his piano. (She smokes, too, but then the whole atmosphere is smoking.) Rachael wears vamped-up versions of the mannish padded-shoulder suits and the sleek, stiff hairdos and ultra-glossy lipstick of career girls in forties movies; her shoulder comes into a room a long time before she does. And if Deckard had felt compelled to test her responses it could have been the occasion for some nifty repartee; she might have been spirited and touching. Her role is limply written, though; she's cool at first, but she spends most of her screen time looking mysteriously afflicted—wet-eyed with yearning—and she never gets to deliver a zinger. I don't think she even has a chance to laugh. The moviemakers haven't learned that wonderful, simple trick of bringing a character close to the audience by giving him a joke or having him overreact to one. The people we're watching are so remote from us they might be shadows of people who aren't there.

The only character who gets to display a large range of emotions is the fourth of the killer replicants, and their leader—Roy Batty (the Crazed King?), played by the tall, blue-eyed blond Dutch actor Rutger Hauer, whose hair is lemon-white here. Hauer (who was Albert Speer in *Inside the Third Reich* on television last May) stares all the time; he also smiles ominously, hoo-hoos like a mad owl and howls like a wolf, and, at moments, appears to see himself as the god Pan, and as Christ crucified. He seems a shoo-in for this year's Klaus Kinski Scenery-Chewing Award. As a humanoid in a homicidal rage because replicants are built to last only four years, he stalks through the movie like an evil Aryan superman; he brings the wrong kind of intensity to the role—an effete, self-aware irony so overscaled it's Wagnerian. His gaga performance is an unconscious burlesque that apparently passes for great acting with the director, especially when Hauer turns noble sufferer and poses like a big hunk of sculpture. (It's a wonder he doesn't rust out in all that rain.) This sequence is particularly funny because there's poor Harrison Ford, with the fingers of one hand broken, reduced to hanging on to bits of the cornice of a tall building by his one good hand—by then you've probably forgotten that he *is* Harrison Ford, the fellow who charms audiences by his boundless good humor—while the saucer-eyed Hauer rants and carries on. Ford is like Harold Lloyd stuck by mistake in the climax of *Duel in the Sun*.

Ridley Scott may not notice that when Hauer is onscreen the camera seems stalled and time breaks down, because the whole movie gives you a feeling of not getting anywhere. Deckard's mission seems of no particular consequence. Whom is he trying to save? Those sewer-rat people in the city? They're presented as so dehumanized that their life or death hardly matters. Deckard feels no more connection with them than Ridley Scott does. They're just part of the film's bluish-gray, heavy-metal chic—inertia made glamorous. Lead zeppelins could float in this smoggy air. And maybe in the moviemakers' heads, too. Why is Deckard engaged in this urgent hunt? The replicants are due to expire anyway. All the moviemakers' thinking must have gone into the sets. Apparently, the replicants have a motive for returning to Earth: they're trying to reach Tyrell—they hope he can extend their life span. So if the police want to catch them, all they need to do is wait for them to show up at Tyrell's place. And why hasn't Deckard, the ace blade runner, figured out that if the replicants can't have their lives extended they may want revenge for their slave existence, and that all he's doing is protecting Tyrell? You can dope out how the story might have been presented, with Deckard as the patsy who does Tyrell's dirty work; as it is, you can't clear up why Tyrell isn't better guarded—and why the movie doesn't pull the plot strands together.

Blade Runner is musty even while you're looking at it (and noting its relationship to Fritz Lang's *Metropolis* and to von Sternberg's lighting techniques, and maybe to Polanski's *Chinatown* and *Fellini's Roma*, and so on). There are some remarkable images—for example, when the camera plays over the iron grillwork of the famous Bradbury Building in Los Angeles the iron looks tortured into shape. These images are part of the sequences about a lonely, sickly young toymaker, Sebastian (William Sanderson), who lives in the deserted building. Sebastian has used the same techniques employed in producing replicants to make living toy companions for himself, and since the first appearance of these toys has some charm, we wait to see them in action again. When the innocent, friendly Sebastian is in danger, we expect the toys to come to his aid or be upset or, later, try to take reprisals for what happens to their creator, or at least grieve. We assume that moviemakers wouldn't go to all the trouble of devising a whole batch of toy figures only to forget about them. But this movie loses track of the few expectations it sets up, and the formlessness adds to a viewer's demoralization—the film itself seems part of the atmosphere of decay. *Blade Runner* has nothing to give the audience—not even a second of sorrow for Sebastian. It hasn't been thought out in human terms. If anybody comes around with a test to detect humanoids, maybe Ridley Scott and his associates should hide. With all the smoke in this movie, you feel as if everyone connected with it needs to have his flue cleaned.

July 12, 1982

Comedy Without Impulse

*I*f you're not in a frame of mind to see the world in a funny light and you're writing, directing, and starring in a comedy, you're lucky to achieve whimsicality, which is what Woody Allen has got in *A Midsummer Night's Sex Comedy*. Having reached a doomy dead end in his last picture, the 1980 *Stardust Memories*, he's attempting to get a new lease on humor—something that isn't easy to do and can't be faked. And Woody Allen has an extra problem, something that he apparently can't help: he looks down on humor. I don't know that I've ever seen such a refined sex comedy; it has a meticulous art atmosphere and Mendelssohn on the track. Even when Woody Allen thinks in terms of boudoir farce, he's looking over his shoulder at Ingmar Bergman. *Stardust Memories* was a terminal movie about Woody Allen; this one is only about Bergman's *Smiles of a Summer Night*. And the characters in the Bergman film had much more at stake.

This time, it's an American weekend in the country, early in the century, and Woody Allen is the host, though you don't feel his presence as strongly as in the other films he has starred in. The host works on Wall Street but dabbles in inventions—small, winged contraptions for flying, and mystical devices such as a "spirit ball" for getting through to the other, unseen world. He and his wife (Mary Steenburgen) have invited her cousin, a world-famous genius professor (José Ferrer) with a grand manner, who is to be married this weekend. Like Bertrand Russell, the professor is known as a man of reason, a pacifist, and a free thinker in sexual matters; his worldly and glamorous young fiancée (Mia Farrow) already shares his bed. The host has also invited his best friend, a doctor (Tony Roberts), who when he can't persuade his mistress to duck out on her husband for the weekend asks the nearest nurse (Julie Hagerty) to accompany him, and though they have never before exchanged a word, she accepts enthusiastically. The couples are, of course, no sooner introduced than they begin to regroup.

If there's a theme, it's the conflict between the professor's contempt for metaphysical speculation (he thinks metaphysicians are "too weak to accept the world as it is") and the host's trafficking in psychic gadgetry like the spirit ball, which lights up and makes sputtering noises when spirits are near. The group is rather amusing, and for a while the film seems saucy and fairly promising (when we learn for example, that the prof and his fiancée met at the Vatican). Viewers may feel that everything must be building toward a big, explosive joke. But nothing really develops—not even the clashes that are prepared for. Nothing busts loose. When the host's spiritualist toy functions as a camera obscura and reveals a pair of ghostly lovers in the woods near the house, the characters' reactions to the vision are so mild and unsurprised you'd think that these people were accustomed to weekends with much more elaborate spook shows. During the apparition, I expected the comedy to be in what each of the six people thought he saw and why, and in who was frightened or upset or delighted. And I expected some of them to see far more in the vision than others did, and thought they might talk and argue about what had happened. Surely the host would be excited, and feel triumphant at having proved his point even to the rigid, pragmatic professor. And maybe the prof would be shaken and try to explain the vision away by claiming it was a hallucination. But the scenes that followed were so limp I didn't know if this was the first time that the host had had results or if these spirits were the usual after-dinner entertainment.

As a writer, Woody Allen doesn't seem to play with the possibilities in the characters. He has written the professor so that he's merely a pompous ass. It's fine if the two younger men think that's what he is, but couldn't there be something else in him for the women to respond to? If this horny eminence hadn't been so formal and manicured—if, perhaps, he'd been a scruffy, paunchy old charmer with dirty fingernails and a seductive line that the prettiest girls always fell for—wouldn't there be more shape to the antagonism? There's no fun in a one-sided contest; like Bergman, Allen makes the man of reason a straw fool. He's Bertrand Russell but a dummy. And once again Tony Roberts is Woody's best friend. The doctor is supposed to fall insanely in love with the prof's fiancée, but there's no depth in his lunacy—he's up there on the screen just to be the star's best friend and to betray him. When the doctor confesses that he has slept with his friend's wife, it's as if material from some earlier Woody Allen picture were being replayed—hasn't Tony Roberts made this confession to Woody Allen before? We're living through Woody Allen's repetition compulsions. The three actresses—Mia Farrow, Mary Steenburgen, and Julie Hagerty (she was the stewardess heroine in

Airplane!)—are all lovely and talented comediennes. But they're all the same soft type—slender and lyrical, breathy-voiced, intimate, quirky. This is a movie with three Annie Halls.

Julie Hagerty has a beautiful naïve deadpan and a way with lines—she presents herself as the most trusting and gullible of all human creatures. At the same time, this nurse is so avid for sex that if the porch swing propositioned her she'd leap for it. Hagerty is able to create more of a character than the two others by staying inside this sweet, warm, and simple façade; she's the best thing in the movie. Mary Steenburgen doesn't have enough to do (she's certainly the least assertive—and least busy—of hostesses), and though she fusses over her husband lovingly, she's handicapped because Hagerty is playing the role Steenburgen usually plays, and also because no one is chasing her. (The scenes in which she's entangled in her long skirts and petticoats while trying to jump on her husband are the sorriest slapstick that Allen has ever put in a movie.) Mia Farrow is the femme fatale of the piece. But the director seems to take it for granted that we all know how ravishing she is, because he doesn't set up her scenes to demonstrate it. We don't even get the radiant closeups of her that could show us the exact second in which the doctor is smitten. The fiancée has lived in Paris and is meant to be highly advanced in her attitude toward sex (she admits to having had perhaps twenty lovers), and the two other women are determinedly uninhibited. These three childless women talk very openly, yet even when the wife asks the nurse for sex information the subject of how to keep from getting pregnant is never mentioned. In a picture in which the host's contraptions are featured, mightn't the women bring out their gadgets, charts, what have you? *Something* is needed to subvert this film's distanced, sherry-sipping tone.

As a director, Woody Allen doesn't appear to have much feel for decisive moments—for the onset of passion, or for midsummer madness, either. We hear the men trying to set up trysts, but, amazingly, the director doesn't give us any clues to why each man wants the woman he does; if the men didn't talk about their infatuations we'd never know of them. Essentially, the game of sexual musical chairs is seen only from the men's point of view: the men make their moves, and there are almost no contrary desires on the women's part. They are willing to oblige, and this easily available sex constricts the film's comic possibilities. (Nobody's frustrated for long.) But why has the professor been made an advocate of unfettered intercourse if the picture isn't going to show that the old goat has had the freedom that the two younger men have dreamed of? In having all three men follow their urges and having all three women so soft and pliable that the only thing they want is sex (they don't care with whom), Allen is pre-Shakespeare—he's pre-everybody. And he nullifies the comic advantages of the costume setting.

The dialogue isn't in period, but it isn't consistently out of period, either. And it isn't dialogue, exactly; it's more like a decoction of dialogue—as if the dialogue had leaked out, leaving only a summary of itself. What the characters say has next to nothing to do with the action; it's somnambulistic talk. Woody Allen is trying to please, but his heart isn't in it, and his talent isn't, either. His writing here may remind you of the sort of intellectual character in a Chekhov play of whom another character would say, ironically, "He's burning with new ideas." When the theme that's set up dwindles away, the picture is left with nothing but a belief in frolicking, happy sex. The message arrives a little late. (This isn't a great time for promiscuity; newly discovered infections are giving it a bad name all over again.)

You feel that there was no pressing reason for Woody Allen to make this film—not even the pleasure that some directors find in making movies. Visually, the film is too studied and painterly to have been made in a lighthearted mood. I began to long for a little of the messiness of his early pictures; who can be funny in tableaux that suggest the Nelson Rockefeller collection of imitation works of art? Woody Allen is so much a man of our time that his comedy seems denatured in this classy, period setting. (The only time he looks at home in the countryside is when he's walking along talking to one of the women with the same sort of conversational closeness that he has in his other movies when he walks with a girl down a city street.) In one scene, he pays homage to Jean Renoir's enraptured *A Day in the Country* by having Tony Roberts sit high in the fork of a tree while a girl leans against the trunk, but in the Renoir film the seduction was momentous—it had fear and trembling in it. This film—with its awful title, like the package label on a generic—is devoid of feeling. There isn't anything in it to react to.

When a Woody Allen film doesn't provide much in the way of jokes to laugh at, there are bound to be people who feel that genius has stepped in. I'd hate to think that he doesn't want to fight this.

$\cdot \qquad \cdot \qquad \cdot \qquad \cdot \qquad \cdot$

*I*f you're in a depressed state and you're playing a lovable, affectionate fellow, you're likely to develop the sickly, slack smile that disfigures Al Pacino in *Author! Author!* I am deducing the depression from the self-conscious smile; I can't think what else could account for that sagging, false winsomeness. At times, his teeth seem to be stranded on the screen, left behind. Pacino has never been one for easygoing, everyday charm; he has played comedy in other movies, but it was bitter or dark-toned or absurdist, as in *Serpico* and the scenes in *Dog Day Afternoon* when he was turned on by the crowds outside the bank and started to strut and show off. Here he's trying to be a playwright who's a genial, normal jokester, and though he reads his lines very skillfully, he can't seem to get the message to his face or his body. He's like a man who's looking for something and has forgotten what; he prowls, distractedly. And when he tries for warmth, his hangdog expression and five-o'clock stubble make him look as if he's going to sink through the cracks in the sidewalk. There are lots of them—this is a New York movie. Actually, all the men in it and some of the women, too, have blue shadows on their faces; you'd have to conduct an extensive search to find a movie with scuzzier lighting. (If people could be locked up for aesthetic crimes, the cinematographer, Victor J. Kemper, would have been put away long ago.)

The director, Arthur Hiller, has made more than twenty pictures, but he must keep his eyes closed on the set. There's no consistency of judgment or taste in a Hiller picture, and often they run downhill, as this one does. *Author! Author!* is blotchy in just about every conceivable way. The script, by Israel Horovitz, has trim, funny lines but also terrible, overingratiating ones, and some of the worst ideas and the most doddering, bonehead situations to be seen on the big screen in years. Horovitz, who has said in interviews that the movie is semi-autobiographical, makes the playwright hero a terrific talent and an object of adoration by children. Horovitz is maudlin about this character based on himself, and the movie is shaped to demonstrate what a wonderful human being the hero is—he has kept his values while achieving success in the corrupt big city. Most of the scenes in which the playwright is shown in his dealings with his producer (Alan King), the director who is fired (André Gregory), the director who is hired (Bob Dishy), and the investors (Bob Elliott and Ray Goulding) have a quick, satirical snap. Alan King has ripened as an actor in the last few years; here he's a shiny-eyed comic dynamo with gleaming choppers. As the blowhard producer, he has an insincerity that immediately communicates itself—his too hearty enthusiasm and too rakish smile bring energy even to his few and flabby lines. But there's a gaping difference in quality between these scenes—in which everybody lies as a matter of course—and the one in which the playwright chases after his wife (Tuesday Weld), who has casually gone off with another man, leaving behind her four children by three earlier husbands. In the first half, the dialogue has a real sense of give-and-take, but then the film follows up on all the stuff we're not interested in. The playwright also has one child of his own, and by the time he is hauling kids onto the roof of his Greenwich Village house to protect them from being dispersed to homes they don't want to go to, *Author! Author!* has turned into a *Times Magazine* article on male parenting.

While enshrining the father, the film scores points against the mother for her hateful selfishness. But since Tuesday Weld (who looks more like a china doll than ever) plays the sort of dissociated person who is poised and appears reasonable but is totally crazy underneath, it doesn't make much sense for the husband to be shocked that she doesn't behave like a responsible person. Hasn't he ever noticed that she's crazy? He says he's in love with her; we certainly don't share his infatuation—as far as viewers are concerned, she's a dead issue once she has left. But she keeps being dragged back into the movie. And whenever Hiller drenches us in sincerity by showing the suffering she causes the children, who crack jokes when their hearts are breaking, the movie becomes a shambles. He must think that audiences will be good-natured enough to laugh when scenes are intended to be funny whether they're funny or not; maybe he hears a laugh track in his dreams. Dating the Hollywood star (Dyan Cannon) who's appearing in his play, Pacino can't have dinner with her at Elaine's without taking some of his children along. *Arthur* got by with scenes almost as dumb as this one, but Dudley Moore brought his elfin élan to them, and it helped to carry the audience over the most dismal moments. Pacino does some very clever things, but his proficiency can't alter the vibrations he gives off. With that depressive, burned-out underlayer in his performance, you don't believe that he's such a madcap and so full of love for the kids that he'd haul them to Elaine's. (It might take more than élan to make you accept that as funny anyway.)

Author! Author! is an indefensibly bad movie, but I didn't mind seeing it. There's something fascinatingly berserk in Horovitz's mixture of good and bad writing. The movie is often cloying, and there are passages of pure muck, such as the one in which our hero explains why he's such a great guy with the kids: he was an orphan. But it does have those fast-moving theatre scenes, and Dyan Cannon, though she drops out too soon, has her big, tough, loose grin (this film has more than its quota of teeth), and she gives her scenes an infusion of spirit; you can feel the audience response when she's onscreen—it's the way people in the thirties used to rouse themselves from apathy when Joan Blondell showed up. There are a few nifty bits, such as a bag lady (Florence Anglin) with a Bronx Irish accent who inspects herself in a mirror on the street, and there's a bewildering oddity: as the playwright's son, Igor, a boy comic (Eric Gurry) gives an accomplished performance of the wrong kind; he's ready to host a roast. And there's the mystery of Al Pacino: What happened to the intensity and the quick rhythms he had just a few years back? You could see emotions smoldering in that dark face. It doesn't even look like the same face anymore. It's pasty, as if he'd vacated it.

July 26, 1982

Texans

As a title for a Western epic, *Barbarosa* is probably meant to strike a chord in our memories. The twelfth-century German King Frederick I, known as Barbarossa, became a symbol of unity to his people, and for centuries after his death it was said that he was alive, sitting in a cave, and would return. The new film is about a late-nineteenth-century American who serves his people, too, or at least his family (though neither the family nor he quite recognizes it), and he returns from the grave more than once. Barbarosa means Red Beard, and in the movie it's the name given a legendary outlaw because of the blood—said to be that of his victims but more likely his own—that dripped onto his beard. The part is played by the legendary red-haired—and, some would say, outlaw—Willie Nelson, whose beard is now gray, with just a few remnants of red. A studio executive once told me that moviegoers would never accept Willie Nelson as a hero, because he was too much like Gabby Hayes. And you can't deny it, he *is* grizzled, and from a distance he does look like a toothless, tobacco-chewing desert rat. Yet up close Willie Nelson has an aura—he's majestic. He is probably the most acceptable noble American in modern movies, and in *Barbarosa*, the first movie to be made in this country by the Australian Fred Schepisi, he has a role that brings out his weathered self-sufficiency and his humor.

In worn fringed buckskins, and with long pigtails hanging down under a sombrero (with a bullet hole) that he wears straight-brimmed across his forehead, Barbarosa is a desert rat mythologized by those who grow up fearing him. They have reason to be afraid: for thirty years, Don Braulio (Gilbert Roland), the patriarch of a Mexican clan, has been telling the young boys about their hereditary enemy and sending the bravest young men out, one at a time, to search the Texas border area to find the gringo outcast Barbarosa and kill him. And for thirty years Barbarosa has had to slaughter one young man after another. He's like the dragon in the fairy tale who threatens the community: Without this external menace, how would the clan be kept strong?

When you see the immense cruel terrain, you get a sense of what it must have been like to be cast out into it. Schepisi is a master of the very wide screen, and he's working with the same cinematographer, Ian Baker, who shot his Australian films (*The Devil's Playground* and *The Chant of Jimmie Blacksmith*). The vistas are overwhelming—the landscapes have a near-hallucinatory, unspoiled dignity. Shot along the Rio Grande, in an area of extremes that's either steep Texas mountains or mustard-colored mesa and desert, *Barbarosa* has some of the psychedelic ambience of Sergio Leone's spaghetti Westerns—the West seen in a fever. But Leone's films are almost abstract; his characters act out the rituals of the Western in a hyper, mock-American setting—a hot, dusty nowhere land. Leone's people aren't rooted in a specific moment of the American past; they aren't rooted in anything but movies. Schepisi takes Willie Nelson, with his frontiersman-Indian-hippie look, and puts him back in the period that that look was derived from. The other gringo characters are also authentic to the West we've seen in old photographs—especially Gary Busey as Karl, a lumpy, raw farm boy, and the families that he's part of by blood or by his sister's marriage. They're of Germanic stock, and some of the elders still have the Old World in their bones and speak with heavy accents. They're duty-bound, hardworking people; dressed up in their Sunday clothes for the funeral of Karl's sister's husband, they're as stiff as the corpse, upright in his coffin, standing among them while an itinerant photographer records the event.

Karl doesn't know his own strength; he hit his brother-in-law with a stick, and, having killed him without meaning to, he has to run off to escape reprisals from the dead boy's father. (George Voskovec may have put a shade too much of Job into the father's Biblical grief and anger.) While hiding out, Karl encounters Barbarosa and—again without intending to—becomes an apprentice desperado. Busey is a magical shambles: he makes a certain kind of American huskiness and uncouthness seem the best part of the national character. His Karl is an outlaw-galoot—Mark Twain might have dreamt him up. The ham-handed boy in torn, sweaty overalls—Busey wears them the way country boys used to, like sacking around beef—learns how to live in the wilds and how to rob canteens, when to shoot interlopers and when to let them pass. His teacher, it turns out, is also an outlaw because of a family feud: the reason Barbarosa stays near the border, despite the fact that this makes it easier for the young Mexicans to find him, is that he has a wife and a daughter in Don Braulio's hacienda. Barbarosa and Karl are both outcasts from their families—it's their in-laws who drove them off. The movie is a comedy about the tragic accidents and the primal, irrational hatreds that unite families in opposition to homesick loners like these two. Barbarosa has triumphed over his family by wrapping himself in his own myth, but that's all he's got until Karl hooks up with him. Then, after all the years alone, Barbarosa once again experiences the wonders of simple fellow feeling. And the blundering, rock-ribbed Karl comes to see the beauty in the myth of Barbarosa the fiery fighter, and he helps to perpetuate it.

The picture may seem a little loose at first, but it gets better and better as it goes along and you get the fresh, crazy hang of it. The script is by the Texas-born William D. Wittliff, who also wrote last year's *Raggedy Man* and was a co-writer of *The Black Stallion* and of the only other film starring Willie Nelson, *Honeysuckle Rose*. In *Raggedy Man*, Sissy Spacek and Eric Roberts and the two boys who played her children had surprising, evocative, believable dialogue, and their vocal inflections and rhythms were lovely, but the story took a literary, gothic turn that seemed to negate the film's best qualities. Wittliff's script for *Barbarosa* is sustained; it doesn't go fancy on us, and it doesn't repeat the ideas of earlier epics. Wittliff must have sat down and thought out for himself (in ironic terms) how outlaw legends started, and what functions they served for the communities where children grew up with a whole folklore about outlaw-monsters. The dialogue that Wittliff then wrote for these men has the feeling of the period—the eighteen-eighties—yet is profane, living language. I don't mean that the two desperadoes use a lot of four-letter words—I can't recall that they use any—but that they never say too much, and each word counts. The characters have their own tang or, at least, Barbarosa and all the Germanic Americans do. (At times the Mexicans sound like stage Mexicans, and Don Braulio's dialogue is no more than functional, but it's a deep pleasure to see that Gilbert Roland's handsome profile, which he first presented to Hollywood cameras in 1925, is as firm as ever.)

Although this film is very different from Schepisi's Australian movies, it's similar in its feeling for landscape and its affection for the characters' individual, screwy ways of reasoning, and it shows the fullness of his approach to moviemaking. All the elements are in balance. The music permeates the images—it's by Bruce Smeaton, one of the few genuinely lyrical composers working in movies. (He scored Schepisi's earlier films, too.) And there isn't a shot that stays on the screen a hairbreadth too long. Schepisi has a total vision of what he wants a film to be. Willie Nelson doesn't need to sing here—the whole picture is a ballad. The latter part of the film isn't quite rounded—a few too many things seem to happen offscreen—and I could have used more footage of Karl and his family (in particular, his father, Emil, who is marvellously well played by Howland Chamberlin). But this is the most spirited and satisfying new Western I've seen in several years, and the only one that achieves a real epic feeling about its hero. I think that probably *Barbarosa* could not have been an epic without Willie Nelson. The qualities that differentiate him from the traditional Western heroes are the qualities that make this movie work. He brings a film gravity. If a big, stalwart actor said, "I don't kill for amusement," you'd probably think, Here it goes—into the morality that divides the good guys from the bad guys and psychopaths. But when Willie Nelson says it, you think, Of course, taking a life is a serious matter to him. Nelson's scruffiness is part of his grace. He knows how to hold the screen by absolute stillness, and he speaks his lines so plainly that you listen for the subtle nuances and watch for the small, precise gestures. He's so unaggressive an actor that you reach out to him emotionally. Singers, like prize-fighters, have often made good actors—they've got the phrasing, the rhythm, the presence. And there's little doubt that Willie Nelson has a great asset that even the most skilled actors often don't have: he knows exactly who he is. That's what gives him the moral authority to play a Western hero.

. . . . .

*D*imples, wigs, bazooms, and all, Dolly Parton is phenomenally likable in *The Best Little Whorehouse in Texas*. As the woman who runs the venerable institution—it's situated in a rural area off the Austin-to-Houston highway—she's a madam doll. Her exterior is completely stylized, yet her manner is natural and easy, and she gives the impression of having lived a bit—of having earned her permissive, tolerant manner. This is only Dolly Parton's second picture, and it was directed by Colin Higgins, whose style is so broad it's flat (he was also responsible for her first film *Nine to Five*, in 1980), but she has become assured; her whole personality is melodious, and her acting isn't bad at all. It's a pity that she's being used as a throwback—a plushier Betty Grable, a riper, more womanly Marilyn Monroe—and given a Gay Nineties look.

The setting is contemporary: the film has been adapted from the long-running Broadway musical based on Larry L. King's 1974 *Playboy* article about a crackbrained crusading TV newsman (played here by Dom DeLuise) who attacked a time-honored brothel with such fervor that the authorities had to force the madam to close it. There's no reason for the tight, hourglass-figure costumes and the cleavage that you could lose a carriage and a team of horses in, except to display what Colin Higgins must regard as Dolly Parton's comedy gifts. Each time she appears in a different gown, her chest seems to have swelled and grown more prodigious; it's the focal point of her scenes—there were gasps and giggles from the audience. It's as if the director, the cinematographer, and the costume designer were out to sabotage her. When she bends toward us, she becomes almost frightening—a cartoon woman—and in one sequence she reclines outdoors under the stars with her longtime pal and lover, the local sheriff (Burt Reynolds), and her chest is cantilevered so that it overwhelms whatever it is that the two of them are saying about God and country. Yet Higgins' tastelessness doesn't defeat her. Dolly Parton has the charm to transcend her own cartoonishness and the additional portion inflicted on her.

Burt Reynolds falls back into the category of leading man, and it's his own fault. He has spent so much time on the Johnny Carson show talking about how he wants to tackle the challenging roles that win other actors Academy Awards that he can't be anything but a stale joke in the snug roles he then selects. He doesn't give an ostentatiously bad performance—just his usual low-key, embarrassed-to-be-up-here-doing-this-dumb-stuff performance. He's still acting as if he's better than his roles, but he may be the only one left who still believes it. While Reynolds, in his big, hollow part, underplays and looks slightly despondent, Charles Durning, who has the relatively minor part of the governor of Texas, steals the honors with his "Sidestep" song-and-dance routine—a demonstration of how a corrupt-to-the-bone politico evades answering embarrassing questions and takes joy in his own slippery skill. It's one of seven numbers that remain from the fourteen that Carol Hall wrote for the Broadway show, and it's a nifty bit of political satire. (Durning's slight resemblance to Lyndon Johnson—in a complacent mood—doesn't hurt.) This sequence, which starts with Durning's feet moving as he sits in the back of a limo, is the only part of the movie that's satisfyingly shaped and has a musical-comedy rhythm.

Whorehouse almost seems intended to be a worse movie than it is; it's as if the moviemakers distrusted anything fresh in the material. With Jim Nabors as narrator (and deputy sheriff), the picture piles on the coy Americana. It passes over the genuine, funny Americana in Larry King's original account. He had details such as the piecemeal construction of the house over generations: with "a room added here and there as needed," it had "more sides and nooks and crannies than the Pentagon." And then "there were all those casement-window air-conditioners—fifteen or twenty of 'em." The movie shows us a conventional picture-postcard mansion. King described the whorehouse as having turned back a goodly percentage of its earnings to local merchants, such as car dealers, but the movie has the working girls, who it might be assumed have been earning a handsome enough living, piling into a bus when the house is closed. In King's account, it's assumed that the girls will then go "on the regular red-light circuit"; the movie gives the impression that they will disperse and will look for other occupations—which goes against the grain of the story as satire. The joke in the material is that this relatively clean, well-run bordello (the actual one was registered with the county clerk as a "ranch boarding house," paid "double its weight in taxes and led the community in charitable gifts") is shut down, while big-time vice in the cities is undisturbed. Higgins, who did the rewrite of the script, by King and Peter Masterson (they also wrote the stage version), doesn't seem comfortable with satire. Even the finish of the "Sidestep" sequence is given short shrift, when the governor hears the results of a poll and hastens to be on the winning side. Higgins has turned the material into your basic flabby old love story: the sheriff has to overcome his prejudice against the life his Dolly has led before he can settle down with her. (It can't be too difficult for him—she doesn't have the gimlet eyes that you often see in photographs of actual madams.)

By tradition, the winning team of the University of Texas–vs.–Texas Aggies Thanksgiving football game spent Thanksgiving night at the whorehouse (courtesy of the alumni), and this series of events, from the locker room to the highway and on to the festivities at the house itself, constitutes the film's musical centerpiece. The house has one black whore, and the football team has one black player; naturally, when the couples go into their rooms these two pair off. What a neat world it is. Higgins must be in love with the smily, cheery "family musicals" of the Deanna Durbin days: the film's rambunctiousness is off-color yet wholesome, in the worst sense. (This is the sort of movie romp in which the frolicking prosties can hardly wait to jump into bed with the fellas.) When the sheriff learns that the publicity-mad newsman is leading a raiding party toward the house, he doesn't pick up the phone to warn Dolly—he drives out instead. And when the raiders break in and catch the football players in bed with the girls the young athletes don't make any attempt to smash the cameras. There's an antediluvian sensibility behind much of the writing and directing. At one point, Jim Nabors tells the madam that he doesn't think he'll be able to visit the house for a while—he doesn't think his bride will approve. Dolly assures him that the cows are delighted to have a rest—they like to see the bull go off on a Saturday night. Who but Colin Higgins would compare Jim Nabors to a bull?

August 9, 1982

Neutered

*J*ohn Irving's big-hit novel *The World According to Garp* uses just about every plot device available to novelists, and even the incidents that seem most random are prefigured by hints, warnings, delayed climaxes, ominous stories within stories. The book is designed self-protectively: everything that happens seems to have its opposite happening, too. Everything is contradictory, parsed, justified. All that holds the novel together is the thin wire of its own mechanics. The disasters that are visited upon the hero-victim, the writer Garp, become the story's texture, its aesthetic weather. John Irving grandstands for his readers. He wants them to be moved—it hardly matters how. Irving isn't interested in character, and the observations that he comes up with aren't insights—they don't add depth to the people or the events. They just keep things bopping along. He uses violence and morbidity the way a hack movie director does—to excite you, and maybe because he has nothing else on his mind. Published in 1978, *The World According to Garp* is a gigantic contraption of a book, loaded with charm, and it gives many people what they want from a best-seller: a family saga; an easy read that's amusing here, gripping there; and the feeling that they've mastered a roller coaster. The novel pretends to be about social issues; it pretends to be a serious piece of writing, too, and Irving may believe that it's a salute to *The Catcher in the Rye* and *Catch-22* and Vonnegut, and that he's making the techniques of John Barth and Günter Grass accessible to the general reader. In *Garp*, he turns their techniques into hooks. It's a triumph of cunning.

It has been reported that the first writers who were asked to adapt the novel to the screen felt that it couldn't be filmed, and I think essentially they were right. None of the actions in the novel are self-explanatory; the events in Garp's life don't make sense—they make litrichoor. And they don't do that without the baroque apparatus that Irving constructed—his wheels within wheels and his elaborate rigging. The movie version that has been directed by George Roy Hill, from a script by Steve Tesich, has no center and no scenes that are developed enough to draw a viewer in; it's a simple series of vignettes, spanning Garp's life from his beginning to his end. This isn't necessarily bad—Hill's pastel, detached, and rather meaningless comedy may, in some ways, be preferable to Irving's convolutions—but in recounting the book's key incidents Hill and Tesich lay bare the pattern of mutilations in the plot. The film, which is a generally faithful adaptation, seems no more (and no less) than a castration fantasy.

Garp's Puritan mother, the New England–bred nurse Jenny Fields (Glenn Close), feels no stirrings of sexual desire and regards men's drives as lust. But she wishes to have a child. It's 1944, and she works in a hospital that's handling war casualties. So she gets on top of a dying soldier who has an erection; once is enough—she is impregnated. That's her first and last sexual experience; Garp is practically a virgin birth. A straight-backed, narrow-minded maternal monstrosity, Jenny is also fearless and independent. She takes a position as nurse in a prep school, and in this institutional atmosphere she raises her son with complete confidence and authority. She cleans the boy's wounds when he's mauled by a vicious dog who bites part of his ear off; she saves him when he's about to fall off a roof. She's not one for physical contact, though. And when Garp (Robin Williams), the struggling young writer, uses her as a character in a story, she informs him that he can't do that—that her life belongs to her. Then she suddenly announces that she, too, is going to write a book, and she churns out a best-selling autobiography, an anti-male tract in which she tells the world about how her son was conceived, so that he becomes a public character—Garp the bastard son of the holy mother. He doesn't express any rage in the movie, and Jenny Fields never goes as far as carrying a scalpel, which the Jenny of the book does (she uses it on a masher in a movie theatre, explaining to the police, "I was trying to cut his nose off"), but metaphorically she's got a knife out, all right. Just after Garp's birth, when one of the prep-school boys gets rid of a girlie magazine by putting it in the baby's crib, she knows intuitively which boy it is, and she marches over and blasts him with "A word of warning, you filthmonger. If you expose my baby one more time to cheap shots like this, I'll inoculate your jock-strap with bubonic plague, and it'll do such a job on you that you'll have nothing left to even scratch down there. Understand?" This gets a laugh from the audience, of course, but it certainly doesn't help a viewer understand the film's later view of the humorless, threatening Jenny as a warm, compassionate woman. (It doesn't help a viewer understand Steve Tesich's reputation as a screenwriter, either. Apart from the drill-sergeant coarseness of the speech, there's the term "cheap shots," which isn't just wrong for the period—it's also misused.)

The castrating Jenny, whose book makes her a great feminist heroine and a founder of the women's movement, goes on wearing her crisp, pure-white uniform long after she has given up the nursing profession. (She remains a nursie at heart.) When she's famous, she is accompanied by a bodyguard named Roberta Muldoon, a transsexual who was formerly a tight end for the Philadelphia Eagles. Played by John Lithgow, the friendly, companionable big bruiser Roberta has more life in him/her than anybody else in the movie. Lithgow (who is six foot four) speaks in a man's voice, but his manner is ineffably wholesome and girlish; he's like a bulkier Joyce Grenfell, but with a faraway look in his eyes. (Who knows what romantic longings that Philadelphia Eagle hoped to satisfy when he convinced himself that surgery could turn him into a woman? Did he ache to be overpowered?) Lithgow's first three or four scenes are startling—he's *pretty* (in a strapping way), and he has the sensual languor of a girl who's waiting to meet her dream man and expects it to happen any weekend now. It's disappointing that he doesn't have any new aspects of the character to show in his later scenes when Roberta has become the faithful old friend of the family to Jenny and the Garps; by then Garp has acquired a wife—Helen, a college professor, played by Mary Beth Hurt—and two small sons. Roberta, who has been mutilated by choice, is presented as levelheaded and stable—in fact, as the only normal person on the screen. We never quite get a fix on Helen (who fades very fast, as if women became mousey at twenty-six), and the others are all eccentrics. Jenny is usually surrounded by a collection of macabre feminists known as the Ellen Jamesians. They have cut out their tongues to protest the rape of an eleven-year-old girl, Ellen James, whose assailants had cut hers out on the false assumption that that would prevent her from telling who they were. The Ellen Jamesians, screwups and hysterics who attempt to dramatize women's victimization at the hands of men, are so hostile to men in general that they treat even Garp as the enemy. I don't know why. Since they accept Roberta, who can be a good person because he had his male organ cut off, why not accept Garp, who was never really allowed to have one?

In this pop nightmare of a world, your worst fears are realized, with bonuses you never dreamed of. But Garp takes so much pleasure in ordinary, daily family life—in looking after his two boys, especially—that he's a happy man. Or so he tells us. From what we see, he's marked for disaster. The horrors that are visited on him as a child are nothing compared to what happens when he's an adult—his wife, Helen, is unfaithful, one son is killed, the other loses an eye, Helen accidentally bites off her lover's penis, Jenny is assassinated, and Garp himself is hounded by fanatic feminists when he's mourning her at a memorial service. He is wearing women's clothes—that's the only way he could get in—but an Ellen Jamesian, a girl who has given him a bad time since they were children, spots him and he has to run for his life. Then this same demented Ellen Jamesian, dressed in crisp nurse's whites—in honor of his mother—comes after him with a gun.

Tongues, ears, penises, eyes, lives—everybody on the screen is losing something, and this universal mutilation is now being described (in complimentary terms) as John Irving's "vision." The novel has an antic tone and plenty of disguises, but it's a poison-pen letter to Mother and the feminist movement. And the film is even more transparent. Glenn Close's Jenny Fields has the burnished look, the well-scrubbed glow, of a Liv Ullmann; she radiates while the character constricts. Jenny holds everything in and remains unfazed, untouchable—Garp himself never seems able to get through to her.

Glenn Close's line readings are reminiscent of Katharine Hepburn's cadences (filtered through Meryl Streep), but she has fine carriage for the role. She's unyielding. Uniformed for battle, her Jenny Fields is a warrior-woman, Nurse Ratched as mother of us all. And that infernal glow of hers makes it impossible to judge whether at any given moment Garp loves her or hates her, or what the film director feels about her. She's a joke, she's a saint. Whatever she is, she's inhuman.

If you look at John Irving on a TV talk show, or even in a publicity photograph, you see a darkly handsome macho man, muscular and moody, with the eyes of a bear—a brooding Heathcliff. If you look at Robin Williams, you see the rubber face that he has developed for the quick transitions and contortions of standup comedy; he's almost too flexible for the camera—his twinkling facial movements are so quick and easy they don't have much meaning. I like Williams as an actor—he feels the meaning of the words he's saying, and he sometimes gives them a delicate twist that makes you perceive the intensity of his emotions. (For example, the way he says, "That's the oldest profession," and after an accident that has left him with his jaw wired and his tongue thick, the way he says to Helen, "I really miss you"—fumbling on "miss" and almost weeping.) Williams is frisky in the role, a sweet, resilient man being tossed about by forces he can't understand. He's crestfallen and sad—like a bland, Gentile Portnoy—and he's very touching. But Williams doesn't bring the film much weight; he's muscular enough for his preppy wrestling scenes, but a chesty imp is still an imp. (And Hill's having given Garp a wife who suggests a wispy version of his mother diminishes Garp, and the movie, too.) The difference between Irving's face and Williams' face is comparable to the difference between *Garp* as a novel and *Garp* as a movie. There's resentment in Irving's face and in the novel; the movie skitters along, as if to say, "There's no reason for anything. That's how life is. You can't win."

The masochistic gifted-victim game has been played in recent American writing on just about every conceivable level, but this is still something special: Irving has created a whole hideous and deformed women's political group (the Ellen Jamesians) in order to have his author-hero, his alter ego, destroyed by it. Yet in the tenth-anniversary edition of *Ms.* John Irving was cited, along with Alan Alda, Phil Donahue, the late John Lennon, and thirty-odd others, as *Ms.* heroes. His citation read, "For integrating feminism as a major philosophical theme; for writing about rape with its true terror and brutality; for creating male characters who care about kids; and for understanding that feminist excesses are funny." And Irving has paved the way for this, too, by making Garp a new-style family man, who likes to cook and take care of the kids. He stays home—househusband in an apron—while his wife works. He, too, changes roles. And in the book he is a defender of wronged women who, as a man, takes some of the guilt for rape upon himself. Look at what happens in the book and the movie, though, and Irving is the opposite of a feminist: it's as if he saw himself as a five-foot-eight phallus, imperilled by women.

The film, like the book, purports to be about the mystery of life, and if you listen to what Garp says, it's about love of family. This may be his one-upmanship over Jenny: Garp wants to be both the paterfamilias missing from his life and the homemaker also missing from his life. But when Freudian buttons are pushed in this movie you can't tell how to follow the signals. Apparently, whatever its psychic sources, Garp's love of family is meant to be the real thing, and the film comes equipped with a message that Frank Capra might have snapped up: As the family sits down to a dinner Garp has cooked, he has a beatific expression, and he says to Helen, "Sometimes you can have a whole lifetime in a day and not notice that this is as beautiful as life gets. . . . I had a beautiful life today." If George Roy Hill helped us feel the beauty of the kids and of ordinary family life (as, for example, Spielberg does in *E.T.*), it wouldn't be necessary for Garp to poeticize his euphoria.

Hill is a very dexterous director; he holds you in a light, firm grip, and moves you along. What's missing from his work is the kind of feeling that makes images expressive and would bring conviction to that dinner scene—sans greeting-card poetry. As a movie, *Garp* is a better piece of work than Hill's jagged *Slaughterhouse-Five*; it has certainly been better cast. But though you see Hill laying out the film's motifs—and undertow is a chief one—the movie has no dramatic pull. Emotionally, Hill doesn't get his feet wet. Except for Roberta, the only character with any mystery is a slutty, almost silent prostitute (played by Swoosie Kurtz); she has a lewd, lopsided grin that tells us far more than she can put in words for Jenny, who hires her in order to quiz her about what men want. In a movie, when people verbalize their emotions but we don't see anything that backs up what they say, the result is hollow. If love isn't made visual, we don't feel it. What we react to at this movie is its breezy dissociation, which feels rather strange, because of the ghoulishness of the material. (This isn't false to the book, though, where Irving keeps laying groundwork for his later effects and you're so thoroughly primed for the accidents that what happens isn't catastrophe, it's farce. And he takes a bow for that effect, too.)

How could the modern feminist movement, which is rooted in the sexual liberation of women, be inspired by a lust-fighter like Jenny (a woman who is grandly contemptuous of all sexual desire), except for the sly purposes of satire? Or the angry purposes of a writer swaddling his rage in trumps and tricks and reversals? It's when writers create straw men to attack that they expose what's bugging them, and Irving creates straw women: Garp's drillmaster mother and the Ellen Jamesians. Irving's hero goes on being mutilated, over and over again, and coming back smiling. (John Irving doesn't smile much.) And finally a hysterical woman polishes off what's left of the wounded, cuckolded, bereaved Garp.

Who is the narrator of this account? Who would celebrate Garp when he's gone? In Ovid's version of the story of the Athenian princess Philomela, after she is raped by her brother-in-law, who cuts out her tongue, she is avenged and turned into a nightingale. If Irving wanted to provide a grace note, the narrator should be Ellen James (played, in a brief scene, by Amanda Plummer)—Ellen grown up, full of words, and writing the novel. (You don't have to think very hard to recognize that having your tongue cut out—losing your voice—is, symbolically, a writer's castration.) But Irving doesn't have the generosity to turn Ellen into a nightingale. And though he may have drawn her story from the legend of Philomela, he probably took the car-accident, big-bite castration scene from Kenneth Anger's *Hollywood Babylon* (where, however, the biter is a homosexual male). There's no feeling of truth in either the book or the movie. Garp is a good boy who loves his mother and his wife no matter how big their teeth grow.

· · · · ·

An Officer and a Gentleman seems to come out of a time warp. I've seen it before, with Tyrone Power. It's a slick, high-pressured, and well-acted variant of the picture that was made fairly regularly in the thirties and forties: the selfish or arrogant fellow with a chip on his shoulder who joins some branch of the military, learns the meaning of comradeship, and comes out purged—straight and tall, a better human being, one of the team. This is not a genre I'm just wild about; the regenerative moral powers of military discipline interest me less, maybe, than practically any other movie subject I can think of. But I have to admit that the director, Taylor Hackford (his only other feature was last year's *The Idolmaker*), has devised snappy and enjoyable variations on this old familiar tune, even though the script, by Douglas Day Stewart, is schematic, in the manner of TV drama, circa 1955. (The minor characters have tragedies so that the major characters can learn lessons. And the people who do what they should are rewarded by happiness, on a good income.) If I wanted a corpse revived, I'd call Taylor Hackford *before anybody else*. Is that a compliment? Yes and no. Somebody who is this astute about jazzing up formula romantic melodrama might be tempted to use the same overcharge even on a live project. He works on us—he fingers the soft spots on our infantile skulls. And he never dawdles: he has a headlong style; he gives the picture so much propulsion that it gains a momentum of its own. It's crap, but crap on a motorcycle.

Hackford has energized Richard Gere—the tightly wound-up loner-hero Zack, who has had to make his way by his street smarts and is determined to become something more than his father is. (Zack's mother took her own life when Zack was thirteen, and his father, who had deserted her, is a good-time-Charlie sailor; his way of being a father was to introduce the kid to booze and women.) The goal that Zack has set for himself is to be a Navy flier, and he has made it over the first hurdle by putting himself through college; the movie centers on his thirteen-week basic-training ordeal at the Naval Aviation Officer Candidate School in the Northwest, near Puget Sound. The hazards include the lean, tough drill instructor, Sergeant Foley (Louis Gossett, Jr.), and the local girls, who, the sergeant cautions the officer candidates, will try to snare them. Gere still uses a blank look too often, but he has got past the facile, mannered performances in which he sounded like three or four fifties stars; you can see an honest effort to go inside the character of Zack and inhabit it, and the picture seems tailor-made for him. It almost seems to be about Richard Gere as an actor: it's about someone empty who has to be transformed. (And we're eager to see what the new, emotionally rich man will be like.) But late in the picture, when Zack is supposed to have changed—after the sergeant has caught him in some petty chiselling and he has been punished and has broken down—you see Gere get up and walk away with that loose, rolling walk of his (like a junior-high kid's imitation of Yul Brynner), and he's still Richard Gere lost in his own placid beauty. He pushes himself to go as far as he can—this is his most wholehearted screen performance. But there's no emotional transformation, though Zack races around doing good deeds and the picture seems to be congratulating itself on what a wonderful person he has turned into. Gere remains a colorless, unexciting actor. Is it a matter of his not trusting his instincts? Or of his being excessively serious? Or reserved? Whatever it is, he's devoid of personality. His face seems all one tone, and he conveys only one emotion at a time. Partly this is because his eyes don't take the camera well (there doesn't seem to be anything behind them), but there's also something more elusive; try as he may to fight it, there's a touch of the Gregory Peck kind of dullness about him. You feel that this is a not very fiery man working with all his might to act fiery—when he remembers to.

Gere has become capable and accomplished, but he doesn't have what Debra Winger has (and she has it right to her fingertips)—the vividness of those we call "born" performers. As Paula, a girl who works in the local paper mill, she's a completely different character from the flushed hot-baby she played in *Urban Cowboy*, but she hasn't lost her sultriness or her liquid style. Paula's tough-chick little-girl insolence plays off the avid look in her eyes that tells you she longs to make human contact—she's daring you to trust her. And what may be the world's most expressive upper lip (it's almost prehensile) tells you that she's hungrily sensual; when she's trying to conceal her raw feelings, her hoarse voice, with its precarious pitch, gives her away. (It helps that Debra Winger has kept her own nose; it's straight with an aquiline hint—just enough to make her look strong and distinguished.) When Paula is nervy and impatient, you feel where her impulses come from. And when she's desperate because she's losing the man she loves you pull for her. You pull for her even if the premise that this is her only chance in life strikes you as hype and you have subversive thoughts about what kind of life she'll have as a Navy flier's wife. Debra Winger makes you accept the important part: that Paula loves Zack, that *she* believes her life would be empty without him. And Hackford does a smashing job of making the whole retrograde love story whiz by with such force that audiences don't have much time to think, "Wait a minute—this is a smart, beautiful young girl who will have nothing in life unless this Prince Charming makes her his princess? And this fellow has to rise out of his father's class and become an officer or he'll have nothing in life?" The movie is stirring, on a very stupid level, and it takes you back: Hackford may convince some people (until they go out into the cool night air) that Zack and Paula have to marry or they'll both go downhill—Zack will be cut off from his feelings, and Paula will be a drudge forever.

It's amazing what this picture gets by with. Lou Gossett is playing every I'm-rough-on-you-for-your-own-good sergeant you've ever seen. I've never been able to believe in these yelling, cursing men who can gauge a recruit's character and bring out the best in him. It's a phony idea made flesh: the wise drill sergeant as surrogate father is about as convincing as the loving, wise shrink played by Judd Hirsch in *Ordinary People*, and has the same plot function—a quick cure for psychic damage. But there's an extra (realistic) curlicue in having him black, and Gossett plays Sergeant Foley bone hard and delivers his lines rhythmically and precisely, giving his words a spin whenever possible. (Douglas Day Stewart's words need more than a spin, but the way Gossett spits them out you hardly notice.) It's a beautifully hammy austere performance—Gossett has the grace never to display Sergeant Foley's soft, warm heart. During the training sessions, he's as definite and beyond question as Barbara Woodhouse is when she's giving orders to dog owners. And he looks as fit as it's possible to look; like the lithe, elegant Woody Strode, at times he suggests a member of a superior race.

Hackford knows how to shape performances for the story he's telling; there are impressive characterizations by David Keith as Zack's innocent friend and Robert Loggia as his cynical father, and there are entertaining flashes of Tony Plana as an officer candidate with a Mohawk haircut and Lisa Eilbacher as a woman candidate. Even the solemn-faced Tommy Petersen, who plays the young boy Zack, is a fine match-up—he looks as if he really could grow into Richard Gere. But it's Debra Winger who holds the picture together—she makes you feel that there's something burning inside her. And she looks different in every shot, which helps to keep your mind off the fact that her character doesn't develop. The only time I cringed for her was in the poorly staged scene with Zack telling off a callous, cold-blooded girl friend of hers, and Paula rounding on the no-goodnik girl with a pitying "God help you." (I've only seen Duse in a silent film, but I'd swear that even she couldn't have brought off that line in that situation.) On the other hand, Hackford has enough howling effrontery to put over the big romantic number, when Zack, having recognized Paula's true qualities, arrives at the mill, dressed in his officer's white uniform, walks through the grime until he finds her, and then carries her out, as the other employees, misty-eyed, applaud. (*Norma Rae* prepared us: workers applaud in mills all the time.) A movie like this, in which no one is like anyone you know and everything is made up, can make *you* feel imaginary, too.

August 23, 1982

Action

The Road Warrior is intense, and it's all of a piece. The Australian director George Miller grabs you by the throat—or lower—and doesn't let go until it's over. The picture probably won't leave you feeling crummy the way junk-food movies usually do, because in visual terms, at least, *The Road Warrior* is terrific junk food. Miller must have the jittery nervous system of an exploitation filmmaker linked to the eyes of an artist. The picture has its own distinctive tautness (there's nothing left to trim) and its own special dark, almost violet light that doesn't suggest either night or day—it's as if the outdoors were lit by torches. The film might be taking place in the lustrous, paranoid dreams of a man who had gorged, happily, on action movies—on *Death Wish* and *Death Race 2000* and *Walking Tall*, on A.I.P. wheelers and samurai epics, on images of Vikings, Apaches, sadomasochists, and hot-rodders, on Bronson and Eastwood, on demolition derbies and medieval jousts. Set in a post-apocalyptic Wasteland, *The Road Warrior* is a mutant, sprung from virtually all action genres. It's an amazing piece of work; it's like "Starsky and Hutch" at switch blade speed. The jangly, fast editing suggests wit; so does the broad blacktop highway that cuts across the desert nothingness. Australia is certainly the right place for this fantasy—the parched horizons tell you why men would turn into motor maniacs. *The Road Warrior*, which is in Panavision and Dolby, could be the prototype of future road movies—perhaps of all action movies. But I didn't find it great fun to watch. The crashes, the flames, and the persistent instant-myth music (you barely need to add water) are rather wearing. (If there were such a thing as Jungian music, this would be it—unless Carl Orff staked an earlier claim.) The picture doesn't mean anything to me—not, at least, what it does for a lot of men I know, especially the ones who haven't had a real fix since the last Sergio Leone picture, a decade ago. (At times, *The Road Warrior* could be a spaghetti Western directed by George A. Romero.)

That *was* Wasteland with a capital W. *The Road Warrior*, which in other countries is known as *Mad Max 2*, is a sequel to Miller's first film, the 1979 *Mad Max*—an openly sophomoric bash. *Mad Max* was a revenge fantasy turned into a futuristic cartoon; the constant car-wrecking had a two-fisted deliriousness. It was of the exploitation genre that the critic David Chute, with no pejorative intention, calls "crash-and-burn," and it was Australia's biggest international box-office success ever (though not in this country: a jarringly dubbed version played here, on the theory that Americans wouldn't be able to understand the Australian vulgate). But Miller—who, as he makes clear in an interview with Chute in the July-August *Film Comment*, looked for the reasons for the film's success and believed he had found them when he was introduced to Jung, via Joseph Campbell's *The Hero with a Thousand Faces*—became convinced that he had unconsciously struck something very deep. And so this new film comes equipped with a prologue describing its hero's past in prose poetry. Sample: "In the roar of an engine, he lost everything . . . And became a shell of a man . . . a burnt out, desolate man, a man haunted by the demons of his past . . . A man who wandered out . . . into the Wasteland . . . And it was here, in this blighted place, that he learned to live again." You can hear those dots, and the words are spoken in fruity, cultivated tones.

Maybe Miller's belief that he has tapped into the universal concept of the hero is what makes *The Road Warrior* so joyless. It isn't simply stupid—it's trying-to-be-smart stupid. It's abstract in an adolescent way. And though Max, the road warrior (Mel Gibson), is mythologized in that prologue, he doesn't have anything particularly heroic to do. *The Road Warrior* is much hipper than a Western such as George Stevens' 1953 *Shane* (which was already in the mythmaking business: Alan Ladd's drifter was meant to suggest Galahad on the range), but it follows the same basic pattern. The boy whose piteous cry "Shane!" clung to people's ears when the picture ended has become the Feral Kid (Emil Minty), a wolf-boy orphan with a deadly metal boomerang for a toy, who attaches himself to the loner Max. And the apathetic Max encounters a new version of the homesteaders: some few decent men and women have survived the Third World War (two big powers fighting over oil) and have banded together in a small, walled encampment around a dinky refinery, where they have been refining the last remaining oil into gasoline and hoarding it, so that they can get in their battered vehicles and make a run to the seashore, two thousand miles away. These homesteaders are under siege by punkish post-nuclear-war bikers—savages on motorcycles, slightly updated from their Roger Corman days. Rampaging vandals who tear people apart for pleasure, they're led by a masked body builder, the Humungus. He wears leather-and-metal straps crossing his muscles, and his men are comic-strip terrors, each accoutred in his own rough-trade style—fashion plates of the newest in nightmare adornment. The huge, garishly strong Wez (Vernon Wells), whose yellow-haired punk boyfriend sits behind him on his bike, sports a fire-red Mohawk strip of hair on his shaved head, plumes and football pads at the shoulders, a studded codpiece, and a hideously businesslike metal crossbow on his gauntlet. His buttocks are bare. These nouveau barbarians, who look ready to storm an s-m bar, are determined to get the homesteaders' gas, and have set up camp just a few miles away from the enclosure.

Miller doesn't show any interest in characterization, except for what can be obtained by astute casting. His performers aren't required to act—only to present their faces and bodies to the camera. Yet he has a gift for placing them in the very wide frame so that even if they are almost silent we respond to them as individuals. The people at the refinery are decked out in what looks like homespun burlap (and, when the weather changes, what looks like homespun fur)—they're clothed in virtue, like early Christians in a De Mille epic—but each face makes an impression, no matter how brief its screen time. And there's a real film instinct at work in Miller's treatment of Bruce Spence, who plays a stork-legged, rotten-toothed aviator who uses snakes to guard his autogyro. The first time we see him, he appears out of the sand, like a trapdoor spider. This fellow looks like an assemblage of hopeless parts, and in most movies he'd bite the dust, yet with his gummy, horsey grin, his overexcited jumping up and down (is there a punk record playing in his head?), and his talking to himself—muttering about the things he remembers from the era when there were arts and traditions—he somehow survives. He's like his ragtag plane and the other pieced-together, souped-up vehicles that can still go. By the end, he has even managed to get himself a pretty girl, with a loyal spirit. Bruce Spence's aviator is more hopeful and tenderhearted and adaptable than Mel Gibson's glum Max, whose parts match up quite handsomely.

Bruised and puffy, Max has no edges, he stands about blandly, uncertainly, on the sidelines—Brutus in leather armor—while others make decisions. His finest moment—and perhaps Miller's most lyric, fairy-tale image—is totally passive: the wounded Max, carried on the tiny autogyro, floats high above the blasted desert landscape and the human debris. This vaguely Wagnerian shot is beautiful on its own; it doesn't have any dramatic meaning, because we don't know what has been going on in Max's mind. And when he is partly healed and has decided to join the homesteaders, who have nursed him, he still seems split—it isn't clear whether he has become fond of the good folk or just wants revenge on the bikers. It's because Mel Gibson is carrying all of George Miller's mixed ambitions on his shoulders that he has no stature as a hero. And it's because of this underlayer of indecisiveness that the action doesn't have a real kick. We're told in the prologue that Max has lost his reason for living; this film is supposed to be about his spiritual rebirth and the first stirrings of a new civilization, but he remains sullen and withdrawn. And civilization may be a long time coming: Miller, following the moldiest Hollywood tradition, cues us to exult along with the good guys whenever one of them kills a baddie. The picture gets whatever charge it has from the spectacle of devolution.

Miller is barely in his mid-thirties (he studied medicine and worked as a doctor while he was making short films that prepared the way for *Mad Max*), yet if you think of him as one of the kinetic moviemakers, such as John Carpenter and Romero, he's a giant. And his chase sequence with Max driving an oil truck makes the comparable truck chase in Spielberg's *Raiders of the Lost*

Ark look lame—as Spielberg, who has expressed admiration for Miller, might be the first to acknowledge. But Miller apparently doesn't see the limitations of the kind of material he's working with, and he has given it an art-film aspect. I don't mean the visionary shots, such as the bikers circling in the dust (as if they had all the gas in the world), riding round and round the enclosure, like old movie Indians on horses terrorizing the fort. Since this is basically a mindless film, I don't fault Miller for sacrificing credibility to beauty. And it's amusingly sloppy that in order to stage the climactic chase and battle, which is a variant of the settlers in their wagon train heading out through Indian territory, Miller asks us to accept a piece of visual idiocy: the refinery is surrounded by flat, dry desolation as far as the eye can see, yet when Max believes he's leading the homesteaders on their run he heads straight for the bikers' campfires, as if that were the only route he could take. What I regret is George Miller's thinking there's mythic depth in sickly-stale elements—the lonely Feral Kid who worships Max, and the aviator's devotion to Max (like Walter Brennan's fealty to Bogart), and Wez's love for his blondie, and Max's not allowing himself to have any fellow-feeling except for his pooch (a great-looking bandy-legged Australian Cattle dog, with a black monocle around one eye, a white around the other), and all the other familiar bits.

Miller gets effects, all right, but they're not the perverse, erotic effects that seem promised; the picture is weirdly not kinky—maybe because he's trying to be seriously kinky. *The Road Warrior* is sappy-sentimental, and, for all its huffing and puffing, it doesn't blow any houses down; it has no resonance of any kind. Something rather solemn comes across in the prologue and the afterword, and in the use of actual documentary shots of warfare to substantiate the film's apocalyptic claims (a terrible mistake in judgment for a comic-strip movie, no matter how elegant), and in the important-person, Charlton Heston–like poses that Max assumes—especially the cantilevered-hip position, with all the weight on one leg. Miller consciously uses Mel Gibson as an icon; that's enough to squeeze the juice out of any actor.

At a point near the end of the picture, after the tanker chase, the limitations of action-genre moviemaking stare right out at Miller: this is when we discover that while we've been watching Max driving, and fighting off the big brute Wez, the important things have been happening elsewhere. The decent folk in burlap have used their heads and planned their strategy; what we were watching was the kid stuff—"action." For once, Miller seems at a loss; he doesn't appear to know whether or not this revelation should be treated as a joke on Max, and so he muffles the scene. The script (by Terry Hayes and Miller, with Brian Hannant) has provided this ironic episode—a twist on *The Treasure of Sierra Madre*—that undercuts Miller's serious approach to the crash-and-burn genre, but as a director he's no longer willing to laugh at himself, and he retreats to the safety of muzzy mythologizing. And so the wolf boy (who is our narrator) grows up and, like many of his kind, learns to talk like a BBC announcer, but with an Australian accent. And Max, who has to remain a loner so he'll fit the Jungian hero pattern, is left behind, brooding. He's like Steve McQueen at the end of each episode of his old bounty-hunter TV series, with nothing to look forward to next week but more killing.

George Miller is enormously gifted as a moviemaker, and he has fused his crazily derivative material; this cultural compost heap has yielded a vision. But when you get caught up in his way of thinking, you can convince your-self that the more indebted to old movies your material is, the richer it is, and the more archetypal—and that junk food is the only true nourishment. There's nothing under the film's clichés—nothing to support the visceral stress that Miller's single, continuous spurt of energy puts on us. And there's no humor, finally, under that incessant music. If Max had it in him to laugh at how he was used—to laugh the way Walter Huston did at the end of *Sierra Madre*—there might be some point to the picture. The introspective Max nev-er gets past his own joylessness. We're supposed to regard him as a hero be-cause he's a fearless driver. Is he fearless because, not caring if he lives or dies, he has less to lose than his enemies? Or is it that he's a survivor because he's alone? Either way, he never acknowledges that he has anything at stake, and he's no hero to me. This is a phony genre picture. Genre pictures are meant to be entertaining; this one wants to be much more. It's an abstract presentation of male paranoid fantasizing, with an air of intelligence. The male audience can think it's prophetic (Max was used); maybe the male audi-ence can even think it's deep. (It's definitely not a picture for heterosexual couples on dates.)

We may not feel crummy after the movie, but we feel hollow. I would think that even those who are elated while they're watching it feel hollow. *The Road Warrior* is for boys who want to go around slugging each other on the shoulder and for men who wish that John Wayne were alive and fifty again.

The film has been greeted by superlatives from reviewers, because of what I think may be a tragic misunderstanding of the appeal of movies in ear-lier periods: the widely expressed idea that what people used to go to the movies for was simply action and fireworks, a basic, easy-to-follow story, and the good winning out over the bad—that all they wanted was genre films. It might be closer to the facts to say that people accepted the routinized genre pictures when they couldn't get something wonderful, because they under-stood that great movies didn't come along every day. It's scary to read critics praising action pictures that are no more than embodiments of male dyna-mism and suggesting that these are the only real movies—what the people want—even after TV has done action to death. I know that I didn't go to the movies to see car crashes or galloping horses or gangsters shooting each oth-er, though I often went to films in which these things happened; I went be-cause I wanted to "see the picture"—to become involved in the characters' intertwined lives and to experience the worlds that all the hacks and crafts-men and artists who worked in the movies could bring into being. We're of-ten told now that moviegoers never sought anything more than they get from

Star Wars or *Raiders*, and I want to testify that this is a falsehood. It's one that movie and TV executives have been known to embrace. When critics in the press and on TV embrace it, they're engaged in another form of shoulder-punching.

September 6, 1982

Buzzers

Susan Sarandon and a young actress new to films, Molly Ringwald, sport beautiful short haircuts in Paul Mazursky's *Tempest*. At one point, they also stand in the surf of a Greek island and sing "Why Do Fools Fall in Love?" like carefree vaudevillians, and they're completely charming. Those are the two best reasons for seeing the film. It also has a pert dizzy blonde called Dolores (Lucianne Buchanan) who seems to thrive in any circumstances—there's nothing in her head to hold her back. And it has a flickering wit that burns brightest in an Athens taverna scene: the camera pans over a group of Japanese tourists (with Arabs behind them) as they listen earnestly to a rendition of the Jewish "Hava Nagilah." Except for these diversions, though, the movie is fairly dismaying. Loosely inspired by the Shakespeare play, it doesn't appear to have any other sources of inspiration. Mazursky, who wrote the script with Leon Capetanos, presses a buzzer marked "mid-life crisis," and that's supposed to take care of why the hero—Phillip Dimitrious (John Cassavetes), a world-famous American architect of Greek ancestry—is sour on everything and does all the nutty, arbitrary things he does. When he insults his actress wife's friends and stalks out of his Manhattan flat, taking his fourteen-year-old daughter, Miranda (the fresh, believable Molly Ringwald), with him, we don't experience his disgust with his existence; sunlight floods through the windows of the house he says he hates. We simply look on as father and daughter whip around Athens, and pick up Aretha (Susan Sarandon) and her wire-haired terrier on a Piraeus street corner, and the three, plus dog, go off to a remote Greek island inhabited only by a goatherd, Kalibanos (Raul Julia, wearing thick, droopy mustachios), who lives in a cave, with his goats and a TV set.

Despite Aretha's lithe, cushiony desirability, Phil takes her off to this lonely spot and then insists on living as a celibate during the year the group spends there. He behaves like a sovereign lord on the island: he dismisses Miranda's complaints that she wants to go home and get back to school, and he almost kills Kalibanos for leching after her. He seems both regal and mad. If you want to know the reasons, you have to push the Freudian buzzer marked "Phil's unresolved sexual feelings for his daughter." But there aren't even any buzzers to push—except the Shakespeare one—to account for most of what goes on. Many of the incidents loosely correspond to events in the play; if they seem unhinged, it's because they aren't connected to any framework of meaning independent of the play. Why does Phil put Aretha and Miranda and Kalibanos to work in the heat, hauling stones to build a Greek theatre on the island? Is it perhaps to construct a temple for the actress wife (Gena Rowlands) he left? Whatever the reason, Phil seems to forget all about the stone theatre; he doesn't even bother to show it to his wife when she—with the others on board her lover's yacht—is cast up on the island by the storm he has (or thinks he has) summoned forth. There are other mysteries, such as Phil's somewhat deranged monologues about baseball, and his sudden decision to slit a goat's throat as a sacrifice, presumably to the gods. What gods? This is just about the first (and last) we hear of them. And we don't want to hear any more. Kalibanos's goats are dainty beauties who have been treated as characters, and to see one killed for a rhetorical flourish is jarringly ugly (even if its death is only simulated). The goat squirms and appears to cry in terror while trying to break free of Cassavetes' hold on it; the picture has a frivolity that the goat can't share. There's also a niggling, flyspeck-size mystery: the yacht owner (Vittorio Gassman) is a Mafia chieftain who travels with an entourage, and among these bodyguards and jesters is a man called Harry Gondorf. Is this an allusion to Henry Gondorff, the character Paul Newman played in *The Sting*? If it's an inside joke, it's too far inside for me.

Mazursky tries for a free, airborne mix of comedy, musical, psychodrama, and dream play—which might have been a marvel if he had found an original tone that the audience could respond to, and if he had hatched a protagonist whose emotions we could share. But he has put John Cassavetes at the film's center. Cassavetes isn't a bad actor, and he has become handsomer with the years; in the island sequences, with his hair gray and close-cropped, he looks remarkably noble. (His haircut is almost as nifty as the girls' bobs.) But he's one of the most alienating of actors. He has a dour, angry presence, and even when he's smiling there's something unreachable underneath—and ominous. Cassavetes can't engage in small talk without its seeming to be a diversionary tactic—an attempt to conceal the obsessions weighing on his dark spirit. And since Mazursky never comes up with anything that might indicate what Phil is suffering from, there's this black void at the center of *Tempest*—Phil's funk.

An actor takes on a ludicrous burden when he attempts to play a genius. How is he to demonstrate his intellectual powers? By canny expressions and sudden heartfelt speeches? By eyes narrowed as if by thought? Those were the old (and hopeless) Paul Muni methods. John Cassavetes goes his own route: he stares at the horizon, and he snarls and glowers like a Doberman guard dog. The only genius he demonstrates is as a party pooper. Mazursky's movies are generally semi-autobiographical, and if he had played Phil himself perhaps the movie wouldn't have had such delusions of pain-in-the-soul glamour. If, instead of the movie's having them, Phil the architect had had them—if he had been half conscious of his grand poses—we could have laughed at him and maybe understood him. There's a suggestion of this: Phil's crisis is set off by his discovery of a white hair on his chest; he quickly plucks it out.

A writer-director isn't always sure what tone he's aiming for until he has the cast assembled on the locations and begins to feel things coming together. And then, if the crew and the actors are buoyant, he can easily be deceived about what he's getting. It's possible that Mazursky, working intuitively, let the film go in several directions, hoping that the footage would fuse and become a mythological comedy-fantasy. From the way the scenes play, it's likely that he hadn't resolved in his own mind whether Phil is a genius who has "sold out" (he has designed a glitzy Atlantic City gambling palace for the Mafia man who takes up with his wife) or is just—suddenly—empty. In the Manhattan scenes, is it meant to be ironic when people speak of their great admiration for Phil—are they in awe of him because of the work that he regards as selling out? Or did he really do great, innovative work, or at least try to, *before* he sold out? We never get a clear impression of what accounts for his fame or of the dissatisfaction that he runs away from or of why he's ready to go back when he is. The picture has no core of motivation. Things just happen, and we're expected to take them at face value. I don't believe that an architect like Phil would express the realization that he hates his life by saying, "The money and the power don't mean a thing." What visionary architect (except maybe Albert Speer) would believe he had money and power? If Mazursky himself came onscreen with all this angst, lines like this would flower and achieve their full fatuity. When Cassavetes says them, he sounds like a great thinker created by Sidney Sheldon. Selling out may be one of the all-time worst movie subjects. (Remember Kazan's *The Arrangement?*) Naturally, Phil, like other American successes who are maddened by the emptiness they feel deep inside, has a vigorous, simple-man father to tell him that he should go back to his roots. (Surprisingly, the role is played by Paul Stewart, who may never in his long career have looked so juicy and strong.)

Sometimes Mazursky comes close to the high madness he must have hoped for—for example, in the scene in which Kalibanos, playing "New York, New York" on his clarinet, calls up the soundtrack voice of Liza Minnelli and a full orchestra, and his goats leap about in ecstasy. This is the kind of joke that makes you like the director for trying it, even though the idea is better than its execution: what you actually see is a group of goats being tossed onto rocks by offscreen hands—a "dance" created in the editing room, like the cat's cha-cha in the Purina commercial. When Susan Sarandon or Molly Ringwald or even Lucianne Buchanan is around, there's some vivacity on the screen, and there's hope for the movie. Sarandon, who was brittle and actressy in her early films, has been softening; maybe the new, warm, braless Sarandon owes something to having worked in two Louis Malle pictures. In *Pretty Baby*, there was still a split between the petulant actress and the lovely, sensual presence, but by the time of *Atlantic City* she seemed to have learned how to give in to her plushness and come alive on the screen. In her early scenes in *Tempest*, she's tanned and has the huge bright eyes and the sheer incredible prettiness of early screen stars, such as Nancy Carroll. Sarandon uses her body on Phil, rubbing against him like a pussycat asking for affection, and you sit there thinking that Phil, who keeps resisting her blandishments, is some kind of control freak. One of the disappointments of the movie is that her role seems to shrivel—Mazursky is so determined to keep Phil faithful to the wife he's hiding out from that he trivializes Sarandon's Aretha. And if you haven't seen Mazursky's earlier films you don't have any way of understanding what's at stake here, because Mazursky doesn't show that Phil is a romantic about marriage; he simply imposes his own romanticism upon Phil's actions. Yet, playing husband and wife, John Cassavetes and Gena Rowlands, who have actually been married for many years, might never have been introduced to each other, and when this stranger woman who has been scouring the seas, searching for the daughter she hasn't seen in almost eighteen months, comes ashore after the storm, she and Miranda don't seem to have met before, either. They don't even have the animal instinct to touch each other.

The names in this movie are tacky: if the Miranda character is going to be called Miranda, why call the Ariel Aretha when—for many of us—there can be only one Aretha? And I take it as a bad omen that Mazursky uses the name Phil again, after his last picture, *Willie & Phil*, evaporated. The actors who played Willie and Phil didn't leave any footprints. Cassavetes leaves prints, all right, but they're too big for his feet. The whole picture is overblown. It's luxuriantly elegant: you feel you should applaud the writers for the complexity of the flashback structure and compliment the composer, Stomu Yamashta, for the modern score—even though neither of these things really works. This is the kind of picture that makes you feel you should ooh and ah the vistas (courtesy of the cinematographer, Don McAlpine). It has a look that I have come to dread—the polished pictorial extravagance of stupe classics, such as Albert Lewin's 1951 *Pandora and the Flying Dutchman*. This *Tempest* even has the swank blue skies that *Pandora* had—the opaque skies that look spread on right from the paint tube. And it's a sophisticated fantasy in the same mode: the images might be used to advertise a new *parfum*. *Tempest* is an absurd movie, but what an artifact! It takes a high degree of civilization to produce something so hollow.

·   ·   ·   ·   ·

*T*he standup comedian Michael Keaton is a human whirligig with saucer eyes and quizzical eyebrows—the face of a puzzled adolescent satyr. At first, you hardly notice that face, because he moves like a hyperactive kid; even when he stays in place he's so wound up that his body is dancing in all directions. It's not as if he were spastic—the movements all seem to have a purpose. You get the feeling that his mind is working so fast that he has to gyrate just to try to keep up with the conversation he's having with himself. While this is going on, his rubbery, questioning face is openmouthed—he's a little perplexed. His moods change so fast that some portion of him is always left in the lurch.

Part hipster, part innocent lost soul, Keaton makes his film début in Ron Howard's *Night Shift*, which isn't much of a movie but manages to be funny a good part of the time anyway, and he gives it a pensive, space-cadet weirdness—a touch of lyricism. Ron Howard, who as an actor in movies and on TV has often played the straight-arrow foil, is one of the few young directors who know how to set up a scene so that gags can blossom. Still, *Night Shift* doesn't quite take off—its central situation holds it down. The picture is based on a newspaper item about two young men who were caught operating a prostitution ring, using a city morgue as their headquarters. This may sound like a terrific premise for a comedy, but where can you go with it? Although the movie has a factual basis, it feels wildly improbable. The script, by Lowell Ganz and Babaloo Mandel, is a string of jokes, and, maybe because the writers come from television, they don't appear to know when the characters need new dimensions, when we in the audience need to develop a stake in what happens to them, and when the material needs to enlarge. The writers exhausted their energy and inventiveness in trying to make the central situation halfway plausible and in working out likable characters for the two night attendants at the morgue who go into the pimping business. Even TV writers eager to get a crack at a movie must have doubts about whether they can stretch their talents when the principal setting is a morgue. Everything considered, Ganz and Mandel (it's tempting to call them Lowell and Babaloo) do pretty well, and Ron Howard manages to suggest a fairy-tale world full of hardworking, honest prosties and two naïve, well-meaning pimps, who are like guardian angels to the girls, dispatching them in city hearses disguised as limousines.

As the two attendants, Michael Keaton and the film's ostensible star, Henry Winkler, play off each other very gently. Keaton's brain is teeming with get-rich-quick schemes, and, talking constantly, he comes up with bizarre solutions to nonexistent problems. He's the idea man, and he seems to have all the screwed-up big-city energy in his jive talk and his jiggling movements. But when he has to carry through on any of his schemes he falls apart; reality stuns him. He's a totally ineffectual dreamer. And that's where Winkler, the nerd, comes in. This is the first movie in which I've been able to tolerate Winkler; he isn't dazzling enough to make me forget his other performances, but he isn't bad, either. As the mild, Milquetoast pimp (or, as Keaton tells him to think of himself, love broker), he has the slightly dazed look of an unworldly man trying to navigate in the New York night world, but he's the quiet, steady one who knows how to carry ideas out—how to organize the business and arrange pensions and health plans for the prostitutes and keep them reassured. There's a mock-bittersweet tone to the scenes between the partners. Keaton is outgoing (he has to be or he'd implode), and he offers a mass of confidences; Winkler, whipped by the aggressions of city life, is thin-skinned, shy, and silent. Fearful of everyone, and sexually frustrated, he's so polite that when he suddenly tells the babbling Keaton to shut up, Keaton is crushed.

Night Shift doesn't have the scale to be a runaway hit, or the focus—the emphasis is on the nebbish, but we're more interested in the hipster. And though the psychopathology of city life is used as the source of the comedy, the film doesn't quite develop that into enough of a theme. About two-thirds of the way through, the situations begin to have the TV blahs, and even the pacing slumps when the two heroes are released from jail. But the film picks up at the end, and there are a lot of attractive performers—especially the one-time Second City comedienne Shelley Long. (She was the blonde with the heart-shaped face who won Ringo Starr in *Caveman*.) As the prostitute hero-ine, she's a newfangled satiric version of the girl next door. But if it weren't for Michael Keaton—the ultimate big-city inhabitant with shady dreams, the man whose body is always talking—the film would seem negligible. Who can resist a hero who has always wanted to dress like a pimp?

September 20, 1982

Actors as Heroes

M*y Favorite Year* is about hero worship, and—surprise!—it's for it. The picture is set in New York in 1954—the year that the live Saturday-night TV series "Your Show of Shows" was at its peak popularity. That was the year NBC divided it into two shows by separating its stars, Sid Caesar and Imo-gene Coca, and created a third asset by signing their producer, Max Liebman, to put on specials. "Your Show of Shows" was followed by "Caesar's Hour," in which big Sid was teamed with Nanette Fabray, and these two series have merged in people's memories, where Sid Caesar has the hallowed status of genius, because of his own gifts and because of the writers who worked on his shows—Neil and Danny Simon, Carl Reiner, Larry Gelbart, Lucille Kallen, Joe Stein, Mel Brooks, and Woody Allen, among others. *My Favorite Year* is a fictional treatment of life backstage during the days when those soon-to-be-famous writers were brainstorming together, shouting ideas into the air or, as in the cases of the shy Neil Simon and Woody Allen, whispering their jokes to a fearless, brass-lunged confederate. It helps to know the legends, because some of the scenes aren't fully shaped, but if you didn't know anything about Sid Caesar or his writing team you could still laugh at *My Favorite Year*—the characters and situations are alive on their own. This show-business farce is the first film directed by Richard Benjamin, and the lighting is gummy, the views of Broadway are a blur, and the staging sometimes creaks—it even klonks. But the film has a bubbling spirit, and I was carried along by the acting and by Benjamin's near-libidinous reverence for his smartass characters. This man is crazy about actors—not a bad start for a director.

As Stan (King) Kaiser, the brawny star of the TV show "Comedy Cavalcade," Joe Bologna suggests an introverted ox. Absent-minded, slugged—like a heavyweight who has just gone ten rounds—he stares down at the small people who work for him as if he couldn't remember what they were there for. He stares down even at people who are taller than he is. What makes Bologna so authentic is that he has a manic force field, and it was precisely the comics with this kind of aggressive aura (Sid Caesar, Milton Berle, Jackie Gleason, the young Steve Allen) who came across the strongest on early, live TV. Somehow, TV filtered out their threat, and viewers didn't register it. (What viewers experienced was simply their energy.) But backstage how could anybody miss it? Bologna's King Kaiser is a looming presence, and there doesn't have to be trouble for him to smell it; violent and depressive, he holds his ground, and if his punches knock someone out he has a self-congratulatory reflex—with a gigantic paw, he shifts the weight in his crotch. An inarticulate comic who has surrounded himself with talker-writer prodigies, King has no awe of them: he knows that he—not the writers—makes people laugh.

One layer of the script, which is by Norman Steinberg and Dennis Palumbo, is about the truculent, half-mad King in relation to the writers in their rumpus-room office. They, of course, think they're the reason he gets laughs. Sy, the senior gagman (Bill Macy), rants about everything they have to do; even his personal grievances are all-encompassing. Bill Macy has a true comic artist's understanding of sleaze, as he proved in *The Late Show* (he was the failed talent agent turned bartender), and he has a gift for bringing unexpected depth and detail to a role, as he demonstrated in the otherwise tinny *Serial* (he was the suicide). When Sy holds forth to the other writers about what he's going to say to King, he sounds as if his life is on the line; when King confronts him, he retreats instantly. He's so smooth it's a transformation—it's on the order of a recantation. This rancorous old warhorse of a gagwriter has all the mechanisms to survive in the business; when he goes home, he probably sleeps like a baby. (He's no saner than King—just more verbal.) As the only woman in the bunch, the nifty Anne DeSalvo makes you understand at once why the attractive but self-deprecating Alice would be accepted, and how much she enjoys being part of this competitive craziness where anyone's best lines may be stepped on.

The youngest of the writers—and the film's protagonist—is a small chipmunk called Benjy, whose actions are probably based partly on the exploits of the young Mel Brooks (his company co-produced the film), with maybe some borrowing from the early life of Woody Allen. The role is played by Mark Linn-Baker, who is dark-haired and has a round face with pointy features—even a pointy chin. His Benjy is button-eyed and shiny—a snookums. He looks as if when he opened his mouth a cheep or a chirp would come out. This Brooklyn worrywart with cultural yearnings and conflicts about becoming a gagwriter is like a Jewish-intellectual version of Eddie Bracken. It's a tricky role; at times Linn-Baker is borderline ghastly, and at other times he seems just what was needed, and quite inventive. Then you may be dubious again—especially in the scenes between Benjy and the producer's assistant, played by Jessica Harper, whom he considers his girl. (Her boss, the teeth-gnashing producer, is played by Adolph Green, who certainly has a lot of teeth to gnash.) You'd never guess what a remarkable performer Jessica Harper can be from what she does here; she has no role to play, and the only time she doesn't seem like a bad actress is when she's telling Benjy why she isn't interested in him—she's saying things you agree with. What finally saves Linn-Baker is that Benjy is given the task of keeping an eye on the week's guest star—a screen star he idolizes—and making sure that this notorious womanizing boozer stays sober. In his first big movie role, Linn-Baker has the good luck to play most of his scenes with Peter O'Toole.

As the guest from Hollywood—the peacock Alan Swann, who is part John Barrymore and part Errol Flynn (maybe the best parts of each)—O'Toole is simply astounding. In recent years, he hasn't had the press he deserves—particularly in England. Maybe, having had the nobility of a certain kind of stardom conferred upon him, he is thought not to have kept his side up. His recent performances seem to be an answer to that; he's saying, "See, I'm not gone—you're just looking in the wrong place." And he has been getting better as an actor. When you watch him work in *The Stunt Man* or on TV in *Masada* or here, it's clear that he doesn't impress himself with what he's doing. And he doesn't hold back a thing—not even what stars usually hold back to make you know they're stars. While others turn into immobile figureheads, he has become a master of physical comedy—a whirlwind on the order of Barrymore in *Twentieth Century*. O'Toole's Alan Swann arrives at the TV production facilities and collapses—apparently dead drunk, but not quite unconscious. He hears King's decision to bump him from the show and hears Benjy make an impassioned plea that they keep him. And when he's on his feet he acknowledges his debt to Benjy. At that moment, we're his, and, as a result, we know why Benjy is his. Drunk, Alan Swann isn't merely swozzled—he's liquefied. But in his woozy eyes you can still see his imagination at play, and you recognize that he exults in his diction and the fine, trained voice that echoes back. Even when Swann is drunk, he's acting a great actor drunk. Self-destructive as Swann is, he still has some control. When we first see this wasted dude, he isn't wearing a watch, but he arrives for rehearsals on the dot. He honors his commitments, as he honors his debt to Benjy. Swann is a pro, and wants to work, just as King Kaiser does. King is a star because he's funny, and so he has got to be funny. Alan Swann knows that as a romantic-daredevil hero it's his job to make people fall in love with him. Each in his own area is a cock of the walk, and in the film's climax they stand together as heroic equals and fight off their common enemy.

The picture is a triumph of casting—not least in giving us Lainie Kazan as the chipmunk's mother. I never thought that I'd be capable of saying anything complimentary about Lainie Kazan; watching her sing and bulge on television, I have sometimes cowered—I've wanted to throw a blanket over the set. But her fleshiness is perfect here; it goes with her fossilized hairdo and her leering smile. Padded (I assume) and stuffed into her dress, this new Lainie Kazan goes beyond shtick; when she talks about what's real, she seems to become a real mother. And, powerhouse comic mama though she is, she's—well, sexy. When Alan Swann, who has accompanied Benjy to Brooklyn for dinner, looks at her, there's tribute in his eyes; his expression says, "This woman is not just this kid's mother." The whole Brooklyn sequence is generous-hearted; everybody is ridiculous but no one is put down for it. And running through the film there are jokes that spin off each other. As a crooked union leader in a pin-striped suit who is trying to kill King Kaiser for repeatedly satirizing him on the show, Cameron Mitchell has great animal noises rumbling out of him. When the live "Comedy Cavalcade" is to start, King Kaiser is dressed in his own version of the pin-striped suit—it has shoulder pads sticking out so far you could fly with them. Then he becomes confused and begins to think it's the Musketeers routine that's coming up. Talking out loud to herself, the wardrobe mistress (Selma Diamond) honks, "He thinks he's in the wrong costume every week." But it turns out that King is right to be confused, because inadvertently the union-crook routine and the swashbuckling skit merge.

The jokes are good, but it's Peter O'Toole's Swann—the film's wild card—who makes it memorable. I can't think of another major star, with the possible exception of Ralph Richardson, who would have the effrontery (about what great actors should allow themselves to do) to bring this sly performance off—and Richardson didn't develop this kind of funky daring until he was too advanced in years for it to be romantically effective. O'Toole and Linn-Baker almost bring off a close-to-impossible-to-play sequence in which Swann takes Benjy to the Stork Club. Swann is asked to speak to an elderly adoring fan (Gloria Stuart, as deep-bosomed as ever, and, except for what looks like a gray, elderly-lady wig, nearly as beautiful). He understands what his romantic persona is, and he plays it immaculately, sweeping the woman into his arms and waltzing with her. Though the Club scenes end in a sloppy bit (the usual tray of pastries gets spilled), O'Toole's tone is so sure that the waltzing episode doesn't become maudlin or self-congratulatory.

Swann is always aware of the impression he's making; when he enters a room, his feelers are out. He enjoys living up to the public's dream of him— his courtliness is part of his sense of the fitness of things. But this same man drinks out of cowardice and is in absolute terror when he realizes that the TV show must be done live, in front of a studio audience and twenty million people at home. Benjy persuades him to go on by telling him that he couldn't have played all those movie heroes if he didn't have some of that courage in him; by the end, Swann has justified Benjy's idolatry. Maybe this movie is so satisfying because it believes in what it's saying: that stars have the heroism to do things most people couldn't do—that there's a reason these heroes are heroes. You can almost see Richard Benjamin (part Benjy himself) grinning, his sheep's eyes wet with admiration for Peter O'Toole, who does the equivalent of pratfalls on his face—smacking himself against walls and floors—and then may do something so foxy-subtle that some of the moments between Swann and Benjy transcend comedy and become fable.

The plot appears to be casual—even a bit scatty—yet when you think the movie over, the layers of reference in the script come together. They chime the way they do in the best-constructed farces, and it's a very pretty sound, especially when they chime ironically. Sy and the other gagwriters who think they're the reason for King's success—how do they feel when at the climax of the TV show everything crashes and the script is discarded, and the studio audience goes berserk with laughter? King gets an ovation. Imagine what it will be like on Monday when he walks into the writers' office and says "Top it."

. . . . .

*A*ctors who have labored to learn the rudiments of their profession must want to kill the potential teen idol Matt Dillon, the open-faced young star of *Tex*. He's a "natural," who takes the camera with the baffling ease of a puppy. He doesn't apply any particular sexual heat in this movie, and he isn't crafty, like James Dean—there are no Method mannerisms, no affectations of any kind. From the way it looks, he just uses the sweet starry radiance that nature gave him, and smiles his relaxed, all-American-sweetheart smile. Even his gift for baby-macho comedy seems part of the package. What Dillon does in *Tex* may not be the result of studying technique, but it works better on camera than most trained acting does. Viewers can feel they're in direct contact with this luminous kid. The only thing his performance lacks is tension—that's what's usually missing in the performances of naturals—but the movie isn't conceived in terms that require it. (I imagine that a director who wanted tension and excitement wouldn't have much trouble getting it out of Dillon if he weren't playing such a nice boy. He wasn't this down-home yokel in *My Bodyguard*, *Over the Edge*, or *Little Darlings*.)

Tex is oddly quiet, tepid, soft. At times, I wasn't sure whether the Oklahoma locations were hazy or the cinematographer (Ric Waite) was in some personal, watery-pastel fog. The movie has no strong images; everything is flattened out. And Tim Hunter, making his début as a director, uses setups that are drably simple. Luckily, his modest, amateurish approach comes across as integral to the material, which is an adaptation that he and his writing partner, Charlie Haas, did of one of the four novels by S. E. Hinton that became favorites of teen-agers in the seventies. When Susan Hinton (who appears here in a bit as the typing teacher) began writing, she used her initials on her books because she was afraid that high-school boys wouldn't accept stories about their adolescent travails if they knew that the writer was a girl. Now in her thirties, she was only sixteen when she wrote the first, *The Outsiders*, which Francis Ford Coppola has filmed, also with Matt Dillon—it is to be released before Christmas. (Coppola is working on a movie based on another Hinton novel, *Rumble Fish*, again with Dillon.)

Tex, an affable, unformed kid, walks with his arms out, away from his body, as if he were slightly muscle-bound (though he isn't). He's a prankish but harmless fifteen-year-old who loves his horse, Rowdy. He and his serious-minded eighteen-year-old brother, Mace (Jim Metzler), are pretty much on their own—their mother is dead, and their father is off on the rodeo circuit. There's no way of citing what happens in this movie (Tex loses Rowdy, Tex becomes involved with a drug dealer, Tex intercepts a letter, Tex learns a secret about his parentage, etc.) without making it all sound like an everything-but-the-bloodhounds-snappin'-at-his-rear-end joke. The plot is just one damn thing after another going wrong for the boys, and a lot of the film's insights are socio-babble, junior division. But an amiable, unforced good humor takes the curse off all this. Hunter's major contribution as a director is that he allows Dillon's mysteriously effortless charm to shine, and Dillon, who has a gift for expressing confused and submerged shifts of feeling, makes us see that Tex is developing into a more definite—and stronger—boy. (We may feel that we're actually seeing the growth process.) The director doesn't do as well by some of the other performers—he keeps them on one emotional key throughout. There's an unrelieved performance by Ben Johnson as the heavy—a rigid-minded, prosperous citizen who doesn't want the no-account Tex hanging around his kids; he doesn't even know that Tex has a crush on his daughter (a lively, smart performance by Meg Tilly). And as the older brother, who takes out his own frustrations on the screwup Tex and is like a strict, nagging parent to him, the promising Jim Metzler (who has the handicap of looking too old for the role) is monotonously harried. If Metzler had been encouraged to lighten up now and then, or even if he were different with Tex from the way he is with other people, he'd be a whole lot more convincing. There's more shading in Pamela Ludwig's scenes as a high-school-age mother and in Bill McKinney's performance as the boys' rodeo-bum father—whom we learn not to judge too harshly.

There are little "life lessons" all the way through—this is an old-fashioned kids' movie (and I'm not sure what it's doing in the New York Film Festival). Yet it creeps up on you—the way, I'm told, Hinton's books do. The naïveté has its own kind of emotional, fairy-tale magic. Too bad that there's nothing in the very likable *Tex* to make it linger in the mind—it's visually so fuzzy that it drifts away like a TV show.

$\cdot \qquad \cdot \qquad \cdot \qquad \cdot \qquad \cdot$

*E*ric Rohmer's *Le Beau Mariage* ended just when I started to get interested, and when I hoped we might find out something about the heroine (Béatrice Romand). A bright young working girl who is studying for her Master's in art history, Sabine has had a considerable amount of sexual experience. At the beginning of the film, she breaks off an affair with a successful painter, because he's married and she is weary of the complications, weary of freedom and insecurity. Twenty-five now, she decides she wants marriage; she wants to be taken care of and to make a home for a man and have children. But she pursues this aim in an inexplicable way: she meets a lawyer who she decides is her type, and she goes after him so briskly and transparently that she might seem a madwoman, except that her obsession is mundane. It's such a dumb little obsession that there's no passion in it, and she's an orderly little campaigner—watching her lay siege to this man is like watching someone arrange his desk. Rohmer, who wrote the script, never gives us a clue to why the attractive Sabine doesn't draw upon her knowledge of men to be more elusive and less forthright about her intentions. Or why she can't read the lawyer's feelings. She puts herself in a pitifully exposed position, and she's so stubbornly determined to marry this man, whom she hardly knows, that she goes through a series of humiliations before she abandons the chase.

What Rohmer is up to is basically cuteness, but with a measured tone. The film is full of glib, precise chatter and the clickety-click of Sabine's high heels; it's a "nicely made film," and you're aware that everything in it is intentional to the last nuance. And during Sabine's hounding of the lawyer his embarrassment is calibrated very skillfully. But Sabine's willful stupidity is preposterous, and the whole conception of the film rests on our recognition that its premise is preposterous. (That's the only kick the film has.) When Sabine abandons her delusion, she smiles at herself as if she'd had a victory—as if she'd shown that man a thing or two. I don't know why she smiles, unless Rohmer is suggesting the old ponderosity that woman's nature can't be fathomed. Béatrice Romand, who was enchanting as the young teen-ager in Rohmer's *Claire's Knee*, is initially disappointing. But as the movie proceeds she regains some of that enchantment. In several sequences, she seems to light up and grow beautiful in front of our eyes. And, since we see her suffering, she becomes poignant—we want Sabine to come to her senses. And at the end, when she does, and there is the suggestion of a new candidate for her affections, I, for one, wanted to see her play the game right. I wanted to see her when she was in control of herself—maybe in counterpoint to what she had done when she was direct and honest and utterly impossible. What we have witnessed seems only the first act. But it's all we get, and though the end has a teeny twist, it's still a letdown. Serio-comic triviality has become Rohmer's specialty. His sensibility would be easier to take if he'd stop directing to a metronome.

October 4, 1982

Up the River

*F*or all the hell that Werner Herzog reportedly went through to make *Fitzcarraldo*, which showed on the closing night of the recent New York Film Festival, the film itself is a leaden variation on his *Aguirre, the Wrath of God*. It's *Aguirre* without the inspired images or great subject. *Aguirre* was about the civilized Europeans who, in their greed for gold, travelled to the Amazon and enslaved and slaughtered Indians. It was about madness. The sixteenth-century Spanish ladies in long gowns, sitting in their sedan chairs and being carried over the face of a cliff in the pale-green Andes, the peaks partly obscured by clouds—that may be historically accurate, and it's as magnificently bizarre as any image on film. When we see the Spanish expedition in that phantom landscape, Herzog seems great. When he takes us closer, he's in trouble, because he hasn't worked out a style of acting to go with his vision. The performers in their bulky, richly textured costumes don't appear to have any idea what's wanted of them; they flex their face muscles and stare at each other significantly. But Herzog was in luck: as Aguirre, Klaus Kinski, wearing a metal helmet that seemed to be soldered to his skull, had so little to do that he kept acting up a grotesque storm. Aguirre's glassy blue eyes didn't blink; they seemed to have popped open and stayed that way. He was like an angry, domineering Bette Davis; he held his mouth like a dowager, pursing his lips and scowling, and he took command of a group of soldiers by the demonic force of his glare. Kinski's Aguirre was a crazy conquistador who always walked at a tilt, and when he stood still he was slanted backward or, occasionally, sideways; he achieved the effect of the angled sets in *Caligari* just with his own body, which told us how off-balance his mind was.

Aguirre even managed to have Gothic political overtones—it could be seen as a parable of Hitler's taking power. The movie is trancelike: we experience the disorientation of the Europeans lost in this primeval lassitude. And the absurd humor is like a wink that you can't quite believe you saw; there's no preparation for it and no follow-up—Herzog never acknowledges it. Suddenly, a Spaniard says of the arrow that has just hit him, "This is not an arrow," or a man's severed head keeps on talking, finishing the sentence he was speaking when it was lopped off. And there are frames that are charged with something that goes beyond what we think of as dream, or even nightmare: abandoned in the jungle, a hooded horse stands immobilized in helpless terror; the camera passes over the remains of a boat, with a tiny lifeboat dangling from its stern, lodged high in the treetops.

Though made in 1972, *Aguirre* wasn't released here until 1977, which turned out to be perfect timing. Until the sixties, American anti-war movies had attempted to be realistic about war, but in the post-Vietnam period the horror of that war was all mixed together with the drug culture, and for many people psychedelic intensification began to seem the only true realism. The imagery of *Aguirre*—visionary, skewed, cuckoo—was a hallucinatory horror trip. The film took the edge off Coppola's still-to-come version of Conrad's dreamlike *Heart of Darkness*; Herzog had made the white-intruders-vs.-the-natives trip first. (Some moviegoers cheered each time an Indian's poisoned arrow hit its mark.) *Apocalypse Now* was clearly influenced by *Aguirre*, and Coppola may have acknowledged the debt in a visual gesture: his image of a wrecked plane nesting in a tree was possibly an homage to Herzog, though it couldn't match the shivery wit of that boat. Coppola's image could be accounted for; Herzog's had the purity of madness.

It may have been the surreal triumph of the boat in the trees that sent Herzog back to the shrouded mountains and mucky jungles of Peru and got him into the five-year mess of making *Fitzcarraldo*. In 1894, an Irishman known to the Peruvians as Fitzcarrald made a fortune in the rubber trade by figuring out how to ship the rubber from an inaccessible stretch of land: he dismantled a riverboat and used hundreds of Indians to carry the parts overland from one tributary of the Amazon to another, where it was reassembled. When Herzog was told this story, he must have visualized the riverboat on a mountain—his earlier image writ large. Of course, a film about that incident wouldn't have much visual excitement if the boat was in pieces. Herzog had been fascinated by the logistical mystery of how the prehistoric stone blocks were brought to Carnac—a feat that probably involved an army of slaves working for many years, like the building of the pyramids. Putting things together, he decided on something that would dwarf the actual Fitzcarrald's accomplishment: *his* Indians would haul a three-hundred-and-twenty-ton steamboat (roughly ten times the size and weight of Fitzcarrald's vessel) up a mountain *intact*, and on a grade twice as steep as the one in the historical account. *Fitzcarraldo* is a movie made for an image. And so perhaps it's not surprising that still pictures of the steamboat on the mountain are more resonant than the film. In a sense, *Fitzcarraldo* wrecks the image by explaining it. The mystery evaporates when we see the impossible made possible—when we see the hauling process.

Movies are based on illusion—movies *are* illusion. The sound of Fred Astaire's taps was added to the soundtrack after his dances were shot; Garbo's laugh is said to have been dubbed in *Ninotchka*; when the tiny Yoda stood in the forest advising Luke Skywalker, they were both actually on a platform built a few feet above a studio floor. The magic of movies is in the techniques by which writers and directors put us in imaginary situations and actors convince us that they are what they're not. Then along comes the G. Gordon Liddy of movies, Werner Herzog, who apparently sees the production of a film as a mystic ordeal.

In making *Fitzcarraldo*, Herzog was proving his uncompromising integrity by housing his actors deep in the jungle and having them go through the hardships of the characters they play—only more so. He christened the jungle camp "Film or Death." Herzog thought that this movie would be a cheat if he used miniatures and mattes. There's some goofball puritanism operating in this man: he treats the challenges he sets up as if they had been imposed on him—as if he had been cursed. He thinks he's producing art because he turns the making of a film into such a miserable, difficult struggle for all concerned. But the art of the motion picture is fakery—even its most ascetic practitioner, Carl Dreyer, knew that. Dreyer didn't burn up the elderly woman who was tied to the stake in *Day of Wrath*, and chances are that the actors who played in *Ordet* didn't even have to down all that poisonous-looking black coffee. Robert Bresson didn't actually drive the girl who played in *Mouchette* to suicide. (Only the audience.) Nothing destroys the spell of dramatic movies so jarringly as the intrusion of violence and pain that clearly aren't faked, such as the slaughter of an animal or the wire-tripping of a horse. Those are the real snuff films.

Fitzcarraldo is embarrassingly—infuriatingly—real; the Indians tugging at Herzog's steamboat are workers trapped inside his misconception of a movie. We may be appalled by the labors that are evident in *Fitzcarraldo*; we may even be impressed by them. But we always see them as exactly what they are: labors undertaken to be photographed. The story he has devised never takes hold; there isn't enough illusion for that. The plot seems no more than a pretext for the central image. At times, the ship slowly climbing the mountain does seem rather magical, but two hours and thirty-seven minutes is a long sit, and the deliberateness of Herzog's pacing can put you in a stupor. A lot of other things happen, but that's all they do; they don't develop and they're not followed through. Herzog has got himself into some zone between documentary and drama where neither works. It may be that his passion for authenticity is more religious than aesthetic, because he can't seem to make the images vivid—it's as if all his energy had gone into meeting the behind-the-scenes tests that he created for himself, his cast, and his crew (and, probably, his backers).

The actual Fitzcarrald, who was content to have his boat transported in pieces, was already rich; he succeeded in his maneuver and got wildly richer from it. Herzog has written his Fitz as a lovable loser, though with Klaus Kinski in the role very little of that comes through. We don't know quite what Kinski's Fitz is, because he's not like anyone else in the world (except maybe Bette Davis playing Rutger Hauer). Herzog has grafted another element onto the story of the historical Fitzcarrald by giving his hero a reason for wanting to get rich in the rubber trade: an obsession with building an opera house in the jungle and bringing Caruso to sing in it. (An opera house was in fact built on the Amazon, in Brazil, in 1896.) This makes Fitz more like a movie director—like Herzog himself, who certainly didn't use the six million dollars that *Fitzcarraldo* finally cost on pleasures of the flesh. Herzog needed the money so he could punish himself and everyone around him—in the cause of art. A man who at fourteen or fifteen decided that filmmaking was his vocation, Herzog has got an army of heathens with painted faces hauling his three-hundred-and-twenty-ton Cross up a mountain—and in the misproportioned narrative this is meant to be merely the first step toward the goal of bringing opera to the jungle. By the time the ship is over the hump, we're prepared to accept any token of a finish, and that's about what Herzog delivers.

In Les Blank's feature-length documentary *Burden of Dreams*, which is about the making of *Fitzcarraldo*, there's a brief scene of Jason Robards in the title role (before amoebic dysentery caused him to leave the picture). Just from Robards' presence in that one bit, it's clear that his Fitzcarraldo might have been a likable, charismatic Irish bum with a dream. And we can tell that Kinski's Fitz is intended to be a generous, good-hearted fellow, because he talks to a pet pig and he likes the native children—he gives them chips of ice, and when they cluster around him in his shack he plays his Caruso records for them (and the pig). But Kinski is megalomania incarnate. Even in a dishevelled white suit and a floppy white straw hat that he looks lost in, he gives off emanations that are far too outré for this role. With his goggling eyes and his big dome and the spikes of yellow-orange hair sticking out of it, he's an icon of stark raving freakishness. Kinski keeps an expression on his face until it looks fixed and mad; he never lets you forget that he's different from other men. If he ever had an ordinary "normal" range, he doesn't anymore. And Kinski only does a single. He's usually a single who gives what's needed, but not this time. Kinski's Fitzcarraldo isn't a man with a dizzy dream—he's a bored, fed-up actor eyeballing the camera. This means that Claudia Cardinale, in the role of Molly, the madam of a fancy whorehouse who finances Fitz's scheme, can't quite come into focus. Cardinale, with her big bright smile, is a warm and jovial Molly, and if Robards were opposite her we could understand why she is so protective of Fitz. Cardinale is ripely alive even in this asexual movie, and she stays in character like a real trouper, even though

Kinski pats her or takes her arm routinely, and so her Molly seems rather too conveniently acquiescent, and somewhat simple.

There is a sequence that might have been a comic heartbreaker and might also have told us what we needed to know about Fitz and his past: At an abandoned railway station where he has gone to pull up some tracks that could be useful for guiding his boat down the mountain, he is greeted by a family headed by a black man, who beams with pleasure at the sight of him. The man is still loyally guarding the rails that Fitz had hired him to guard six years earlier, when he was involved in an abortive bringing-in-a-railroad venture. Almost unbelievably, Herzog doesn't shape the meeting so that Fitz has some response—perhaps becomes shamefaced about past failures and forgotten pledges, maybe promises to pay the man some of his back wages. The scene is just dropped. And nowhere is there a suggestion of when or how this scrounging dreamer developed his passion for Caruso. Herzog has always been great at flooding huge landscapes with music, and when Fitz stands on the prow of his ship with his head flung back and with Caruso's voice coming out of the phonograph next to him, it's obvious that he feels he's the king of all he surveys. But Herzog has said that he himself doesn't like opera—that he went once and walked out. (A bummer of a first opera bored him and he never went to another. Suppose somebody's first movie is *Fitzcarraldo* ...) The one opera-house scene (it was staged by Werner Schroeter) is insulting to Caruso and the aged, crippled Sarah Bernhardt, whom it purports to represent. For no apparent reason, Bernhardt is played by a female impersonator. Or perhaps there is a reason—to make Fitz's obsession ludicrous. He sees the plump singer and the tottering old tart in the same performance that we do, and he's ecstatic.

The tone that Herzog is after in this film must be romantic irony; he looks at Fitz's passion from the outside and sees Fitz's goal—opera in the jungle—as something of a joke. The film is a parody variation of *Aguirre*: this time the protagonist doesn't want to rule—he just wants to be an impresario. And he isn't meant to be a madman—just a little nutty. In the documentary, when Herzog rages against the beauty of the wilderness—when he says that he hates it, that it's all vileness and fornication, and that "the trees here are in misery, the birds are in misery, they don't sing, they just screech in pain, even the stars up here look like a mess"—surely he means us to laugh at his ranting intensity? He's playing the obsessed clown, and that's what he must have had in mind for Fitz, whose big accomplishment is worthless, and who finally relaxes and enjoys himself with a bit of bravura that is his way of making good on his vow to bring opera to the banks of the Amazon. Yet while we're watching the movie it just seems to be an inept attempt at a heroic spectacular, and when we get to the ramshackle finish it's as if *Lawrence of Arabia* had dissolved in giggles.

The biggest disappointment in *Fitzcarraldo* is Peru. After a visually promising beginning, Herzog seems to lose interest in the external world (and no one in this movie has much of an internal world, either). The shots are repetitive and are held too long, and though they're lovely, they don't have the ghostly, kinky expressiveness of the great images that sustain one through the dragginess of *Aguirre*. And probably because of Herzog's ironic intentions the steamboat being towed up the mountain loses any metaphorical meaning. In some shots, it looks so fake I guess it has to be the real thing. The sight that we wait for turns out to be a bust: when the ship is poised at the very top, it looks like a big toy.

The moviegoers who attend Herzog pictures probably perceive his Sisyphean labors as a metaphor for how every artist is tested, and think the labors crazy but grand. And sometimes they are: at the end of *Aguirre*, when the madman is on the raft and the camera circles him, it's as if he were strangling within the circumference of his own hysteria. (He's like the thrice-encircled poet of "Kubla Khan.") But the visual grandeur has gone flat in *Fitzcarraldo*. There may be limits to the results an imaginative moviemaker can get if he keeps rejecting imaginative techniques. A man who has to do everything the hard way raises the suspicion that he's simply a hardhead. Herzog says things like "If I show a plastic ship going over a plastic mountain, it will be just a Hollywood movie, a cheap movie, and everyone will know it." Does Herzog actually go to the movies? (He seems to want only the torment of making them.) No one could deny the persistence of tacky-looking pictures, but even fifty years ago craftsmen in Hollywood (and at UFA, in Germany) were creating effects more than equal to Herzog's needs in *Fitzcarraldo*. It can't be that he's afraid of a plastic look; he knows better than that. He could have controlled the quality of process shots much more easily than he controlled the maneuvers of that ship, and he wouldn't have risked other people's lives doing it or put his co-workers through misery. He would have been free to work as a film artist—instead of playing Pharaoh. Herzog puts his effort in the wrong place. Is it that he's afraid of *not* being tested, of *not* having his ordeals? He needn't worry; these days nobody makes big, ambitious movies without passing through fire.

The footage of Herzog himself in the Les Blank documentary, standing and addressing the camera (though with eyes averted), is stronger than anything in his own movie. (He does have an inner life—and it's frightening.) If you see *Burden of Dreams*, you may not be able to think of *Fitzcarraldo* without remembering Herzog's almost priggish dissociation from his own acts. *Burden of Dreams* isn't a major work on its own, but it has an unusual effect: it makes *Fitzcarraldo* crumble in the memory—it merges with it. In the documentary, Herzog acknowledges the injuries and fatalities that occurred during the making of his picture, but he regards them as the unavoidable results of his commitment to film; they're setbacks—obstacles to the profession of moviemaker. A sainted liberal, he's deeply concerned about the Indians' sufferings over the centuries, and he assures us of his care not to contaminate them with Western culture. His tone is mournful as he rambles on about the terrible exploitation that has been killing them off, and it's bad enough to watch hundreds of them in the mud pulling at his damn steamboat without listening to him lament their tragic history. At one glorious point in his monologues to the camera, this humble fellow tells us that his dreams are the same as ours—that "the only distinction between me and you is that I can articulate them." This puts him in a class with the movie queen in *Singin' in the Rain* who dimpled prettily as she said, "If we bring a little joy into your humdrum lives, it makes us feel as though our hard work ain't been in vain for nothin'." Herzog *is* an artist, but he's also a faker—the most dangerous kind, possibly, because he doesn't know how to use his fakery except to make himself seem more holy than other people.

October 18, 1982

Rice Krispies

Watching *Fast Times at Ridgemont High*, I was surprised at how notbad it is. It may fall into the general category of youth-exploitation movies, but it isn't assaultive, and it's certainly likable. The title appears over a shot of a California shopping mall—which makes sense, because new California high schools, with their separate buildings for art and music and whatever, are more and more like shopping malls. And the mall is where the Ridgemont kids go right after school—to their jobs. (It's also where they spend the money they earn.) *Fast Times* is like the *Beach Party* movies at a later stage—as if they'd evolved and gained a higher form of consciousness. What makes it appealing (yet may upset some parents) is that the kids rely on one another. They've gained independence from the adults at home. The kids are there to catch each other after the falls, and to console each other—they function as parents for each other.

It's not surprising that the movie is a success: for the kids in the audience, the feeling of being in an autonomous world of high-school kids must be wonderful. *Fast Times* isn't like the films about teen-age gangs, and it isn't one of those movies that say the kids are smart and the teachers are stupid—as if the only thing that corrupts people is the aging process. It isn't concerned with adults' anxieties about colleges and careers, either. The world of this film is a kids' network, where their choices, whether surfing or studying or just getting stoned, aren't judged. Directed by a young woman—

Amy Heckerling, making her feature-film début—the movie has an open, generous tone.

Fast Times follows the course of several kids' lives by means of short takes, vignettes, and montages of gags. There are no big crises, in which a boy or girl feels totally alone. If the film has a theme, it's sexual embarrassment. Sex fouls the kids up—they seem to know about drugs before they've got into sex—but even sex isn't the kind of problem it used to be. The girls talk about it as a matter of technique that they can learn, and they're hoping to find a boy who's a good lover. Though it's obvious that what they'd really like is romance and a boy to hang out with (who might turn into a sex partner), they manage to be fairly humorous about their miserably botched attempts at coupling. When the fifteen-year-old Stacy (Jennifer Jason Leigh) is worried about not knowing how to perform oral intercourse, her closest girl friend, the tall and knowing Linda (Phoebe Cates), a luscious specimen of Valley Girl, instructs her, and, using a term they probably picked up in class, they discuss the "variables." Stacy, proceeding as if she were doing lab work, makes the mistake of experimenting with Mike (Robert Romanus), a fast talker who believes that the way to impress women is to have a certain attitude— "You never let on how much you like a girl," "Act like wherever you are that's the place to be," and so on. He turns out to be a fast lover, too—a scared, fumbling, teen-age premature ejaculator. Mike is the most verbal of the kids; the others talk in their own sneering slang. The dialogue throughout seems uncannily accurate: the kids sound as if they were sending each other telegrams, but with every second or third word in italics (and with "awesome" and "bitchin' " as the only words of praise).

The characters emerge from the gags. Stacy's older brother, Brad (Judge Reinhold), a senior, is proud of his finesse behind the counter at the most popular burger joint in the mall, and he takes such pleasure in his car that he washes it with some of the same caressing motions he uses when he's wiping the grease off the griddle at work. Little Ratner (Brian Backer), who takes tickets at the movie house in the mall, has a scene so recognizably primal that kids in the audience must squirm for him: the pragmatic Stacy invites him into her room and sits him on the bed next to her, and he's afraid to make a move. Half a dozen or so of the young actors have roles of roughly the same importance, but Sean Penn—in the role of the surfer-doper, Jeff Spicoli—becomes the film's star. He has the kind of talent that bites you on the nose and makes you laugh, and he inhabits his part totally. When the history teacher confiscates a pizza that Spicoli has had delivered to him in class, he is hurt and astonished—he can't believe it. But you may get the feeling that a moment later he'll have accepted the disciplinary insult as if it were some sort of special attention—a compliment. Spicoli, with his red-rimmed eyes, his tangled yellow hair, and his big, baffled double takes, is the most pleasant stoned kid imaginable. He has a giggle that comes from far inside—in his amiable state, whatever mishaps there are in the world are funny.

Sometimes you can see that the ideas in the script, by Cameron Crowe (it's adapted from his book about the year he spent at a California high school, impersonating an adolescent), are potentially better than the way they've been carried out. But Amy Heckerling has a light hand, and the gags that miss don't thud. Some of the jokes may be treated too glancingly—for example, the bit with a classful of students automatically sniffing the solvent on their Ditto paper isn't pointed, and it goes a little flat. Yet if this errs, it's in a graceful direction. (There's only one really bum scene: on the night of a school dance, Ray Walston—the teacher who seized the pizza—shows up at Spicoli's house to force a history lesson on him.) When Heckerling falters at the end of a sketch and the actors are just on the verge of losing their characters, the music—a collection of some nineteen pop songs—saves them from humiliation. The music isn't obstreperous; it doesn't underline things—it's just always there when it's needed.

In this movie, a gag's working or not working hardly matters—everything has a quick, makeshift feeling. If you're eating a bowl of Rice Krispies and some of them don't pop, that's O.K., because the bowlful has a nice poppy feeling. Neither the film's bad moments—nor its good ones—stay with you. Jokes such as the "assassinate Lincoln" buttons that are passed out before the big game between Ridgemont and Lincoln High aren't exactly memorable, but they're not meant to be, either—only enjoyable. Jennifer Jason Leigh has a bloom that makes the scenes in which she's a very weary teenager all the more convincing. Heckerling has taste—she doesn't milk pathos out of the rough spots Stacy gets into. She doesn't make a big deal out of things—this is a gentle, blackout-style comedy. At times, it's a comedy with an eye for a particular kind of California beauty: there's an evocative shot of Phoebe Cates seen through lawn sprinklers as she walks toward the camera. Too bad we don't get more of Phoebe Cates' Linda. Stacy is the normal girl of the past, with her biology speeded up, but Linda, who takes all her cues from pop culture, may represent a new, jaded, sullen mood. Nothing causes a light to flicker in her huge, shining eyes, and she doesn't look ahead much. She doesn't seem fully alive. Yet the friendship of the two girls—the matter-of-factness of it—is lovely. Linda may not know a whole lot about sex, but what she knows she shares. And she sees the comedy in her own blank bordeom.

•　　•　　•　　•　　•

*I*f a moviemaker is a Freudian, his most "personal" films are likely to be forever looking back. They'll center on the protagonist's past—his childhood. And no matter whose childhood is pawed over, Freudian pawing tends to be of limited interest on the screen, because, of course, we know pretty much what will be exhumed. In the Spanish writer-director Carlos Saura's *Dulces Horas*, or *Sweet Hours*, the past is a riddle to Juan (Iñaki Aierra), the playwright hero. It's melancholy in a special, hooded way. The long-faced Juan is so obsessed with memories of the massive furnishings in his family's apartment, of the elderly father who skipped off and the young mother who committed suicide, that he has written a play, *Sweet Hours*, which contains the key scenes of his early life. The play is in rehearsal, and he attends the sessions watchfully, rapt. He's searching for something. (Can it be the clue to what's always missing from Saura's films—the final burst of energy that would make everything count?)

Saura is a fine craftsman, and the movie is a graceful, measured, Freudian-fantasy game, with Juan slipping in and out of the actors' reconstructions and his own memories. Except for some initial confusion about who the regulars at his family dinner table are (at first I wasn't sure whether a dark-haired man with a mustache was Juan's father or uncle) and an episode about a hammy actor in military uniform which interrupts the story of Juan's early life, the transitions are formally very pleasing. And finally, as it must in the art work of all conventional Freudians, the light dawns on Juan. He dredges up the repressed material, and his Oedipus complex is resolved: he comes to see that as a boy he tried to break up his parents' embrace because he wanted his mother to himself, and he sees, too, what a seductive witch his beautiful mother was, and how deeply she implicated him in his father's flight and her own death.

Saura has given the gentle, rather passive Juan a bonus—a perfect wish fulfillment—by having him fall in love with Berta (Assumpta Serna), the stunning young actress who is rehearsing the role of his mother. Since Assumpta Serna plays both the actress in the reënactments and Juan's mother as she appears in his memories, this lucky fellow manages both to resolve his Oedipus complex and to marry his mother. I wish I could say that this trick is brought off like an exploding Buñuelian joke. But the whole movie is on gliders, and the shifts from the present to the theatrically performed past and to the remembered past are smoothly and intricately choreographed—it's all very dignified. Saura is romantic about his hero's past and present, and the lilting soprano voice of Imperia Argentina in the soundtrack song "Recordar" ("To Remember") is yummy icing on Juan's yummy life. (The film's title comes from the lyrics.)

Even the shocking revelations about Juan's parents are languorous and sensuous; there's no messiness from below deck to soil this cultured Freudian dream. Every detail is symbolically right; Juan's home life was stuffy and bourgeois, so the site for the home he and Berta will build is away from the city—open and breezy. This movie has the kind of subtle obviousness that is generally described as "literate." What it comes down to is that Carlos Saura has a feeling for dark, autumnal elegance, and a dexterous technique that he puts at the service of tired ideas. What saves him from pedantry is that his films have occasional moments of erotic vibrancy. Scenes that aren't explicitly sexual in content are sexualized, so that they become ambiguous and disturbing—even haunting. There are no satisfying dramatic revelations, and the meanings remain vague, but from time to time the images have an erotic tingle. In a Saura film, something more directly sexual is often impending; it hovers in the atmosphere. Fernando Rey and Geraldine Chaplin, for example, looked superb as the father and daughter in Saura's 1976 puzzle-movie *Elisa, Vida Mía*; their closeups seemed about to tell us something—but, of course, it never broke through. If this new picture is quite tolerable, it's because of the shots of the wide-eyed Assumpta Serna, who, when she smiles, has a teasing elusiveness a bit like that of Vanessa Redgrave. She makes the atmosphere hum. Tall, with a loose-limbed, modern-woman stride, and with her soft light-brown hair worn free and easy, the apparently straightforward Berta uses a ruse to make the first date with Juan, and she's always coming after him; she knows he's shy, and she's not about to let him get away. It seems right that Berta is a little taller than Juan—she's his mother. And perhaps Saura means us to perceive that the bland Juan will never know that he didn't pursue Berta. Maybe Saura means us to see that the cycle is inescapable; that could be why Berta calls Juan Juanico, just as his mother did, and bathes him like a child. But the tone of the ending is optimistic, and as Juan and the pregnant Berta hug each other, the child Juan (who had wanted to separate his parents) appears from out of the past and kisses them both. It's a Freudian benediction on their union. Can the picture, with all its refinements, be this sappy? Can Saura be saying that Juan got his mother and it's bliss? Or, to put it differently, is he saying that once Juan has had his psyche straightened out and knows that he must inevitably marry his mother, he can relax and enjoy being infantilized? Beats me. The enigma of Saura is his addiction to enigma.

•   •   •   •   •

*I*t has been a while since I saw a movie in which a man's sadistic rottenness was established by having him be mean to a cat. In *Jinxed!*, the mistreater of cats (and women) is played by Rip Torn, and so the character—a gamblin' man—has elements of parody built in, but the director, Don Siegel, doesn't pick up on them. He doesn't pick up on much of anything. The star of the film is Bette Midler, as Bonita the cat-lover—an entertainer who works in the casinos at Lake Tahoe and Reno. The picture gives Midler one good, frantic routine: between the stanzas of a fast, rowdy medley that Bonita is singing onstage, she bumps and grinds her way to the wings where her lover (Ken Wahl), a young blackjack dealer, is standing, and she hisses out the procedures of a plan to murder that hateful sadist, who has been whacking her around and psyching out the dealer—jinxing him. Bonita does her fast grind back and forth across the stage, delivering a stanza of instructions for every stanza of song, without losing her rhythm. The movie is on to something here: slapstick black comedy with a beat. But it isn't developed. *Jinxed!* goes back to being a grotesque imitation of a screwball romance, and the skinny plot is stretched out to the length of a feature film by such insulting devices as a treasure hunt. Even the movies *Jinxed!* was lifted from are bad. (It has a strong aroma of *The Only Game in Town*, along with a sprinkling of James M. Cain novels.)

The battered singer is supposed to be heartsick in the beginning, because the scummy gambler treats her like dirt, and then buoyant at the end, when she's with the decent young dealer. But Siegel doesn't appear to have charted the film's emotional progression. Midler starts out strong and ends up subdued and frazzled. And the relatively inexperienced Wahl isn't in the same picture with her. He has no technique to draw upon, nothing to respond with. Ken Wahl began acting just a few years ago, and he probably had considerable help from his directors on *The Wanderers* and *Fort Apache, the Bronx*. He's cruelly exposed here: the camera seems to zero in on his handsome, clear-eyed face and bare chest just when he's pleading for guidance. He has been turned into a TV-style hunk.

Midler has some lines that are real swifties and she turns even moderately amusing ones into zingers, but the situations don't go anywhere. And though she has got her spandex pants and her great wiggle-walk (her thighs seem to be tied together) and the lewd twinkle in her eyes, she isn't colorful here. She has gone deathly blond. The platinum hair bleaches out her rosiness and her radiance. She needs the soft blurry warmth of pink and orange and gold; with her hair whitened, her face seems to lose its planes—to be flattened out. (She has said that making this film was "the worst experience of my entire life," and you can just about touch the tense, drawn face muscles.) Though Midler's specialty is being smart and on top of things, Bonita is a silly ditz—the type of helpless dumb blonde whose affectations Midler as a stage performer usually satirizes. And the character has been so thinly conceived that all Midler can do is play comic mannerisms. She's drawing upon externals only—shtick. That's what Goldie Hawn has had to do in pictures such as *Foul Play*, but it may be riskier for Midler: the cartoon mannerisms she resorts to are extreme, and her energy level has to be extra high (high even for her), because there's nothing—absolutely nothing—going on around her. She keeps Bonita rushing about double-quick—so fast that when she stops she has the shakes. Midler ransacks herself and invents like a crazy dynamo just to give *Jinxed!* some artificial respiration. She turns it into a one-woman comedy show, but you can see what the effort is costing her, and she carries only part of the picture.

She's wasting herself, because she selected a stupid script, by Bert Blessing (a pseudonym for Frank Gilroy, who wrote *The Only Game in Town*), which was then reworked by David Newman, and then she picked a director who's wrong for her. Bette Midler is caught in a new bind: stars of her magnitude can generally choose what they want to appear in, but often they don't take the time or the trouble to make intuitive decisions—the kind of decisions that Midler learned to make in her stage material. It's unlikely that she would have signed to work with Don Siegel if she had looked at even a couple of his recent pictures—say, *The Shootist* and *Escape from Alcatraz*—and he was never the right director for a musical-comedy star. This worst experience of her life was predictable.

The debacle probably didn't faze Rip Torn, who has a trick up his sleeve: he saves his sliest blinks and changes of expression for when he's meant to be a corpse. He gives a more entertaining performance dead than alive.

November 1, 1982

The Magician

*R*obert Altman's *Come Back to the 5 & Dime Jimmy Dean, Jimmy Dean* shouldn't work, but it does. Every idea and line of dialogue in Ed Graczyk's play, which centers on the reunion of a James Dean fan club on the twentieth anniversary of his death, is derivative in a fake-poetic, fake-magical way; it reeks of the worst of William Inge, of Tennessee Williams misunderstood. In structure, it's a Texas-small-town, women's version of O'Neill's *The Iceman Cometh*, with each woman forced to reveal her hideous truth—what her whole pitiful system of pretensions has been covering up. And it has its Iceman: a member of the group who left town and now returns to blast the lid off these cowardly lives. I doubt if a major film director has ever before voluntarily taken on as thoroughgoing a piece of drivel as this one. Yet when Altman gives a project everything he's got, his skills are such that he can make poetry out of fake poetry and magic out of fake magic. When he'd finished this film, he went off to the University of Michigan to stage Stravinsky's *The Rake's Progress*, which features a machine for converting stones into bread.

Altman had a humiliating defeat when he directed *Come Back to the 5 & Dime Jimmy Dean, Jimmy Dean* on Broadway early this year; afterward, he restaged the one-set play in a New York studio with basically the same cast and shot it in Super 16-mm. in nineteen days, at a cost of nine hundred thousand dollars—put up by Mark Goodson Productions and Viacom (which acquired the right to show the film on its cable division, Showtime). When *Come Back* was blown up to 35-mm., there may have been a small loss of vibrancy (the peach-pink tones seem to have grayed out a bit), but it still has a glow. Discussing his plans to film plays for cable TV, Altman told *Newsweek*, "There has to be a new style—not a play, not a movie," and *Come*

Back is somewhere in between. The material develops like a well-made the-atre piece: the playwright withholds crucial information about the characters' past experiences, then gradually strips away their lies. And although Altman has trimmed the text of the Broadway version, the dialogue retains the over-explanatory quality that is typical of the stage. There's a lot of talk. But he uses an unusually fluid camera style. The movement inside the 5 & Dime set-ting is delicately purposeful—he keeps us aware of the women's faces and shoulders, of how they stand or touch or hover over one another. While Graczyk's dialogue is coming out of them, the camera peruses the ones who are speaking and the ones who are listening. We're physically close to them, as we're physically close to the actors in Bergman's films. But Altman doesn't burrow into a character the way Bergman does, starting in closeup and push-ing farther and farther in. Altman's camera doesn't have that relentlessness; the characters don't look pinned down—they appear to be caught in passing, on the wing, and that's part of what makes this film seem so magical. Moving in apparent freedom, the principal actresses go at their roles so creatively that, I think, they've found some kind of acting truth in what they're doing. They bring conviction to their looneytunes characters.

When you come out, you may be saying to yourself, "If Robert Altman can do that with a piece of sausage, think what he could do with a good script." But it's possible that Sandy Dennis, Cher, Karen Black, and, in a lesser role, Marta Heflin are able to do so much with their parts because of the cheesy mythmaking undertones of the material. If the roles made better sense, the actresses might not be able to plunge so far down into themselves or pull up so much emotion. It's *because* this glib, religioso play is so deriva-tive that the actors have found so much depth in it. When actors peel away layers of inhibition, they feel they're uncovering "truth" and it's traditional for directors and acting teachers to call it that. But this truth may be derived from their stored-up pop mythology—atrocity stories from sources as diverse as comic books, TV, and Joan Didion, and tales of sacrificial heroes and hero-ines that go back beyond the birth of movies to the first storytellers. "Truth-ful" acting may be affecting to us because it represents the sum total of everything the actors have been affected by. It comes from areas far below conscious technique; it's true to their psyches. To use the theatre term, the performers here have made the roles "their own." They may think they're finding meanings in the material, but actually they're adding them. If they didn't—if they stayed with the surface of this play—they'd be dead.

As the more than slightly mad Mona, Sandy Dennis is the linchpin of the production, and if you're not fascinated by the way Mona tries to distance herself from the life about her and from her own sensuality you might find the film intolerable. Sometimes it may seem that not much separates a superb Sandy Dennis performance from an irritating one, since she uses some of the same mannerisms in both. But when her tics are right for a role she can zoom off and come up with things no one else would have dreamt of. I found her impossible in her starring vehicles (the 1967 *Up the Down Staircase* and the 1968 *Sweet November*) but a droopy joy in the 1970 *The Out-of-Towners* and unfailingly funny in the 1977 *Nasty Habits*. And she brought something weirdly human to last year's *The Four Seasons*. (She was the only person in it I could have any feeling for.) Mona is her most extravagant creation: nervous and nostrilly and ladylike, a woman who hides in dowdy clothes yet can't resist wearing her thick, curly red hair soft and loose—floating about her, aureole style. Even Mona's affectations—which center on how fine-grained and sensitive and asthmatic she is—are of the flesh. She's compellingly strange and repressed, yet carnal, and, I think, very beautiful (she's a little like Piper Laurie in *Carrie*), and when she's angry she's frighteningly bossy. She gets "burned up," and you can see why the people around her don't challenge her stories: Mona's grip on her fantasies is the strongest thing about her. I admired the performance that Sandy Dennis gave in Altman's 1969 *That Cold Day in the Park*, but it was a much more held-in character; Mona—a delusionary romantic—is far more stirring. And Sandy Dennis takes more chances as an actress now. The way the role is written, Mona is a hand-me-down from Tennessee Williams; complaining of the small-minded small-town people, she's a cow-country Blanche DuBois. She has some of Blanche's frailty; that's why it's so shocking when she yells—you don't expect her to be able to sustain that much emotion.

The town that the 5 & Dime is in is close to the site where parts of *Giant* were filmed in 1955, and it's Graczyk's conceit that working as extras in the crowd scenes was the biggest event in the lives of the local people, and that for the hyper-impressionable Mona, the boyish young star of the movie, James Dean, was a Christ figure. When she gave in to her desires and had sex with a boy one hot summer night, she convinced herself that it was James Dean the Saviour who came into her body, that she was "chosen," and that the son she bore—Jimmy Dean—was his.

The action flashes back and forth between 1955 and the reunion year, 1975, without any attempt to make the actors appear younger or older: it's as if Altman had said, "There's so much illusion hopping around in this material, let's not play games with makeup—let's treat the audience as adults who can accept the convention that the actors are meant to be both young and old." And so the actors are liberated, and the décor takes on the job of telling us which period we're in, and does it easily, painlessly. Actually, the camera's frequent scanning of the 5 & Dime—a variety store with a soda fountain—is oddly pleasurable. The set has a mirrored wall, and Altman uses mirrors for the illusion of space (and for time changes, too, and tricks of memory). The action even passes through them. In Louis Malle's *My Dinner with André*, which also uses a large mirror, there are times while André is talking when the movie seems to transport you, and this happens in the Altman film, too. Its modulations are transporting, and Pierre Mignot's cinematography is airy and lyrical without any show-biz glitter. Although the action is all in the store, there seems to be plenty of room, and the movie breathes as if it were shot outdoors. Altman keeps looking at the world, and it's never the same; what we're responding to is his consciousness at work (and play). The sunlight coming through the shop's glass front and the dusty pastel colors are part of the film's texture, along with the women's hair and heads and hands, which are always touching, moving. Present and past interpenetrate, and Altman keeps everything in motion. (The closeups are pauses, not full stops.) His feeling for the place is almost as tactile as his feeling for the performers. When the characters' passions well up, the camera is right there, recording the changes in their neck muscles, their arms, their cheeks. But it never crowds them.

As Sissy, the waitress at the 5 & Dime—a strutting good-time girl, who's the opposite of Mona—Cher is direct and simple in her effects, as if it were the easiest thing in the world to slip into the character of an aging small-town belle with a Texas accent. When Sissy and Mona fight, you feel the emotional violence in these two women who can't help being contemptuous of each other. And though Sandy Dennis is amazing in these scenes, Cher holds her own. Cher could play Arletty roles—at least, she could if Altman were directing her—and not just because her fine cheekbones and long, slender arms suggest Arletty's particular type of dark patrician beauty (the look of an archaic figure on a vase) but because she has the funny tough-broad quality to go with it. There was a richness in Arletty's whory elegance—she made you feel she'd learned even from the things she wished she could forget. Cher doesn't seem rich in experience that way, but without any of the kook fiddling about that she did on TV—staying completely in character, without tricks or reminders of who she is—she's stunningly unself-conscious.

Karen Black, who makes a late, carefully prepared-for entrance (like the Iceman), has the showiest role, and she plays it with spectacular tawdry world-weariness; her Joanne is like a gay-bar version of Angie Dickinson, tailored white suit and all. Joanne, with her low voice and the stiff hairdo of a TV anchorwoman, is heartsick and past hope, yet still loving. She's the most sinned-against—a living hard-luck story. And her masochism is presented as glorious gallantry. Slinking around—prowling the 5 & Dime—she embodies all the ironies that Ed Graczyk could pile onto her, and damned if Karen Black doesn't bring them all off. (The material develops an edge when she appears.) Joanne is the third—and the most "hurting"—of the film's three mutilated goddesses. And Karen Black keeps the mawkishness from splashing all over the set. I think this isn't just the best performance she has given onscreen—it's a different kind of acting from what she usually does. It's subdued, controlled, quiet—but not parched. When she and Cher get a little drunk and laugh uproariously, there's a healthy raucous feeling in it.

Two of the former members of the club have driven from Dallas for the anniversary. Marta Heflin's Edna Louise, a mousey blond mother of six (and pregnant again), submits to the bullying of her hefty, richer friend, Kathy

Bates's Stella Mae, who has a brassy voice and wears a cowgirl hat. It's a Laurel & Hardy relationship, with the puny and timorous Edna Louise becoming rather endearing. Perhaps because Edna Louise allows Stella Mae to walk all over her, she's the only character who's exempted from exposure; Edna Louise is a dishrag, and so she's meant to be the happy one of the bunch—touched by grace. Graczyk's schema is offensive (and so obvious you may find yourself moaning), but Marta Heflin's performance is sweetly, appealingly meek. Kathy Bates has a good prurient bit toward the end (before it becomes labored), but her loud belligerence seems too practiced. Altman doesn't appear to have shaken the stage rhythm out of her delivery. This fault is even more pronounced in Sudie Bond's performance as the crabby fundamentalist Juanita, the widow who runs the 5 & Dime. Juanita isn't well integrated into the camera rhythms, either; her expressions and her words seem frozen—as if she had worked up the character long before and had nothing more to bring to it. But Altman handles the only male actor—Mark Patton, as Joe (who looks a little like James Dean)—with fine discretion, using him as a partly hallucinatory figure; he materializes as Mona thinks of him.

Altman's overall directing is a model of tenderness and tact. His touch seems as sure here as it was wobbly in most of the pictures he has made since *Nashville*, in 1975. He's a great director. But there is still the puzzler: it's not just the actors who have swallowed Graczyk's big, windy ironies—Altman bit on them, too. A banner welcoming the club members who have returned for the 1975 anniversary tells us the name of the group: the Disciples of James Dean. The 5 & Dime has two enshrined portraits—one of Christ, one of Dean. Altman lightens these ironies; his humor doesn't fail him. There are a few clinkers, though. One of the women makes the flat-out statement that the group knew all along that Mona wasn't telling the truth; surely "suspected" would have been more felicitous? And there's a symbolic notion that's too ripe even for parody: the 1975 scenes take place during a drought, and the storm that's expected passes over—there's no rain. Graczyk's play is actually much worse than the material of Altman's most forgettable films. Its only advantage is that it has given him a cast-iron structure. Though the opening scenes that set up the characters and the time shifts seem very free and flimsy (and are initially off-putting), every detail is pinned in place. I think Altman may have been attracted by the trashy play because it's a remote variant of his 1977 film *Three Women*, which he himself wrote (and which disintegrated in solemnities). He's drawn to archetypal American figures, and to characters who represent our well-known warped and impoverished values. Mona, to whom a movie star is God; Sissy, who thinks her chest is her passport to glory; Stella Mae, the boastful materialist; Juanita, the tight-faced hypocrite—they're all designed to muckrake themselves, and Altman may have felt that the play was "saying something." But he has made it effective by going way beyond its prosaic intentions. Yes, the characters are warped by their illusions, but Altman has a poetic intuition of the way illusions wrap around people's lives, and his technique—all the artifice he brings to the staging—becomes one with the themes of illusion and deception. And the pop mythology that the actresses bring to the film can be startling in its intensity, because where the lines are written for pathos, he tops it with a satirical twist. His comedy and artifice save the day.

Commercial failure can affect an artist's judgment as badly as overconfidence can; his tastes may regress. When Altman came to New York last year to work in the theatre, he told the *Times*, "I think I've been too isolated." His wanting to stage *Come Back* is proof of that. But whatever has gone flooey in Robert Altman's choice of material, he's in his prime as a director. Actually, he's in too good form for this play: he outclasses it. People who are caught up in the performances and the style may be appalled by the text, and those who are keen on Graczyk's writing will probably wish the film were done in the head-on-collision, blurting-out manner of, say, *On Golden Pond*. The movie is a genuine oddity—like *The Night of the Iguana* performed by a company of seraphim. The rake's machine for converting stones into bread is, of course, a devil's trick—a fraud. Altman's magic is the real thing.

November 15, 1982

Designs for Living

*T*he title of Marco Bellocchio's *Leap Into the Void* (*Salto nel Vuoto*) probably refers to risking new experiences and to suicidal jumps, but it might also describe the bafflement that a viewer feels during the opening of the picture. Bellocchio isn't eager to offer a helping hand; we have to find our own way in. At first, I was enthralled by what was going on—which was morbid, yet farcical—without quite grasping it. And then I remembered feeling almost exactly the same way, back in the late sixties, when I saw Bellocchio's first picture *Fists in the Pocket*. (A fluent, wild man's movie about bourgeois inbreeding, it was made in 1965, when he was in his mid-twenties, and opened here in 1968, as did his second film, *China Is Near*; those two and *In the Name of the Father* are the only Bellocchio films to have got commercial openings in this country until now.) The relatively new *Leap Into the Void*—it was made in 1979—isn't as convulsive and furiously intense as *Fists*, but it has the same seductive undertone. When Bellocchio fantasizes about family life, he makes me feel that I should be horrified, but in some sneaky way I'm having too good a time.

The protagonist of *Leap*—a judge, Mauro Ponticelli, played by the usually suave French actor Michel Piccoli—is mean in perverse, Buñuelian ways. Mauro has always been protected and cared for by his older sister, Marta (Anouk Aimée), now middle-aged and a menopausal virgin. They are a couple, and their relationship is so fetid that it would be a relief to discover that it's incestuous; it isn't—it's infantile. Mauro can't eat dinner until Marta cuts his meat. When he's with his mistress, she has to do it for him. He has no intention of growing up—we know because at night, when the respectable judge is sleeping, the child he was rolls out from under his bed and joins the solemn-faced young Marta and the other Ponticelli children, in their long white nighties. This troupe may remind you of the little people in *Freaks* scrambling under the circus wagons; these magical children who come to life at night might be spilling out of the unconscious or a dream.

The madness of Mauro and Marta suggests a projection of ordinary feelings into an overheated atmosphere. Often we're not sure whether what we're seeing is "really happening" or is only being thought about; then it becomes apparent that it doesn't matter. Mauro is bored with his domestic situation; he idly imagines that he'd like to be rid of Marta, who is beginning to act a little crazy. He has a case before him in court involving a handsome, cynical actor (Michele Placido)—a petty criminal and sociopath who has taken money from a rich woman and driven her to suicide—and he introduces this dashing sleazo to Marta. He daydreams of this bearded outlaw type causing Marta's death. And Marta is indeed drawn by the actor's sexual magnetism; she's caught up in his romantic contempt for everything her brother stands for. What Mauro has probably been concealing from himself is that Marta's unusual behavior has actually been a sign that she is rebelling—that she's struggling to free herself from her deathly bondage to him. She's curing herself; he's the one who's in bad shape. When he's eating and Marta leaves him alone for a minute—she goes to talk to their peasant housekeeper—he can't stand being ignored; he rattles the things on the table to attract the women's attention, and when that fails he drops his utensils on the floor, and standing as if crucified he says piteously, "I don't exist."

The movie is about family entanglements and the functions of madness. At one point, Marta hysterically throws her clothes out the window. Mauro instructs the servant to go down and pick them up, and, suddenly, at the sound of Mauro's voice—the pompous voice of reason—Marta and the servant laugh and hug each other. And we know that Mauro is the crazy one. There's a tense, frightening sequence with Marta becoming distraught during a christening. The whole tribe is assembled, and she, as the godmother, is holding the terrified, yowling infant. And she can't endure the crying sound. In the middle of the ceremony she is so panicked that the mother grabs the baby from her. Marta bolts from the church and becomes helpless and confused; she has led such a confined existence that she doesn't know how to get home. Mauro, the proper, considerate brother, the one who argues for a private sanatorium when her other relatives want her sent to a state institution, catches up with her and guides her—into the trap he imagines will finish her off.

The film is poised between farce and tragedy. I won't say that it's rejuvenating, exactly, but it does seem to clear passages in the head. What's flabbergasting is that it's Bellocchio's creepiness that opens things up. There are distinctive sequences that suggest a sort of post-Freudian jokey frenzy, such as one with Mauro throwing a rock at the barge that the actor and his firebreathing hippie friends are on, singing and carousing.

Michel Piccoli wears his hair parted low on one side and combed across his head, like a vain bald man, and he makes himself seem almost plumply self-satisfied. He's a superb comedian, and for the role of Mauro the spoilsport he has transformed himself from the inside out: it's a surreptitious kind of acting—he lets us see the hidden essence of the character. Mauro the judge is a worm: a spoiled worm wriggling in its comfortable nest. In public, he is perfectly groomed and behaves impeccably; he's a complacent man who believes in order. It's only in darkness or at home that his resentments show. Piccoli plays Mauro as a stick but a soft, sly stick—cruel and frightened. He tiptoes around the apartment; his apprehensiveness gives him a depth that most prigs don't have. He often looks as if he'd just stepped in something—and his face tells you what. Yet he's condescending at the same time. It's just about impossible to take your eyes off him, because you never know what slimy expression he'll have next. He's a craven fraud—a distant cousin to the characters W. C. Fields used to play. Piccoli is able to give this mesmerizing performance despite the fact that he and Anouk Aimée are dubbed into Italian. In an interview that Bellocchio gave to the leftist newspaper *Paese Sera* in 1980, he supplied a partial explanation of their effectiveness: "The two leading characters are both bourgeois, and there is nothing more bourgeois than certain French actors." (All the well-preserved, worldly-wise French stars should be in this kind of movie.)

Anouk Aimée is usually strikingly beautiful and a little blank—not quite in contact; I've never felt I knew her characters any better at the end of a movie than at the beginning. But she's a magnificent camera subject, and her remoteness fits the situation here. She's playing a rather simple role—a woman trying to come to life. Bellocchio and his co-scriptwriters (Piero Natoli and Vincenzo Cerami) view Mauro satirically and with a microscope, but they look at Marta neutrally or, at times, very sympathetically. She is meant to represent an emerging healthy person, and so she enjoys the company of the peasant servant and puts her arms around the servant's lovely, ticklish, giggly five-year-old boy (played by the director's son, Piergiorgio). It might be better if we did not see Marta's opening her heart to the peasants as a way for her to find redemption from bourgeois sickness. Bellocchio builds class structures into his movies—he might be described as an avant-garde social realist. Mauro is so fully realized as a spiteful monster-dreamer that he transcends his theoretical function; Marta doesn't quite. I'm not sure that any performer has ever triumphed over the requirement to embody hope for the future. And, restrained and tentative a hope as Marta is meant to represent, the character is somewhat washed out by her good-humored wholesomeness.

Hope doesn't quite go with Bellocchio's feral sense of the ridiculous or his snake charmer's style. He has the technique of a master; he had it when he made his first feature. And he keeps this movie in slippery chiaroscuro—it all might be taking place in a dark dream. Bellocchio's wildness plus his formality add up to a distinctive, irrational kind of irony. We come out shaken, maybe, but also, possibly, grinning, because he's so knowingly mean-spirited and his technique sings. Except for Buñuel, he's the only director I can think of whose morbidity is exhilarating. And he's an elegant moviemaker—though he may be contemptuous of this gift, considering it bourgeois. Bellocchio never hurries; he seems to have a finger on our pulse. *Leap Into the Void* is a film about people who are out of control made by a director who's in as close to total control as a moviemaker is ever likely to be. I'm not sure if it should be considered a great movie, but there's greatness in it.

·   ·   ·   ·

*C*urly-red-haired Angie (Sara Botsford) is built big; she's rangy and good-looking, with an uptilted nose and a hell raiser's smile. Brown-haired little Helen (Patty Duke Astin) is pretty in an old-fashioned way, and she's a serious, down-to-business person. When these two face the camera in *By Design*, we're confronted by four bright-blue eyes, and a quandary. Angie and Helen are in love and they live and work together happily—they design women's clothes and run their own fashion business in Vancouver. There's only one thing that's wrong with their relationship: Helen yearns to be a mother. Whenever she sees a child, she tunes out on what she's doing, and her face goes soft. Now that she has only a few childbearing years left, she's practically in mourning for the possibility of motherhood. Angie is younger and tougher. She doesn't go all mushy about kids, but she loves Helen, and if Helen can't feel fulfilled without one she's willing for them to become parents.

By Design is a buoyant, quirky sex comedy, in which the two women explore the possibilities open to them, and the director, Claude Jutra, takes a look around the whole modern supermarket of sex. There are a lot of options: a light dawns and people try something out, and if it doesn't work they try something else—the light keeps dawning. *By Design* takes in the bars and beach houses, fast-food restaurants and discos, and the sexual patterns of those who inhabit them, with a glance at the home of a cigar-smoking businessman whose Japanese wife pads around like a servant. Jutra—whose best-known work, the 1971 *Mon Oncle Antoine*, is probably the most plangent movie ever made in and about Canada—has a light, understated approach to farce. His sensibility suggests a mingling of Tati and Truffaut; he never makes a fuss about anything. The scenes are quick and they're dippy, but with a pensive, melancholy underlay. If the openness of the situations seems a bit strange, that may be because Jutra, a Québécois, whose earlier movies were in French, is working in English here, yet his acceptance of the various characters' attitudes and hangups seems "very French"—which in this case means insouciant and tender, too.

The script for *By Design*, which was written by Joe Wiesenfeld, Jutra, and David Eames, seems to skip along from one incident to the next. What holds the movie together is the bond between the two women, who couldn't be more unlike. The outgoing Angie enjoys horsing around with men, while Helen is a homebody who wants nothing to do with them. Angie is casual, and maybe even shallow—she takes things in her big stride. Helen is the deep one. When you first see these two walking together, with Angie towering over Helen, they may seem a goofy mismatch; it takes a while to see that this goofiness—which they accept—is what's mysteriously right about them as a couple. When they're swaying on the dance floor at a lesbian bar, Sister Moon, their tall and short bodies seem welded together. Dignified little Helen may be matronly and withdrawn when she's with other people, but she's all there for Angie. She provides the solidity and depth that Angie needs; she anchors the raw, funky Angie who smiles faraway smiles to herself. Nothing that happens in the movie ever makes us doubt that these two love and need each other.

The movie's relaxed, omnisexual spirit allows for easygoing slapstick when the women check out an adoption agency and listen to an intense young social worker (Clare Coulter) who is all wound up about the sexual politics of their situation. It doesn't take long for them to reject the possibility of artificial insemination and to begin looking men over, considering them as studs. (Those four blue eyes are very discombobulating to the men they stare at.) They decide to shop around in a singles disco, but Helen, who is offended by the idea of going to bed with a man anyway, hates the place and goes outside to wait for Angie. Eventually, they settle on Terry (Saul Rubinek), a photographer who works for them; he's gaga over women, and—conveniently—he has a crush on Helen. Rubinek, with his wet brown eyes, and eyebrows like semaphores, plays Terry as part Chaplinesque innocent, part Groucho. He's a girl chaser and squeezer and gooser who so far has had his best luck with impressionable teenyboppers. (They hope he'll make them stars.) Angie and Helen are no doubt the only women who have ever thought of Terry as a stud, and he is so flattered he begins to grow up. These three major characters all get what they want, but not in the way they'd planned.

The picture has its oddities. Near the beginning, Angie and Helen turn down a business deal because it requires them to use synthetic fabrics, but then their business problems are dropped until the end. Early in the film, there's also a bewildering display of their designs: the garish evening gowns in which their models parade might have been created for the women of the Shanghai red-light district in the thirties. (Does Jutra know something about Vancouver designers that we don't?) These gowns look as if they *should* be made of synthetics. And sometimes Jutra's playfulness and the bits of unstressed slapstick wilt. But most of the time the picture has a freshness that's very surprising, given the subject: a couple who want a child. Maybe it's fresh because, unlike most sex comedies, it's grounded in biology. And the performers in the smaller roles—Suzie the model (Sonia Zimmer), a dimply Swede (Alan Duruisseau), and a teen-age cowgirl (Jeannie Elias)—make you feel that if the story veered off and began to follow their lives you'd have a good time with them, too. At the center of the movie, there's a sex sequence, cutting back and forth during a phone conversation between the occupants of a bed in an apartment and the occupants of a bed in a motel, that is near to being irresistibly funny. It's what everything was leading up to, yet it took me by surprise.

When *Mon Oncle Antoine* opened in Washington, D.C., in 1972, Russell Baker wrote a column saying that it was "the most extraordinary movie," and adding, "It is almost impossible to explain why." He came close, though, when he said, "It is like walking into one of Wren's small London churches just when you have come to believe that the entire world looks like the Pentagon." *By Design* has some of that same quality: the beginning sets up false expectations, but once you're into Jutra's rhythm, the film is thoroughly unaffected. He uses the music—by Chico Hamilton—sparingly. And though the film was lighted by the French cinematographer Jean Boffety, who had a lot to do with the whirling lyricism of Claude Sautet films such as *César and Rosalie* and the delicacy of Altman's *Thieves Like Us,* Jutra has settled on a simpler, bold look. It's almost harsh: you can read the grain of the faces—you can see that Helen's jaw is beginning to set, you can see Angie's pores and wrinkles. They don't need to be protected by makeup—you accept them as they are.

By Design is so matter-of-fact in the way it tells its story that it may invite ridicule; some people may think that the absence of melodrama and "art" is a sign of ineptitude. Jutra isn't as well known as he deserves to be, because he's trying to get past most of what impresses people. He's a cheerful ironist (with the possible exception of Robert Towne, what other director would risk lesbianism as a subject for comedy?), and Jutra is so unassuming he makes this film seem smaller than it is. Even his most daring scenes (such as the crosscut sex) aren't punched up. He doesn't whisper in your ear, "Look how terrific these two actresses are." He stands back and allows you room to think—he lets you discover the spectacular Sara Botsford for yourself. Her freewheeling, provocative Angie gives the film its zip, and as a conventional woman in an unconventional situation Patty Duke Astin gives it a core of emotion. Despite a few facile acting habits she has picked up, her performance is unemphatic and rounded. As a pair, the two of them help make *By Design* one of the most likable movies around. (It has already opened in Boston and Los Angeles, and is due here shortly.) It isn't bubbly while you're watching it, but it effervesces when you think it over. It's like a Lubitsch sex comedy stripped of the glamour but not of the fun.

·   ·   ·   ·   ·

*P*aul Bartel's *Eating Raoul* just doesn't have enough going on in it—not even enough to look at. It's about a couple of prissy squares—the Blands, of Los Angeles (played by Bartel and his five-foot-eleven star, Mary Woronov)—who consider sex disgusting and want to open a nice, clean country restaurant. They raise the money they need by murdering swinging singles, who they feel will never be missed; in their eyes these swingers deserve to be punished. This skeletal spoofy black-comedy idea could support a lot of gags, but there are only a few here. Mary Woronov has glimmers of perversity (she's an innately kinky presence), and as Raoul, a handsome Chicano who tries to cut in on the profits, Richard Beltran brings some energy to his role, but the picture is thin-textured—it's like watching a stretched-out, slowed-down episode of "Mary Hartman, Mary Hartman." This isn't accidental: Bartel is a flaky, eccentric moviemaker who knows what he's doing—even his own phlegmatic performance is deliberate. The nothingness of this movie is supposed to be its droll point, and Bartell must mean the Blands' candy-colored existence and their moral double-bookkeeping to be audaciously funny. But *Eating Raoul* seems sedated. Watching it, I felt as if I were experiencing sensory deprivation.

November 29, 1982

Raunch and Reticence

*S*lender-faced Margot Kidder has a witty curl to her lips, and she clearly took delight in the role of the deranged siren in Brian De Palma's 1973 *Sisters*. But she can be an irritant on the screen. There's an obstinacy about her: often she doesn't seem to yield to the roles she's playing. When she's in a "Boo!" picture like *The Amityville Horror*, her holding back may make her seem the only smart person in the cast. But when a performer walks through movies with a stare of indifference, it doesn't do much for the audience, and in the *Superman* films Margot Kidder comes across as gritty and unfeeling. It wasn't until I saw her in the new Canadian movie *Heartaches* that it occurred to me that her balkiness on the screen might have represented a gifted woman's dissatisfaction with what she was caught up in. Might she in those movies have been saying, like a Godardian sleepwalking hooker, "I sell my body but my soul belongs to me"? (She was certainly soulless on the screen.) Or was she so untouched by the material that she was handed that she simply had nothing to express? As the brazen, pushy Rita of *Heartaches*, Kidder has the depth that was missing from her other roles; this is the first full performance I've ever seen her give, and she's something to behold. Her Rita is one of those characters—like Barbara Stanwyck's Stella Dallas—who are coarse yet sensitive. They appall you at the same time that they win you over. They're preposterous creations—sentimental, gutsy, possibly even tearjerking—yet they're played with so much honest emotion that they become intensely likable.

Heartaches, which was directed by Don Shebib, has some of the appeal of the Hollywood romantic comedies of the thirties in which a couple of working girls meet up and help each other out. One might be a naïve, pretty waif, the other older and more knowing but a fool for a handsome man. In this updated version, which took off from the novel *The Bottle Factory Outing*, by the English writer Beryl Bainbridge, and then went its own way in a script by Terence Heffernan, the waif—dark-eyed Bonnie—is played by Annie Potts, and Rita is the kind of pushover who used to be called a tramp. She has a frowzy dried-out dye job—so bleached it looks grayish-yellow—and the first time we see her, in the Ontario countryside on a bus heading for Toronto, she's wearing boots, jeans, a tight T-shirt with "J' ♥ LES HOMMES" emblazoned across her chest, a cowboy jacket, and big beads. She dresses like a bad dream, and her voice is as loud as her clothes. On the bus, she meets the quiet, pregnant Bonnie, and her efforts to help Bonnie—who is running away from her husband—are so raucous and foulmouthed that the bus driver throws them both out onto the highway. Rita gets misunderstood a lot.

Shebib, whose *Goin' Down the Road* played here a little over a decade ago, has his own loose style of Canadian picaresque; you find yourself looking at his characters' messy lives with smiling, relaxed good will. Toronto itself seems idyllic when viewed in New York, and it's an inviting magical kingdom to the two women. They take an apartment together in a building that's owned by an Italian immigrant, go to work in his mattress factory, and become part of an Italian community. The movie is a pastoral ramble in the big city, with shaggy, unforeseeable details. Bonnie's garage-mechanic husband (Robert Carradine) arrives and begins to shape up, but essentially the story is about the friendship of Bonnie and Rita. At first, Bonnie is woozy and remote; she doesn't talk much, and when she does it's in a cracked warble of a voice. She whines like a cuddly puppy with a stomach ache—she sounds so forlorn she's funny. Rita helps her get her feet on the ground, and by then Bonnie understands (as we do) that it's the hard-bitten Rita who's the innocent one. Her head is full of romance.

As soon as the two of them walk into the mattress factory, Rita is convinced that she has met the man of her life—the boss's nephew, Marcello (Winston Rekert), a shy fellow who is fresh from the old country and is bewildered by her brashness. Shebib himself is one of the least pushy of directors, and you can almost feel him recoil from Rita's belligerent outfits and her raunchy, single-minded pursuit of Marcello. Shebib keeps giving closeups to the subdued Annie Potts, as if he were seeking sanctuary. This is actually lucky for Kidder, because Rita is a big role, and if Shebib had tried to show off her performance he might have encouraged her to overdo it. But the frequent celebrations of Annie Potts's lustrous dark hair and huge eyes are practically saying to Kidder, "Sister, you're not my type." The theme of the movie must have been acted out on the set. Rita has to fight for everything, even the camera, and so she's always in motion and we never get too much of her. It's Margot Kidder's picture, though, every step of the way, and she moves with her head and arms thrust out, as if she were ready to take a swing at the world.

$\cdot$ $\cdot$ $\cdot$ $\cdot$ $\cdot$

Still of the Night is reticent and soft where it should be tough. The writer-director, Robert Benton, is unquestionably intelligent, but he doesn't seem to have the twisted savvy that's needed for the job at hand. The film shows almost no evidence of the nasty streak that's part of the pleasure of a good thriller, or of the manipulative skills that might give us a few tremors. In the early part, when Josef Sommer is onscreen, we do get a few prickly sensations. As George Bynum, who works in an art-and-antiques auction house that resembles Sotheby Parke Bernet, Sommer is like a snide and slightly dirty Trevor Howard. We see him at his analyst's office; he arouses the doctor (Roy Scheider) by telling him stories about an icy hot woman he has been having an affair with. She works at the auction place, too, though she's wealthy, and Bynum indicates that he's afraid of her, because she has already killed a man. Bynum is a trickster, a psychological-game player, and we can't imagine why he's going to this therapist—is it to get under the doctor's guard, to put one over on him? During the sessions, Bynum sits all hunched up, and his confidential voice seems to sneak in through the crack beneath the door. He has a murderous gleam in his eye; he doesn't look like a victim. But Bynum is knocked off. And the movie is about the doctor's infatuation with that hot-number mystery woman—played by Meryl Streep—who he, in turn, thinks may be trying to kill him.

Meryl Streep's performance is all about her hair. It isn't pale gold here; it's platinum white, parted low on the side, and it hangs bone-straight. She keeps her head tilted down, her face turned away under the white curtain, and then, peering up, she shakes it back a little. This is Veronica Lake's kittenish act, but without her teasing, kitty-cat charm. There's a glimpse of Streep looking up at Sommer with a silent giggle—it's a good naughty moment. In most of the rest of this movie, she doesn't resemble a living person; her face is gaunt, her skin has become alabaster. She seems to have chosen to do a Meryl Streep parody; she's like some creature from the moon trying to be a movie star. We get the impression that the heroine is meant to be guileful and slinky—a woman with neurotic wiles. But Streep's high-strung emotionality isn't fun in the way that Faye Dunaway's has often been. Streep has been falling into the trap of selecting noble roles—the martyrs, the drippers. And she makes this femme fatale seem more zombified than anything else. I liked Streep on the stage (in comedy, especially), but I have come to dread her reflective manner and flooding tears—she could give pensive a bad name. If only she would giggle more and suffer less—she keeps turning herself into the red-eye special.

A mystery that's deeper than who killed George Bynum: Why is Roy Scheider so dull? He isn't an incompetent actor, and he's actually rather accomplished here—he's at least restrained. But he has no visible personality. Roy Scheider may be as close as one can get to being a *tabula-rasa* actor; he brings his role nothing of himself except his physical frame—some sinews, a profile. In *Jaws*, as the tenderfoot from the big city who was openly scared of just about everything to do with the water, he was an amusingly sane Everyman. And in Bob Fosse's fantasy autobiography *All That Jazz* he was taut and jumpy—strung out. Dressed in black and wearing an extra-pointy Vandyke on his pointy chin, he looked like Basil Rathbone as Robin Hood's enemy Sir Guy of Gisbourne, and he made you feel you were watching Fosse himself. It wasn't an impersonation; it was as if Fosse had taken over his body, from the inside. That's the only role in which Scheider had an exciting presence, and it wasn't his; we seemed to be looking right through him to Fosse. As the shrink who's frightened of the woman he is falling in love with, Scheider may be embodying Benton—his decency and refinement and conscientiousness. I doubt if Benton means Scheider to be exciting here; he probably wants him to be the stable force—our man on the screen. But this colorless thinker hero represents everything that's wrong with Benton's moviemaking. He wants to work in an entertainment genre that's free of "meaning," but he disdains jokes, punch lines, cheap flash. He glosses them over.

If everybody in the movie were as lively (in a creepy-crawly way) as Josef Sommer and Sara Botsford—she appears as one of the women who work at the auction house—the scuzz in the air would be thick; it would be vibrating in all directions, and the movie might be sleek yet impenetrable in the silly, satisfying manner of *The Big Sleep*. Benton seems to have misplaced the sense of fun that he had in *The Late Show* and in his earlier scriptwriting days. Benton (who worked out the story with his old writing partner, David Newman) certainly knows that a thriller set among people who never appear to be short of money requires a satiric edge. Maybe the success of his *Kramer vs. Kramer* has thrown him off, so that he has become too discreet. The clean, sterile look that the cinematographer, Nestor Almendros, gives the New York City locations and the studio interiors doesn't seem to have a thing to do with the story. It's as if Benton couldn't really get down to dirtying his mind with the genre he's working in. He tries for something ultra-sensuous in a scene where Streep attempts to talk while she's being massaged; it's nifty on its own, but it doesn't play off anything. The gags here are isolated; there's even dead space around the dialogue. In one sequence, the therapist and his mother (Jessica Tandy), who's also a therapist, try to solve the murder mystery by checking each other out on the Freudian symbolism of a dream that Bynum once reported; it's a dry, smooth routine—the mother-and-son shrinks might be playing patty-cake. But this, too, needs to connect with something more. The sequence isn't a joke—it's almost a joke. Benton seems to have a dilettante's fondness for other directors' touches—everything from a screaming big bird to the Hitchcock-style mother of the hero. They don't really work for him; they're not satiric, and they don't express his sensibility. They're vacuous, yet he keeps dropping them in all through the movie, probably because he doesn't have the temperament to whip up freak touches of his own.

Was the plot so clear in Benton's mind that he trimmed away the explanations, thinking we would be able to figure it all out? He seems too solid a literary craftsman to have conceived something this spotty and elliptical. But even if the plot all came together and formed a pattern that we could keep in our heads and take home, the picture might be static. As a director, Benton seems unable to find any rhythm in the scenes, and maybe that's because he hasn't heated up the various obsessions and set them in motion. We don't feel the tug of the doctor being drawn to the inscrutable blonde, and we never shudder for the danger he's in. All the way through he's on the wrong track, and this isn't even comic, because we don't know why. The most dramatic thing about the movie happens offscreen: Meryl Streep switches the part in her hair from one side to the other.

December 13, 1982

Tootsie, Gandhi, and Sophie

Tootsie began with Don McGuire, who wrote what is said to have been a wild screenplay. After it was sold and Dick Richards was set to be the director, Robert Kaufman was hired to do a new draft. When Dustin Hoffman read Kaufman's version, he agreed to play in the picture, and brought in his playwright pal Murray Schisgal (with whom he had once tried to concoct a movie about a man impersonating a woman) to rework the material. Then the director, Dick Richards, was replaced by Hal Ashby, and Larry Gelbart was hired for yet another version. After that, Hal Ashby was replaced by Sydney Pollack, and Elaine May (who chose to be anonymous) was signed to do a rewrite; after her came the team of Barry Levinson and Valerie Curtin, and after them, Robert Garland. And with some of these people doing more than one draft, when the screenplay had to be submitted to the Writers Guild for arbitration over the issue of who should get the screen credit, three large cardboard boxes were needed to transport the more than twenty scripts. Pollack must have saved whatever he could of the best in each of them—*Tootsie* sounds as if one superb comedy writer had done it all. There is talk in Hollywood now of forming the I Also Wrote/I Almost Directed *Tootsie* Club. (The writing credit went to Larry Gelbart and Murray Schisgal.)

One of the things that Hollywood used to be good at was producing enjoyable, seemingly effortless entertainments, such as the Hepburn-Tracy *Pat and Mike*, Jean Harlow in *Bombshell*, Claudette Colbert in *Midnight*, Jean Arthur and Ray Milland in *Easy Living*, the Hepburn and Grant *Bringing Up Baby*, and later on, *Some Like It Hot*—films that were factory products and commercial as all hell but took off into a sphere of their own. Those movies continue to give so much pleasure that they have a special glamour. *Tootsie*— a modern addition to this company—has what the best screwball comedies had: a Can-you-top-this? quality. (And they often got it from relays of top writers—who were on the payroll, anyway, in those days.) Paying off this project's earlier writers and directors added heavily to its cost, and it took a rather scandalous one hundred shooting days—some of them, according to press and TV accounts, given over to squabbles between Hoffman and Sydney Pollack. But when the result is a *Tootsie* the expenses seem justified. And when Hoffman delivers the kind of performance he gives here, the talk in the media about his being overpaid seems beside the point. This movie is inconceivable without him. Once Hoffman was committed to the project, the scriptwriters began to shape the central character to fit him, and then they went further. In its final form, *Tootsie* is based on Dustin Hoffman, the perfectionist; he's both the hero and the target of this satirical farce about actors.

The central character, Michael Dorsey, is a brilliant, "uncompromising" New York actor whom no one wants to hire, because he makes things hell for everybody. A stickler for the "truth" in an actor's performance, he overcomplicates things. He's a nut—acting is his mania. So, despite his gifts and his reputation among the young actors whom he coaches, at thirty-nine he's still frustrated—scrounging for a living and finding jobs as a waiter. At the start of the movie, he hasn't had any acting work in two years, and when his girlfriend (Teri Garr) goes up for an audition for a role in a soap and is rejected as the wrong type, he decides to try for the part himself. Made up as a woman, he presents himself as Dorothy Michaels, and lands the job.

Michael is dressed in skirts for about half the movie. This isn't a simple female impersonation, on the order of *Charley's Aunt*. Michael finds himself when he's Dorothy—not because he has any secret desire to be a woman but because when he's Dorothy he's acting. He's such a dedicated, fanatical actor that he comes fully alive only when he's playing a role, and you can see it in his intense, glittering eyes. There are always several things going on in Hoffman's face. He lets us see that Michael's mind is working all the time, and that he's making an actor's choices. Michael is thinking out Dorothy while he's playing her—he's thinking out what a woman would do. When he's giving a performance as Dorothy, he feels a freedom that he doesn't have when he's just Michael. Dorothy, in her fussy, high-necked dresses, has a definite personality—we in the audience become fond of her. She's a flirt, a joker: *she* doesn't have to take herself as seriously as Michael, the artist (who's all nerves), takes himself. She has a much less knotted personality than he has—he allows her to have the charm he denies himself. She also has a Southern accent, and a rather troubling voice; it slips around in a hoarse, neuter sort of way. But Michael is a meticulous actor: Dorothy's vocal patterns and her phrasing are very different from his. And when she's at the TV studio, playing the role of Emily Kimberly, the hospital administrator in "Southwest General," she takes on a brisk huffiness. Hoffman's performance works at so many different levels in this movie that when Michael is in women's clothes you keep watching his crooked, lipsticky smile and his mascaraed eyes, to see what's going on in his head. And when Michael is only Michael, you miss Dorothy, and Emily, too. You can believe that Michael would be a hit playing Emily Kimberly, because this scrappy woman, with thick wrists and oddly sharp, crooked teeth and a bouffant red hairdo, is more eccentrically, believably alive than anyone you're likely to see on the soaps. The performers I've caught (in my limited exposure as I flick from one channel to the next) have been a glazed, strangely slowed-down race of people, plagued by uncertainty; they move as if they were under water and seem to spend their lives on the telephone. Emily, who's fast-talking, overexcited, and absolutely sure of everything she says, would be bound to stir things up.

It's the film's notion that when Michael plays Emily he is driven to depart from his scripts and improvise whenever he feels that the lines she has been given aren't true to her character, and that his improvisations—his peppery rejoinders when the male head doctor is being condescending to Emily—endear him to women viewers. It would be easy to say that the movie was itself being condescending to women—that it was suggesting that it took a man to be tough and forthright enough to speak up for women's rights. Dorothy does seem to be bringing enlightenment into her co-workers' lives, and there's an element of self-congratulation (and self-aggrandizement, too) in the way Michael delivers his spontaneous feminist speeches. But it's also perfectly in character for Michael, experiencing male condescension for the first time, to feel it as an insult to Emily, his creation, and have her erupt in anger.

Michael loves his characters more than he loves himself—Emily has to be fearless, a standard-bearer. Michael compulsively embroiders on the role of Emily and enlarges it; even in a hospital soap he's on a quest for the truth of his character. Michael isn't adaptable; he's a total, egocentric idealist. That's what has made him too cantankerous to be a working actor.

When Dustin Hoffman smiles—as Dorothy—he may be more sheerly likable as a movie star than he has ever been before. He gives a master actor's performance: he's playing three characters, and they're shaped so that Dorothy fits inside Michael, and Emily fits inside Dorothy. Even Hoffman's self-consciousness as an actor works in this performance; so does his sometimes grating, rankling quality (which is probably his idea of sincerity). The climactic scene that ends Michael's imposture isn't as well thought out as the rest of the picture, and the cutaway is abrupt; the scene needs reverberations or an aftermath—it's just shucked off. And there's an undercurrent that I could do without: the suggestion that Michael, through playing a woman, becomes a better man—more in touch with himself and all that. This doesn't come through strongly enough to do the movie much harm. It's the kind of increment of virtue that actors and directors speak of proudly, though, when they're giving interviews to papers or on television; they can make it sound as if this were why they made the picture—to improve our characters and their own, too.

What's good about Michael's playing Dorothy is that it enables Hoffman to show a purely farcical side of himself, and he has some inspired moments. After Michael has fallen in love with Julie (Jessica Lange), the star of "Southwest General," who has become very much attached to Dorothy, he has a scene in which he eagerly agrees to babysit with her infant, without having the faintest idea of what he may be letting himself in for. We can see Michael's harried mind clicking along inside Dorothy even during the babysitting. He tries everything he can think of to amuse the child, and after he has been sitting on the floor trying to quiet the kid by stuffing food into her, he falls back in exhaustion. With his legs spread out under his skirt and his big, fluffy head of hair sunk on his small body, he looks like a broken doll. And there's a brief gag scene with Michael, whose career has just been shattered, walking by a mime in Central Park who's in a precarious pose and knocking him over with a malicious touch—no more than a finger. This is the only time Michael ever shows any doubt about his vocation, and it's a passing, aberrant impulse—as if his head didn't quite know what his hand was up to.

Sydney Pollack, who was an actor in his earlier years, originally went to Hollywood (in 1961) as a dialogue coach for John Frankenheimer; essentially he's still a dialogue coach, and this works better for him here than it ever has before. Having dealt with stars most of his life, he knows how impossible they can be, and he has been able to make *Tootsie* something practically unheard of: a believable farce. The picture has more energy than anything else he has done; it's almost alarmingly well cast, and the lines of dialogue collide with a click and go spinning off. Pollack himself gives some jabbing, fast readings; he plays a major role—that of Michael's agent—with zest. Teri Garr has developed a shorthand style of comedy that's all her own, and the audience has such strong empathy with her that she can get her flighty, pent-up character across to us in a few terse movements and phrases. The actress she plays dramatizes her reaction to everything; she's always shrieking or on the verge of shrieking—in disbelief at what is happening to her. Yet Teri Garr always takes us by surprise; she has become the funniest neurotic dizzy dame on the screen. As Michael's roommate, an avant-garde dramatist, Bill Murray keeps dropping into the movie and making an observation or a comment, and his inflections break up the audience every time. (He is said to have ad-libbed his role.) As a lecherous, foolish old ham who plays the head doctor in the soap, the veteran performer George Gaynes has a small comic triumph: once you've laughed at him, even the sight of him triggers more laughs. Dabney Coleman, as the director of the soap, doesn't seem to have come up with anything fresh, but Charles Durning, who plays Julie's farmer father, does some shrewd underplaying, especially in a scene in which you can feel how badly he wants to wallop Michael.

When Jessica Lange appears, the movie changes from the crackling, rapid-fire presentation of the hopes versus the realities of out-of-work actors' lives to something calmer, and perhaps richer. She has a facial structure that the camera yearns for, and she has talent, too. Her face is softer here than in *Frances*; her Julie is a dream girl, and she's like a shock absorber to Michael. When he, dressed as Dorothy, sees her, some of his irascibility melts away. Julie has honey-colored hair, and a friendly smile; she looks freshly created—just hatched, and pleasantly, warmly spacy (enough to be deeply impressed by Dorothy's high-principled talk about the theatre). Jessica Lange helps to keep the movie from being too frenetic. There is none of the usual actress's phoniness in her work; as Julie, she says her lines in such a mild, natural way that it makes perfect sense for Michael to stop in his tracks and stare at her in wonder. The picture is marvellous fun.

·　　·　　·　　·　　·

*L*eaving the theatre where I saw *Gandhi*, I felt the way the British must have when they left India: exhausted and relieved. Directed by Richard Attenborough, the film (which runs three hours and eight minutes) has no dramatic center; perhaps in compensation, the action all seems to take place in the dead middle of the screen. In his interviews, Attenborough appears to have an instinct for the telling detail, the anecdote that reveals character, but that's part of what he lacks as a moviemaker. *Gandhi* is reverential and holy, like the pictures that used to be made about Jesus. Gandhi, too, goes by in a cloud of serenity, and everyone who sees him knuckles under (with the exception of a few misguided fellows, of course). Ben Kingsley, the English actor of half-Indian extraction who plays the Mahatma, looks the part, has a fine, quiet presence, and conveys Gandhi's shrewdness. He has also mastered a smile that's part compassion, part wince of pain. Kingsley is impressive; the picture isn't. It isn't a disgrace—it just isn't much of anything. The first half builds up considerable interest in Gandhi; the second half is scattered—as if it had been added to or subtracted from at random. And Kingsley can't give his role a core, because it has been written completely from the outside. During the picture, we never feel that we know Gandhi, and when it's over we still have no insight into what went on in his head. All we get to take home is the shine in Kingsley's eyes.

Members of the press have been congratulating Attenborough for making an old-fashioned movie, but that was hardly a matter of choice for him. Attenborough works in the tradition of orderly, neat imagery: in his India even poverty is clean and barbered. His sensibility is conventional, like that of the studio heads of three or four decades ago. The picture is respectable. It skitters over some of the principal events in Gandhi's public life and tidies up his rather kinky domestic relations. Spanning fifty-five years, it's a schoolbook Life of Gandhi, and can be regarded worshipfully.

There are many famous performers in the cast: the British brigade includes John Gielgud, Trevor Howard, John Mills, Michael Hordern, John Clements, Ian Bannen, Ian Charleson, and villainous Edward (twisty-face) Fox; Athol Fugard plays General Smuts, Candice Bergen is supposed to be Margaret Bourke-White, and Martin Sheen is a reporter, though he can't have much to report, because when historic encounters are going on in front of him he's looking down at his feet. Several of the Indian actors are look-alikes for the figures they're playing, but the Nehru look-alike (Roshan Seth) doesn't have Nehru's elegant presence, and Gandhi's enemy Jinnah (Alyque Padamsee), who wants India to be divided into two countries (as indeed it was), is too obviously a decadent bad guy. There are some amiable people on the screen such as the round-faced Saeed Jaffrey as Patel, but except for Gandhi there are no characters of any consequence, and the material is unshaped—you can't tell what goes on in *anybody's* head. The film's Gandhi is a one-man independence movement; he doesn't discuss nonviolence with other Indian leaders or with his own aides—he lays it down as a decree. And the only drama is in his courage and the courage of his nameless followers, as they carry out acts of civil disobedience and allow themselves to be beaten, maimed, killed. Nonviolent resistance can be very appealing to movie audiences—nonviolent rebels pose no threat to us. And, of course, audiences here can make the association and recall that this policy worked for Martin Luther King, Jr. It worked for King as it had for Gandhi—because he, too, was able to publicize the confrontations, and thus to shame white Americans, as Gandhi shamed the British. But in countries where movements for freedom don't have access to television and the press, nonviolent resistance isn't a political maneuver—it's just a morally superior way of getting yourself mangled.

(The soldiers who attacked the refugees in the Lebanese camps were probably delighted that their victims were unarmed, and the Nazis who ran the death camps took pains to insure that theirs wouldn't put up a fight.)

There's a great subject here—a man without any public office, or even a clerical title, who becomes the leader of a nation by sheer force of spiritual authority. But can Gandhi's story be told without a trace of irony? Gandhi didn't use his fasts and his emaciated body just to embarrass the British; he used them against his own people, too. And here is his replica on the screen using his own martyrdom as a tactic—pushing guilt on everybody and getting his way. Basically, he's using the same diabolical tricks as the Jewish mothers that TV comics complain about. And Gandhi had a manipulative genius for timing and publicity. He made a virtue of what was practical. He was also often rigidly impractical—a side of him that, understandably, is omitted from the film. Many scenes break off as if they'd been cut before they were played out. Possibly, the script, by John Briley (there was an earlier version, by Gerald Hanley, and another, by Robert Bolt, and some rewrite work by Donald Ogden Stewart), suggested more of what formed Gandhi and set him apart. Still, it must have been written basically as the life of a saint. When the film's Gandhi says things like "All through history, the way of truth and love has always won," we must be meant to take them straight, be uplifted, and burn incense.

Attenborough himself is no slouch when it comes to publicity—the *Times* alone has had at least eight articles and news stories about the movie—and the accounts of his twenty-year struggle to get it made sit heavy on reviewers' heads. I don't think these accounts are necessarily false, or exaggerated; he has probably gone through some gruelling bad times to make this movie, and the subject may very well have become an obsession with him. But that doesn't mean that he's an obsessive artist. He steered a middle course so that the picture wouldn't offend people. What this amounts to is an empty, schoolboy's (or actor's) form of hero worship. Attenborough seems, more than anything else, infatuated with Gandhi. (Attenborough to a *Newsweek* correspondent: "I adore courage.") The movie is, as he hoped, generally inoffensive, but, apart from those scenes in which the unarmed Indians wait to be attacked by their armed adversaries, it's also, I think, unaffecting. This has to do with the kind of moviemaker Attenborough is. He has scenes with crowds of perhaps hundreds of thousands, but his images are less expressive than the footage we could see on television every night when masses of Iranians gathered in the streets to do obeisance to Ayatollah Khomeini. You have to read about Attenborough's deep commitment to the subject, because you couldn't guess it from what's on the screen. There is no trace of a point of view; the film feels as if it were directed by a committee. The movies that Satyajit Ray has made and the ones that Louis Malle shot in India in the late sixties—the feature-length documentary *Calcutta* and the seven-part series *Phantom India*—have the spirituality that this officially approved, laundered *Gandhi* doesn't have. When I've seen the Satyajit Ray films or those by Malle, I've felt that I was beginning to perceive something of the torpor and beauty of India; *Gandhi* makes me feel that I've been on a state visit.

•　　•　　•　　•　　•

Sophie's Choice, an unusually faithful adaptation of William Styron's Holocaust Gothic, is, I think, an infuriatingly bad movie. It comes to us stuffed with literary references and encrusted with the weighty culture of big themes: evil, tortured souls, guilt. The director, Alan J. Pakula, did the screenplay himself. He didn't write it, he penned it, and the film tells us that (1) survivors of the death camps carry deathly guilt within them and (2) William Styron is right up there on Parnassus with Thomas Wolfe, Walt Whitman, Emily Dickinson, and Hart Crane.

As Sophie, Meryl Streep is colorful in the first, campy, late-forties scenes, in a Brooklyn house divided into apartments and known as the Pink Palace, when, red-lipped and with bright-golden curls, she dimples flirtatiously and rattles on in Polish-accented, broken English, making her foreignness seem zany. This giddy, triste Sophie charms Stingo (Peter MacNicol), a young Southern writer—the stand-in for Styron—who has moved into the room right under hers. And there's an oddly affecting (though stagey) comic scene when Sophie and her lover, Nathan (Kevin Kline), babble to Stingo at the same time, seemingly unaware that each is drowning out the other. But once the flashbacks to Sophie's tormented past start up and the delayed revelations are sprung on us, and we know we're supposed to feel the lurid thrill of everything she did to survive, I felt more sympathy for Meryl Streep, the actress trying to put over these ultimate-horror scenes, than I could for Sophie herself. Streep is very beautiful at times, and she does amusing, nervous bits of business, like fidgeting with a furry boa—her fingers twiddling with our heartstrings. She has, as usual, put thought and effort into her work. But something about her puzzles me: after I've seen her in a movie, I can't visualize her from the neck down. Is it possible that as an actress she makes herself into a blank and then focusses all her attention on only one thing—the toss of her head, for example, in *Manhattan*, her accent here? Maybe, by bringing an unwarranted intensity to one facet of a performance, she in effect decorporealizes herself. This could explain why her movie heroines don't seem to be full characters, and why there are no incidental joys to be had from watching her. It could be that in her zeal to be an honest actress she allows nothing to escape her conception of a performance. Instead of trying to achieve freedom in front of the camera, she's predetermining what it records.

Meryl Streep's work doesn't hold together here, but how could it? Sophie isn't a character, she's a pawn in this guilt-and-evil game played out by Sophie the Catholic, Nathan the Jew, and Stingo the Protestant. Styron got his three characters so gummed up with his idea of history that it's hard for us to find them even imaginable. And, with Sophie as the careworn flirt and Stingo as the heir to Southern chivalry, Nathan *has* to be unpredictable, or nothing would happen. (Maybe that's the reason for psychotics in fiction.)

MacNicol, in the usually lifeless part of the onlooker who's going to write the story we're seeing, gives the best and the only sustained performance: his auburn hair is cut very short, and he looks the twenty-two-year-old he's meant to be; he keeps an intensity going—he's right there, completely involved in the lovers' sadomasochistic trials. In the ads for the movie, Meryl Streep and Kevin Kline are posed like Garbo and John Gilbert—older Endless Lovers. But Kline is saddled with the kind of flamboyant role that never works—the brilliant, suffering genius. What is a poor actor supposed to do when he's given florid, tortured speeches to deliver? I kept waiting for him to cry "O Bright Ironic Gods!" It's an unplayable part—there's not a single believable moment in it.

What Pakula never figured out was how to get all this crazed romanticism in motion. There's nothing to move the picture forward during the scenes in which Nathan discovers that Sophie has *Look Homeward, Angel* in Polish, or Stingo receives *Leaves of Grass* as a present from Sophie and Nathan, or Stingo recites Emily Dickinson to Sophie, or the three of them are having an epiphany on Hart Crane's Brooklyn Bridge. The movie is a novel being talked to us. And Styron's novel is all come-on. The book has the kind of plotting that points relentlessly at a character's secret and then has to have the character lying constantly, so that the lies can be stripped away. Styron does a dance of a thousand veils with what he regards as the Mystery of Our Time. The movie, following the book, is a striptease. Styron builds the novel toward momentousness, but it's a structure of titillation. And maybe he's afraid we might be tired of the Nazis, so he works to nab us: he sweetens things along the way, throwing in Gothic goodies like the Pink Palace. (Was it inspired by the 1963 movie *What a Way to Go!*, with Shirley MacLaine trying to cheer up her husband, Pinky, by having the rooms in their mansion all painted pink?) The whole plot is based on a connection that isn't there—the connection between Sophie and Nathan's relationship and what the Nazis did to the Jews. Eventually, we get to the Mystery—to Sophie's Choice—and discover that the incident is garish rather than illuminating, and too particular to demonstrate anything general. When you read the book, you can see that there are no unmarked cards in Styron's deck, and you feel you're being played for a sucker. The inert movie takes the book so seriously that you may feel it's Pakula who's the sucker.

December 27, 1982

The Cool and the Dead

Walter Hill's action comedy *48 Hrs.* socks it to the audience. The picture is a roller coaster that hurtles along—*The French Connection, Dirty Harry, The Defiant Ones, In the Heat of the Night, Butch Cassidy and the Sundance Kid* all put in a compactor, smashed, and pressed into cartoon form. It's "dynamite" entertainment—punches, exploding guns, and two men snarling obscenities at each other. Friends who say they loved it qualify that in the next breath, with "I mean I loved Eddie Murphy." There's really no distinction: Eddie Murphy is the movie. It has been shaped around him, and the white actors in the cast, including Murphy's co-star, Nick Nolte, have been turned into rabid honkies so that he can be the black underdog hero and deliver the zingers.

The action is set in a semi-imaginary San Francisco, where Nolte is a rough-and-ready police detective chasing after a pair of killers—pure evil scuzz—who have broken out of prison. The only person who knows enough about the pair to guide him is a young hipster thief (Murphy) who's in jail, with six months left to serve on a three-year sentence. Nolte springs him for forty-eight hours; freed, he puts on his civvies—a Giorgio Armani suit—and looks as pretty as a pimp, and they set out together at breakneck speed, brawling and cursing each other but destined, of course, to become guffawing pals. In order to keep the black-and-white insults rowdy, the movie is pushed into a phony, racist time frame. It isn't now, and it isn't any believable then; it's an eighties minstrel show, in which bigoted whites (which is to say all whites) get their comeuppance from the bitingly clever black man.

Making his film début, Murphy, the young star of "Saturday Night Live," has been cast in the Richard Pryor role—the role that Richard Pryor created for himself—and Murphy is too good at it. At twenty-one, he has his own sleek style. Murphy doesn't imitate Pryor; he doesn't need to—he has digested him. A dapper child of the disco age, he controls the tone of his scenes with Nolte. He's in charge—or, rather, his reflexes are in charge. He's swift as a shark—a Mack-the-Knife comic—and he barely gives Nolte the time of day. This smooth-faced kid takes over the screen, because he's playing black all the time. He's always calling attention to his blackness, but there's no fear and craziness behind his swagger, as there has been with Pryor. Murphy starts his movie career as the beneficiary of Pryor's wild flailing about. Fastidious, and with timing so precise that it seems almost surgical, he uses blackness as a pose. It's Pryor's comedy made cool.

The film itself may reflect a new kind of cool. When racial epithets are used in *48 Hrs.*, the joke is in the sublimation of shock—it's as if the jokes weren't about "coons" but about coon jokes. Black people in the audience don't seem to mind. They may be ecstatically happy to witness the birth of a black star (and one who keeps getting the better of the white man), and some of them may believe that this film represents how whites in general think anyway. The racial infighting between Nolte and Murphy is presented very knowingly, as though we were all in on this dirty ambivalence, if only we'd admit it. It's as though any evidence of blacks and whites getting along together were such a candy-coated lie that only saps could fall for it. Amazingly, people I know come out of this picture and don't say anything about the exploitation of racism—they're scandalized about the film's treatment of women as whores or nags, which in terms of what goes on in this movie is a relatively minor aberration.

48 Hrs. uses the clichés that it mocks, starting with its basic stratagem—the black-and-white pairing of the TV cop shows. Nolte, the gruff, dedicated, maverick cop, is probably meant to represent traditional American heroism—the solid values that Steve McQueen and John Wayne are supposed to have had at their core. Each time Nolte gets behind the wheel of his beat-out sky-blue 1964 Caddie convertible, he turns into a comic-strip driver; he starts it up with a roar, like a teen-age kid with his first motorcycle—the louder the better—and he can't turn a corner without the car's screeching: he's the white people's finest, and he's a honkie clown. The movie is blatantly cartoonish, but that doesn't mean it isn't saying anything. I think we're meant to believe that its profane badinage and even its most exaggerated racial animosity have a deep, gritty truth in them, and that because it's a comedy it can go deeper than "serious" movies. I think we're meant to believe that this paranoid fantasy of race relations is what the TV shows with black and white buddies don't have the guts to let you see. It's as false as they are, but in a hip way. This movie says, We're so hip that we can be ugly with each other. (The insults probably indicate the limits of the four writers' ingenuity; the script is by Roger Spottiswoode, Hill and Larry Gross, and Steven E. de Souza.)

48 Hrs. is excitingly paced; it hooks you at the start and never lets up. But I didn't enjoy it. Hill packages black rage and then throws in a night-club-in-the-Fillmore sequence in which the black musicians—the Busboys—are used to heat things up. In closeups, they put on the kind of sexy big grins that James Agee described, in revulsion, as "niggery," and the sequence is edited orgiastically—the way these things were done in the "daring" movies of the twenties and thirties, when jazz was considered "primitive." Hill's community sings in his other pictures (*The Long Riders, Southern Comfort*) served the stories he was telling; this time the picture comes to a stop so that we can goggle at black sexuality or admire the director's flash.

Most of the time, he isn't doing anything special—even the car chases aren't much fun. He does what other action directors have done, but he does it faster, and with tumescent instrumental music blending with city noise and whipping up the audience's emotions. And he loads some of the scenes with style because they have no other weight. The style feels random and imposed on the material—not that the material would be better without the imposition. I'm thinking, for example, of the use of an extreme telephoto lens to capture the shimmering, up-and-down-the-hilly-road effect of the truck in the prison-break opening, and the variations of this imagery on the San Francisco streets, and of the smoky neon colors of Chinatown in the showdown in the fog, with men looming up out of the miasma. There are also clever empty touches: the killers are a mismatched pair, like the heroes—a handsome, hulking big Indian (Sonny Landham) and a lean, wiry white psychopath (James Remar), who shoots people for diversion. And there are Freudian potency games about losing and getting guns. Some sequences come out of the blue: Nolte and Murphy have a whamming, bloody fistfight for no apparent reason except sheer macho exuberance. And in the scheme of the film how does each of them prove his courage? By shooting when he isn't expected to. (This movie is like a commercial for guns.)

Nick Nolte has a great weathered face (and, from some angles, a creepy resemblance to Pat Hingle). With the extra weight that he's packing here, his features have sunk into the mass, and he looks and acts thick, as if he needed to catch up on a whole lot of sleep. Eddie Murphy has no rough edges—he's polished; Nolte seems unfinished. At times, his rumbling bass voice startles you—it seems to be changing, going down farther and farther. Does Nolte feel so uncomfortable with what he has to say that he's trying to replace the lines with a growl? He gave impressive, charged performances in *Who'll Stop the Rain* and *North Dallas Forty*; he's an ideal screen actor—believable, and with a much larger range than McQueen or Wayne. He gives a picture body—physicality—but he was never just beefcake (except in his first big-studio movie, *The Deep*, in 1977), and so it's a surprise to see him doing a buddy picture. It's probably an even bigger surprise to him—you can see him struggling for something more. He has a searching, protean presence here that's a little embarrassing: he's an honest actor looking for a character that hasn't been written. The police detective is no more than an out-of-shape Neanderthal with shaggy corn-silk hair; he's a foulmouthed slob so that Murphy the dude, in his narrow tailoring, can outsmart him by his hustler's verbal finesse and his black man's sense of irony. (When there's danger, Murphy—always the comic—parodies fear; Nolte plays it straight.) It's only at the climax, with fog drifting through the Chinatown passageways, that the hunched-over Nolte finally stands upright, and is huge and powerful. He is thrown away in this movie, just as Annette O'Toole, who plays the girlfriend that the detective doesn't know how to talk to, is thrown away. (I assume that her part was chopped; in what's left, she's there to be stood up—an insulting role.) So is

Frank McRae, as the black police officer who is Nolte's superior; he's made an uncouth boob.

The picture represents what in L.A. is called professionalism: its only goal is box office, and it appears to have been pared down to just what it can sell. What's left in, of course, is Nolte defending Murphy against McRae's complaints, and yelling, "He's got more brains than you'll ever know. He's got more guts than any partner I've ever had!" And in the film's biggest scene, in a redneck country-and-Western joint (just your everyday San Francisco hangout), Eddie Murphy, using the badge Nolte has handed him, intimidates a mob of angry crackers by shouting, "I'm your worst f——g nightmare, man. I'm a nigger with a badge!" The audience has been so hyped up by then that it roars with laughter, as if white men really were terrified of omnipotent black cops. Murphy is a whiz of a performer; he has concentration and intensity, and he's so young that there's an engaging spirit in what he's doing. But this picture is plastic paranoia all the way through, and it has handed him a dubious victory. Pryor made white people understand his resentments, and it felt good to have that stuff out in the open. *48 Hrs.* brings out invented, distorted hostilities, and is being cheered for it, as if it were doing us a service.

·   ·   ·   ·   ·

The Verdict is a brown and anguished movie about a once trusting and idealistic man—Frank Galvin, a Boston Irish lawyer, played by Paul Newman—who was hurt by those closest to him and became a booze-soaked failure. But Galvin still retains a faith in the judgment of the ordinary people who sit on a jury, and that faith enables him to redeem himself. It's a Frank Capra setup given art-film treatment; everything looks gaslit and under layers of heavy varnish. The exteriors are covered in drizzle, and the interiors are dark-panelled rooms and high-ceilinged institutional halls and offices where Galvin, shot from a distance, with the camera angling up from floor level, seems dwarfed, insignificant. I don't think there's a white wall in all of this picture's Boston. The powerful forces of society are arrayed against Galvin, and the movie never lets you forget it. He has filed suit against the Archdiocese of Boston, which owns the hospital where the comatose woman on whose behalf he is suing was given the wrong anesthetic during childbirth. The little lawyer is a sad and aging David battling a cynical, manipulative Goliath—James Mason as Concannon, the opposing attorney, the head of a powerful law firm, with a squad of fifteen or so evil young aides to do his research. When they sit at a conference table during strategy sessions with him, the group suggests junior devils being coached by the unctuous old master, and Concannon is described to us by Galvin's only friend (Jack Warden) as "the Prince of F——g Darkness." And the judge (Milo O'Shea) is grossly prejudiced—he plays footsie with the Church. Directed by Sidney Lumet, from a script by David Mamet that derives from a novel by Barry Reed, the movie is so impressed by its own high seriousness that it has a hushed atmosphere. It strives for gloom.

Paul Newman plays the role for all it has got, and, making himself look softer and heavier, and even a little slack and jowly, he gives a fine performance, but he has been giving much livelier and more varied fine performances for the past several years (*Slap Shot*, *Fort Apache, the Bronx*, *Absence of Malice*). He doesn't need the halo Lumet puts on him. (You almost expect it to light up and spell "This is an Academy Award performance.") Lumet's admiration of his acting weighs Newman down; so does Mamet's (deliberately) stale and repetitive language. Newman has a limited palette here; he removes the confidence from his voice (he sounds shaken, frightened), but his lines work on only one level—at times, this makes him seem like a cartoon trying to think. It's a bowed-down, sorrowful-sot performance—a tired old show-business view of "a good man."

When Lumet gets serious, his energetic, fast-moving style falls apart, and he photographs scenes from fifty yards away. The camera just sits like Death on these dark, angled images. Lest anybody miss the point, Lumet puts dirges on the soundtrack; they serve as accompaniment to Galvin's heavy breathing and to the uninflected voice of Charlotte Rampling, the mysterious woman who shows up to complicate Galvin's life. Lumet pours on the melodrama, and he stretches the suspense over a long, long period, keeping the audience palpitating for the turn-around—the arrival of the surprise witness (Lindsay Crouse, showcased as a colleen). In its own sombre, inflated terms, the picture is effective, but it's dragged out so self-importantly that you have a lot of time to think. Would you hire this lawyer? Galvin rejects the bishop's cash-settlement offer without discussing it with his clients—the comatose woman's sister and brother-in-law, who need the money to have her cared for and to make a fresh start themselves. Galvin thinks he can do better for them in court, and that the "truth" of what happened must come out. But he's poorly prepared when the trial opens, and it's only a lucky fluke—the surprise witness—that saves the day for him. Galvin seems a hopelessly naïve, incompetent, and untrustworthy lawyer; he risks leaving his clients penniless because of his faith in the common man. He regards a settlement out of court as cowardly and dishonorable—as "selling out." He explains why he can't accept the bishop's offer: "If I take the money, I'm lost—I'll just be a rich ambulance chaser." This lawyer appears to be going into court to strengthen his own character. It's no wonder he has no other cases. *The Verdict* is presented in the guise of a realistic view of the corruption of our institutions, but it's about a sensitive hero's struggle to regain his self-respect. Mr. Smith went to Washington and Mr. Galvin goes to court. It's the story of a man who was disillusioned and became a drunk; by the end he has regained his illusions.

January 10, 1983

Hopeless

*T*wenty years ago, I watched Emmanuèle Riva in *Thérèse Desqueyroux*, the Georges Franju film of the François Mauriac novel, and I felt I knew exactly why Thérèse was attempting to poison her husband. He was a dull lump of a man, and Philippe Noiret played him to perfection. Since then, I have seen Noiret in many roles and have often admired his performances, but whenever he's at the center of a movie my thoughts return to Thérèse and her poison. Dull lumpiness is Noiret's specialty—his métier. He plays tired, apathetic men, and I know no better reason for not going to a movie than that he's the crestfallen, half-asleep star of it. This year, France's official submission for the Academy Award for Best Foreign Film is *Coup de Torchon* (*Clean Slate*), the seventh feature directed by Bertrand Tavernier, and his sixth with Noiret, who is its star. He functions as this director's spokesman and alter ego; Tavernier calls Noiret his "autobiographical actor," and they have a big, bearlike resemblance to each other. Noiret is the incarnation of Tavernier's spiritual funk. They stand jowl to jowl.

Coup de Torchon takes place in some sort of French colonial Dogpatch in Africa in 1938, just before the start of the Second World War. Tavernier invents an antic, off-kilter world, indolent and itchy—the world of a domestic farce with jungle rot. Noiret is Cordier, the only officer of the law in the area, but a cuckolded, henpecked weakling, who lets his wife (Stéphane Audran) keep her sulky clod of a lover in the house and pass him off as her brother. Cordier doesn't fight back; he allows himself to be played for a fool, and whenever he can he gets away to see his mistress—Isabelle Huppert, who's married to a brute who beats her. Huppert, who waggles her naked bottom at the camera, is the only really amusing performer in the cast. When her bottom is covered, Cordier, with mangy stubble on his face, has his hand up her skirt. They're figures in a cartoon idyll. Learning that she has become a widow, this spiteful sweetie strips and frolics. And when she has an orgasm it barely ruffles her blank surface; she announces it in a bemused, impartial tone, like a kid spotting an ant in his sandwich. The picture's comic lechery suggests a small fable, and Noiret, with his crafty, hangdog expressions, is a shrewd comedian, especially in the scenes in which he's jeered at by the local pimps and the other brutal white men who exploit the natives. But that's only one dimension of this long, ambitious movie, which has a leaden spirit even in these sequences that aim at sly farce. When Noiret is funny, you can almost feel Tavernier waiting for that to be over so he can move on to heavyweight matters of conscience. And the farce scenes are propelled by ironic tango music, which contributes to the film's funereal atmosphere by alerting you to what's coming. Clearly, the Europeans in this crummy village in the late thirties don't know what we in the audience know about the evils of colonialism, and the film, which is both facetious and sententious, relies on our complacency about our received wisdom.

Based on an American pulp novel, *Pop. 1280*, by the late Jim Thompson (which was set in the American South), the picture is about how the abject, grovelling Cordier, who is sensitive to the suffering of the blacks, proceeds to clean up the area by secretly killing off the exploiters, using his reputation for being cowardly and ineffectual as a coverup. The script is by Jean Aurenche and the director, who collaborated in 1975 on *The Judge and the Assassin*; this time they have combined the two characters, and piled on the ambiguities. They keep casting doubts on Cordier's motives. When he goes to the nearest large town and we hear the European police administrator in the billiard parlor saying that "niggers have no souls," we're getting the preparation for Cordier's shooting spree. The administrator follows this declaration by kicking Cordier in the behind. The bad guys who abuse blacks (and women of all races) also abuse Cordier. So he has personal reasons for murder as well as the big moral ones. And one of the varmints that Cordier kills is, conveniently, the husband of his mistress.

Cordier's grizzled face seems so slack and comic and his antagonists are such nasty, awful people that the audience doesn't take his shooting them very seriously; when he dispatches his first victims, two pimps in soiled white suits, there's no shock in the scene. It's a joke, a device in a farce, like Cordier's sanctimonious expression as he furtively cops a feel of his mistress's thigh when they're outdoors in what would be the village square if this village had a square. Tavernier doesn't make his intentions known for quite a stretch, and viewers may accept the twists of plot without realizing how much they're being asked to swallow. In an interview in the *Times*, Tavernier, a former film critic, jokingly described *Coup de Torchon* as "the first African *film noir*." But this phlegmatic demonstration of what drives a chicken-hearted man to violence is a French academic's idea of a dark thriller. (Can a man who wears baggy pants be a *film noir* hero?) Cordier doesn't just knock the bad guys off—he thinks about it. A pure, intelligent woman—a new schoolteacher—comes to the village, for the sole purpose, it seems, of allowing him to unburden himself of his rationale for passing judgment and turning executioner. She is made an unwitting accomplice—that's the punishment for her virtue. And the idea is introduced that Cordier has become a killer out of pity. Tavernier doesn't mean that ironically; he doesn't mean self-pity—he means compassion for the victims of injustice and brutality, one of whom just happens to be Cordier himself. (Even his faithless wife and her clod get bumped off.)

The audience may enjoy Cordier's ridding the area of its exploiters, but the film's thesis is that even such drastic and half-mad cleanup jobs are hopeless. *Coup de Torchon* means to be astringent—it means to clear away humanist self-deceptions, and it sets out to prove that nothing good can happen. (With Noiret as protagonist, you know that from the start.) And it proves it, of course. When a black man learns that Cordier has killed someone, and realizes that Cordier may kill him, too, to conceal the crime, he pleads for his life. Cordier makes a speech to him about the *merde* of *existence* and then shoots him. An American *film noir* director would simply have had Cordier pull the trigger (and we might have been horrified); the French pedant gives us his philosophical song and dance, so we'll know that it isn't merely Cordier who's a rotten bastard—the world is rotten, and everything is pointless.

But Cordier, revealing himself to the schoolteacher, also lets us know that he thinks he is Christ returned, and his character changes—he becomes very austere. *Coup de Torchon* is the story of a saintly madman. (Suggested alternate title: *Maybe He Is Jesus.*) The longer the movie goes on, the worse it gets. First, it's a farce, then it's a *Dirty Harry* for liberals, and then it moves into Christ mythology, and it's so torpid that Isabelle Huppert's flitting about looks like energy. (Even that is denied us when the film, which benefits from her affectlessness, uses it against her and shows her to be a cold little butcher at heart.) For Tavernier, dispiritedness is about the same thing as social concern. He appears to believe that a man of feeling is necessarily a weakling, a Cordier who spends his life getting dumped on while worrying about justice in the abstract. The film indicates that for this man of feeling compromise and sloth and rot are inevitable. Tavernier's conscience (it's a disease) leads him to make ponderous announcements that don't seem to relate to Cordier's colonial fleapit. Tavernier's "truths" are grotesque in this setting. He keeps going until he's got so many rationales for killing that you can take your pick. By the end, Cordier is telling us that he just helps people realize their true natures. (Apparently, it was the true nature of the black man to be dead.) And then Tavernier moves on to the real beaut—the same one that Chaplin (to his shame) pulled out of the hat in *Monsieur Verdoux*. The war in Europe is just beginning, and Cordier, who is the director's mouthpiece, as Verdoux was Chaplin's, tells us that murder is nothing compared with the horrors of the world.

With this stroke, Tavernier cancels out even the one potentially affecting scene in the movie—Cordier's execution of the black man—in order to lecture us. He may think he's bringing out the rage behind despair, but all he brings out is his sense of futility. *Coup de Torchon* is saying horrible, senseless, inexplicable things, such as that whopper that killing on a small scale is less immoral than killing on a big scale. (Tavernier must mean it, because he said practically the same damn thing at the close of *The Judge and the Assassin*.) I have heard Tavernier's films lauded as "the cinema of ideas," but *Coup de Torchon* chokes on its own unresolvable ambiguities. It's saying that Cordier is crazy and his philosophizing is the rationalizing of a madman. It's also saying something to this effect: if Jesus had come back forty-odd years ago he wouldn't have been able to save the world—he could only have participated in its horrors. Or, to put it at its crudest, he'd have been a paranoid schizophrenic.

·　　·　　·　　·　　·

Best Friends is a Velveeta comedy, processed like a Neil Simon picture, with banter and gags and an unctuous score. All its smart talk is low-key and listless. It stays on the surface, yet it's dissatisfied with the surface; it's a deeply indecisive movie. The script raises the question: Why is it so much easier for two people to live together harmoniously if they're not married—or, to put it the other way, why does formalizing a living-together relationship often make it tense and nerve-racking, so that both partners feel trapped? Millions of us must have sweated over this question during the past several decades—it's a great subject for a modern comedy of false expectations. But the scriptwriters, Barry Levinson and Valerie Curtin, who have raised the issue (and who, according to press accounts, have sweated it out themselves), have nothing but sitcom answers. In the movie, Burt Reynolds asks his L.A. screenwriting partner, Goldie Hawn, to tie the knot, and though she's fearful that it will spoil things between them, he seems so deeply mortified by her reluctance that she agrees. They marry and embark on a wedding trip back East to meet their new in-laws, and it isn't just the marriage that collapses—their personalities decay.

The script probably reads fine, but it plays all wrong. The dialogue is too neatly worked out; there's no way to speak it without making us aware of how clever it is—how flip yet knowing. Nothing in this picture really feels right; you sense the discomfort of honest effort going awry. My guess would be that the director—Norman Jewison—and the stars hoped for a depth that would give the lines poignancy. But the writers, trying for truth, have achieved no more than self-consciousness: the lovers are unreconstructible me-generation types—childish and narcissistic. Neither shows any particular interest in the other's background, or even any instinctive rapport with the other's parents. These lovers have been made so lightweight that there's nothing at stake when they recoil from each other, and there's no tragic, absurdist comedy in their parents' lack of any real bond with them. Goldie Hawn tries to create a giddy, bright woman who suddenly feels overwhelmed by bad luck—sunk. But acting benumbed doesn't do much for the audience, and neither she nor any other performer should ever again be asked to fall asleep by dropping his or her head face forward into a platter of food. I don't think

Burt Reynolds is ever in character here; he gives a flabby, mildewed perfor-mance. (Maybe it's time for him to start playing mean, grinning sonuvabitch roles—he might get some drive back that way.) What has gone wrong, I think, is that the movie starts escaping its subject as soon as the pair go off on their trip and into a series of comic nightmares. The test of the change in their relationship would have come if they had stayed right where they were.

January 24, 1983

Memory

The Night of the Shooting Stars (the original Italian title is *La Notte di San Lorenzo*) is so good it's thrilling. This new film by Vittorio and Paolo Taviani (who made the 1977 *Padre Padrone*) encompasses a vision of the world. Comedy, tragedy, vaudeville, melodrama—they're all here, and insep-arable. Except for the framing-device scenes that take place in a blue-lighted, fairy-tale present, *Shooting Stars* is set in a Tuscan village and its environs dur-ing a summer week in 1944, when the American troops were rumored to be only days away, and the Germans who had held the area under occupation were preparing to clear out. But this setting is magical, like a Shakespearean forest; it exists in the memory of Cecilia, who is telling the story of what hap-pened that August, when she was a sultry six-year-old hellion (played by Mi-col Guidelli), and her family was part of a group of a few dozen villagers who had decided to disobey official orders. Convinced that the Germans, who had mined their houses, meant to destroy the whole town—San Martino—that night, they stole out after dark and went to find the Americans. The directors (who also wrote the script, with Giuliani G. De Negri) are great gagmen—they aren't afraid to let Cecilia exaggerate. She remembers herself as a tiny six-year-old who is independent of adults and smarter than life. It doesn't take much stretch of our imaginations to grasp that accidents that befell the child—such as tumbling onto a basket of eggs—have become enlarged. The basket itself has assumed heroic proportions, and, having been blamed for what she couldn't help, the little girl takes a demonic joy in smashing the two eggs that are still intact. The Cecilia we see never complains and always finds ways to amuse herself; when she has witnessed an on-the-run wedding (the groom is AWOL, the bride's pregnancy is close to term) even the hops she takes, out of sheer pixilated excitement, are a bit higher than life. At this rushed wedding, an old man drinks a ceremonial glass of wine and gives a recitation about what happened to Achilles and Hector as if the Trojan War had taken place in his own lifetime. I think you could say that *Shooting Stars* is about how an individual's memories go to form communal folklore, and vice versa, so that we "recall" what we've heard from others as readily as what we've actually seen or heard. And the myth becomes our memory—the story we tell.

The Tavianis' style here is intellectualized, but their effects are unaccountable and gutty. Right at the start, in the chaos of a war that's lost but not yet over, and with Army deserters making their way home and hiding out from the Germans and the local Black Shirts, and with families split between Resistance fighters and Fascists, and nobody sure what the Germans will do before they pull out, San Martino is victimized by a practical joker who plays "Glory, Glory Hallelujah" on his phonograph. It's a marching version, with drums and woodwinds, of the old camp-meeting hymn that became "John Brown's Body" and later the "Battle Hymn of the Republic," and it begins softly, as if John Brown's brigades were at a distance and coming closer, and the townspeople, who have been cowering in their cellars, think that the Americans, their liberators, have arrived, and rush out to greet them. One boy is so sure of it, he sees them.

Galvano (played by Omero Antonutti, the powerful father of *Padre Padrone*) is the leader of the group that sneaks away in the night; at times he's like a theatre director. He tells his people to wear dark clothes for camouflage, and the whole troupe scrambles into black coats and coverings at the same time—it's like backstage at the opera, with everyone getting ready for the masquerade scene. And then there's another, quicker routine: the dogs who must be left behind, because their barking would betray the group, bark because they're being left behind. At last, Galvano's villagers are out in the country. They have been told that the Germans will blow up the town at 3 A.M., and when it's close to three they stand still and listen. We hear their thoughts, and then, exactly at three, distant shelling can be heard, and we see closeups of ears, like enlarged details of paintings by Uccello. The villagers listen to the destruction of San Martino—the only world they know—and we see their hands clenching their house keys, and see their expressions. Galvano doffs his hat and weeps for San Martino; a man throws his key away. It's an unostentatiously beautiful passage. The people mourn, but they're too excited to feel crushed: they're out on the road looking for Americans. In the morning, they take off their black clothes. The August landscapes are golden, and Cecilia is proud of her pleated, red print pinafore. It's made of the same material as her mother's sundress; they're wearing matching mother-daughter outfits.

Shooting Stars keeps opening up and compressing as it cuts back and forth between what happens to the group in the hills and what happens to the others, back in San Martino, who believed the authorities when they told them that they'd be safe if they took refuge in the cathedral. The elderly bishop, who has collaborated—has done what he was told—offers bland assurances to everyone while praying to God that he will really be able to protect his flock. (His prayer has a note of apprehensiveness; life is making a skeptic of him.) So many townspeople gather inside that the bishop runs out of wafers, but the people have brought loaves of bread with them and they break these into bits. He consecrates the bread, and everyone is given the Host— the ritual has never seemed more full of meaning. When the crowded cathedral explodes, the door blasts open and smoke pours forth; two priests bring the bishop out, and, dazed, he slumps in the square. The pregnant bride had become too ill to go on with the trekkers in the country, and her mother had hauled her back on a litter and taken her into the cathedral; now the mother tries to carry the mortally wounded, unconscious girl out, and the bishop, pulling himself to his feet, helps her. For a minute, they're both slightly bent over, facing each other and tugging at the helpless girl; they're forehead to forehead, and their eyes lock. It's an insane, cartoon effect—"This is what trusting in God and the Fascists gets you!"—and it makes the pain of the situation more acute. *Shooting Stars* is so robust that even its most tragic moments can be dizzyingly comic. When Richard Lester attempted black humor on the horrors of war (in the 1967 *How I Won the War*), the scenes were jokey and flat, and the people were no more than puppets. In *Shooting Stars*, black humor is just one tonality among many, and the exhausted mother and the double-crossed bishop aren't diminished by being revealed as dupes; having shared their rock-bottom moment, we feel close to them. Many voices are joined in these memories, and though the people who have headed out for freedom may look more courageous, the film doesn't degrade the ones who stayed behind. They had their reasons—children, old age, fears. In one way or another, they're all like that woman with the pregnant daughter.

Out on the roads, a Sicilian girl who has been shot by German soldiers—who is already dead—flirts and makes small talk with some stray G.I.s, Sicilian-Americans from Brooklyn, before she accepts her death. The only other movie director I know of who could bring off an epiphany like this is the Ukrainian Dovzhenko, the lyrical fantasist of the silent era. The Tavianis present their wildest moments of fantasy in a heightened realistic form; you believe in what you're seeing—but you can't explain why you believe in it. I think that we're eager to swallow it, in the same way that, as children, we put faith in the stories we heard at bedtime, our minds rising to the occasion, because what happened in them was far more real to us than the blurred events of our day. And for the grown woman Cecilia the adventures that she took part in have acquired the brilliance and vitality of legend.

San Martino is probably much like the town of San Miniato, between Pisa and Florence, where the brothers were born (Vittorio in 1929, Paolo in 1931), and which was the site of a massacre carried out by the Germans. (Their first short film—*San Miniato, July 1944*, made in 1954—was about this massacre.) The full fresco treatment they give the events of that summer in *Shooting Stars* is based partly on wartime incidents that they themselves witnessed when they were adolescents; they have said that everything they show actually happened—that the events they didn't witness they picked up "one by one . . . from all kinds of sources, official and otherwise." It's this teeming, fecund mixture, fermenting in their heads for almost forty years, that produces this film's giddy, hallucinated realism.

The movie is not like anything else—the Taviani brothers' pleasure in the great collection of stories they're telling makes it euphoric. It's as if they had invented a new form. In its feeling and completeness, *Shooting Stars* may be close to the rank of Jean Renoir's bafflingly beautiful *Grand Illusion*, and maybe because it's about the Second World War and Renoir's film was about the First, at times it's like a more deracinated *Grand Illusion*. Trying to pick the name by which he'll be known in the Resistance, a man who sings in church decides that he wants to be called Requiem. A married couple who belong to Galvano's group are out in the middle of nowhere, listening to the sounds of a warplane overhead, and the man holds his wife's compact up so she can see to put on her lipstick. Galvano's hungry people come across a watermelon patch, and the film becomes a bucolic festival; one girl can't wait for a melon to be cut open—she smashes it with her bottom. At night, all of them sleep piled on top of each other in a crater—a shell hole—as if their bodies had been flung there in a game of pick-up-sticks. And the image is so vivid that somehow you don't question it. Was this crater with its groundlings conceived as a secular joke on the seraphic figures floating in the painted domes of churches? You don't boggle at anything in this movie. The Tavianis have the kind of intuition that passeth understanding. An era is ending, the society is disintegrating, but they take a few seconds to show us Galvano, who has gone to a stream to bathe, standing still in the water, completely at peace—his mind a blank. It's a transcendent image. He could be anywhere and the water would renew him; he has a sense of balance. Galvano gets to consummate his lifelong dream, but before he goes to bed with the woman he has loved for forty years—the woman who hasn't been accessible until now, because she became part of the landed gentry—they kiss, and he tells her apologetically that his kiss would be better if he hadn't lost three teeth. What he's saying is "Do you know what you've made us miss?"

The film's greatest sequence is hair-raisingly casual—a series of skirmishes in a wheat field. Still looking for the American troops and spotting nothing but Germans, the villagers come to a wheat field and meet up with a group of Resistance fighters who need help with the harvest (or the Fascists will get it), and the villagers lend a hand. And suddenly all the ideological factions that have been fighting in the country are crawling around in the tall wheat. There's a civil war taking place in the fields, with men who all know each other, who in some cases are brothers or cousins, going at each other with clubs and guns and pitchforks. These are not noble peasants. Two old friends wrestle murderously, each demanding that the other surrender; the gentle bridegroom kills a fifteen-year-old Fascist, who is grovelling in terror, and the kid's father falls to the earth and scoots in a circle like an animal in agony. Scenes from this battlefield could turn into Anselm Kiefer's huge straw landscapes, which are like windswept, overgrown memorials that have come up out of the past—out of war and mud and destruction. At one chaotic moment, a couple of people who are tending a wounded old woman reach out at arm's length for the flask of water that a couple of other people have just given to a wounded man, and then, realizing that they're enemies, both pairs start shooting at each other—from a distance of about three feet. It's a pure sick joke, like something Godard would have tried in *Les Carabiniers* if he'd thought of it. In *Shooting Stars*, you're never reminded of a filmmaker who isn't a master.

The Taviani brothers say that if there is a theme running through their movies it's "From silence to communication," but they try to spoof their own theme, too. When Cecilia and another little girl meet up with two G.I.s, Cecilia's friend picks the one she likes, and he gives her a chocolate bar, but Cecilia's G.I. indicates that he has nothing to offer her. Silently, she makes funny ugly faces at him, and he replies in kind, and then, wanting to give her some token, he improvises—he blows up a condom as if it were a balloon, and she dances off with her prize. This, like several other scenes in the movie, is reminiscent of Rossellini's 1946 film *Paisan*; the Tavianis, who saw that film when they were university students in Pisa, say that it was *Paisan* that made them decide to become moviemakers. And so maybe this G.I.-condom scene can be passed over—it's effective in the thin, overcooked manner of *Life* journalism in the forties. It's an amusing parody of a whole batch of romantic encounters in wartime movies, but it's also a dismayingly pat little number.

In a sense, everything in *Shooting Stars* is a theatrical routine (but not on that level). The Tavianis' style keeps you conscious of what they're doing, and, yes, the technique is Brechtian, but with a fever that Brecht never had. The Tavianis make stylized unreality work for them in a way that nobody else ever has; in *Shooting Stars* unreality doesn't seem divorced from experience (as it does with Fellini)—it's experience made more intense. They love style, but it hasn't cost them their bite—their willingness to be harsh and basic. During the brief period when a movie is actually being shot, a director often wishes that he had someone to help him—someone who knew what was inside his head. These two do, and that may account for the calm assurance of the film and its steady supply of energy. Every sequence is a flourish, but there's heft in the Tavianis' flourishes, and no two have the same texture or tone. The shaping of the material is much more conscious than we're used to. The movie builds, and it never lets up—it just keeps channelling its energy in different directions. Even when *Shooting Stars* is at its most emotionally expansive, you're aware of the control the directors have. What they're controlling is exaltation. That's the emotional medium they're working in.

They use sound in a deliberately primitive way: the sound here—whether it's from nature or Verdi or the score by Nicola Piovani—makes memories flood back just as odors sometimes bring things back. It's sound of great clarity, set against silence. (A superb fanfare is heard during the film's main title—a fanfare followed by cannon fire and then, for a moment, nothing.) The memories the sound brings back come up out of the muck and are heavily filtered; they're distorted, and polished until they gleam. And the directors' visual techniques—their use of dissolves, especially—keep you conscious of the processes of memory etching in and eroding. The film's impassioned style is steeped in nostalgia. Cecilia's mythicized memories are her legacy to her own child, to whom she is telling this story at bedtime. For the Tavianis, as for Cecilia, the search for the American liberators is the time of their lives. For an American audience, the film stirs warm but tormenting memories of a time when we were beloved and were a hopeful people.

February 7, 1983

Torrid Zone

*P*eter Weir's *The Year of Living Dangerously* is set in Indonesia in 1965, during the political upheavals that shook President Sukarno's unstable government, and at the start of the film the traditional Javanese silhouette puppets, slinky and sinister, quarrel and berate each other to the music of a gamelan orchestra. We're being briefed that we see only the shadows of the threatening interchanges that are going on somewhere else. And that's what we get: intimations, fragments, hints and portents, and on a very wide screen—the characters are surrounded by forces they can't control. Shadow dancing is Peter Weir's specialty, and for the first half of *Living Dangerously* he keeps us entertained by the obliquity of his style. The gamelan music is replaced by babble in many languages and the clatter of typewriters and electronic machines; in scene after scene there's some kind of communication going on that we're not privy to. The camera lingers for just a quick look at turmoil that isn't explained—transactions that are furtive, seedy. We have a guide: a half-Chinese, half-Australian cameraman, the goblinlike Billy Kwan. (This male role is played by the actress Linda Hunt.) Billy introduces himself in a voice-over monologue, and he tells us about the culture and the people we meet. There's nothing casual in his narration; it's cryptic, polished, and very literary—he's like a novelist playing God, and he talks about the characters in the movie as if they were his creations. Mostly, he talks about what can't be seen directly—the shuddering unease in the capital which he accounts for in terms of shadow and substance.

Living Dangerously, which centers on the Caucasian community in Djakarta—journalists and diplomats—recalls *Casablanca* and a batch of other Warners tales of international intrigue set in studio versions of Istanbul or Shanghai or wherever. But Weir's images are much more arresting and detailed, and though the Indonesian settings had to be faked (in the Philippines and Australia), they're faked convincingly. They're exotic enough for the film to have that air of estrangement that Antonioni's *The Passenger* had. (It's also Nicolas Roeg's long suit.) *Living Dangerously* suggests the same sort of unknowability, but Antonioni uses this atmosphere as a metaphor for emptiness—it becomes thick and metaphysical, and the fun goes out of it. Weir keeps the fun in *Living Dangerously*; he doesn't stiffen on us and become forbidding. In *The Passenger*, paranoia goes so far that it becomes affectless: the whole world is governed by conspiracy, and the landscape has an impenetrable secret. In *Living Dangerously*, the things that are mysterious can at least be glimpsed.

Movie squalor has its glamour, especially when there's plenty of sweat and malaria. And there are particulars that tease—such as the nature of the pink beverages followed by vibrantly green ones that are served to Mel Gibson, as an Australian foreign correspondent who has just arrived in Djakarta, and to Sigourney Weaver, as the assistant military attaché at the British Embassy. Billy Kwan, who befriends the Australian and becomes his partner, has played matchmaker and arranged for the two to meet. In the first half of the film, nothing is center stage, but indirectly we get a sense of what's going on: a first view of the famine victims as Gibson comes out of a hotel bar, a flash of Sukarno (played by an actor) in a limousine, the beggars who come into a restaurant, a Communist-led anti-American demonstration. And a new-style old-time "dangerous" steaminess builds up as Gibson and Weaver eye each other. When he watches her dancing to a record of Jerry Lee Lewis's "Whole Lotta Shakin' Goin' On" and one of her spaghetti straps keeps slipping off her shoulder, or when they're running together in the rain and she's giggling like crazy, the movie has "hot stuff" written all over it. Weir knows what's spectacular about Sigourney Weaver: her brainy female-hunk physicality—her wide-awake dark eyes, the protruding lower lip, the strong, rounded, outthrust jaw, and her hands, so large that when she embraces Gibson her five fingers encompass his back. Weaver has practically no character to play—she's the proud beauty, the headstrong princess of the puppet play. But she suggests a privileged woman who feels perfectly free to enjoy her prerogatives, and that's a turn-on for the audience, because what a set of prerogatives! She uses her face and her body, and pours on the passion and laughter; she has the kind of capacity for enjoyment that the young Sophia Loren had. (These women were never innocent.)

When the handsome young reporter picks up the challenge and goes after the beauty, the audience silently cheers him on. In this, at least, he's a hero. The title *The Year of Living Dangerously*, which was Sukarno's prophetic term for 1965, applies more specifically to the reporter's pursuit of big stories and of this lusty big woman (who may be an agent). The allusive treatment of these two and of the six or eight other principal characters appears to be all you need; Weir provides concrete details (in a Hemingway manner), leaving you to figure out what goes on in between. The score is entertaining, with records that range from Richard Strauss to Little Richard, and background music by Maurice Jarre, in which the gamelan bell sounds are never far away. And though there's a lot you don't understand, the picture has been building, the love affair has been set atingle, and you assume that it's going to develop and everything will become clear.

Instead, in the second half the plot seems to become slapdash and rather hysterical, with Weaver disappearing for far too long while Gibson chases around trying to corroborate something she has told him, and with Billy, our guide, becoming disillusioned with just about everyone and everything. *Living Dangerously* goes slack at the exact point where Weaver (overacting for the only time, her eyes popping) tells Gibson about a shipload of munitions that the Communists are bringing in for an attempted coup. Peter Weir has been doing fine with the shadow play, but now he tries for the thing itself—the political power games going on—and as a melodramatist he's a fizzle. When he's operating on just one level, he doesn't seem practical-minded enough to unravel the plot. Actually, the plotting isn't careless; it must have been worked out very complexly on paper. But you have to think the movie over to know that, because while you're watching it the action seems to wander. We assume that Gibson sent out the crucial information, but are we meant to think that this precipitated the reprisals against the Communists? We don't find out what the British Embassy (where Weaver got the news) intended to do with it, or whether the British, in fact, did anything at all. And Billy's political anguish would make more sense if we knew how to take it—is he posing, even to himself? Weir must think the audience cares only about the swirl of action and eroticism, and doesn't want to understand the specifics. He appears to have an Australian version of sixties counterculture hipness. The movie displays left-wing attitudes, but it shows no particular interest in politics—not even enough to help us understand why Billy, who likes to dress up as Sukarno, identifies with him, and then feels betrayed by him. Billy, the pivotal character, is eager for acceptance by the white community, yet he worships Sukarno as the voice of the Third World. Billy is both a party crasher and a party pooper; he's a little dictator, but he also carries on as if he were St. Francis of Assisi. The picture shows us his phoniness—he has a shamefaced adolescent grin when he's caught enjoying himself—yet it also endorses his sanctimoniousness. In the only really stupid scene, a big-bellied, fiftyish journalist (the marvelous Australian actor Noel Ferrier, who drapes his bulk in a toga-like print shirt) makes a pass at a slim native boy and is reprimanded by Billy's stern glance, while we're thinking, Let the boy speak for himself—this old gent might feed him and, if he takes a fancy to him, get him out of this starving country.

Living Dangerously, which, considering its scale and the thousands of extras, was made remarkably cheaply (under six million dollars), is a much more sophisticated film than the ads may indicate: you have to keep your eyes and ears busy to catch everything that's going on in it. It's when Weir slows down that he's in trouble. A scene of the reporter eying the door to the airport runway and then slipping out while customs guards are taking his tape recorder apart is the sort of movie escape that requires speed and confusion. A few extra seconds here kill it. (Watching the reporter doubt for too long whether he can pull off the trick, we doubt everything about it.) This bungled scene is followed by a perfectly timed image of the runway crew, who have just removed the stairs from a Royal Netherlands plane, seeing the foreigner coming and automatically moving them back for him. It's a neat visual comment on the last vestiges of colonialism.

There are performances, too, that are perfectly calibrated in the editing, such as that of Bembol Roco—the Filipino actor who plays the hero's assistant, Kumar—particularly in his final, giving-in-to-laughter scene. And there's the striking, bald Bill Kerr, who has a remarkable voice. He shone in Weir's 1981 *Gallipoli* as Uncle Jack, who read aloud to the children, and he shines again as a testy Britisher, Colonel Henderson, whose white man's burden seems to have given him a ramrod-straight back. But most of the foreigners seem designed solely to document Billy's conviction that their aggressiveness is a violation of the Indonesians, and no one more than the vicious, disgruntled member of the press played by Michael Murphy, who is jealous of the scoops that Gibson gets (with Billy's help), and is a rotten exploiter of teenage native girls so supple and narrow-hipped they're like children. Murphy does possibly his best acting in this man-you-love-to-hate salacious-villain role, except that he plays the same kind of vermin in every scene he has. Some minuscule trims might have made him look brilliant. A little lightening up in the script—by David Williamson, Weir, and C. J. Koch, whose highly readable 1978 novel it's based on—would have helped, too. These Westerners are too priggishly eager to set up other Westerners as bastards. (I wish that they had found more humor in the contradictions of the hero's position as an ambitious, instinctive liberal in a poverty-ridden country.)

To a degree, Weir is the victim of his own skill at creating the illusion of authentic Third World misery, rioting, and chaos. The earlier, studio-set films about international intrigue were so obviously hokey that the backgrounds (with their picturesque natives) were perfectly acceptable as backdrops for romantic melodrama. Here when the backgrounds are used that way it's a little obscene; the emaciation of the natives overwhelms the made-up problems of the Caucasians. Documentaries, TV coverage, print journalism, and modern history itself have changed audiences' responses, and when fake dilemmas about "involvement" are cooked up for the hero they're an

embarrassment, like his final dash to join the heroine. The conventions of forties romantic adventures look childish here, and at the end we don't quite
know how to feel when the hero, having had his consciousness raised, and
recognizing that he can't master the situation, clears out, though he's in the
midst of the journalistic opportunity he has been looking forward to for a decade. Even the film's suggestion that when he's wounded during the reprisals
against the Communists he pays for what he has done—or that he (metaphorically) gains new vision by losing an eye—is a literary convention from
another time.

Still, this film that goes partly flooey is Weir's most exciting moviemaking; it's alive on the screen. His *Gallipoli* was a well-executed academic exercise on the subject of the waste of war—an "artistic" film, full of familiar
pathos and irony. (With its two runner heroes, it was at least a well-made
Chariots of Fire.) I watched it dutifully, without pleasure. Scene by scene, I
was fascinated by *Living Dangerously*; I was held by it and had a very good
time, though I didn't believe any of it. And I was held despite my aversion to
its gusts of wind about destiny, truth versus appearance, and so on. Weir has
a penchant for the Major Arcana, and in *Living Dangerously*, though Billy
Kwan is a bit of a bum and a fantasizer, he's also the same sort of in-on-the-
mysteries-of-the-cosmos character that the aborigine actor Gulpilil played in
Weir's 1977 *The Last Wave*. Gulpilil's line "A dream is a shadow of something
real" fits right in with Billy's conversational style. So does the line from Edgar
Allan Poe that's quoted in Weir's 1975 *Picnic at Hanging Rock*: "All that we
see or seem is but a dream within a dream." Intellectually, Weir is in a rut,
and Billy's mystical understanding of Indonesia might be boiled down to the
mysticism of L.A.: "Go with the flow." But never has movie blather been spoken more affectingly.

Linda Hunt has been in only one earlier movie (she was the prize-fight-
er's mother in *Popeye*), but she has had an impressive series of stage roles
and is currently appearing as Joan of Arc in a new play at the American Place.
This tiny woman—she is only four foot nine, and is very slender—may be an
acting genius. The concentration and lyric intensity she brings to her acting
seem selfless, and this makes it possible for her to purify the lines she speaks;
she puts little quote marks signifying ambiguity around much of what she
says. She has an otherworldly quality, and her voice might have come from
the moon; it's magnetically odd and simple—the voice of a seer, a fraud, or a
loner. Like Julie Harris's, it carries an aura of silence. And whether it seems
male or female hardly matters. Linda Hunt can't totally scrape off the romanticized spirituality that's written into the role of Billy, who says he believes in
"giving with love to whomever God has placed in our path." And she can't
redeem Billy's forlorn, angry speeches to the correspondent: "I gave you my
trust. I created you!" Right from the beginning, it's apparent that Billy is this
movie's walking conscience and higher moral purpose. (Weir seems afraid
that we might find the scumminess of Java as pleasurable as he does.) But the
tough yet delicate solitariness of Linda Hunt's Billy Kwan gives this film dis-

tinction. Her dedicated acting raises the picture up to where the air is thin but clear.

The atmosphere is muggy for Gibson and Weaver—they give the movie its earthy, old-Hollywood kick. Mel Gibson is a highly accomplished screen actor; that was apparent in *Gallipoli*, too. But he's very young (twenty-seven), and something bland and ordinary seems to be poking through the sullen, burned-out fellow he plays in *The Road Warrior*. Here Gibson's being too young for his role isn't a disadvantage. When the reporter sees Weaver across a room, he's agog—he has a puppyish look. He's like Henry Fonda staring at Barbara Stanwyck in *The Lady Eve*: he's moony, a bumbler. And his openmouthed gawking at Weaver amuses her; she's so wild about him she's charmed by his callowness—she laughs at him the way Stanwyck laughed at the mesmerized Fonda (and made him fall all over himself). Gibson still doesn't have a very distinctive personality as an actor, but his character's jangled nerves are good for him; he uses his eyes more here—he has more tension and dash—and he brings a spunky, romantic-comedy quality to his role. Except for the postcoital conversation about that damn Communist ship, every scene he has with Weaver plays as a love scene. When they're together, the movie has the hectic, under-the-surface energy that is Weir's brand of magic. When Gibson and Weaver are out in the rain, drenched, it excites them. When they cause a scandal by leaving a party at the Embassy, they get in a car and he drives, hellbent, as if nothing could stop them, and he plows right through an army roadblock; the guards shoot at them, and the gun bursts are like applause for their sexiness.

February 21, 1983

Jokers

*P*utting a grossly insensitive, coldhearted deadhead at the center of a movie is a perverse thing to want to do, and Martin Scorsese's *The King of Comedy* isn't an ordinary kind of bad movie. It's so—deliberately—quiet and empty that it doesn't provide even the dumb, mind-rotting diversion that can half amuse audiences at ordinary bad movies. It's too enervated for that, yet the silence and emptiness are mesmerizing, and the scenes—frequently with just two people talking and nothing going on around them—are so extended and spooky that the audience, overprepared to laugh, grabs at any possibility of release. The plot is small-scale—material for a sketch, dragged out. Rupert

Pupkin, the fan played by Robert De Niro, is a New York messenger who is determined to become a TV star like his idol, the comic Jerry Langford (played by Jerry Lewis), the host of the country's most popular late-night talk show. Rupert rehearses alone in his mother's basement for the time when he will make his guest appearance on that show, and when all his efforts to ingratiate himself with Langford fail he kidnaps him and negotiates for a ten-minute spot as ransom. Scorsese must have wanted the film to be very intense and intimate, because there's almost no casual, everyday life. Rupert, Langford (he may have been named for Fritz Lang and John Ford), and the third character—the rich hysteric Masha (Sandra Bernhard), who helps Rupert with the kidnapping because she fantasizes having sex with Langford—are all loners.

The camera thrusts Masha at you, emphasizing her curved nose and pulpy lips; she's like a drag-queen terrorist in an Andy Warhol film. She certainly gets your attention: you want to run for cover. It's obvious that Scorsese means us to feel that way. Masha's stridency, Rupert's aggressive stupidity, Langford's black bile—Scorsese feels he's doing something salutary by rubbing our noses in this ugliness. It's *The Day of the Locust* in the age of television, but with a druggy vacuousness that suggests the Warhol productions of the sixties. It might be an homage to John Cassavetes.

Robert De Niro's Rupert Pupkin is Jake La Motta without his fists. In *Raging Bull*, De Niro and Scorsese had things boiled down, so that Jake's entire character was the chip on his shoulder. This time there's no chip. If De Niro, disfigured again here, has removed himself from comparison with other handsome young actors, it's not because what he does now is more than acting. It's less; it's anti-acting. Performers such as John Barrymore and Orson Welles and Laurence Olivier have delighted in putting on beards and false noses, yet, no matter how heavy the disguise, they didn't disappear; they still had spirit, and we could feel the pleasure that they took in playing foul, crookback monsters and misers—drawing us inside and revealing the terrors of the misshapen, the deluded. A great actor merges his soul with that of his characters—or, at least, gives us the illusion that he does. De Niro in disguise denies his characters a soul. It's not merely that he hollows himself out and becomes Jake La Motta, or Des the priest in *True Confessions*, or Rupert Pupkin—he makes them hollow, too, and merges with the character's emptiness.

In most of De Niro's early performances—in *Hi, Mom!*, even in *The Gang That Couldn't Shoot Straight*, and in *Mean Streets*, *The Godfather, Part II*, *Taxi Driver*, and *New York, New York*—there was bravura in his acting. You could feel the actor's excitement shining through the character, and it made him exciting to watch. But, for all his virtuosity, his Monroe Stahr in *The Last Tycoon* was lifeless, and his Michael in *The Deer Hunter* heroic yet never quite human. And then he started turning himself into repugnant, flesh effigies of soulless characters. Rupert is chunky and thick-nosed, and he has a foul, greasy mustache; is it so De Niro can remove himself further from the character and condescend to him even physically? Rupert waves his arms when he talks; they work in pairs, as if he didn't have the brains to move them independently of each other. De Niro cunningly puts in all the stupid little things that actors customarily leave out. It's a studied performance; De Niro has learned to be a total fool. Big accomplishment! His Rupert is as boring to us as he is to Langford. What De Niro is doing might be based on the Warholian idea that the best parody of a thing is the thing itself.

Rupert doesn't really talk to or listen to anyone else in the movie; whatever he's doing, he's always in rehearsal, trying out his new moves. Scorsese and De Niro close him in, just as Hal Ashby and Jerzy Kosinski closed in the Peter Sellers character in that dim, prolonged one-joke satire *Being There*, and for the same purpose: to tell us that TV is making such fools of us that we'll accept a moron—as a statesman in *Being There*, and as an entertainer in *The King of Comedy*. Sellers' stillness, his unhappy expression, his stately misery in those itchy old clothes, and the Oriental-sage formality of his speech didn't make much sense—how could these be the effects of a simpleton's watching TV? But Sellers did create a solemnly dull character: a baffled, easily hurt, wanting-to-please moron. Pupkin is a nothing.

De Niro's performance—from the Nobody's-Home school of acting—is of a piece with Scorsese's whole conception of the film. *The King of Comedy* could have developed an emotional charge if we were pulled inside Rupert Pupkin and felt that we shared the envy and craziness of this pesky fool—if we, too, began to feel that Jerry Langford the star owed us something. But Pupkin, in his loud synthetics, and with a hideous haircut (an imitation of Langford's hideous haircut), inspires no empathy. We don't feel any anxiety for him even when he performs his act, and we're not meant to. He is presented as a man who cares for no one. He crashes Langford's country mansion, accompanied by a beautiful black woman, Rita (Diahnne Abbott), who was a cheerleader when he knew her in high school and is now a bartender; he has told her that they are invited for the weekend, and he probably isn't just trying to impress her—he's probably hoping that she'll wow Langford and it will help him win acceptance. (Rupert doesn't understand that Langford isn't given to partying on weekends.) When he and Rita are ordered out, he's totally indifferent to the humiliation she experiences. She's furious at herself for having trusted Rupert when she knew better, and she tries to explain to Langford, but he's too pigheaded and incensed to respond to her need to dissociate herself from Rupert's scheme, and Rupert, eager to get in solid with Langford, brushes her off as if he barely knew her. Everybody comes off horribly in this sequence, Rita included—she gets even with Langford by stealing a small, perhaps valuable box from a table.

The minds behind this picture come off the worst. They've set it all up for us: the cheerleader with no cheer left in her life; Langford, a relaxed, clear-faced child in a photograph displayed among his mementos but now puffy and implacable; and Rupert, annoyed with them both, because his attempt at pimping fails. I hate most that detail of the petty theft: this movie reduces everybody to crud. It's almost as if Rita were being punished for looking so smashing in the pale-peach-colored gown she bought specially for this big weekend; the possibility that our feelings might be engaged—that we might think we were at an ordinary movie—has to be stepped on.

Except for Diahnne Abbott's scenes, and a bit of pathos when the screaming gargoyle Masha sees her dream man leaving her and for a minute the camera relents and lets her be soft and attractive, the only emotions that come across are Langford's meanness and his contempt for Pupkin. Jerry Lewis is the only real thing here; his performance has the weight of authenticity—we can feel Langford's physical need for solitude. Lewis doesn't make an extra gesture in the entire film; Langford uses up so much energy when he's doing his show that he conserves himself by the economy of his off-camera movements. Even the sterility of his huge New York apartment serves a purpose for him: bare vistas, no one to be entertained. Out for a stroll in the city, he walks head first, sniffing the air; his body seems to dangle from that head. It's all pantomime, and it's the best scene in the movie—perhaps the only imaginative one—and it doesn't suffer from the visual chill of most of the interiors. When Langford is hounded by Pupkin, and when the sanctity of his mansion is violated, he glares at this cockroach Pupkin and he swells with impotent rage. There's something believable here: it's in Jerry Lewis's bullying face and his solid slab of a body—you feel he has reserves of rage to draw on. With a minimum of dialogue, Lewis lets us understand that Langford believes he earns his peace and isolation. Lewis doesn't try to make the off-camera Langford likable; the performance says that what the off-camera star feels is his own damn business.

Scorsese may believe that he has made a cautionary fable—that in telling us we're worse morons than Pupkin because we laugh at Pupkin's jokes he's doing us a service. A lot of people actually accepted the bit of pipsqueak irony in *Being There* as a serious warning, but that film had a deluxe, deep-toned prettiness, and it was clear; it didn't make people feel stranded the way *The King of Comedy* does. Scorsese must have decided to give us the creeps. The shots are held so long that we look for more in them than is there. Langford's apartment, his offices, with their long corridors, and most of the other settings seem designed to death, because almost nothing happens in them, and their few inhabitants don't look at ease or in the right place; even Shelley Hack, who is cool and smooth as an efficient secretary, walks across an office reception area as if it were something she was called upon to do just once an eon.

In interviews that have been printed recently, Scorsese talks about his own shift in identifications—how he has gone from being a Pupkin to being a Langford. He appears to be playing the latest director (and sometimes star) game of discussing each new movie as if it had come out of his loins. No doubt he believes what he's saying—at least, while he's saying it—but the script of *The King of Comedy*, by Paul Zimmerman, isn't about a person of talent who's driven to find the expressive forms he needs or about an artist trying to gain a foothold. It's about a devious, unfeeling nerd with a stale, jokebook mentality—the kind of fan who thinks he should be in the star's place.

In an inchoate, under-the-surface way, the material (which Zimmerman wrote in the early seventies) is affected by an offscreen presence: John W. Hinckley, Jr. The story has a basic, generic resemblance to *Taxi Driver*. I don't think there is any great mystery about Hinckley's fixation on that movie: the character of the assassin Travis Bickle in *Taxi Driver* was partly modelled on Arthur Bremer, the diarist who shot Governor George Wallace, and it may be a modern anomic archetype. But, having struck a nerve once, Scorsese may have squirmed when he realized he might hit another one, because he seems to have backed away.

This director, whose specialty (except for *Raging Bull*) has always been getting inside his characters' manias and making us know from the inside how they felt, stays on the outside this time. The Scorsese whom we expect to love junk culture—who used it rapturously in *Mean Streets* and *Taxi Driver* and parts of *New York, New York*—is suddenly crucifying people for their bad taste. The camera fixes on Rupert's cheap clothes and mad Masha's distorted expressions with the punishing scorn of a John Schlesinger. The pop music that Scorsese used to get us drunk on has been replaced by post-industrial-malaise music—the Muzak in elevators and offices which we're hardly conscious of. Except for the opening song, "Come Rain or Come Shine," which has a nostalgic quality here—it recalls a time when there were idealistic heroes and heroines in movies, a time when there was the promise of sexual fulfillment—the music is just neutral stuff in the background.

The King of Comedy is a chore to watch, but it's much buggier and more worrying than most dead films, because its deadness must be intentional. I don't believe that Scorsese's identification has shifted to the Langford-Vegas axis, but something has gone sour. You can feel it in the mistiming. He designs his own form of alienation in this movie—it seems to teeter between jokiness and hate. The forward-looking, energetic young lovers who used to be at the center of movies are sometimes replaced now by confused, desperate characters; Scorsese replaces them with characters who are pitifully incapable of sustaining our interest, and that leaves a vacancy. Like Coppola in *One from the Heart*, Scorsese puts "little people" who are mountains of clichés at the center, and then italicizes everything around them. He does it in a style that's so domineering it's screwy. When Rupert and his old high-school cheerleader sit in an almost empty Chinese restaurant, a man sitting alone behind Rupert imitates his ridiculous hand-waving gestures; the scene comes across as a joke on conventional-movie background shots. When Rupert fantasizes being a star and sitting at a table in Sardi's with Langford, a caricaturist is seen drawing them both. Everything that happens seems to be mimicked or repeated elsewhere in a different form, and the effect is to robotize people. Rita's lifting the box from Langford's table is prefigured by a roll of microfilm being snitched from a purse in a scene from *Pickup on South Street* that is glimpsed on one of the three TV screens in Langford's apartment.

As often as possible, Scorsese creates little pockets in the frame and slips in talismanic, souvenir effects. People associated with Scorsese—agents, friends, family—are placed in strategic spots or turn up as life-size cardboard cutouts. They're Scorsese's own version of the photographs that Langford keeps around to document his life. And Scorsese has had so much press coverage that some people in the audience catch the personal references, and they may even laugh. But these details (which are probably full of meaning for Scorsese) don't really have any meaning in the picture. With an audience that's squirming, wanting something to respond to, Scorsese can get a few laughs from the comic rhythm of repetition: an office receptionist looks up at Pupkin at intervals, always in exactly the same way—another reminder of old, conventional-movie techniques. And when the director, who frequently keeps us staring at the austere, neo–Art Deco functionalism of Langford's office, places a camera on an empty doorway, Rupert soon comes rushing out, followed by two security men who are trying to eject him; it's a basic comedy chase. In this sequence, a storyboard strip can be seen hanging from an office wall. Maybe Scorsese needs to play tricks of style to fuel his interest in this movie. Maybe, having got into a project that was wrong for him, he started manufacturing little inflatable pool toys: floating bars of soap, swim fins— anything to distract him. But there isn't an ounce of fun in his playfulness.

And though the film turns indecisive and fumbling toward the end, there's no getting around it: the ironic little punch built into the material requires that Rupert Pupkin achieve fame and fortune as a result of kidnapping Langford. The movie would have no point at all without that. *The King of Comedy* is the tale of a no one who becomes a someone who is still really a no one. This film despises its own protagonist and the culture that produced him. There's no aesthetic rule that says an artist has to like his characters, or his culture, either; as John Osborne has demonstrated, an artist can bring both to life by the passion of his hatred. But Scorsese's hatred has no fire in it; what he's rubbing our noses in finally is a glaring emptiness, and it's his, not ours. Just in case we missed the film's subtext that even sex is dead, poor crazy Masha starts singing "You're going to love me . . . come rain or come shine" to the trussed-up, kidnapped Langford. Despite Scorsese's pulling away from the implications of the plot, it's pretty hard to watch this movie without, in the back of your mind, thinking of Johnny Carson and other celebrity performers, and of the loonies out there with their hawklike determination to get at the stars. You can't help thinking: *The King of Comedy* is a training film for pests, and worse.

•   •   •   •   •

*T*here were psychoanalysts en masse at the convention in *High Anxiety*, and there were sizable numbers of them in *Spellbound* and *The Cobweb* and other films set in sanitaria, but I doubt if there have ever been as many psychoanalyst characters in one movie as there are in the light, romantic comedy

Lovesick, which was written and directed by Marshall Brickman. Starting with the hero, played by Dudley Moore, and including such eminent analysts as Selma Diamond, Wallace Shawn (snappier here than usual), Alan King, Stefan Schnabel, Richard B. Shull, and John Huston, and the shade of a trim, urbane Sigmund Freud (Alec Guinness), they're an amusing crew, given to collecting professionally sanctified art—tiny African sculptures that suggest fertility. The story is perhaps too simple: Moore inherits a patient, a young playwright (Elizabeth McGovern), from an analyst friend (Shawn) who has fallen in love with her and died of guilt. Of course, Moore falls in love with her, too. Luckily, she has the opposite effect on him: she brings him to life. (This isn't hard to believe, because as the playwright the rosy-cheeked McGovern is like a walking announcement of spring; she's endearingly child-like—you can almost hear the whirring hum of her mind working.)

As he did in his first film as writer-director, the 1980 *Simon*, Brickman parodies the craziness of the highly educated and compulsively self-aware. His touch and his pacing are much more sure this time—he has a dapper, weird precision of tone that's funny. He knows how to tell jokes visually with deadpan timing, and he can write dry, shiny, casually funny dialogue. What (on the basis of these first two films) he can't do is provide a structure for a movie. He starts with a promising (if flimsy) situation and then wanders away from it, while the dramatic tension dribbles out. This may be partly because he doesn't bite off enough to chew for an hour and a half; in *Lovesick* the invention flags after the initial rush. He doesn't even give himself any subsidiary situations to cut away to, and this puts too much of a burden on Dudley Moore, who is always in danger as a performer, because he's so eager to oblige. Moore is too engaging here right from the start. The hero should be a Freudian pedant so the girl can humanize him. Moore is too familiar and likable to get away with playing a tight-faced prig, even if Brickman had set it up. Moore is very skillful, but Brickman may not have found the right, distinctive actor for his hero yet; Alan Arkin wasn't it in *Simon*, either. (Brickman may need someone who isn't an all-purpose comedian but will discover his comic resources when he starts delivering Brickman's lines.)

There's a comic sensibility in this movie, and it comes from Brickman's functioning as both writer and director. But two movies have gone limp on him; someone who isn't as emotionally committed to the material as he is can easily see the point at which the script starts falling apart. (It happens here when Moore and McGovern have a quarrel that pops up out of nowhere.) Brickman may come around to the idea that he could use a collaborator on the writing—someone with a tougher-minded instinct for plot development and perhaps something a little more vital on his mind. (On occasion, artists are freed to be themselves when they collaborate, as Brickman must have learned when he worked with Woody Allen on the scripts of *Sleeper*, *Annie Hall*, and *Manhattan*.) Brickman has his own comic grace; it's sustaining energy—and a subject—that he lacks.

But there is some good, trick casting—the painter Larry Rivers, his great-bird head held high, plays the painter whom Moore's wife leaves him for. And there are terrific bits: the analyst Shawn, holding the knife with which he's supposed to cut his birthday-party cake, is suddenly frozen by the associations in his mind; a hard-bitten interviewer at a Social Security office (that inspired comedienne Anne DeSalvo) is completely impervious to the stress she's putting on the raging paranoiac (David Strathairn) who's applying for help; a homosexual analysand (Kent Broadhurst) leaps to interpretations of his comatose doctor's silence; another patient (Gene Saks) lives in a state of perpetual crisis, while a wealthy woman (Renée Taylor) goes to an analyst because it helps fill her days. The plot also involves Ron Silver (who in *Best Friends* played a movie producer resembling Jon Peters) as a Hollywood star resembling Al Pacino—a star who comes back to the New York theatre to renew himself in the playwright McGovern's first opus. The twenty-one-year-old playwright from out of town is not only lucky enough to land a sumptuous apartment and have her first play produced by Joe Papp—she has the blissful good fortune to have a Lincoln Center theatre for rehearsals. This fantasy aspect of *Lovesick* is rather appealing; Brickman is attempting a modern fairy-tale version of a comedy of manners—a Lubitsch film for the eighties. What isn't appealing is the "niceness" in his approach—the tasteful sprightliness that keeps the movie from being about anything. Somebody as sharp as Marshall Brickman shouldn't try to make a virtue of innocuousness.

March 7, 1983

Night Life

*T*he Scottish comedy *Local Hero* is misleading in the most disarming way imaginable. Experience at the movies has led us to expect a whole series of clarifications, but they don't arrive. After a while, their non-arrival becomes a relief, and we may laugh at ourselves for having thought we needed them. The film also offers a special pleasure to those of us who grew up listening to the recording of Sir Harry Lauder singing "Roamin' in the Gloamin'." We finally have a chance to experience that Scottish form of entrancement when the gloaming—an opalescent twilight—is made visible to us; night is magical in this movie, as it should be. In the opening section, set in a Houston sky-scraper that houses the headquarters of Knox Oil, an ace mergers-and-acquisitions executive, Mac (Peter Riegert), is being sent to Scotland to buy Ferness, a fishing village on a bay which the conglomerate (headed by Burt Lancaster) has decided should be the site of a new refinery. It's a cheesy, coy opening, with poorly timed satirical gags, but there's a hint of something more subtle and original when Mac uses a phone to talk to someone who's only a glass partition away. And even before Mac reaches Ferness—when the tall Danny (Peter Capaldi), a young Scots employee of Knox, is driving him to the coast, and fog swirls around their car and causes them to hit a rabbit—the atmosphere, the tempo, everything changes. The two men, who spend the night in the fogbound car, seem becalmed. And by the time Mac and Danny (with the stunned rabbit in the back seat) reach the village, Mac, the fireball master of the telex, with a beeper watch and a briefcase that has a battery-powered lock, has internalized the fog. He's stunned, too; he has gone soft in the head.

The writer-director Bill Forsyth observes the people in the movie—and especially his young heroes—as if they were one-of-a-kind creatures in a peculiarly haphazard zoo. Riegert brought off some stoned double takes as the amiable, sponging friend of the hero in *Chilly Scenes of Winter*; here his role requires him to sustain one big, rapt double take for the whole picture. He's the butt of Forsyth's humor, and at the same time he's the person we empathize with. That may be part of the film's seductiveness, and it helps that Forsyth is rarely explicit about anything—the picture is like one of those lovely Elizabethan songs that are full of tra-la-la-la-la-las. Riegert's tranced-in Mac never formulates his infatuation with the villagers, the crescent of beach, the glistening bay, the starlight, and the good, dark beer; we see the effect it all has on him in his wistful, stupefied face. He's experiencing something new to him: happiness. And he doesn't know what to make of it—for Mac, happiness is indistinguishable from lunacy. Capaldi's Danny, who observes what's going on around them—that the practical-minded villagers are secretly holding meetings to discuss how they can get the highest prices out of Mac— doesn't intrude on Mac's preoccupation. Danny, with his child's head smiling from on top of his galumphing body, as if it weren't quite sure how it got up there, grabs his chances to go off and spend time in the bay with a marine biologist (Jenny Seagrove), who also works for Knox. Danny has a stiff, jerky walk; when he makes a getaway from Mac he hunches his shoulders, pulls his elbows in close to his body, and takes off at a run, his lower arms gyrating. He's like a big, floppy gooney-bird. The enticing biologist, who seems to live in the water, has a hint of iridescence about her; the possibility that she's a mermaid doesn't faze Danny any more than anything else in life does.

The other young hero—the most relaxed actor of a large, relaxed cast— is Denis Lawson, as Gordon, the village innkeeper, pub owner, accountant, unofficial mayor, and great lover. Lawson plays Gordon's functions as different aspects of his personality. Gordon the pub owner is a genial companion, but Gordon the innkeeper is brusque and formal: he will do exactly what is required of an innkeeper, and not a hairbreadth more. Gordon the accountant is a slippery fellow—he oozes insincerity. Gordon the leader of the community is frank and good-humored. And Gordon the man-of-the-world lover is smugly pleased with himself when he's alone with his bride (Jennifer Black). There's something of the dandy in Denis Lawson's approach to comedy; he makes each of Gordon's functions funny in a suavely different high style—each has its own tics and gestures, its own type of self-satisfaction. Dark and intense, he's an ideal screen actor—he draws the camera by the control inside his ease.

The exchanges among these three men are low-key and very odd, with Gordon handling the negotiations for the villagers and sizing up Mac, figuring out how far he can push him, and Danny taking sidelong glances at Mac and vaguely wondering if he's as out of it as he seems. (Danny is too giddy to give it a lot of thought.) The humor is dry, yet the picture is romantic in spirit, and Burt Lancaster has something to do with that. He doesn't have a large role, and he's at a disadvantage because most of his scenes are in crosscuts back to unenchanted Houston, but Lancaster is convincing as a sturdy, physically powerful man, and even more convincing as a man of authority whose only intimacy is with the stars above. In his penthouse office-apartment in the Knox skyscraper, this tycoon presses the button that opens the sliding dome of his planetarium and he stands under the constellations. Lancaster has an imperial romantic aura; he belongs there, on top of a tower under the stars, and I doubt if there are many actors who could convey so much by just standing there. The tycoon's telescope has an echo effect in moviegoers' memories: Lancaster was also devoted to astronomy in Visconti's *The Leopard*, and Forsyth may have carried that theme over. But there's something more deeply right about the image here. A stargazing reserve has become apparent in Lancaster's recent performances: it's as if he finally felt free enough to be himself on the screen—to let us see that he has thoughts he feels no need to communicate. The welcome familiarity of his speech rhythms tells us something: he, too, is one of a kind. There's nobody else in the world with a voice like that—the smoothness with the remnant of roughness underneath. Forsyth, by glorying in the plumage of each person's singularity, somehow makes one-of-a-kindness seem infinitely wonderful and absurd.

This young (thirty-five) writer-director has invented his own form of poetic comedy. His style is far more personal and aberrant than that of the popular British comedies of the fifties, which, in general, were made from tightly knit, cleverly constructed scripts. Forsyth seems to go where impulse and instinct guide him; he's an entertainer-filmmaker who gives free play to his own sense of the ridiculous and his own sense of beauty. He gets a lyrical performance from the silvery surf at night, and there are great happenings in the luminous skies—the aurora borealis and a whizzing meteor shower. The village and the bay live up to the dream-stricken expression on Mac's face. Mac has found paradise, and in a place where English is spoken—a transformed English, made softer and more lulling by cadences that drift upward.

Local Hero isn't any major achievement, but it has its own free-form shorthand for jokes, and it's true to itself. No conflict ever emerges in this film (though one is clearly seething inside Mac's head); nobody even throws a punch. Forsyth's understatement—his muting of effects—creates a delicately charged comic atmosphere. There are no payoffs to gags; you get used to some oddity and then it disappears. The humor is in people's idiosyncratic behavior, and once Forsyth gets into his stride everything is unexpected and nothing is forced. (The only thing that isn't distinctive about *Local Hero* is its prosaic title, which doesn't seem to refer to anyone in particular.) Sometimes Forsyth's ideas are close to quaint—as in the character of Victor (Christopher Rozycki), the captain of a Russian trawler, who is as robust as all getout. But Forsyth carries out even this idea in a way that redeems it—the Russian's accent is just what's needed at a Ferness celebration when he sings "Lone Star Man" with The Ace Tones, a group of adolescent local boys whose country rock has a slightly woozy cross-cultural sound. (One of the musicians is John Gordon Sinclair, who was the hero of Forsyth's last film, *Gregory's Girl*.) You may hear yourself laughing at jokes you can't really explain, such as Mac's unwitting violation of protocol: he's talking to a group of village men who hang out together, and, pointing to an infant in their midst, he asks "Whose baby?" Nobody answers.

In the scene that I like best, Mac, alone on the misty beach, takes off his watch, so that he can stick his hands into the water and scoop up shells. He puts it on some rocks and moves a small distance away. And the forgotten watch, inundated by the tide, beeps underwater to the sea creatures swimming by. That's an almost perfect example of how Forsyth handles the theme of the collision of cultures. It isn't the Scots who are offended by the American hotshot's business equipment; it's the fish.

．　　　．　　　．　　　．　　　．

*E*very once in a while, the highly accomplished Ben Gazzara gets a film role that he's itching to play and a director who's in love with that marvellous oily, enigmatic face of his. Gazzara is handsome yet guarded, like an armadillo. He could be a survivor of an ancient (and untrustworthy) race. As Charles Serking, the drunken, permanently hung-over, semi-famous poet in the Italian director Marco Ferreri's *Tales of Ordinary Madness*, he gets to cut loose and do things onscreen that he has never done before—that probably nobody has done onscreen before. Ferreri is known for carrying ideas to extremes (*The Ape Woman*, of 1964, *La Grande Bouffe*, of 1973, *The Last Woman*, of 1976), and his script is based on the stories and the spirit of the American poet and novelist Charles Bukowski, a master of rut who writes about the gutbucket pain and elation of being human. The specific story drawn on for this movie (made in English) is "The Most Beautiful Woman in Town," from the City Lights book *Erections, Ejaculations, Exhibitions and General Tales of Ordinary Madness*. The story is written in the first person, and that's who Gazzara is playing—his Serking is an interpretation of Bukowski.

Tales of Ordinary Madness isn't for people who are disturbed by four-letter words or sexual acts performed with lewd gusto. That should still leave quite a few of us. It's a startling movie, partly because it's so simply presented. Though it's about many of the same themes as an Ingmar Bergman picture, it isn't stark—it has the matter-of-fact, one-thing-after-another plainness of an Abbott and Costello movie. Serking, a skid-row scrounger with a gray beard and with seat-sprung pants hanging down from his shrunken body, swigs from a bottle in a brown paper bag and sniffs like a stray dog at a succession of fat, mean, and sleazy women. The sleazier they are, the more he likes them. He sees the brutish comedy in what he's doing, and that's part of why he does it. (At times, he's a lot like Mailer the grizzled challenger.) Between sexual bouts, he reads his poetry at a college, raises hell at a foundation that tries to treat him as an artist-genius, drinks until he pukes, and then drinks some more. The movie, with its artist-bum as hero, has a slight resemblance to the 1970 *Tropic of Cancer*, in which Rip Torn played Henry Miller, but this bum Serking is also a sufferer, and the picture is far more sexually explicit. It goes beyond raunchiness—it's naked. And the bare, functional filmmaking intensifies our awareness of what the coupling human beings on the screen are doing to each other—there's nothing else to look at. Visually, the film seems washed out at the start, and then it becomes brighter; sunlight seems to become one of Ferreri's themes. It isn't likely that anyone imagined that Joseph Strick, who directed *Tropic of Cancer*, shared Miller's excitement about women of any age or shape. Here you feel that Ferreri, who has his own wild man's understanding of comedy, has also got right down inside Bukowski's self-mocking lust and self-dramatizing temperament. Certainly Gazzara has felt his way in—his reptilian eyes shine with the mischief his role makes possible. They almost pop out in his scenes with Susan Tyrrell, as a loco who's perhaps the gamiest and funniest of the women he has bouts with. (She yells so violently during sex he has to cover her mouth.)

Except for side excursions to the college, to the foundation in New York, and to the ocean, the movie is set in Bukowski's old habitat, Los Angeles, where he has spent most of his life. (His books sell moderately well there and spectacularly well in Europe, especially in Germany, and he now lives a more stable and prosperous existence in San Pedro, California.) Serking's L.A. is mostly Hollywood at its crummiest—flophouses, rooming houses, cheaply built garden apartments, and bars where broken-down hookers hang out. It's in one of these bars that Serking meets Cass, "the most beautiful woman in town." Ornella Muti, who plays the role, fully lives up to the description; she's as lithe as a cat, and has the soft radiance of the young Hedy Lamarr in the coital scenes of *Ecstasy*. And Ferreri, who has worked with her before (in *The Last Woman*), lights her to perfection. (He appears to take more care with her scenes than with the rest of the film.) Ornella Muti's Cass is sloe-eyed, dark-haired, and high-waisted, with the long legs of a Balanchine dancer. Convent-bred, she's mysteriously, uncannily beautiful—a carnal Madonna who punishes herself by working as a prostitute. Cass, whose beauty would open any doors, picks up men in the cheapest sour-smelling dives. This degradation isn't enough: she mutilates her flesh. She's intelligent but crazy, and she has nothing binding her to life.

This beautiful woman, with her inverted narcissism—she costumes herself in dramatic, mood-fitting ensembles, with special attention to the neck she has sawed away at—is like a mad nun. Cass is a trite, preposterously overdramatic creation—a fallen angel with crosses dangling from her ears and a faraway look in her eyes—and yet something about her rings true. She has elements of every self-destructive Catholic girl I've ever known or heard of; her self-love and her self-hatred aren't just a made-up subject. And her ringing true helps to validate Serking's attitudinizing and his despair. Cass is a sex goddess, she's walking poetry—and Serking, who loves her, can't hang on to her. He gets her out into the sun, but he can't infuse his own love of life into her.

The early parts of this movie have a shocking comic power (and sometimes the comedy drains away and leaves a deliberately sad tawdriness), but the sequences don't have much impetus. After Cass's story takes shape, though, the picture develops its own kind of rhythm. And by the end Serking, whose pants are always about to fall down to his knees, begins to seem—well, valiant. He's resigned to failure, but he keeps trying—he wants to believe in the dream he had of a life with Cass. Meanwhile, there are all those Hollywood locos, and even a fresh young thing who asks him "Where does poetry come from?" That heartfelt question may call for a half grapefruit in the face, but the vain Serking, touched, responds very tenderly. After all, for him women hold the mystery of creation.

At the beginning of the movie, when Serking is speaking in a deep voice in an ornate, sparsely filled college auditorium, he says, "To do a dangerous thing with style is what I call art." It's a dangerous thing for Ferreri (who wrote the script with Sergio Amidei and Anthony Foutz) to use that line. Inevitably, it leads to thoughts of: Is *Tales of Ordinary Madness* art? A lot of skepticism wells up in me when poets go into their living-on-the-edge, deep-in-the-lower-depths boogie. From time to time, Serking does a voice-over narration, and it could be a parody of the tough-guy narration in the Raymond Chandler detective movies, with Serking on a quest for truth and beauty. He says things like, "the defeated, the demented, and the damned—they're the real people of the world, and I was proud to be in their company." Since the director doesn't appear to have the best grasp of how Americans talk, it's sometimes hard to tell whether this kind of flatulence is meant to be taken straight. Chances are it is, but it also fits the character Gazzara is playing. Ferreri uses his deadpan simplicity to bring out the infantilism of middle-aged macho clowns who know they're being infantile and getting high on excess but don't know how to grow up, and don't want to, anyway. There's genuine audacity and risk-taking in this movie. It may not have the energy of great art, but its nakedness has an aesthetic force. When you come out of the theatre, you know you've seen something; it wasn't just another picture.

The great thing about Marco Ferreri is that he gets to the point. In one image—Serking rams an enormously fat woman's crotch with his head—the film sums up what a number of Rabelaisian writers have struggled to say about their desire to go back to the womb. That image cuts through the fake profundities that the film falls for. And even when Gazzara is lamenting bourgeois stultification and crying out "Can't we awaken? Must we forever, dear friends, die in our sleep?" he knows that these are the words of a poseur. He makes Serking a big enough poseur to be a macho-clown artist.

·   ·   ·   ·   ·

La Nuit de Varennes, a creakingly cultured historical pageant set in the time of Louis XVI, is a French-Italian co-production and it was directed by Ettore Scola, but it's almost the essence of the Old Wave. Here they are: the worldly, no longer young, but very sensual women—the women so mature that a half smile is always playing on their faces (Hanna Schygulla as a countess who is lady-in-waiting to Marie Antoinette, and Andrea Ferreol as the wealthy, beautiful widow of a winegrower). And here they are: the civilized old libertines (Marcello Mastroianni as the exhausted Casanova, and Jean-Louis Barrault as the scandalously popular, often pornographic writer Restif de la Bretonne). There are also assorted historical and fictional personages (Harvey Keitel as Thomas Paine, Daniel Gelin as an arms manufacturer, and Jean-Claude Brialy as the countess's homosexual hairdresser). For diverse reasons, they're all travelling by carriage or stagecoach to Varennes. What makes the trip significant is that it's 1791, and the King, whose freedom has been curtailed since the Revolution in 1789, has fled with the Queen and is also on the road, in a coach ahead of them, hoping to make it to the border, so he can organize an army and return to fight the Revolution. (He failed, of course; he was arrested at Varennes.)

And what do the ladies and gentlemen who are trailing behind the King do in their carriages? They talk wisely and wittily about the great political issues of the day, and they talk and they talk, the royalist countess arguing with Tom Paine, and so on, while I, for one, sit there reading the subtitles, my eyes gradually glazing over. For two and a half hours, these people look knowingly at each other and talk literately. Once, after Casanova's carriage breaks down and he has been invited to join the others in the big coach, they all get out and walk for a bit in a forest—the grade is too steep for the horses to handle the load—and it's like a holiday for the audience. This interval is actually the high point of the proceedings, because one of the passengers is a jolly middle-aged touring opera singer (Laura Betti, who has a gift for playing eccentrics; a sense of fun bubbles up in her), and as this singer and Casanova walk up the grade together they sing an aria from *Don Giovanni*, the opera about a lover much like Casanova which Mozart composed just four years earlier—with a helping hand on the libretto from the paradigm himself, it is said. For a minute or two, the music and the playful doubling up of Casanova legends are a restorative. But then back to the coach and all that wit and wisdom. Scola is an accomplished, sometimes remarkable director, but he has got himself into an arch and soggy genre. At the end, when a dismaying, lesson-for-today twist is sprung, there were unmistakable let-me-out-of-here groans from the audience.

It's a pleasure to see Barrault, who (like Gielgud) looks stronger and more human now than he did in his hollow-cheeked youth. (His profile, which Scola calls attention to, is an achieved work of art.) But the role of Restif has been written to make him a darling old reprobate. In the opening sequences, we're tipped to smile at his naughtiness when he gets into bed with his adoring young daughter; this movie descends from a long line of "Gallic romps." Casanova has been made to seem the toweringly tall figure that he was, and Mastroianni, looking suitably ruined, and with his blotchy face pasty-white where he powders it, has at least one superb bit. Though impoverished and desperate (he faces arrest for debt), Casanova declines the offer of the widow, who, declaring herself passionately in love with him, wants him to come live on her estate. He declines gallantly and with supreme tact; then, as he leaves her, we see his eyes, and he looks hounded, as if he wanted to cry out, "Does she really think I could make love to her?" And Brialy, whose fussbudget hairdresser is almost a comic archetype of the snobbish priss, manages to give his character scintillating, stylized gestures—he flutters like a mechanical doll. But the hairdresser's attachment to the countess has more devotion and feeling in it than anything else in the movie, and it's too facile a ploy for Scola and his co-writer, Sergio Amidei, to have made this relationship the only model of reciprocal affection. Quel irony. It's on the same level as the countess's look of recognition when she sees the poor limping, decaying Casanova; it turns out he was her first love. Quel big news.

March 21, 1983

Saved!

---

*S*ay *Amen, Somebody* features Thomas A. Dorsey, an eighty-three-year-old hepcat whose long fingers always seem about to snap. His singing voice is soft but deep, and he appears to find the sounds that come out of him as wondrous as we do. (There's a kind of objectivity about Dr. Dorsey's view of himself and of everything else.) He's still bouncing to the jazz rhythms that he brought into black people's churches in the late twenties and early thirties—the Depression years—when he fused their profane and their sacred music and called the result gospel. Until then, Dr. Dorsey, the son of an itinerant revival-show preacher, was a blues composer and Ma Rainey's pianist and bandleader. But he felt a lack in the music: it didn't have the inspirational lift of spirituals. When he combined the forms, the strong beat made the lift more intense than it had ever been. For a few years, some of the black churches fought to keep gospel out, but its combination of rhythm and spirit was too powerful for them. This music born of the Depression (and of city life) was accepted by black people so readily and joyfully that most of us, I imagine, have grown up assuming that it came from way back.

A bantamweight, Dr. Dorsey flies with the beat as he conducts. (He is choral director emeritus of the Pilgrim Baptist Church in Chicago and also presides over the annual National Convention of Gospel Choirs and Choruses, which he founded in 1933.) Waving his arms, he's in orbit, the way the great grasshopper Stravinsky used to be when he conducted *his* jazzy music. You can see the roots of gospel when Dorsey performs; his gestures are full of show-business fervor. At times, he's a bit like George Burns when Burns gets going in a patter song, but he's as physically active as Burns is deadpan and fixed in place. Among the many songs Dorsey has composed is the majestic "Take My Hand, Precious Lord," and when he sings it he gives it a simplicity that seems to go right to the wellsprings of art. This old trouper—his lower lip is loose and distended from all the years of singing gospel—is still in the midst of things. Each time a gospel song is performed, it's newly created by the antiphonal interaction between the lead singers and the congregation. It's a call-and-response, dialogue music, and the spontaneous yea-saying interjections by the members of the unofficial chorus help to charge up the soloists. This pattern of mutual encouragement is hypnotic for all concerned; in the movie it carries over even to casual, at-home conversations. Dr. Dorsey has become so conditioned to being spurred on by black audiences that when he talks to the film crew and there's silence, he wants to bring them to life. "Say amen, somebody!" he calls out.

Gospel music keeps its singer-evangelists young, radiant, hearty. That's the unspoken message of *Say Amen, Somebody*. The women (of several generations) have troubles with their husbands and children; their families don't like their being off on tour so much. But the women have the slickest answer that any woman who felt the need to get out of the house could come up with: the Holy Spirit is in them—they're doing the Lord's work. When you watch Delois Barrett Campbell, the featured singer of the Barrett Sisters, who acts out her songs with her face and her hands, you can't help smiling at the plight of her minister husband, arguing forlornly that he'd like her to be there for *his* church—not gallivanting off to Europe to spread the glad tidings of salvation.

Now seventy-eight, Willie Mae Ford Smith, the matriarch of gospel (she's like a black Margaret Mead), got into it before the churches accepted it—the churchmen didn't want that "coonshine stuff," she says—and she has been touring most of her life. Her contralto voice is astonishingly firm and strong, but, of course, it may have been much larger once—we can't tell, because she didn't make her first recording until she was sixty-eight. (She has a loose lower lip, too, and remarkable low tones.) George T. Nierenberg, the young filmmaker, shows Mother Smith's middle-aged children talking about the effect her vocation has had on their lives, and a grown-up grandson condescends to her: he's not a chauvinist, he says—he just doesn't think it's right for women to be preachers. In one scene, Willie Mae Ford Smith disagrees with the way the eighty-seven-year-old Sallie Martin, a former singer and Dr. Dorsey's business manager, remembers events of a half century earlier. These elderly women are as smart as can be, but they obviously don't care for each other, and their thick wigs give them a disoriented, comic look; they're like bickering dolls in a Punch-and-Judy show. (Sallie Martin has a pendulous lower lip, too.)

The movie is never less than absorbing, but it doesn't develop in its second half. The three Barrett Sisters—dramatic, physically striking women with ample figures in shiny, clinging blue gowns—sing so exhilaratingly that they create a problem. Nierenberg (who is known for his earlier documentary *No Maps on My Taps*) isn't making a concert film; he's doing something rather more difficult—he's documenting the lives of the pioneers of gospel music. Yet the film reaches an emotional pitch when we hear the Barrett Sisters singing, and, much as we may enjoy the pioneers' reminiscences and be amused by the griping of their families, we feel let down when we get more and more talk and only snatches of song. (There may be a little too much of a good thing with Mother Smith.) So much emotion builds up when we listen to the triumphantly alive Barretts that we expect more full-scale numbers. We want to go on soaring, and though there are appearances by the O'Neal twin brothers and by a sensationally attractive young St. Louis singer, Zella Jackson Price (she looks better than she sounds), the film pulls us back to history and human-interest sociology.

Members of the congregations on the screen often react to the ecstatic singing with smiles of happiness and coursing tears. And I gather that people in theatre audiences are doing the same thing. It's a profoundly joyous craziness, this gospel music. The low range that both the men and the women seem to develop has a special, heartbreaking tonality. (There's a brief clip of Mahalia Jackson, whose deep contralto clears your head of any small thoughts.) And the high range of the Barrett Sisters has a piercing, shrieking beauty that's very different from the emotional qualities of other kinds of soprano singing. I know it can be said that the greatness of this music is in its earthiness—that the singers acknowledge their sensuality, that the music is both sexual and spiritual. But there is something more frightening in gospel. Just once, for a few frames, we see Delois Barrett Campbell's immaculately groomed Reverend husband carried away: he could be having a seizure, and he suddenly talks "in tongues." It's only at the very end of the film that, under the closing titles, we glimpse others in violent spasms.

Nierenberg has a very clean act. He recoils from the natural shape of the material. What isn't acknowledged in the movie is that most of what we see and hear is the buildup to these scary communal fits—the convulsive writhing and muttering of religious possession. The parishioners come in dressed in their respectable Sunday outfits. There are strict regulations about what can be worn; they have to look proper—in order to go nuts. It's easy to make fun of those stuffy church leaders of the past who wanted to keep their hymns draggy and their spirituals pure, who didn't want the sexy rhythms and beat of ragtime and jazz and blues brought into the church. But they may have recognized that for a lot of people rhythmic excitement and spiritual uplift make an overpoweringly pleasurable combination, and that their exuberance leads to something uncontrollable and orgiastic. For many people, that's what the singing is *for*. It works them up to be "saved"—to get out of themselves, to have a seizure. I wish that Nierenberg had constructed this movie so that the music built to the climax that Sundays in these churches actually build to, and hadn't protected us by nipping things off. He's a very sensitive and talented documentarian, and this is a lovely piece of work, but he's too genteel for his subject.

. . . . .

At twenty-two, Sean Penn can get by with playing Mick O'Brien, the sixteen-year-old hero of *Bad Boys*. He's probably the best actor in American movies who is still young enough to play adolescents. Penn made his film début in 1981 as the overwrought cadet's levelheaded roommate in *Taps*, then played the friendly surfer-doper in *Fast Times at Ridgemont High*. He's the star of *Bad Boys*, and he holds the picture together. He gets so far inside a role that he can make even a sociological confection such as this hero, Mick—a proud, tough juvenile delinquent who commits crude, reckless crimes—someone an audience can care about. Each time, Penn comes as a complete surprise; so far, there's no residuum that carries from role to role. He's small and pale, and in *Taps* he caught viewers' eyes by the understanding in his face as he witnessed his roommate's galloping neurosis and tried to get through to him. As Spicoli, in *Ridgemont High*, he walked lurching from side to side, like a rooster; Spicoli couldn't spring on the balls of his feet, the way Mick does. As Spicoli, Penn widened his eyes and lifted his face up; that gave him a look of stoned surprise and made his head seem squarish. There isn't so much as a trace of that goggle-eyed expression of pleased incredulity in Mick's wary, squinting look. When Mick gets bad news—and he gets lots of it—he doesn't set his jaw, he lets it drop. His face sobers, becomes longer, more handsome, and more adult. Mick's auburn hair, which he wears down to the middle of his neck, Pre-Raphaelite length, emphasizes his pallor. It's a sad, reticent face.

The script of *Bad Boys*, by Richard DiLello (from an idea by the producer, Robert Solo), doesn't grant the character much in the way of humor or interaction with other kids on the streets or in the reformatory to which he's sent. Penn is given so little to work with that it's practically a pantomime performance: he holds us by the depth of Mick's grief over the way things have worked out in his life. He sits in his cell—hypersensitive, intelligent, and bitter. There's unextinguishable blazing energy in that face—it may be part resentment, but there's nothing mean or petty about it. Mick knows that he has made a mess of his life; he doesn't try to blame anyone else.

Mick is emotionally isolated from everyone in the world except his teen-age girlfriend (and lover), J.C., played by Ally Sheedy, with whom he's completely trusting. Then he's locked up in the grimy, hellishly noisy reformatory and has no one—except us. Penn draws us into Mick's isolation. Brando and James Dean drew us in, too, but not as simply as Penn does it. His body is often quite still when his face is at its most revealing, and though he has moments of strutting there are no big flourishes. He's not wound up, like James Dean; he's not crouched over his center. This is one of the least mannered magnetic performances I can recall. Penn's acting is open and fluid—we enter directly into the intense melancholy that Mick feels at being separated from J.C. When he's about to be attacked and he thinks he has got to kill or be killed, he burns her photograph, and his eyes mourn her.

Bad Boys is about how Mick gets out of the trap he's in, and possibly even without any hunks in the cast it will attract young audiences, because Mick and J.C. are as true to each other and as imperilled as Romeo and Juliet. But the only artistry in it is in Penn's performance. The film isn't stupid; it has been thought out by very bright people. But it's a singularly unimaginative j.d. movie—a *Pixote* spoils you for pictures like this. Directed by Rick Rosenthal, it's fairly proficiently made, in a brutal, realistic, neo-Warners style, with shock cuts, a pungent visual surface (using Chicago locations and Illinois correctional institutions), and Bill Conti's snazzy, aren't-you-lucky-I'm-here music, which gets anxious and excited for us, whipping itself into snits and furies. The suspense is of a very primitive kind: you know early that things are going to get worse, and you have a fascinated dread of what's coming. But even when episodes are powerful they're banal.

The moviemakers are so aware of the flimsiness of their contrivances that they keep preparing us, trying to convince us that the events are plausible. We're put in the position of watching tragedies being set up—which can make you want to hoot. It's so carefully explained why a little Puerto Rican boy is out on the street at night that, of course, we recognize he's really out there so he can get killed. There are relevant-to-nothing inserts of J.C. all by herself on deserted streets, so we won't ask what she's doing out alone in a dangerous spot on the night that she is raped. When a Puerto Rican gang leader (the older brother of the dead boy) is sent to the same correctional facility as Mick, who had inadvertently killed the child, we are assured that the authorities know that the Puerto Rican—Paco (Esai Morales)—has sworn vengeance against Mick, and that they are planning to transfer him as soon as there's an opening in another institution. And when the transfer comes through, it's not immediate, of course—it's for the next day, so we know that Paco has to make his move that night. Each time something horrible happens in this movie, it could almost be a relief, because we've been primed for so long. If it isn't, it's because the violent scenes go on and on. No doubt the director believes that these scenes are morally justified, because the picture comes out so strongly against brutality, but they're not aesthetically justified—he has no talent for violence. They're low-grade moviemaking, and they slow the picture down.

The film's one attempt at a comic-relief character is the brainy little Jewish sociopath Horowitz, Mick's cellmate. Eric Gurry, the boy comic who played Al Pacino's son in *Author! Author!* as if the kid had been tutored in Las Vegas, has some of the same whorish facility here, but he does have a few scenes in which he breaks through to something boyish and genuinely funny. When a vicious bully is injured by a bomb that Horowitz has made in the cell, the authorities assume that Mick was in on the scheme. Horowitz has a proud, sweet smile when he says he made the bomb by himself; it's not that he's being honorable and taking the heat off Mick—it's that he wants the full credit. The other performers offer few surprises. That includes Ally Sheedy. The moviemakers have given Mick an adult's idea of a fine girl—no makeup, no rebelliousness, no punkish attitudes. J.C. is a clean-cut, natural-looking Juliet with immaculate middle-class speech and mid-calf skirts who just happens to be completely and openly in love with this young thug, and he's in love with her honor-roll qualities. J.C. is like the true-blue girls that the G.I.s in Second World War movies were going to come home to. Most of her scenes are set to sweet, tasteful semi-classical music. Mick can't fail to become an upstanding citizen. He has got the love of a good woman, junior division.

April 4, 1983

Gents and Hicks

*T*he Swedes must have their own terms for the suppressed hysteria and the male obsession with proving oneself by great, daring achievements which we associate with Victorianism. In Jan Troell's *The Flight of the Eagle*, an account of the 1897 North Pole expedition by balloon undertaken by the Swedish engineer S. A. Andrée and two colleagues, Andrée himself (played by Max von Sydow) is a classic case of raging fears hidden under a stoic, "manly" exterior. Andrée has brushed aside the judgments of experts that such a trip can only fail and has convinced the press and the public that he is an intrepid hero and the big, ballyhooed adventure a matter of national honor. He has raised money for the gigantic balloon—christened the Eagle—from the richest men in Sweden (including King Oscar II and Alfred Nobel). His only setback has been a humiliating postponement of the flight, first scheduled for 1896, because the winds weren't favorable. So in July of 1897, when weather conditions aren't really favorable, either, but don't seem too bad, the balloon house is torn down and the three pitifully inexperienced aeronauts go up.

The lift-off is a calamity. The Eagle—over a hundred feet high, with a hundred and sixty-nine thousand cubic feet of hydrogen—rises, then starts to fall into the ocean. Andrée orders ballast thrown overboard, and the balloon rises again, but in the confusion all three guide ropes are lost, and he and the other two men know that they will now have no way to control the thing. They will drift, at the mercy of the winds. They could save themselves, call off the expedition, and face the jeers of the well-wishers and journalists who have been celebrating the great occasion and are still waving, down below. But Andrée's fear of losing face is much stronger than his fear of losing his life, or his sense of responsibility for the other men's lives. The moment to admit failure passes, and the balloon floats northward. In a few days, it's heavily encrusted with ice and snow, and despite the struggles of the men, who throw out their provisions and manage to stay aloft for sixty-six hours, the winds force them down. The Eagle collapses on an ice floe five hundred miles from the Pole and about two hundred miles from land. Beached in the Arctic desolation, the amorphous, still partly swollen balloon looks like something horrible that has crept up from the sea and died.

Andrée's fantasy had already been deflated, in the chaos of the lift-off, when the other two men realized that he didn't know what he was doing—he had actually been up in balloons only a few times and never for more than three and a half hours. Even before they fall, all three of them recognize that they don't stand much chance of making it back. But—and this is certainly part of the Victorian spirit—Andrée never allows himself to appear discouraged. If he can't achieve the glory of planting the Swedish flag at the Pole, he may still make some scientific contributions. The others calculate the direction of the nearest land; they hope to go south. But Andrée decides that the group should head toward an unexplored region in the east.

They trudge over the shifting ice floes for almost three months, getting nowhere. Andrée, absorbed in his cataloguing of data, seems more than a little mad. He keeps scrupulous records of the thickness of the ice, the temperature of the air, and everything they see—even the hardships that they finally succumb to. In 1930, when the bodies of Andrée and his companions were found, his records were intact, preserved in his clothing where he had carefully stored them, and the negatives of the photographs taken were also re-covered. Thirty-four of them turned out to be of good quality, and many of these can be seen in the movie. Periodically, the action is transformed into a black-and-white still; the effect is of a memento mori, and it helps to give *The Flight of the Eagle* a disturbing visual texture—a poignancy that goes beyond that of the usual epic film. We seem to be both inside this expedition, watching the interactions of the three men, and outside it, seeing it as something in the past. As the film goes on, its color palette contracts: warm colors disappear, and we are left with the glittering white of packed snow, the blue-white of snow casting shadows on itself (like eggs in a carton), and silvery grays, charcoal grays, dull, icy grays. When the men rip open a polar bear, its red flesh is a visual shock; the film has been turning into the black and gray and white of the photographs.

Jan Troell is both cinematographer and director here, as he was on his two-part epic *The Emigrants* and *The New Land*, and is also, once again, the film editor and one of the collaborators on the script. (It's based on the 1967 book by Per Olof Sundman.) Troell goes right at his subject. He doesn't pamper the audience, and his actors don't stand out in a theatrical way. There's no coyness, no ingratiation, and none of the usual dramatic devices to alert us that big things are happening up there on the screen. There's no pressure, either. *The Flight of the Eagle* develops its own momentum.

Andrée's determination to make something extraordinary of his life is treated without romanticism, but is given its due. Von Sydow seems to get into a realm of almost mystic creativity, and he's scarily convincing; as he plays Andrée, we grasp why this man can't ever do the sensible thing to save his hide, and why he can't acknowledge his fears. Courage, gallantry, will power, and self-control mean far more to him than the physical passion of his mistress does. Andrée never sacrifices his unquestioned authority as the leader of the expedition. He doesn't lose his air of inquiry or his formality when he and the others are eating raw polar bear. (He isn't shaken until a polar bear gnaws on human flesh.) When he writes in his log that everything is fine, he's doing what he believes is an explorer's duty: to be hopeful, no matter what. He's a man of another century, and in some ways he seems remote from us even when we feel his pain and when we feel we see right through him. His two partners have more of a capacity for enjoying themselves, but initially, at least, they share his crazed vision. Nils Strindberg (Göran Stangertz), a gentle young physicist who loves music and his pianist fiancée, leaves her and the other good things on land to sail in the clouds (and fall through the ice). And the huge, burly Knut Fraenkel (Sverre Anker Ousdal), who is Andrée's spiritual adversary during the whole ordeal—a funny roughneck with an ironic twist to his hostility—blinds himself to the insanity of the expedition until it's too late. All three breathe the spirit of the age. Gentlemen of their time, they're interested in science and technology and the arts; they're eager to know whatever there is to be learned. At the last of the send-off parties given for these amateur aeronauts, Andrée dances with Lachambre (Clément Harari), the roly-poly, bearded little Frenchman who manufactured the Eagle, and who has dressed himself up as Mother Balloon. In costume or out, Lachambre is like a dreaming child who has turned into Kris Kringle. It's the age of Jules Verne.

Troell brings these characters from another time so close that by the end they're like possibilities inside us. And the big, black balloon, which represents so much folly and hope, is itself a character. At the beginning of the film, with the titles, we hear a restrained, percussive sound, premonitory and chilling; later, it's mixed with the sprightly tunes at the parties. It could almost be the voice of the monstrous dark blob on the ice—the warning that the three Victorians don't listen to. Troell's moviemaking here is a one-of-a-kind mixture of stolidity and lyricism, with a touch of the uncanny. The film is steady and evenly paced, whether it shows the men exercising to strengthen their bodies for the trip or posing as they are reproduced in wax for posterity. Andrée takes a replica of his head to his mother—presumably to comfort her in his absence or to remember him by if he doesn't return. This leader of men, with his gaunt dignity, and his pale-blond eyelashes and soft, carrot-blond hair, is at his most anxious and uncertain with his mother. When she objects to the beard on the replica, he explains that polar explorers need beards for warmth, but one by one he carefully pulls the whiskers out of the wax face, so she won't be distressed by them. The film shows us Nils Strindberg suffering in the cold and desperately ill on his birthday, and the other two trying to cheer him up with a gift: a tiny packet of candies. (Fraenkel says, "With true altruism, we only licked half of them.") Strindberg, who has the friendliest nature of the three, is physically the weakest; when the misery is too much for him he seems to begin living in the past—or an imagined future—with his fiancée. In the icy wastes, when the men think of erotic and happier times, the flashback fantasies are unnaturally bright and luminous and almost stiff—as if the men's memories were freezing, too. When Fraenkel and Strindberg do a festive little dance to celebrate the sick joke that the ice floes have changed direction so many times that Andrée has been leading them south without knowing it, the scene suggests the world of Beckett. Loneliness and suffering burn out both Fraenkel's and Strindberg's hopes, but Andrée, like those madmen in literature who go on classifying specimens when their world has fallen apart, keeps making the meticulous entries in his journals that will, long after his death, bring him the acclaim he sought: S. A. Andrée has become one of Sweden's national heroes—a great, mythic figure.

Troell's straightforward methods aren't novelistic; they're almost the opposite of the Masterpiece Theatre techniques. As a cinematographer-writer-director, he has a unity of image and idea which has rarely been attained since the silent era. He does what young film enthusiasts dream of doing—uses film as a painter uses paint, a writer uses pencil and paper. But *The Flight of the Eagle* gives you the feeling that you've got into a beautiful, whopping big book and are opening your mind and imagination to what it presents. When the balloon falls, the movie takes off, and it has the emotionally devastating effect of a great novel. There's a heft to Troell's sensibility. His landscapes are palpable, and the people in them are part of a magnificent visual sensuousness. He doesn't try to subdue nature; he accepts the rawness and the austerity along with the vernal lushness. In *The Treasure of Sierra Madre*, we saw the developing personalities of three men; here we see three men gradually bleached of their differences. In their last days, they're all in such terrible shape that they turn into joking pals. Toward the end, it's as if they shared one memory and had become one person. The final, reconciliation scene between Fraenkel and Andrée is, in its way, peerless. When Fraenkel has been mauled by a polar bear and is dying, Andrée pleads with him, "You can't go now. . . . You've got to stay with me." Fraenkel whispers "I'm sorry" with his last breath. Then Andrée lays him out in the pink silk scarf and the white gloves that Fraenkel had brought with him for the victory celebration when they were all going to be presented to the Czar. The movie earns the emotions that it brings forth. Troell doesn't tell you what happens; in his attentive way, he makes it happen right in front of you. These Victorians turn into modern man.

·   ·   ·   ·   ·

*I*n *Tender Mercies*, Robert Duvall, as Mac Sledge, a legendary country-and-Western singer and song-writer who has become an alcoholic wreck, begins to recover through the kindness of Rosa Lee (Tess Harper), the young widow of a soldier killed in Vietnam. She lets him stay at her motel and gas station on the desolate Texas prairie, and he does handyman jobs to pay for his keep, but they haven't actually exchanged much more than a few yups and nopes when, about half an hour into the picture, he says, "I guess it's no secret how I feel about you. A blind man could see that." Which is quite a surprise, because nobody could see it. There hasn't been the slightest interplay between them—not so much as a soft expression or a good hot look. And I'm afraid that I was further confused because Rosa Lee has been so blank-faced and terse that I'd thought she was meant to be—well, simple, dim-witted. So it took me a while to get into the film's conception and realize that in this scheme of things simple meant deep, and that this woman of few words is supposed to represent frontier-woman steadfastness and true, enduring values. She's patience, normality, perfection. (What she isn't is a character.) Once I got it straight, I knew how I was supposed to react to her faint smile of gratification as she watches Mac—now her husband—getting himself dunked, along with her nine-year-old son, in the baptismal tank at her church. Mac is born again. Being with Rosa Lee and the boy has healed him. And he ends her loneliness, and provides the boy with the father he never had. (Mac's conversion, like his falling in love, takes place off camera; that could be one of the mercies referred to in the title.)

It used to happen that you paid to see a movie and you got back your weight in homilies. A lot of people must miss this; tired of the new junk, they want the old junk—like the stuff they used to get from the alleged Golden Age of Television. Audiences appear to be deeply moved by this barebones picture, which is said to be honest and about real people. Duvall's Mac is pure, wrinkled granite; he's such a recessive personality that the few seconds of emotion he lets come through seem to convince some viewers that they're seeing great acting. But it may be that Duvall puts too much emphasis on the integrity (i.e., the shell) of the character: his integrity as a performer means that we lose out. For example, I think he needed to give more to the scene in which Sue Anne, his eighteen-year-old daughter by his first marriage (to a high-powered country-music star), comes to see him, hoping for the understanding she doesn't get from her mother. Sue Anne is played by Ellen Barkin, whose few scenes are the high points of the movie. She has something rare in a young actress: power. And she has a great face for acting—her eyes are about a mile apart. Her lines aren't any more expressive than the rest of what the scriptwriter, Horton Foote, master of arid realism, provides, but she makes you feel Sue Anne's messy hopes so acutely that when this girl asks her father if he remembers a song he used to sing to her and he stands there, impassive, it's bewildering. After she leaves, he recites the lyrics of the song so we'll know he remembers everything, and that he is—in the language of this movie—hurting. I don't understand why he couldn't have given her a sign of acknowledgment that he remembered—he can see that she needs it. Duvall appears to operate on the premise that the less Mac Sledge shows the more he feels. (I've never seen a star performance so dependent on a squint; Mac's T-shirts should read "Life Makes Me Wince.")

I kept waiting for *Tender Mercies* to get started—to get into something. I was still waiting when it was over and I was back out on the street. The Australian director Bruce Beresford, who makes his American début with this inspirational film, has shot it in bright sunshine out in the middle of nowhere; the motel–gas station is as isolated as the mansion in *Giant*. (It's a mystery how Rosa Lee ever expected to make a living from it.) I was grateful when a van pulled up and several local young men—musicians—piled out; they've come to pay their respects to Mac, and though they seem like the kind of guys who can spit watermelon seeds real far, they serve to populate the screen and provide a few minutes of affability. And it helps to see Betty Buckley, who stirs things up a bit in her role as Dixie—Mac's first wife, the red-haired singer whom he had brutalized in the days when he was a mean drunk. Onstage, Betty Buckley's Dixie is a brassy trouper—a hardworking second-rater; too bad that offstage she has lines like the complaint about her daughter: "I gave her everything in the world she ever wanted." (I didn't make that up, but then neither did Horton Foote.) Mostly the picture consists of silences; long shots of the bleak, flat land, showing the horizon line (that, too, gives a film integrity); and Duvall's determination to make you see that he's keeping his emotions to himself, and Tess Harper staring out of her corn-flower-blue headlights. These two have matching deep-sunk eyes; the theme song—which Duvall sings in a dry, unmusical voice—is called "It Hurts to Face Reality." *Tender Mercies* is proof that a movie doesn't have to be long to be ponderous.

May 16, 1983

Fun Machines

Some of the trick effects might seem miraculous if the imagery had any lustre, but *Return of the Jedi* is an impersonal and rather junky piece of moviemaking. There doesn't seem to be enough light, and the editing isn't crisp (particularly in the first third). *Jedi* features a tribe of potbellied woodland creatures, the furry, cuddly Ewoks, who suggest a cross between koala bears and puli dogs; the Ewoks help their friend Princess Leia (Carrie Fisher) by toddling about the forest bashing her enemies—one fiercely determined Ewok scrambles into an aircraft that looks like a kiddie car, and he becomes a daredevil ace. The sequence should be magical, because God only knows how all this was done, but the images are muddy and the slapstick is repetitive. The forest is unenchanted and, like the other settings, in the desert, all too earthly. And though we want to be able to remember this glade full of raffish little Teddy bears, the effects are gruelling; they tend to cancel each other out. This is partly because of what has become recognizable as the George Lucas approach to fantasy: it's bam bam pow—he's like a slugger in the ring who has no variety and never lets up. This third film of the *Star Wars* trilogy (which, we are told, constitutes the middle section of a nine-film cycle) is, except for a slow beginning, paced like its predecessors and like *Raiders of the Lost Ark*, which Lucas also produced. But I think that the groaning exhaustion that had me sighing with relief when *Jedi* was finished can also be blamed on its British director, Richard Marquand (*Eye of the Needle*, the TV series "The Search for the Nile"). Every time there's a possibility of a dramatic climax, a chance to engage the audience emotionally with something awesome, Marquand trashes it—and not deliberately, as Richard Lester might, to show us that he's too hip for that, but out of what appears to be indifference yet may just be a weak visual imagination. Even the scene that should be the emotional peak of the whole mythic trilogy—the moment when the young protagonist, Luke Skywalker (Mark Hamill), removes the black visor and the helmet that have concealed Darth Vader's face—has no thrill. There isn't a gasp to be heard in the entire theatre. Luke looks into the eyes of his nightmare father, and he might be ordering a veggieburger.

In *The Empire Strikes Back*, when Han Solo (Harrison Ford) was frozen into sculpture—his face protruding from a bas-relief, the mouth open as if calling out in pain—the scene had a terrifying grandeur. Though *Empire*, released in 1980, didn't have the leaping, comic-book hedonism of the 1977 *Star Wars* and, as the middle, bridging film of the trilogy, was chained to an unresolved, cliffhanger plot, it was a vibrant, fairy-tale cliffhanger. The director, Irvin Kershner, brought the material a pop-Wagnerian amplitude; the characters showed more depth of feeling than they had in the first film, and the music—John Williams' variations on the *Star Wars* theme—seemed to saturate and enrich the intensely clear images. Scenes from that movie linger in the mind: the light playing on Darth Vader's gleaming surfaces as this metal man, who's like a giant armored insect, fills the screen; Han Solo saving Luke's life on the ice planet Hoth by slashing open a snow camel and warming him inside; Luke's hand being lopped off, and his seemingly endless fall through space; Chewbacca, the Wookie, yowling in grief or in comic fear, his sounds so hyper-human you couldn't help laughing at them; the big-eared green elf Yoda, with shining ancient eyes, who pontifically instructs Luke in how to grow up wise—Yoda looks like a wonton and talks like a fortune cookie. The effects in *Empire* appeared to be integral to the story and the characters; in *Jedi* the effects take over. Everything has lost its tone: when Leia finally frees Han Solo from his living death as sculpture, the scene has almost no emotional weight. It's as if Han Solo had locked himself in the garage, tapped on the door, and been let out.

Probably the most difficult thing facing the director of a fantasy that is dependent on mechanical effects is how to make the images flow. George Lucas couldn't do it when he directed *Star Wars*, but he kept the movie hopping, by cutting it into short, choppy scenes. Kershner is a master of visual flow, and, joining his own kinks and obsessions to Lucas's, he gave *Empire* a splendiferousness that may even have transcended what Lucas had in mind. Maybe because of the cascading imagery of *Empire* (which was almost as impassioned as John Boorman's *Excalibur*, and was also funny), Marquand's work looks especially klunky and drab. The characters seem to be robbed of their essences. Chewbacca's personality has drained away. The spark is gone from Yoda's eyes; the little green sage looks swollen and baggy—he has been given horrible fuzz all over, as if he were a peach—and the way he's lighted he isn't even green. Billy Dee Williams' Lando, the gambling man, has been made a general in the rebel forces; perhaps the high rank is meant to compensate for his being on the margins of the movie. (He checks in now and then to remind us of a war that's supposed to be going on somewhere.) Worse, the bravado is gone from Han Solo; this sad palooka is so callow he seems to have regressed. Leia, older and sleeker now, looks at him affectionately, like an indulgent mother who has learned to live with her son's dopeyness. The director doesn't appear to have any use for him: when Han Solo is freed from the block of stone, he's blind, and the picture doesn't even bother to emphasize the moment when he regains his sight. This must be the only movie ever made in which the romantic lead has his sight restored to him in an aside.

Leia herself has acquired more importance in the scheme of things, but in a rather unsatisfying way. We've been assuming that men become knights because of their valor, and Luke, striving to become a Jedi, has been tested over and over. Yet Leia becomes strong and wise—a fighter—because of her lineage. The scriptwriters (Lawrence Kasdan and Lucas) remove the trilogy's moral underpinnings when they tell us that you can become a Jedi knight, with the Force to do good, by heredity. (It's a very un-American notion.) Throughout *Jedi*, we can see that Luke is meant to be maturing and gaining wisdom, but, like Han Solo and Leia, he's colorless. In *Empire*, these three seemed capable of real exhilaration and real suffering. In *Jedi*, they're back to being comic-strip characters wandering through a jokey pastiche of the Arthurian legends.

The movie is openly silly, with obvious parody references to *The Wizard of Oz*, *The Adventures of Robin Hood*, *King Kong*, *Tarzan, the Ape Man*, and everything else, including itself. Some of the silliness is in the ingenious manner of L. Frank Baum, and it's wonderful: the Ewoks fighting off the Empire's soldiers by the strategies that Robin's men used in Sherwood Forest; the Ewoks taking the chatterbox C-3PO, in his gold-colored casing, for a god and putting him on a throne, whereupon he proceeds to draw upon his memory bank and tell them the story of everything that has happened in the three movies—he turns it all into bedtime stories for drowsy Teddy bears. (That's the most endearing idea in the trilogy; it's like something Mark Twain couldn't quite work into *A Connecticut Yankee in King Arthur's Court*.) A batch of new creatures turn up, and one of them, an ogre, Jabba the Hutt, might have come out of a woodcut by Tenniel: he has a walruslike body, a pyramidal head that merges with it, and—superb touch—the wrinkled eyelids of a dowager. And he has a tiny companion perched on him—a parrotlike monkey, or is it a winged Chihuahua? But most of the new critters—monsters that the epicene Jabba has gathered around him at his underground castle—haven't been given much semblance of life. Some, such as the minotaurs, are drooling, cartoon heavies in masks; many have opaque, shoe-button eyes or seem Muppety; others haven't waited to be adapted by toy manufacturers—they're stuffed animals to start with.

Although the dialogue of the first two films also alternated gee whizzes with flat exposition, I don't remember the construction being so bald a series of "Meanwhile, back at" episodes, and I don't recall broken promises, such as solemn pronouncements about Luke's "destiny" which turn out to be all wet. In this kind of movie, in which practically everything is foretold, shouldn't we be able to trust the prophecies that are intoned? Why else include them? And when Luke, dressed in a Hamlet getup, tells Darth Vader's master, the Emperor of the dark side—who's shrouded like Death in *The Seventh Seal*—"Soon we'll both be dead," it's gibberish, an embarrassment. This Emperor, who commands legions of Storm Troopers, is an embarrassment anyway. He's photographed too close in, so our time with him is spent staring at the variations in his makeup and the black liquid that the actor is sloshing around his teeth, trying for a ghastly look. There's also an oddly callous development. In one scene, Luke, bargaining with Jabba for Han Solo's life, casually offers the ogre a present: C-3PO and R2-D2. It's as if Dorothy offered the wicked witch a swap—the Cowardly Lion, the Scarecrow, and the Tin Woodman in exchange for Toto. Luke's apparent willingness to betray his loyal friends comes across as mean, even if he intends it only as a tactic.

Chances are that none of this will make any highly visible difference to the children who are clamoring to see the picture. *Empire* left kids dangling; this one has the payoffs. And Lucas may be on to something: that for children (and some adults) a movie that's actively, insistently exhausting can pass for entertainment. Lucas produces the busiest movies of all time; they're made on the assumption that the audience must be distracted every minute. *Return of the Jedi* is packed with torture scenes, and it bangs away at you; it makes you feel that you've seen it all before. I don't mean to suggest that Lucas intends to shortchange audiences; quite the reverse. He gives them a load of movie—so much that their expectations are rammed down their throats. But by now it's clear that his conception of a good show for kids is junky at heart. *Return of the Jedi* is a fun-machine movie. It's the new form of pulp, and when it's made on the scale of *Jedi* slovenliness is an inevitable part of it. A picture with as many special effects as *Jedi* costs a major fortune, and to make it so that the tricks are not just approximations of what was hoped for could double that cost. One answer might be to plan films with fewer tricks, better scripts, and directors who love to see the sparks that actors can give off. Lucas's answer is to pile on the effects—and, with the rumbling noises of things blowing up in Dolby, you're physically under bombardment. There's no blood in the killings in *Jedi*, but is killing without blood really preferable? The picture is indecently affectless: it ends with the triumph of the good guys and the grand celebration of a (bloodless) nuclear explosion—with no worry, no aftermath, no fallout.

The performers aren't encouraged to bring anything to their roles, and they become dispirited: their faces go slack. Denis Lawson, the jack-of-all-trades innkeeper of *Local Hero*, is one of the featured performers in *Jedi*, and you'd never know he was anything special; if the young Alec Guinness or Peter Sellers were in the role, you'd never know he was bursting with talent, either. (Returning to the role of Obi-Wan-Kenobi, even the elderly Guinness, with all his sly skill, barely makes an imprint on this picture.) The cast may be full of comic marvels who were never allowed to do anything but put on masks or sit behind a mockup of the controls of a bomber so that sound-effects wizards could fit the racket in. I can believe that kids will be excited by *Jedi*. They have lived their imaginative lives with the Star Wars characters for six years; each three-year wait has had to be filled with imagination, and so the characters have acquired depth. (Children may not have had such prolonged experiences with any other characters unless they've got into, say, the Oz books.) But I can't believe that *Jedi* will give kids any deep pleasure, because there's no quality of personal obsession in it, or even of devotion to craft. What a director like Richard Marquand does is take the fantasy out of fantasy.

It's one of the least amusing ironies of movie history that in the seventies, when the "personal" filmmakers seemed to be gaining acceptance, the thoughtful, quiet George Lucas made the quirkily mechanical *Star Wars*—a film so successful that it turned the whole industry around and put it on a retrograde course, where it's now joining forces with video-games manufacturers. If a filmmaker wants backing for a new project, there'd better be a video game in it. Producers are putting so much action and so little character or point into their movies that there's nothing for a viewer to latch on to. The battle between good and evil, which is the theme of just about every big fantasy adventure film, has become a flabby excuse for a lot of dumb tricks and noise. It has got to the point where some of us might be happy to see good and evil quit fighting and become friends.

· · · · ·

Blue Thunder is a better piece of visual design than most of the other new fun machines, and its night shots of Los Angeles might pass for *film noir* poetry if the picture didn't star a monster helicopter. This sumptuous test model, with the deceptively romantic name Blue Thunder, is lovingly photographed, but it's only a gadget. Still, it might give Roy Scheider a run for it in a personality contest. Scheider plays an L.A. police-officer pilot, and the battle between good and evil rages in the glaring, dirty looks he exchanges with Malcolm McDowell, as a racist Army colonel—he's one nasty pussycat. Apart from these skirmishes, the picture is all stunt work and atmosphere—there's electricity in the air, and the city has a psychedelic, futuristic quality, like Godard's Alphaville. The plot is no more than hints and eavesdroppings about a sinister right-wing conspiracy within the government—something opaque about secret plans to build more Blue Thunders to use in the cities for surveillance and against "armed insurrection," which seems to mean any rioting by blacks or Hispanics. Scheider is up against all this single-handed, except for his rookie co-pilot—Daniel Stern, who gives the only engaging performance in the film, with the exception of the late Warren Oates in a brief appearance as a scowling good-guy police captain. The scriptwriters (Dan O'Bannon and Don Jakoby) may be able to write concise dialogue, but they obviously don't do people. There are no characters, apart from whatever the performers can whip up. McDowell comes through with a bit of smart-alecky obnoxiousness; most of the other right-wingers are just stick figures. Scheider might be more fun if he could stop exuding so much decency, but he can act, and he has the wary, kinetic qualities the role requires. If he seems a stand-in rather than a star, it's because when Roy Scheider is imperilled, there just isn't much at stake.

The director, John Badham, does a clean, smooth, and very showy job—you can feel his justifiable pride in his finesse. The picture is solemnly, elegantly kicky, and, what with all the stunt flying and the hair-trigger editing (by Frank Morriss and Edward Abroms), this is the sort of action film that can make you feel sick with excitement. Though it isn't at all brutal, it tries for the high-powered suspense that made a huge box-office hit of *The French Connection*. Badham and his team may appear to have the skills to bring it off, but something is missing. This picture is *The French Connection* without Gene Hackman and without dope. It's all technique—suspense in a void. Working with the cinematographer John A. Alonzo, Badham provides the glamour for a romance or a musical comedy. You sit there admiring the dark-blue tropical-city nights and feeling your stomach tighten as the helicopter, pursued by police cars, Army planes, assorted missiles, and the mad-twit colonel, swoops down over the freeways full of cars and zigzags among the office buildings. But all you've got to think about is: How did the movie people get permits to fly so low?

May 30, 1983

Ingmar Bergman's Family Reunion

*I*ngmar Bergman's *Fanny and Alexander* is a festive and full-bodied dream play—a vision of family life as a gifted child might spin it around, turning himself into a hero, a magician, an actor. In what Bergman says is his final movie, his obsessions are turned into stories, and he tells them to us—he makes us a beribboned present of his Freudian-gothic dream world. To start with, Ingmar Bergman should not have been born a clergyman's son; Alexander Ekdahl is born into a large, prosperous theatrical family. And at the opening of the movie the dark-eyed, ten-year-old Alexander (Bertil Guve) has his head in his toy theatre; he looks at us pensively, dreamily, over tiny, blazing footlights. We see him then in his family home, stealing from his parents' wing into his grandmother's rich, glowing rooms—the image framed as if we were looking through a proscenium. In the next scenes, it's Christmas Eve, 1907, and the whole troupe of Ekdahls, who have been busy putting on their annual Nativity play in the big Ekdahl theatre, which is just across the square from the house, come in hugging, gossiping, kissing, scrapping: a mammoth entrance scene. Aunts, uncles, cousins, servants—it takes a while for them all to arrive. It takes us much longer to sort out the two dozen or so characters, and that's part of the point. They're a bawdy, physically affectionate clan, they eat and drink huge amounts, they indulge children indiscriminately. They're an organic unit, a body of people.

Alexander's widowed grandmother, Helena Ekdahl (Gunn Wållgren), has retired from the theatre, but she is still the head of the family, and seated next to her at the table is the man whom the children call Uncle Isak. He's her former (and longtime) lover, Isak Jacobi (Erland Josephson), a Jewish antique dealer and moneylender, who is her closest confidant. Alexander's real uncles aren't in the theatre, but they're both clowns. Carl Ekdahl (Börje Ahlstedt), a professor at the university in the town and a masochistic mess, is married to a German woman. He regularly gets drunk and performs for the children: he runs up and down the stairs to get limber, then he drops his pants, they hold lighted candles close to his bottom, and he blows out the flames. (It's a scene we usually get in frat-house movies.) The other uncle, Gustav Adolf Ekdahl (Jarl Kulle), whose restaurant on the square gets the theatre trade, is a snorting, friendly bull—he's always pawing the ground amorously. This loudmouthed lech is so openhearted and unembarrassed that he's irresistibly likable. His complaisant wife, Alma (Mona Malm), who's like a plumper, gigglier Elizabeth Taylor, is as happy as a bird—his affairs don't bother her in the least. Nobody is really religious, nobody is in any way spiritual; in fact, Alexander's idealized family is so hearty and indulgent it's gross. But not his parents. The theatre is his father's religion—Oscar Ekdahl (Allan Edwall), who manages the large, successful company and plays roles such as the Ghost of Hamlet's Father, is a frail, middle-aged man with nothing carnal in his nature. He's almost disembodied. Alexander's mother, Emilie (Ewa Fröling), is, of course, young and beautiful, and the leading actress at the theatre.

The picture is scaled big; it runs for three hours and ten minutes, and the glistening Christmas scenes, which go on for perhaps an hour, have a quality of fantasy and communal memory intertwined. Returning to work in Sweden, Bergman (who in 1976 had left his home terrain in anger at the undeserved humiliation of being accused of tax dodging) is collaborating once again with his chosen family—the extended family that he has created. The cast includes an ex-wife, a couple of his children, and performers who have worked with him on the stage and the screen over a period of almost forty years; the crew is headed by Sven Nykvist, his cinematographer (and right hand). The movie is a family reunion, and Bergman is reasserting that this is the world he belongs to. *Fanny and Alexander* may really be his final movie; he's sixty-four, and he says that the physical strain of making movies is too great. But he intends to go on working in the theatre and in television. "They'll have to carry me out feet first before I quit the stage," he says, and *Fanny and Alexander* confirms it. The theatre is the world he's happiest in. It's not accidental that Bergman, who was born in July, 1918, has placed the film in 1907, when Alexander is ten; that way, he can imagine himself to be a man born in the nineteenth century. He's acknowledging that he doesn't love the technology of movies in the way he loves the less pressured and more companionable life of the theatre.

Fanny and Alexander is at its weakest when it's explicitly a tribute to theatre—when Alexander's father, tears in his eyes, makes this humble backstage speech to the company:

My only talent, if you call it talent in my case, is that I love this little world inside the thick walls of this playhouse. And I'm fond of the people who work in this little world. Outside is the big world, and sometimes the little world succeeds for a moment in reflecting the big world, so that we understand it better. Or is it perhaps that we give the people who come here the chance of forgetting for a while the harsh world outside. Our theatre is a small room of orderliness, routine, conscientiousness, and love.

The father's small mustache and the way he combs his hair are unfortunate; they give him a resemblance to Hitler, which couldn't have been intended. And his humility seems pathetic and false. For one thing, his playhouse is a flourishing large, many-tiered theatre and has just been packed full with a dressed-up audience. And that guff about helping people to forget the harsh world outside: Bergman wouldn't have the face to deliver those lines himself—not the Bergman who put us through *The Virgin Spring*, *Winter Light*, *The Silence*, *The Passion of Anna*, *The Serpent's Egg*, and even the gray, bleak *From the Life of the Marionettes*. Yet we're clearly meant to take those lines straight, and Bergman returns to them at the conclusion; the message of this farewell movie is his view of theatre as distraction for the tired businessman.

But *Fanny and Alexander* is at its strongest when it's most theatrical. There wasn't a moment when I wasn't held by the Christmas material; the pacing of these scenes is relaxed, assured—they almost seem to be happening in real time, yet Bergman sustains a tone of wonder and expectancy. His offhand technique is masterly—from time to time the images seem ceremonial, like prized photographs of family occasions. Still, I didn't feel any ping of excitement during those scenes; the evocative images (Alexander with his hand on the frosty window he's looking out, Alexander with his magic lantern) only evoke earlier Bergman films, and the large, generous-hearted family is a bit sticky. There's an element of self-applause in the wonderful-family-of-the-theatre scenes. The picture didn't really begin for me until the shock of Alexander's action at a crucial moment. His father, Oscar, has collapsed onstage during a rehearsal of *Hamlet*; the actors can't get a cab, and they take him home on a cart—hauling it, like horses. The cathedral bells are pealing—it's a remarkable sequence, presaging a change in the film. At home, Oscar lies in bed, making his farewells to his family, while Alexander and his younger sister, Fanny (Pernilla Allwin), sit in the kitchen doing their schoolwork—they're comforted by the presence of the servants. (It's a fine image. You think, "Of course—that's just where they'd be.") Then their father sends for them. Alexander goes reluctantly—everything in him fighting against what he is forced to do. First, Fanny is taken to the bed, and her father says goodbye to her. Then he calls for Alexander, who tries to crawl under the bed. But he isn't allowed to, and his hand is forcibly put in his father's. Oscar is holding tight to Alexander's hand when death grabs at him and his mouth opens in a rattling sort of choke—and Alexander pulls his hand free and runs away. That instant of Alexander's recoil was the first image in the movie that had any real potency. It was followed by another: Fanny and Alexander, hearing screaming at night, go to investigate. It's coming from the room where their father is laid out; the door is open just enough for them to see his body and see their young mother walking back and forth, screaming her loud, wailing scream rhythmically, as if to a metronome. The kids, hand in hand, just stand there in the next room, listening, staring, their faces unchanging. It's pure theatre, and the stylized image is eloquent, inspired. Bergman has put the precision of our childhood memories into these simplified compositions.

The movie plunges then into gothic horror, and it's a little goofy and very entertaining, but I don't think it ever again achieves the full authority of those two scenes. The funeral procession, with Alexander trudging along, head down, and muttering all the swear words he knows (not enough to relieve his feelings), doesn't quite come off. But the movie gets rolling into its second-act extravaganza when the ghost of Alexander's father, dressed in a spiffy white suit, begins making appearances, playing the spinet and talking to the boy, and the prelate who officiated at the funeral, Bishop Edvard Vergérus—a dread name in Bergman films, where a Vergérus is always a villain—begins courting the widow. An actress to the heart, Emilie starts fancying herself in a new role, and the woman whom we have just watched pacing and wailing is soon telling the bishop—in all sincerity—that she's never felt anything as strong as her love for him. (The choice of Ewa Fröling for the actress mother with the strong lungs results in some rather disconcerting scenes, including this one. It isn't at all clear why this tall, blond young woman married the flabby, vaporous, and much older Oscar, and Ewa Fröling has a striking modern look—she's bold, direct. The staring eyes, the thick dark brows, even the large mouth—they all seem out of period. She's fascinating but remote, as if she'd walked onto the wrong stage.)

The action is much faster in these sequences. The handsome, tense, puri-

tanical bishop (Jan Malmsjö) is a blood-chilling and very actory villain—
Christopher Plummer crossed with George Grizzard. When he starts giving
Alexander moral instruction, it's like a new Inquisition. And it's apparent from
the start that this ascetic—an apostle of discipline—will never understand the
boy. To Vergérus, it's a sin that Alexander told his schoolmates that his mother had sold him to a circus. And Emilie, who is present during the boy's inter-
rogation, doesn't laugh; her role change is total, and she takes the fib as
seriously as Vergérus does. Then, in an eerie image that might be Alexander's
dream of Claudius and Gertrude and the grieving Prince, the bishop flirts
with Emilie while Alexander's head is right next to their heads. It's a poisonous, unholy trinity. The scenes have a real creepiness after Emilie tells the two
children that she's going to marry the bishop. And he delivers the crushing
news that he wants her and her children to come to him naked, leaving all
their possessions behind—bringing no toys, nothing. It's a masterstroke of
wickedness. Bergman goes whole hog on horror, and it's terrific fun, because
he pulls us in. We get it all: the isolated, dungeonlike house; the mystery of
how the bishop's first wife (and children) drowned; the bishop's scrawny
mother and prune-faced sister, with their Spartan rules; the sullen menacing
servants. One of them—the ratlike kitchen maid Justine, who has a sallow
face and listless, stringy hair—is played by the great Harriet Andersson and
becomes a classic mad, spying, tattling enemy of children. Her scenes have a
nightmare intensity, especially when she claims that the house is eating her;
she mutters that the doorknob eats her skin, and she's picking at her palm,
keeping it raw and bleeding.

We become imperilled children, and it's frightening, but it's also a relief,
because now we understand the film's mechanisms better. When Alexander
refuses to break down, as the bishop is determined to force him to, we perceive how the boy (Bergman) has split his actual life into a grandiose vision
of the bright, cheery days with his "true" theatrical family and the dank miseries of being oppressed by a puritan stepfather, who locks you and your sister
in a bare room with barred windows. In this ogre's household, the sensory
deprivation makes you feel as if your soul were being depleted, and—horror
of horrors—you must finish everything on your plate. The difference seems
to turn on the contrasting visions of Hans Christian Andersen and the Brothers Grimm, and there's a shift from the "natural" time of the Andersen scenes
to a disorienting telescoping of time, so that we don't know how long Emilie
was a widow before she married the bishop, or how long the children are
prisoners. We're hustled along, and the action is pell-mell. Bergman lets his
imagination run wild in these Grimm scenes: Uncle Isak, the mysterious Jew,
comes to the rescue with his black-magic arts; Emilie, restored to her senses
and trying to escape, puts a sleeping potion in the bishop's broth. The picture
falls apart for a while when the children are hiding out in Isak's antique shop.
In these scenes, Isak and his young relatives are crafty and slimy; they display
the stereotypical traits that anti-Semites ascribe to Jews. Presumably, this is all

Alexander's vision. It's an incoherent one: Alexander, wandering around at night, is ushered into a barred room where a dangerous, mad youth is kept, and is inducted into mysteries (which remain mysteries) by this young man, who seems to be a young woman. But Bergman takes hold of things again after Alexander, who has been taught to use second sight, sees the bishop's obese, bedridden Aunt Elsa in flames.

I enjoyed *Fanny and Alexander* enormously, but I wanted to love it the way I loved Bergman's *The Magic Flute*, and I couldn't. This may be because, although I can perceive what's happening when a boy's fantasies are being worked out, I don't feel the tingle of recognition that the material may have for men. The movie is all Alexander's fantasy life. Fanny isn't really in the picture at all; she's merely a blond, blue-eyed presence, and her name's being in the title is probably vestigial—Bergman may have meant to do far more with her than he did. (The script, just published here, was written in 1979, and it includes a third child, older than Alexander. There are other deviations in the film. In the script, Alexander and Fanny aren't actually Oscar Ekdahl's children but the result of Emilie's extramarital liaisons, and that would certainly be consistent with the way the role of Oscar is cast and played. And in the published version there's the suggestion that the grandmother came from a Jewish family, which helps to explain her attachment to Isak.)

My inability to respond to the film with more abandon isn't only because it's a male fantasy, though. The film is certainly a culmination—a warm-spirited summing up—but it's also a willed masterpiece, and that may be part of what causes the trouble. It's scaled so ambitiously that I kept waiting for it all to come together, but it's somewhat misshapen. After the holiday richness of the first section, there's almost nothing left for the final, Dickensian celebration—the return to the safety and sensuality of the bustling Ekdahl household (where one of the servants has just had a baby, by the unembarrassed Gustav Adolf). The irony that has been set up for the Paradise Regained conclusion—that this warm, yielding family makes no distinction between its legitimate and illegitimate offspring—is a shade self-congratulatory. Too much is made of the Ekdahls' tolerance and of how the servants are really part of the family. And Bergman doesn't trust the material to reach us emotionally; he explains it—not only in that banal speech of Oscar's but by giving the grandmother a passage from Strindberg's *A Dream Play* to read to us at the end (while Alexander is curled on her lap). There are times in this movie when Bergman kills the magic by showing his hand. Surely he has made so many dream-play films already—*Wild Strawberries*, for one—that he doesn't need to present the decoding information from Strindberg, unless he's worrying about the future, television-trained audience. (He has prepared a five-hour version for Swedish TV.) I flinched when Emilie told Alexander to stop thinking he was Hamlet. Bergman sets up the metaphors and puts in the paternal ghost, and then he undercuts his own handiwork with Emilie's brusque line. (Was he worried that some people in the audience might not get the idea of the boy's being highly suggestible if he didn't come right out and explain it?) Fortunately, at the end he couldn't resist a good laugh scene, and gave Alexander another ghost to haunt him.

The passion that was in *Shame*, the sense of discovery that was in Bibi Andersson's great monologue in *Persona*, the elation that was in *The Magic Flute*—they're not here. Bergman may truly have gone past his excitement about moviemaking; *Fanny and Alexander* is a more distanced work. If it calls any film besides Bergman's own earlier ones to mind, it's probably *Children of Paradise*—that other epic about life in the theatre. I don't think *Fanny and Alexander* achieves comparable romantic heights, but it's a cornucopia of a movie, with marvellous things in it. There's an amazingly wide-ranging and vital performance by Gunn Wållgren (who's almost seventy) as the matriarch Helena, the presiding spirit of the movie—her pale-blue eyes, weary but still eager, see into Alexander with complete love. It makes sense that he leaps into her unmade bed, and it's apparent why he pokes around her rooms—her things have a sense of history about them. And there's a lovely, soft-toned performance by Pernilla Wållgren as the Ekdahls' young servant girl Maj (who allows Alexander to keep her company in her bed when it isn't otherwise occupied). The movie also has many oddities; some of them (such as the boy illusionist's being a girl) link up with motifs in other Bergman films, and perhaps with whatever was behind his original use of them. And there are great loony details: Erland Josephson plays the exotic Jew to the medieval hilt, and in the scene in which he's trying to trick the wicked bishop and save the children, he lets out the grandest "Oy" I've ever heard. When the bishop, under the pretext of disciplining Alexander out of love, gives him ten strokes of a cane (raising weals across his back), the bishop's insidiously calm mother holds on to the boy's neck; she has a silver thimble on one finger of the hand grasping his flesh, and that bit of metal gives the scene an extra touch of sadism. Gunnar Björnstrand, in the suitable guise of a distinguished elderly actor, turns up at the Ekdahls' table on ceremonial occasions; making the movie was clearly a ceremonial occasion in itself.

The most obviously appealing thing about *Fanny and Alexander* is its sanity. It's a learning-to-live-with-your-craziness movie. (That may be as good a definition of sanity as any other.) Bergman isn't punishing the audience with his obsessions; he's using his consciousness of his own absurdity to turn them into entertaining fairy tales. (That could be another definition of sanity.) If he has also constructed a picture that's a rationale for his own role as the patriarch of a theatrical clan, this self-acceptance is rather jolly to contemplate—at a safe‘distance. And there is genuine affirmation in the film: it's in the lighting and in the way that he revels in the actors' faces. There's no airbrushing of their weaknesses and wrinkles. But the parts of *Fanny and Alexander* that remind you the most of other Bergman movies don't remind you of the good parts of those movies. And this film has almost none of Bergman's great wit. What it has is lovingly placed warm gingerbreading, which I fear will lead audiences to take it as a healing experience. They can come out of the movie beaming with pleasure at the thought of Ingmar Bergman's finally achieving harmony with himself. But the conventionality of the thinking in *Fanny and Alexander* is rather shocking; it's not modern conventionality—it's from the past. And that may have a lot to do with why the film seems healing. It's as if Bergman's neuroses had been tormenting him for so long that he cut them off and went sprinting back to Victorian health and domesticity. The picture is an almost sustained flight of Victorian fantasy, and it may win Ingmar Bergman his greatest public acceptance. Coming from Bergman, banality is bound to seem deeply satisfying—wholesome. It can pass for the wisdom of maturity.

. . . . .

*T*he people who made the nuclear-scare movie *WarGames* had half an idea. The first part is a sly, affectionate comedy centering on an American middle-class high-school student who, like many others, is caught up in the technology of computers and video games. The Seattle computer-freak hero, David, played by Matthew Broderick, has a gentle, childlike face and surprisingly large, competent hands. He has all this miracle-working technology and not a thought in the world about what to do with it. He just goofs off, the way kids a few decades back goofed off with ham radio sets, and in the seventies with CB equipment. About the only practical thing David has found to do with his new prowess is to tap into the school's computer to improve his grades, and he performs a similar service for a girl he likes. He has taste: Jennifer (Ally Sheedy), who delivers some of the movie's best lines, is straightforward and funny. The two kids have an easy manner, and the director, John Badham, seems to know just what he's doing. He leaves the picture in Matthew Broderick's capable big mitts, and it has a core of comedy and excitement. The publicity has tipped us to where the film is heading, but we're charmed by the kids and the details.

WarGames gives the impression of having been thought out in human terms. David, who might be a Seattle cousin of the California kids in *E.T.*, is only one of the young computer nuts around; there's Jim (Maury Chaykin), who designs games, and there's Malvin, known as Mr. Potato Head (Eddie Deezen), who is possibly the first example on the screen of a new species—computer nerd. What for David is presumably no more than a phase is already Malvin's whole existence. And there's a little boy who hangs around the video arcade—eight or nine years old, he's a miniature version of David. (David's father, too, seems linked to these weirdos, if only by his blank expression and his Southern-style method of buttering his corn.) The influences on Badham are fairly clear: there's more than a suggestion of the Spielberg of *Close Encounters* in the way the shots are edited at the beginning of this picture (and in the opening of Badham's other new film, *Blue Thunder*); David is also probably the closest we've come to an American equivalent to Truffaut's young Antoine Doinel. He's the life in the movie; it's dead when he's offscreen. The moviemakers seem to know this—up to a point.

There are premonitions of solemnities to come when David, who is trying to crack the codes of new video games that aren't yet on the market, accidentally plugs into the Defense Department's war-games system, based in Colorado. He thinks he's playing just another game—Global Thermonuclear War—and we're whacked over the head to grasp the irony that indeed he is. Then the movie is thrown to the machines—to the Defense Department's master computer, a huge box of flashing lights that makes horrible noises. It sounds like an eighteen-wheel truck rumbling down the highway—it's loud even for the sound of doom. When David realizes that he is the cause of the President's announcement of a nuclear alert, he doesn't know how to stop this big contraption from playing out the game automatically. He asks the computer whether what they're engaged in is a game or for real, and the computer answers, "What's the difference?" For a computer, there isn't any. It's a neat touch that this Armageddon computer is tended by an expert (Irving Metzman) who's a grown-up Mr. Potato Head. Before David can do anything to stop the game, he's tracked down, arrested by the F.B.I., and taken to Colorado. There, he's grilled by the specialist in charge of the computer system (Dabney Coleman), who doesn't believe him and simply can't register that the master computer has begun the countdown for the big cataclysm; he thinks that the kid is part of a Communist conspiracy, and the general who's in command of the war room (Barry Corbin) has him locked up. There are echoes of *Dr. Strangelove* here, but the picture doesn't go all the way to satire. It presents almost straight what we laughed at twenty years ago. Still, David has to improvise at each step of his dealings with the military men, and it's fun watching him, and Badham and Broderick and Ally Sheedy have built up so much good will that the movie doesn't go completely flooey until David, who picks the lock of the room where he's being held, and Jennifer—who has joined him—set off for the island where the scientist who programmed the big computer lives.

If you've been starved for movies about mad geniuses and Kevin Kline's thrashing about in *Sophie's Choice* didn't quite satisfy you, you can get your fill with *WarGames*, where John Wood plays the hermit computer scientist, Professor Falken, as a falconlike fellow who's so brainy and bitter that he rolls his eyes from side to side and wears his hair in bangs. The professor may suggest a tall, potty Fritz Weaver, but his intensity is all his own. His blue eyes are popping and smoking; they're the only things left alive in his witch's face. This is a real baroque clinker of a performance, but the audience doesn't laugh. Professor Falken is a saint driven mad because the government wouldn't stop its gamesmanship—the top men in the Defense Department believed there were "acceptable losses." Stanley Kramer has returned to us, lugging leftover dialogue from *On the Beach*. David and Jennifer have now become the Voice of Youth, and when Jennifer announces, "I'm only seventeen years old—I'm not ready to die yet," David's rejoinder is something like "I always thought that there would be plenty of time. I really wanted to learn how to swim." And the reason the audience doesn't throw candy wrappers and stale popcorn at the screen is—I'm guessing—that the movie is so full of itself that it demands to be cheered for voicing the fears of people in the audience and getting its message across.

The actual message of the movie (from a script by Lawrence Lasker and Walter F. Parkes) is simply that computers, being subject to whim, error, malfunction, and misinterpretation of data, shouldn't be trusted to launch nuclear missiles—that human judgment is needed to protect us from the flukes of mechanization. But once the speeches have started, the moviemakers go on to make their "personal statements," the picture loses all its humor, and the actors start acting all over the place. The audience I saw it with didn't seem to mind. After all, it's the master computer itself—indistinguishable from God—that speaks the key line: "The only winning move is not to play." *WarGames* is this year's *The China Syndrome*—the kind of cautionary melodrama that succeeds or fails at the box office for reasons that have almost nothing to do with its quality.

A lingering question: Isn't it time for moviemakers who aren't trying for a satirical effect to recognize that four-star generals are not likely to be barnyard louts? And that maybe the high-level officers in the war room might be soft-spoken, articulate, and knowledgeable—might be at least as aware as we are of the lunacy of the operations they're involved in? A movie in which the adolescents (and even the child video-games addict) are presented as bright, civilized, and resourceful and the adults (except for the mad professor) are presented as thickheaded droids may be suspected of (a) catering to the young movie audience and (b) falling back on TV-style cartoon characters. The men in the war room are puff-cheeked macho dumb, and Dabney Coleman's face is overworked. There's no way for the halves of this picture to come together, because the first half is about how wonderful kids are and the second half is about how stupid and corrupt adults are. It's as if nobody had ever told the moviemakers where adults come from.

June 13, 1983

Index

Eyre, David, 213
Eyre, Peter, 221, 222

Fabian, 115
Fabray, Nanette, 394
Falstaff, 187
Fame, 30, 290
Family Circle, 188
Fancher, Hampton, 361
Fanny and Alexander, 486–93
Fantasia, 299
"Fantasy Island," 357, 358
Farnsworth, Richard, 117
Farrow, Mia, 240, 365, 366–67
Fast Times at Ridgemont High, 407–9, 473
Faust, 339
Faye, Herbie, 77
Feiffer, Jules, 119, 122
Feld, Fritz, 216
Feldshuh, Tovah, 115
Fellini, Federico, 65, 87, 88, 125, 296, 299, 450; dir., *8 ½*, 65, 87, 89; *Nights of Cabiria*, 251; *I Vitelloni*, 252, 320; *Fellini's Roma*, 364
Fellini's Roma, 364
Fernandez, Wilhelmenia, 328, 329
Ferreol, Andrea, 469
Ferrer, José, 365
Ferreri, Marco, 466–69; dir., *Tales of Ordinary Madness*, 466–69; *The Ape Woman*, 466; *La Grande Bouffe*, 466; *The Last Woman*, 466, 467
Ferrier, Noel, 453
Ferriol, Caroline, 67
Ferris, Barbara, 43
Feuillère, Edwige, 150
Feydeau, Georges, 174, 176
Field, Sally, 288, 289
Fields, W. C., 99, 157, 197, 221, 344, 420
Fiesta, 357
Film Comment, 111, 335, 385
Filmways, 39
Fink, Margaret, 61
Finney, Albert, 253, 254, 291, 293, 295, 338, 345
First a Girl, 332
First You Cry (TV movie), 80
Firth, Peter, 136
Fisher, Carrie, 211, 481
Fisk, Jack, 354; dir., *Raggedy Man*, 350, 354, 372
F.I.S.T., 289
Fists in the Pocket, 418

Fitch, Robert, 275
Fitzcarraldo, 401–7
Fitzgerald, F. Scott, 269
Fitzgerald, Geraldine, 232
Flaherty, Joseph P., 225
Flanders, Ed, 244
Flash Gordon, 124–27, 184
"Flat Foot Floogie with the Floy Floy," 175
Flaubert, Gustav, 183
Flea in Her Ear, A, 174
Fleischer family, 123
Flight of the Eagle, The, 475–79
"Flintstones, The," 197
Floyd, Joey, 41
Flying Down to Rio, 299
Flynn, Errol, 396
Focal Point, 156
Follow the Fleet, 275
Fonda, Henry, 269, 270, 272, 456
Fonda, Jane, 162–63, 270, 271, 293, 310
Foolin' Around, 11
Foote, Horton, 480
Ford, Harrison, 208, 209, 361, 362, 364, 482
Ford, John, 137, 141; dir., *Fort Apache*, 137; *Cheyenne Autumn*, 357
Forman, Miloš, 175, 263–66; *One Flew Over the Cuckoo's Nest*, 77, 179, 292; *Taking Off*, 175; *Ragtime*, 263–66; *Hair*, 264, 265, 266
Forrest, Christine, 199
Forrest, Frederic, 297, 298, 329
Forsyth, Bill, 463–66, dir., *Local Hero*, 463–66; *Gregory's Girl*, 466
Forsyth, Frederick, 168
Forsythe, Drew, 159
Fort Apache, 137
Fort Apache, The Bronx, 151–55, 288, 289, 412, 441
Fortune, The, 3
48 Hrs., 437–40
Fosse, Bob, 427; dir., *All That Jazz*, 180, 345, 427
Foster, Jodie, 29
Foul Play, 163, 412
Four Friends, 283–86
Four Seasons, The, 207, 208, 415
Foutz, Anthony, 468
Fowle, Susannah, 61
Fowles, John, 237, 238, 239
Fox, Edward, 433
Fraker, William A., 96; dir., *The Legend of the Lone Ranger*, 231

Matthews, Jessie, 332
Matuszak, John, 194, 195–96
Mauriac, François, 442
May, Elaine, 429
"Maybe," 344
Mayron, Melanie, 310, 311
Mazursky, Paul, 46–50, 216, 320, 323, 389–92; dir., *Willie and Phil*, 46–50, 392; *An Unmarried Woman*, 47, 49, 135; *Alex in Wonderland*, 47; *Blume in Love*, 48; *Harry & Tonto*, 49; *Next Stop, Greenwich Village*, 320; *Bob & Carol & Ted & Alice*, 320; *Tempest*, 389–92
Mead, Margaret, 472
Mean Streets, 109, 153, 457, 460
Meatballs, 225
Medak, Peter, 232–33; dir., *Zorro, the Gay Blade*, 232–33
Meet Me in St. Louis, 348
Melato, Mariangela, 126, 240
Méliès, Georges, 124, 125
Melnick, Daniel, 14
Melville, Herman, 98
Melvin and Howard, 71–78, 292, 294
Melvin Simon Productions, 69
Mendelssohn, Felix, 365
Mephisto, 337–40
Meredith, Burgess, 243, 346
Merman, Ethel, 344
"Merv Griffin Show, The," 248
Metropolis, 364
Metzler, Jim, 284, 399
Metzman, Irving, 240, 494
Meyer, Nicholas, 355–60; dir., *Time After Time*, 75, 355; *Star Trek II: The Wrath of Khan*, 355–60
Meyer, Russ, 198
Meyers, Nancy, 94
Mezzogiorno, Vittorio, 316, 319
M·G·M, 14, 99, 198, 234, 278, 297, 353, 357
Michael Dunn Memorial Repertory Theatre Company, 353
Middleton, Charles, 126
Midler, Bette, 42, 43, 95, 97, 229, 411, 412
Midnight, 429
Midnight Express, 20, 122, 188, 290
Midsummer Night's Sex Comedy, A, 365–68
Miéville, Annie-Marie, 104
Mignot, Pierre, 415

Mikado, The, 124
Mildred Pierce, 236, 237
Milius, John, 98, 127
Millais, Hugh, 168
Milland, Ray, 429
Miller, Ann, 275, 357
Miller, Dick, 193
Miller, George, 384–89; dir., *The Road Warrior*, 384–89, 456; *Mad Max*, 384, 386
Miller, Harvey, 94
Millholland, Bruce, 240
Milligan, Spike, 216
Millöcker, Karl, 337
Mills, John, 433
Mind Benders, The, 129
Miner, Jan, 49
Minnelli, Liza, 109, 231, 232, 391
Minnelli, Vincente, 348; dir., *Meet Me in St. Louis*, 348
"Minnie the Moocher," 27
Minty, Emil, 385
Mirren, Helen, 185
Miss Lonelyhearts, 87
Missing, 309–12
Missouri Breaks, The, 283
Mr. T., 346
Mitchell, Cameron, 397
Molinaro, Edouard, 164–67; dir., *La Cage aux Folles II*, 164–67; *La Cage aux Folles*, 164, 165
Moment by Moment, 32
Mommie Dearest, 233–37
Mon Oncle Antoine, 421, 423
Monroe, Marilyn, 32, 157, 330, 373
Monsieur Verdoux, 217, 444
Montalban, Ricardo, 356, 357, 358
Montez, Maria, 125
Monty Python and the Holy Grail, 183
Moonwebs, 262
Moore, Dudley, 99, 231, 232, 333, 370, 462, 463
Moore, Kenny, 304
Moore, Mary Tyler, 78, 80, 81
Moore, Roger, 11
Morales, Esai, 474
Morante, Laura, 313
More American Graffiti, 33, 209
Morgan, Donald M., 100
Morgan, Helen, 329
Moriarty, Cathy, 107, 108
Moroder, Giorgio, 188, 335
Morris, Desmond, 308

Quaid, Dennis, 156, 157, 196
Queen, 125
Quest for Fire, 307–9
Quinn, Aileen, 344, 345

Rachel, Rachel, 78
Radio City Music Hall, 297
Rafelson, Bob, 21, 175, 178–82; dir., *The King of Marvin Gardens*, 175; *The Postman Always Rings Twice* (1981), 178–82, 190, 191
Rafelson, Toby, 76
Raggedy Man, 350, 354, 372
Raging Bull, 106–12, 190, 191, 457, 460
Ragtime, 263–66
RAI, 316
Raiders of the Lost Ark, 207–12, 348, 351, 386–87, 389, 481
Railsback, Steve, 63, 66, 68
Rain, 96
Rainmaker, The, 173
Rains, Claude, 194
Raise the Titanic, 73, 114
Rake's Progress, The, 413
Rall, Tommy, 275
Rambaldi, Carlo, 350
Ramis, Harold, 225
Rampling, Charlotte, 89, 441
Randall, Tony, 11
Rashomon, 141
Rathbone, Basil, 427
Ravel, Maurice, 141, 196
"Rawhide," 26
Ray, Satyajit, 151, 434, 435
"Ready to Begin Again," 96
Real Paper (Boston), 190
"Recordar," 410
Red Mill, The, 70
Red Shoes, The, 338
Redbook, 236
Redford, Robert, 16, 20, 24–25, 42, 78–82; dir., *Ordinary People*, 78–82, 207, 383
Redgrave, Michael, 237
Redgrave, Vanessa, 411
Reds, 278–83, 314, 334
Reed, Barry, 440
Reed, Carol, 153, 328; dir., *The Third Man*, 156
Reed, Pamela, 75, 172, 260
Reeve, Christopher, 223–24, 326, 327
Reid, Kate, 173, 175
Reiner, Carl, 394; dir., *The Jerk*, 195

Reinhold, Judge, 408
Reinking, Ann, 345
Reiser, Paul, 322
Reisz, Karel, 212, 237–41; dir., *Saturday Night and Sunday Morning*, 84; *Isadora*, 212; *The French Lieutenant's Woman*, 237–41; *Who'll Stop the Rain*, 439
Reitman, Ivan, 224–26; dir., *Stripes*, 224–26; *Meatballs*, 225
Rekert, Winston, 426
Remar, James, 439
Remick, Lee, 132
Reno, Kelly, 349
Renoir, Jean, 71, 72, 76, 145, 151, 368, 449; dir., *A Day in the Country*, 368; *Grand Illusion*, 449
Resnick, Patricia, 162
Resurrection, 117–19, 153
Return of the Jedi, 481–85
Rey, Fernando, 411
Reynolds, Burt, 11, 374, 445, 446; dir., *The End*, 214
Reynolds, Debbie, 357
Reynolds, Freddy, 56, 58
Reynolds, Naida, 77
Rhoden, Harold, 72
Rhys, Jean, 294
Rhys-Davies, John, 209
Rich and Famous, 247–48
Richard Pryor Live in Concert, 96, 323, 325, 326
Richard Pryor Live on the Sunset Strip, 323–26
Richards, Dick, 428, 429
Richardson, Ralph, 221–22, 397
Richardson, Tony, 300–302; dir., *The Border*, 300–302
Richter, W.D. (Rick), 156
Ridgely, Robert, 77
Riefenstahl, Leni, 338
Riegert, Peter, 464
Rififi, 189
Riggs, Rita, 117
Riley, Jack, 216
Riley, Terry, 253
Ringwald, Molly, 389, 391
Ritchie, Michael, 76, 77, 95–97; dir., *Smile*, 77–78; *Divine Madness*, 95–97
Ritter, John, 11
Riva, Emmanuèle, 442
Rivers, Larry, 237, 463
Road Warrior, The, 384–89, 456
"Roamin' in the Gloamin'," 463